New Gill History of Ireland 6

Twentieth-Century Ireland

Revolution and State Building

REVISED EDITION

New Gill History of Ireland

1. *Medieval Ireland: The Enduring Tradition*
   Michael Richter

2. *Sixteenth-Century Ireland: The Incomplete Conquest*
   Colm Lennon

3. *Seventeenth-Century Ireland*
   Raymond Gillespie

4. *Eighteenth-Century Ireland*
   Ian McBride

5. *Nineteenth-Century Ireland: The Search for Stability*
   D. George Boyce

6. *Twentieth-Century Ireland: Revolution and State Building*
   Dermot Keogh

The Gill History of Ireland originally appeared in eleven volumes between 1972 and 1975. It was succeeded by a proposed six-volume series entitled New Gill History of Ireland in 1990, although in the event only five volumes were published. Now the revised and re-written series is published in its entirety.

New Gill History of Ireland 6

Twentieth-Century Ireland

Revolution and State Building

REVISED EDITION

Dermot Keogh
with **Andrew McCarthy**

Gill & Macmillan

Gill & Macmillan Ltd
Hume Avenue, Park West, Dublin 12
with associated companies throughout the world
www.gillmacmillan.ie
© Dermot Keogh 1994, 2005
0 7171 3297 8

Index compiled by Cover To Cover
Typography design by Make Communication
Print origination by O'K Graphic Design, Dublin
Printed in Malaysia

This book is typeset in 10.5/13 pt Minion.

The paper used in this book comes from the wood pulp of
managed forests. For every tree felled, at least one tree is
planted, thereby renewing natural resources.

A CIP catalogue record for this book is available from the British
Library.

5 4 3 2 1

The extract from 'The Statue of the Virgin at Granard Speaks' by
Paula Meehan is used by kind permission of the author and The
Gallery Press, Loughcrew, Oldcastle, County Meath, Ireland, from
The Man Who Was Marked By Winter (1991).

For my mother, Maureen Keogh, for Ann, Aoife and Clare, Eoin and Niall, and for Edward and Angela Cahill

Contents

Preface

This book has been researched over six years in Ireland, in a number of European countries and in the United States. I have accumulated many debts of gratitude to people who helped me with their scholarship and friendship during this period of investigation. A number of institutions, at home and abroad, provided financial support which allowed me to research extensively in the United States. The head of the Department of History at University College Cork, Joseph Lee, has proved ever helpful over the past twenty years. His major work, *Ireland 1912–1985: Politics and Society*, was a source of great stimulation. The friendship of Joe and Anne Lee has meant much to myself and my family.

I was given study leave by President Michael Mortell and the Governing Body of UCC, while the Arts Faculty fund enabled me to research specific aspects of this volume. The Registrar of UCC, Aidan Moran, was always very supportive. Among my departmental colleagues I thank Elizabeth Steiner Scott and Brian Girvin. I am also grateful to many colleagues in Ireland and abroad who helped me with the writing of this work. In particular, I would like to thank Professors Brian Farrell, Tom Garvin and Ronan Fanning of University College Dublin. My thanks also to Deirdre McMahon and Neil Buttimer. Professor Patrick Lynch and Tom Barrington made an important contribution to my knowledge through their writings and advice. The late Professor T. Desmond Williams was an excellent teacher and a friend whose intellectual generosity was much appreciated.

I owe a deep debt of gratitude to Dr Mary Harris, Senior Lecturer, Department of Irish Studies, University of North London, particularly for her scholarly advice on the issue of Northern Ireland and for her expertise in the researching and drafting of the section on the Boundary Commission. She also made many valuable suggestions as a reader of the various drafts of this book and helped with sources in Irish.

My close friends, Matthew and Madelaine MacNamara, were supportive, and their home was a welcoming port during the many squalls of university life which are designed to throw the working academic off course. Professor MacNamara translated a number of French sources and introduced me to many new ideas and approaches. Father Kevin Kennedy's wide knowledge and culture was always a source of great stimulation. Bill and Miriam Hederman O'Brien's friendship and encouragement over many years should not go unrecorded. Brian and Laura Lennon are close friends who have been very helpful to me on many occasions, as were Angela and Edward Cahill. My former *Irish Press* colleague, Michael Mills, was very encouraging and often pointed me in the right direction. Liam Moher commented on the first draft of this book and suggested many changes. His late father, John, who was a Fianna Fáil TD for Cork in the 1950s, helped me greatly to understand the political personalities and the events of those earlier years. My thanks also to Seán Dunne, who guided me towards a number of important sources and was ever willing to discuss my developing ideas and theories. John Banville, a friend from our time in the Irish Press in the early 1970s, helped with his advice and by providing me with a plentiful supply of Irish history books to review. The annual Patrick MacGill summer school was a source of great personal stimulation and Dr Malachy McCloskey and the committee were very hospitable to my family on our annual visits to Glenties. My thanks also to Annie and Joe Mulholland. Terence Brown of Trinity College Dublin was also very helpful and supportive.

The staff of the UCC library made the life of the researcher much easier. I am indebted to Tom Crawshaw, Edward Fahey, Helen Davis, Trudy Ahern, Ann Collins, Jill Lucey, Valerie Fletcher and Virginia Teehan. Richard Haslam, head of the Department of Public Administration at UCC, was an excellent guide to the labyrinthine world of local government in Ireland. My thanks also to Ruth McDonnell, UCC Information Officer, who helped me on many occasions. I also thank the staff of the Cork County and City libraries.

Dr Garret FitzGerald was very helpful to me over two decades of research, as was his colleague Peter Barry, who arranged for me to see certain files at the Department of Foreign Affairs. Brian Lenihan gave me a number of interviews. Many members and former members of the staff of the Department of Foreign Affairs were very helpful over the years. I am grateful, in particular, to Noel Dorr, Ted Barrington, Pádraic MacKernan, Thelma Doran, Billy Hawkes, Philip McDonagh, Bernadette Chambers and Declan Kelleher. Máire Mhac an tSaoi and Conor Cruise O'Brien, former Irish diplomats, were generous with their time. Richard Stokes, Department of the Taoiseach, championed the opening of state archives when it was neither fashionable nor profitable. I am grateful to him for his persistence and professionalism. Dr David Craig, Ken Hannigan and Aideen Ireland of the Irish National Archives have all played an important role in facilitating the speedy processing and opening of official archives. I thank them for their assistance during my many long visits. The paper keepers in the National Archives provided a speedy and expert service which made working in Bishop Street a genuine pleasure—fire alarms notwithstanding.

I also wish to thank the staff of the government departments who answered my many queries. Commandant Peter Young, Director, Irish Military Archives, and his staff helped locate relevant material. I am grateful to the staffs of the Archives Department, UCD, the National Library and Trinity College Dublin. Denise Moran and Mary Guckian of the library of the Institute of Public Administration, Dublin, were very helpful. I am also grateful to the staff of the British, French, Swiss, Italian, Dutch and German embassies for their help in the preparation of this manuscript. My particular thanks to the Spanish Ambassador, Fermín Zelada.

The later Cardinal Tomás Ó Fiaich gave me access to the Armagh archives and arranged for me to work in the archives of the Irish College, Rome. I am also grateful to Bishop Michael Murphy of Cork for access to the Daniel Cohalan papers. I am grateful to David Sheehy, Dublin Archdiocesan Archives. The Dominicans Austin Flannery and Bernard Tracey were generous with their time and help. The Jesuits gave me access to the Edward Cahill papers. The Franciscans made available a section of the Éamon de Valera papers on the framing of the 1937 constitution; I am particularly grateful to the archivist of that important holding, Dr Breandán Mac Giolla Choille. Brother Paul, the former editor of *The Word*, was very helpful in recalling his many contacts and interviews with leading Irish politicians and ecclesiastical figures. Father Gearóid Ó Súilleabháin CM advised and read parts of this manuscript. Father Thomas Davitt CM very kindly let me read his father's memoirs. On the question of church-state relations, I am indebted to Peter Hebblethwaite, Louis McRedmond, Seán MacReamoinn and Father Michael O'Carroll. The Conference of Major Religious Superiors helped my research on certain aspects of this book. My thanks also to John Cooney. Tony O'Malley gave me an extended interview; my thanks also to Jane

O'Malley, who received Ann and myself very warmly in their home in Callan, Co. Kilkenny. My thanks to Barbara Dawson and Liz Foster of the Municipal Gallery of Modern Art in Dublin. Charles Clarke gave me a number of important references to articles on twentieth-century Irish painting. My thanks also to Tim Pat Coogan and Martin Mansergh.

Part of this book was researched and written while I was a fellow at the Woodrow Wilson Center for Scholars in Washington DC in 1988, and again as a visiting scholar in 1990. My thanks to the many academics with whom I made friends during those stays and to Michael Haltzel, Director, West European Program, and his wife, Helen, for their help and support. I also thank Mike Lacey, Director, North American Program and his wife, Kath, for their friendship, hospitality and use of their library on my frequent visits to Washington. Ann Herpel, David Jonas Frisch and Courtney Slater worked with me as research assistants during my two stays at the Wilson Center. Charlotte Thompson, West European Program, helped me complete a section of the research. Susan Nugent typed part of the manuscript and made many helpful criticisms of the drafts. Marguerite and Tom Kelly were my hosts in Washington on two occasions when I enjoyed a home away from home. I would also like to record my thanks to the staff of the Library of Congress, the National Archives in Washington DC and at Suitland, and the librarian at the Woodrow Wilson Center, Zdenek Davis.

My thanks to the Department of History, Cornell University, where I taught summer school in 1989. Our friends Walter and Sandy LaFeber made my family welcome in Ithaca. The excellent Cornell library and the stimulating company helped advance the research for this book. Professor Jim Walsh, Dean of Social Sciences, San José State University, and his wife, Ann, were very helpful to me when I was doing research in San Francisco. I would also like to thank Barbara Dubins and other members of the staff of the San Jose Department of History for their hospitality.

When my research took me to Brussels, Alan, Ortensia and Maureen Hick were my generous hosts. The Irish Colleges in Rome and Paris kindly put me up while I was in those cities on research trips. I would like to thank the rectors of the Irish College, who helped me during my various stays in Rome.

I used material from personal interviews with the following as background to the writing of this book: Frank Aiken, Peter Barry,

Frederick Boland, Gerard Boland, John Bruton, Con Cremin, Alan Dukes, Garret FitzGerald, Justin Keating, Seán Lemass, Brian Lenihan, Jack Lynch, Seán MacEntee, Máire Mhac an tSaoi, Seán MacBride, Maurice Moynihan, Tommy Mullins, Conor Cruise O'Brien, Ruairí Quinn, Dick Spring and T. Desmond Williams.

My thanks to Frances Kelly, who gave me access to the papers of her husband, Frederick Boland. I would also like to thank Ita Cremin for allowing me to read and prepare for publication the memoirs of her late husband, Con Cremin.

I have been enriched by my contact with UCC postgraduates, many of whom are working on various aspects of the history of twentieth-century Ireland. In particular, I would like to thank Dr David Ryan, De Montfort University, Leicester, Mervyn O'Driscoll, Wolfson College, Cambridge, Dónal Ó Drisceoil, Patricia Dromey, Helen Callanan, Maria McKnight, Robert Patterson and Maurice Fitzgerald. Nigel Moriarty, Aengus Nolan and Finín Ó Drisceoil were a great help during the latter stages of this book's preparation.

My thanks to Norma Buckley, Deirdre O'Sullivan and Charlotte Holland. Veronica Fraser typed the many drafts of this book and I am very much in her debt. Donal Kingston was always available to help me overcome problems with computers.

Fergal Tobin, of Gill & Macmillan, commissioned this book in 1986. I am grateful to him for his encouragement and his help. My thanks to Finbarr O'Shea. My thanks also to Hildegard Penn. Jonathan Williams copy edited the text of the first edition and corrected the proofs. He has earned my gratitude and deep respect for his professionalism.

My mother, Maureen Keogh, and family, to whom this book is dedicated, deserve great praise. The research for this volume required long trips away from home. Ann was ever supportive, as were Aoife, Clare, Eoin and Niall.

Dermot Keogh
University College Cork

My colleague, Dr Andrew McCarthy, coauthored the new chapter in this revised edition and helped me prepare the text for publication. I am grateful for his help and generous cooperation, as I also am to Margaret Clayton for her support and expertise.

Professor Dermot Keogh
Head of Department of History
University College Cork, June 2005

Note on the use of terms in Irish

On 21 January 1919 Sinn Féin deputies, elected to Westminster in the British general election of 1918, established a constituent assembly in Dublin called Dáil Éireann. The members rejected the use of the British abbreviation MP and used instead TD (Teachta Dála). The Provisional Government came into existence under article 17 of the Treaty. On 6 December 1922 the Free State (Saorstát) was formally established. The Lower House of the parliament became known as An (the) Dáil. The Upper House became known as Seanad Éireann. The 'prime minister' was called President of the Executive Council. The 'cabinet' was called the Executive Council. With the introduction of Bunreacht na hÉireann (Irish Constitution) in 1937, the Irish Prime Minister was called Taoiseach (plural Taoisigh), and the deputy Prime Minister, Tánaiste. Oireachtas means parliament. The Ceann Comhairle is the Speaker of Dáil Éireann; the Cathaoirleach is the Speaker of Seanad Éireann.

Éire was the name given to Ireland in the 1937 constitution. The term was used outside the country, and by the British in particular, to denote the southern Irish state.

Fianna Fáil, meaning Soldiers of Destiny, was founded in 1926 by Éamon de Valera. (De Valera usually signed his name Éamon de Valera. There is no accent on his last name in Spanish and that form has been used throughout this book.) Fine Gael, meaning Tribe of the Gael, succeeded Cumann na nGaedheal (League of the Gael). Sinn Féin (Ourselves) was founded by Arthur Griffith in 1905. After the 1916 Rising, Sinn Féin was the term used by the British to describe the insurgents. This name came to be used to describe the Irish radical nationalist movement after 1917. Following the civil war, the anti-Treatyites retained the name Sinn Féin; this party was the political wing of the IRA from the 1920s.

The office of President (Uachtarán na hÉireann) was established under the 1937 constitution. The President (An tUachtarán) is elected by popular ballot for a seven-year term. She or he is eligible for re-election once and only once.

The Irish police force is known as An Garda Síochána, or the gardaí.

The Gaeltacht (plural Gaeltachtaí) means Irish-speaking area; these are situated in Counties Cork, Donegal, Galway, Kerry, Mayo, Meath and Waterford.

Introduction to the First Edition

I don't believe that a period of history—a given space of time, my life, your life—that it contains within it one 'true' interpretation just waiting to be mined. But I do believe that it may contain within it several possible narratives: the life of Hugh O'Neill can be told different ways. And those ways are determined by the needs and the demands and the expectations of different people and different eras. What do they want to hear? How do they want it told? So that in a sense I'm not altogether my own man, Hugh. To an extent I simply fulfil the needs, satisfy the expectations—don't I?[1]

Archbishop Lombard, in Brian Friel's play *Making History*, has alerted the historian to the danger of trying to quarry the 'one true' interpretation of the past. The relatively short history of the Irish state has shown just how limited a doctrinaire approach to interpreting the past can prove to be and how sterile is the conflict between 'schools' of history, which are usually short on research based on primary sources and long on ideology. Father Francis Shaw caricatured such a rigid approach to the writing of history in a memorable article, which was deemed by the editor of *Studies* to be too controversial to publish in 1966:

In the right corner virgin Éire, virtuous and oppressed, in the left the bloody Saxon, the unique source of every Irish ill and malaise; round eight, the duration of each round a hundred years: this might be said to be the accepted *mise en scène* of the Rising of Easter Week, and it may be added that the seconds in the English corner are usually degenerate Irishmen. It is a straight story of black and white, of good 'guys' and bad. The truth of course is different; there are many qualifications and complexities. . . .[2]

Father Shaw challenged the orthodoxies of nationalist historiography at the time of the fiftieth anniversary of the 1916 Rising when simplification of the past by the official mind was thought necessary in order to rekindle a sense of lost patriotism. The 'one' interpretation was simply that of a virgin Éire versus the bloody Saxon, with a significant but not a total victory going to Éire in 1921/22. There was a confidence at the official political level in the 1960s about interpreting the country's past. That reflected the self-confidence of the decade. But over thirty years later such self-confidence was nowhere in evidence. There was a certain diffidence about celebrating the 1916 Rising and Ireland's revolutionary nationalist past.[3] There are a number of reasons why that has come about. Firstly, the carnage in Northern Ireland, which has claimed over 3,000 lives, has sensitised the official mind to the dangers of the oversimplification of the past. Secondly, the work of the New Ireland Forum, which reported in 1984, posited the pluralism and the diversity of the Irish tradition. Thirdly, the mystique of violence definitely lost its appeal in the 1970s and 1980s as members of the historical profession looked at the past from the perspective of having to live at a time when paramilitary violence in Northern Ireland heaped atrocity upon atrocity.[4]

Revisionism was employed very often as a term of abuse to describe the writings of a younger generation of Irish historians. In 1986, in his essay 'We are all Revisionists now', Roy Foster bravely surveyed the debate at the time and wisely concluded that to say '"revisionist" should just be another way of saying "historian"'.[5] Eight years later Tom Dunne made a good contribution to the same debate in his 'New Histories: Beyond Revisionism'.[6] The nationalist academic tradition was not slow to take up the challenge.[7] Many historians felt obliged to take sides and it was lonely for those who chose to occupy the no-man's land between the two poles. A number of important general histories of Ireland have been published in the context of a debate which proved on more than one occasion to be more polemical than enlightened. These works show a diversity of approach and a richness of interpretation which make a nonsense of putting historians into either a revisionist or a nationalist camp. Roy Foster's *Modern Ireland 1600–1972* has covered some of the territory which is central to this work (see pages 431–596). The relevant pages (213–338) in his edited *The Oxford Illustrated History of Ireland* also make an important contribution to the process of reinterpreting the recent Irish past. Ronan Fanning's *Independent Ireland* made excellent use of the limited primary source material available at the time of writing. Part III of K. Theodore Hoppen's *Ireland since 1800: Conflict and Conformity* provides an excellent overview. My colleague Joseph Lee's *Ireland 1912–1985: Politics and Society* has surveyed the twentieth century with characteristic scholarship, brio and verve.

John A. Murphy's *Ireland in the Twentieth Century* was first published in 1975 as part of the Gill History of Ireland. It has whetted the appetite of many generations of students for the study of Irish history. My book, written nearly 20 years later, has been in a position to take advantage of the cornucopia of new primary source material which has been released over the past six years. In writing this volume, I have drawn heavily on the files of various government departments, personal political papers and archives in London, Paris, Rome and in the United States. It is up to the discerning reader, if she or he is so inclined, to determine whether the work is revisionist, nationalist or otherwise. It is time to attempt to go beyond revisionism in order to write a 'narrative of inclusion'.

This book does not deal with the politics of Northern Ireland, except in so far as they impinge on life in the Saorstát, later called Ireland or the Irish Republic. Detailed attention is paid to the Boundary Commission in the 1920s, to the IRA's anti-partitionist activities and to the conflict after 1969.

This volume has nine chapters which take the reader chronologically from 1922 to the early 1990s. It examines the development of Irish party politics from William T. Cosgrave to Albert Reynolds. The book focuses on the growth of Éamon de Valera's Ireland and demonstrates that Fianna Fáil was a coalition rather than a unitary party. In particular, the divisions between Seán Lemass and Seán MacEntee are highlighted. It explores the reasons for the long-term popular appeal of Éamon de Valera and analyses the ultimate poverty of Fianna Fáil populism and the demise of its most determined exponent, Charles Haughey. The book also shows that the early generation of Irish politicians, in both Cumann na nGaedheal (Fine Gael) and Fianna Fáil alike, possessed a form of idealism and commitment to the development of the country which was not shared uniformly by a number of prominent politicians from the 1960s onwards.

But the country was well served throughout by the permanent civil service. The opening of state archives has enabled the historian to study in greater detail the interaction between ministers and their respective departments. Bureaucratic politics are examined in this book, and the failure of the state to modernise, particularly the Oireachtas and local government, is put forward as an argument for the decline of government, which became most evident in the 1980s. The state failed to develop the structures necessary for its ethical well-being and efficient running. Far too much latitude was left to influential political leaders to privatise government decision-making.

The new primary source material permitted me to examine a range of new topics in detail. There was an opportunity to consider official attitudes to women in Irish society. The writing of inclusive gender balanced history has only just begun. The growth of the literature and the culture of the new state has been traced and interwoven into each chapter. In particular, stress has been laid on the pioneering role of women in the world of painting and the visual arts. The new archives, too, helped provide insights into the writing of 'history from below', with special emphasis being laid on the themes of poverty, unemployment and emigration.

My research also examined the interaction between church and state and investigated the relations between leading churchmen and the political elites of the different parties. In particular, the personality of Archbishop John Charles McQuaid has been studied and set in a broader political context. His close and sometimes troubled relationship with Éamon de Valera has been investigated. The impact of Vatican II on Irish society is traced, as is the social role played by church people in housing action campaigns in the 1960s and 1970s. The role of the new right in the 1980s is also analysed. This work has also tried to examine the attitude of the Catholic hierarchy towards the minority churches. Particular attention has been paid to the emergence of anti-semitism in Irish society in the 1930s and the ungenerous attitude of the Irish government towards the admission of Jewish refugees during and after World War II.

The development of Irish foreign policy is also a central theme in this work. Extensive use of the archives of the Department of Foreign Affairs has cast new light on de Valera's external policies in the 1930s, the origins of neutrality and the conducting of the diplomacy of survival during World War II, and the politics of the cold war. The background to the declaration of the Republic in 1949 and to Frank Aiken's China policy has been examined with the assistance of the papers of the diplomat Frederick Boland. This research was supplemented by personal papers and archives from Washington and London. Entry into the European Community and growth within the EC are also examined, as is the state's Northern Ireland and Anglo-Irish policies.

In the chapters written on the period after 1962, the absence of primary source material has been supplemented by extensive interviews with the senior politicians of the time. I was fortunate to have a wide range of contacts who gave generous help to me in the researching and writing of the later period. On occasions, I was able to consult official memoranda and files. This material was given on a confidential basis and has not been acknowledged in any detailed way in the footnotes.

This book was written at a time when the country had more than 300,000 people unemployed and there was growing public cynicism over major financial scandals and over the apparent failure of the political system to reform itself. It was completed before the 1992 general election which returned a Fianna Fáil/Labour partnership government.

Introduction to the Second Edition

I have avoided the temptation to rewrite large sections of the first edition in the light of the changes that have taken place in Irish society since the mid-1990s. Instead, the text remains intact with the addition of minor changes and corrections.

Since this book was published in 1994, there have been two very distinctive developments propelling change that is as profound as it is concentrated in a mere decade. First, Irish society has been transformed politically, socially and economically. In the twenty-first century, Ireland increasingly resembles the secular world of the older member states of the European Union. In another sense, that society has been 'globalised' and/or 'Americanised'. It is no longer a question of being torn between the Atlantic and European cultures. The Tánaiste, Mary Harney, formulated the Irish position as follows in a speech she made on 21 July 2000:

> History and geography have placed Ireland in a very special position between America and Europe. . . . As Irish people our relationships with the United States and the European Union are complex. Geographically we are closer to Berlin than Boston. Spiritually we are probably a lot closer to Boston than Berlin. Ireland is now in a very real sense the gateway to Europe.[1]

However, Ireland and Irish people feel quite comfortable in their new position as part of a common Euro-Atlantic culture. There is a new-found self-confidence and self-belief in early twenty-first century Ireland. Fear of outside influences—a defining characteristic of the country in its early decades of existence—is hardly evident any more as literary and film censorship is most relaxed and the state no longer plays an intrusive role in the lives of individual citizens.

Second, there is now a much clearer understanding of what Tom Garvin has described in the title of his book as *Preventing the Future —Why Was Ireland So Poor For So Long?* He ascribed much blame to an educational system that was other-worldly and that only altered in the 1960s in time to foster radical change. Let me leave to one side my difficulties with this thesis. Ireland's membership in 1973 of the European Economic Community, now the European Union, also was a transforming agent as was the 'victory' of the peace process in Northern Ireland.

However, much has emerged in recent years of the hidden histories in Irish society relating to political and administrative corruption, sharp practice in the banking sector, child sexual abuse in state-owned schools run by religious stretching back for decades. The media —television, investigative journalism, etc.—has delivered an incisive, emotive, and oftentimes sensationally panoramic picture of aspects of Ireland's hidden past. Those revelations have done much to explain the retardation of modernity in Irish society. They have also helped to cure Irish society of any feelings of nostalgia about 'a world we have lost'. The public has witnessed, with varying levels of bewilderment, the harrowing abuse scandals, and the impact that a small minority of clerics has had on victims. And the public has wondered how all this could have happened. To borrow a phrase from the late *Irish Times* journalist John Healy, nobody shouted stop. Notwithstanding the impact of education, the level of corruption of a petty personal and more organised corporate kind shows why Ireland remained poor for so long.

Never has the case been stronger for a multi-disciplinary approach to understanding the issues of Irish society than in the midst of the revelations about that hidden past. Historical judgement requires a thorough understanding of the options open to society and not just the road taken. History is about choices: it is about understanding the past in the light of circumstances of the past, not the values and practices of the present. The tendency towards, and prevalence of 'presentism', distorts historical understanding. We are now in a period of mass communications when many broadcasters in their professional work never had or have lost a sense of history. Our multi-media age often demands speedy—almost instantaneous—answers and explanations and neatly packaged information couched in terms and values with which today's society can relate. This is where the historian must try to counteract the impact of the reduction of complex issues to a few seconds of background in a media report. The historian needs to adopt the role of outsider. Moreover, there is little point in the historian being an *âme sensible* ready to shift to the study of certain topics because of a developed sense of political correctness.

In the introduction to the first edition of this work, I maintained that 'the country was well served throughout by the permanent civil service'. In light of the revelations of the 1990s, many will wonder how incidents—like the Garda 'Blue-Flu', Armed Forces deafness compensation claims, etc.—bear down on my positive perception of the public services. I believe that there has been a weakening of the civic culture which produced so many idealistic senior civil servants from the 1920s to the 1970s. I argue that that culture has been weakened. It has not disappeared. I would broadly stand over that hypothesis for a number of reasons. The whole of the public service in Ireland—embracing the civil service too—is approximately 300,000 employees in 2005, engaged in specialist and generalist roles in delivering the broad range of public service functions. The civic culture which helped form the Irish state since 1922 was reflected very strongly in the ranks of the public service. Control, accountability and transparency will always be desired alongside satisfactory service delivery. Any organisation that large will, almost inevitably, develop negative characteristics and a tendency to espouse a model of closed government. The civil service is caught in a struggle between a desire for modernity and the comfort of the old system of closed government and anonymity.

Civil servants also face the challenge of exercising their role in an increasingly complex society where specialist knowledge is required to handle difficult issues. Increasingly, the public services have come under criticism in recent years because of greater scrutiny and rising expectations of 'improved' public service. In order to meet the challenge of change, modernising the public services will remain an ongoing goal. But that will require a greater vote of confidence in the role of the civil service to discharge its duties.

Ireland is still 'well served' not just by the civil service but also by the other institutions of state. It is important to distinguish between the small number of politicians who have been indicted for corruption and the even smaller number of public officials who succumbed to the temptations of making easy money. This view is based on the findings of a decade and more of tribunals and investigations. Ireland is not a kleptocracy. Nevertheless, the all-too-cosy relationship between private sector money and political institutions was, and is, a real danger to the health of Irish democracy.

But much has come to light about the fabled private sector, and particularly the financial institutions. What has been the resulting cost for the country of a culture of deception? The state has been cheated of revenue that might have made the difference in the conversion, for example, of the Irish general medical service into a system all might view with pride. The care and treatment of those suffering from disabilities and the care of the aged are high priorities for any society. The idea of trusting the care of the aged and the running of nursing homes to the private sector is an abdication of state responsibility in the same way as it was to give over the care of children in institutions to members of religious orders, virtually without effective checks and balances. The thesis presented in the final chapter of this book implicitly warns against the scaling down of the public sector, through acts such as the sale of Aer Lingus, the creation of more public/private partnerships and the road to greater and more extensive privatisation. It strikes at the communitarian value system on which the original state was so imperfectly founded.

The challenges to the history profession have grown since the first edition of this work appeared in 1994. The resources available to the historian have increased dramatically. For example, the internet has provided an abundance of new sources. Without listing all of them, the availability of the historical debates of both Houses of the Oireachtas on the internet has brought a wealth of sources to the desktops of all on-line researchers. Thanks to the efforts of the CELT project in UCC, these historical records extend back to the revolutionary period to include the proceedings of the First Dáil from 21 January 1919. Now the public may consult the primary documents for themselves.

The decision to make the debates of the Oireachtas available was an enlightened one taken by the former Minister for Finance, Charles McCreevy. However, this historian's gratitude is tempered by the knowledge that Mr McCreevy reined in the scope of the Freedom of Information Act, cutting off a vital artery to areas of official documentation and denying society the right to examine areas relating to cabinet documentation. But such are the processes of Irish democracy with which academics must grapple and circumvent if not overcome and reverse. Nothing should be taken for granted.

Historical perceptions have been transformed in Ireland, too, since 1994. In the first edition I argued in favour of an inclusive history, at a time when debates on revisionism—political and historical—were still occupying the minds of many academics. The focus of debate was on a very narrow subject band. There was a greater need to research the period than to pronounce and declaim on it. However, the 'success' of the Northern peace process in the mid-1990s, and its general endorsement by the vast majority in the Republic, may have redirected perspectives on Irish history.

The revelations regarding the 'hidden histories' have forced historians to accept the challenge of opening up new areas of research. In Ireland we simply have not reached the end of history.

In conclusion, this edition appears at a time when the thirst for the reading and study of history in Ireland and abroad appears to be growing. Against international trends, there are signs of a revival of history as a leaving certificate subject in Ireland. The Irish government introduced a new history curriculum early in the new century and this may partly explain the increase in the number taking the subject of history. However, the rising quality of the teaching in secondary schools is the basic reason for the revival of the subject. Those who have prophesised the end of history as a school subject are gravely mistaken if Ireland is taken as the example. Additionally, there appears to be a growing market for history books, reflecting the need to understand the history of a relatively young state in its broad chronological and international context. There is also a great intellectual curiosity about the Irish diaspora and the role of the Irish in many receiving countries like the United States, Canada, Argentina, Australia, New Zealand, Britain and other countries of the European Union.

A solid understanding of Irish and international history is not a mere optional embellishment in a liberal arts education; it is a vital component of citizenship which provides the skills to help understand and analyse social, cultural, political and economic trends in an age of unprecedented global change coming to be known as the Information Revolution.

Ireland: political and administrative divisions

A War without Victors: Cumann na nGaedheal and the Conservative Revolution

C
ivil war overshadowed the birth of Saorstát Éireann (Irish Free State). In Northern Ireland the minority Roman Catholic community had to learn to live with institutionalised sectarianism. Both states came into existence as a result of enforced compromise. The new political elites in Belfast and Dublin did not regard this outcome as ideal, but pragmatism determined that imperfect solutions had to be made to work. There was unfinished business on both sides of a disputed border.

The passage of the Government of Ireland Act on 23 December 1920 provided the legal basis for the setting up of Northern Ireland. Comprising the six north-eastern counties, it was 5,452 square miles in area and constituted 17 per cent of the land area of the whole island.[1] Belfast was its capital and the seat of the new Northern Ireland parliament. Northern Ireland also had thirteen seats at Westminster and twelve after 1948 when the university seat was abolished. (The figure is now 18.) Events between the summer of 1920 and mid-1922 did not augur well for Northern Ireland's Catholic minority. During this time, over 450 people died in violence, termed 'pogroms' by nationalists. About two-thirds of those killed were Catholics. Thousands more were expelled from their jobs and many were driven from their homes. Nationalist fears of sectarianism had been further increased by the plan to establish a local police force. The Bishop of Down and Connor, Joseph MacRory, wrote to the Bishop of Southwark, Peter Amigo, in September 1920: 'Just now we are threatened in Belfast with Carsonite police, most of whom would be taken from the very men whose awful bigotry has victimised our poor Catholic workers for the past ten weeks.'[2]

But the establishment of the state proceeded despite widespread nationalist opposition north and south of the border. There was an 89 per cent turnout in the Northern Ireland elections of 24 May 1921, where intimidation and violence were widespread.[3] The Unionists got forty seats, with six each going to the abstentionist Sinn Féin and the Nationalists. King George v opened parliament on 22 June 1921 with a plea to all Irishmen 'to pause, to stretch out the hand of forbearance and conciliation, to forgive and to forget, and to join in making for the land which they love a new era of peace, contentment, and goodwill'.[4] Sir James Craig became prime minister. Cardinal Michael Logue of Armagh predicted: 'If we are to judge by the public utterances of those into whose hands power is fallen in this quarter of Ireland, we have times of persecution before us.'[5]

Violence also marked the birth of Saorstát Éireann. For the President of Dáil Éireann, Éamon de Valera, the Treaty signed on 6 December 1921 fell far short of what the country could have got. He told a private session of Dáil Éireann on 14 December: 'I was captaining a team and I felt that the team should have played with me to the last and that I should have got the last chance which I felt would have put us over and we might have crossed the bar in my opinion at high tide.'[6] For de Valera the Treaty meant an acceptance of colonial status with all the trappings of imperialism—an oath of allegiance, a governor general, British bases, and partition. As the debate progressed, he said despairingly on 6 January 1922: 'There is no use in discussing it. The whole of Ireland will not get me to be a national apostate and I am not going to connive at setting up in Ireland another government for England.'[7]

For Michael Collins, the architect of the Sinn Féin military campaign against the British between 1919 and 1921, the Treaty was 'a stepping stone' and 'freedom to achieve freedom'. Aware of the terrible alternative of renewed war with Britain, throughout the debates Collins expressed impatience with suggestions to renegotiate: 'I have done my best to secure absolute separation from England. . . . I am standing not for shadows but for substances and that is why I am not a compromiser.'[8] Collins justifiably felt that Dublin had got a good deal. But it was a compromise 'without the supportive symbolic system'[9] of the Republic, which the purists like de Valera claimed as their own.

On 7 January 1922 the Treaty was carried in the Dáil by 64 votes to 57. De Valera resigned as President and was replaced on 10 January by Arthur Griffith. The former wrote to his close friend, the rector of the Irish College in Rome, Monsignor John Hagan, on 13 January 1922:

A party set out to cross the desert, to reach a certain fertile country beyond—where they intended to settle down. As they were coming to the end of their journey and about to emerge from the desert, they came upon a broad oasis. Those who were weary said: 'Why go further—let us settle down here and rest, and be content.' But the hardier spirits would not, and decided to face the further hardships and travel on. Thus they divided—sorrowfully, but without recriminations.[10]

With sentiments of that kind in mind, the historian T. Desmond Williams wrote of the civil war many years later:

All wars are the product of indecision, chance, misunderstanding, and personal will. They come from the environment in which people work and the conviction of those in power. . . . Perhaps the extremists on both sides alone knew their own minds and the contingent situation better than those of more moderate opinions.[11]

Ideology, conviction, accident, personality and geography all helped divide much of the country into Treatyites and anti-Treatyites, and into different camps within the blocs. The Irish political world in 1922 remained a kaleidoscope of shifting emotions and ambivalences. It took the violence of civil war to force many finally to take sides.

The vote in the Dáil on 7 January was not the formal act of

ratification required under Article 18 of the Treaty. Nicholas Mansergh writes that members elected to the House of Commons of Southern Ireland, as established by the Government of Ireland Act, were the designated body. The assembly was summoned to ratify the Treaty on 14 January in Dublin's Mansion House. It did so unanimously and then set about selecting a Provisional Government. This was not to supplant the Dáil ministry, under the presidency of Arthur Griffith. The two existed in parallel, with overlapping membership: Griffith was not in the Provisional Government, but Collins, W.T. Cosgrave and Kevin O'Higgins were in both. The Irish Free State (Agreement) Bill was not enacted until 31 March 1922.[12]

In the months between the establishment of the Provisional Government and the outbreak of civil war, there were three tiers of power in the country. Firstly, there was the cabinet of the Second Dáil, presided over by Arthur Griffith. Secondly, there was the cabinet of the Provisional Government, of which Michael Collins was chairman and Minister for Finance. Thirdly, there was Michael Collins the burgeoning politician, who grew in stature and influence as the months progressed.

The first task confronting the Provisional Government was to secure military control of the country. Michael Collins set about achieving that objective, in which he was helped in particular by two members of his general headquarters staff, Gearóid Ó Súilleabháin and Seán MacMahon. Collins's charismatic personality helped win converts to the side of the Provisional Government, and his radical attitude towards the Northern Ireland state revealed that he had not abjured the revolutionary goal of unity.

The Irish Republican Army (IRA) had split over the Treaty: nine members of general headquarters staff were in favour and four were against. That split was also evident in the rank and file, where the decision of a local leader often determined the direction loyalties took. On 18 January 1922 the Provisional Government agreed— unwisely as it turned out—to allow the holding of a special IRA convention on 26 March, but permission was revoked as the general situation in the country deteriorated. Dissident IRA members regarded Michael Collins and General Richard Mulcahy as traitors. Rory O'Connor and Liam Mellowes emerged among the leading militarists on the anti-Treaty side. Mellowes, for example, had said during the Treaty debate on 17 December 1921: 'I stand now where I always stood, for the Irish republic. . . . The Treaty is a denial of the Republic. . . . We are defending it.'[13]

In early 1922, as the situation looked like developing into a shooting war, the British evacuation was slowed down. In March Limerick became the centre of conflict, and a brokered peace narrowly averted civil war. An armoured car, sent to help secure the defence of Templemore, Co. Tipperary, was seized on 20 March by anti-Treatyites. Despite the cancellation on 15 March of government permission to hold the army convention, the IRA went ahead, in defiance of that order. Over two hundred delegates were in attendance. Rory O'Connor hinted at a press conference on 30 March that any attempt to hold a general election would be stopped by force. Asked if that meant the establishment of a military dictatorship, he replied: 'You can take it that way if you like.'[14]

The pro-Treaty *Freeman's Journal*, a newspaper which had courageously reported the excesses of British rule in Ireland during the War of Independence, published an account of the convention's proceedings and had its offices and printing presses attacked with sledgehammers. The *Clonmel Nationalist* earlier had seen the IRA smash the press, melt down the type and threaten the editor. *The Cork Examiner* was also threatened. These acts of intimidation and vandalism prefigured what was to happen in fascist Italy and Nazi Germany during the 1920s and 1930s. There was more than just a passing resemblance between the IRA and the proto-fascist movements in Europe at that time. The radical authoritarianism of the IRA was evident when a proposal to set up a dictatorship was discussed at the convention. Todd Andrews, a young anti-Treatyite, wrote in his memoirs: 'I did not see anything wrong with an IRA military dictatorship but I resented the breakdown in discipline.' Andrews believed that the indecision at the convention meant that 'from that moment we Republicans were beaten'.[15]

The proposal to set up a dictatorship was defeated, but the army convention moved to the right. A new executive with the Limerick-man, Liam Lynch, as chief of staff was appointed, and Éamon de Valera and other Sinn Féin political leaders were marginalised. An anti-Treatyite party, Cumann na Poblachta, had been founded, but de Valera proved more incapable than unwilling to exercise control over doctrinaire and intransigent anti-Treatyites. The 'chief', as he was still known to his followers, toured Munster in March. He was under great personal strain and may have suffered what would be known today as a nervous breakdown. That may help explain the content of some of his speeches, which one cannot excuse on the grounds of bad reporting. At Thurles he was reported as having said that if the volunteers of the future tried to complete the work the volunteers of the previous four years had been attempting, they 'would have to wade through Irish blood, through the blood of the soldiers of the Irish Government, and through, perhaps, the blood of some of the members of the Government in order to get Irish freedom'.[16] In Cork, Collins called the various speeches the 'language of madness' and may have been unwittingly correct in the literal sense. A subsequent attempt by de Valera to refute the editorial interpretation of his words was not very convincing, and he never denied in a plausible way that he had used those words.[17]

Meanwhile there were widespread seizures of arms and explosives throughout the country by the anti-Treatyite IRA. Raids were conducted on public houses and shops to acquire provisions. For example, money was seized from 323 post offices in the three weeks from 29 March to 19 April. Rory O'Connor and his followers captured the Four Courts on 14 April and the anti-Treatyites began to fortify the building. They also took the Masonic Hall in Molesworth Steet, and later published a list of members of the lodge found in the building. To the surprise of many, a number of Catholics were masons and one, a Catholic baker in Rathfarnham, almost went out of business. Kilmainham Jail, the Kildare Street Club and the Ballast Office were also taken over in Dublin. The 'irregulars', as government sources termed the opposition, were engaged in armed attacks in the capital and in other parts of the country. On 25 April Brigadier General Adamson was shot dead in Athlone in a skirmish with republicans who had taken over a hotel in the centre of the town. On 27 April there was fighting in Mullingar.[18]

The Labour Party and the trade union movement, having decided to contest the forthcoming June general election, held a fifteen-hour general strike 'against militarism' on 24 April. Meetings and pro-parliamentary demonstrations were held in eleven large towns and cities.[19] Labour, having rejected social radicalism for social democracy, went 'the whole hog and accepted all the trappings of An Saorstát'.[20] It was fortunate for the new state that Tom Johnson, the Labour leader, remained such a strong parliamentarian.[21] The growing violence and the stridency of the language on the opposing sides surprisingly did not prevent a political accommodation between Collins and de Valera in the June election. They agreed in May on a pact whereby the two sections of Sinn Féin would be represented on a national panel in proportion to their existing Dáil strength; there was further agreement on the division of ministries afterwards. This was a last desperate effort by Collins to enable de Valera and the moderates to break with Liam Lynch and Rory O'Connor.[22] The strategy did not please many of Collins's followers, including Griffith, and it satisfied militant anti-Treatyites even less. Many would have preferred an election with a straight fight between the two sides.

The success of the pact—already in a state of terminal decay by polling day—was not helped by the publication of the draft constitution on the morning of the election. In another political context, that document might have been praised for its liberal tone,[23] but to the anti-Treatyites, it had the king stamped all over it. The poll, which took place on 16 June, showed that there was a majority in the country in favour of the settlement. Out of a total of 128 seats, 58 pro-Treaty Sinn Féin and 36 anti-Treatyite Sinn Féin candidates were returned. The Labour Party took 17 seats, the Farmers' Party won 7 and independents got 10. The outcome was a victory for the Provisional Government.

The garrison in the Four Courts was intent upon armed confrontation. On 18 June an IRA convention narrowly rejected a motion to declare war on the remaining section of the British garrison in Dublin. Four days later Sir Henry Wilson, who had become MP for North Down after retiring as Chief of the Imperial General Staff in February 1922, was shot dead outside his home in London. It is now accepted that the assassination had been ordered by Collins some considerable time before and had never been countermanded.[24] Two men were hanged for the crime. Wilson's death was not universally mourned in Ireland, where one semi-literate anti-Treatyite wrote on 24 June: 'Have you heard of the shooting of that cur, Sir Henry Wilson? He is a good scoundrel out of the way, if they be able to get at Craig, Coote and McGuffin, they will have got the best of the Devil's pigeons.'[25]

Prime Minister David Lloyd George held the anti-Treatyites responsible and issued the Provisional Government with little short of an ultimatum to act against the Four Courts garrison. Fearful that his coalition government might disintegrate as a consequence of the assassination, the British prime minister wrote to Collins on 22 June stating that he and his colleagues regarded 'the continued toleration of this rebellion defiance of the principles of the Treaty [and] incompatible with its faithful execution'. He continued: 'the ambiguous position of the Irish Republican Army can no longer be ignored by the British army'. Lloyd George's letter was summarised as follows for the Irish cabinet: 'Letter . . . stating that documents found upon the murderers of Sir Henry Wilson clearly connected them with the Irish Republican Army and revealed the existence of a definite conspiracy against the peace and order of Britain.' Lloyd George also related that information had reached him that 'active preparations were on foot to resume attacks upon British subjects'. The British government felt that it 'had a right to expect that the necessary action towards the occupants of the Four Courts would be taken by the Provisional Government without delay'. Pieces of artillery were offered to help in the attack.[26] It was further understood that the British were in possession of proof 'revealing the existence of a conspiracy on the part of certain elements in Ireland to undertake attacks against life and property in England and in this country'.[27] Diarmuid O'Hegarty, secretary to the Provisional Government, wrote to Lloyd George requesting that the information at the disposal of the British government should be placed in the hands of the Provisional Government when the newly elected Dáil—due to meet on 1 July—would be called upon to support such measures as might be considered adequate. O'Hegarty explained the strategy of the government for dealing with the anti-Treatyites:

> The Government was, however, satisfied that those forces contained within themselves elements of disruption which given time would accomplish their complete disintegration and relieve the Government of the necessity of employing methods of suppression which would have perhaps evoked a certain amount of misplaced sympathy for them.

The British were not willing to share the information. Winston Churchill, Colonial Secretary, sent a telegram to Arthur Griffith and Michael Collins on 23 June stating that the information in possession of the British government was 'at present of a highly secret character, and cannot be disclosed'.[28]

The British cabinet discussed a response from Collins on 24 June. It appeared that he was not in a hurry to take action. Matters would receive his 'personal attention', but there was no promise that the 'immediate action demanded by the prime minister would be taken'.[29] As the Provisional Government saw their room for manoeuvre disappear, the British prepared to send sufficient ships to Dublin to house 400 prisoners. Churchill was requested to draft a proclamation to be issued after the attack on the Four Courts. The decision was taken by the British government to surround the Four Courts on 25 June. However, the British commander-in-chief, General Sir Nevil Macready, balked at the idea of taking unilateral action without giving the necessary 72-hour notice to signify the breaking of the Truce. There was a danger that a British attack would fail to capture the leaders of the revolt and possibly drive the two wings of the IRA back together again. Macready decided to wait and see.[30]

On 26 June the irregulars raided a garage in Dublin and commandeered sixteen cars. Their commanding officer was arrested and, in retaliation, the Four Courts garrison kidnapped Collins's assistant chief of staff, J.J. 'Ginger' O'Connell. The Provisional Government discussed an ultimatum from the Four Courts at its meeting on 27 June that O'Connell was being held 'as a hostage pending the release of Leo Henderson who had been arrested in connection with the raid on Ferguson's garage, Baggot St.' While members of the Executive Council regarded the kidnapping as a provocation which could not go unchallenged, Collins remained reluctant to fight.[31] But what was the alternative?

Diarmuid O'Hegarty, in a handwritten note, recorded that the government's ultimatum to the occupants of the Four Courts had been ignored, and artillery fire was opened by government troops on the building about 4 o'clock in the morning of 28 June 1922.[32] The garrison surrendered on 30 June. Among the prisoners were Rory O'Connor, Liam Mellowes, Dick Barrett and Joe McKelvey. Fighting also took place in the city centre, but O'Connell Street was in the hands of government forces by 5 July. Collins, despite the obvious personal distress caused to him by having to fight against close friends and former comrades, pressed the military initiative and drove the anti-Treatyite forces back into the countryside. On 8 August, troops arrived in Cork by sea and secured the state's second city. The irregulars were forced to flee all the major cities. It was now a guerrilla war, but one that the government appeared confident it could win.

The Irish army stood at 10,000 and it rose dramatically in numbers until it was over 40,000 by the end of the civil war.

Michael Collins had resigned his position as chairman of the Provisional Government on 12 July, the better to devote himself, as commander-in-chief, to the crushing of the military uprising. It has been argued that the emergence of William T. Cosgrave as acting chairman of the Provisional Government signified the 'sidelining' of Collins. Nothing could have been further from the truth. If anything, the physical force challenge enhanced his personal power and dominance over his jittery colleagues.[33] Collins made a significant difference to the government's military effort. The decision to land troops from the sea in the south and south-west wrong-footed the irregulars. Landings in Cork and Kerry provided an element of surprise which helped restore the military initiative to the government forces.[34]

In contrast, de Valera proved unable to exercise significant influence over the military wing of the anti-Treatyites either before or after the outbreak of hostilities. He was on his way into Dublin by car when he heard news of the Four Court bombardment. His immediate reaction was to blame the British: 'England's threat of war—that, and that alone—is responsible for the present situation. In face of England's threat, some of our countrymen yielded.'[35] De Valera rejoined his old battalion. The armed conflict relegated the importance of politics to a low level and de Valera simply lost his role. (The Dáil was not reconvened and TDs were left without a forum.) De Valera went on the run and made his way to the south where he joined his besieged colleagues. While anti-Treatyite forces regrouped in Fermoy barracks in August, de Valera was told of the killing of his close friend Harry Boland. Kathleen O'Connell, who was de Valera's long-serving secretary, recorded: 'He felt it terribly—crushed and broken. He lost his most faithful friend.' As he was preparing the evacuation of the last anti-Treatyite stronghold, de Valera recorded that it was 'one of the most miserable days I have ever spent'.[36] The tragedy was that Michael Collins, too, had lost one of his closest friends. He wrote to his fiancée, Kitty Kiernan, on 2 August: 'I passed Vincent's Hospital and saw a small crowd outside. My mind went into him [Harry Boland] lying dead there and I thought of the times together. . . . I'd send a wreath but I suppose they'd return it torn up.'[37] That was the tragedy of civil war.[38]

Arthur Griffith died suddenly on 12 August 1922. The personal strain on him had been very great that summer and he had had a difficult time with a number of his colleagues.[39] Ministers lived in a state of panic. The political situation was worsened by the animosity among the most senior members of the Executive Council.[40] Had Collins not been in the background, it might not have been possible to sustain the unity of cabinet. Ministers faced that terrifying prospect when Collins was shot dead in an ambush at Béal na mBláth, Co. Cork on 22 August. Not yet 32 years of age, Collins had grown in stature and had come to tower over his contemporaries on both sides of the civil war divide. It is idle to speculate about what he might have achieved had he lived, but it is certain that his death temporarily removed the ballast from the Irish ship of state. No leader could have replaced him adequately, but there could not have been a more cruel contrast than that between Collins and William T. Cosgrave, the new chairman of the Provisional Government. Cosgrave, at 42, was *a primus inter pares*. Collins had been a national leader and the country had not merely lost in him a commander-in-chief; the Provisional Government and, some would have said, the country, had been orphaned.

Failure to keep discipline in an expanding army was almost inevitable without Collins. Mutiny was the ultimate outcome, and there was an earlier breakdown of discipline on the government side. The activities of the 'Oriel House gang', as they were known, introduced a sinister element into the prosecution of the civil war. Known as the Protective Corps or CID (Criminal Investigation Department), these loyal followers of Collins operated in plain clothes and were given something of a free hand. They lived in Oriel House near Dublin's Amiens Street and there were allegations that prisoners and anti-Treatyite suspects had been maltreated there.[41] 'Chivalry and humanity were early casualties on both sides in the civil war,' commented the Free State Officer Niall C. Harrington, in his memoirs.[42] There was cause for concern over the behaviour of government troops, particularly in Kerry. This brought about considerable conflict between the new GOC, Richard Mulcahy, and Kevin O'Higgins, Minister for Economic Affairs.[43] Were extra-judicial killings condoned or tolerated by the Provisional Government? The answer to that question is emphatically in the negative, but there was a certain indulgence shown by elements in the military. That was particularly so in Kerry where there were extra-judicial killings of prisoners by government forces at Cahirciveen, Ballyseedy, Countess Bridge and Killarney.[44] In July 1923, the body of Noel Lemass, the brother of a future Taoiseach, was dumped in the Wicklow mountains.[45] But despite these extra-judicial killings, the Irish military were usually kept strictly under civilian discipline, compared to the experience of civil wars in other countries.

It was the view of an older Seán Lemass, who was to become Taoiseach in 1959, that the civil war should have ended after the fall of Fermoy.[46] There is evidence to suggest that de Valera was also of that opinion. John Hagan, the rector of the Irish College in Rome, was at home in Wicklow on holiday in early September 1922. A political supporter and strong influence on de Valera, Monsignor John Hagan set out to help end the hostilities. His friend Seán T. O'Kelly had been jailed in Kilmainham. O'Kelly had written to the rector requesting his intervention as soon as possible 'for the good of the country'.[47] He had also prevailed upon Oscar Traynor, a future Fianna Fáil minister, and the IRA leader from Cork, Tom Barry, to try to halt the fighting. Barry wrote to the Minister for Defence, Richard Mulcahy, who sent the chief of military intelligence, Liam Tobin, to interview the men in question. Unfortunately the encounter ended in 'hot words on both sides' after Tobin, according to O'Kelly, attempted to bully Barry and place obstacles in the way of the talks: 'they are going the right road to secure a continuance of the war till the very last bit of ammunition of the republicans has been expended and the last of their men imprisoned or shot', he wrote.[48] O'Kelly, writing to Hagan before he had left for Ireland, had suggested that two of the bishops, Michael Fogarty of Killaloe and Edward Mulhern of Dromore, should be invited to act as intermediaries.

In Dublin, Hagan put O'Kelly's suggestion to Mulcahy. The Minister for Defence facilitated the peace moves, but he was not too hopeful of success. The rector received a disappointing reply from Rory O'Connor and Liam Mellowes in Mountjoy jail. There was no willingness to compromise. Both men wrote on 6 September that they hoped that the 'day of good intentions will never set in Ireland'. With 'passionate longing' they hoped, too, that

> . . . the section of the countrymen now in arms against the republic should end the senseless and criminal strife and unite with us in its defence against the common enemy whose devilish

machinations have, by the aid of the powerful and corrupt press in this country, stampeded them into continuing the war which the British forces hitherto failed to make effective.

Despite the promise to hand on the rector's letter to their superiors outside the prison, Hagan did not feel that the two men showed 'anything like eagerness to arrive at an understanding'. He urged both O'Connor and Mellowes to meet the two men from Kilmainham (Barry and Traynor) since they would be 'giving away no principles'. Mulcahy gave permission for the meeting, but Barry escaped from jail in the meantime, and a note from the minister to Mellowes and O'Connor went unacknowledged.[49] Mulcahy had met de Valera, without cabinet approval, on 6 September, but the minister came away with the feeling that there was 'no room for discussion'.[50] Hagan contacted de Valera, only to be told that 'nothing will be gained by seeing us at the moment'.[51] Further peace efforts by the leader of the Labour Party, Tom Johnson, and the trade unionist William O'Brien had the same negative results.

The time for talking was over. Mulcahy requested the cabinet in mid-September to introduce emergency powers, the extension of capital punishment and the establishment of military courts for soldiers or civilians found guilty of a range of crimes. The Dáil approved the draconian legislation on 28 September by 48 votes to 18.

Was de Valera in a position to halt the civil war at that stage? It appears that he was unwilling even to try. A meeting of the anti-Treatyite army executive was held on 17 October and a decision was taken to set up an 'emergency government' of the 'republic', with de Valera as president. Austin Stack was nominated as Minister for Finance, P.J. Ruttledge was given Home Affairs, Seán T. O'Kelly got Local Government, Robert Barton was given Economic Affairs and the jailed Liam Mellowes was made Minister for Defence. Meanwhile, Hagan had returned to Rome. In November he received a letter from Bishop Thomas O'Doherty of Galway: 'Things are not very hopeful here. De Valera has allowed himself to be hoisted into the "presidency" on the remaining bayonets of Rory O'Connor's squad.'[52]

The Provisional Government had approached the Catholic hierarchy on 4 October 1922 to secure a condemnation of the anti-Treatyites. The hierarchy published a statement on 22 October censuring the campaign of destruction which had resulted in murder and assassination and 'wrecked Ireland from end to end'. Those involved were 'guilty of the gravest sins, and may not be absolved in Confession, nor admitted to Holy Communion, if they purpose to persevere in such evil courses.'[53] De Valera was crestfallen by the words of condemnation of the bishops: 'Never was charity of judgement so necessary, and apparently so disastrously absent', he wrote on 6 November 1922 to the Archbishop of Melbourne, Daniel Mannix. He remained convinced that the 'Free State agreement must go' because it had 'brought nothing but disaster'. He warned that the government could either banish people who thought like him or execute or murder them.[54]

Erskine Childers was arrested four days after de Valera had written his letter to Mannix. He had been caught in possession of a pistol which Michael Collins had given him as a gift. On the morning when Erskine Childers stood trial at Portobello Barracks, 17 November 1922, four men who had been caught in possession of weapons were executed. (The first death sentences had been handed down in Kerry but they had not been carried out.) Childers was sentenced to death by firing squad on 18 November and the sentence was carried out six days later.

Childers had been born in London on 25 June 1870. His mother was a Barton of Glendalough House, Co. Wicklow. He was Clerk of the House of Commons from 1895 until 1910 when he resigned to devote himself to the cause of Irish nationalism. In 1914, his yacht *Asgard* landed a consignment of German guns at Howth for the Irish Volunteers. Joining the British navy in 1914, he won the DSC. Childers resumed his activities on behalf of Irish Home Rule after demobilisation. He was elected Sinn Féin TD for Wicklow in 1921 and served in Dáil Éireann's Ministry of Propaganda. He was secretary to the Irish plenipotentiaries in the Treaty negotiations of 1921. His cousin Robert Barton was a member of the Irish delegation. Both took the anti-Treaty side. Amongst all the anti-Treatyites, a particular animus was reserved for Childers by a number of government ministers.

His execution evoked great revulsion in the Dáil and gave rise to the utterance of at least one expression of anglophobic vindictiveness.[55] The execution of Childers shocked and outraged many citizens who did not support the anti-Treatyites. For example, the coadjutor bishop of Armagh, Patrick O'Donnell, wrote to John

Hagan: 'No event of recent years has saddened me in the same way as the execution of Erskine Childers. Since I heard of it I think of little else.' He had reluctantly intervened, but had 'nothing for my pains'. O'Donnell found: 'All the executions are deplorable especially that of poor Childers. I said Mass for him today. . . . Up to then the Irish government seemed to me to have done well on the whole and then, I can judge, wisdom left them. I trust it may soon return. . . . Our Cardinal and the Archbishop of Dublin are against the executions.'[56] (The government carried out three other executions on 30 November.)

On the anti-Treatyite side, Liam Lynch stated on 27 November that all TDs who had voted for Mulcahy's 'Murder Bill' would be shot on sight. A captured order, purporting to be signed by Thomas Derrig as 'adjutant-general' of the anti-Treaty forces (later Minister for Education), was sent to Cahir Davitt in the army command's legal staff. (Davitt, who had served as a judge in the Sinn Féin courts, was appointed a judge-advocate general in the Adjutant-General's Department of the Irish army.) It provided for the execution of all members of the Provisional Government, all members of the Dáil who had voted for the Army (Special Powers) Resolution, the members of the Army Council and most if not all of the army command's legal staff. Davitt recorded: 'We were generally sceptical as to whether this wholesale "execution" order was to be accepted at its face value when our doubts were tragically resolved on 7 December.'[57] Seán Hales, a distinguished west Cork military leader in the War of Independence, was shot dead as he left the Ormond Hotel on his way to Leinster House. A second deputy, Pádraig Ó Máille, who had been travelling in the same side car, had been seriously wounded.

This crisis eclipsed the formal coming into being of Saorstát Éireann (Irish Free State) on 6 December 1922. Davitt was summoned to the adjutant-general's office where the Army Council had been meeting on the evening of 7 December. Mulcahy told him that they had decided to set up a system of military committees to deal summarily with persons arrested in possession of arms, ammunition or explosives, while retaining the military courts to deal with cases other than those of persons caught red-handed. Davitt saw the committees as being in the nature of a drumhead court-martial. He agreed to draft the communiqué which appeared under Mulcahy's name the following day in the press.[58] At a government meeting that evening, a decision was taken to execute Rory O'Connor, Liam Mellowes, Dick Barrett and Joe McKelvey. Mulcahy and Eóin MacNeill were believed to have proposed and seconded the motion. Kevin O'Higgins accepted the decision only with great reluctance when he allowed himself to be persuaded that there was no other way. The following morning the four were executed in Mountjoy as a 'reprisal' for the assassination of Hales and as a 'solemn warning' to those 'engaged in a conspiracy of assassination against the representatives of the Irish People'. Archbishop Byrne, who had sought to dissuade the government, wrote in dismay to Cosgrave on 10 December that the term 'reprisals' had been used in the army communiqué: 'Now, the policy of reprisals seems to me to be not only unwise but entirely unjustifiable from the moral point of view. That one man should be punished for another's crime seems to me to be absolutely unjust. Moreover, such a policy is bound to alienate many friends of the Government, and it requires all the sympathy it can get.'[59] The superior general of the Calced Carmelites, Peter Magennis, a friend of Mellowes, reacted in a vigorous fashion: 'I know these fellows [ministers] were contemptible curs, but it never occurred to me they were such vampires. Drunk with this sudden greatness their one idea is to revel in human blood.'[60]

While there were no further executions of Dáil members, the anti-Treatyites embarked upon an intensified campaign of wholesale destruction in December. The property of prominent government supporters was destroyed. On 10 December the home of Seán McGarry was set on fire by a party of armed men who failed to allow the family time to reach safety. His wife and two children were injured, one of the children dying later as a result of the burns. The premises of Mrs Nancy Wyse Power in Camden Street and the offices of two firms of Dublin solicitors were destroyed in December by arson. Lord Glenavy's eldest son, Gordon Campbell, had his home burned down on 18 December. Bombs were thrown at the offices of the *Irish Independent* in Middle Abbey Street. The premises of Denis McCullagh were wrecked by an explosion. On 20 December, a day when news of seven further executions was released, a party of armed men seized the Dublin to Belfast mail train, forced the passengers to leave and set it on fire. They then compelled the driver to crash his train into another train carrying government troops and military supplies. In another incident, two unarmed soldiers were fired on in

Dublin. One was killed and the other was seriously wounded. It was in this fashion, Davitt noted, 'we saw the old year out'.[61]

Confronted by such widespread violence and loss of life, elements on the government side took the law into their own hands. Towards the end of the month a party of armed men, who described themselves as 'the authorities', called at the lodgings of Francis Lalor, a de Valera sympathiser, and took him away by force. His body was later found near Milltown golf course. Davitt commented: 'This killing had all the appearance of being an "unofficial execution" carried out by some members of the Government's forces.' While the fighting continued until 27 April, the outcome was in little doubt; the government was conducting a war of reconquest. The executions continued without any reservations over the moral justification or expediency of the policy. Cahir Davitt explained in his memoirs:

> . . . I was not in favour of the execution policy; but I never doubted the right of the Government to adopt and enforce it. . . . The reprisal execution of O'Connor, Mellowes, McKelvey and Barrett was not merely the most justly deserved of all the executions, it was also the most justifiable. As a drastic means of ending the incipient campaign of assassination of Dáil Deputies its success was immediate and conclusive.[62]

In the view of William T. Cosgrave's son, Liam, the policy cut short the war: 'The government considered the executions shortened the Civil War and saved more innocent persons being killed by the Irregulars. My father accepted responsibility for the actions of his government.'[63]

The last executions were carried out in June 1923 over a month after Frank Aiken, who had succeeded Liam Lynch as anti-Treatyite 'chief of staff' gave the order to 'dump arms'. When the shooting stopped, it was evident that there were no real victors: 'In civil war, alas, there is no glory; there are no monuments to victory or victors, only to the dead', Todd Andrews wrote in his memoirs.[64] The civil war had driven Monsignor John Hagan to wonder if the previous two years had justified his 'theory that there was never such a thing as genuine Irish nationality, and that we really are an amalgamation of clans, each well pleased with itself if it secures a job or prevails in some similar way over the other.'[65] Hagan's undue pessimism did highlight the difficulties facing the new Irish political class in the construction of the modern Irish state; the sizeable anti-Treatyite faction had yet to accept the legitimacy of the state. The civil war cost the state about £17m and material destruction was estimated at about £30m. Estimates were £10.5m in 1923/24 for an army which came to stand at over 40,000. The Dáil was told in April 1923 that a deficit of over £4m had accumulated over the previous year and this had been met by borrowing.[66] In 1923/24, 30 per cent of all national expenditure went on defence and 7 per cent more on compensation for property losses and personal injuries. In 1926/27 state expenditure was £28m, of which £1.7m was paid in compensation.[67] Government sources spoke of 800 army deaths between January 1922 and April 1924, according to Hopkinson.[68] When the anti-Treatyite casualties are added to those of the army, the figures have been estimated at between 4,000 and 5,000 military deaths. In the absence of further research, this estimate appears to be much too high.[69] But whatever the financial burden and the loss of life, it was difficult to quantify the measure of bitterness which the Treaty split had injected into the political bloodstream of the new state. Although the fighting stopped in April 1923, the government still had to house about 10,000 internees, some of whom went on hunger strike. There was no official willingness, despite protestations from prominent clergymen, to allow an early mass release. A general election was held on 27 August while the country was still in an unsettled state. The anti-Treaty Sinn Féin won 44 out of 153 seats. The Labour Party retained only 14 seats. The government party, Cumann na nGaedheal, which had been founded in March 1923, took a disappointing 63 seats in a Dáil which had been enlarged from 128; that was a gain of only five seats. Éamon de Valera had been arrested on an election platform in Ennis, Co. Clare on 12 August, only to be released in July 1924. Nevertheless, he polled 17,762, to his Cumann na nGaedheal opponent's 8,196.[70] He had to wait until 1927 to demonstrate that he had the potential to lead his followers to electoral victory.

De Valera's rival, William T. Cosgrave, did not give inspiring leadership, but he had a safe pair of hands and was intent upon providing popular legitimacy for the Free State. Cosgrave held the position of president of the Executive Council until 1932.[71]

The struggle to provide the state with popular legitimacy between

1922 and 1932 placed enormous strains on personal relations between ministers. The civil war had thrown men together who differed in temperament and ideology. The country's transition to political normality helped expose the suppressed tensions and personality conflicts in the Executive Council and within the army.

THE ARMY MUTINY AND THE SEARCH FOR LEGITIMACY

One of the most pressing tasks confronting the government in 1923 was to reduce the army to peacetime requirements and recruit more members to the gardaí. Eoin O'Duffy (aged 30) had been named chief commissioner of the gardaí in August 1922.[72] Under the direction of the Minister for Home Affairs, Kevin O'Higgins, the first batch of gardaí had occupied 19 stations in September and the force was gradually extended to the rest of the country by the end of 1923. About 3,000 had joined by the end of 1922 and the authorised strength was brought up to nearly 4,500 in the first half of 1923. The gardaí and the Dublin Metropolitan Police (DMP) were amalgamated in 1925. O'Higgins told a parade of recruits in February 1923: 'The internal politics and political controversies of the country are not your concern.'[73] While it was difficult to re-establish the rule of law in the country, it was soon possible to ensure that debts could again be collected, court orders enforced and summonses served. O'Higgins reorganised the Oriel House-based DMP G Division. Colonel David Neligan was assigned the task of leading the new detective unit, to be called the Special Branch, and excesses gradually became a civil war memory.

The army proved more difficult to reorganise. Richard Mulcahy was the Minister for Defence.[74] Seán MacMahon was chief of staff, Gearóid Ó Súilleabháin was the adjutant-general, and Seán Ó Murthuile quartermaster-general. Together they made up the Council of Defence. There were about 49,000 men in the army in June 1923, of whom about 3,000 were commissioned officers. The immediate peacetime objective was to reduce the army to about 20,000, of whom 1,400 would be commissioned officers. There was incipient revolt in July 1923 among a group of officers identified with the old IRA organisation. They felt that Mulcahy was much more sympathetic to the advice of Irish Republican Brotherhood (IRB) members in the high command. Nevertheless, about 400 officers retired in August 1923 with either a lump sum or in the knowledge that there were jobs reserved for them in the public service. Mulcahy pressed on to secure his twin objectives of demobilisation and reorganisation before the end of the financial year, March 1924. However, progress was slow and the work of government remained one of 'compromise, vacillation and inconsistency'.[75] The Minister for Industry and Commerce, Joseph McGrath, was sympathetic to the old IRA. Kevin O'Higgins remained a critic of Mulcahy. Cosgrave, out of sympathy with Mulcahy's tactics, attempted to mollify the old IRA, but without success. Mulcahy was informed on 9 January 1924 that an attempt might be made within days to take over certain barracks in different parts of the country. The minister briefed Cosgrave about the deteriorating situation on 13 January and was highly critical of his colleague Joe McGrath. A few days later there were further alarming reports that the old IRA planned to assassinate prominent officers and seize barracks. Michael J. Costello, who was in army intelligence in 1924, recalled that the idea of the mutineers was to rebuild a strong old IRA group in the army; he felt that those officers had the 'encouragement' of McGrath, who had 'the special confidence of Cosgrave'. The dissidents were led by Colonel Frank Thornton, Major-General Liam Tobin and Colonel Charles F. Dalton. Fortunately for Mulcahy, one of the conspirators was a member of army intelligence; the officer was conveniently given an office and telephone to himself. Unknown to the conspirator, conversations in the room and on the telephone were recorded by relays of shorthand-takers.[76]

With the enforced retirement of a large number of pre-Truce officers imminent on 7 March, a letter was delivered to Cosgrave on the previous day. Signed by Dalton and Tobin, it was an 'Ultimatum to the Government of Saorstát Éireann' from the old IRA, making two demands: the suspension of army demobilisation and the removal of the Army Council. The government was given until 12 noon on 10 March 1924 to reply. What were the consequences for non-compliance? 'In the event of *your* [my emphasis] Government rejecting those proposals we will take such action that will make clear to the Irish People that we are not renegades or traitors to the ideals that induced them to accept the Treaty.'[77] McGrath, who had acted as an intermediary between the old IRA and Cosgrave, resigned from government on 7 March 1924. The military raided his home later that day. As reports came in from around the country of acts of rebellion in army barracks and of arms going missing, Eoin O'Duffy was appointed on 10 March as general officer commanding the forces of Saorstát Éireann. In the Dáil on 11 March both Cosgrave and Mulcahy appeared resolute and used the strongest language to condemn what had happened. However, in private, Cosgrave sought to defuse the situation and instructed McGrath to see both Tobin and Dalton. A letter of apology was received from the two men, making clear that they recognised the civil authority as being in absolute control of the army. That appeared to mollify Cosgrave and on 17 March he told McGrath to relay to the mutineers that they had until 20 March to surrender, together with all stolen property.

However, senior army officers took a much more serious view of the mutiny. Army intelligence, according to Costello, got information by tapping the Crown Alley telephone exchange; they discovered that the ringleaders of the mutineers were going to meet on 18 March in Devlin's hotel, Rutland Street. Costello stated that the higher army staff had decided that the hotel should be surrounded by troops on the night of the meeting. That decision was taken without consulting O'Duffy, the Minister for Defence, or any member of the Executive Council. Tobin arrived late, noticed that the hotel had been surrounded and fled. Colonel Hugo MacNeill, who was in charge of the troops, did not feel that he had the authority to enter the hotel or to arrest the officers who were meeting there. Costello had a number of telephone conversations with MacNeill and higher authorities in Portobello barracks. It was decided not to move.

Costello returned later to Portobello barracks where he found the adjutant-general, Gearóid Ó Súilleabháin, and the secretary of the Executive Council, Diarmuid O'Hegarty, in discussion. A long exchange of views took place. The objections to a raid were that it might result in bloodshed and compromise Mulcahy, but it was agreed that the raid should go ahead. The minister was not consulted because, as O'Hegarty said, it would take two days to get a decision from Mulcahy. Costello returned to Rutland Street at about 1 a.m. Colonel MacNeill led his troops into the hotel and found the mutineers hiding on the roof. The arrested officers, including Frank Thornton, were removed in lorries to Arbour Hill barracks. Troops opened fire on an arrested mutineer who had jumped out of one of the lorries on O'Connell Bridge. He was not wounded, but was recaptured.[78]

The Executive Council met twice the following day. Mulcahy submitted his report. It contained, for example, phrases like 'troops were dispatched,' 'orders were given,' 'developments were reported' and 'instructions asked for'.[79] He did not sound like a minister in charge of events. The minister then withdrew from the discussion. In the absence of Cosgrave, who was ill, the Executive Council quickly agreed to request the resignation from their administrative posts of MacMahon, Ó Súilleabháin and Ó Murthuile, to place O'Duffy in full control, and to request the removal of Mulcahy from his position as minister. As Vice-President of the Executive Council, O'Higgins communicated the decision to Mulcahy. Before resigning office, Mulcahy was instructed by O'Higgins to ask the three most senior officers in the army for their resignations. That was a particularly distressing task. In the interim, Cosgrave was to take over as acting Minister for Defence.

A committee of three had been named on 15 March to inquire into the origins of the mutiny.[80] It reported on 17 June 1924. The attempted barracks' revolt resulted in the resignation of two ministers, three major-generals, seven colonels, nearly 30 commandants, 40 captains and 19 lieutenants. One study of the episode concludes: 'Mulcahy, MacMahon, Ó Murthuile and Ó Súilleabháin were the chief victims of the mutiny, and they were the men most responsible for creating a disciplined, non-political army.'[81] The burlesque aspects of the so-called mutiny unfairly detracts from the contribution of the three senior officers who had done the state some service—even if early retirement from the force was the high price that they individually had to pay for their steadfastness in the face of incipient rebellion against the lawful civil authorities.

THE FREE STATE'S NORTHERN POLICY
Antagonism to partition had been part of the rhetoric of the army mutineers, but it is surprising how much of a non-issue the North proved to be in the early years of the new state. Indeed, the outbreak of the civil war may well have prevented serious hostilities between North and South. By June 1922 two pacts between the prime minister of Northern Ireland, James Craig, and Michael Collins—the first signed on 21 January 1922 and the second on 30 March—had broken down.[82] A dangerous situation had developed when the British army and the IRA clashed in the Belleek-Pettigoe part of County Fermanagh

in early June.[83] There was also much tension along other border areas. Collins's policy of supporting IRA activity in the North was seen to legitimise unionist attacks on Catholics in Belfast, which were, in turn, seen to call for the defence of Catholics by the IRA. With the withdrawal of the IRA from the North, this danger was averted.

Nevertheless, the situation that Cosgrave inherited was a difficult one. The northern state seemed capable of survival, contrary to the expectations of Cosgrave's predecessors. While the state had been set up under the Government of Ireland Act, disparagingly known as the 'partition act' and generally ignored by nationalists, the Treaty had provided for the continued existence of Northern Ireland. Nevertheless, acceptance of it had been a purely tactical affair. The day after the Treaty was signed, Eóin MacNeill met a northern deputation and discussed plans for a campaign of non-recognition, embracing courts of law, juries and education in the northern state.[84] Of these plans only a campaign for boycotting the northern ministry of education materialised, but Collins's interest in undermining the northern state continued.[85] The outbreak of the civil war deflected Collins's attention and his military from the North, and his aggressive northern policies were abandoned. In August 1922 a committee of five was appointed to consider the question of a northern policy.[86] A northern Presbyterian and member of the Executive Council, Ernest Blythe, who was a member of this committee, produced a memorandum urging a more peaceful approach towards the northern question. Such a strategy was adopted and the payment of northern Catholic teachers by Dublin ceased soon afterwards. But there appears to have been little support in Dublin for Blythe's recommendation that 'Catholic members of the Northern Parliament who have no personal objection to the oath of allegiance should be urged to take their seats and carry on a unity propaganda'.[87]

Article 12 of the Treaty had provided for a less taxing way of dealing with the partition question. This permitted the government of Northern Ireland to opt out of the Free State within a month. If the northern government so decided, the provisions of the Government of Ireland Act would continue in force where Northern Ireland was concerned, and in this case

> ... a Commission consisting of three persons, one to be appointed by the government of the Irish Free State, one to be appointed by

the government of Northern Ireland and one to be appointed by the British government, shall determine in accordance with the wishes of the inhabitants, so far as may be compatible with economic and geographic conditions, the boundaries between Northern Ireland and the rest of Ireland, and for the purposes of the Government of Ireland Act, 1920, and of this instrument, the boundary of Northern Ireland shall be such as may be determined by such Commission.[88]

An unsuccessful attempt had been made to avoid this in a pact signed by Collins and Craig in January 1922. The two leaders had agreed to decide on behalf of their respective governments on future boundaries between the two states. This proposal, however, was abandoned on 2 February when the leaders again met and serious differences in expectations emerged.[89] While Craig argued that only minor rectifications of the boundary were envisaged, Collins argued that 'the majorities must rule and in any map marked on that principle under the above headings we secure immense anti-Partition areas.'[90] While the Dublin government was threatened by civil war, it was not in a position to become involved with a boundary commission. Nevertheless, it could not afford to let matters slide. There were signs of a movement among northern Catholics in favour of recognition of the Belfast government. In August 1922 Captain L. MacNaghten, sent by the Executive Council to investigate the climate of opinion among nationalist politicians and businessmen in Northern Ireland, reported considerable support for recognition of the Northern parliament. The pressure for action on the Northern question increased in September 1922 when the mayor of Derry called for a conference of all those elected for Northern constituencies in 1921.[91]

Over the next three years the Dublin government's Northern policy was geared towards controlling Northern Catholic politics, emphasising the Northern government's subordinate status and trying to move towards Irish unity. On 2 October 1922 the Provisional Government appointed the North-East Boundary Bureau (NEBB) which was to be involved in gathering information and publishing propaganda over the next few years; Kevin O'Shiel, assistant law officer, produced a memorandum on the Northern situation on 6 October. He was clearly aware of the divisions among Northern Catholics and stated that Dublin would have to rely on Northern Sinn

Féin for the maintenance of its policy in Ulster. He viewed both extremists and Devlinites—the rump of the old Irish Parliamentary Party—with alarm. Recalling meetings with members of Northern advisory committees earlier in the year, he said: 'Whilst I was arguing a policy of peaceful do-nothingness in Northern Committees the two branches of the IRA were actually making united preparation'. On the other hand, he warned that the supporters of the Northern nationalist politician Joe Devlin were pressing for entry to the Northern parliament and feared that if they did so, they would secure the release of Northern political prisoners.[92] He advocated a conference of nationalists, with a majority of government supporters. On 11 October O'Shiel, Cosgrave and O'Higgins met a deputation of Northern nationalists. O'Shiel assured them that he had been working on a scheme for gathering information in connection with the Boundary Commission.[93]

On 21 and 22 November, a conference took place in Dublin, attended by O'Shiel, six MPs elected for Northern constituencies and a number of leading political figures. An advisory committee was set up to coordinate the activities of the NEBB and its legal agents in the North.[94] The legal agents appointed included three men who played a prominent part in Catholic politics—J.H. Collins of Newry, Alex Donnelly of Omagh and T.J. Harbison of Cookstown.[95] The danger of Northern Catholics developing an independent policy was thus averted. The Provisional Government again became involved in Northern politics when, in an attempt to prevent a Devlinite victory, it supported the Sinn Féin campaign during the November election for the imperial parliament.[96] On 7 December Northern Ireland formally contracted out of the Free State, and Craig stated that the Boundary Commission was *ultra vires*.[97] O'Shiel proceeded slowly with the boundary preparations. In a memorandum to each minister in May 1923, he had urged a policy of *festina lente* and had emphasised national unity, rather than the securing of more territory, as the main objective. He explained: 'hence the Boundary Commission must be regarded as a weapon, probably *the* most important weapon in this diplomatic war for National Union.' He also felt that the Boundary Commission should be allowed to take its course to the bitter end only as a last resort.[98] Furthermore, O'Shiel was concerned that Lloyd George's replacement as prime minister by Bonar Law in October rendered unlikely a settlement favourable to the Irish Free State. He felt that 'the tory Die-hards were not only in complete sympathy with the aim and objects of Northern ascendancy but were in many instances directly connected by blood with the great aristocratic, commercial and landlord families in the Six counties'.[99] He feared that an unfavourable settlement would cause unrest among Northern Catholics, and that if such unrest spread south, the Dublin government might fall.[100] However, in December 1923 a further election brought about a change in the British government, and O'Shiel felt that a considerable obstacle to the Free State's success either in conference or with the Boundary Commission had been removed.

In July 1923 the Irish Free State had appointed Eóin MacNeill as its representative on the Boundary Commission. The following month the Executive Council provided for propaganda and public relations. Hugh MacCartan was to be sent to London to keep in touch with the press there, and Labour and Liberal organisations were to be contacted.[101] O'Shiel had already informed the members of the Executive Council that he considered that the success of the boundary negotiations 'would depend enormously on the quality and persistence of our Propaganda'.[102] The NEBB's views were most clearly expressed in its *Handbook of the Ulster Question.*

On 10 May 1924 James Craig formally refused to appoint a commissioner for Northern Ireland. To bypass this difficulty, legislation was introduced at Westminster to empower the British government to appoint a third member of the Boundary Commission.[103] On 28 November 1924 the commission advertised in the press, inviting submissions to be sent before 31 December.[104] In all, 130 representations were received.[105] Evidence was heard from 585 witnesses between 3 March and 2 July 1925.[106] The NEBB's secretary, E.M. Stephens, worked closely with Northern Catholics on the preparation of evidence in support of the transfer of Northern territory to the Free State. The NEBB received the support of the majority of the clergy in the disputed areas, a support which it considered influential.[107] While no transfers from the Free State to the North were envisaged, the Free State had hoped that the northern state would be so diminished that it would be too small to be economically viable.[108]

While the sittings were underway, Craig announced a general election for 3 April 1925. Cosgrave provided both financial assistance and organisers to assist the nationalist election campaign and sent a representative north to consult the northern bishops on the election issue.[109] Hugh MacCartan, on behalf of the Dublin government, helped convene a meeting in Belfast to decide on election strategy. Nationalist candidate A.E. Donnelly, who was also one of the NEBB's legal agents, said that the next election in Tyrone and Fermanagh would be for the Dáil. Nationalists won ten seats, Sinn Féin two. Cosgrave sent telegrams of congratulation to the successful nationalist candidates, much to the annoyance of the *Belfast Newsletter*, which referred to the telegram to Joe Devlin as 'direct interference by the head of one state in the internal affairs of another'.

A leak in the *Morning Post* on 7 November 1925 predicted that the Boundary Commission would make minor transfers of territory to both the Free State and Northern Ireland. The prospect of territory being lost caused outrage in Dublin, and Eóin MacNeill resigned. Leaders of the Free State, Northern Ireland and British governments met in London to discuss the crisis. The British prime minister, Stanley Baldwin, read out details of the Boundary Commission's proposed transfers. It recommended the transfer of 183,290 acres and 31,319 people to the Free State. Of these, 27,843 were Catholics and 3,476 Protestants. Northern Ireland was to receive 49,242 acres and 7,594 people, of whom 2,764 were Catholics and 4,830 Protestants.[110]

An agreement signed in London on 3 December 1925 revoked the powers of article 12 of the Treaty in regard to the Boundary Commission and released the Free State from liability to service the United Kingdom's public debt. The Free State agreed to assume liability in respect of malicious damage in the Free State since 21 January 1919. The powers allocated to the Council of Ireland under the Government of Ireland Act were to be transferred to the government of Northern Ireland.[111] Cosgrave issued a statement to the press expressing the belief that the agreement laid 'the foundation of a new era in Irish history'. O'Higgins also expressed his satisfaction.[112] In the Dáil, Cosgrave defended the agreement, arguing that the Boundary Commission's award would have 'sown the seeds of distrust and disorder', would have bankrupted County Donegal and would have involved the transfer of 'thousands of unwilling citizens'.[113] As regards the Northern minority, he stated that there was only one real security for minorities and that was the goodwill and neighbourly feeling of the people among whom they lived; he argued that 'next to this, written guarantees are scraps of paper, and irritating scraps of paper which kill in spirit what they profess to secure in words.'[114]

There were many outraged reactions to the settlement. A meeting in Omagh, Co. Tyrone on 7 December 1925, attended by leading Northern politicians, clerics and others, issued a statement denying that they were bound by the settlement, and stating that the Free State had surrendered its trusteeship of the Northern Catholics. Notwithstanding the chorus of protests, the agreement was passed by the Dáil on 15 December and was rushed through the Senate the following day on the grounds that it was necessary for the preservation of peace and public safety. Cosgrave attempted unsuccessfully to secure the recognition of the Northern parliament by Northern nationalist MPs by sending H.A. Bradstreet, a representative of the *Morning Post*, to Northern Ireland to interview nationalist representatives both individually and collectively.[115] Cosgrave and Craig never met again. The next time leaders of the two states met face to face was when Seán Lemass visited his northern counterpart, Captain Terence O'Neill, in Belfast in 1965.

CHURCH, STATE AND CULTURE

The failure of the Boundary Commission was a tragedy foretold. The Irish Free State quickly came to accept the permanence, in the medium term at least, of partition. Religious homogeneity south of the border contributed to relative political stability, while politico-religious rivalry in the North was the cause of an endemic sectarian tension. The vitality of the various churches in Ireland in the 1920s was manifest in the thriving missionary movement which sent clergy and religious to various parts of the world. The Columban Fathers, founded in Maynooth in 1916 for the conversion of China, was a leading example of that outward-looking spirit.[116] But, at home, Irish Catholicism in the 1920s sought, as one of its major objectives, to help reinforce the legitimacy of the new state. Indeed, the political climate of Saorstát Éireann suited and reassured members of a Catholic hierarchy which had lived through the dangers of the revolutionary period. William T. Cosgrave was a devout Catholic and a close friend of Archbishop Byrne of Dublin, who had gained special permission from the Holy See to have an altar built in Cosgrave's home where Mass could be said for his family. (The Minister for Finance, Ernest

Blythe, was the only non-Catholic in the Executive Council.) Cosgrave, however, never quite succeeded in converting—and neither did he particularly wish to do so—the Irish hierarchy into Cumann na nGaedheal at prayer. John Dignan was the first bishop to break ranks and in 1924 openly identified with de Valera's anti-Treatyites. When he was consecrated in June, he predicted that 'the Republican Party is certain to return to power in a short time'. His prediction was realised in 1932.

There was general political approval for the censorious attitude of the hierarchy towards sexual morality. Modern dancing and foreign fashion were frowned upon by bishops, who feared that continental moral laxity might reach Irish shores through the medium of cinema, radio and the British yellow press. Archbishop Harty of Cashel said on 25 April 1926 that the quantity of such horrible papers circulating in the country was simply appalling.[117] On 9 May 1926 Archbishop Gilmartin of Tuam condemned foreign dances, indecent dress, company-keeping (this term was clerical code for even the most innocent kind of relationship between males and females beyond the age of puberty) and bad books. He spoke of a 'craze for pleasure—unlawful pleasure' and warned that family ties were weakened, and in other countries where there were facilities for divorce 'the family hardly existed'.[118] The same prelate admonished his flock on 8 December 1926:

> In recent years the dangerous occasions of sin had been multiplied. The old Irish dances had been discarded for foreign importations which, according to all accounts, lent themselves not so much to rhythm as to low sensuality. The actual hours of sleep had been turned into hours of debasing pleasure. Company-keeping under the stars of night had succeeded in too many places to the good old Irish custom of visiting, chatting and story-telling from one house to another, with the Rosary to bring all home in due time.[119]

A joint pastoral, issued a year earlier on 6 October 1925, warned against the 'occasions of sin' which were attendant on night dances in particular:

> To say nothing of the special danger of drink, imported dances of

an evil kind, the surroundings of the dancing hall, withdrawal from the hall for intervals, and the dark ways home have been the destruction of virtue in every part of Ireland. The dancing of dubious dances on Sunday, more particularly by persons dazed with drink, amounts to woeful desecration of the Lord's Day wherever it takes place. . . .[120]

The hierarchy somewhat innocently believed that native dancing had redemptive powers: 'Irish dances do not make degenerates'.[121] Sex was therefore a matter of considerable concern to church and state alike in the 1920s.[122] There was a naïve popular belief that, left alone, Ireland would be a paradise. This is expressed by one of the characters in David Thomson's *Woodbrook*:

Tommy said that the English were damned. . . . All Protestants were. However well they behaved on earth, they could not get to heaven, only to purgatory at the best and most of them to hell for the terrible crimes they continued to commit of which he mentioned some that had been reported lately in the papers.

It astonished me to hear him talk as if serious crime did not exist in Ireland. He believed there had been in Ireland no rape, no murder, no abuse of children in his or his father's time.[123]

Legislative initiatives on censorship, the curtailing of drinking hours and the blocking of divorce were not taken under pressure from the bishops. Bishops and politicians had a conservative Catholic outlook which would have been shared, in the main, by the leaders and members of other churches. An Intoxicating Liquor Act, which limited opening hours, was passed in 1924, and in 1927 measures were taken to reduce the number of public houses. The question of divorce revealed a pattern that was to repeat itself in church-state relations. The government sought the ruling of the hierarchy on the matter.

Before 1922 a divorce was obtained by a private Bill in parliament. Soon after independence, three private divorce Bills were introduced. The Attorney General, Hugh Kennedy, sought a decision from the Executive Council as to whether legislation would be promoted to set up the necessary procedures. Cosgrave sought the advice of Archbishop Byrne and the bishops as a body. The hierarchy meeting in October 1923 stated: 'The Bishops of Ireland have to say that it would be altogether unworthy of an Irish legislative body to sanction the concession of such divorce, no matter who the petitioners may be.' Cosgrave took note of this advice. In 1925 he wrote to a bishop concerning the situation: 'I was a child so far as my information and knowledge of the subject [divorce] was concerned.' Standing orders were suspended to prevent such a Bill being introduced in the Dáil. Despite a spirited opposition in the Dáil, the measure was upheld. Professor William Magennis summed up the contradictions in the debate: 'You cannot be a good Catholic if you allow divorce even between Protestants.'[124] There the matter rested until the introduction of Bunreacht na hÉireann in 1937. Since the foundation of the state, the Catholic Truth Society and a number of prominent clergymen had campaigned for stricter censorship laws. The Minister for Home Affairs set up a Committee of Enquiry on Evil Literature in 1926. A Censorship Bill was introduced in the summer of 1928. Three leading Irish literary figures—William Butler Yeats, George Bernard Shaw and George Russell—all condemned the legislation,[125] but their collective wrath and reputation were not sufficient to prevent the passage of the Bill, and the first censorship board was established on 13 February 1930. The committee had the power to prohibit the sale and distribution of 'indecent or obscene' books. The publishing, selling and distribution of literature advocating birth-control was also deemed to be an offence under the Act.

Theatre in the Saorstát in the 1920s enjoyed freedom from censorship. However, when the Abbey Theatre performed a new play by Seán O'Casey, *The Plough and the Stars*, in February 1926, there were vocal protests against the bringing of the tricolour into a public house in the second act. Objection was also taken to the presence in the pub on stage of a prostitute, Rosie Redmond. The play ran for two weeks, but with the lights on in the theatre and with gardaí lining the passages at the sides of the pit.[126] The social realism of the play caused deep offence, just as earlier Lennox Robinson's short story in *To-morrow* had caused upset; it concerned an Irish farm girl who had been raped and then imagined herself to be the Madonna. For his literary efforts, Lennox Robinson was sacked from his job as secretary of the Carnegie Library Trust.[127]

There were many other examples of popular intolerance. For example, Brinsley MacNamara published *The Valley of the Squinting Windows* in 1918. It was considered unacceptable by many people in the village of Delvin, Co. Westmeath. The result was the public burning of the book and the humiliation of the author. The author's father, a local schoolmaster, was boycotted and driven into exile. This was followed by a bitter legal battle in 1923. MacNamara was made registrar of the National Gallery of Ireland in 1925—a post he continued to hold until I960.[128]

The publication of James Joyce's *Ulysses* in 1922 was also a shock to romantic nationalists. Molly Bloom's luxuriation in her own sensuality did not meet with universal approval in Ireland or abroad;[129] paradoxically, the book was never banned in Ireland. But Seán O'Casey did not fare quite so well and his work was not viewed with favour by the Abbey. His plays *The Shadow of a Gunman* (1923), *Juno and the Paycock* (1924), *The Plough and the Stars* (1926) and *The Silver Tassie* (1928) did not set out to flatter the revolutionary generation of 1916–23. Liam O'Flaherty's *The Informer*, which was first published in 1925, examined the themes of betrayal and repentance. The title story in Frank O'Connor's collection *Guests of the Nation* (1931) treated the Irish nationalist struggle from the point of view of ordinary soldiers on both sides, who were the ultimate casualties. Peadar O'Donnell did not idealise the recent political past in *The Gates Flew Open* (1934) any more than he had romanticised rural life in *Islanders* (1928). Tomás Ó Criomhthain's *An t-Oileánach* was no rural pastiche. The poetry of Austin Clarke also stood in contrast to the idealised view of contemporary Ireland and her 'heroic' past; Daniel Corkery's *The Hidden Ireland* (1925) sought to define the Irish spirit in terms of 18th-century Gaelic literature.[130] The latter was much more warmly celebrated by his contemporaries than the work which sought to portray the recent Irish past in a less heroic mode.

Developments in the visual arts in the 1920s brought the non-representational revolution to Ireland. Denied due place in Irish society, it was appropriate that two women painters would be responsible for bringing Cubism to a stronghold of classical art like Dublin. Mainie Jellett and Evie Hone mounted a joint exhibition in 1924. The former had had two of her abstract works severely criticised when she had showed them in the capital the previous year.[131] They continued to run the gauntlet of the critics for many years until local provincial prejudice was finally overcome and well-deserved recognition followed.[132]

A young London-born Jewish painter, Harry Kernoff, had made his home in Dublin in the 1920s. He was influenced by the *Neue Sachlichkeit*, or New Objectivity movement, which was a reaction against Expressionism. Kernoff's early work was a quest to understand reality in the style of this new movement.[133] Jellett, Hone and Kernoff were three of a group of younger Irish painters who sought to develop their talents in the wider framework of contemporary developments in European art. Some members of the younger generation had a role model in the individualism of Jack B. Yeats. The continued hostility to innovation was a feature of Irish society in general. Similar tensions were also to be found in the world of Irish architecture.[134] Conservatism remained a feature of most aspects of Irish administrative, cultural and social life in the 1920s. The emphasis was on the need for continuity.[135]

Unfortunately, the government failed to provide adequate funding for such institutions as the National Gallery, the National Museum and the Dublin Metropolitan College of Art. However, the role of government in the patronage of culture and the arts was not negligible; the work of Dr Thomas Bodkin was before its time.[136] The latter, who was director of the National Gallery from 1927 to 1935, had been active in promoting the idea of a ministry of fine arts in early 1922. While the Saorstát did not appoint a minister for fine arts, it did fund An Gúm in 1926, an Irish-language publishing branch of the Department of Education; at first its activities were restricted to the production of school books, but that was extended to cover general works. In post-civil war Ireland, parsimony rather than philistinism was the reason for the failure to fund the arts.

Economic stringency, the close relationship of the government with the Catholic Church and a state philosophy of minimal interference have been identified as three constraining factors on the development of educational reform in the 1920s, when the main emphasis was on curriculum rather than structural change.[137] The Minister for Finance, Ernest Blythe, cut national teachers' salaries by 10 per cent in 1923. However, despite the limited state resources during their respective tenures, the two Ministers for Education, Eóin MacNeill (1923–25) and John Marcus O'Sullivan (1926–32), were responsible for significant administrative initiatives:

The department was created and its procedures established, systematic investigations were launched into various issues, a new secondary examination and curricular structure was devised, a primary certificate was introduced, a network of preparatory colleges was established and legislation was successfully promoted in the late twenties on school attendance, the universities and vocational education.[138]

Ó Buachalla argues that the policies pursued by the Cumann na nGaedheal government were 'singularly important in that they established a model which the education system followed with minor modifications for almost forty years.'[139]

The Saorstát viewed sport as an extension of the educational process and as a means of building character and national identity. The idea to hold the Tailteann games was first advanced at the Irish Race Convention in Paris in 1922 where it was proposed to stage an Irish Olympic Games. The plan was to run the games in July and this was pushed back to August, but the civil war ended that idea. The Tailteann games were held in 1924. Aonach Tailteann, as it came to be called, was also held in August 1928.[140]

The Gaelic Athletic Association (GAA) emerged as the strongest sporting and cultural organisation in the country. There was a ban on its members playing nominated garrison games: soccer, hockey, cricket and rugby. There was also a prohibition on its members attending 'banned' games. This was not a universally popular measure, but it prevailed until 1971.[141] However, the ban *mentalité* continued into the early 1990s. Few rules in any sporting organisation have produced such acrimony; the most extreme example was the removal of the head of state in 1938 as patron of the GAA for his attendance in his official capacity at an international soccer match in Dalymount Park.[142] This dispute was finally resolved in 1945 when de Valera intervened and the GAA guaranteed that no future President of Ireland would ever be so embarrassed again. On 16 April 2005, the GAA amended Rule 42 with the requisite two-thirds majority to allow, in certain circumstances, the central Council of the GAA to permit other sports in Croke Park.

Despite the establishment of the two states, the GAA remained a 32-county organisation. It retained very close relations with the Cosgrave government through the Garda Commissioner, Eoin O'Duffy, a noted sporting enthusiast. When the Minister for Posts and Telegraphs, J.J. Walsh, resigned from politics in 1927, the government lost an important link with the association. It was always going to be difficult for Cumann na nGaedheal to maintain the loyalty of GAA members; the civil war had made its own inroads into the unity of the association. The most serious split in the GAA arose as a result of the feelings provoked by the execution of two prominent and popular Clare players, Con MacMahon and Patrick Hennessy, in Limerick in 1923. According to Marcus de Burca, there were resignations in Clare when a meeting failed to carry a motion of protest against the executions. The county split and a year later anti-Treatyites, representing about 25 clubs, set up a rival county board. Unity in the county was restored in the summer of 1925.

Although the GAA had supporters in the two rival political blocs in the early 1920s, there was little danger of the association opting for one side or the other. Its financial situation was far from being solvent and the GAA had to work with the Cosgrave government to help it get its books back in order. For example, the GAA refused to pay an entertainment tax, which had been introduced by the British in 1916. Persisting in its refusal, the organisation was given an exemption in the 1925 Finance Act, together with a number of other sporting groups which played 'British' games. That was not very pleasing to GAA headquarters. It complicated relations and weakened the bonds of friendship between the government and the GAA. The Association's refusal to pay income tax, despite being notified by the Revenue Commissioners of liability, also remained a matter of some contention with Cumann na nGaedheal after 1922, but, owing to the perilous nature of the GAA's finances, the Revenue Commissioners did not pursue their claim. The Finance Act of 1927 exempted the GAA— alone among sporting organisations—from having to pay income tax. That arrangement lasted for 50 years, according to the historian Marcus de Burca.

But the relationship between Cosgrave and the GAA remained ambivalent. In the latter part of the 1920s, the GAA recouped its strength. Between 1924 and 1932, the number of affiliated clubs rose from 1,000 to 1,700. In 1928, Leinster had 600 clubs, Munster 400, Connacht 160 and Ulster 200. It was a formidable sporting and cultural organisation, which in later years was to be described as 'Fianna Fáil at play'.

Happily the unity of a number of sporting organisations had survived partition. Rugby and hockey continued to field all-Ireland national teams. This helped develop an island-wide sporting identity among the players and followers of both sports and it led to regular cross-border contact. There were no signs of disunity when, for example, the 'green jersey' was worn at Lansdowne Road on the day of a rugby international. In contrast, soccer, which was one of the sports which might have brought large sections of the poorer unionists and nationalists together, was a victim of political tensions. The Football Association of Ireland was established in June 1921. That left two rival soccer capitals, Belfast and Dublin. There was a strong following in Cork, Limerick, Waterford, Sligo and Dundalk. The two rival associations in the two states fielded two 'national' sides. Soccer, which was supported by working-class sections of urban Ireland, was partitioned. FAI clubs in the Saorstát maintained a high standard and had a strong following. Politics and sport had occasion to mix during the 1922 cup final when Shamrock Rovers played St James's Gate and the latter won in a replay. Fisticuffs broke out after the game. One Shamrock Rovers player followed an opponent into the James's Gate dressing room. IRA-man Jack Dowdall, brother of one of the players, produced a revolver and the Rovers man left in haste. However, most of the excitement was usually reserved for the pitch in the 1920s and teams like Bohemians, Athlone Town, Shelbourne and Fordsons of Cork were prominent. For a fortunate minority of the urban poor, soccer was a means of upward social mobility. The game was played with passion, and internationals in Dublin and Belfast were loyally supported.

ECONOMY AND SOCIETY

A Gaelic utopia did not rise from the ashes of 1916, 1919 or 1923. That could not be guaranteed simply by the departure of the British.[143] But the official perception of the state's progress was inflated. The *Saorstát Éireann Official Handbook* (1932) spoke glowingly about the new attractions of the country since independence. It was described as a motorist's paradise: 'Roads as good as man need desire lead from Dublin to Belfast, to Derry, to Sligo, to Galway, to Limerick, to Cork, Waterford, Wexford; and these are nobly supplemented'.[144] With its colourful cover in Book of Kells-like script, this handbook was a self-confident and assertive review of the first decade of the new state's existence. It depicted the scenic beauties of the state through the landscapes of Paul Henry, Maurice MacGonigal, Mary Duncan and

Estelle Solomons, while the art of Harry Kernoff and Seán Keating respectively provided two social realist images of a busy Dublin port and the construction of the dam for the Shannon Hydro-Electric works.[145] The Minister for Industry and Commerce, Patrick McGilligan, championed this latter undertaking, which became a symbol of the new state's road to modernisation and was captured officially for posterity on canvas by Seán Keating.

The harnessing of the Shannon was achieved in spite of the hostility of the Department of Finance, the diffidence of McGilligan's ministerial colleagues, the hostility of the parliamentary opposition and the sniping of de Valera and his associates. The contract was signed with the German firm Siemens on 13 August 1925 and Ardnacrusha power station was officially opened on 29 July 1929. The Electricity Supply Board (ESB) had been formally established by order of the executive council on 11 August 1927.[146] Despite the many difficulties, McGilligan should be given the credit for ensuring that an ambitious state electrification scheme actually got off the ground.

The establishment of a national radio station was the second and final modernising image of the new state in the 1920s. Broadcasting began from the Dublin station, 2RN, on 1 January 1926 and gave listeners 'an almost undiluted diet of live music' in the early days. About 80 per cent of transmission time was devoted to recitals. The remainder of the time was given over to language classes and programmes on gardening, poultry-keeping and history. There was a five-minute news bulletin each day, based on information taken from newspapers and foreign stations. The socialising impact of Marconi had to await later developments in the field of current affairs. A second station was opened in Cork city, but was closed down and used as a relay station only. The opening of the Athlone transmitter in 1932 enabled a listener with a valve set in any part of the country to pick up the transmission.[147] The setting up of the Agricultural Credit Corporation in 1927 was another enterprising action by the government, as were the establishment of the First Banking Commission (1926) and the Currency Commission (1927).

With certain exceptions, therefore, the government of Saorstát Éireann was far from being innovative. The emphasis was on trying to keep the administration running. In the phrase of Patrick Lynch, there was 'little use for idealism and less scope for utopianism in the Irish Free State of 1923'.[148] The secretary of the Department of Finance recorded: 'The passing of the State services into the control of a native Government, however revolutionary it may have been as a step in the political development of the nation, entailed, broadly speaking, no immediate disturbance of any fundamental kind in the daily work of the average Civil Servant.'[149] Professor Frederick Powell has argued that the Free State was 'a socially conservative regime rooted in traditional Catholic values and wedded to the interests of the large farmers, professionals classes and businessmen who supported Cumann na nGaedheal.'[150] But Professor Powell would agree that the external economic environment, a backward economy burdened by civil war debts and overwhelmingly dependent on agriculture, was unlikely to have anything other than a conservative outcome. The country's industry was based mainly on the processing of the output of agriculture—food, drink and footwear:

> Of a population of 2.97 million, the work force came to 1.3 million, and of this, 670,000 were engaged in agriculture. The estimated net output of agriculture was £49m—more than twice that of industry. The distribution of the population reflected this economic structure; 2.01 million people lived in rural areas and 0.96 million in towns. The population also had a high dependency ratio (the ratio of those above and below working age to those of working age), 38:62, reflecting patterns of continuing heavy emigration.[151]

Emigration in the period 1921–31 averaged 33,000 per annum.[152] Unemployment rose dramatically, particularly at the end of the decade when the Wall Street Crash left many Irish people with no option but to return home. Only 9,000 emigrated in 1931, 801 of whom went to the United States. The number of Irish who left for New York in 1932 was 256.[153]

But even the harshness of the times cannot account for the swingeing economic cuts made on the poorer sections of the community during the 1920s. The reduction of the old age pension in 1924 provides the classic example of such meta-political behaviour. In 1922/23 the cost of pensions to the exchequer was £3.3 million, out of total estimates of £20m.[154] The original proposal was to reduce the pension from 10 shillings (50 pence) to 8 shillings (40 pence) per week.[155] But the loss of a shilling was as draconian as the members of the government would tolerate. Despite the obvious unpopularity of the decision, Blythe made no apology to his party. He wrote: 'I find that Cumann na nGaedheal and its branches, so far from trying to realise the position and appreciating the needs of the case, has joined in the ignorant and irresponsible chorus of criticism.' The minister felt that the government was entitled to look to well-informed and responsible citizens for support and encouragement. Criticism of the government's decision was 'somewhat deplorable', he added.[156]

Official attitudes to women in the 1920s provided yet another example of the political conservatism of the new state; although women had played a very important part in Irish revolutionary politics, the return to normality in the post-civil war period closed down many aspects of Irish life to women, who were dutifully expected to revert to the conventional role of housewife and home-maker. No woman served as a government minister between 1922 and 1979. As far as the civil service was concerned in the 1920s, there was a preference to keep women out of posts, beginning at the junior executive grade. But that was not legally possible.[157] A marriage bar lasted until 1973.[158] A marriage bar against women national teachers was introduced in 1934 and lasted until 1958.[159] That policy was to deny the state access to a major reservoir of talent.

But this did not mean that women were unable to make a mark in the Irish patriarchy. The role of Evie Hone and Mainie Jellett in the world of the visual arts has already been noted. Louie Bennett and Helena Moloney contributed to the unionisation of women in Ireland.[160] Hanna Sheehy Skeffington (1877–1946) fought throughout her life for civil and women's rights. Mary Hayden (1862–1942), professor of modern history at University College Dublin, was very much a minority in the male-dominated world of academia. The glass roof, referred to in feminist literature in the 1980s, was pitched very low in the Saorstát.

Fortunately for Cosgrave, the trade union movement was involved in its own civil war in the mid-1920s and was therefore not as free to engage a conservative government in industrial combat; division radically reduced the ability of organised labour to respond in a unified manner to the government challenge to the interests of their members. The return of James Larkin to Ireland in 1923 had set in train a struggle for the control of the leadership of the union he had helped to found in 1909.[161] The largest union in the state, the Irish

Transport and General Workers' Union (ITGWU) had been run by William O'Brien in Larkin's absence.[162] Larkin, who had been jailed for his political activities in the United States, had never been the easiest of colleagues. He was even more difficult upon his return to Dublin in April 1923. The conflict proved impossible to contain within the ITGWU. The outcome was the foundation of the Workers' Union of Ireland in July 1924.[163] This conflict poisoned relations within the trade union movement for many years.[164]

Tom Johnson and the Labour Party led the opposition in the Dáil up to 1927. De Valera and Sinn Féin continued the policy of abstentionism throughout 1924 and 1925. A divided opposition left the governing Cumann na nGaedheal to go effectively unchallenged up to the foundation of Fianna Fáil in 1926. A Cork politician, Liam de Róiste, aptly diagnosed in 1924 the political vulnerability of Cumann na nGaedheal:

> The 'pro-Treaty' party is not a cemented political party. It is a combination of diverse elements held together for the time being by the opposition of the anti-Treaty section. Pro-Treaty consists of Sinn Féin, Old Unionists, sections with diverse outlooks. The binding force is acceptance of the Treaty. Otherwise there is great divergence of opinion.[165]

The lack of party unity and discipline opened the way to political recovery for de Valera and his followers.[166]

DE VALERA AND THE RISE OF FIANNA FÁIL

Éamon de Valera and his colleagues were in no mood to give any credit to Cumann na nGaedheal for the solid work of running an Irish government. There was nothing particularly heroic about the mundane tasks of day-to-day administration. The received wisdom of the anti-Treatyites of a later generation reviewed the 'dark outlook' at the end of 1925 thus:

> The Treaty position appeared consolidated. The English king's representative styled 'Governor General' occupied the Vice-Regal Lodge in Dublin. Irish ports were in the hands of the British navy, and the Irish Free State was bound to give Britain any facilities demanded in time of war. Every member of the Dáil was required

by the Constitution to take an oath of allegiance to the British King. Free State Ministers, attired in court dress, attended a levee at Buckingham Palace: British imperialism had re-established itself in Irish social life.[167]

There were two very distinct responses to the position of political impotence in which the 44 abstentionist Sinn Féin deputies found themselves. Mary MacSwiney represented the diehard republican element who refused to compromise and give in to the demands of what she disparagingly termed 'potato politics'. Addressing the leader of the Labour Party, Tom Johnson, she said: 'Man as a spiritual force will ever in the last analysis enthuse on the things of the spirit rather than on those of the stomach. Mistake not, sir, potatoes for principles; and worse, do not exalt potatoes and attempt to pass them off as the highest and noblest principles of nationhood.'[168] That 'not an inch' approach was in contrast to the radical pragmatism of those members of Sinn Féin who were represented by Seán Lemass. In a series of articles in the anti-Treatyite *An Phoblacht*, he had written in 1925: 'Who would walk through the streets of Dublin and see what squalor foreign domination has brought and console himself with grandiloquent Philosophy? . . . We must win and soon. Give them the promise of victory.'[169]

De Valera had been released from jail in July 1924. He was in poor health and quite dispirited. Rumours circulated at the time about his retiring from political life. He was not to do so until 1959. De Valera and Seán T. O'Kelly remained in close contact with their respected adviser, Monsignor John Hagan, the rector of the Irish College in Rome. O'Kelly had resided at the Irish College in 1920 and had lobbied the Vatican with the help of the rector. Hagan had provided intellectual, moral and material support for de Valera and his family in those difficult years. During that crucial period Hagan had been one of de Valera's main theological and political advisers. He had also played an important role the previous summer in helping de Valera to orientate his political thinking. Archbishop Daniel Mannix of Melbourne, another supporter of de Valera, led an Australian pilgrimage to Rome in May and June 1925. His arrival in Europe did not please either the British or the Irish governments. Mannix had not set foot in Ireland since he had left for Australia in 1912. He had opposed the introduction of conscription in Australia during World

War I. In 1920, he set out to return to Ireland. Visiting the United States, he delivered a series of fiery nationalist sermons which angered the British government. The British government prevented him from landing in Ireland. He took up residence for a number of weeks in London. His movement to other cities in England was restricted. Later that year he travelled to Rome where he had an opportunity to inform the Holy See of his views on British activities in Ireland. Mannix went back to Australia without being allowed to return home to visit his family near Charleville, in north Cork. The prelate's mother had died in January 1925 and de Valera had attended the funeral. Mannix was unable to be present. In correspondence de Valera must have indicated that he wanted to explore new political options with the archbishop and the rector. Hagan discussed matters with Mannix and wrote to de Valera on 31 May: 'My Dear President . . . I inclined to gather that he [Mannix] would not be disposed to balk at it [the abandonment of abstentionism] in the circumstances, provided there was no danger of a split.' Hagan indicated to de Valera that there was the possibility of a split in Sinn Féin arising sooner or later, even if the existing policy of non-entry into the Dáil was maintained.

These matters were considered sufficiently pressing for de Valera to decide to travel to Rome for a meeting with his clerical advisers. The reasons for the trip were threefold: he was in poor health and needed a rest; details of Mannix's proposed visit to Ireland had to be arranged and the archbishop educated in post-civil war politics; and, finally, de Valera was anxious to discuss the future direction of Irish politics with him. De Valera visited Blackrock College where he borrowed the cassock and passport of his friend Father Patrick Walshe. Dressed as a priest, he set out for Rome in the company of Seán MacBride, whom he brought along as an interpreter. MacBride, who was to serve as chief of staff of the IRA between 1936 and 1937, was the son of the executed 1916 leader, Major John MacBride, and Maud Gonne. Born in 1904 in Paris where he received his early schooling, he later attended UCD, joined the Irish Volunteers and during the War of Independence was active in the IRA. MacBride opposed the Treaty and was imprisoned for his role in the IRA during the civil war. Forced to flee to Paris for a time, MacBride kept up his membership of the IRA. Unlike de Valera, he remained a hardline opponent of political compromise. On 2 June, from Florence, de Valera sent a note to

Hagan: 'Mr Seán MacBride . . . will himself explain the object of his visit if you find it possible to accord him an interview.' De Valera came clandestinely to the Irish College and was hidden in the rector's rooms, where talks took place in the presence of Peter Magennis, Michael Curran and John Hagan. Seán MacBride, who attended some of the time, was opposed to any form of compromise.[170]

Hagan had prepared a memorandum which he circulated to his small Roman 'republican' group before de Valera had arrived in the Italian capital. On the basis of his historical and theological analysis, Hagan made the clear recommendation that there was no theological objection to taking the oath of allegiance and suggested that de Valera should enter the Dáil: 'As to the rest, may not the present situation be likened to a ship carrying Ireland and its fortunes but managed by a crew of madmen who are driving the vessel straight on to the rocks, while the doomed passengers refuse to step in and pitch the madmen overboard, on the pleas that even that much contact with them would soil their hands?'[171] De Valera returned to Dublin aware that he had the historical, intellectual and theological framework in which to discuss a new departure. At the Sinn Féin *ard fheis* de Valera proposed the following motion: 'That once the admission oath of the 26-county and six-county assemblies is removed, it becomes a question not of principle but of policy whether or not Republican representatives should attend these assemblies.'[172] Father Michael O'Flanagan tabled an amendment to the effect that it was incompatible with the principles of Sinn Féin 'to send representatives into any usurping legislature set up by English law in Ireland.' The amendment was carried by 223 votes to 218. De Valera resigned as President the following day.[173]

On 13 April 1926, de Valera announced that he was setting up a new political party, Fianna Fáil (Soldiers of Destiny). The inaugural meeting was held in La Scala theatre, Dublin, on 16 May. A statement on 17 April had outlined the objectives of the new organisation: the reuniting of the Irish people and the banding together of them for the tenacious pursuit of the following ultimate aims, using at every moment such means as are rightfully available: 1) securing the political independence of a united Ireland as a republic; 2) the restoration of the Irish language and the development of a native Irish culture; 3) the development of a social system in which, as far as possible, equal opportunity will be afforded to every Irish citizen to live a noble and useful Christian life; 4) the distribution of the land of Ireland so as to get the greatest number possible of Irish families rooted in the soil of Ireland; 5) the making of Ireland an economic unit, as self-contained and self-sufficient as possible—with a proper balance between agriculture and the other essential industries.

It was no accident that Hagan visited Dublin in April 1926. He usually took holidays in the late summer. Now his presence was required to help ensure that Fianna Fáil gained maximum support. He had the influence and prestige to sway some who might have doubted the wisdom of the new departure. He visited the de Valera home and left a gift of a sum of money. Mrs Sinéad de Valera wrote to Rome thanking Hagan 'not only for your generous present but for the very thoughtful way it was given'. She added: 'But at present we have no anxiety about financial affairs and it would be selfishness and covetousness on our part to personally accept such a great gift. Many, many thanks. You have been kindness itself to us all along.'[174] That letter was written between the break with Sinn Féin in March and the foundation of Fianna Fáil.

De Valera, in his inaugural address to the Fianna Fáil party at the La Scala theatre, quoted the executed 1916 leader James Connolly's protest: 'Ireland, as distinct from her people, is nothing to me'.[175] In an early handbill, Fianna Fáil urged—'Stop Emigration, End Unemployment, Ní neart go cur le chéile' [Strength in unity].[176] Fianna Fáil managed to attract most of the prominent anti-Treatyites: Seán T. O'Kelly (vice-president), P.J. Ruttledge (vice-president), Gerard Boland and Seán Lemass (both honorary secretaries), Dr James Ryan and Seán MacEntee. Among the members of the national executive were Frank Aiken, Tom Derrig, Dan Breen, Patrick J. Little and Dr Con Murphy. There were six women on the committee: Countess Markievicz, Mrs Tom Clarke, Miss Dorothy MacArdle, Mrs Hanna Sheehy Skeffington, Miss L. Kearns and Miss Margaret Pearse.

Great energy was put into the building up of a national party. When asked about the success of these efforts, Seán Lemass said that it was the result of 'very hard work, but it was facilitated by the existence of the survivors of the IRA who were interested in getting back into some form of action'. He attributed the success of Fianna Fáil as a political party to the very large volume of public support for its general policies and the growing ineffectiveness of the Cosgrave administration.[177] De Valera went to America in February to give evidence in the case taken by the Irish government to gain possession of the remaining funds collected on bond certificates in 1920 and 1921. The court returned the money to the subscribers. De Valera toured the USA raising money for Fianna Fáil and returned in May 1927 with sufficient funds to help build the organisation. A party newspaper, *The Nation*, was established. Fianna Fáil employed full-time organisers. The party's first *ard fheis* had been held on 24 November 1926, the fourth anniversary of the death of Erskine Childers.

Cumann na nGaedheal called an election for 9 June 1927. But Cosgrave and his colleagues were unprepared. They knew and cared little for constituency structures. Party leaders did not play an organised role in local government. Little was done to build up a local party machine or to establish a fighting fund to be used at election time. Fianna Fáil, on the other hand, saw from the outset the necessity to construct an active and adequately funded national organisation. De Valera and his new party were prepared. Large advertisements appeared in the national press stating 'Fianna Fáil is going in; Fianna Fáil is going to win' or 'Vote for Fianna Fáil and put in a government which will give the poor and struggling a chance to exist.'[178] The Labour Party—and not for the last time—accused Fianna Fáil of stealing its policies; Tom Johnson challenged de Valera on 4 June to state whether he intended to enter the Dáil.

The Irish Times and the *Independent* attacked Fianna Fáil. On 4 June 1927, the latter paper suggested that if de Valera 'got a majority of seats an immediate attempt would be made to precipitate a *coup d'état*. . . . Fianna Fáil is asking the country to endorse a policy that carries ruin and desolation in its train.' Every vote cast for de Valera, argued the *Independent*, would be a vote for the 'shipwreck of the state'. The provincial press, with rare exceptions, was hostile to Fianna Fáil.[179] Political exchanges were robust. For example, there was a heated argument between a priest and a government minister in May. The *Independent* reported on 27 May 1927 that a Cumann na nGaedheal election meeting had proceeded almost without interruption until a Fianna Fáil meeting began beside it. Father Coyle presided at the Fianna Fáil rally. Pointing to the other platform, he said that six months before 'those people' did not know whether Fermanagh was in Northern Ireland or in the Free State. The priest could be heard telling people not to vote for those who had consented to the permanent partition of the country. The Cumann na nGaedheal speaker replied: 'It is all very well for a priest to come out now and tell you about the Boundary, but how are you going to get rid of it? Are they going to fight? A priest, according to a rule of the Church, has not the right to fight' (cheers, boos, groans). Pointing to the other platform, Father Coyle replied: 'There is an arch-traitor, the Minister for Finance—he thinks he will hold the purse again, but he never will.' Father Coyle, gesticulating fiercely, told his audience that it was the last time Blythe would appear in County Monaghan as their representative.[180]

The election, however, was not a two-horse race. The Labour Party had supported the Treaty and had won 14 seats in the previous general election. Despite civil war in its own ranks between the followers of James Larkin and the followers of William O'Brien, it was expected to increase its number of TDs in 1927. The Farmers' Party, which had first made its appearance in the 'pact' election, when it had won six seats, had returned 15 TDs in 1923 and these usually supported Cumann na nGaedheal; but shortly before the 1927 election, the party was divided between protectionists and free traders. Fianna Fáil had its attractions as the champion of 'self-sufficiency'. William Redmond's National League had been founded in 1926. The party of William Redmond, a son of John, might have been expected to take the votes of the residual supporters of the Irish Parliamentary Party. Many ex-servicemen in World War I might have been expected to vote for the National League, as would moderate protest voters like the members of the Licensed Vintners' Association, outraged at government policy to change opening hours. Sinn Féin was also in the field, together with a range of independent candidates.

In the end, the voting went very much in Fianna Fáil's favour: de Valera's party returned 44 deputies, only three less than Cumann na nGaedheal. Labour had 22 TDs and the Farmers' Party got 11. Redmond's party got eight seats and there were 21 others, amongst them five abstentionist Sinn Féin deputies. De Valera had an opportunity to topple the government if his Fianna Fáil members were to enter Leinster House.

Fianna Fáil issued a statement on 17 June that their 44 deputies would 'claim' their seats, but under no condition would they take the oath. The following day Fianna Fáil suggested that it was 'ready to form a government with the cooperation of all progressive non-imperialist persons.'[181]

On 23 June, the day the new Dáil assembled, the *Independent* carried a Fianna Fáil advertisement with the legal opinion of three constitutional lawyers to the effect that deputies could take their seats without taking the oath before the election of the President. That morning de Valera attended mass at Westland Row and later addressed a crowd outside Fianna Fáil headquarters in Middle Abbey Street. He led his deputies to Leinster House. The clerk of the Dáil showed them into a room where he said he had a little matter for them to attend to before they could take their places in the chamber. Seán T. O'Kelly, acting as spokesman for the group, refused to take the oath. The clerk said that he had better things to attend to and made to leave the room. At that point, de Valera attempted to enter the chamber, but was prevented from doing so because the doors had been locked.

Fianna Fáil faced considerable criticism in the press in the days following their Dáil débâcle. The *Leader* attacked de Valera: '. . . a Don Quixote is no use to it [Saorstát]. We want to harness the Shannon rather than attack windmills.'[182] Aware of the possible damage to Fianna Fáil, de Valera took a new course of action. Article 47 of the Saorstát constitution provided for the introduction of Bills by plebiscite and article 48 provided for a referendum, 75,000 signatures being required. Fianna Fáil immediately announced a nationwide campaign to force the government to submit the question of the oath to a referendum.[183] There the matter rested until all was changed by the terrible events of Sunday, 10 July; the Vice-President and Minister for Home Affairs, Kevin O'Higgins, was shot dead while on his way to mass in Booterstown, Co. Dublin. He was unarmed and did not have a bodyguard. His attackers were IRA men who happened to see him while they were on their way by car to a GAA game in Wexford. Apparently the attack was not premeditated. It was simply unlucky for O'Higgins that his murderers had happened to find him alone. His death was a tragedy for the government and for the country.[184]

Cosgrave told the Dáil on 12 July that the killing was 'a political assassination against a pillar of state'. He said the crime would fail in its object: 'We will meet this form of terrorism as we met other forms of terrorism and we shall not falter till every vestige of it is wiped out from our land.'[185] De Valera said that the shooting was murder and 'inexcusable from any standpoint. . . . It is a crime that cuts at the root of representative government.'[186]

There was a danger that the cycle of violence of 1922/23 might repeat itself. Tom Johnson was told by the Minister for Finance, Ernest Blythe, who was on his way from a meeting of the Executive Council on the evening of the murder, that there was a grave danger of unauthorised violence by the police and the army. The ensuing political crisis brought about a series of talks between the leaders of the major parties; the Labour Party met the Ceann Comhairle, Michael Hayes. He had come to 'make soundings and evoke discussion', according to Johnson. At a time when the strongest member of the minority government had been struck down, with two ministers (John Marcus O'Sullivan and Desmond FitzGerald) seriously ill and at least two others on the verge of physical and psychological collapse, the Labour leader told Hayes that he was prepared to recommend membership of an all-party coalition. A meeting was fixed between Johnson and Cosgrave for 19 July, but the evening before that, Johnson was invited to see the President. He was informed that the government intended to introduce a Public Safety Bill and an Electoral Amendment Bill; the latter would deny abstentionist TDs their Dáil seats by requiring candidates to swear an affidavit before formal nomination that he or she would take the oath on being returned to the Dáil. Cosgrave told Johnson that he proposed an election within a month for the 51 seats held by abstentionists. Both men agreed that Fianna Fáil would lose most of its seats. Johnson was of the view that the majority would go to Cumann na nGaedheal. Cosgrave failed to secure an agreement from Labour that the two parties would divide up the seats of the abstentionists. He had argued that ministers were physically unable to conduct a strenuous election campaign so soon.[187] Was this a ploy to get Fianna Fáil into the Dáil?[188] Despite Labour opposition, the Constitutional Amendment Bill, the Electoral Amendment Bill and the Public Safety Bill went through the Dáil on 4 August after an all-night sitting.

A few days before the passage of the legislation, Johnson received a message from de Valera via Gerard Boland that the Fianna Fáil leader would like to meet him. Fianna Fáil had decided on 6 August that its members would enter the Dáil. A meeting was held between the leaders of the two parties that evening, but little emerged other than de Valera's statement that the Fianna Fáil members would enter the Dáil but would not take the oath. Johnson and William O'Brien met

Boland, O'Kelly and Frank Aiken to discuss future strategy. A memorandum was tabled by O'Kelly on behalf of Fianna Fáil, requesting Labour support on a range of issues. Johnson drafted a general statement of the Labour position on 10 August and the parliamentary Labour Party unanimously supported a motion the following day that the party should form a coalition government with Fianna Fáil support. On 11 August the Fianna Fáil TDs took the oath, and their seats, in the Dáil without incident.[189]

A motion of no confidence against the government was immediately tabled. It was agreed that it would be taken on 16 August. In the meantime, Johnson had secured the support of Redmond's party to form a government that would not include members of Fianna Fáil. On 13 August the leader of the Labour Party sat down in secret with William O'Brien and R.J.P. Mortished to pick a cabinet. The latter was a trade union activist who later enjoyed a distinguished career in the International Labour Organisation (ILO). They met in the Powerscourt Arms Hotel, Enniskerry. The names of the ministers were listed on a single sheet which was afterwards torn up and thrown into a wastepaper basket in the hotel. The cabinet was to be made up of Labour, National League and independents. By chance, the editor of *The Irish Times*, John Edward Healy, saw the three men at a bus stop on their way back to town. He returned to the hotel, found the bin, pieced together the torn sheet and the following day printed the entire list in his newspaper.

Cosgrave appeared to be heading for inevitable defeat on 16 August in a debate which lasted for over four hours. The President was so sure of his fate that he had given a farewell party for his staff,[190] but Johnson failed to request T.J. O'Connell to return from Canada where he was attending a conference. When the vote was finally taken, a Sligo deputy, John Jinks, was not in the chamber. That made it a tie at 71 each and the Ceann Comhairle gave his casting vote in favour of the government. The pro-Saorstát correspondent of the *Round Table* Commonwealth journal wrote of 'high Jinks in the Dáil'. There were many rumours around the city that the alderman from Sligo who, earlier in the day, had attended a party meeting where he had not voiced any objection to the no confidence motion, had been 'spirited away' by a number of Cumann na nGaedheal supporters who had put him on the train home in a far from sober condition.[191]

In September, Cosgrave risked calling a snap general election.[192]

The gamble paid off and Cumann na nGaedheal returned with 62 seats to 57 for Fianna Fáil and 13 for Labour. Tom Johnson lost his seat to James Larkin, a member of the militant left. He was a severe loss to the parliamentary Labour Party and his incisiveness in the Dáil was missed.[193] The Farmers' Party got six seats and Redmond two. There were 12 independents and one independent Labour. In the absence of Johnson, de Valera was the undisputed leader of the opposition and he played that role effectively through the latter part of the 1920s. Seán Lemass accurately described Fianna Fáil as 'a raw lot' when the party first came into Leinster House, but five years in opposition before the next general election provided the apprenticeship that the leaders of a party who were restless for power needed so badly.

THE FOREIGN POLICY OF THE FREE STATE
The Free State had showed enterprise in the management of Irish foreign policy. The Treaty was registered as an international instrument with the League of Nations in Geneva on 11 May 1924.[194] The Saorstát had joined the year before and became the first Commonwealth country to establish a permanent delegation in Geneva. Canada followed a year later.[195] Despite a diminished staff at the Department of External Affairs, Saorstát foreign policy was conducted in a lively and professional fashion under the watchful eye of the assistant secretary, Joseph Walshe.[196] Desmond FitzGerald was the minister in charge until 1927.

It appears that External Affairs suffered more dramatically from the split over the Treaty than any other government department. Many of the more prominent Sinn Féin envoys who served in the first Dáil between 1919 and 1921 took the anti-Treaty side. These included Seán T. O'Kelly, Leopold Kerney, Robert Brennan, Seán Nunan and Art Ó Briain. Among those who stayed were Frank T. Cremins, Michael Mac White and Seán Lester. The small group of overworked diplomats performed very well and kept the Saorstát to the fore in Commonwealth affairs. The contribution of Kevin O'Higgins was particularly effective at the 1926 Imperial Conference.[197]

Saorstát representation abroad came rather slowly. Geneva has already been mentioned. An Irish high commissioner was appointed to London in 1923. Professor T.A. Smiddy was officially informed in October 1924 that he could regard himself as a permanent official of the Free State government in Washington. By 1927 he enjoyed the title of envoy extraordinary and minister plenipotentiary.[198] The Irish government appointed Seán Murphy as commercial attaché to Paris. That office also had responsibility for Brussels, where Count O'Kelly de Gallagh was the Saorstát commercial representative. The Saorstát was slow to appreciate the potential of this department. External Affairs remained the 'Cinderella' of all the government departments, but there were significant achievements. However, as Conor Cruise O'Brien has mentioned, they failed to make the rafters ring in Roscommon.[199]

Patrick McGilligan was the new driving force in a Cumann na nGaedheal government devastated by the loss of O'Higgins. He took over as Minister for External Affairs on 12 October 1927. A widely respected figure in Irish political life, he had first come to national prominence in 1924 when he was appointed Minister for Industry and Commerce.[200] McGilligan held the two portfolios until 1932. He found a strong ally in Joseph Walshe, secretary of the Department of External Affairs, and both men quickly laid the foundations for the expansion of the Irish diplomatic service. A memorandum drafted in the department in June 1928 called for sweeping changes in Irish diplomatic representation abroad. Concern was expressed over the ambiguous situation in which Irish envoys found themselves *vis à vis* the British representatives: 'There can be no doubt that the appointment of Ministers to one or more of the great European Powers would very clearly establish the fact, which is not at the moment appreciated, that the Saorstát must be regarded as a unit in international affairs in no way subservient to Great Britain.'

McGilligan sought to follow the example of the Canadians, who had sent envoys to both Tokyo and Paris. It will be remembered that Dublin had a high commissioner in London, and an envoy in Washington from 7 October 1924.[201] On continental Europe, McGilligan sought to establish a legation and consulate in Berlin, enlarge the Paris office into a legation and consulate, close the Brussels office and extend the Geneva office. He also wanted to appoint a representative in Ottawa, to open a consulate in New York and to increase the size of the Washington legation.[202] The administrative battle was hard fought, but by 1929 the Executive Council had decided to send delegates to Berlin and Paris. Approval later followed to exchange envoys with the Vatican. Count Gerald O'Kelly de Gallagh was appointed envoy extraordinary and minister plenipotentiary to Paris. A fluent French speaker, he had been a long-serving Sinn Féin envoy. He was not terribly bright and, on occasion, had the talent of being able to misrepresent his country fluently in two languages. The appointment to Berlin proved much more fortunate. Daniel Binchy was 29 and was Professor of Jurisprudence and International Law at UCD. He had spent time in Germany as a student and spoke the language fluently. Binchy retired from the diplomatic service after three years, but in that short time he made a significant impact in diplomatic circles in Berlin.[203] McGilligan also secured, with some difficulty, an exchange of envoys with the Holy See in 1929. The Irish bishops were not enthusiastic about the idea of having a resident nuncio in Dublin, but, despite such a relatively minor problem, McGilligan succeeded in pursuing the 'freedom to achieve freedom' strategy in foreign policy. On 27 August 1928 President Cosgrave signed the General Pact for the Renunciation of War (Kellogg Pact). McGilligan told the Dáil that this was the first time there had been an international agreement signed by any member of the Commonwealth other than Britain as a separate instrument of ratification: 'It is the first time we negotiated and ratified an international agreement of this kind.'[204]

In 1929, McGilligan signed the optional clause of the Permanent Court of International Justice at Geneva. Under this clause, member states agreed to submit their international disputes to the compulsory jurisdiction of the Permanent Court.[205] The Irish Free State continued to demonstrate its independence of action from the British at the League of Nations. Dublin responded favourably to the initiative of the French Foreign Minister, Aristide Briand, in 1930 to establish a European Federal Union.[206]

The Irish delegation played an important role at the Commonwealth Conference of 1930. The year 1931 ended with the enactment of the Statute of Westminster, whereby it was agreed that no law enacted thereafter by the parliament of the United Kingdom should extend to a Dominion unless the Dominion had requested and consented that it should do so.[207] The Treatyites had been proven correct: Commonwealth membership meant the capacity to achieve freedom within a developing system which would result in the establishment of 'autonomous communities'. Writing from London in October 1930, Desmond FitzGerald summed up the situation:

Knowing the history of these last years as I do I am amazed at the way we have changed the situation . . . the Free State is (or will be in a couple of years—without even a vestige of any form even to mar it) just a constitutional monarchy—with only that to make the difference between it and an Irish Republic. In the matter of independence and sovereignty there is no whittle of difference. But accepting the Treaty we certainly are getting all that the most perfervid supporters were claiming for it—and more.[208]

That may have been the reality. But constitutional battles which yielded slow but steady results did not capture the popular imagination.

DE VALERA, COSGRAVE AND THE 'RED SCARE'

Nineteen twenty-nine found the government in growing difficulties. Part of the problem sprang from the perceived inadequacy of the existing law to deal with a recrudescence of IRA activities. Intimidation of juries was widespread, and the IRA left people in no doubt as to what would happen if a 'guilty' verdict was returned in cases involving its members. A state witness was murdered on 20 February 1929 and a juryman was seriously wounded about the same time. The IRA weekly journal, *An Phoblacht*, published 'a continuous stream of seditious language, justification of past crimes, and incitements to future crimes'.[209] In the absence of an adequate law, the authorities conducted 'cat-and-mouse' arrest tactics to harass known members of the IRA. But in March 1930 a number of people appeared before the circuit court in Dublin and recovered damages for illegal arrest and false imprisonment. The Department of Justice recorded earlier: 'This procedure seems to have been planned and financed by Seán MacBride.'[210] (He became Minister for External Affairs in 1948.) There were eight similar cases pending at the beginning of 1931. In four cases the plaintiffs recovered £10 each and in four other cases £5 each. That placed the government, according to a Department of Justice source, 'in an almost ludicrous position of helplessness'. By early 1931, the police authorities and the Minister for Justice were agreed that the existing law was inadequate to deal with the threat of subversion.[211] On 30 January 1931, the IRA killed a police agent called John O'Carroll in Dublin and two months later a garda superintendent [Curtin] was murdered in County Tipperary. The

Wolfe Tone ceremonies at Bodenstown on 20 June 1931 were likely to be turned into a provocative show of force by the IRA. This event had become an annual ritual of defiance by the IRA to the authority of the Saorstát. The government cancelled all trains to Sallins, Co. Kildare and gardaí took up positions around the cemetery on the previous evening. Seán Russell, who was to have delivered the graveside oration, was imprisoned. Peadar O'Donnell took his place. He told detachments of the IRA from nineteen counties: '. . . all the powers in their hands we must take into our hands and in the final phase we must be prepared to meet force with force.'[212]

The IRA 'army convention' decided in February 1931 to found Saor Éire, an organisation of workers and farmers which would provide the movement with an alternative political outlet to the moribund Sinn Féin. It came into existence on 3 May. A month later Peadar O'Donnell, a left-wing republican, told a parade that the days of active service were over for the present. He saw the pressing need for a republican workers' party to help set up a peasants' republic. The first Saor Éire congress was held on 26 and 27 September 1931 and about 150 attended. The following members of the general headquarters staff of the IRA were elected to the executive: Seán MacBride (adjutant-general), Michael Price (director of intelligence) and Peadar O'Donnell (member of the army council).

According to the Department of Justice, Saor Éire's outlook was 'frankly communistic'. The organisation's draft constitution advocated the abolition without compensation of landlordism in lands, fisheries and minerals; the establishment of a state monopoly in banking and credit and the setting up of a state monopoly in export and import services and to promote cooperative distribution.[213] The Garda Commissioner, Eoin O'Duffy, sought an immediate strengthening of the law. He reported on 27 June 1931 that 'members of the Irregular Organisations and their followers treat the gardaí with absolute contempt; criminal suspects refuse to answer any questions and the ordinary citizen in the affected areas who, under normal conditions, would assist the gardaí to the utmost of his ability is through fear driven into silence.'[214]

The country witnessed a third IRA murder on 20 July 1931. *An Phoblacht* had stated on 20 June that the CID should be treated as 'social pariahs' and that the same treatment was to be extended to 'Judges and District Justices, to uniformed police—to every individual who is a willing part of the machine by which our Irish patriots are being tortured.'[215] On 20 July John Ryan was killed in County Tipperary after he had given evidence in an illegal IRA drilling case. His body was found with a placard around his neck: 'Spies and Informers beware. IRA.' He had first received a threatening letter on 29 April from the 'adjutant, South Tipperary Brigade, IRA', stating that he had been found guilty of treachery; it warned him that if he were found in the country after 17 May his life would be forfeited. On 12 September, a new garda barracks at Kilrickle, Co. Galway, was blown up. On 13 September William McInerney of Kilrush, an outspoken opponent of Saor Éire and the IRA, was seriously wounded by revolver fire while examining a notice, 'Spies Beware', which had been posted on his hall door.[216] The authorities took particular note of an interview given to the *Daily Express* on 24 August where Frank Ryan, a member of the IRA who was to become even better known in the late 1930s, justified the killing of O'Carroll, Ryan and Curtin and boasted of the organisation's power to operate on a still larger scale.[217]

A Department of Justice report, dated August 1931, estimated that there were about 1,300 officers and 3,500 rank and file in the IRA. The names of the most important members were known to the gardaí, but for reasons of weakness in the law, they remained at large. There were a range of related organisations which worried the authorities: Cumann na mBan, Fianna Éireann, Irish Friends of the Soviet Union, Irish Working Farmers' Committee, Workers' Revolutionary Party of Ireland, the Irish National Unemployed Movement, the Workers' Defence Corps, and the Irish Labour Defence League. It was also reported that many of the leaders of the revolutionary forces in the country had visited Moscow. The same Department of Justice memorandum argued that Seán Russell, Seán MacBride (described as the 'principal travelling organiser' of the IRA) and T.J. Ryan had, among other members of the IRA executive, been 'gained over *[sic]* to the Communist movement'. The memorandum concluded that recent developments marked 'the definite union of the Irish Republican Army with Communism in this state'. In return for the military support of the IRA, the communists supplied every man to the IRA who, 'whether from poverty or principle or mere love of agitation, is anxious to see the system of private property and private enterprise destroyed in this state.'[218]

So seriously did Cosgrave take the warnings from security sources that he sought an immediate meeting with Cardinal MacRory. Joseph Walshe of External Affairs was used as an intermediary. He was sent to Armagh to brief MacRory. Cosgrave met the cardinal outside Dublin because he feared that he was under IRA surveillance. Less than a month later, a memorandum was sent to every bishop in the country. It spoke of 'the existence of a conspiracy for the overthrow by violence of state institutions'. There was 'definite evidence of contact with the International Communistic Organisations which have their headquarters in and are controlled by Russia'. On 14 October 1931 a Public Safety Bill was introduced into the Dáil banning twelve organisations, including Saor Éire and the IRA. Military tribunals were introduced to counter the difficulty of jury intimidation. On 18 October the hierarchy issued a joint pastoral denouncing Saor Éire as a 'frankly communistic organisation' that was seeking to 'impose upon the Catholic Dáil of Ireland the same materialistic regime, with its fanatical hatred of God, as now dominates and threatens to dominate Spain'. (This was a reference to the recent flight of King Alfonso XIII and the establishment of the Second Spanish Republic.)

Fianna Fáil appeared not to be particularly perturbed by government alarm over the spread of communism. De Valera argued in the Dáil that 'if men are hungry, they will not be too particular about the ultimate principles of the organisation they would join, if that organisation promises to give them bread.' He sought the removal of the causes of poverty. At the same time, he stressed that he did not want to see the doctrines of Bolshevism take root in Ireland. De Valera did not let it be known in the Dáil that a friendly bishop had sent him a copy of the memorandum which had been circulated to the hierarchy. The leader of Fianna Fáil, with an eye on the next general election, secured an appointment with Cardinal MacRory to discuss the 'red scare' and to state the opposition of his party to communism.[219]

Cumann na nGaedheal also had to begin to worry about the general election. The recent Immoral Literature Bill had lost the government—or so ministers felt at the time—valuable support from members of the Church of Ireland. There was pressure from the Catholic bishops to close legal loopholes which permitted the sale of contraceptives in Ireland. The government agreed to establish a committee to investigate reform of the Criminal Law Amendment Acts 1880–85. Thus the need for action on that matter was delayed until after the general election. The politically vulnerable position of the government also made it amenable to episcopal representations while the Legitimacy Act (1930) was being drafted. The Vocational Education Act (1930) was also drafted with due deference to the views of the hierarchy.[220]

However, all Cosgrave's careful efforts not to alienate Protestant opinion were jeopardised in 1930 by the Letitia Dunbar-Harrison case. Miss Dunbar-Harrison had been appointed to the post of librarian for County Mayo after winning an open competition. She was a Protestant and an honours graduate of Trinity College Dublin. When the local library committee refused to approve the appointment—a stand supported by Mayo County Council—the government stood by the decision of the Local Appointments Commission, disbanded the council and kept Miss Dunbar-Harrison at her post. Local clergy were against her. A Christian Brother, M.S. Kelly, argued that 'her mental constitution was the constitution of Trinity College.' Monsignor E.A. D'Alton, dean of Tuam, told the local library committee that it was not appointing a 'washerwoman or a mechanic but an educated girl who ought to know what books to put into the hands of the Catholic boys and girls of this county which was at least 99 per cent Catholic.' There was a renewed sensitivity between the Catholic and Protestant communities following the Lambeth Conference decision on contraception in 1930. Resolution 15 condemned the use of contraception for motives of selfishness, luxury or mere convenience. It argued that where there was a clearly felt moral obligation to limit or avoid parenthood, the method had to be decided on Christian principles. The primary and obvious method was complete abstinence from intercourse:

> Nevertheless in those cases where there is such a clearly felt moral obligation to limit or to avoid parenthood, and where there is a morally sound reason for avoiding complete abstinence, the Conference agrees that other methods may be used, provided that this is done in the light of the same Christian principles.

That measured statement was in no sense a charter for licence. But the Lambeth decisions of 1930 did establish another source of serious division between the two churches. For that reason, D'Alton stressed the difference between the two churches on birth control: 'supposing there were books attacking these fundamental truths of Catholicity, is it safe to entrust a girl who is not a Catholic, and is not in sympathy with Catholic views, with their handling?' he asked.[221]

The appointment of Miss Dunbar-Harrison as librarian was really only a minor concern in comparison to the fears expressed in certain extremist Catholic journals about the employment of Trinity graduates as dispensary doctors. The *Catholic Bulletin*—never regarded by the bishops as automatically reflecting the views of the hierarchy—spoke out against Trinity and questioned whether any distinction could be made between the Protestant and Catholic graduates of that college: 'Is not the title of Catholic, assumed and used by such a Catholic Medical Graduate of Trinity College, Dublin, simply an added danger for the morality of our Catholic population, rich and poor?'[222]

Soon after that article appeared, the Minister for Education, John Marcus O'Sullivan, had an interview with Archbishop John Harty of Cashel. The archbishop assured the minister that the bishops were not going to make any pronouncement on the librarian question, but the bishops did not want to have the issue formally raised at a meeting of the hierarchy. It was a matter for the local ordinary, Thomas Gilmartin of Tuam, whom Cosgrave met on 25 February 1931. Gilmartin urged Cosgrave to sign a concordat with the Holy See.[223] That was not a position with which many members of the hierarchy would have agreed.

By March 1931 Cosgrave had secured strong backing within the Executive Council for a tough stance. A memorandum was prepared for Cardinal MacRory on 28 March: 'We feel confident that Your Eminence and their Lordships and bishops appreciate the effective limits to the powers of government which exist in relation to certain matters if some of the fundamental principles on which our state is founded are not to be repudiated.' He regarded as unconstitutional any attempt to impose a religious test on a candidate for the post of dispensary doctor. Cosgrave drew attention to the delicate question of marriage dispensations on grounds of non-consummation which were granted by the church and 'of which the civil authorities receive no notification'. He warned:

> That these and other difficulties exist is not open to question. That in the present circumstances, they are capable of a solution which

could be regarded as satisfying, at once, the requirements of the church and the state is, I fear, open to grave doubt. Any failure following an attempt to solve these problems would only add to the difficulty, and if it came to public knowledge, might prove a source of unrest, if not a scandal.

Aware of the gravity of the situation for future church-state relations, Cardinal MacRory saw Cosgrave in mid-April. The details of the meeting are not available, but Cosgrave and O'Sullivan met Archbishop Thomas Gilmartin within days of seeing the cardinal. The archbishop, in whose ecclesiastical province the dispute was located, was on the defensive from the outset. He meekly suggested that Cosgrave might consider transferring Dunbar-Harrison at a suitable time. (She was moved finally in January 1940 to become librarian in the Department of Defence.) The outcome was, according to the Irish correspondent of the *Round Table*, 'fair to the lady, soothing to the Mayo bigots and good for the government'.[224]

However, Fianna Fáil had capitalised on the government's embarrassment in Mayo. Local Fianna Fáil had opposed the appointment of Miss Dunbar-Harrison. De Valera made great play of the fact that she did not speak Irish in an area where there were many native speakers. De Valera conveyed to a meeting in Irishtown, Co. Mayo, that he was on their side.[225] The leader of Fianna Fáil was an adroit soother of people's concerns and that was no more clearly in evidence than during the Mayo librarian's case. He so hedged his thinking with qualification that his own followers might have been forgiven for thinking that they, too, did not know exactly where he stood. De Valera knew exactly where he stood: nothing was allowed to transpire which would upset Fianna Fáil's plans for victory in the next general election; and if that meant leaving Cumann na nGaedheal to twist in the wind, then so be it. There was little need for concern; Cosgrave had become adept at making a bad political situation worse for Cumann na nGaedheal.

The adverse economic situation forced Cosgrave to introduce a supplementary budget in early November 1931. Petrol went up by fourpence a gallon and income tax by sixpence in the pound.[226] The government also felt obliged to reduce the wages of teachers and the gardaí. While these measures did not amount to a particularly astute electoral strategy, Cosgrave and his government deemed the state finances as being too serious a business to be the subject of partisan political considerations. This was an era of relative innocence. The Constitutional (Special Powers) Tribunal operated between 20 October 1931 and 18 March 1932. It made orders which declared certain issues of publications such as *An Phoblacht, Irish World, Workers' Voice, Irish Worker* and the *Republican File* to be seditious. It dealt with 60 trial cases which yielded 52 convictions and 8 acquittals. A hearing opened on 25 January 1932 before the special tribunal; there were four charges of seditious libel against *The Irish Press* and its editor Frank Gallagher. The charges arose out of the publication of articles alleging ill-treatment of prisoners while detained in a garda barracks. The newspaper was given two fines of £100, but costs were not allowed. The words of the judgment showed that the tribunal was not satisfied that the insinuations made by the paper against the conduct of certain police officers were entirely baseless.[227] The Department of Justice's summary of events describes the outcome as a 'drawn battle'.[228]

Absorbed in the management of government to the point of exhaustion, neither the Cumann na nGaedheal ministers nor the party machine were in a fit condition to take on Fianna Fáil. In contrast, morale was high in the main opposition party and Fianna Fáil was as anxious to fight a general election as members of the government were loath to do so.

DE VALERA AND THE ELECTION CAMPAIGN OF 1932

W.T. Cosgrave dissolved the Dáil on 29 January 1932. The timing of the election, announced for 16 February, was not particularly good for the government. The supplementary budget had forced a reduction in the wages of teachers and the gardaí. The military tribunal had attracted criticism, and a Fianna Fáil-supported campaign had already begun to have 'the prisoners' released. Fianna Fáil had a fine propaganda tool in the daily *Irish Press*.[229]

Cosgrave could have waited until after the summer, but that would have given Fianna Fáil more time to prepare. What appeared to concern Cosgrave most was the risk of 'politicising' the 31st International Eucharistic Congress, which was to be held in Dublin in June.[230] Such other-worldly considerations belonged to an innocent 'pre-stroke age' in Irish politics, but Cosgrave was also convinced that the prevailing 'red scare' atmosphere was an opportunity to skewer Fianna Fáil.

Cosgrave launched the Cumann na nGaedheal manifesto at the Mansion House, Dublin, on 29 January and spoke of 'the conspiracy solemnly condemned by the hierarchy'. The emphasis in his speech was on law and order. He was followed by the ever colourful Lord Mayor of Dublin, Alfie Byrne TD, who vowed that 'the disciples of paganism would never again find either Dublin city or any part of Ireland an easy prey to their anti-God preaching.'[231] Cumann na nGaedheal's *Fighting Points for Cumann na nGaedheal Speakers and Workers* provided arguments and quotations for speakers to bring out in the campaign that Fianna Fáil was a communistic, pro-IRA, state socialist party intent upon Bolshevising the structures of the Irish state. It was also argued that Fianna Fáil 'would like to erect a Chinese wall around this country—develop a sort of a Hermit Nation.'[232] The law and order rhetoric was supported by the use of a public relations company; one election poster showed de Valera being marched along by a gunman, with the title 'His Master's Voice'. Another was entitled 'The Shadow of a Gunman'. All depicted Fianna Fáil as being under the power of the subversives.[233] *The Irish Press* struck back with a series of front-page cartoons; one drew a connection between freemasonry, Unionism and Cumann na nGaedheal. Other cartoons ridiculed Cumann na nGaedheal.

Fianna Fáil speakers gave as good as they got at church gate meetings. Under the slogan 'Speed the plough', Fianna Fáil pledged to increase tillage and move towards self-sufficiency in the country's requirements of wheat, oats and barley. That would increase the earnings of agricultural workers and small farmers by £3,130,000. The burden of taxation could be reduced by £2m, according to the literature, which also promised to create 84,605 new jobs in the industrial sector under a new policy of autarchy. Fianna Fáil promised to establish a state housing board which would build 40,000 new houses within a maximum period of five years: 'The first concern of a Fianna Fáil government will be to provide suitable dwellings for working-class families at rents which they can afford to pay.' Imported building materials were to be substituted by goods manufactured in Ireland, and the 2,250 unemployed skilled building workers were guaranteed permanent employment over a five-year period. Fianna Fáil also made specific commitments to revamp the national transport system, speed up the work of the Land Commission, reorganise the sea fisheries, eliminate all political tests for employment in the public service and guarantee equal opportunities to all, privileges for none, amend the old age pensions act and prepare a scheme of pensions for necessitous widows and orphans.[234] In June 1930 Fianna Fáil had taken a seat in Longford-Westmeath and a second at a by-election in Kildare the following year. Fianna Fáil's director of elections, Seán Lemass, took full advantage of having in de Valera the person who was for many the living embodiment of the Irish revolutionary tradition. *The Irish Press* reported on 8 February that the 'chief' had been greeted in Clare and Limerick 'by enthusiastic thousands at the chain of meetings which he addressed. Bands and torchlight processions, attentive crowds who waited for hours to hear him speak, were striking features of his wonderful reception.' He pressed home the view that the principal task confronting any government was to tackle unemployment, which stood at 80,000. In Kilkee, de Valera focused on emigration, which had resulted in 250,000 young Irish people having to leave since independence at an estimated cost in lost wealth to the country of between £125,000 and £200,000.[235] The constitutional questions were also debated on the hustings, but Fianna Fáil preferred to focus on the economic issues.[236] Very little went right for the government in the campaign. Letitia Dunbar-Harrison made a front-page appearance in *The Irish Press* when she denied reports that she was resigning her job as librarian in Mayo: 'It's a fabrication, like the silly lies circulated a few weeks ago by an English newspaper', she told a reporter.[237] That case had uncomfortable echoes for Cosgrave and Cumann na nGaedheal.

What *The Irish Press* called the 'hardest fought general election for years' concluded on 16 February with Lemass being optimistic about victory.[238] De Valera's party increased its vote from 35.2 per cent to 44.5 per cent; that gave Fianna Fáil a total of 72 seats, compared with 57 in September 1927. Cumann na nGaedheal dropped from 62 to 57 seats.[239] However, when the sums were completed, Fianna Fáil was five short of an overall majority. The Farmers' Party had four and there were 13 independents. A split in the Labour Party had contributed to its weak performance. It had seven deputies, compared with 13 in the previous election. There were two members of Independent Labour: Richard Anthony (Cork Borough) and Dan Morrissey (Tipperary).[240]

William Norton, who became Labour Party leader after the 1932 election, had expressed his opposition to the idea of a coalition with Fianna Fáil during the campaign,[241] but the party was in broad agreement with de Valera's social programme and the pledge to repeal the Constitutional Amendment (Military Tribunal) Act.

Representatives of the two parties met on 8 March, the day before the Dáil reconvened, to explore the basis for cooperation. The Labour Party was represented by Tom Johnson, William Norton and William Davin; de Valera, Seán T. O'Kelly and Gerard Boland represented Fianna Fáil. Over the previous ten years, the Labour Party had failed to convert Cumann na nGaedheal to any of its policies. The Labour delegation was able to secure a commitment from Fianna Fáil for the introduction of a maintenance scheme for the 80,000 unemployed, the building of 40,000 houses, a pension scheme for widows and orphans, the reorganisation of the transport industry and measures against profiteering in the flour-milling industry.[242]

Fianna Fáil now had the necessary number of votes in the Dáil to come to power, but there were rumours that force would be used to stop de Valera from taking office. At a meeting in Wynn's Hotel, Dublin on 10 February 1932, a decision was taken to organise ex-national army officers and men who had pre-Truce service with the IRA. A convention was subsequently held on 17 March, a week after the Dáil had reconvened, and the Army Comrades Association was founded. Dr T.F. O'Higgins presided at the original meeting. General Mulcahy had also attended. *The Irish Press* had come to hear of this first meeting.[243] In an editorial on 26 February, the paper claimed 'that two Ministers, a well-known member of the Cumann na nGaedheal Party, and some others are engaged in a movement to obstruct the transfer of Government to Fianna Fáil. They are alleged to have formed a secret organisation for this purpose among Free State Army pensioners, to whom they appeal, it is said, on the ground that a Fianna Fáil Government would be committed to the revision of Army pensions.'[244] Cosgrave dismissed the suggestion as being 'grotesquely untrue' and 'mischievous'. The outgoing President said that the Minister for Justice considered the rumours unworthy of serious consideration.[245] The emphatic nature of Cosgrave's denial indicated that he was not fully in touch with the activities of all his ministers. But if there were Cumann na nGaedheal ministers who were inclined to the use of force, there was no question of Cosgrave lending weight to any attempt to stop de Valera from coming to power.[246] He respected the institutions of the state.

The pro-Fianna Fáil *Catholic Bulletin* wrote an ungracious political obituary of Cosgrave. He was compared to John Redmond and was described as having 'accommodated himself in a generous way to the requirements of alien institutions. He will be remembered by the Masonic brethren as one who struggled "manfully" to make Capitalistic Imperialism and English Protestantism respectable to the Irish people'.[247] The Irish correspondent of the *Round Table* was more benevolent. He saw Cosgrave as the quiet, almost unknown, man who had been accidentally called to control the destiny of his country ten years before: 'That he has done so is a tribute not only to his personal qualities of courage, shrewd political sense, and determination, but also to the colleagues who gave him loyal support, and the people who were wise enough to place and renew their trust in his wisdom and integrity'.[248] T. Desmond Williams summed up William Cosgrave's contribution thus:

> The Irish tradition is a mixed one; it has been influenced by ingredients deriving from Protestantism and Catholicism, republicanism and monarchism. . . . It was Cosgrave's achievement that, right at the very beginning, he understood the mixed nature of Irish society, and appreciated the role played in its evolution by Irishmen of different racial origins and possessing varied religious and intellectual convictions. To set the ship in motion, it was necessary to achieve reconciliation.[249]

However much that assessment may need to be qualified in the light of new evidence, it remains substantially accurate to conclude that Cosgrave and his colleagues had secured the popular legitimacy of the liberal democratic state during their turbulent ten years in office.

De Valera and Fianna Fáil in Power, 1932–1939

Éamon de Valera took office as President of the Executive Council on 9 March 1932 with a Labour Party-supported majority of only 13 votes. For many, the victory of Fianna Fáil was a triumph for what Seán Moylan had described as 'the owners of the donkey and cart over the pony-and-trap class'.[1] On 20 February an editorial in *The Irish Press* stated that the party had drawn its 'strongest support from the farming community, the most stable element in our population'.[2] The Fianna Fáil victory had, according to the same editorial, 'inspired the people with new hope and new courage' and had kindled an enthusiasm in the country not witnessed since 1921. But leading members of Cumann na nGaedheal felt far from confident about handing over the reins of power to de Valera and his 'slightly constitutional' band of erstwhile revolutionaries. It has to be assumed that the party believed its own election rhetoric. Cumann na nGaedheal shared the fears of Northern unionists that the extremists in the IRA, who had given tactical support to de Valera, might push him to one side when the time was opportune for a *coup d'état*. 'It will be well', warned the *Belfast Newsletter*, 'if the people ringing their bells today are not found wringing their hands tomorrow.'[3] *An Phoblacht* gave due cause for concern when it stated triumphantly: 'Cosgrave's rule is as dead as the Tsar's and Kerensky is in power.'[4] But de Valera did not see himself ever playing the role of a green Kerensky. He intended to hold onto power, albeit with the support of the Labour Party. Cosgrave has been deservedly praised for his role in the democratic transfer of power.[5] But it would not have been unreasonable for frontbench members of Cumann na nGaedheal to have felt that they would soon be back in office, so untried and inexperienced as administrators were Fianna Fáil. In fact, Cumann na nGaedheal had to wait another five elections and sixteen years before entering Government Buildings again as a party in power.

Fianna Fáil ministers, despite the opposition's wishful thinking, did not buckle under the strain of office. De Valera took on the additional burden of External Affairs, a portfolio that included the handling of North-South relations, and one which he continued to hold without interruption until 1948. He made his loyal friend Seán T. O'Kelly Vice-President and Minister for Local Government and Public Health. Frank Aiken, who had been chief of staff of the IRA in 1923, was made Minister for Defence—a shrewd move, calculated to test the loyalty of the army while at the same time mollifying radical republicans. Paddy Ruttledge was made Minister for Lands and Fisheries. Dr James Ryan, who was to become one of de Valera's closest colleagues on the Executive Council, was given the Agriculture portfolio. Tom Derrig was given charge of Education and James Geoghegan received the Justice portfolio. Two men of note, Gerry Boland and Dr Con Ward, were made parliamentary secretaries (junior ministers) in the departments of the President and Public Health respectively.

The two men who were to emerge as great rivals, representing different ideological wings of the party, were the new Finance Minister, Seán MacEntee, and the Minister for Industry and Commerce, Seán Lemass. MacEntee grew into his role as the resident high Tory in the Fianna Fáil cabinet. Lemass was much more inclined to want to take calculated risks. While the philosophical conflict between the two men became acute in the late 1930s, the differences were not quite so obvious in 1932. In reality, de Valera presided over a coalition where the conflict between radicalism and conservatism became more pronounced. First impressions, however, revealed the radical face of Fianna Fáil.[6] The Public Safety Act was suspended, thus automatically abolishing the military tribunal, and lifting the ban imposed on the IRA and kindred organisations. All 'political' prisoners were immediately released from jail. Easter week 1932 witnessed many large 'republican' demonstrations. De Valera confined the Irish army to barracks in order to avoid any chance of friction. Privately, de Valera and Aiken attempted to get the IRA to moderate its 'irreconcilable attitude', but, the Irish correspondent of the *Round Table* commented, 'they are not likely to be satisfied with any concessions he can offer.'[7] Nor were they.

Within days of coming into office, de Valera found himself the recipient of conflicting advice in closely related policy matters— Anglo-Irish relations, in particular, and external relations in general.

Seán MacEntee was one of the first senior Fianna Fáil members to push de Valera to 'pursue a more vigorous diplomatic policy in the Department of External Affairs'. On 18 March 1932 he wrote that Ireland should endeavour to 'isolate Great Britain, not merely amongst the States not members of the Commonwealth Group, but even the latter itself'. As a first step, he proposed the appointment of diplomatic representatives to Canada, Australia and South Africa. That might give Ireland Commonwealth allies when it came to discussion over the oath. MacEntee saw the possibility of forming an anti-British bloc inside the Commonwealth which could bring the British to the point where the government might 'willingly see us secede altogether from the group'. He also raised the possibility of mobilising the Irish in various Commonwealth countries.[8]

Three days before MacEntee had penned his letter, de Valera had had his first interview with the secretary of the Department of External Affairs, Joseph Walshe. The latter may have felt that he had due cause for apprehension: he had 'taken the Treaty side' during the civil war. A somewhat relieved Walshe returned to his department to tell his colleagues: 'He's charming, absolutely charming.' (That was the experience of senior civil servants in almost all departments. The secretary of Justice was the only one to be replaced in 1932.)[9] There was a general ripple of relief in External Affairs at the reaction of the secretary. That sense of relief was soon experienced throughout the civil service as the administration was allowed to get on with its job. Nevertheless, Walshe—unlike MacEntee—argued in favour of continuity in Anglo-Irish policy. Walshe argued that a radical shift by the government might provoke the imposition of economic sanctions by the British government:

> A boycott of our goods could be engineered. The Argentine could
> replace our meat in six weeks—Denmark could replace our butter
> and eggs with hardly any interval. Large elements of the people at
> home would then begin to turn against the government and say
> we had made a mess of things.[10]

Domestic pressure from within Fianna Fáil, and from the wider
'republican' movement, may have been responsible for the hardline
Anglo-Irish policy which de Valera drifted into within weeks of
coming to power. That was against the best advice of the most senior
member of the Department of External Affairs.

Charles Alphand, the experienced French envoy in Dublin,
reported in April to Paris that de Valera's programme—for the
moment—did not include leaving the Commonwealth.[11] The
diplomat identified Seán Lemass as being a force for moderation.[12]
Alphand outlined the economic constraints on the action of any Irish
government:

> ... Great Britain has at its disposal substantial means of financial
> pressure. The Irish currency is exclusively linked to sterling and,
> even if the republican party dreams of freeing itself from this
> subjection, one cannot see how they can do it. The whole Irish
> banking system is dependent on the bank [of England]. The
> Irishman does not invest his money, and above all he does not
> invest it in Ireland: he leaves it on deposit in his bank which puts
> it to use in England. ... Much more than by the oath taken by
> deputies, by allegiance to the King or by the payment of the
> agricultural annuities, England holds Ireland by economic chains
> which bring to converge on London, as if towards the real capital,
> all the interests of the country.[13]

That realisation in the Departments of Finance and of Industry and
Commerce may well have helped stay de Valera's hand.

Nevertheless, on 23 April the Constitutional (Removal of Oath) Bill
was published; it took over a year to get it through Leinster House
because of the intransigence of the Senate—an upper House which de
Valera quickly determined to disband as soon as it was feasible.

The British government had not welcomed the arrival of de Valera in power. *The Times* attributed his victory to the 'adventurously romantic' ideals of a younger generation.[14] Because of the fact that Fianna Fáil depended upon the Labour Party for a majority, it may have been felt in London that Cosgrave's return to power was not far off. On 22 March the National Government, comprising Labour and Conservatives, had reconstituted the cabinet Irish Situation Committee. The Dominions Secretary, James Henry Thomas, had advised his cabinet colleagues that no action should be taken 'which would enable Mr de Valera to say that we were forcing him out of the British Commonwealth'.[15] Thomas visited Dublin in June to discuss the outstanding issues in Anglo-Irish relations. The most serious of all was the threat by de Valera to withhold the land annuities. De Valera made a return visit to London, accompanied by Seán T. O'Kelly, Joseph Walshe and another civil servant, Seán Moynihan. There was tough talking on both sides. However, de Valera was prepared to allow adjudication on all financial payments not covered by formally ratified agreements, provided the composition of the tribunal was not restricted to Commonwealth personnel.[16] The diplomacy finally gave way to a trade war when de Valera held back disputed annuities. In retaliation, the British imposed a 20 per cent *ad valorem* duty on live animals, butter, cream, eggs, bacon, pork, poultry, game and other meats. On the basis of 1931 figures, this affected £26m out of £36m of Irish exports to Britain. It was an outcome neither side had wished for.

The worsening Anglo-Irish situation inevitably embroiled the hapless governor general, James McNeill—due to retire in 1933—in conflict with the government. He was the victim of a series of ignorant snubs by two cabinet ministers. So intolerable had the situation become for McNeill that he felt compelled to publish in the press on 10 July 1932 his correspondence with de Valera which chronicled the discourtesies to which he had certainly been subjected by gauche cabinet ministers. His appointment was—on the advice of the Executive Council—terminated by King George V on 9 September. De Valera replaced him on 25 November with an old friend, Domhnall Ó Buachalla, who continued to live in his own home with Irish-speaking gardaí in attendance. According to the *Round Table* correspondent, Ó Buachalla 'fulfils all Mr de Valera's requirements and reduces the position of governor general to that of a Gaelic rubber stamp for affixing to Acts of the Oireachtas'.[17] McNeill might have gone sooner had it not been for the fact that de Valera had to preserve due decorum during the great international showpiece of his first administration—the 31st Eucharistic Congress, held in Dublin in June 1932.[18]

EUCHARISTIC CONGRESS

Fianna Fáil did not wish to interrupt the zealous preparations for the Eucharistic Congress which the Cosgrave government had so assiduously pursued in the last years of its term of office. On the contrary, de Valera grasped the opportunity with enthusiasm to publicise internationally 'the nation's loyalty to Catholicism and to Rome'. Fianna Fáil's relations with the Catholic Church had improved before the general election. If residual anti-clericalism had continued to exist in the ranks since the time of the civil war, it was eclipsed by the carefully crafted confessional strategy pursued by Fianna Fáil from the late 1920s. Todd Andrews described de Valera as being 'a deeply religious man but not evidently pious'. He did not want to 'evangelise anyone'. Andrews knew that de Valera was aware of the fact that many of his colleagues did not forgive the hierarchy as easily as he had done. But 'the chief' did not tolerate gratuitous displays of anti-clericalism, as when Andrews made an off-the-cuff remark privately to a group of TDs during an election meeting in Kerry: 'You will have no peace until you get rid of the clerical managers and give the national teachers full responsibility to run their own schools.' Dev made no comment, but 'froze me with a look'.[19] The church-state situation remained far too delicate for de Valera to allow such undisciplined comments to become a commonplace.

The early months in office for Fianna Fáil were a time for concentration upon confidence-building measures between church and state. In April, the Executive Council had favoured suspending the sitting of the Houses of the Oireachtas on Catholic Church holidays. In October, the Minister for Justice was instructed to see whether it would be possible to alter the dates of public holidays to coincide as far as possible with Catholic Church holidays.[20] The Eucharistic Congress (Miscellaneous Provisions) Bill went through with as little difficulty as if Cosgrave had been in power. Nevertheless, de Valera had still to prove definitively his bona fides to the bishops. Todd Andrews recalled how de Valera had to bear the 'personal hostility of the bishops, thinly disguised at the time of the Eucharistic Congress, with a patient shrug'.[21] The archives do not reveal, however, any noticeable tension between the President and the most important members of the hierarchy. Nevertheless, some of the rural bishops— like a number of leading members of Fianna Fáil—had long memories.

The cost of the Congress was subscribed to generously during a national collection at all masses on 30 November 1930. There were also generous subscriptions from overseas. The cost of the Congress came to over £75,000, exclusive of the help provided by the state. There was a credit balance of £5,421.14 which was donated to Archbishop Edward Byrne's Dublin cathedral fund. If the material and organisational preparations were thorough, the spiritual arrangements were quantitatively very impressive indeed. A single issue newspaper, *The Congress News*, was produced on 26 April 1931; it recorded the fact that by 21 March the number of masses, benedictions and holy hours, and other acts of piety and devotion was a total of 85,673,432; this was in preparation for the Congress in Dublin. By the end, the figure had reached 315,460,345.

The Eucharistic Congress began on 20 June with the arrival of the papal legate in Dún Laoghaire. All went well, except for the fact that Cardinal Lauri almost mistook de Valera and the Executive Council, who were there to meet him at the end of the gangplank, for members of the special branch! Fianna Fáil was allergic to wearing court dress. There was a triumphal entry into the city and on to the pro-cathedral. Later that evening, there was an official state reception in Dublin Castle. The women were advised discreetly to wear wraps lest too much flesh might be on display. This may have been in deference to the cardinal and other members of the hierarchy, who felt that the country was still suffering from moral laxity.[22] Clergy and laity alike survived the state reception to attend a garden party organised by the hierarchy in the grounds of Blackrock College the following day. There were 14,000 in attendance. De Valera remained very much in the debt of his friend, John Charles McQuaid, who was president of the college, for the way in which he ensured that the governor general, James McNeill, and the members of the Executive Council did not have to cross paths that day.

On 23 June there was a mass meeting of men in the Phoenix Park. The following night it was the turn of the women. The highpoint of the ceremonies was the open-air mass in the Phoenix Park, attended by over one million people, at which the tenor John McCormack sang. That was followed by a procession and benediction on O'Connell Bridge. Eoin O'Duffy, the Garda Commissioner, was the chief steward.

The Eucharistic Congress brought to Dublin representatives from all over the Catholic world. The power of the Irish in the Catholic Church was manifest. More importantly, the Irish Catholic diaspora reassembled to celebrate the 'resurrection': the victory of the two halves of the one struggle—Catholic emancipation and national independence. Thus, an editorial in *The Irish Press* stated: 'The union of the Christian ideal and the national endeavour has been manifested in every great moment in our history.'[23] The Eucharistic Congress in Dublin was not simply a religious celebration. It was a manifestation of Irish Catholic nationalism.[24]

THE SHAPING OF DE VALERA'S 'REPUBLIC'

Fianna Fáil also manifested its sensitivity towards religion in a more direct way. Criminal law amendment remained one of the unresolved matters to which the hierarchy wished the government to turn its attention immediately. The report of the Committee on the Criminal Law Amendment Acts (1880–85) and on Juvenile Prostitution had been in the Department of Justice since 20 August 1931.[25] That report presented a picture of Ireland which was the reverse image of the idealised, pious country of the Eucharistic Congress.[26] Take the recorded number of illegitimate births: 1922, 1,520; 1926, 1,716; 1927, 1,758; 1928, 1,788; 1929, 1,853. The latter figure represented 3.1 per cent of total births registered in that year. The conclusion was that illegitimacy had been increasing throughout the country since 1925 'at an unprecedented rate'. But the report concluded that those figures represented 'only part of the actual situation'. The high numbers had so strained the accommodation of the county homes that the authorities were faced with 'the objectionable fact that unmarried mothers of first-born children cannot be maintained apart from the other inmates (the decent poor and sick)'. It had been found necessary for the Poor Law bodies in the district of Dublin Union and in the counties of Clare and Galway to provide auxiliary institutions for unmarried mothers. The Department of Local Government was making similar provisions in other counties.[27] One witness said that only 25 per cent of illegitimate births were registered in Limerick. That was also the opinion of a priest who gave evidence on behalf of Bishop Patrick Morrisroe of Achonry. The report provided statistics from the Catholic Protection and Rescue Society (950 cases in 1929 and 1,026 cases in 1930). St Patrick's Guild had dealt with 495 cases in 1929 and 432 in 1930. The figures for unmarried expectant mothers who had gone to England to have their children were also high—105 cases handled by the Crusade of Rescue, belonging to the archdiocese of Westminster, in 1930.

The report commented that the testimony of all the witnesses— clerical, lay and official—was striking in its unanimity that 'degeneration in the standard of social conduct has taken place in recent years'. Various reasons were advanced for this situation: loss of parental control and authority during a period of general upheaval, unsupervised and unlicensed places of popular amusement, commercialised dance halls, picture houses and the opportunities 'afforded by the misuse of the motor cars for luring girls' were the chief causes for the 'present looseness of morals'. John Flanagan, parish priest of Fairview, Dublin, said in his memorandum that 'conduct that in other countries is confined to brothels is to be seen without let or hindrance on our public roads'. In his testimony Canon Lee, PP of Bruff, Co. Limerick, deplored the decay of morals and blamed it on 'the dance hall craze'. Such halls were, he said, unsupervised, unlicensed 'schools for scandal'. The representatives of the bishop of Achonry laid equal stress on dance halls and referred to 'a sinister feature of these dances, namely, that they were attended by strangers who travelled from distances in motor cars and were accustomed to take the country girls they met there for a "night drive"'. Other clerical witnesses spoke of girls being drugged and doped at dance halls.[28]

The Garda Commissioner, Eoin O'Duffy, gave evidence and said that the moral climate of the country had changed for the worse in recent years. There had been an alarming amount of sexual crime increasing yearly, a feature of which was the 'large number of cases of criminal interference with girls and children of 16 years and under, including many cases of children under 10 years'. The police estimated that not 15 per cent of such cases were prosecuted because of the anxiety of parents to keep them secret, the desire to protect the child from the ordeal of a public court appearance, and the difficulty of proof. The figures supplied by the gardaí for offences against girls under 18 (including children) were 169 (1924–26), 268 (1927–29) and 93 (1930). The figures for offences against or between males (including children) were 76 (1924–26), 174 (1927–29), and 69 (1930). The police estimated that the number of girls between the ages of 16 and 21 engaged in prostitution was about 100 in the Dublin area.

In response to the problem, the committee recommended the raising of the age of consent to 18, partially on the grounds that,

> Generally speaking, Irish girls of 16 to 18 years of age, by nature, habits and training, possess less knowledge and experience of the moral and physical dangers to which they are sexually exposed. They are less capable of protecting themselves against such dangers than are girls at the same period of life in England, for these are mostly brought up from childhood accustomed to live in gregarious surroundings, which, it may be said, instil in them instincts of 'canniness' and self-discipline that the conditions of Irish agricultural life do not foster.

Such rhetoric was a distortion of a more complex reality, and when legislation was being drafted in 1933, a memorandum from the Department of Justice took issue with the report and suggested that it should be taken 'with reserve'. It left the impression that the authors did not face their task in a judicial and impartial frame of mind. The recommendations were invariably to increase penalties, create offences, and remove existing safeguards for persons charged. Their main concern seemed to be to secure convictions, yet they did not consider the case of a man charged in the wrong. The memorandum argued against publication. Commenting on some of the statements by the clergy, the official in the Department of Justice concluded somewhat tongue in cheek:

> ... unless these statements are exaggerated (as they may easily have been owing to the anxiety of the reverend gentlemen concerned to present a strong case to the committee), the obvious conclusion to be drawn is that the ordinary feelings of decency and the influence of religion have failed in this country and that the only remedy is by way of police action. It is clearly undesirable that such a view of conditions in the Saorstát should be given wide circulation.[29]

The heads of the Criminal Law (Amendment) Bill were drafted and circulated in November 1933. The Act was passed in 1935.

Part of that draft Act dealt with dance halls. When the Minister for Justice met a delegation of the bishops in December 1932, it was stressed that an amendment to the law covering dance halls was 'very urgent'. An episcopal subcommittee had made a number of impractical suggestions, including one that young girls should be admitted to dances only when accompanied by their parents. A garda was to be at the entrance at all times. Ownership of dance halls was to be vested in the clergy or in the people of a parish.[30] The Dance Hall Act was also introduced as a separate piece of legislation, largely to satisfy the bishops. It provided that a licence from a local district court was necessary in order to hold a public dance. This piece of legislation was far from being successful.[31] It commercialised entertainment in the countryside and created the institutions captured so well in William Trevor's short story 'The Ballroom of Romance'. Flann O'Brien poked fun at the way in which some district justices had the 'habit of taking leave of their senses' at the annual licensing sessions:

> They want Irish dancing and plenty of it, even at the most monster 'gala dances'. They believe that Satan with all his guile is baffled by a four-hand reel and cannot make head or tail of the Rakes of Mallow. I do not think that there is any real ground for regarding Irish dancing as a sovereign spiritual and nationalistic prophylactic. If there is, heaven help the defenceless nations of other lands.[32]

There was another side to Irish society which has yet to be explored, the side which Brian Friel speaks about in *Dancing at Lughnasa* where the five sisters together look after the child 'born out of wedlock' and take care of their returned brother, Father Jack, who had been a missionary in Ryanga. He believed in ancestral spirits and offering sacrifices to the Great Goddess of the Earth, Obi. He extols the virtues of a society where what could be considered a bastard in Ireland was considered a 'love child' in his part of Africa. Women there wanted to have many 'love children'. Father Jack saw the practicality of polygamy. He explained how the Ryangans loved dance. They were a remarkable people with no distinction in their culture between the religious and the secular: 'And of course their capacity for fun, for laughing and practical jokes—they've such open hearts! In some respects they're not unlike us', he says. Father Jack was right, but the women in *Dancing at Lughnasa*, as was the case with many Irish women of the 1930s, felt too inhibited to exhibit the Ryangan side of their character. It simply slipped out in those very occasional moments of exuberance which could not be found in the highly chaperoned ballrooms of romance.[33]

Fianna Fáil's conservatism in the moral sphere was reflected in de Valera's handling of literary and film censorship. Some 1,700 books were banned by 1943, among them outstanding names in literature. These included titles by Graham Greene, Ignazio Silone, Alberto Moravia, Miguel de Unamuno, Andre Malraux and Robert Graves. The best of the Irish writers were added to the list: Kate O'Brien, Seán O'Faoláin, Frank O'Connor, Austin Clarke, Liam O'Flaherty, Seán O'Casey, Samuel Beckett, George Bernard Shaw and James Joyce.

De Valera quickly turned into a bitter disappointment for those members of the Irish literary establishment who thought that Fianna Fáil promised something different to Cumann na nGaedheal. Seán O'Faoláin, the author of two biographies of de Valera, saw him as a politician rooted in feelings rather than thought, who had an 'urban sentimentality about the land' and the Gaeltacht. De Valera, according to O'Faoláin, allowed himself to be dominated by 'race memory' and a nostalgia for the land of north Cork and south Limerick. When de Valera attempted to formulate his ideal image of life, he saw 'something so dismal that beside it the Trappist rule of Mount Melleray is a Babylonian orgy'. Many intellectuals felt themselves ground to bits in de Valera's new Ireland, according to O'Faoláin. Fianna Fáil was creating, he wrote, a new middle class familiar to those who had read the novels of Balzac:

> They were not very different to what you see any day at Baldoyle [racecourse] or in the Dolphin Restaurant, except that the new middle-classes were much more cultivated in France. Our replacement society was, mainly, a lot of well-meaning, good hearted, good humoured, not unidealistic, cute chancers with about as much cultivation as the heel of your boot.[34]

Perhaps O'Faoláin gives a somewhat one-sided representation of the new Irish entrepreneurial class that was emerging from behind the tariff wall imposed by Fianna Fáil. The Control of Manufacturers Act 1932—so repugnant to the outgoing secretary of the Department of Industry and Commerce, Gordon Campbell—was not sufficiently radical to meet 'the demands of the more vocal native industrialists'.[35] There was clearly a strong lobby for the creation of an autarchic industrial class, some of whom were certainly 'not unidealistic, cute chancers', as O'Faoláin had termed them. But the nationalists, who wished to reduce radically the number of foreign subsidiaries, failed to persuade Fianna Fáil to take such a decisive step. When Seán Lemass introduced new industrial legislation in 1934, it proved to be 'a comparatively moderate reaction to popular demands rather than something foisted on the public by the Fianna Fáil government.'[36]

If Fianna Fáil was to disappoint the young Irish writers of the 1930s, Irish business people, too, had cause to feel some frustration. By the autumn of 1932, the farming community had felt the impact of the trade war with Britain. Hostility to Fianna Fáil had led to the formation of the Army Comrades Association, led by Dr T.F. O'Higgins (brother of Kevin O'Higgins), in February 1932. Made up mainly of ex-servicemen, it had grown to about 30,000-strong within a few months. Employed as a quasi praetorian guard by Cumann na nGaedheal, it clashed on occasion with a triumphalist IRA—many of whose members had been released by de Valera immediately after he came into power. 'No free speech for traitors' was the fascistic slogan of the IRA that autumn as it sought to harass Cosgrave's party. It also sought to intimidate people into buying, and drinking, Irish products. The high priests of Irish nationalism deemed it unpatriotic to drink Bass and this resulted in commando-like assaults on pub signs and kegs of beer. The loss of thousands of gallons of Bass was perhaps the IRA's only clear-cut major victory since 1921.

It was irksome for Fianna Fáil to have to depend upon the support of Labour to maintain its majority in the Dáil. William Norton, an ex-post office worker, was a poor substitute for Tom Johnson as party leader. He was no match for de Valera as a political tactician, and Fianna Fáil successfully continued to pilfer Labour policies throughout the early 1930s. The budget, introduced by MacEntee on 11 May 1932, placated Labour since it was 'calculated to give relief to the poor at the expense of the rich'. There were provisions for increases in housing grants, old age pensions, pensions for the blind and milk for children in need. The standard rate of income tax was raised from 3s. 6d. to 5s.[37] Tom Johnson was made a member of a housing board, and of a Cost of Living Commission of Enquiry set up by the government.

While conservative on socio-sexual matters, Fianna Fáil began with a sense of social radicalism: 'We were outraged by the sight of children with bare feet in winter living in tenements', Frank Aiken once explained. But the daily demands of government meant that the radical reform, which some members of Fianna Fáil sought, could not be achieved. The 'economic war' with Britain forced de Valera to take measures of retrenchment. At the end of December, the government announced that it was planning to reduce the cost of living bonus of all civil servants by one-thirteenth at the beginning of the new year. That would affect the lower paid civil servants in particular. Members of Norton's Post Office Workers' Union were directly threatened. A concession to reduce the cut by 50 per cent in the case of the lower paid was rejected by Labour on 30 December and the party announced that its continued support of the government in the Dáil was under active consideration.

Before examining the snap election of January 1933, it should be stressed that de Valera had gained personal prestige by comporting himself with some skill on the international stage since coming to power. He had sent a delegation to the Commonwealth economic conference in Ottawa at the end of July. A complicated exchange of views between Dublin and London took place in the following months. In October, de Valera, MacEntee, Geoghegan and Conor Maguire, the Attorney General, travelled to London to take part in a conference on the financial dispute and the annuities question. Although the talks ended in failure, de Valera dispatched Joseph Walshe to London ten days after his return to continue the search for a solution. Lemass was pressing for a quick settlement to the economically ruinous trade war, which was so subversive of the efforts of the Department of Industry and Commerce to foster rapid job creation.[38] Supporters of the opposition also sought to end the silly one-sided war, and the latter months of 1932 presented de Valera with a growing problem as the economic situation in the country deteriorated.

De Valera succeeded in counteracting some of the adverse publicity at home by his performance as president of the council of the League of Nations. He opened the League assembly on 26 September with a speech which had been written by a young Irish diplomat, Frederick Boland, who had entered the department only in 1929. It was clear and candid and, while it took the delegates by surprise, its honesty won de Valera much praise. 'It is a tragedy that his mental blindness prevents him from applying the principles which he enunciated at Geneva nearer home', commented the correspondent of the *Round Table*.[39] The same writer provided an explanation for de Valera's decision to call a snap election for 24 January 1933:

> Pressed by Labour on the left, sniped at by the IRA in the rear, and harried by the more conservative elements amongst his own followers on the right, his position had become intolerable to a man of his autocratic mentality.

ELECTION VICTORY AND THE IRA THREAT

The decision to go to the polls had less to do with pique than with a keenly developed sense of political timing.

De Valera did not want to give the opposition parties the opportunity to unite against him. Cumann na nGaedheal had seen the necessity to regroup and reorganise swiftly. Overtures had been made to the leader of a new National Centre Party, Frank MacDermot; but he had turned his back on the proposition of national government with Cumann na nGaedheal. Representing the larger farmers, he had found little to inspire him in the performance of Cosgrave. The electoral campaign further reinforced MacDermot's ambivalence towards Cumann na nGaedheal. In an effort to outbid Fianna Fáil, Cosgrave pledged that he would end the economic war with England within three days, reduce the land annuities by one-half and suspend the payment of the annuities for two years. The only thing Cosgrave had not promised, commented one humorist, was to offer to pay annuities *to* the farmers.[40] Meanwhile, in London, there were expectations that Cosgrave would be returned to power 'with a surprising majority'. But the British government also had its sceptics.

In his election campaign, de Valera blamed the British for the weak state of the Irish economy. Despite the fact that unemployment had risen from 30,000 in March to 80,000 in October, he refused to modify his Anglo-Irish policy. In the Executive Council, Lemass, MacEntee and Ryan favoured the early ending of the economic war.

When the ballots were counted, Fianna Fáil had an overall majority of one, with 77 seats; Cumann na nGaedheal had 48 (a loss of nine). Labour increased its representation by one to eight, while the Centre Party won 11 seats and independents got the remaining nine seats.[41] It was not all that de Valera would have wanted but, at least, he had a working majority and the confidence that the Labour Party had more in common with Fianna Fáil than with any of the main opposition parties.

De Valera did not find that there was any need to make radical changes. His ministers were performing well.[42] The efficiency of many of them had surprised the opposition. The predicted army coup had not taken place either in 1932 or in 1933. De Valera had not manifested any signs of extremism in his handling of government policy. Quite the reverse. Showing no desire to declare himself a green *duce*, he quickly assumed the role of conservative statesman, using a firm and restraining hand on his more radical colleagues. He did not fulfil the prophecy that he would be a Kerensky-like figure, who would allow himself to be manipulated by the IRA.

Speaking in the Dáil on 29 May 1935, de Valera admitted to disappointment at the failure of the IRA to accept peaceful government by majority rule. 'Political' murders continued. Hugh O'Reilly had been attacked and died of gunshot wounds in December 1933. On 9 February 1935, Richard More-O'Farrell had been shot dead following a raid on his family home. Vice-Admiral Henry Boyle Somerville was shot dead by the IRA at Castletownshend, Co. Cork, on 24 March 1936. His crime: that he had written references for locals who wished to join the British forces. On 26 April 1936, John Egan was shot dead in Dungarvan, Co. Waterford by members of the IRA for giving information to the police which had led to the discovery of an arms dump. De Valera had thought that he could co-opt the IRA, but the tactic of bringing 'retired' IRA members into the local defence force, the special branch and the army had only limited success.

A left-wing section of the IRA continued to lay stress on the need for social agitation and class-based urban/agrarian movements. Peadar O'Donnell, George Gilmore and Frank Ryan were among those who wished to make common cause with other fringe revolutionary groups on the left in Ireland. In an atmosphere of strong anti-communism, such moves were not likely to have had much success. Two examples of popular intolerance for the activities of the left will illustrate this point. In March 1933, a workers' college in Connolly House in Dublin was attacked by a mob whipped up to a frenzy by a priest during a religious retreat.[43] On another occasion, James Gralton, an Irish Marxist who had returned from the United States, was a victim of mob violence. He ran free dances in a hall in County Leitrim which was attacked and fired upon. Peadar O'Donnell, who went to speak on his behalf at Drumsna, Co. Leitrim had to climb out of danger when the local priest threw the second clod at him. He got away with 'a few bruises and two cracked ribs'.[44]

The minutes of the general 'army convention' of 17 March 1934 provide an important insight into the basis of the ideological division which ultimately split the organisation. George Price proposed that the IRA redeclare its 'allegiance to the Republic of Ireland, based upon production and distribution for use and not for profit in which exploitation of the labour of human beings with all its attendant miseries and insecurities shall not be tolerated. . . .'[45] Tom Barry of Cork opposed the motion on the grounds that 'if we were able to seize power we would have to hold it'. He felt that it would mean having to keep factories open. Barry argued that the communist bogey was one that created 'great difficulties' for the IRA. Countering, O'Donnell felt that they had to have a plan which would bring about the unity of the country: 'We have about 12,000 people in the IRA. There are 100,000 adults behind us. That 100,000 is being shut out.' O'Donnell wanted to build a national network and seemed to hint at the idea of a popular social uprising.

Seán MacBride opposed the motion on the grounds that it would ultimately mean having to contest elections: 'I have very little faith in the mass of the constitutionalist republicans nor in the opinion of the mass of the people.' (Those same sentiments were echoing through fascist Europe at the time.) On the other side, Frank Ryan saw no future for the IRA if it did not adopt the motion: 'The whole people are looking to us for a lead and we are not leading.' Fianna Fáil had once sought an alliance with the IRA and 'now they treat us with contempt'. He accused MacBride of wanting inactivity to continue. MacBride, in turn, said that the IRA should be the guiding influence of the mass of the people. The meeting ended in acrimony as the motion was defeated. A second motion, introduced by O'Donnell, to establish a Republican Congress was also defeated and there was a general walkout by left-wing delegates.[46] 'Court martials', expulsions and resignations followed.

About 180 delegates of the breakaway group met at Rathmines town hall, Dublin on 29 September 1934. The appearance earlier in the summer of a new paper, *Republican Congress*, had provided the ideological direction for the meeting. Edited by Frank Ryan, it was denounced by many members of the clergy as a communist organ. At the Rathmines meeting, the delegates were split between those who sought to establish a workers' republic and those who wanted a left-wing, republican, anti-de Valera, popular front. The latter carried the day by ninety-nine votes to eighty-four. The movement was split at birth and soon entered into decline. One of its only notable actions was to carry out an attack on the Savoy cinema, Dublin, where a film of a British royal wedding was being shown. Lack of funds and internal divisions ended the life of the Republican Congress. A young County Waterford teacher, Frank Edwards, was dismissed by the clerical manager of his school because of his attendance at the Congress.[47] The 1930s were not a time when left-wing sympathisers could expect tolerance in Ireland.

The government, however, was much more concerned with the threat from the physical force movement than from the Irish social revolutionary left. On 18 June 1936, the IRA was declared an illegal organisation by the Executive Council under article 2A of the constitution. The IRA march to Bodenstown on 23 June was banned. Maurice Twomey, one of the leading IRA men, was arrested and jailed. Many of those who remained in the organisation after 1936 were of a green fascist mentality and it was no coincidence that they sought to collaborate with Nazi Germany during World War II.

FASCISM AND THE BLUESHIRTS

The threat to freedom of speech from the IRA had been the suggested cause for the emergence of the Army Comrades Association (ACA) in February 1932. The economic war provided the context of social threat in which such a movement might develop. In 1933 the crushing electoral defeat encouraged usually staid members of Cumann na nGaedheal to become reckless. The successes of fascism in many Catholic countries in Europe made that ideology attractive. De Valera's sacking of Eoin O'Duffy as Garda Commissioner on 22 February 1933 provided the embryonic movement with a charismatic leader. The 'green *duce*' took over his new post as leader of the ACA on

20 July 1933 and had the organisation renamed the National Guard. The blue shirt was adopted as a uniform and the flag of St Patrick was chosen as an emblem. National reunification was the organisation's first aim. The National Guard was also committed to oppose 'communism and alien control and influence in national affairs and to uphold Christian principles'. To be a member, one had to be Irish or have parents 'who professed the Christian faith'.[48] Jews, therefore, were not eligible to apply for membership. A new publication, *The Blueshirt*, denied on 5 August 1933 that the movement was anti-semitic, but that was not the case. Members of secret organisations were also prohibited from joining the Blueshirts. This was a movement which could be described as being clerico-fascist.

O'Duffy was vain enough to consider himself to be a Celtic version of Mussolini. He presented himself to one Italian visitor, who reported him as saying that 'he did not fear the use of the word dictator nor the word fascism'.[49]

The United Irishman, a Cumann na nGaedheal paper, carried an article on 17 June 1933 which gave advice to the members of the ACA— not in any sense a pacifist organisation:

It is not, therefore, pledged to confine itself to verbal methods. If a comrade is subjected, because of his membership of the association, to gross abuse, his reply should be a swift blow or series of blows. When for any reason this dignified and effective type of rejoinder is not possible, the comrade should preserve a studied calm and contemptuous silence.[50]

O'Duffy left Dublin on a countrywide recruiting campaign, threatening to return to lead a march to the Dáil on 13 August—the annual day of commemoration for Michael Collins and Arthur Griffith. Frank Aiken, the Minister for Defence, believed that O'Duffy was planning a Mussolini-style march on Leinster House. He had had reports that O'Duffy had been trying to infiltrate the army, and the minister knew that O'Duffy had had success among discontented reserve officers.[51] Seán Lemass did not know whether the army and the police could be trusted. He, too, felt that O'Duffy was trying to emulate Mussolini's march on Rome and to take over by force the parliament and government offices.[52] The meeting was proscribed. Gardaí on duty at Leinster House were armed and their number increased to 300. Swoops were carried out on the homes of known Blueshirts and all firearms were confiscated. O'Duffy was forced to abandon the idea of a meeting. It is not possible to know what O'Duffy would have done if he had found himself at the head of a large crowd in the grounds of Leinster House, but the likelihood is that he would have tried to seize power.

On 23 August, the government banned the National Guard. De Valera employed the full force of the Offences against the State Act to deal with the threat to law and order. Military tribunals sat to administer justice. The same military personnel were used as had been first employed in 1931. De Valera had already set up an auxiliary police force of ex-IRA men who had fought in the civil war on the anti-Treaty side. These became known as the 'Broy Harriers', after Colonel Eamon Broy, the new head of the gardaí. A police raid was carried out on the headquarters of the National Guard in Dublin on 30 August. Three days before, O'Duffy had been prevented from holding a meeting at Béal na mBláth, Co. Cork (the place where Michael Collins had been killed).

The perceived persecution of O'Duffy by the government temporarily blinded opposition politicians to his many glaring faults as a leader. Determined to oust de Valera, three opposition parties— Cumann na nGaedheal, the Centre Party and the National Guard— fused into the one organisation, the United Ireland Party (Fine Gael), under the leadership of the mercurial O'Duffy. The Irish *Duce*, who was not a member of the Dáil, became its president. However, Cosgrave remained the leader of the parliamentary party and one of its three vice-presidents. (The other two were Frank MacDermot and James Dillon, the son of John Dillon, the Irish Parliamentary Party leader.) Lemass, somewhat cruelly if not aptly, called the new party 'the cripple alliance'.

O'Duffy announced the setting up of the Young Ireland Association to replace the banned National Guard. The government again intervened. On 14 December 1933, the League of Youth was established to replace the proscribed Young Ireland Association. Certain parts of the countryside were in a state of high agitation in 1934. The refusal of some farmers to pay land annuities led to the seizure of cattle. Special police stations were set up in particularly troublesome areas where provision was made to sell the seized cattle. At each centre a number of court messengers were employed, who operated under the protection of special police escorts for the serving of warrants. Attempts were made to intimidate purchasers, but the government ensured that the people who came forward to buy cattle were given safe passage out of the area. Blueshirts then resorted to sabotage—blocking roads, cutting telegraph wires and interfering with the railways. Firm government action against O'Duffy was matched with an increasing stridency and a violence of language which was a cause of embarrassment to people like MacDermot, Dillon and Cosgrave. For example, O'Duffy was quoted by Dillon as having been reported as saying in September 1934:

> His followers could allow no person to say they were traitors. They could not have that. *They must break the skull* of anyone who said they were traitors. [my italics.]

Dillon also quoted another newspaper account, which reported O'Duffy as saying:

> . . . if Mr Norton could name one labour man living in Germany or Italy who would vote against Hitler or Mussolini he would retire from public life . . . no power in the world could induce the people of Germany or Italy to change. *Hitler had done more for Germany* than any other leader in the world had done for his country. [my italics.]

Dillon called this *ráiméis* (rubbish).[53]

That was written at a time when O'Duffy's antics had exasperated many members of the Fine Gael leadership, yet there was no doubting the popularity of the general. In early February, in Dublin, O'Duffy was enthusiastically acclaimed by about 1,600 delegates at a convention of the United Ireland Party. His long speech had obviously been vetted and approved by the more staid members of his party; the mark of Professors James Hogan of University College, Cork and Michael Tierney of University College, Dublin was apparent in the text.

In response to O'Duffy's growing militarism, the government introduced the Wearing of Uniforms (Restriction) Bill on 23 February. This prohibited the wearing of uniforms and badges and the use of military titles in support of a political party. It also forbade the carrying of weapons, including sticks, at public meetings. The Bill was roundly attacked by a number of people who ought to have known better.[54] James Fitzgerald-Kenney, a former Minister for Justice, felt that a law that gave gardaí the power 'to tear the clothing off a respectable, decent Irish girl, to tear off her blouse in the public street or the public place, is a monstrous power to put in any Bill'.[55] It passed all stages in the Dáil on 14 March, but the Senate rejected it on 20 March by 30 votes to 18—thus delaying the implementation of the Act for eighteen months. A week later, de Valera introduced a Bill to abolish the Senate.

The Blueshirt threat continued and there were many disturbances throughout the country. One of the worst occurred in Cork in August when a crowd of about 3,000 farmers gathered outside Marsh's Yard, where a sale of seized cattle was taking place. A lorry, containing a number of men armed with sticks, was driven through the police cordon and a gate leading to the sale yard. The special branch men who were guarding the buyer opened fire and wounded seven of the men on the lorry. One of them, Michael Lynch, from Carrignavar, Co. Cork, died of his wounds. At his funeral on 15 August, O'Duffy described him as a 'Blueshirt martyr who had set an example for all to follow'.[56]

The previous month, on 9 July, MacDermot had written to O'Duffy from his sickbed in London. The time had come, he said, when he felt obliged to make a more formal protest than he had yet done against

. . . the tendency of certain speakers and writers of our party to attack the Parliamentary system of government, and to imply that it is our official policy to replace it by a Blue Shirt ascendancy modelled on Fascism.

MacDermot reminded the general that the party convention at the Mansion House had committed them to the experiment of forming economic corporations and the training of youth to ideals of voluntary public service. At the same time, they had pledged themselves to maintain democracy and the supremacy of parliament. Moreover, they had explained how they had wanted not to overturn the parliamentary system but to strengthen and improve it: 'I am fully prepared to defend "Kangaroo Democracy" on its merits',[57] he wrote.

O'Duffy replied on 13 July that 'far from having any desire to overturn the parliamentary system we wanted to strengthen and improve it'. He wanted to maintain parliament but to set up, at the same time, a national economic council to advise parliament on agricultural and industrial questions. That explanation did not satisfy MacDermot, who had determined that O'Duffy had to go. However, illness prevented him from being more active in Irish politics at the time. Fine Gael realists had gained a glimpse of the future when O'Duffy failed to lead the party to victory in the local government elections held on 26 June 1934. O'Duffy was rash enough to state during the campaign that his party would secure a majority on every county council. They did so in only eight out of twenty-three. Fianna Fáil retained control over the remaining fifteen. In all, Fianna Fáil won 728 seats, Fine Gael 596, Labour 185 and others 371. Of the independents, 118 were said to favour Fianna Fáil and 253 Fine Gael. That meant that the government bloc held 946 seats, against 934 held by its opponents. Four county councils—Tipperary South Riding, Kilkenny, Queen's County (Laois) and Waterford—all with anti-government majorities, were suspended before the election by the Minister for Local Government, Seán T. O'Kelly, on the grounds of maladministration. No elections were held in those areas. To add insult to injury, the elections were held on a register of rated occupiers—the last not to be held under full universal suffrage.[58] However, if the vote increased the lobby inside Fine Gael to get rid of O'Duffy, it was not sufficiently strong to prompt de Valera to call an immediate general election.

It was apparent that the marriage of Blueshirtism and the conventional opposition parties was under severe strain in the early autumn of 1934. Dillon explained to MacDermot on 25 September that he was convinced that O'Duffy had 'made up his mind after the local elections that constitutionalism did not pay' and that he had prepared the ground to split Fine Gael and the League of Youth. According to that theory, O'Duffy wanted to win control of the League of Youth[59] and press for more radical policies. He may have been encouraged to pursue that line by his lieutenant, Thomas Gunning, who operated as his spy during subsequent discussions of the national executive of Fine Gael. However, on 30 August, the executive met in Dublin and a long discussion on the general policy and its internal organisation took place. The Blueshirts' 'no rent' manifesto was vetoed and it was agreed that TDs would be invited by the divisional officers of the League of Youth to their monthly meetings. It proved to be a very acrimonious meeting and Dillon recorded that there were 'disgusting scenes' between O'Duffy and James Hogan, in the course of which O'Duffy abused the professor 'like a fishwife'. The latter had been vehemently opposed to O'Duffy's wild scheme to try to organise the Blueshirts in Northern Ireland.[60] Rashly, O'Duffy resigned from Fine Gael and public life a few days later. According to Dillon, he was prepared to come back in six months if called upon, but insisted that it would be 'on his own terms'. The national executives of the League of Youth and Fine Gael were called into session. A Dublin publican, Paddy Belton, tried to split the two movements. Gunning left the room periodically to report developments by phone to O'Duffy. In the interval during the meetings of the two executives, Belton let it be known that O'Duffy was now prepared to withdraw his resignation. Dillon believed that, at that stage, when O'Duffy realised that he could not split Fine Gael and the League of Youth, he had given instructions to Gunning to split the League itself. He was further of the opinion that O'Duffy might have succeeded had he not already resigned. Dillon admitted that he had been extremely reluctant to face the parting of the ways, but he had been convinced that it had been made inevitable by O'Duffy's conduct after his resignation and by the content of his recent speeches. He felt, however, that good would come out of 'what seems at first glance to be evil'.[61] His resignation was accepted. O'Duffy's tactic had backfired. He did not leave gracefully and showed no willingness in the following weeks to stay out of public life. He tried to claw his way back to the leadership of the League of Youth. Tierney described as 'grotesque' the general's efforts to regain power.[62] He founded the National Corporate Party in 1935 and a year later tried to re-enter Irish politics via Spain.

Slowly Fine Gael sought to rebuild. But Michael Tierney did not think that the troubles in the party were over. He felt that the return of Cosgrave to the leadership 'quite blasts all chance of beating Dev. in any measurable time'. The departure of O'Duffy, he argued, meant that the party had 'become Cumann na nGael [sic] all over again, without becoming very much inclined to extremism'. Tierney thought that Blythe and E. Cronin (the new leader of the League of Youth) would be easier to talk to than O'Duffy: 'It is quite true, I am afraid, that he has become impossible, but it's equally impossible without him.'[63] Finally, Tierney advised MacDermot to 'abandon politics'. The former said that he had 'lost hope in the old gang completely. They will never move until the electorate exterminates them.'

COSGRAVE AND IRISH FOREIGN POLICY

On 3 October 1935, Italian troops invaded Abyssinia. They moved southwards from the colony of Eritrea and northwards from Italian Somaliland. The war was over in seven months and Mussolini was victorious. De Valera had warned the Assembly of the League of Nations in Geneva on 16 September: 'Make no mistake, if on any pretext whatever we were to permit the sovereignty of even the weakest state amongst us to be unjustly taken away, the whole foundation of the League would crumble into dust.'[64] He supported the imposition of sanctions against Italy. In the aftermath of the failure of that policy, de Valera told the League on 2 July 1936 that financial measures could be made effective only 'if we are prepared to back them up by military measures'. He deplored the fact that no one, apparently, was prepared to risk a war that would be transferred to Europe for the sake of a nation in Africa.[65] The Labour Party supported de Valera, leaving the remainder of the parliamentary opposition in some disarray. For example, Sir Osmond Grattan Esmonde, Fine Gael TD for Wexford, felt that Haile Selassie was more likely to be the descendant of King Herod of Jerusalem than King Solomon: 'I think that in this war Signor Mussolini is the Abraham Lincoln of Africa, and that he is out to abolish the slave trade in spite of the sentimental sympathy of Great Britain.'[66] Who was really at fault in the eyes of Paddy Belton? None other than the Jews, who, he said, were 'there or thereabouts in Abyssinia, too'.[67] Eoin O'Duffy, who had just returned from the world fascist conference at Montreux, assured his followers that Italy had taken steps 'to end an intolerable situation and defend her prestige among the civilised nations'. He said that several Blueshirts of his party had volunteered their services in the fight.[68]

When William Cosgrave tried to articulate his party's position, he linked Irish support for sanctions with the securing of economic concessions from the British in the trade war.[69] Further speeches of that nature were made by O'Higgins and Cronin.[70] Disquiet in Fine Gael ranks with such a crude policy line led to the resignation of one of the party's vice-presidents, Frank MacDermot.[71] He felt that the Fine Gael policy position offended against 'common sense and decency'. This brought immediate support from the former Irish envoy to Berlin, Daniel Binchy, who congratulated MacDermot on 3 November 1935 on his 'stand for political decency and common honesty, of which your late colleagues seem to have forgotten the meaning'. It was what Binchy had expected of MacDermot: 'It must be of some consolation to you to feel that every word uttered by you in the course of this controversy will be heartily endorsed by decent people of all parties.' He added:

> I have had more first-hand experience than most people of their 'international [sic] policy' when they were in government and accordingly I know that in the present case they are merely running true to type. The loss is their own.[72]

Fine Gael lost political ground on the Ethiopian issue, particularly because 'on the whole, indeed, Irish public opinion may be said to be quite solidly behind him [De Valera] in the attitude he has taken up.'[73] A subsequent effort by Cosgrave to retrieve the situation in a speech at Navan, on 11 October, met with little success. He still had to claim that it would not have been irrelevant to have dealt with the Anglo-Irish dispute at Geneva. Cosgrave's maladroit handling of the Ethiopian crisis had simply highlighted the continuing state of disarray inside Fine Gael. De Valera had yet again been allowed to use a foreign policy issue to embarrass Fine Gael.

DE VALERA'S SEARCH FOR AUTARCHY

Fianna Fáil remained very vulnerable over the retarded performance of the Irish economy. The government did not secure rapid economic growth for the country. The great depression and US immigration restrictions meant that more Irish people were forced to remain at home in the 1930s. The total population rose from 2,927,000 in the first half of the 1930s to 2,971,000 in 1935. By 1939 it had fallen again to 2,936,000. Emigration averaged 14,000 a year in the 1930s—there was a small net inflow in 1932—compared with 35,000 in the early years of the state's existence.[74] Emigration, which was now mainly to Britain rather than to the US, increased again in the latter part of the 1930s, reaching 26,000 in 1937.[75]

The economic war had been one of de Valera's most costly diplomatic gaffes. Neither London nor Dublin wanted to continue, but it was difficult to see how it could be ended. A manifestation of goodwill was shown by both sides on 3 January 1935 when the Coal-Cattle Pact was signed. The British government agreed to increase the quota of imports of Irish cattle by one-third. The Irish government reciprocated by agreeing to buy its coal from Britain, thus taking the wind out of the sails of the Jonathan Swift slogan which had been purloined by the IRA: 'Burn everything British but their coal.'[76] But there were 145,000 on the unemployment register in January 1936. Precious energy had been deflected into fighting mythical battles with the British, which had little to do with hard economic issues, and much more to do with trying to salve wounded 'national' pride. The Guinness company, which exported nearly three-quarters of its output, built a new brewery in Park Royal, London. It opened in 1936, contributing directly to the decline in Irish exports from 1.3 million barrels in 1935 to 0.8 in 1938.[77] Would this diversification have taken place had there not been an economic war?

Clearly, Fianna Fáil did not preside over an 'economic miracle' between 1932 and 1936, but there was something refreshingly innovative about the government's administrative style. Seán Lemass, in particular, was no respecter of economic sacred cows. He had difficulty dealing with the idolators, who could not see beyond the golden calf of *laissez-faire.*[78] But despite his failure to nationalise the Irish transport system, the semi-state sector was dramatically expanded in other important respects. Cumann na nGaedheal had set up the Electricity Supply Board, the Agricultural Credit Corporation and the Dairy Disposal Company. In 1933, Comhlucht Siúicre Éireann was founded to manufacture sugar from home-grown beet. The Industrial Credit Company was founded in 1933. The Turf Development Board was established in 1934 (it became a statutory body, Bord na Móna, in 1946). A chemicals manufacturer, Ceimicí Teoranta, was set up in 1934. The Irish airlines, Aer Lingus, was founded in 1936 and cross-channel services to London, Liverpool and Bristol were up and running before the war. The Irish Life Assurance Company and the Irish Tourist Board were both established in 1939.[79] Reviewing progress in April 1937, Lemass told the Dáil that 800 new factories and workshops had been started since Fianna Fáil had come to power, including fifty large factories in the previous year. He said that in September 1936 78,000 people had been employed in protected industries.[80]

Lemass was very much a Roosevelt-style New Dealer. That American Democratic spirit had much more influence on Fianna Fáil than the meanderings of continental Catholic authoritarians. While Lemass espoused the cause of protectionism and put up with the silliness of the economic war, he refused to make excuses for inefficiency. The Minister for Industry and Commerce told an annual dinner of the Federation of Saorstát Industries in 1937 that there was no national ground for the maintenance of an inefficient concern—the type that feared competition—no matter who owned it. On the contrary, he said, there were many grounds for putting it out of existence as quickly as possible. The minister was referring to an agitation for the limitation of the number of firms in certain industries on the plea of overproduction and undue competition. Internal competition was largely relied on to check possible abuses of protection, secure efficiency and keep prices at a reasonable level, he said.[81] Lemass wanted no truck with green gombeenism.

The government's record on progressive legislation was not unimpressive. The extension of unemployment assistance was carried out. Widows' and orphans' allowances were increased.[82] An average of 12,000 houses per annum were built in the country between 1932 and 1942. The figure had been 2,000 per year during the tenure of Cumann na nGaedheal.[83] A large-scale school building programme was undertaken in the vocational sector in 1936.[84]

Religion continued to be included in the curriculum of the vocational schools. The Minister for Education, Tom Derrig, was a less than inspiring choice for that portfolio. Unlike Lemass in Industry and Commerce and Jim Ryan in Agriculture, Derrig did not have an innovative mind. Perhaps that was what de Valera wanted—a safe pair of hands. Derrig's relationship with the Irish National Teachers' Organisation was needlessly testy. It was not helped by the salary cuts introduced in 1933 for teachers and public servants.[85] There was a strong emphasis on the teaching of Irish. The marginalised children of inner city Dublin may have found an unlikely ally in a snobbish parish priest, who spoke of 'reviving the language that was only the vehicle of expression for bog-men'.[86] The tragedy was that bad teaching, the rural-based imagery of textbooks and an elitist attitude among the new Gaelic Irish of Dublin officialdom and Fianna Fáil combined to make the language alien to city children. The richness of that tradition was denied to generations of the urban poor. But that did not mean that some success was not recorded in the revival of the language in the 1930s. The number of all-Irish primary schools increased from 228 in 1931 to 704 in 1939.[87] Ó Buachalla estimates that 12 per cent of the national schools and 28 per cent of the secondary schools in English-speaking areas were using Irish as the medium of instruction by the early 1940s. De Valera was a conservative influence in most facets of education and listened attentively to clerical experts in that field. While he was Minister for Education from September 1939 to June 1940, he established the Dublin Institute for Advanced Studies. But, overall, de Valera's Fianna Fáil failed to respond to the educational challenge of the 1930s and missed an opportunity to be innovative.

THE REALITY OF THE RURAL IDYLL

Rank poverty in the countryside in the 1930s continued to force young men and women to suffer the indignities of the 'hiring fair', so poignantly described by Patrick Kavanagh in *The Green Fool*.[88] Others sought seasonal work abroad. About 9,500 went to Britain in 1937 and, of that number, some 1,787 from west Mayo and west Donegal set out to work in the Scottish potato fields.[89] On 17 September 1937, *The Irish Press* carried a headline: 10 ACHILL YOUTHS PERISH IN HOLOCAUST. Three were sixteen, two were fifteen and the others were thirteen, seventeen, eighteen, nineteen and twenty-three. One family lost three sons and two other families lost two sons each. A bothy which housed the males had caught fire in Kirkintilloch, Dunbartonshire, Scotland: The doors were locked' was the only coherent, pitiful statement that the twelve girls who had escaped from the inferno could make to the *Irish Press* reporter when he arrived afterwards.[90] The editorial in the same paper commented that the very nature of the work the victims were engaged in added to the 'sentiments of pity and compassion which the holocaust in a Scottish bothy must excite'. Peadar O'Donnell, an ex-IRA activist and talented novelist, wrote a feature describing the circumstances of the tragedy:

Indeed there is little puzzle in what happened in Kirkintilloch. It was shifting day. The workers came from a far-away farm, as like as not in a different shire. As like as not they travelled in an open lorry packed in with their boxes. As like as not they got there around dusk. Probably the bothy had not been used since around this time last year. There would be no fire. The beds would be risky as the best thing to do would be to drag in plenty of good dry straw and make two big shake-downs. A fire, a drink of tea. Sleep. . . .[91]

Was this an acceptable image of a nation spiritually exalted by de Valera and Fianna Fáil? It was a metaphor of failure. Diarmuid Breathnach mentions that the bodies of the islanders were among the last passengers to travel by rail to Achill Sound: the line was closed on 30 September 1937. Ironically, the first train to run on this line as far as Mulrany in June 1894 had carried the bodies of 38 Achill islanders who had been drowned on their way to Scotland.[92] De Valera and other government ministers attended the heart-rending funeral service on 20 September. Archbishop Gilmartin of Tuam, in a sermon, described it as a time 'not so much for words as for silence and grief'.[93] He compared the lives of the victims to that of Christ the worker and said that they were 'martyrs to duty', the duty of having to earn 'your bread by the sweat of your brow'. An appeal, opened by *The Irish Press*, reached over £1,000 within days of the disaster.

Professor J.B. Whelehan wrote trenchantly about the event and castigated comfortable middle-class society for being too complacent:

Those of us whose lives are in the Ireland of easy-chairs, of cinemas and canned music, of golf and tennis, of jazz dance and autocars; those of us who so avidly chase every new sensation, who are at such pains to try new methods of 'killing' time; how can we realise the day-in, day-out struggle for bread by the victims of materialism and selfishness who live on barren rocks by the Atlantic. . . . No, we can know nothing of Western life nor can anyone who has not lived it realise its appalling tragedy of suffering slavery, starvation and disaster. Realise it! Why, we have not time to think of it! Our bridge-parties might suffer and our sherry-parties might cease to attract if we thought too much!

He viewed the measures taken by the government as 'half-hearted' and argued that it was no longer possible for the Irish to salve their consciences by blaming the Saxon:

Now that we are masters in our own land, are spectacles like those of Arranmore and Achill to be symptomatic of the use of our much-vaunted freedom? What matters political freedom to people who know not whence the next meal will come? What matters political freedom if our finest lads must still slave for the foreigner, and return, caskets of ashes?[94]

An interdepartmental committee, under Seán Lemass, met and reported its findings in 1938, but there was little to recommend beyond cataloguing the plight of those caught up in the annual migrations to England and Scotland. Trade union organisation was seen as being the only remedy.[95] Little that Fianna Fáil did after 1932 succeeded in removing the roots of radical poverty in areas where the party's strength remained firmest.

DE VALERA AND THE SPANISH CIVIL WAR

Fianna Fáil populism was strengthened by the party leader's adroit use of radio during the 1930s. The national station's attitude to political elites was rather deferential. It did not exactly pioneer the era of investigative journalism.[96] In an atmosphere of relative docility, de Valera became the first party leader in the history of the state to use the radio extensively. The attention paid to serving a mass audience enhanced de Valera's mystique and the strength of Fianna Fáil populism. Despite a poor speaking voice, he was an effective communicator to both his home constituency and to the Irish diaspora in Britain, Canada and the United States. Moreover, *The Irish Press* ensured that 'the chief's' message was reported without a comma out of place.

The Spanish civil war years tested de Valera's skills as a communicator and innovative political strategist. Spain was the continental foreign policy issue that most divided Irish society in the 1930s. The fight was popularly perceived as a straight conflict between communism and Catholicism. RED RULE IN SPAIN read a headline in the *Irish Independent* following the victory of the Popular Front coalition in February 1936.[97] RED DAWN IN SPAIN predicted the *Independent* on 14 July as the paper, four days later, welcomed the military revolt of General Francisco Franco.

The Irish Christian Front was set up in Dublin by supporters of Franco on 21 August 1936. Pledged to fight against the 'menace of communism' in Ireland and to aid the 'Christians in Spain in their fight against the new paganism', Paddy Belton—who had supported Mussolini in 1935—carried forward a crusade for the victory of international corporatism.[98] A series of 'monster' meetings were held throughout the country in the late summer, as many well-intentioned lay Catholics and former luminaries in the Blueshirts sought to show that the hour of corporatism had come at last in Ireland. Eoin O'Duffy was persuaded, through the intervention of Cardinal MacRory, to go to Spain to meet Franco. The acerbic Irish correspondent of the *Round Table* described him as belonging 'to that rather dangerous category of second-rate men of action to whom thought is abhorrent'. He felt that Spain was the best place for 'our Irish Don Quixote'.[99]

Plans for the establishment of an Irish brigade were accepted with alacrity by Franco, and O'Duffy returned to Dublin to recruit a promised 20,000 volunteers with the help of the minuscule Corporatist Party.[100] Meanwhile, the Irish Christian Front had been putting pressure on an all-too-compliant Catholic hierarchy to hold a special national collection for Spain. Following a meeting at Maynooth on 16 October, Cardinal MacRory issued a statement on behalf of the bishops. He described Spain as 'fighting the battle of Christendom against the subversive powers of communism'. The country had been made to endure 'the tragedy of ruin and shame . . . at the hand of an infamous minority under foreign dictation'.[101] Irish Catholics gave over £40,000 in a national church collection. The money was spent by the Irish Christian Front to purchase first-aid equipment for the insurgents and the remainder got into the hands of General Franco's side.[102]

In July 1936, the Spanish civil war appeared to present a major threat to the future of the Fianna Fáil government, faced as de Valera was with having to go to the polls within a year. *The Irish Times, The Irish Press,* the liberal journal *Ireland To-day,* and the republican and left-wing press varied in their positions, from hostility to the insurgents to outright support for the beleaguered republic.[103] There obviously had been some degree of sympathy for the Irish Christian Front expressed in Fianna Fáil ranks as a consequence of intense constituency pressure on TDs. Several local authorities in the country had passed resolutions calling upon the government to recognise General Franco's claims. However, de Valera had not made life easy for rural deputies by supporting, on 23 August 1936, the non-intervention principle in the Spanish conflict advocated by the French government. The government statement, issued on 25 August, said that Ireland was 'profoundly shocked by the tragic events' in Spain. It hoped that peace would soon return to that country and said that it 'would gladly participate in any practical effort directed towards that end'. Non-intervention and a refusal to interfere with the diplomatic status quo in relation to recognition remained the two principles of Irish foreign policy throughout the Spanish civil war. Twenty-seven countries eventually agreed to the principle of non-intervention. The Irish government prohibited the export of arms to either side in the conflict.[104] The Spanish Civil War (Non-intervention) Bill, which followed later, made participation in the war by Irish citizens punishable by a fine of not more than £500 or two years in jail.

In two major debates on the Spanish civil war, in November 1936 and February 1937, the government showed no willingness to yield to Fine Gael's demands to give recognition to the *de facto* position of Franco as 'ruler' of Spain.[105] *The Irish Press* accused the opposition on 25 August 1936 of being 'more Catholic than the Pope'—a reference to the fact that the Vatican had continued at the time to recognise the Madrid government as the *de jure* government.[106]

After many vicissitudes, O'Duffy succeeded in getting over 700 volunteers to Spain by the end of 1936. The rector of the Irish College in Salamanca, Alexander J. McCabe, wrote in his journal after a visit to Cáceres, where the brigade was stationed:

> In modern Ireland there seems to be a lot of talk, claptrap and codology and this Irish brigade has been a regular frost and a complete washout. . . . It is a pity that Jack Doyle, the comedian-boxer, did not join the brigade. It would help to make it complete. All crusades are like this . . . they begin to reckon up in pence what they have won or lost.[107]

O'Duffy was not an inspiring leader. His brigade was poorly trained and even more poorly led. There was conflict between the Irish and Spanish officers. Ordered to the front in early 1937, the brigade was involved in a tragic exchange of fire with its own side. After a few months in a relatively quiet part of the front line, the brigade returned to Dublin in a welter of acrimony and recrimination.[108]

O'Duffy, a pathetic figure, was a spent political force. He died, a broken man, in 1944. His young aide, Thomas Gunning, remained on in Spain, where he worked with the Germans. A true believer in Nazism, Gunning played a role in the drawing up of charges against Frank Ryan. The latter was one of about 200 Irishmen who had fought on the republican side.[109] Ryan was charged with commanding republican firing squads. There was also a reference in the charge sheet to his alleged part in two murders in Ireland. Gunning later admitted that he had tried unsuccessfully to have Ryan shot, but Ryan survived jail in Franco's Spain and escaped with German help in July 1940.

The Irish envoy to Spain, Leopold Kerney, was ordered back to Madrid in April 1939. Franco was the *de facto* ruler of Spain.

BUNREACHT NA HÉIREANN

The political turbulence of the mid-1950s did not deflect de Valera from the task of writing a document which was to be his most enduring and problematical legacy to Irish society; Bunreacht na hÉireann was the embodiment of the Catholic nationalist tradition which he personified in his public life. His object was to replace what he considered to be the 'dictated' constitution of 1922 with a document 'freely' chosen by the Irish people. The writing of Bunreacht na hÉireann became de Valera's homework for almost a year before it was published in May 1937. The Executive Council formally took the decision to prepare a new constitution on 5 June 1936. The legal officer in the Department of External Affairs, John Hearne, had been chosen by de Valera in April to draft the heads of a Bill. The Irish high commissioner in London, John Dulanty, delivered a memorandum to King Edward VIII that same month, outlining the intentions of the Irish government. The abdication crisis, later that year, enabled de Valera in one Bill effectively to write the monarch and the governor general out of the existing constitution. The External Relations Bill provided for the continuance of existing diplomatic relations, whereby all foreign diplomats in Dublin would continue to be accredited to the British sovereign.[110]

The table on the next page traces the progress of the document through the final drafting stages in 1937.

Introduced in Dáil...10 March
Provisional draft (limited circulation by de Valera)
....10–15 March
First draft circulated...16 March
First revise circulated..1 April
Second revise circulated...10 April
Third revise...23 April
Published and circulated..1 May
Second Reading..1–13 May (69 votes to 43)
Third Reading (committee stage) ....25 May-3 June
Fourth Reading (report stage)..9–14 June
Approved by Dáil, and recommended for
adoption...14 June (62 votes to 48)
Enacted by the people..1 July

For 685,105

Against 526,945

Majority 158,160

Date of coming into operation.........................29 December 1938
Senate met...27 April
President elected..4 May
President entered office..25 June

On 12 March 1937, the Executive Council met to discuss general procedure in regard to the enactment of the new constitution. On 16 March, the printed text was distributed confidentially by de Valera to members of the Executive Council and to other selected persons, including the president of the High Court, Conor Maguire, a High Court judge, George Gavan Duffy, James Geoghegan of the Supreme Court and a small number of senior civil servants—one of whom was Joseph Walshe of the Department of External Affairs. The reaction to the private viewing of the draft constitution appears to have been generally favourable. However, the draft religious clause was dropped from the version that was formally circulated to all heads of departments in the civil service on 16 March.

One of the few comprehensive replies came from J.J. McElligott, secretary of the Department of Finance and a veteran of the GPO in 1916. He found what was to emerge in the final version as articles 2 and 3 to be somewhat irredentist in tone. The claim to territory 'which does not belong to us' gave, according to McElligott, a 'permanent place in the constitution to a claim to *Hibernia Irredenta*'. He was struck by the parallel with Mussolini's attitude to the Adriatic beyond its recognised seaboard. McElligott's comments were not heeded, but they have a present-day ring in view of the political debate on these two articles which has continued ever since.

De Valera set up a small drafting committee made up of Maurice Moynihan, John Hearne, Philip O'Donoghue, the legal adviser in the attorney general's office, and Michael McDunphy, assistant secretary, Department of the President. This committee was in constant touch with the President and met without a break up to the end of April, some of the sittings lasting until midnight or later. A separate committee worked on the Irish version, which was to become the official text. However, one serious problem remained. There was a major disagreement over the wording of the religious article, which was very confessional and had appeared only in the version privately circulated by de Valera on 10 March.[111] It reads as follows:

1. The state acknowledges the right of Almighty God to public worship in that way which He has shown to be His Will.

2. Accordingly, the state shall hold in honour the name of God and shall consider it a duty to favour and protect religion and shall not enact any measure that may impair its credit.

3. The state acknowledges that the true religion is that established by Our Divine Lord Jesus Christ Himself, which he committed to his Church to protect and propagate, as the guardian and interpreter of true morality. It acknowledges, moreover, that the Church of Christ is the Catholic Church.

4. The state recognises the Church of Christ as a perfect society, having within itself full competence and sovereign authority, in respect of the spiritual good of man.

   (i) Whatever may be ranked under the civil and political order is rightly subject to the supreme authority of the perfect society, the state, whose function it is to procure the temporal well-being, moral and material, of society.

(ii) The state pledges itself, therefore, in virtue of this sovereign authority conferred on it by God within its temporal sphere to enforce respect, by its just laws, for the inalienable rights of the citizen and the family, and to preserve, as best it can, conditions of right social and moral well-being.

(iii) In cases where the jurisdiction of Church and state requires to be harmoniously coordinated, the state may come to a special agreement with the Church and other religious bodies upon particular matters, civil, political and religious.

6. The state guarantees to its citizens freedom of religious conviction and liberty to practise their religion in private and in public, having due regard however to right order and morality.

7. The state pledges itself not to impose any disabilities on the ground of religious conviction that would be contrary to natural rights and social justice.

8. Every religious association, recognised by the state, shall have the right to manage its own affairs, own, acquire and administer property, movable and immovable, and maintain institutions for religious and charitable purposes.

9. The property of a religious denomination shall not be diverted save for necessary works of public utility and on payment of just compensation.

10. Legislation providing state aid for schools shall contain no discrimination against schools under the management of a particular religious denomination.

The month of April 1937 had been taken up with delicate negotiations with church leaders of all faiths. The following minute of discussions left by de Valera reveals the intensity of the shuttle diplomacy:

April 3	Called on the Nuncio, Paschal Robinson *(Saturday)*
April 5	Saw Cardinal Macrory at the Nunciature *(Monday)*
	Called on Archbishop Byrne
April 10	Saw the Nuncio, who promised to see Cardinal *(Saturday)*
	Saw Archbishop Edward Byrne
	Saw Dr J.A.H. Irwin (Presbyterian)

April 11	Saw the Nuncio at Seán T.'s *(Sunday)*
April 12	Called on Archbishop John Allen Gregg [Church of Ireland] *(Monday)*. Called on the Nuncio. Saw Dr Irwin
April 13	Phoned the Nuncio *(Tuesday)* Saw the Rev. W.H. Massey, head of the Methodist Church in Ireland
April 14	Saw Dr Irwin *(Wednesday)*
April 16	Saw Dr Irwin, the Moderator, and the Moderator Designate, who travelled from Belfast *(Friday)* Saw the Nuncio at Seán T.'s J.P.W. [Walshe] went to Rome *(Friday evening)*
April 22	Called on the Nuncio *(Thursday)*
April 23	Nuncio phoned to say Cardinal approved Christian Churches *(Friday)*
April 24	Saw Nuncio and Cardinal *(Saturday)*
April 26	M. Moynihan saw Archbishop Gregg and D. Robinson got letter from Archbishop Gregg to Archbishop Charles Frederick D'Arcy of Armagh *(Monday)*
April 27	Robinson goes to see D'Arcy *(Tuesday)*[112]

De Valera sought to avoid a church-state crisis. While he found the archbishop of Dublin accommodating, he was disturbed to learn that the Cardinal archbishop of Armagh, MacRory, was hardline and wanted—like McQuaid—to have a 'one, true church' formula included as of right.

Joseph Walshe was sent to Rome in an effort to break the deadlock and avoid a serious crisis between church and state. He saw the cardinal secretary of state, Eugenio Pacelli, who was later to become Pius XII. It was obvious that the Vatican had been advised by the apostolic nuncio in Dublin to remain uncommitted in the affair. Pacelli explained patiently how the Holy See could not give approval unless the Catholic Church was recognised. On two occasions he suggested to the alarmed Walshe that the Irish might be in heresy, but that was perhaps a special form of humour displayed by the ultra-serious cardinal. In the end, Pacelli told Walshe that the pope's position was *ni approvo ni non disapprovo, taceremo,* meaning: 'I neither approve nor do I disapprove, we'll maintain our silence.' That was good news for Walshe. He could now write to Dublin that it would be possible to use the term *churches* for the other Christian bodies. The neutrality of the Holy See also meant that de Valera could avoid a serious church-state crisis, which almost certainly would have meant defeat for the constitution in a referendum.

The constitution was published, together with the final wording of the religious article [44], on 1 May. It read in part:

(i)   The State acknowledges that the homage of public worship is due to Almighty God. It shall hold His Name in reverence, and shall respect and honour religion.

(ii) The State recognises the special position of the Holy Catholic Apostolic and Roman church as the guardian of the Faith professed by the great majority of the citizens.

(iii) The State also recognises the Church of Ireland, the Presbyterian Church in Ireland, the Methodist Church in Ireland, the Religious Society of Friends in Ireland, as well as the Jewish Congregations and the other religious denominations existing in Ireland at the date of the coming into operation of this Constitution.

(i)   Freedom of conscience and the free profession and practice of religion are, subject to public order and morality, guaranteed to every citizen.

It was approved by the Dáil and recommended for adoption on 14 June by 62 votes to 48.

Less than half-an-hour after the Dáil rose on 14 June, de Valera dissolved the Oireachtas and declared a general election and the holding of a referendum on the new constitution. It was clear from the outset that the governing party intended to run on the issue of the constitution; de Valera said in a broadcast to the United States on 15 June that the document was 'the spiritual and cultural embodiment of the Irish people' and dismissed opposition allegations that he wished to establish a dictatorship.[113] The choice was between approval of 'our own constitution or a badge of subjection', he told a rally in Dublin.[114]

Fianna Fáil again built its campaign about its leader. He traversed the countryside and spoke at 24 major rallies. His campaign began in the west and then went south. De Valera toured the midlands and the north-west. According to *Irish Press* reporters, he made 'triumphal' entries into every town, where he was accorded 'magnificent' receptions. His arrival in the capital of his own constituency, Ennis, had the town in 'tumult'. *The Irish Press* reported that his 'great cavalcade of motors' made its way from Scariff along the roads dotted with bonfires, and crowds blocked his way when de Valera reached Ennis. There, fifty horsemen were drawn up to lead him to his hotel. The 'air resounded to the noise of exploding rockets and the music of bands' as he reached Carmody's Hotel, 'amid scenes of unparalleled enthusiasm'.[115] That same political liturgy was repeated elsewhere. At Dungloe, Co. Donegal, de Valera said:

> Not since the time that the great Irish chiefs, O'Neill and O'Donnell, left these shores have we arrived at the position we have got today. We are as certain as we are alive that in a relatively short time this country will be one united whole.[116]

Fianna Fáil fought with the energy of a party faced with the possibility of defeat. The passions stirred by the Blueshirts, the rage engendered by the enforced sale of confiscated cattle, and the general sense of economic turmoil in the countryside were factors which told against Fianna Fáil. The Spanish civil war had added another negative variable for de Valera, as had his policy of non-intervention, but fortunately for Fianna Fáil, Cosgrave and the opposition fought a lacklustre campaign. The constitution was de Valera's trump card, to which Cosgrave had no counter. To make matters even worse for Fine Gael, O'Duffy and 633 members of his faction-ridden brigade arrived home from Spain on 21 June. They did little to enhance opposition chances of victory. When the votes were counted there was a majority for the constitution: Fianna Fáil won 69 seats, Fine Gael 48, Labour 13 and independents got eight. Two ex-ministers, Richard Mulcahy (beaten by James Larkin) and Desmond FitzGerald, lost their seats. There were two women TDs in the new Dáil. They were Mary Reynolds (FG Leitrim) and Bridget Mary Redmond (FG Waterford). (There had been three women TDs in the previous Dáil (two Fianna Fáil and one Fine Gael) and two in the one before that. In June 1927, four women TDs had been elected and two were returned in September of that year.) Thirty-one deputies failed to secure their seats, and there were fifteen new members.[117]

The writing of a new constitution was a risk-laden political strategy. The idea had been greeted with less than enthusiasm by a number of de Valera's closest cabinet colleagues, but the risk had been worth it. A confrontation between church and state had been avoided. The country had a new charter, infused with Fianna Fáil philosophy. De Valera had wrong-footed the opposition by turning the general election into a plebiscite on the constitution—an Irish document for the Irish people.

De Valera was left to put in place the new Seanad, the second house of the Oireachtas. That had been the subject of vigorous debate within Fianna Fáil. The Commission on the Second House of the Oireachtas had reported to government on 1 October 1936. Two minority reports had also been presented.[118] Seán MacEntee had fought a vigorous campaign against the idea of Dáil members being used as an electoral panel. So upset was the Minister for Finance about this idea that he drafted a note to de Valera:

> If I must accept proposals I believe to be so ill-advised as these are or resign from the government, I prefer to resign, and accordingly I place myself at your disposal to make that resignation effective at your convenience.

MacEntee saw the danger of Fianna Fáil becoming involved in naked patronage. In another draft he wrote that certain proposals represented 'machine control in its most blatant and absolute form'. The system, he felt, would return a Senate 'composed mainly of party hacks', who would be 'ill-fitted indeed to fulfil the important functions conferred on it by the constitution so that the system of checks and balances on the legislative powers as is embodied in that will be destroyed.' MacEntee thought also that the reaction of 'our fellow countrymen in the North to this failure in constructive statesmanship will be definitely bad and will further defer any hope of reunion.' He felt that an effort was being made to buy back the support of the Labour Party: 'Those who buy in such a transaction will have to sell also. In this case what is being sold is the independence of our party and, for the reasons which I have already given, its honour as well.'[119]

MacEntee had to be satisfied with the compromise which emerged in the constitution; a chamber of 60 members, 11 of whom were to be nominated by the Taoiseach. Graduates of Trinity College Dublin and the National University of Ireland each elected three members. The remaining members were elected by vocational panels, over which county councillors and TDs had a major influence. The Seanad limped along very much under the control of Fianna Fáil. It was Mr de Valera's poodle. It could be argued that the composition of the Seanad was a victory for the outspoken vocationalist lobby. It was much more accurately the fulfilment of MacEntee's prophecy—a monument to the politics of patronage.

De Valera placated the Catholic integralist lobby by setting up the Commission on Vocational Organisation on 10 January 1939. The temperamental Bishop of Galway, Michael Browne, was made chairman. 'There was nothing like a group of self-declared experts getting on with the job of proposing solutions', commented MacEntee many years later.[120] That was one way to deal with a difficult and persistent lobby. It reported in 1943.

THE ANGLO-IRISH AGREEMENT

De Valera reached the height of his political power in 1938. The economic war was brought to an end and he regained possession of the Treaty ports. Article 7 of the Treaty bound the Free State in time of war to provide such harbour and other facilities as Britain might require for its defence.[121] The British had retained possession of Berehaven, Cobh, Belfast Lough and Lough Swilly, with depots at Rathmullan and Haulbowline. After a long period of secret diplomacy, on 7 January 1938 the Irish cabinet authorised the sending of a delegation to London for the purpose of discussing a number of issues of mutual interest. Britain's prime minister, Neville Chamberlain, felt that he got on excellently with de Valera.[122] The feelings of friendship and respect were reciprocated by de Valera. A new Anglo-Irish agreement was signed on 25 April 1938, followed by a lunch at Downing Street, during which Chamberlain returned to de Valera a pair of field-glasses taken from him when he had surrendered at Bolands Mills in 1916.[123]

The new agreement had sections on defence, finance and trade. The senseless economic war was at an end. The Irish government paid a £10m lump sum for the annuities. The Anglo-Irish agreement was a ready-made platform for de Valera to go to the people. Announcing that polling would take place on 17 June, de Valera claimed that opposition irresponsibility had driven him to the country. The government had been defeated by one vote on a private member's motion to establish compulsory arbitration in disputes concerning civil service pay and conditions. At his first election meeting in Blackrock, de Valera told his audience that neutrality would be impossible without the possession of the ports.[124] 'I can say to you that I have far greater hope of seeing in my lifetime a united Ireland than I had in 1932', de Valera told a meeting in Tullamore on 6 June. He added that the task of getting the six counties in was now merely a task of converting a relatively small number of those who claimed not to be Irishmen to recognise that the island and the whole of the people of the island could be far happier, more prosperous, and more contented in a single state than divided, as they were at present. In Sligo, de Valera said that if the government had been defeated in the Dáil three months earlier, no agreement with Britain would have been possible. He stressed that it was particularly dangerous for the government not to have a majority when dealing with the British.[125] At Castlecomer, Co. Kilkenny, according to the *Irish Press* correspondent, farmers, coal-miners, and agricultural labourers united to give de Valera an enthusiastic welcome. He pledged that a free Ireland would undertake to defend herself: 'We who fought for six or seven centuries to secure freedom and, having secured it, are we not prepared to take the measures that common sense dictates in order to retain that freedom?' That would not be done in the interest of the British, as the opposition had asserted, de Valera said.[126]

In a show of military strength, two thousand men of the regular army and 600 volunteers moved north from Gormanston to the south bank of the river Boyne on manoeuvres. 'A miracle of mobilisation' was how it was described by an *Irish Press* special correspondent.[127] Fianna Fáil was made to look even better by yet another poor opposition campaign performance. There were claims that Fianna Fáil had stolen Fine Gael policy and thus ended the economic war. The main opposition party promised to apply de-rating to agricultural land, to stabilise farm prices, and to reduce taxation and the cost of living.

The Labour Party, led by William Norton, feeling confident that it would hold the balance of power in the next Dáil, promised to secure increases in social benefits, to decrease working hours and to institute a general rise in the wages of workers. Fianna Fáil made an extra effort to target the Labour vote, but there was some evidence of behind-the-scenes tension between leading Fianna Fáil strategists. The philosophical differences between Seán Lemass and Seán MacEntee had increased during their years in government and became evident during the election campaign. Lemass wrote on 5 May 1938 reminding his colleague that the election was taking place in thirty-four constituencies, MacEntee's Dublin Townships being only one. He complained that Fianna Fáil speakers had been concentrated on that one constituency, thus being unable to give urgently required assistance to other constituencies. Lemass concluded:

> I trust that today's bout of oratory will prove sufficient for the electors in Dublin Townships, and that these speakers will be available on next Sunday and during the week in the constituencies where we may gain seats.[128]

MacEntee spluttered an unrepentent reply on 5 June, defending his electoral strategy. But whatever happened behind the scenes, Fianna Fáil got the strategy right and returned 77 deputies, to 45 for Fine Gael, nine for Labour and seven independents. That gave the government a comfortable working majority: 'Now it is possible to pursue a steady course', de Valera said.[129]

De Valera's prestige was further enhanced when he secured all-party agreement for the candidature of Dr Douglas Hyde (Dubhghlás de hÍde) as the President of Ireland. A Protestant, a scholar and a cultural nationalist, Hyde was installed on 25 June 1938. Before the ceremony, the Protestant members of the Oireachtas had attended a special service at St Patrick's Cathedral, Dublin, while de Valera and the Catholic TDs and senators were present at a solemn votive mass in the pro-cathedral. An *Irish Press* correspondent allowed his historical imagination full scope on the occasion:

> Hurled fort of the Danes, moated stronghold of the Normans, but always unchanging symbol of the oppression of the Gael. Kernel of Ireland's political history, it has seen the whole bloody pageant of warring policies. Rebellion and Confiscation, Plot and Conspiracy. Its dungeons crammed with noble Irish hostages and luckless Armada refugees. Its battlemented walls spiked with their tarred heads. It has seen Lords Deputies sailing up the Liffey, hot with the latest edict. Geraldines passing to their doom. York and Lancaster, Cromwellian and Royalist, Dutch King and Scottish King, Viceroys of later years. All now have passed, and the storms that they raised

in their time have settled down to a murmur in the dust.

The writer continued that the thread of freedom had been picked up where it was broken at Kinsale when the Taoiseach hailed the President of the resurgent nation as 'the successor of our rightful princes'. The breach was closed at last, added the *Irish Press* correspondent, who then reflected on the imprisoned Red Hugh O'Donnell, dreaming of freedom, gazing out over the same city which was now festooned with tricolours. De Valera said in his speech:

> Not all the territory of Éireann is at the moment under your sway, a Uachtaráin fhiúntaigh [Honourable President], but the justice of our claim and the tenacity of the Gael in holding to what is his own are our assurance that that, too, will also be set right.

On his way to the Viceregal Lodge, now called Áras an Uachtaráin, the President briefly stopped en route opposite the GPO as a mark of respect to those who had fallen in the 1916 Rising.[130]

De Valera took over the Treaty ports on 11 July 1938. As the tricolour flew over the returned territory, ceremonial parades were held in army barracks throughout the country. That was another important psycho-political moment for the Taoiseach as the country faced a deteriorating international situation. The basic instinct was one of self-preservation. Neutrality was the preferred foreign policy option.

In Time of War: Neutral Ireland, 1939–1945

On 3 September 1939 Kilkenny beat Cork 2–7 to 3–3 in the All-Ireland hurling final at Croke Park. A thunderstorm swept the ground at a crucial point in the game.[1] The outcome was a matter of vital significance for the 40,000 who saw the match: 'Gods make their own importance.' It was only a year after 'the Munich bother', as the poet Patrick Kavanagh called it.[2] Elsewhere, the great powers of Western Europe were at war. The Irish government had decided that neutrality was the best path to follow to protect the national interest. In his poem, 'Settings', Seamus Heaney captures the womb-like sense of security which neutrality brought to the country:

> Terrible history and protected joys!
> Plosive horse-dung on 1940s' roads.
> The newsreel bomb-hits, as harmless as dust-puffs.

The motivation for the policy of neutrality was most realistically expressed by the secretary of the Department of External Affairs, Joseph Walshe: 'Small nations like Ireland do not and cannot assume the role of defenders of just causes except their own.'[3]

The historian John P. Duggan somewhat understated the Irish state of military preparedness in 1939: 'The country was almost defenceless when the Second World War broke out.'[4] The ill-fated Polish cavalry stood a better chance against the mechanised Nazi war machine than the Irish armed forces would have done had Hitler launched a full-scale invasion against the country in 1939—nostalgic reminiscences about guerrilla prowess during the Anglo-Irish war notwithstanding. The strength of the army was 7,600, and 18,000 upon mobilisation. The two brigades were under strength, as were the five garrison battalions. The army had no 'strike force' necessary to resist the invader.[5] During the 'phoney war' the figure dropped to 13,335. By late 1940, the strength of the army had risen to 37,000 and it had gone to 40,535 by December 1942. But there continued to be a serious shortage of weapons, ammunition and explosives.[6] Anti-aircraft equipment was in short supply. The army was particularly fortunate to have at its head Lt Colonel Daniel McKenna, who replaced Michael Brennan as chief of staff in January 1940. He was a reliable, cool and capable officer—an ideal choice for the war years and one on whom de Valera came to rely heavily at moments of crisis.

In 1939, the navy was still being formed. By early 1940 there were two ex-fisheries patrol vessels, *Muirchú* and *Fort Rannoch*, in service. Each was armed with a 12-pound gun, two Vickers machine guns and a supply of depth charges. The three motor torpedo boats each had two 18-inch torpedoes, a heavy machine gun and a hydrophone for detecting submarines.[7] Captain T. McKenna recalled that 3 September 1939 was the day 'realisation dawned in Ireland that the country *was* surrounded by water and that the sea was of vital importance to her'. He argued that neutrality had been declared 'with just nothing whatever to defend it with in the internationally vital area of the territorial sea'.[8] The Irish Air Corps was marginally better off than the navy, but it had nothing like the strength necessary to police the skies, even over Dublin. The equipment was very light and more suitable for training than for dogfighting.[9] Ireland was far from being an armed neutral in September 1939.

De Valera had no other policy choice than to declare the country's neutrality when the Dáil met on 2 September. The Taoiseach introduced two Bills—the First Amendment of the Constitution Bill and the Emergency Powers Bill. It was necessary to amend article 28.3.3 of the constitution to provide for the declaration of a state of emergency during a time when armed conflict was taking place without the participation of the state.[10] De Valera told the Dáil that it was only natural that the Irish people 'should look at their own country first and should accordingly, in looking at their own country, consider what its interests should be and what its interests are'. Once de Valera had received the support of the Dáil for the emergency legislation—which gave the government access if needed to draconian powers—he made a number of strategic changes in his cabinet. Gerry Boland was switched to the Department of Justice; Frank Aiken was made the Minister for the Coordination of Defensive Measures— effectively minister for censorship; Oscar Traynor moved to Defence and Seán Lemass took over the new Department of Supplies. He was succeeded in Industry and Commerce by Seán MacEntee, but Lemass took back that portfolio on 18 August 1941 when MacEntee was moved to Local Government and Public Health. Seán T. O'Kelly was Tánaiste and Minister for Finance. James Ryan held on to Agriculture, while Education passed from de Valera to Tom Derrig in June 1940.[11]

A cabinet committee on internal security was established in mid-September. Elaborate plans were laid to carry on the government of the country from hiding in the event of invasion. Safe houses outside the capital were located, from which government departments would continue to operate for as long as possible. The danger of a reversal to the 1919–21 underground system of operation was ever present.

Ireland sought to implement neutrality strictly by the book at the beginning of the Emergency. Belligerents were notified of Ireland's status. The Department of External Affairs kept a close watch on the actions of the other neutrals, but the legal officer at Iveagh House, Michael Rynne, sought to discourage his superior, Joseph Walshe, from adopting an excessively legalistic interpretation of neutrality. Rynne argued that each new historical situation called for developing a new interpretation of the law if it so suited Irish needs. Despite an outward appearance of rigidity, Irish neutrality was applied ultimately in a very indulgent manner towards the Allies. Ireland has even been described as an 'unneutral neutral'.[12]

IRA, AXIS DIPLOMACY AND NAZI COLLABORATION

In the early months of the war the real threat to the security of the island came from the enemy within. Explosives had been unsuccessfully used by IRA men to blast their way out of Mountjoy jail. There were raids on a post office and a bank in November 1939. The IRA carried out a raid on the Magazine Fort, in Dublin's Phoenix

Park, and got away with explosives and over one million rounds of ammunition.[13] The Dáil met on 4 January 1940 and introduced internment. An IRA man who had been released following a hunger strike was rearrested following the shooting dead of two detectives; he and his accomplice were sentenced to death and executed. Four other IRA men were to share the same fate by the end of the war. The government allowed three others to die on hunger strike. In all, more than 500 IRA activists were interned without trial during the war. Hundreds were rounded up for questioning under the Offences against the State Act. In England, two men were sentenced to death for their part in an IRA bombing and were hanged. The then Minister for Justice, Gerry Boland, said that drastic measures were needed at the time because the very existence of the state was threatened.[14]

However, the outbreak of the war revealed a new and even more sinister dimension to the IRA threat. Irish military intelligence, G2, had suspected that the first IRA contacts with Nazism dated back to the time when Seán MacBride had been active in the organisation. Colonel Dan Bryan had been to the fore in the fight against the IRA since the 1920s. He was among the most intelligent, influential and pro-Allied officers to serve in the Irish army during World War II. Born in 1900 in Dunhill, Gowran, Co. Kilkenny, Bryan joined up in June 1922 and worked for most of the 1920s in G2. Transferred to the defence planning division in 1928, he later worked in the office of the chief of staff between 1931 and 1934. He returned to G2 and served as assistant director of military intelligence until he took over as director from Liam Archer in June 1941. He held that post until March 1952. Very little passed his notice during the war years. He had an unrivalled capacity to penetrate fringe groups and subversive organisations with his agents and informers. Bryan was known to be very sympathetic to the Allies and retained the closest professional working relationship with British and American intelligence during the war years. He kept a particularly close watch on the activities of the pro-Nazi IRA.

Oscar Pfaf was the first of a line of German spies to arrive in Ireland. He was in Dublin in February 1939 and made contact with Liam D. Walsh, a close ally of Eoin O'Duffy, who was recruited to the spy network. Before leaving for Germany, Pfaf had made contact with the general and with the IRA.[15] G2 also maintained an interest in the activities of the novelist Francis Stuart, before his departure for Germany in 1940. Stuart broadcast regularly to Ireland from Germany until 1944. He was assisted by one John Francis O'Reilly. Two Germans, Hans Hartmann and Ludwig Muelhausen, read the news in Irish on the same channel.[16] Charles Bewley, sacked from the Irish diplomatic service in 1939, was also involved in intelligence work for the Germans from his base in wartime Rome, but he could never have been described as an IRA sympathiser.

Berlin sought, with the help of Irish collaborators, to prepare the ground for a possible invasion of the island. About fifteen spies were known to have been sent to Ireland during the war and G2 tracked them all down. Only Hermann Goertz, who parachuted into the country in early May 1940, successfully evaded capture and remained free until 27 November 1941. He spent most of his time hiding in a remote Kerry farmhouse. The Germans had little success in building the IRA into a coherent force likely to be of use in the event of invasion, but leading IRA men were taken to Berlin. Jim O'Donovan and his wife had visited Germany in April 1939. A short-lived radio contact was established with O'Donovan's controllers upon his return. Seán Russell was taken to Berlin to be schooled in the latest bomb-making techniques. Conor Cruise O'Brien met a former *Abwehr* agent, Kurt Haller, after the war and got the impression that Berlin 'valued their IRA helpers more as decoy ducks for use in relation to the vital area of American aid for Britain, than for any very serious plans in relation to Ireland itself.'[17]

Germany operated a two-track policy towards Ireland during the war years. Berlin's covert contact with the IRA was kept from the German Minister in Dublin, Eduard Hempel. He had held the post since 1937 and Iveagh House was convinced that he was not a Nazi; he was viewed as a professional and honourable diplomat. The same could not be said for his press attaché, Carlheinz Petersen, who was a committed Nazi. The other Axis diplomat in Dublin, Vincenzo Berardis, was a diplomatic lightweight. A fascist, he terrorised Italian tradespeople in Dublin, demanding that they display a portrait of Mussolini in their shops. The Japanese envoy gave little trouble since he spent much of his time playing golf. Overall, the Axis legations hardly constituted a formidable phalanx capable of infiltrating and subverting Irish political circles and winning over public opinion, but certain distasteful developments came about with the help of both the Germans and the Italians. The People's National Party (PNP) was founded in early 1940. It produced two issues of a newspaper, *Penapa*, which was nothing more than an anti-semitic rag.[18] Liam Walshe, aide to Eoin O'Duffy, was a member, as was the general himself. There appeared to be overlapping membership with the Irish Friends of Germany, and one member of PNP published *German War News*—a propaganda sheet. PNP met in the Red Bank restaurant in Dublin, and G2 reports on a number of their meetings reveal strong anti-semitic feelings within the party.[19]

Ailtirí na hAiséirighe was another fascist accretion. Founded in March 1942 by an ex-civil servant from Northern Ireland, Gearóid Ó Cuinneagáin, it had among its objectives the establishment of a single authoritarian government and the introduction of the corporative system. Ailtirí na hAiséirighe had, according to an estimate of the Department of Justice, about 30 or 40 members in Dublin after six months in existence, with very few followers outside the capital.[20] In the run up to the 1943 election, it acquired some members in Cork, Waterford and Dundalk, but it never really took off as an organisation. It suffered much the same fate as other corporatist movements in Ireland in the 1930s:[21] it was confined to the margins of Irish society.

The failure to develop a mass fascist movement in Ireland during the early part of the war did not mean that there was not a nucleus of would-be collaborators in the country ready to take advantage of a German invasion. With the help of the IRA, most of the country would have been turned into a Gaelic Vichy had the Nazis taken control.

THREAT OF INVASION

On 10 May 1940 Germany invaded the Low Countries. Two days later de Valera said in reaction: 'I think I would be unworthy of this small nation if, on an occasion like this, I did not utter our protest against the cruel wrong which has been done them.' Ireland had to see to it that an attack on the country 'from any quarter' would find 'a united people ready to resist it'.

That was an indirect warning to London not to contemplate invasion.[22] However, the real threat was from Germany. Since France was fighting a losing battle, the threat of the invasion of the British Isles mounted. A raid by gardaí on a house in the Dublin suburbs owned by a German, Stephen Held, yielded a haul of a large quantity of money and maps. On 1 June British intelligence let Dublin know that an IRA-supported German invasion was imminent. The plan was that an airborne attack on Ireland was to precede the invasion of England. The plans had been found by Dutch officers on a captured member of the ss. At the same time British intelligence reported the stepping up of IRA-German activity in the south and around the Clare coast.

The British evacuation of Dunkirk was completed by 3 June. Italy entered the war on the side of Germany on 10 June and France signed a humiliating armistice on 22 June 1940. León Ó Broin recalled listening to the news of the collapse of France on the radio with a number of his colleagues from the Department of Finance. An Englishman who was working in Finance, Charlie Almond, heard the news and said: 'That's the effin end.'[23] There were many who thought like him, including the secretary of the Department of External Affairs, Joseph Walshe. Fearing the consequences of the Irish government coming to accept that the British were about to lose the war, Chamberlain—who had ceased to be prime minister on 10 May—invited de Valera to London for talks. The British Minister of Health, Malcolm MacDonald, was sent over to convince the Taoiseach of the imminence of a German attack. The unification of Ireland was put on the table. Lemass, according to one source, was tempted to take the offer and go in on the side of the British. Aiken was resolute in his opposition. In the end, the offer was rejected. It was felt that the British would not be in a position to deliver. De Valera rejected the offer and argued in 'a serious, friendly vein that in any case a neutral Irish Free State would serve Britain's interests better than an allied one'. MacDonald wrote later: 'He could scarcely have promised more benevolent cooperation short of declaring war against the enemy.'[24] But that was not how the failure of the talks was perceived by Churchill in London. He was needlessly mistrustful of the Irish government. On the other side, a less doctrinaire approach to the talks might have secured for de Valera a long-term commitment to Irish unity. It was a missed opportunity.

Those talks had to be kept secret because prominent members of the opposition, James Dillon to the fore, wished to end Irish neutrality. That matter had been discussed in mid-June at the Defence Conference—a body which had been set up to include the opposition. Richard Mulcahy tended towards the view that it was better to invite the British, in anticipation of a German invasion. The timing of de Valera's reply—13 July—is important. It was presented to the opposition while the country was awash with rumours of an imminent German invasion. The opposition was told privately by de Valera:

> We are fully aware that this policy does not guarantee the country immunity from attack. There is always the possibility of attack should one side or the other decide, during the progress of the war, that the circumstances are such that the resultant advantages to that hostile invasion need be feared from one side only. But, so long as we are neutral, there is a possibility that the danger of attack may be averted; whilst, if we invite military assistance from one side, immediate attack by the other side, with all its consequences, will be almost inevitable.[25]

The emphatic tone of de Valera's response belied the debate which continued to take place in the Department of External Affairs, where Joseph Walshe had reached a point of near breakdown in early July owing to the pressure of work. The policy option, as Walshe saw it, was how Ireland should respond to Britain's inevitable defeat. He wrote in early July:

> Britain's defeat has been placed beyond all doubt. France has capitulated. The entire coastline of Europe from the Arctic to the Pyrenees is in the hands of the strongest power in the world which can call upon the industrial resources of all Europe and Asia in an unbroken geographical continuity as far as the Pacific Ocean. Neither time nor gold can beat Germany.[26]

Walshe could hardly have been blamed for feeling so gloomy. Irish envoys, with the exception of Seán Murphy in France, had tended to confirm that view. But the temptation to tack tactically closer to Berlin, in anticipation of a German victory, was rejected. The senior official in the Department of the Taoiseach, Maurice Moynihan, recalled that he had never accepted the inevitability of a German victory. He felt that the English would somehow muddle through the crisis.[27] The most senior Irish officers may also have held the same view, based on the calculation that the United States would soon enter the war. However, reports of Irish defeatism had been sent to London in early July by the United Kingdom representative in Dublin, Sir John Maffey. Despite the diplomatic complications, the new British

Dominions Secretary, Anthony Eden, had considered it prudent to recommend the sending of a 'representative' to Dublin after the outbreak of war. Educated at Rugby and Christ Church, Oxford, Maffey had served on the North-West Frontier of India. In 1925 he was made governor general of Sudan and permanent under secretary for the colonies in 1933. With such an education and professional background, he was likely to have been regarded with suspicion by de Valera and by Walshe. Paradoxically, he proved to be an inspired choice. He was reserved, discreet, trustworthy, and he understood de Valera better than any other foreign diplomat resident in Dublin. Maffey's coolness was a major asset in the panic-stricken early summer of 1940. Was de Valera to turn to Berlin in anticipation of a German victory?

The fear that de Valera was about to base Irish policy on the premise of a German victory was reinforced by events in Madrid. British intelligence were made aware that the Irish envoy in Madrid, Leopold Kerney, was being aided by German intelligence to arrange the release of the republican Frank Ryan. Wolfgang Blaum, the chief *Abwehr* agent in Madrid, was in charge. Ryan 'escaped' into German custody on 25 July, whereupon he was taken to Paris and on to Berlin. The British were further alarmed when Hitler's *coup d'etat* specialist, Edmund Veesenmayer, met Kerney in Madrid. The meeting had been arranged by Helmut Clissmann, a German intelligence officer married to an Irish woman. Kerney reported the meeting to Iveagh House on 24 August.[28] This matter became the subject of controversy in the 1950s when Desmond Williams wrote a series of articles on Irish neutrality.[29] Boland, in 1954, sketched from memory the background to what had gone on during the war years:

> For some time prior to his return, there had been uneasiness about Kerney on security grounds. He appeared to be in touch with Frank Ryan and others considered dangerous to the State, but there was a feeling that the information he furnished to the Department about these contacts lacked amplitude and candour. Warnings about Kerney's discretion and contacts also reached us from Dan Bryan.[30]

Perhaps Kerney has been judged too harshly.[31]
    In reality, Veesenmayer did not get what he wanted from Kerney.[32]

Upon his return to Berlin, he recommended to his superiors that 120 picked parachute troops should be made available for operations in Ireland in conjunction with the IRA.[33] But British intelligence was aware of what was happening in Madrid. Initially, they may have read too much significance into Kerney's encounter with Veesenmayer and the German role in the release of Ryan. But the timing of the meeting could not have been worse from an Irish point of view. British pressure on Ireland to shift its policy was mounting in the middle of July. There was a strong military argument to be made to invade then rather than later. A strategy of tension may have included a wide-scale dress rehearsal of invasion plans. But there was little support in the British cabinet for that drastic course of action, no matter how much it may have been favoured by some senior military officers. It is much more likely that the major scare in mid-July was precipitated by British intelligence reports that a German invasion would occur on 15 July. British forces were put on full alert. That included an operation to engage, if necessary, German troops which had landed on Irish soil.

However, much credit must go to Chamberlain in London and Sir John Maffey in Dublin for arguing against extreme action. Chamberlain had said to the Irish high commissioner in London, John Dulanty, on 5 July when asked about a possible invasion: 'Good God, haven't we enough trouble already?' He felt sure that such apprehensions were 'groundless'.[34] A speech by Churchill in the House of Commons on 6 November set in circulation a further cycle of invasion rumours in Dublin. He had said that it was 'a most grievous and heavy burden that we cannot use the south and west coast of Ireland to refuel our flotillas and aircraft'. But Maffey had sought to assuage any fears of military intervention. He was fundamentally opposed to such a move. On 23 December 1940, he advised the Secretary of State for Dominion Affairs, Lord Cranborne:

> Every argument points to the exercise of patience at this juncture, difficult though it may be. It must be realised that in the minds of people here there is no feeling of having let England down, no admission that England can make demands as of right and justice. A show of resentment on our part merely stirs the old passions and works against us. . . . A friendly and reasoned approach will serve us best both here and elsewhere whatever form the final solution may take.[35]

Cranborne recommended this approach to cabinet. He described Ireland as 'a sort of Gideon's Fleece in a devastated continent, immune from the misfortunes that afflict the other peoples of Europe'. He knew that it might have to come to invasion. But there was another option: Ireland 'is entirely dependent on us. We should take every means of opening the eyes of the Irish people to this fact.' He advocated a policy of 'silent sanctions' in order to keep 'her lean'.[36] That was exactly the course adopted by the British. Great pressure was exerted when Ireland tried to establish a merchant marine. The economic screw was turned tighter and tighter as the war ebbed and flowed in favour of the Allies.

DAVID GRAY AND IRISH-AMERICAN RELATIONS

If Maffey proved to be a reliable friend to de Valera, the American envoy, David Gray, was a troublemaker of the first order, who failed to understand the complexities of Irish politics throughout his stay in Dublin. Married to Franklin Roosevelt's aunt, he sent a series of personal reports to the US president throughout the war, usually addressed: 'My dear boss', or 'My dear Franklin'. For example, he wrote to the president's wife, Eleanor, in February 1941:

> In regard to relations with the outside world, especially England, even the Prime Minister lives in a dream-wish world. He and those who follow him cannot see that a small nation without coal, iron or means of defense can live across a sort of East River from Britain and be free and independent in the sense that a continent-wide state or federation of states can be independent and free. They feel that if they are willing to die for this end, it is their right to attain it as if I should say that if I were willing to die for it I could be eight feet tall. Mr de Valera defends this illusion with the genius of a Jesuit attorney always shifting his ground in argument to a position in which he is unassailable on moral grounds.[37]

On 30 November 1940, Gray sent Roosevelt an *aide-mémoire* written by James Dillon:

> Personally I have always felt that the policy of neutrality was a grave mistake and that we would have more effectively vindicated our moral position in the world and protected our material interests by declaring war in September 1939.

Gray called Dillon 'the real leader of the opposition'. He felt that the best bet the British had of getting the ports was 'to play to this Opposition and try to split the country'.[38] That was a high risk strategy and one unlikely to succeed. It was never formally attempted by the us government. Fortunately for Washington, at least two experienced American intelligence officers spent sufficient time in Ireland to provide their superiors with a very different point of view. E.R. (Spike) Marlin and Martin Quigley worked under cover in Dublin.[39] Unfortunately, the fact that Gray had back-channel access to Roosevelt and his wife gave an importance to his reports which they ought otherwise not to have enjoyed. Roosevelt developed a strong personal hostility to the Irish stance and Frank Aiken experienced the coldness of the us president's attitude when he visited Washington in 1941.

 Gray reported to the State Department on 7 March that Aiken had 'likeable qualities and a certain political shrewdness, but what Dillon, who despises him, describes as a mind "half way between the ape and the child".'[40] The head of the Office of Strategic Services (oss), Bill Donovan, who had visited Dublin, described Aiken as of the 'extreme left' in Irish politics. He felt that Aiken may have wanted to visit the us 'for other motives'.[41] The assistant secretary of state, Sumner Welles, saw Aiken on 19 March and formed an equally negative impression of the Irish minister. He was described as having the 'narrowest Irish point of view', advocating 'no cooperation with England while the Ulster question remains unsettled'.[42]

In an interview with Dean Acheson, the assistant secretary of state, on 2 April 1941, Aiken argued that the Germans might not invade Ireland as part of an invasion of England, but as an independent action designed to cut British communications. He thought that the Germans might be able to land about 100,000 men by air and submarine. Their first target would be the Shannon estuary. Aiken insisted that an armed Ireland could deal with the situation until British help arrived. An uninvited British intervention would lead to civil disturbance. Aiken also insisted that the British had greatly exaggerated the utility of Irish ports since the convoy routes were around the north of the country. He learned very quickly from Acheson, however, that the Americans were at one with the British and would not act independently of their Atlantic partners.[43]

Aiken's interview with Roosevelt was tempestuous; he refused to leave the president's room until he could get Roosevelt to say that he would bring pressure to bear on the British regarding Irish unity. Roosevelt had his tea brought to him on a tray. Aiken still did not move. In a fit of exasperation, Roosevelt swept the tea tray from the table. Aiken left as White House domestic staff rushed into the room.[44] He returned to Ireland empty-handed.[45]

De Valera was well aware of the bipartisan approach of London and Washington to neutral Ireland, but relations were far from being as fraught as the encounter between Roosevelt and Aiken suggests. De Valera described Ireland as having an unchanged policy when the United States formally entered the war in December 1941: 'We can only be a friendly neutral.'[46] De Valera returned to that theme on 25 December 1941—about two weeks after the government feared the possibility of a German landing: 'And now, as I said in our own language at the beginning, God's blessing be on you, friends of Ireland, this Holy Night, and despite this terrible war, God's peace be in your hearts.'[47]

On 27 January 1942, American troops landed in Northern Ireland without prior consultation with the Irish government. De Valera simply used the occasion to assert the government's opposition to partition. For about 240,000 GIs, Northern Ireland was home before they were shipped to North Africa or mainland Europe. Thus American troops were incorporated into the contingency plans to participate in the defence of the south in the event of a German invasion.[48] Despite Gray's irresponsible reporting, neutral Ireland worked out a series of secret arrangements for cooperation with the Allies.

HELPING TO WIN THE WAR
The release of new archival material continues to show the extent to which Irish neutrality was prepared to be friendly towards the Allies. The findings to date can be summarised as follows: regular liaison between Allied and Irish military authorities and the preparation of joint plans to defend the Irish state; intimate cooperation between G2 and Allied intelligence services; exchange of meteorological reports and the forwarding of all information to Britain concerning the movement of Axis planes, ships and submarines in the Irish Sea; and permission given to Allied aircraft to overfly a corridor of Irish territory in northern Donegal for easier access to the Atlantic.

Irish policy towards captured German and Allied servicemen was far from being even-handed. G2 recorded that 141 Allied and 16 German planes made forced landings or crashed in Irish territorial waters between the outbreak of war and 30 June 1945. The number of crew from both sides involved was 788, of whom 222 were killed. Some 480 were released, 97 were interned and 27 others were set free after internment. Out of the 788, 50 were Germans, of whom 17 were killed. The remaining 33 airmen were interned for the duration of the war. Only one was repatriated, on 11 October 1943.[49]

At first, the Irish government sought to apply the rule that whenever belligerent military aircraft made a landing within Irish jurisdiction, the crew was interned for the duration of the hostilities. In reality, that did not apply for very long. The Irish government drew a distinction between *operational* and *non-operational* flights and between planes being used *in action* and for *training* or *testing*.[50] In that way, most British and American planes and their crews were handed back.

It was unlikely that a German plane would make a non-operational flight over Ireland during the war. The British usually repaid the Irish for the supplies of fuel received by Allied crews to enable them to return to base. On 27 October 1942, Gerry Boland minuted that he had reminded the British about whether they would soon expect a return of the quantities of petrol which had been supplied out of Irish military stores. About a week later he was told that 2,550 gallons of aviation spirit had been delivered by the Shell Oil Company. This was a gift from the British.

The bias towards Allied airmen did not escape the attention of Hempel. He complained about this to Boland and de Valera. Boland was forced to explain that other neutrals were not interning airmen. On 10 May 1943, Walshe explained to the German Minister that the Irish were continuing to intern crews who were actually on an 'operational' flight at the time of a forced landing. British and American fliers, he added, were more likely to be in that situation than Germans: 'He did not dispute that', minuted Walshe.[51] This policy continued throughout the war.

In September 1940, a memorandum from the Cabinet Committee on Emergency Problems stated that there were no international conventions specifically governing the treatment of belligerent internees.[52] The Irish authorities had to make up the rules on the basis of experience. Some members of the German legation had felt in late 1940 that the regime under which the men were confined was unduly rigorous and unsympathetic. No official complaint was lodged. There was a report that a guard had shone a torch in the faces of sleeping internees. Fred Boland, in the Department of External Affairs, took exception to this practice. He told a committee meeting on 3 February 1941 that internees should be granted all possible concessions consistent with the necessary precautions against their escape. A few weeks earlier, three of the most senior German officers had attended a joint Department of Defence/External Affairs conference where they had put forward suggestions and proposals to improve their conditions.

The conditions of German internees were immeasurably better than what their colleagues were to experience on the Eastern Front later that year. They were allowed parole to exercise for two hours daily. When they objected to their army escort, the internees were told that it was there to 'keep them in view on account of the danger to them from subversive elements'. The internees were allowed to visit swimming baths, the local Curragh golf links and a tennis club. They could go to the cinema twice a week, alternating between Newbridge and the Curragh. By June 1941 internees were being invited to the Irish officers' mess. Both the Germans and the British had their own army cook for their respective canteens. The parole area was extended to include the nearby town of Naas. The internees were also allowed to visit their German diplomatic representative monthly instead of quarterly. Towards the end of the war, seventeen German internees received long-term parole to live in Dublin and pursue courses of study at UCD and other institutions of higher education. Internees were also allowed to take up employment.

It was of mutual benefit to both the Allies and the Irish to facilitate the migration of tens of thousands to England for war work. Although the British were not permitted to advertise, the Irish authorities did not impede the steady supply of workers to England. There are no emigration figures available for the war years, but, based on the number of travel permits issued by the government, the numbers were 25,964 in 1940, 35,131 in 1941, 51,711 in 1942, 48,324 in 1943, 13,613 in 1944 and 23,794 in 1945.[53] The comparatively low figure in 1944 was due to the severe controls which were imposed in that year. Under British legislation, from September 1939 persons of sixteen years of age and over entering Britain or Northern Ireland had to produce a valid document of identity. A British visa was necessary for entry into Britain. The Irish government introduced a system of travel permit cards, which were valid for 12 months and were issued by the Department of External Affairs. Applications were made to the local garda station. About 200,000 went to work in the factories in Britain during the war. Fear of bringing in typhus from Ireland resulted in the government having to hire Tara Street baths in Dublin and oblige everyone going to England to bathe and wash their hair. Women who had their hair set before leaving home found the enforced ablutions in Dublin a tiresome imposition.[54] There was a similar exodus from Northern Ireland; Cardinal MacRory described it as conscription by starvation.

The Irish government helped the Allied war effort by not actively preventing thousands of its citizens from going to Northern Ireland or to England to enlist. The figure again is difficult to estimate, but it may have been as high as 30,000. Desertion from the Irish army was a particular problem. Pay in the Irish army was not very good. A private's pay per week in 1942 was 14s. A private first class received 2s. 6d. per day. After compulsory deductions were taken out for a haircut, laundry and social welfare, a soldier took home less than 13s per week. Soldiers were awarded a one shilling per week increase in 1942. They were paid half, and the remaining sixpence was deferred until after the Emergency. G2 made the following estimate of desertions in 1945:

> There are at present almost 5,000 non-commissioned officers and men of the Defence Forces in a state of desertion or absence without leave. Of these, approximately 4,000 are absent for more than 12 months, many of them for as long as 3 or 4 years. There is little doubt but that the majority of them are or have been serving in the British Forces or are in civilian employment in Great Britain and Northern Ireland.[55]

Neutrality had one obvious benefit. The Irish Free State was saved the experience of having to face the full horrors of war—the indiscriminate bombing of cities. Belfast was heavily bombed on 15 and 16 April 1941. De Valera immediately despatched to Northern Ireland all the fire-fighting assistance that could be mustered.[56] On 31 May, parts of Dublin were bombed by German planes, leaving 34 dead, 90 injured and 300 houses destroyed or damaged.[57] North Strand was the area that suffered the most. German bombs also damaged the South Circular Road, Terenure and Sandycove.[58] Shortly afterwards, a W. Megan wrote to the Irish High Commission office, in London, that the British Research Station, to combat night bombing, was indirectly responsible for the North Strand attack. They had interfered with the wireless ray or beam which the bombers used to locate their targets at night, causing the Germans to believe that they were over their target when they were in fact over Dublin.[59] This was confirmed after the war by the British Air Ministry, and reports were carried in Dublin newspapers on 23 February 1946. The Germans admitted responsibility and £327,000 compensation was paid to the Irish government in 1958.

On 26 August 1940, a German plane bombed a creamery at Campile, Co. Wexford, killing three girls and injuring a number of others. The railway station was also damaged. Compensation was claimed to the value of £18,822.4s.8d. The government submitted a claim for nearly £14,500 and the Germans adjusted it to £12,000.[60] The forced landing of a German plane on Inishvickillane, Blasket Islands, brought claims for compensation for loss of livestock. Hempel issued two cheques, but they were returned to him by the Department of External Affairs. Boland did not feel that payment was warranted. There is evidence that both the Germans and the Allies acknowledged liability for damage to Irish property during the war and compensation was duly paid.

WARTIME CENSORSHIP

The strict censorship regime in Ireland kept many members of the public in a state of near ignorance about what was going on in continental Europe. Frank Aiken was a worthy choice for the job of presiding over wartime censorship. Rigid and unyielding—as Roosevelt had come to realise—he was determined not to allow anything past his gimlet eye. 'Unfortunately,' Frederick Boland commented, 'good judgment was not Frank Aiken's long suit.'[61] The Minister for the Coordination of Defensive Measures outlined his thinking on the question of democracy and censorship in a memorandum on 23 January 1940:

There are some self-styled democrats who would hold on to the peace time liberalistic trimmings of democracy while the fundamental basis of democracy was being swept from under their feet by the foreign or domestic enemies of their democratic State. Wise men, however, discard these trimmings when necessary in order successfully to maintain the fundamental right of the citizens freely to choose by whom they shall be governed.[62]

Aiken argued that 'whoever says he is not satisfied with such a system of democracy in "time of war" is either a very foolish democrat or an *agent provocateur* for those who want to overthrow democracy or to embroil us in civil or foreign war'.[63] Censorship, therefore, was justified on the grounds that it was necessary to stop all communications endangering the security of the state or prejudicial to its good relations with other states. Secondly, censorship was considered necessary on the grounds that it was possible to obtain information which would contribute to the safeguarding of the national interest and the maintenance of good relations with other states.

Censorship was organised into three divisions, postal, telegraph and press. Each branch was controlled by a chief censor, who had the equivalent grade of a principal officer. Recruitment was conducted exclusively within the civil service and all personnel chosen for the job were seconded to the Department of Defence. The key personnel were identified for that service before the outbreak of war. The government appointed the controller, the assistant controller and the three chief censors. The chairman of the Board of Works, Joseph Connolly, served as controller of censorship up to September 1941 when he was replaced by one of his assistant controllers, Thomas Coyne, formerly of the Department of Justice. Gerry Boland claimed that Coyne had a good sense of humour and was inclined to let things through which Aiken would have stopped.[64] A former journalist, Michael Knightly, was chief press censor; E. Cussen was chief telegraph censor and J. Purcell served as chief postal censor.

The bulk of the staff was employed in postal censorship. They were located in Exchequer Street, Dublin. The large staff was instructed to prevent the disclosure of information concerning the organisation and activities of the state's military forces or the state of the country's defences. Secondly, staff were to prevent the dissemination of matter that might prejudice the state's foreign policy or endanger internal security. Thirdly, staff were to stop information which might have interfered with the production, purchase or disposal of supplies, endangered shipping or otherwise affected the trade or commercial relations of the state. Finally, the staff was to collect and distribute to the various government departments any information affecting national interests.

All letters and packets to and from any destination outside the state were liable for censorship. While most correspondence with continental Europe and the rest of the world was opened and the censor's pen used liberally, the sheer bulk of correspondence between Ireland and Britain meant that opening this had to be partial and random. There was, however, cooperation between the respective censorship operations on both sides of the Irish Sea. Mail between Northern Ireland and the Republic was subject to spot-checks.

Telegraph censorship extended to all telegrams, inland and foreign. It also covered all wireless transmitting stations, ships, aircraft and private stations. To facilitate the work of the censor, all traffic was routed through the central telegraph office in Dublin. The press censorship office was located at Dublin Castle, as was the office of the controller. An extensive list of directions to the press was prepared, based on particulars provided by various government departments. There were fifty-five named categories, which included weather forecasts. Newspapers and periodicals were obliged to submit for censorship all matter specified in these directions or other instructions issued during the course of the war, e.g. relating to atrocity stories, and articles on anti-semitism and hunger strikes. *The Irish Times*, in particular, fell victim to the press censor. But other publications, such as *The Standard, Irish Golf, The Wolfe Tone Weekly and Annual, Old Moore's Almanac* and *The Irish Workers' Weekly*, had copy removed. On one occasion, the newspapers were refused permission to publish a section from the lenten pastoral of Bishop Morrisroe of Achonry, which clearly implied the hope that Germany would not win the war. A section from *L'Osservatore Romano* was also prevented from being republished by the censor in early 1941.[65] Even references, in reports of football matches, to weather conditions and the state of the pitch were removed to deprive Berlin or London of such vital information. Boland cites the instance of an evening when Aiken saw a notice for a meeting to be held at Kingstown Presbyterian Hall. He stopped its publication on the grounds that Kingstown no longer existed. The proper name for the town was Dún Laoghaire. On another occasion, Aiken wanted to change the name of the Royal National Lifeboat Institution. He argued that it was either royal or national, but that it could not be both: 'He seemed to think that if we called it RNLI we were being unneutral,' Boland commented. Coyne intervened to save the day, as he was to do on many occasions throughout the war.[66] He persuaded Aiken to let the matter drop.

Books, pamphlets, leaflets, board games, posters, postcards, records, plays and films all fell foul of the emergency censorship. In relation to films, the official film censor had his powers extended to enable him to reject a film which, in his opinion, would be prejudicial to the maintenance of law and order or to the preservation of the state, or would be likely to lead to a breach of the peace or to cause offence to the government or people of a friendly foreign nation. Aiken took a personal interest in film censorship. Films considered unsuitable were Charlie Chaplin's 'The Great Dictator', 'Sergeant York', 'Target for Tonight', 'Soviet Songs and Dances' and a George Formby film, 'Bell-bottom George'. Aiken himself ordered the deletion of the song 'Bless 'em all' from the Columbia film, 'Community Songs—no. 61'. Presumably Aiken was offended by such lines as

Bless all the sergeants we have to obey,
Bless all the corp'rals who drill us all day.[67]

Censorship decisions ranged from the farcical, like the examples given above, to the highly serious, such as the suppression of reports of concentration camps and even the massacre of Irish missionaries in the Philippines. There was a general prohibition on all discussion and debate on neutrality, Ireland's foreign policy and opinions on the course of the war. Freedom of speech was severely curtailed. Aiken, who was profoundly mistrustful of the British, may have considered that a 'time of war' allowed a government to curtail the 'liberalistic trimmings of democracy'. Many of these actions were ignorant, excessive and a grotesque infringement of civil liberties.

G2 also had a strong interest in the operations of the censorship system. Designated individuals, who were of interest to Bryan for one reason or another, had their mail intercepted and opened. Clearly Francis Stuart, Charles Bewley and others known to have Axis connections were on a priority list. In one case, Bryan was ordered to intercept correspondence going to a serving Irish diplomat abroad. Without any initiative from himself, Leopold Kerney in Madrid was being used as a conduit for mail from the relatives of Charles Bewley in Dublin. He also received letters for Frank Ryan which were supposed to have been forwarded to him. Bryan, sometimes with the help of the British censor, intercepted any such letters and they were placed on a file in the secretary's office in the Department of External Affairs. Photographs of other letters relevant to the work of that department were supplied by Bryan. This demonstrated just how thorough G2 was in cooperation with the office of the censor. There is also evidence that diplomatic cable traffic was intercepted and read by G2. However, it bears repetition that G2 listened to the phone calls of a number of legations in Dublin, including the French, German and Italian. This operation was conducted from a room at the top of the GPO in O'Connell Street. Boland went there one evening to observe the operation and listened to an American journalist filing a report from the Gresham hotel to her home office. Little else happened that same evening. Boland recalled how the rest of the evening revealed only tradesmen ringing up the female domestics in the American embassy.[68] But that reminiscence confirms that the phones of Axis diplomats were not the only ones to have been 'tapped' during the war years.[69]

THE STATE, CATHOLICISM AND THE HOLOCAUST

Blanket censorship helped desensitise many Irish people to the atrocities of war. The Catholic hierarchy—in contrast to its counterpart in England—did not feel called upon as a body to speak out about what was happening in Europe. Indeed, the Irish censor usually refused to allow the sermons of Cardinal Hinsley of Westminster to be published. Irish bishops, it appears, were not very well tutored in international politics. There was a tendency to concentrate on local pastoral concerns, rather than the larger Catholic canvas. In the opinion of the leader of the Catholic Church in Ireland, Cardinal MacRory, the war was going to be won by Hitler and he encouraged the Americans to 'try to make peace with him now, because you may have to do so later on.' Writing to the US envoy, Gray, on 20 October 1941, MacRory said:

The only case in which you can escape making peace with him is if you win out yourselves. But is this likely? When can you hope to be able to invade Germany and defeat the German army on its own soil? And suppose that did ever happen, is there the ghost of a chance that there would be a *just peace then*?

The cardinal also admonished the Allies for the 'systematic injustice' against Germany 'before ever Hitler began to misbehave'.[70] Gray sent that letter to Roosevelt. It could hardly have impressed the US president.

The emerging leader of the Catholic hierarchy, John Charles McQuaid, the son of a Cavan doctor, had become archbishop of Dublin in November 1940. Theologically conservative and hierarchical in his thinking, he did not prove to be an alternative voice to the elderly cardinal on the moral questions of the war. Neither was he particularly enlightened in his opposition to Jewish-Christian dialogue in Dublin during the years of the holocaust.[71] But he shared that narrow-mindedness with a number of senior officials in the Departments of Justice and Industry and Commerce. Writing in 1945, S.A. Roche, secretary of the Department of Justice, reviewed Irish policy towards the reception of Jewish refugees:

> The immigration of Jews is generally discouraged. The wealth and influence of the Jewish community in this country appear to have increased considerably in recent years and there is some danger of exciting opposition and controversy if this tendency continues. As Jews do not become assimilated with the native population, like other immigrants, any big increase in their numbers might create a social problem.[72]

The same source wrote to Maurice Moynihan in the Department of the Taoiseach on another occasion; the crude word 'assimilate' was chosen again when 'integrate' might have been less offensive.

> Our practice has been to discourage any substantial increase in the Jewish population. They do not assimilate with our own people but remain a sort of colony of a world-wide Jewish community. This makes them a potential irritant in the body politic and has led to disastrous results from time to time in other countries.[73]

The Irish government's policy towards the admission of foreigners had been very restrictive in the 1930s. That continued to be the case throughout the changed circumstances of the war years when Europe faced an unprecedented refugee problem. The Irish response was ungenerous. The particular circumstances of Jewish refugees were simply not acknowledged. However, the Jewish Representative Council defended the Irish government from charges of anti-semitism which had appeared in a New York paper *PM*: the council repudiated 'as false, irresponsible and mischievous any suggestion that the government . . . is anti-semitic or that there is any organised anti-semitic movement in Éire. . . . No Irish government has ever discriminated between Jew and non-Jew.' Robert Briscoe, a Jewish Fianna Fáil TD, also issued a statement denying that the 'people of Ireland or the present or any government of Ireland are or have ever been anti-Semitic'.[74]

Nevertheless, there were vulgar displays of anti-semitism in Ireland during the war. The writer Elizabeth Bowen reported to the British Foreign Office after a visit to Dublin in autumn 1940 that 'anti-semitism in Éire is considerably on the increase'.[75] At least two putative anti-semitic groups have already been mentioned. Certain TDS were under the spell of fashionable continental ideas. For example, Dan Breen—a hero of the War of Independence—was a regular visitor to the German legation. He was a strong critic of Briscoe, his party colleague. Oliver J. Flanagan, a newly elected opposition TD, asked the Dáil why the government had not directed any special orders against 'the Jews who crucified our Saviour 1900 years ago and who are crucifying us every day of the week?' He wanted the Jews routed out of Ireland.[76] Longford County Council unanimously passed a resolution in 1943 protesting to government that many foreigners—mainly Jews—were having their names changed to names of Irish origin.[77] De Valera received a letter on the same topic mockingly signed: 'Brian Boru (late Abraham Goldstein)'. The anonymous anti-semite said that he had noted several recent example of Jews changing their names:

> At this rate the Irish people will very soon be known by their characteristic noses and olive complexions, not to mention their thieving propensities. Do you not think the time has come to give up the study of Irish and replace it in the schools by Yiddish, as

undoubtedly the latter is going to become the language that matters in Ireland?[78]

Such repugnant sentiment was always a cause for concern in government. De Valera did what he could to ensure that Axis legations were prevented from spreading racism. *Radio War News from Italy*, a newsletter distributed by the Italian legation, was acted against by the Department of External Affairs in 1941. The issue on 18 March had written about the alleged 'swift subordination to American Jewry' of English politics since 1918. The 21 April issue referred to Jews as 'these rodents'. Berardis was called into Iveagh House on 7 May and informed that in recent issues of the bulletin 'your comments on the distinguished head of the American people, the American people themselves, and on the Jews, are not merely in the worst of bad taste, but they display an attitude towards the government of this neutral country which can only be described as a gross breach of the privileges of hospitality which you enjoy.' A formal complaint was lodged with the Italian government.[79] The Irish government adopted an equally tough attitude towards one member of the staff of the German legation who was a Nazi propagandist. But these measures did not entirely prevent Axis propagandists from spreading anti-semitic ideas in Dublin. The government, although vigilant, had to cope with a range of major problems to keep the country supplied with the basics of life.

DOMESTIC WARTIME POLITICS

The external threat brought about a forced consensus on many important issues. The very existence of the state was in jeopardy. It was difficult for an opposition to be perceived as playing politics with the future of the country. But political life continued apace and two general elections were held during the war. The trade union movement—not the opposition political parties—offered the most severe challenge to de Valera and Fianna Fáil in the early war years.

A strike by municipal workers in Dublin in early 1940 was the occasion, rather than the cause, for the sense of urgency with which the Department of Industry and Commerce undertook an immediate review of industrial relations. The strike involved over 2,000 corporation workers. It caused major disruption in various essential municipal services—the waterworks, bin collections, street cleaning and in the fire brigade.[80] A claim for an increase of eight shillings per week had been made by the Irish Municipal Employees' Trade Union (IMETU), on behalf of the workers. The corporation was willing to offer an increase of 3s. 9d. a week, but a meeting of the cabinet on 26 January decided otherwise and the city manager was informed that no increase was to be granted 'without full regard being had to the prevailing rates of wages in comparable employment outside the corporation'. The government pledged to give 'such assistance as might be necessary with a view to the maintenance of essential services'. The corporation offer was duly reduced to an increase of two shillings per week. A strike ensued, with the Dublin Trades Council pledging full support on 6 March. There were rumours that other unions were prepared to take 'sympathetic action'.[81]

The Minister for Industry and Commerce, Seán MacEntee, met a delegation of the ITUC and the trades council on 9 March, armed with a clear mandate from the cabinet which had met the previous day; the minister had been empowered to encourage the city manager to take 'an unyielding attitude'. All necessary steps were to be taken to ensure the continuation of the country's normal import and export trade. However, the government had turned down one of MacEntee's proposals: that a warning was to be issued to workers that if they did not return to work within 48 hours, their jobs would be declared vacant and steps would be taken to fill them.[82] Government pressure eventually brought the strike to an end.

The municipal workers' strike highlighted the government's sense of vulnerability when faced with an industrial challenge. The dispute eloquently made the Department of Industry and Commerce's case for the need for new legislation to govern strikes. This was not a case of overreaction, as Finbarr O'Shea has pointed out.[83] The minister and his senior departmental officials felt very strongly about the need for radical action. MacEntee sent a note to R.C. Ferguson on 17 March 1940 detailing the principles that ought to underpin legislation which dealt with irresponsible and unjustifiable strikes: 'Thus we have come to the position in which a body of Trades Union members can do here what no Government would dare to do, that is, at their own sweet will to paralyse our whole productive economy without any advertence whatsoever to the loss and suffering which may be inflicted upon other sections of the community and with no regard for the public interest.' MacEntee proposed that unions should be fined one pound for each member who participated in a strike in contravention of the terms of the forthcoming Act. He also argued that if an individual who was engaged in an essential industry chose to take part in an unjustifiable strike, the community, in retribution for such action, might and should relieve itself for a definite period of its social obligations to that individual.[84]

Draft heads for a bill were placed before the cabinet in April 1940, very much based on the principles outlined by MacEntee. When strikes threatened essential public services, the government was empowered to declare a state of emergency. Employees were to be listed and called upon, in the name of the people, to perform the services. A refusal could mean dismissal, fine or imprisonment; loss of social welfare and pension rights might also ensue. Traders were to be debarred from providing goods to the said individuals. There were also other draconian proposals regarding incitement or picketing and a minimum of one month's notice for a strike was necessary. There was also a proposal to issue a licence to all associations of workmen and employers engaged in setting wages or negotiating conditions, upon receipt of a fixed sum of money.[85]

Notwithstanding the difficulties of the time, a majority in cabinet felt sufficiently concerned to reject the draft headings. The attorney general had questioned the constitutionality of certain aspects of the draft Bill. The Department of Finance had expressed outright opposition. On 28 May 1940 the cabinet—already preoccupied with international military events—decided to follow the line advocated by Lemass and restrict the legislation to 'lightning strikes'. The outcome was the division of the legislation. Emergency Order 83—which became known as the Wages Standstill Order—was the ultimate response to inflation and spiralling wage increases. This was introduced under the Emergency Powers Act. The Trade Union Act 1941 confined itself to regulating the trade unions. It was quite different from what MacEntee had envisaged in March 1940.

Lemass's return to Industry and Commerce in August 1941 helped relations between the government and the trade unions. Following consultations with union leaders, he introduced a new Trade Union Bill in 1942. This pleased Congress and removed—in the view of the ITUC—in several details 'some of the objectionable provisions of the Act of 1941'.[86] Lemass also showed a willingness to meet the leaders of the trade union movement in regard to the Wages Standstill Order which had so antagonised many of the workers. He received a delegation from the ITUC on the matter in November 1941, and a memorandum was submitted to him by Congress in January 1942. Despite objections from the Department of Finance, Lemass won cabinet approval for the introduction of the Emergency Powers (No. 166) Order, 1942.[87] There were four reasons why Lemass favoured conciliation: 1) the government had ensured that the trade union movement was prepared to tolerate stringent measures because of the war; 2) the military dangers of 1940 and early 1941 had passed with Hitler's lurch to the east; 3) Lemass was ideologically more sympathetic towards the plight of labour; 4) a general election was on the horizon and Fianna Fáil needed every vote it could muster in the unpredictable political climate of wartime and shortage-ridden Ireland. At least, the trade unions had been notified.

Nineteen forty-three was the fiftieth anniversary of the Gaelic League. In his St Patrick's day speech, de Valera exhorted people to learn the Irish language and use it in their daily lives.[88] Ridiculed by his opponents and lionised by his supporters, de Valera had said:

> Acutely conscious though we all are of the misery and desolation in which the greater part of the world is plunged, let us turn aside for a moment to that ideal Ireland that we would have. That Ireland which we dreamed of would be the home of a people who valued material wealth only as the basis of right living, of a people who were satisfied with frugal comfort and devoted their leisure to the things of the spirit—a land whose countryside would be bright with cosy homesteads, whose fields and villages would be joyous with the sounds of industry, with the romping of sturdy children, the contests of athletic youths and the laughter of comely maidens, whose firesides would be forums for the wisdom of serene old age. It would, in a word, be the home of a people living the life that God desires that man should live.

It may be coincidence, but de Valera's speech echoed the words of the poet Máirtín Ó Direáin's poem 'Cuireadh do Mhuire' (Invitation to Mary) which appeared in December 1942:

> Do you know Mary
> Where you will go this year

Seeking shelter
For your Holy Child
When every door is
Closed in his face
By the hatred and price of the human race?

Accept
An invitation from me
To a sea island
In the distant West:
Bright candles will be
Lit in every window
And a turf fire
Kindled in the hearth.[89]

In retrospect, the imagery and sentiments of de Valera's speech read more like the words of a 'lay cardinal' than of a politician. However, it is not generally pointed out that de Valera did not confuse image with reality in the speech cited above. It was the 'Ireland which we dreamed of'. The Ireland of 1943 was a country where, in de Valera's words, 'a section of our people have not yet this minimum (of comfort and leisure). They rightly strive to secure it, and it must be our aim and the aim of all who are just and wise to assist in the effort.'[90] People were much more likely to identify with Maguire, the County Monaghan small farmer who is the central character in Patrick Kavanagh's poem *The Great Hunger* (published in 1942) than with de Valera's ideal. In thrall to the land, Paddy Maguire's words in one stanza mockingly prefigure the romanticism of de Valera:

The world looks on
And talks of the peasant:
The peasant has no worries;
In his little lyrical fields
He ploughs and sows;
He eats fresh food,
He loves fresh women,
He is his own master
As it was in the Beginning
The simpleness of peasant life.

The birds that sing for him are eternal choirs,
Everywhere he walks there are flowers.
His heart is pure,
His mind is clear. . . .

But Maguire finds that there is no escape, no escape from land,
mother and church:

But the peasant in his little acres is tied
To a mother's womb by the wind-toughened navel-cord
Like a goat tethered to the stump of a tree—
He circles around and around wondering why it should be. . . .

He stands in the doorway of his house
A ragged sculpture of the wind,
October creaks the rotten mattress,
The bedposts fall. No hope. No lust.
The hungry fiend
Screams the apocalypse of clay
In every corner of this land.

There was, as has been pointed out, a way out for many Irish people
during the war years: emigration to Britain. That was the route that
over 200,000 took during the Emergency. Thomas McCarthy has
captured the mood of their leaving in his poem 'The Emigration
Trains, 1943':

A pound-note was the best kind of passport
In those days, so I held my pound tightly
After my mother turned away. . . .

I felt like a vagrant, destitute, until
At Waterford Station I realised
My good luck: I owned a suitcase of card
While others carried mere bundles of cloth. . . .

We were heading for England and the world
At war. Neutrality we couldn't afford.
I thought I would spend two years away
But in the end the two became twenty.[91]

Given the problem of high unemployment in Ireland, the 'vent' of emigration removed a large number of voters who might otherwise have punished the government for its lacklustre domestic performance. Moreover, the agricultural sector had suffered a major reverse in the spring of 1941. Foot and mouth disease was discovered in February and within ten months 19,000 cattle and 5,000 sheep had to be slaughtered. The disease was mainly confined to Munster and south Leinster, but it placed the severest restrictions on the movement of farm animals, and of people. Fairs were cancelled and so, too, were major sporting fixtures. In the end, the GAA had to nominate Dublin and Cork to play in the hurling All-Ireland final owing to the fact that so many games had to be called off. Such disruptions were part of wartime life in Ireland, but that did not mean that the electorate was automatically well disposed towards the party in power. De Valera was justifiably reluctant to face the people, but his efforts to prolong the life of the Dáil by a year came to nought in the teeth of strong parliamentary opposition.[92]

The next election was held on 22 June 1943. Petrol shortages made campaigning particularly difficult. The rationing of newsprint had reduced the national papers to a fraction of their normal size. *The Irish Press* was four pages and the anti-Fianna Fáil *Irish Independent* and *The Irish Times* were equally restricted. It was difficult for de Valera to run on the government's immediate record. Rationing and the general shortage of sugar, tea, butter and potatoes in the urban areas gave an initiative to the opposition, which was exploited by Cosgrave of Fine Gael and Norton of the Labour Party.[93] There were proposals for a national government. Fine Gael finally settled upon the idea of a coalition as an alternative to Fianna Fáil. De Valera attacked the inherent instability of coalition government which could be held to ransom by a minority. But that 'core value' underwent a metamorphosis in the late 1980s.[94] MacEntee was the most extreme of the Fianna Fáil ministers in his rhetoric. He accused the opposition of trying to introduce a dictatorship:

> Were the old Blueshirt ambitions still alive? Were the men who were proclaiming a few years ago that 'the Black Shirts were victorious in Italy, the Hitler Shirts in Germany, and as assuredly . . . the Blue Shirts will be victorious in the Irish Free State,' still hoping that one day they would get the chance to overthrow the democratic system altogether here.[95]

Switching his criticisms to the Labour Party on 4 June, MacEntee told a Dublin audience that the Comintern might have been abolished in Russia, but the Muscovites were active in Dublin. He might say, he continued, that they were triumphant in Dublin since they had captured Norton and were holding him as a hostage while the Dublin Communist organisation was infiltrating its advance elements into the Irish Labour Party:

> Honest men of the Labour Party had been trying to keep the Labour movement here in line with Irish tradition, to keep it Irish and Christian. As God-fearing, honest workers they had no use for those pagan totalitarian systems being imported from abroad.[96]

Not for the first time Lemass had good reason to be disturbed by the content of MacEntee's verbal pyrotechnics. His attacks on Labour were particularly unwelcome to other Fianna Fáil candidates who were trying to gain Labour transfers. On 16 June 1943, Lemass wrote to MacEntee making that very point and adding that Ryan, O'Kelly, Traynor 'and some other ministers' agreed. In his own constituency, Lemass also found that the Labour vote would go in the majority to Fianna Fáil 'unless we irritate them by unduly severe attacks on the Labour Party'. He did not think it 'wise' that MacEntee should speak at Crumlin, a Labour stronghold. He added delicately:

> I know you have your own views and methods but you have a different type of constituency to others and, on this account, I think you may perhaps overlook the reactions of your campaign elsewhere.

Lemass told MacEntee that Jim Ryan had intended to phone him to make a similar point, but instead had asked Lemass to drop MacEntee a note. 'I hope it won't cramp your style' Lemass ended tartly.[97]

MacEntee responded in his usual civil manner, reminding Lemass that elections were not won 'by billing and cooing at your opponents and Labour has gone out much stronger against us in this election than they have against Fine Gael.' He charged that Labour had sent in 'organised squads of interrupters' into his meetings, 'but these have now been silenced' and his meetings were 'quiet and orderly'. His constituents included a large proportion of working-class voters who were 'not of the same mind as your workers are in regard to this matter' (attacks on Labour). He agreed willingly to get out of the meetings mentioned by Lemass if that were possible.[98]

MacEntee changed his tone as Fianna Fáil engaged in damage limitation. *The Irish Press* carried a story on 17 June under the headline: 'Labour's tribute to Dr Ryan recalled'. This was an effort to undo the harm inflicted single-handedly by MacEntee. Fianna Fáil concentrated its attack on the inconsistency of Fine Gael policy on coalition.[99]

Just how much trouble Fianna Fáil felt it was in can be seen from the front page of *The Irish Press* on 21 June where a panel entitled 'National Government—Moryah' allegedly documented the opposition of Fine Gael to coalition at a time of national crisis in 1922, 1925, 1932, 1934, 1939, 1940 and 1941. But this was not enough to save Fianna Fáil from taking a severe drubbing at the polls. At an eve of poll rally, Lemass had predicted a complete victory, more in hope than in expectation. The Fianna Fáil seats were reduced from 77 to 67 and Fine Gael from 45 to 32. Labour did dramatically well, rising from 9 to 17. The farmers' party, Clann na Talmhan, won 14 seats and there were eight independents. De Valera managed to form the next government with a relatively unchanged team and to limp on for another year. There were many who felt that Fianna Fáil had been the architect of its own near-downfall and much of the blame was directed at MacEntee. In a draft letter on 28 June 1943 MacEntee offered his resignation to de Valera following a meeting of ministers at which de Valera had passed 'strictures' on him over the manner in which he had conducted the recent election. He had no other option than to retire from government 'unless I strip myself wholly of honour and self-respect, and I am not prepared to continue to serve in the Government at that price.' However, MacEntee was not prepared to go without first stating his reasons for quitting since he had never been 'selfish nor anything but sincere and singleminded' as far as the Fianna Fáil party was concerned. He added in the frank manner to which his colleagues had long become accustomed:

It will surprise none, I am sure, that a party which has suffered a reverse at the hands of the electorate should look for a scapegoat. I venture to say, however, that it will surprise many to learn that the person chosen as the vicarious delinquent is myself. . . . It is usual to censure men for losing elections, but not for winning them.

MacEntee was not surprised, however, because he had experienced such a reaction in 1938. In the past he had excused such criticisms from de Valera on the grounds that he had been misinformed by *others.* That was not the case on this occasion. Gerry Boland had been particularly critical, and there was a reference to the loss of a seat in Roscommon. MacEntee listed the seats where Fianna Fáil had lost constituencies and defended his record at the hustings. Attacks centred on the Trade Union Act and the wages standstill orders; MacEntee took full responsibility for these unpopular pieces of legislation. He was going to forward copies of his speeches to de Valera and ended his letter as follows:

> I shall not, of course, be at the government meeting tomorrow, but shall go to the Department to clear up my private papers, of which there is one way and another some accumulation. I shall, however, be at your disposal to fulfil whatever formalities may be required of me on relinquishing my office.[100]

De Valera did not accept his resignation and MacEntee did not retire from his last ministerial post until 1965.

MacEntee was reappointed Minister for Local Government and Public Health in a cabinet which showed very few changes except for the appointment of Seán Moylan to the Department for Lands. But it was a cabinet which knew that it faced the prospect of having to fight another election at any time.

Cosgrave called it a day and resigned the leadership of Fine Gael. He was replaced by Richard Mulcahy, who had lost his seat in the Dáil and had to lead the party from the Senate. James Dillon might have been much more effective, but he was in exterior darkness as a consequence of his anti-neutrality stance.

If Fine Gael had failed to take advantage of the short interval to regroup and rebuild, the Labour Party was even more unfortunate. The real winner in 1943, Norton, had an opportunity to strip Fianna Fáil of further votes and seats. But Lemass's tactics helped partially to open up the division between Irish- and British-based unions, divisions which were fanned by MacEntee in particular during the framing of the Trade Union Bill. William O'Brien helped found National Labour with the assistance of a number of ITGWU Dáil deputies. The outcome of such Labour factionalism was a political windfall for de Valera.[101]

Defeated on 9 May 1944 on the second reading of the Transport Bill, by 64 votes to 63, de Valera called a snap general election which the opposition parties did not particularly want.[102] (*Dublin Opinion* made some fun of the fact that the names of the two independents who had voted against the government were Cole and Byrne.)[103] De Valera was in a position to exploit the theme of responsibility without power and he asked the electorate to give the party a clear mandate.[104] Lemass said on 12 May 1944 that the defeat of the government had been carefully planned in secret. Dick Mulcahy offered the electorate the prospect of a coalition of his own party together with Labour and Clann na Talmhan.[105] Aiken called such a proposal 'crazy' and so the debate went on. Unlike 1943, the campaign was very short and Fianna Fáil kept MacEntee on a tight rein. The campaign was made all the easier because of the Labour Party split.

De Valera described the rhetoric of the opposition as being picturesque, particularly the portrait of him drawn in the Dáil on the night of the dissolution:

> I was pictured as being in the tantrums, frightfully angry, and they drew a picture about me next day in the Dáil as a man like Galloping Hogan flying off to the residence of the President with my cloak streaming out in the wind, and froth and fire from the nostrils of my horse. One of my colleagues, who was listening to it, said that they made a very nice combination of Paul Revere and Dick Turpin.

It was a pity to spoil such a colourful story, he said, but the reality was a much more sober affair.

Fianna Fáil put up 100 candidates to Fine Gael's 55. Labour offered 31 candidates and National Labour nine. Clann na Talmhan, other small groups and independents put up 57.[106] Surprise worked to Fianna Fáil advantage, as it had done in 1933 and 1938. *The Irish Press* on 25 May reported de Valera as saying in Limerick that the opposition merely wanted 'bedlam'. This was accompanied by a front-page cartoon showing the Dick Mulcahy band all playing out of tune.

Another cartoon on 29 May showed the coalition as three-card tricksters, under the heading 'find the Taoiseach'. The opposition was blamed for dragging the country unnecessarily to the polls. When the votes were counted, Fianna Fáil had 76 seats to Fine Gael's 30. Labour had eight and National Labour four. Clann na Talmhan got eleven and there were nine others.[107] De Valera was voted Taoiseach by a comfortable majority on 9 June 1944. He won by a comfortable majority.[108] His cabinet remained unchanged until the end of the war.

CULTURAL LIFE IN WARTIME IRELAND

On the more light-hearted side, the wartime censor did everything to prevent the stoking of the Irish libido with racy images. Kate O'Brien's *The Land of Spices*, published in 1941, was banned a year later on the grounds that a single sentence in the entire book—intimating homosexual practices—was likely to offend against common decency.[109] That same year Eric Cross's *The Tailor and Ansty* was banned. The earthiness of the hidden Ireland, as told by the tailor and his wife, was deemed to be too much for 'right-thinking' Irish people. There was a lot of sense and much learning in the tailor's comment on the rise of fascism: 'There wouldn't be half this trouble if more people fell to breeding.'[110] In the epilogue to this volume, the tailor composed a new final verse to the song 'The Buttermilk Lasses':

Now all you young maidens,
Don't listen to me
For I will incite you to immoralitee
Or unnatural vice or in similar way
Corrupt or deprave you or lead you astray.[111]

While Europe was at war, the Senate debated the life-and-death subject of censorship at length in November and December 1942.[112] Brian O'Nolan's novel, *An Béal Bocht*, published in 1941, provided catharsis for the saner brand of cultural nationalist who felt nothing but nausea for the new, official, government-approved, sanitised, *Iosa milis*, Gaelic revivalism. Censorship acted as a spur to many Irish intellectuals to struggle against the complacency induced by the policy of cultural autarchy. *Dublin Opinion* continued to provide a more gentle assault on the sacred cows of the new state while *The Bell* (founded in 1940) was a journal of literary, political and social criticism of the highest standard. As its first editor, Seán O'Faoláin set a very high standard. It very quickly became the most important cultural magazine in the country.[113] *Comhar* began to publish in 1942, a year after James Joyce died. The new Irish magazine broke through many taboos with considerable journalistic courage. Both *The Bell* and *Comhar*, edited by the inter-university group An Comhchaidreamh, gave an outlet for the publication of material which would not have been so easily placed in existing journals. The conventions of civilised intellectual discourse were imposed by both editors. But the ideal was apparently not always achieved. For example, Máire Mhac an tSaoi wrote an article on 'Na Dánta Grá San' in late 1944. Sending up the ultra-pious, one reader, 'An Cat Mara', described how the article was written 'go ró-mhaith aici'. He took exception to Máire Mhac an tSaoi's theme:

> Sin é an sort stuif atá á moladh ag Máire. Amour courtois adeir duine amháin; idealized adultery, adeir duine eile. Ach thuig an dochtúir diadha Aodh Mac Aingil, thuig seisean an scéal níosa fearr; 'Dánta salcha ghluaiseas do chum drúisi,' adeir sé.[114]

Naturally, the shortage of paper during the war years meant a reduction in the number of novels and books of poetry that were published. Mary Lavin published her first collection of stories, *Tales from Bective Bridge*, in 1942. Seán O'Casey's *Purple Dust* and Frank O'Connor's *Dutch Interiors* both appeared in 1940.

It is a mistake to depict wartime Dublin—albeit suffering under a severe régime of censorship—as an intellectual wasteland. As one of Europe's unoccupied capitals, it attracted a number of emigré academics and painters. Their presence added to an already lively atmosphere, particularly in the visual arts, with Evie Hone, Mainie Jellett, Nora McGuinness and other members of the White Stag Group leading the way. The latter group of artistic 'bohemians' came under the watchful eye of the Special Branch and G2, but there was no cause for concern. While members of that particular artistic group were very concerned about the issues raised by the war, their more immediate interests were to maintain close contact with the major trends in European art and to help close the gap between artist and society. The refusal of the Royal Hibernian Academy to hang the pictures of Louis le Brocquy and other living Irish artists in its annual exhibition led to the establishment of the Irish Exhibition of Living Art in 1943.[115] It was an exciting departure and one which showed that there were painters in Ireland who were very much influenced by contemporary mainland European trends. More than any other Irish artist of her generation, Mainie Jellett helped gain acceptance for the 'modern' in the country: '. . . the only way to carry on a live tradition is to understand and venerate the great works of the past and to realise the unchanging artistic laws which must be reinterpreted by each period in turn so as to express its needs and character.'[116] Jellett abhorred the division which had grown up between artist and society: 'The present enforced isolation from the majority is to be deplored and, I believe, is one of the many causes which has resulted in the present chaos we live in.'[117]

The controversy over the refusal by the advisory committee of the Municipal Gallery of Modern Art, Dublin to accept the gift of a Georges Rouault painting in 1942 will help illustrate the complexity of the response in Irish society to modern, continental European art and culture.[118] 'Christ and the Soldier' had been purchased by the Friends of the National Collection for £380. Echoes of what was discussed at the meeting of the advisory committee can be found in a letter from the art-lover and collector C.P. Curran, who was well positioned to have known what transpired. He noted that the Friends of the National Collection had been warned by the gallery's curator, J.F. Kelly, that Mrs Kathleen Clarke, the ex-Lord Mayor of Dublin, regarded the painting as a 'travesty' and an offence to Christian sentiment[119] and that some other members of the advisory committee were unwilling to accept the painting even before it had been purchased. Nevertheless, the Friends of the National Collection had gone ahead and bought it since it was in accordance with policy and 'in the best interests of the public'. Curran asked whether the city manager was well advised in rejecting the picture on the grounds that it was either not a work of art or blasphemous, or both.[120] Dermod O'Brien, president of the Friends of the National Collection, who was also a member of the advisory committee, told *The Irish Press*:

> I understand that the objection was that members of the Committee thought the picture was blasphemous; that it was not their idea of how Christ should be depicted. I personally cannot see that. It was not intended to be naturalistic.[121]

The distinguished artist Seán Keating did not consider the Rouault painting to be a work of art; it was 'naïve, childish and unintelligible' he said.[122] Another member of the committee, Sarah Purser, who had not been at the meeting, refused to express an opinion on the controversy. However, she said that Sir Hugh Lane—to whom the gallery owed most of its valuable pictures—had been in the thick of controversy all his life. Many people had said that the pictures Lane had bought were worthless, but time had proved that he was right. She thought that greater consideration should be given to the opinion of the Friends of the National Collection.[123]

The young poet Patrick Kavanagh decided against the Rouault, but condemned those who rejected it, if they confined their objection to that kind of art as a religious work, and made no protest when tradition and harmony were cast aside in secular things.[124] On the other hand, the art critic Thomas MacGreevy took the other side and confirmed that the Irish artist Thomas Healy had been very moved by Rouault's art.[125] Curran made a spirited defence of Rouault, as did Professor Liam Ó Briain of Galway.[126] Evie Hone and Mainie Jellett also sided with the modernists, as the pro-Rouault side was called.[127] The former said that the artist was expressing, in the idiom of his period, the great traditional truths that were eternal. The latter said it was a very moving piece of religious art.[128] Myles na gCopaleen launched a savage attack on the anti-Rouault group:

> The picture is executed in the modern manner, and could not be expected to please persons whose knowledge of sacred art is derived from the shiny chromo-lithograph bondieuserie of the Boulevard Saint Sulpice, examples of which are to be found in every decent Irishman's bedroom.

He felt that a representational portrait of a bishop, such as was carried out so embarrassingly often, could be assessed by merely mechanical standards—the best judge being a child of three who could say authoritatively whether 'it is like him'. But no two people would react in the same way to a Rouault painting. The attitude of each person to the picture was personal and was not necessarily related to any conventional artistic criteria. For that reason, nobody wanted to be bothered with Seán Keating's opinion. 'We can form our own,' Myles wrote:

Impertinent as the expression of individual opinion must be in such a situation, it is a gross outrage that this Board of the Municipal Gallery, having apparently formed opinions desperate and dark of hue, should decide that the citizens of Ireland should not be permitted to form any opinion at all. By what authority does this bunch take custody of the community's aesthetic conscience?

The members of the Corporation are elected to discharge somewhat more physical tasks, such as arranging for slum clearance and the disposal of sewage. Here there is scope for valuable public service, a vast field of opportunity confronts the eye. Why must the members trespass in other spheres where their intellectual equipment cannot be other than inadequate?[129]

The Friends of the National Collection invited the distinguished and humanitarian Holy Ghost priest, Father Edward Leen, to deliver a lecture on Rouault at which the painting would be displayed. Leen silenced the 'blasphemy' school of thought when he asked:

Is the picture blasphemous? The truth cannot be blasphemous even when it lays bare relentlessly, even cruelly, the inner sense of a reality which crashes through our miserable conventionality.[130]

Leen regarded Rouault as among the great leaders of the modern movement '. . . and whether his work appeals or repels, it cannot be ignored, because it is alive and sincere'.[131] This assessment stands in marked contrast to the view of the curator of the National Museum, Liam S. Gogan, who said that the picture had its interest as completing the evolution of recent French art, but only in the direction of its decadence and complete failure. He told a meeting of the Academy of Christian Art in Dublin that the rejected picture was of a piece with the rest of Rouault's work, much of which reflected the degradation which had affected the life of France and other countries, thanks to the materialistic teaching of the nineteenth century. He argued that the influence of the Rouault school could only vitiate and destroy, and at best be an example of faithlessness in things that made life and art of value. Ireland wanted the art of hope, not despair.[132]

The row over the Rouault painting was settled in a novel and definitive way; the national seminary in Maynooth was delighted to take the painting on loan, where it was hung in the library. Today the painting hangs, where it ought to have done from the outset, in its rightful place in the Municipal Gallery. The controversy reflected the radical divisions in Irish society concerning much more than the matter of aesthetics. Above all, it highlighted the danger of trying to reduce the intellectual conflicts in Irish society to a lay/modernist clerical/traditionalist cleavage.

CHURCH, STATE AND SOCIETY

Domestic politics proved to be a little more robust and troublesome in the last year of the war. De Valera was personally very unhappy when Archbishop McQuaid made controversial statements in his 1944 lenten pastoral concerning the education of Catholics. With reference to 'Protestant Trinity College', he ordered that no Catholic could attend—and then only for grave and valid reasons—without the permission of the local ordinary, that is, himself: 'Any Catholic who disobeys this law is guilty of mortal sin and while he persists in disobedience is unworthy to receive the Sacraments.'[133] Ironically, McQuaid's personal doctor, who was a brother of Frederick Boland, was a Trinity graduate, as was the assistant secretary of the Department of External Affairs. (Upon retiring from the diplomatic service, Frederick Boland was appointed chancellor of TCD.)[134]

It ought to be noted that McQuaid also regarded the National University of Ireland, with its three constituent colleges, as 'a neutral educational establishment' which had to be regarded by Catholics as 'failing to give true acknowledgment to the One True Faith'. However, in view of the measures taken by the ecclesiastical authorities in the archdioceses, he regarded University College Dublin as being 'sufficiently safe for Catholic students'.[135] That attitude was consistent with McQuaid's stance on the drafting of the religious article of the 1937 constitution (see chapter 2). But the typecasting of TCD did not go without strong refutation by prominent Catholics. It was thought that the archbishop—although entitled to his view—had gone too far. That was certainly the opinion of Sir Thomas Molony, vice-chancellor of Trinity since 1931, who wrote to the Irish high commissioner, Dulanty, to complain about the archbishop's case against Trinity which was answered in the following way: the Catholic vice-chancellor, fellows, professors and staff sent through the papal nuncio a declaration of their devotion to the pope and the Church and said that they had offered 100 masses for the pope 'that he might be spared all suffering and the Vatican City and Rome preserved'. The TCD statement had been sent by the nuncio to the cardinal secretary of state: 'I presume that is not a breach of neutrality' commented Molony. One of the Catholic professors on the staff, R.A. O'Meara, saw de Valera, but to no avail.[136] The ban remained to be lifted only in 1970.

Meanwhile, the 'last hurrah' for catholic integralism came with the publication of the report of the Commission on Vocational Organisation, chaired by the bishop of Galway, Michael Browne, in August 1944. The committee had finished its work the previous year. Despite the difficulties of wartime travel, it had sat in plenary session on 164 days, on 49 of which oral evidence had been taken. The chairman had missed only one meeting in that time. He had attended 83 out of the 84 meetings, 301 out of 312 sessions. Browne had been in the chair for 160 out of a possible 164 days.[137] Evidence was taken from 174 bodies. A questionnaire was issued to 333 bodies and replies were received from 150. The report proposed the phased introduction of vocationalism. The first and primary stage involved the building of the occupational associations, the trade unions and the employer groups to establish a complete nationwide system covering all sectors. This could be done, the report argued, without any additional cost to the taxpayer, as could the next stage when employers' and workers' associations would come together in vocational groups to deal with common problems. The higher stage of vocational organisation comprised the establishment of functional councils, such as those of law, education and public health; the inter-vocational council of industry; the national conferences and offices of industry, agriculture and commerce; the national councils of transport and finance, and finally the national vocational assembly. The commission recommended that those on the functional councils should not be paid a salary. The same principle was to apply to national bodies controlling the professions, agriculture, industry, commerce, transport, finance and the national vocational assembly. The commission argued that the introduction of its recommendations would curtail the level of *bureaucracy* in the country, reduce the size of the civil service since certain officers or services would become redundant, and provide protection for the 'small man' from monopolies and pressure groups.

A pamphlet published by Browne in 1945 argued that vocational organisation was the means by which people could establish the values of justice, order, efficiency and brotherhood, in permanent institutions 'and by which they can train themselves in the spirit and practice of union, cooperation and brotherhood'.[138] Browne had done very little to win support for the findings of the committee. However, his robust chairing of proceedings and abrasive handling of the civil service during the lifetime of the commission did little to provide a receptive atmosphere for a report where one entry in the index read insultingly: 'Civil Service, see also Bureaucracy'.[139] Joe Lee has correctly identified what he describes as Browne's pathological revulsion for civil servants and pathological veneration of the professions.[140] While his condition certainly was not clinical, it was a combination of attitudes which was shared by many members of the Catholic hierarchy. The Mother and Child crisis was to provide the most obvious and public manifestation of such a complex.

When Moynihan sought departmental reactions to the report in February 1945, he found that his peers were uniformly hostile. The secretary of the Land Commission, M. Deegan, wrote on 21 February from his sick bed that his recovery had not been hastened by the contents: 'I don't think I have ever come across a report which annoyed me more.'[141] That was precisely how Lemass felt about the report. He told the Seanad, on 21 February 1945, that it was a 'slovenly document', written in a 'querulous, nagging and propagandist tone'.[142] The previous October, the Minister for Agriculture, James Ryan, had made a strong defence of civil servants.[143] Even the Minister for Finance, Seán T. O'Kelly, whose friendship with Browne went back to the 1920s, defended the substance of Lemass's comments, but felt that he might have chosen different language to express his views.[144] Bishop Browne responded with a spirited defence of his report and an attack on Lemass.[145] The Minister for Industry and Commerce replied strongly.[146] The report, and vocationalism with it, was effectively buried in an unmarked grave by the deluge of political and administrative opposition heaped upon it in early 1945. Whatever the temptation might have been for radical political experiment in the 1930s, there was no mainstream political support for a radical change in the structure of the Irish state during the latter months of the war.[147]

Browne was not the only long-standing ecclesiastical supporter of

Fianna Fáil to have his work rejected out of hand by a combination of civil servants and government ministers. The bishop of Clonfert, John Dignan—the first bishop to support Fianna Fáil openly in the 1920s—published a pamphlet, *Social Security: Outlines for a Scheme of National Health Insurance*, on 11 October 1944. He had a long-term interest in the subject, and the government had appointed him chairman of the National Health Insurance Society. His pamphlet was originally read at one of the society's meetings. This was an attempt to apply Catholic social principles to health insurance and to other facets of the social services.[148]

The minister in question, Seán MacEntee, dismissed the proposals out of hand, stating in the Dáil that they were 'impracticable, and that accordingly no further action on the basis of the paper would be warranted'.[149] He might have been more civil in his response if he had not first read details of the plan in the national press. The chief medical officer in the department, James Deeny, felt that the Dignan scheme could have been drawn up at the Clongowes Social Order summer school. He considered it a purely 'corporate approach' and the 'only place where I found this philosophy in my travels was in Eastern Europe, particularly the USSR.'[150] The bishop, who had been numbered among the strongest of Fianna Fáil supporters, was not reappointed to the chair of the National Health Insurance Society.[151] MacEntee took on priest or prince of the Church with all the assurance of the self-confident lay Catholic who had God on his side.

He had been equally forthright in his opposition to non-means-tested children's allowances, dole and what he termed dismissively as Beveridgeism.[152] The latter, MacEntee found, had 'gravely disturbed' Catholic opinion in Britain. He therefore argued that the moral objections to a scheme of family allowances were greatest: (a) if the scheme is non-contributory in character, (b) is universal in application and (c) if the distribution of allowances is not related as strictly as possible to the actual need of the recipients.[153] MacEntee proved ever combative in government, switching the grounds of his arguments from the moral to the practical to suit himself.[154] But he could not prevent the introduction of a non-means-tested children's allowance in 1944 (2s. 6d. per week payable on all children except the first). However, MacEntee's confrontational style should not blind the reader to the positive work of his departmental officials and of his parliamentary secretary, Dr Con Ward. Health, in particular, was a pioneering department.

The quirkiness of MacEntee may have helped discredit what otherwise might have been considered a perfectly reasonable position in cabinet. Lemass found it easier towards the end of the war to outmanoeuvre MacEntee. The case of Irish tourism serves as an excellent example of this development. The Irish Tourist Board had been established shortly before the war broke out in 1939. A sum of £600,000 was made available for productive investment in tourism. The board undertook a general survey of tourist areas and formulated preliminary plans for the development of certain existing holiday resorts. It had also prepared training schemes for the industry, worked out a marketing strategy, and a plan for inspection of hotels and guesthouses. Although the war effectively killed off the Irish tourist industry until 1945, some progress was made on designated schemes. In 1944 the board drafted a memorandum for government to prepare for the anticipated post-war expansion in the industry. But the content was undiscriminating when it reviewed favourably the leisure policies of fascist Italy, Nazi Germany and dictatorial Japan, which laid strong emphasis on state-organised and enforced recreation. The Minister for Local Government and Public Health, Seán MacEntee, took particular pleasure in playfully excoriating the naïvety of the board's recommendations. With heavy sarcasm, he wrote:

> The Tourist Board would feel almost at home in Japan, for the Celto-Jap régime they propose is just a variant of the above. It is to consist of work, eating, sleeping, compulsory recreation *[sic]*, but no 'idleness'. But what a mind is disclosed by the passage underlined. [This is a reference to their recreationless lives.] The Fathers of the Desert, the anchorites and the hermits, those who sought solitude that they might in 'mere idleness', as the Board's phrase is, meditate on the great mystery of the solitary Godhead and contemplate His infinite and timeless Majesty, would have had short shrift from the authors if they would not herd it and pig it like the gregarious Japs.

MacEntee wrote sarcastically on the board's efforts on Mexico:

> Doubtless the members of the Tourist Board are highly familiar with Mexico, know all about the social and economic conditions

prevailing in that country as they have been recorded by competent observers. If, however, they are only quoting the 'ballyhoo' of some subsidised propagandist publication, they might with advantage read, as a corrective thereto, Graham Greene's *The Lawless Roads* or Kirstein's *For My Brother*, or even a popular novel like *The Power and the Glory*.[155]

While the content of the memorandum was ignored, it was decided in 1945, with the support of the Department of Industry and Commerce, to expand the budget of the board from £600,000 to £1.25m.[156] Lemass, who was to become Taoiseach in 1959, continued to press for expansion in tourism.[157]

ALLIED DIPLOMACY

The successful Allied invasion of Europe had begun on 6 June 1944. The war was entering its final phase. While preparations were being made for the opening of the much-talked-about second front, there was considerable anxiety in London and Washington about the possibility that a fatal intelligence leak might be made through Dublin. The British had been particularly worried about the presence of a radio transmitter in the German embassy which had been used earlier in the war by the staff—sometimes from a car on the outskirts of the city. Maffey made repeated representations—almost on a weekly basis—about it to the Department of External Affairs.[158] With the imminent opening of a second front, Maffey's representations became all the more insistent and he warned de Valera of the danger. Walshe spoke to Hempel about the transmitter on 15 December: 'I could tell him quite frankly and in the most friendly way that the presence of a wireless transmitter in the German Legation was giving us more worry in our relations with the British and American Governments than any other factor in our many-sided dealings with these two governments.' While Walshe stated that the transmitter had not been used for a long time, its presence in the legation 'constituted a positive danger to our neutrality'. The danger was all the more acute because the 'supreme crisis of the war was at hand' and 'the whole world was talking about a second front'. Hempel was instructed to hand over the transmitter, a fact which Maffey recorded somewhat archly in a letter to Walshe on 22 December 1943:

After my call at your office yesterday I informed London that the German Minister had been instructed to hand over his wireless transmitter set in the presence of an Irish expert, that the set would be lodged in a bank in a safe requiring both of two keys to open it, that the German Minister would retain one key as sign of title while the Éire Government would hold the other, that the bank would have special instructions denying access except to the Éire Government and that the set will be removed this week. I said that I had accepted this solution.[159]

Walshe was stung by the tone of the letter. It implied that the Irish had acted at the behest of the British. He minuted that Maffey 'was not asked to accept. He was simply told because of his representations to the Taoiseach. I made it quite clear that the matter was concluded before he made representations.'

Nevertheless, fears persisted in London and Washington about the danger of a leak concerning the preparation of Operation Overlord, the code name given to the planned landings of Allied forces in Normandy on 6 June 1944. Gray proved to be more jittery than Maffey. The Americans, after consultation with the president, the joint chiefs of staff and the Department of State, finally decided to send notes to de Valera requesting the removal of Axis representatives from Ireland. Gray delivered his letter on 21 February 1944 and Maffey signified British support for the démarche the following day.[160] On 28 February, the Irish Minister in Washington, Bob Brennan, called to the State Department without an appointment and stated that he personally interpreted the note as an ultimatum 'and that he felt that if the Irish Government should refuse our request, Ireland would be invaded by American forces'. Brennan was assured that the note was not an ultimatum and that no invasion was contemplated. Roosevelt's assurance, given in 1942, still stood.[161] De Valera sent his outright refusal to the proposal on 7 March and an answer was prepared and approved by Roosevelt which reiterated the demand to refuse Axis personnel. In the meantime, however, Brennan had visited the State Department again and had stated that Ireland was prepared to give prompt cooperation in adopting whatever security safeguards the British and Americans desired. Washington had already learned of this offer from an official of the oss.

Brennan had stressed that American officers who had visited

Dublin in 1943 had expressed their satisfaction with the measures which had been taken by the Irish authorities. The minister was told that, while the American service authorities might be glad to take advantage of the offer of improved cooperation in security matters, it was still believed that only the removal of Axis representatives would satisfy Washington that Ireland was cooperating adequately in security matters.[162] Winston Churchill had sent a telegram to Roosevelt on 19 March outlining a course of action. It was proposed to halt all Irish shipping to the continent but not to the United States. Meanwhile, the British prime minister stated: 'we should let fear work its healthy process. Thereby we shall get behind the scenes a continued stiffening up of Irish measures which even now are not so bad, to prevent a leakage.'

De Valera made full political play of the situation. In public, he stood firm against the demands of the Americans. In private, he sought to compromise and accommodate himself to something less than the main demand. He was agreeable to the stationing of a US security officer in Dublin.[163] In the changed circumstances, Washington temporised about sending a second note. On 1 May oss agents Will and Marlin arrived in Dublin for a joint conference with a British security officer and with Irish intelligence. The Allied representatives restated the British and American position to Irish intelligence after calling on Gray and Maffey for briefings. The representatives 'were impressed with Irish anxiety to prevent espionage and with the good faith of the Irish officials'. The various possibilities for leakage were discussed 'and our men pointed out what seemed to them the weak points in Irish coverage'. There was the impression that the Irish officials themselves were aware that they were working at a serious disadvantage with a German mission in their country enjoying diplomatic privilege.[164] Marlin and his colleague went away satisfied that Bryan would continue to be as efficient as he had been in the past in countering Axis espionage in Ireland. Of course, the public were never made aware of the level of cooperation between the respective security services. Meanwhile, de Valera emerged from the 'American note' episode with enhanced prestige. He had won, in popular political terms, the last major diplomatic exchange of the war.

There remained in 1944 one other issue on which the Irish government was very active diplomatically: the appeal for the safety of Rome. Mussolini had fallen in July 1943 and the Allies had invaded Italy in September. But victory did not come as swiftly as might have been expected. Rome was bombed, but suffered only relatively light damage. There were fears, however, that the Italian capital might be destroyed in the fighting. In February 1944, the Allies bombed the Benedictine monastery of Monte Cassino. De Valera became very active in trying to secure the safety of the city. The Irish government petitioned both the British and the Americans to refrain from bombing Rome. Other Catholic countries also added their voices to the campaign. In the end, Rome was spared, but not because the Irish government had sought a reprieve for the city. The Allies remained singularly unmoved by a plea to make an exception of Rome when London and so many other cities had been devastated from the air. They simply found it expedient to make Rome an exception.[165] The fixation with the safety of a city may appear to be something of a luxury when the destruction of the Jews was taking place at the same time, but the two concerns were not mutually exclusive. De Valera did show considerable concern for the suffering of the Jews in 1944 and made diplomatic representations on their behalf through the Vatican. Yet it must be stated that the holocaust—the details of which had been kept from the Irish public—did not arouse the same degree of concern in Irish church circles as the threat to the architecture of Christian Rome.

IRISH 'FELLOW TRAVELLERS' AND THE RETREAT FROM BERLIN

As the war drew to a close, the Irish government experienced a certain coolness among the victorious Allies towards an erstwhile neutral. General Charles de Gaulle and the Free French had occupied Paris on 25 August 1944. Joseph Walshe, who was strongly Vichyite in his leanings, communicated on 29 August to the Free French envoy in Dublin that the Irish government was prepared to give recognition to the *de facto* French government. This was a source of considerable irritation at the Quai d'Orsay. When Seán Murphy, the Irish envoy who had been based in Vichy during the war, returned to Paris, he discovered that the French foreign ministry did not want to receive him. Walshe refused to have him replaced. With some difficulty, the French made an exception and Murphy—who was never pro-Vichy— was allowed to remain until he was transferred to Canada in 1950. He was received by de Gaulle on 25 March 1945; the interview proved to be cordial, but Murphy was never allowed to forget in the post-war years that he had served at Vichy.[166]

Ireland's international image at the end of the war was not enhanced in the eyes of the Allies by the capture of William Joyce (Lord Haw Haw), Francis Stuart and Charles Bewley. Joyce was tried and executed, while the other two escaped with their lives. Stuart had remained under suspicion in Dublin for his wartime activities. In 1942, the Irish authorities refused to renew his passport and he was obliged to use 'some sort of identity document issued by the German authorities'.[167]

Stuart turned up in Paris in August 1945 and presented himself at the Irish legation. Boland instructed Seán Murphy to give him £15. He was to be left in no doubt that 'his conduct in 1940, at a particularly dangerous moment of our history', had not been forgotten in Dublin. Two things were to be pointed out to him: first, his services to a foreign country in time of war had placed him 'outside the diplomatic protection of his own government'; and secondly, he was to be interviewed in Dublin about certain events in 1940. Boland described Stuart's claim to Irish citizenship as of a 'rather technical character'.[168] Nevertheless, Stuart was allowed to return to Ireland in 1959.[169]

Charles Bewley was fortunate to escape the hangman's noose. He had 'posed as the Irish Minister to Berlin or Rome and used visiting cards bearing these titles'.[170] What was more worrying was that there was definite proof that Bewley was working for a right-wing Swedish news agency which was, in reality, a German propaganda organisation directed by Goebbels.[171] At the end of the war, Dan Bryan came into possession of certain information that Bewley had used the alias of Dreher during the war and had received a salary of 1,000 marks per month directly from Berlin.[172] It seems that Bewley was transferred in 1943 to the jurisdiction of Goering, about whom Bewley later wrote an uncritical biography.[173] In 1945, Walshe wrote the following damning minute:

> Bewley was an ass—but only an ass. He wasn't a criminal—least of all a dangerous criminal. It was notorious that he was a complete coward and would not risk his skin for any cause or nation.[174]

It was embarrassing for the Irish to discover that 'the words *passeport diplomatique* had been forged on the Irish passport issued to him in Berlin in August 1939.'[175]

Bewley was picked up by the British in Merano, northern Italy, on 26 May 1945. He was taken to a prison camp in Terni. Walshe saw Maffey on 25 July and argued that the British ought to consider not making the Bewley case into a *cause célèbre*. He explained that it would be ridiculous to make too much of Bewley's part in the 'German Drama'. There was also the risk of provoking anti-British comment while 'in blackening B. they would involve, in a sense, the good name of nearly all the Quaker families in this country—to whom he was related by blood—and who were good citizens of this country' and well disposed towards Britain.[176] Walshe argued that the best punishment for Bewley was to show him how unimportant he was, to release him with a kick in the pants and let him make his way back to Ireland. No charges were brought against Bewley and he was released unconditionally on 18 December 1945. William Warnock, who worked under Bewley as a young diplomat, recalled in 1954 that he could not close his eyes to the fact that 'his activities during the war were, to say the least, strange.'[177] Bewley continued to live in Italy and died in Rome in 1969.

The cases of both Bewley and Stuart were little more than footnotes in the history of Anglo-Irish relations at the end of the war. No fair-minded person would believe that the actions and the views of either of those two gentlemen reflected in any way the official policy of Éamon de Valera and the Irish government towards the Allies during the war. Nevertheless, Ireland had been neutral, much to the continuing annoyance of London and Washington. A *modus vivendi* had been worked out between the Allies and de Valera. That was not sufficient to overcome the sense of distaste left by the belief that British and American sailors had died unnecessarily in the Atlantic war owing to the fact that the Irish ports were not open to the Allies as bases of operation. The poet Louis MacNeice captured that sense of revulsion in his poem 'Neutrality', written during the London blitz:

> The neutral island facing the Atlantic,
> The neutral island in the heart of man,
> Are bitterly soft reminders of the beginnings
> That ended before the end began.

Look into your heart, you will find a County Sligo,
A Knocknarea with for navel a cairn of stones,
You will find the shadow and sheen of a moleskin mountain
And a litter of chronicles and bones.

Look into your heart, you will find fermenting rivers,
Intricacies of gloom and glint,
You will find such ducats of dream and great doubloons of
    ceremony
As nobody to-day would mint.

But then look eastward from your heart, there bulks
A continent, close, dark, as archetypal sin,
While to the west off your own shores the mackerel
Are fat—on the flesh of your kin.[178]

Those lines represented an undercurrent of resentment towards
Ireland which de Valera would find difficult to eliminate in a world
shaped by the victors.

4

Seán MacBride and the Rise of Clann na Poblachta

D e Valera had handled Irish foreign policy during the war years with calmness and tact. Then, within sight of the end of the conflict, he committed what Frederick Boland described as a 'ghastly mistake'. When news reached Dublin of Hitler's suicide, the Taoiseach decided that, in accordance with the dictates of protocol, he should go and condole with the German Minister, Hempel. Boland, in his reminiscences, said that it was the 'one thing I profoundly disagreed with him about'. Walshe, too, was opposed: 'Literally on bended knees, we asked him to remember all the Irish-Americans who had lost their lives, but because he had been up to the United States Embassy two weeks previously to condole on the death of Roosevelt, he was afraid of being accused of being partisan.'[1] The Minister for the Coordination of Defensive Measures, Frank Aiken, and the head of the Government Information Service, Frank Gallagher, both told De Valera to go. Seán T. O'Kelly had also been influential in persuading him to make the visit.[2] Writing to Robert Brennan, his close friend and the Irish envoy in Washington, de Valera explained that he might have had a diplomatic illness, but 'he would scorn that sort of thing'.[3]

Hempel told Boland afterwards that 'he was aghast [at the de Valera visit]; he didn't know what to say.' Hempel was delighted to be rid of Hitler.[4] The US envoy, David Gray, wrote to Washington that the British envoy, Sir John Maffey, feared that London might take unilateral action and order his withdrawal at once. Maffey, according to Gray, felt that the immediate joint withdrawal of all representatives from the United Nations might be the most effective form of protest to the de Valera visit. Withdrawal was really Gray's own wild idea. It was reported to President Truman by the acting Secretary of State, Joseph T. Grew, on 7 May. Upon examination of the files, Grew found that de Valera had taken all necessary steps to honour Roosevelt on his death in April 1945. It was discovered that in the Hitler case, the secretary to the Irish President had called in person on the German Minister, but it was explained that that action may have been taken because the Irish President had had no one to telegram in Berlin: 'The President of Ireland is a very insignificant figure and I believe we should not attach too much importance to the failure of his secretary to call upon Mr Gray [at the time of Roosevelt's death]' commented Grew. Truman took the advice to leave Gray in Dublin. On 16 May, Washington replied that the withdrawal of Gray was not warranted. No change would be made to the United States policy of 'leaving Ireland severely alone'. In a draft of the telegram, the words *and will not be readily forgotten* were crossed out.[5] The response was not as drastic as Gray would have liked, but the contents of the telegram illustrate just how cool were official relations between Washington and Dublin.

If de Valera thought that he could allow that particular storm to pass over, he was mistaken.[6] Other events in Dublin at the beginning of May helped reinforce the mistaken view that Ireland was pro-Axis. On 8 May, with the announcement of the German surrender, thousands of Dubliners thronged the streets to celebrate the defeat of fascism and Nazism. The Union Jack was flown widely in the city. At Trinity College, students celebrated by singing 'God save the King', the French national anthem and 'It's a long way to Tipperary'. According to a Department of Justice report, TCD students hauled down the Irish tricolour and hoisted the Union Jack. They then burned the Irish flag. The provost subsequently called upon the Taoiseach to express the apologies of the college authorities for the insult. Amid reports that a group of students had burned the tricolour, there were rowdy scenes in College Green in which a number of University College Dublin students were prominent. Windows of the college were broken by stones and a crowd later marched to the Wicklow Hotel and Jammet's restaurant carrying the Irish and papal flags. Stones were thrown and more windows were broken.[7] These events were also widely reported in the international press.

In two other less publicised incidents about the same time, separate groups in Dublin sought leave to have masses celebrated for Mussolini and Hitler. In the case of the mass for the *duce*, a Franciscan priest had celebrated it before the authorities could get the ecclesiastical authorities to intervene. But in the case of the proposed mass for 'the repose of the soul of Herr Hitler and the welfare of the German nation', the circular fell into the hands of G2. Military intelligence passed it on to the Department of External Affairs, and the archbishop of Dublin, McQuaid, was informed. Boland minuted on 1 June: 'His Grace told Secy. that he had stopped the Mass.'[8] The 'ghastly mistake' of De Valera's visit to the German Minister, coupled with the unseemly incidents in Dublin on the day of the German surrender, provoked the strongest reaction from Churchill. On 13 May 1945, he said:

> This was indeed a deadly moment in our lives and if it had not been for the loyalty and friendship of Northern Ireland we should have been forced to come to close quarters with Mr de Valera or perish forever from the earth.[9]

Churchill later explained the reason for his remarks to his son, Randolph:

> . . . it was a speech which, perhaps, I should not have made, but it was made in the heat of the moment. We had just come through the war, and I had been looking around at our victories; the idea of Eire sitting at our feet without giving us a hand annoyed me.[10]

On 16 May, de Valera made a national broadcast in reply to Churchill. This was one of those moments of high drama in which de Valera excelled. According to Maffey, Churchill enabled de Valera to assume the pose of the elder statesman and he was, as a consequence, 'as great a hero as is the Irishman who scores the winning try at Twickenham'.

De Valera had seen his opportunity, 'found the authentic anti-British note and did not put a foot wrong'. His speech, in what Maffey described as 'the land of the unpredictable', would be 'printed in the history books'.[11] But that was not how Maffey's superiors saw the episode and the envoy was criticised roundly—and not for the first time—for his views.[12] Sir Eric Machtig of the Dominions's office wrote to him outlining the views of the Secretary of State for Dominion Affairs, Lord Cranborne. The latter stated that all sections of opinion with whom he had come into contact were 'revolted'. The prime minister's remarks were accepted 'as a salutary rap over the knuckles'.[13] Perhaps there has been too much focus on the high theatre of the de Valera-Churchill exchange of May 1945. That tends to overlook the good working relationships between Dublin and London which were established at a number of levels during the war. Maffey accurately summarised what had actually transpired during the war in his annual report for 1945/46:

> Consequently when any German activity developed we were promptly informed and all relevant material was handed over to us. Gradually, a certain geographical interpretation of neutrality was developed. We procured the non-internment of our RAF personnel. That was a stiff one, but we got over it. Assistance from the Éire Government included rigid surveillance of the German legation, the impounding of their wireless transmitter and close understanding with the British intelligence service. In this underground of espionage and intrigue a British authority could never achieve what was achieved by a native authority.

Maffey wrote about de Valera in positive terms as not being 'anti-British and that there was no doubt of his wish to see Hitler defeated'. But the British envoy felt that the Irish leader was 'the slave of his own past' and neutrality was for him 'proof-positive to Ireland, England and the world at large that independence was real and that no loyalty was due of right to an English cause'. He added:

> Yet when the account comes to be made up, there will be some grounds for maintaining the view that England was lucky to have, in this excitable country during these dangerous years, a man whom Irishmen trusted, who knew how best to navigate the ship

through the storm [and] who has been careful not to break with the United Kingdom.

There was now the secret hope, argued Maffey, that Ireland would 'quietly discard' the bitter dictum of Arthur Griffith, who, when asked to define the foreign policy of his country said—'Find out on which side the English stand. Ireland will be found on the other side.'[14] Maffey, by this stage, was reporting to a Labour government led by Clement Attlee. Ernest Bevin was Foreign Secretary and Lord Addison was Dominions Secretary. This development eased the relationship between Dublin and London.

F.S.L. Lyons has written thus of the effect of the war years on Irish society:

> It was as if an entire people had been condemned to live in Plato's cave, with their backs to the fire of life and deriving their only knowledge of what went on outside from the flickering shadows thrown on the wall before their eyes by the men and women who passed to and fro behind them. When after six years they emerged, dazzled, from the cave into the light of day, it was to a new and vastly different world.[15]

It is, of course, true that the war insulated Irish society and threw people back on their own resources. The extremes of wartime censorship reinforced that sense of isolation. *The Irish Times* mercilessly exposed the stupidity of Irish censorship by publishing a series of hitherto banned photographs in the middle of May. One showed the Minister for Posts and Telegraphs, P.J. Little, ice-skating in Herbert Park, sometime during the war.[16] In an editorial on 12 May, *The Irish Times* complained that it had been forced to live and work in 'conditions of unspeakable humiliation' and that it had been alone among the dailies in having been compelled to 'submit to the autocrats of Dublin Castle every line that we proposed to print, from the leading article down to the humblest prepaid advertisement.'[17] But while censorship may have helped stultify a heightened awareness of what was actually happening in the international arena at the popular level, there is little evidence that de Valera and many of his ministers were victims of having had to live in Plato's cave. The war years, if anything, sensitised men like Ryan, Traynor, Lemass and

Boland to the realities of power politics. De Valera had learned many political lessons from the world of high diplomacy between 1939 and 1945. That realism was very much in evidence in Anglo-Irish relations. Dublin's relations with the British Labour government remained cordial between 1945 and 1948.

The post-war years were not without major setbacks in foreign policy for de Valera. Despite having the support of the British and Americans, he failed to gain membership of the United Nations for a country which had derived so much status from the League of Nations. This situation was not remedied until 1955. However, this did not result in foreign policy stagnation for the country. Ireland was in a position to join a number of UN-sponsored bodies, the World Health Organisation (WHO) and the Educational, Scientific and Cultural Organisation (UNESCO). The diplomatic service was extended to include representatives in Sweden, Argentina and Australia. At Iveagh House, Boland replaced Walshe as secretary in 1946. Ireland had made a fairly self-confident start to its role in the post-war era. Between 1946 and 1948 the country normalised its relations with the former Allied powers and became an exemplary upholder of cold war values.[18]

DOMESTIC POLITICS

The war had been over only a few weeks when Fianna Fáil faced a major electoral test. Seán T. O'Kelly was chosen by the party to stand for the Presidency. De Valera had, in that way, killed two birds with the one stone. The 'chief' had rid himself of a loyal but difficult colleague and had, at the same time, furnished Fianna Fáil with a candidate who could win against an opposition hungry for victory.

The diminutive Dubliner was enormously popular. The campaign was raw and robust and redolent with civil war rhetoric. Fine Gael fielded a former chief of staff of the army, General Seán MacEoin. He proved to be a strong candidate, as did the independent republican, Patrick McCartan.[19] The election took place in the middle of June. Among the more colourful speakers, as usual, was Seán MacEntee. He raised MacEoin's Blueshirt past and said on one occasion that if the Fine Gael candidate had his way people would not get a ballot paper when they went to the polls but rather a Blueshirt baton on the tops of their heads.[20] Seán Lemass attacked the anti-Irish foreign press which now supported MacEoin, who had voted against the constitution in 1937 and for the retention of the trappings of national subjection.[21] De Valera returned repeatedly to the 'unfounded' charge that Fianna Fáil was attempting to establish a dictatorship. Such a charge, he said, was an echo of the 'vile campaign' carried on against the country during the war years.[22]

McCartan denied a charge that he had spent all his time in the United States selling Irish sweep tickets in the 1920s; he accused O'Kelly of being in Paris on a salary of £500 plus expenses 'when the guns were going' between 1919 and 1920.[23] McCartan promised to take only £5,000, and £2,000 expenses, and to spend all his money in the interests of the country. The campaign, as can be judged from the above, rarely got to discuss issues at a high philosophical level. Voting took place on 14 June in the presidential, county council and urban district council elections. On the first count, O'Kelly got 537,965 votes to 335,539 for MacEoin and 212,834 for McCartan. When the votes were distributed, O'Kelly's total was 565,165 to MacEoin's 453,425.[24]

The new President was inaugurated at a ceremony in Dublin Castle on 25 June 1945. Afterwards, O'Kelly was driven through the streets in an open carriage where he was warmly received by Dubliners who saluted one of their own made good. 'Put him up on your lap so that we can see him,' one woman is alleged to have shouted to his amply proportioned wife. In fact, Seán T.'s diminutive stature—usually accentuated by a top hat—was to remain a subject of fun throughout his tenure as President from 1945 until 1959. When he was presented to the Irish rugby team before a match, some of the Northern players were heard to say: 'Will you cut the grass so that we can see him?'[25] Re-elected unopposed in 1952, O'Kelly proved not the easiest of presidents for a government to deal with; he could be obstinate and unreasonable at times. But he was always sociable and remained—despite his wife's best efforts—a believer in the Pauline view that a little wine was good for the stomach.

There were difficult times ahead for Fianna Fáil. Although O'Kelly had won the presidential election, party officials had cause to look with some apprehension at the excellent performance of Patrick McCartan. O'Kelly had got only 27,200 of McCartan's transfers, while 67,748 were non-transferable.[26] But there was some consolation in the fact that Fianna Fáil had gained eleven seats in the expanded Dublin Corporation (FF 19; FG 12; Labour 11; independents 3).[27] However, Fianna Fáil appeared to have grown a little complacent with the habitual exercise of power for thirteen consecutive years. Yet de Valera retained a reputation for being particularly slippery. The leader of the Irish Labour Party, William Norton, said: 'He can throw a somersault on the edge of a razor blade and, when you express amazement, he will say there is heaps of room for everybody to do it.'[28]

Scarcity and rationing did not end with the unconditional surrender of the Germans in May 1945. The Emergency Powers Act, which had been introduced in 1939 and under which wages had been controlled since 1941, was due to expire in September 1946. The divided trade union movement was not likely to accept the continuation of the Wages Standstill Order beyond that date. Yet the adverse economic circumstances which had been a feature of the war years were likely to prevail for some time to come. The shortage of raw materials during the war had severely undermined the industrial sector of the economy. Industrial production had fallen during the course of the war by almost 30 per cent, while industrial employment had declined by 15 per cent.[29] A series of bad harvests— particularly the wet summer of 1946—exacerbated an already grave social situation. Bread rationing had to be reintroduced. In March of the same year the butter ration was reduced by half—from four ounces to two ounces—per week. The margarine ration of two ounces was doubled to offset that move. In the autumn of 1947 a mini-budget was introduced which raised taxes to pay for increased food subsidies. Almost everything remained in short supply. Fuel was so scarce that the government was forced to cut rail services to a minimum; motor travel remained practically impossible. Even government ministers were hit by the cuts. It was a case of wartime conditions without a war.

The Department of Industry and Commerce reported to government in December 1945 that there were 62,000 men and 8,000 women registered as unemployed and that that figure was likely to rise when the wartime workers returned from England and Northern Ireland and were demobilised from the British and Irish armies. A cabinet meeting was told in December 1945 that since 1940, 133,584 men and 58,776 women had received permits for work outside the state. There were members of government, such as Seán MacEntee, who had been rash enough to talk about an unemployment rate of 'almost 400,000' as far back as 1941.[30] Although no longer in Finance, MacEntee was never one to see the positive side when there was an opportunity to speak of doom and gloom. Beleaguered, besieged and exhausted by the exertions of the politics of survival, many Fianna Fáil ministers sought only to hold the line of power.

The deluge of returning Irish never took place. In fact the trend was quite the reverse. Emigration, mainly to Britain, rose substantially between 1945 and 1948. It increased from about 24,000 in 1945 to over 30,000 in 1946 and 1947 and 40,000 in 1948.

The problem troubled the Irish bishops, and emigration was a subject of prolonged discussion at the meeting of the hierarchy in Maynooth on 7 October 1947. In a public statement, the bishops viewed with 'great alarm' the excessive rise in emigration in recent years and were 'especially perturbed' by the fact that such large numbers of 'our young are leaving Ireland to take up employment in circumstances, and under conditions, which, in many cases, are full of danger to their religious and moral well-being.'[31] However, the bishops also passed unanimously a resolution to send a private submission to de Valera on the same subject.[32] The resolution referred to 'foreign agents' being 'allowed to enter the country to attract girls abroad with promises of lucrative employment, the fulfilment of which no one in this country could control.'[33] De Valera passed the matter immediately to the Departments of Industry and Commerce and Social Welfare. The latter department replied on 17 October and explained that a liaison office of the British Ministry of Labour and National Service had been established in Dublin in 1942. That was a mechanism to avoid indiscriminate recruitment; both men and women had been subject to interview by the liaison officer. On 1 July 1946 restrictions on the emigration of women were removed by the government and from that date women had been free to emigrate to employment without restriction. The liaison officer had continued to interview women for the nursing profession and for institutional employment. After 31 October 1947, Irish people required no visa to enter the United Kingdom. The Department of Social Welfare informed de Valera that there was no other authorised arrangement for recruitment of persons to work abroad. The French government had sought facilities to recruit workers for employment in France, but 'were not encouraged and the project was abandoned'. However, there was no legal ban on agents recruiting workers in Ireland if they so wished.

De Valera sent a reply to the bishops on 16 February 1948. The delay was undoubtedly due to the Taoiseach's reluctance to contact the hierarchy on the issue, which was also raised at the October meeting of the hierarchy—section III of the 1947 Health Bill which dealt with the welfare of mother and child. But on the question of emigration, de Valera expressed deep concern at the numbers of young men and women who had been leaving the country for employment abroad, 'in many cases without having experienced real difficulty in finding suitable employment at home'. The increase in the number of young women emigrating was causing the cabinet particular anxiety. But the government sought to counter this by expanding employment in the agricultural and industrial sectors:

> The denial to individuals of the opportunity to seek a livelihood or a career abroad would, in the Government's view, be the restriction of a fundamental human right which could only be justified in circumstances of great national emergency.

As regards the activities of employment recruiting agents, 'careful inquiry throughout the state had not revealed any evidence that emigration was caused to any important extent by the efforts of agents from other countries.' The government, moreover, had no existing powers to control such activities, De Valera wrote, but would seek such powers from the Oireachtas to provide the necessary legislation if agents were a major cause of emigration.[34]

While both church and state were terribly exercised by the problem of emigration after the war, there was a somewhat mixed reaction to the idea of Ireland becoming a refuge for displaced people from continental Europe. There was considerable resistance, particularly from the Departments of Justice and Industry and Commerce, to the idea of the government adopting a liberal refugee policy, but the Departments of the Taoiseach and External Affairs ultimately secured a more open approach. That did not mean that many refugees came to Ireland in the end, but, at least, the policy was not the closed door that certain bureaucratic elements had wanted. Maurice Moynihan and Frederick Boland played a prominent part in securing a victory for relative generosity.[35] Ireland's role, however, remained far from exemplary.

THE CATHOLIC CHURCH AND THE NATIONAL TEACHERS' STRIKE

While de Valera remained under pressure from the Catholic hierarchy on the question of emigration, he faced a formidable challenge to his authority from the archbishop of Dublin in 1946. The souring of the McQuaid-de Valera relationship in that year was all the more ironic because the Taoiseach had used his good offices at the Vatican to suggest that the archbishop ought to be given the 'red hat'. McQuaid and the Taoiseach parted company with some acrimony on the issue of a strike by national teachers in 1946. The wartime wage standstill had imposed considerable hardship on already very poorly paid teachers, and the government had refused to relax its policy sufficiently a year after the end of the war. Teachers had been particularly offended by the government's decision in 1944 to grant civil servants increases in their ordinary cost of living bonus, ranging from between 7s. 9d. to 23 shillings per week. National teachers only got one shilling a week bonus. Traditionally regarded as part of the backbone of Fianna Fáil, national teachers felt compelled to go on strike in Dublin on 20 March 1946. The action was terminated on 30 October 'on a note of abject defeat', according to Séamas Ó Buachalla.[36] But this was the pyrrhic victory where wiser elements in Fianna Fáil might have prudently reflected on the line: 'One more such victory and we are lost.'[37]

This strike deserves to be examined in some detail in view of its significant impact on the later political fortunes of Fianna Fáil. Speaking at the *ard fheis* on 6 September 1946, de Valera appealed to the teachers to return to work:

Is there anybody here who does not realise that it is much easier for a government to say 'yes' to the demand made upon it, particularly when these demands are made by friends, than to say 'no'? The great difficulty where government or parliament are concerned is to get them to say 'no' when they believe in their hearts it is 'no' they should say in the common interest. Do you think it pleased us to have the standstill order in regard to wages? I assure you it did not. . . . It would be a great mistake to think that they could isolate one body of public servants and give them increases and that they could deny the demands of other public servants.[38]

De Valera had remained unusually intransigent from the beginning of the dispute. A month after the strike had begun, the Taoiseach had written to a friend in the Holy Ghost Order, Father Patrick O'Carroll, who had agreed to mediate. He replied on 16 April: 'We all regret that the teachers have taken up their present attitude. There is, however, nothing, so far as I can see, that the Government can do in the matter.'[39] It was impossible for de Valera not to have realised just how deep feelings were running on the matter.

However, many Irish National Teachers' Organisation (INTO) supporters of Fianna Fáil felt betrayed. For example, a retired teacher with 51 years' service, Mícheál Ó Slatarra, wrote to de Valera on 14 April 1946 stating that he was existing on a pension of £4 per week. He was writing as 'one of your oldest and most sincere friends in Éire for the past 30 years, and as a veteran in the Sinn Féin ranks since 1900.' Praising de Valera as a politician who 'never did a small act', he asked him to do 'one great act' and personally put an end to the teachers' strike: 'I want you to ask why did the Dublin teachers strike. The only answer that can be truthfully given to this question is—They were forced to do so by downright *want*. My idea is that Poverty knows no law.' Mr Ó Slatarra wanted de Valera to settle the dispute by striking a mean between the offer made by the department and the salaries asked by the INTO.[40] Another teacher, Riobárd Ó Caoimh, who was about to retire on a pension of about £20 a year after 50 years' service, urged de Valera not to have the 'faith and loyalty of the people of this country undermined for the sake of money'. As a GAA official, he met many teachers at matches:

> . . . and they all talk of the treatment they are getting. It is rankling and cankering their hearts. I have heard teachers say shocking things about the government. . . . Can you realise it before it's too late, that you are bringing the best body of servants in the world to this state for *money*? How can these teachers teach as I have outlined above with hate rankling in their hearts? They will teach as they feel, they will sow the seeds of discontent in their pupils. A teacher has marvellous power over a child—he can make them into devils or angels.[41]

Fianna Fáil supporters in the teaching profession felt betrayed.

The tragedy was that this was a strike that could have been avoided.

The teachers' struggle for higher wages had received support in October 1944 from the National Conference of Bishops.[42] Intensive discussions had taken place throughout 1945, but the final government offer was rejected at the end of the year. In a letter to the Minister for Education, Tom Derrig, on 10 December 1945, the INTO said that it would call the Dublin teachers out on strike on 17 January if there was not an improved offer: 'The executive do not wish that this should be regarded as in any sense a threat,' the INTO secretary, TJ. O'Connell, wrote. But that was exactly how it was interpreted by Derrig. The archbishop of Dublin, John Charles McQuaid, had been sent all correspondence by the INTO. The union's executive followed McQuaid's advice and wrote a conciliatory note to Derrig, unreservedly withdrawing the offending paragraph in the letter of 10 December. Their letter went unacknowledged.[43] The INTO and the minister did, however, meet on 20 and 21 December. Derrig also had a meeting with the INTO on 18 January 1946, at which he told the union delegates that no further improvements could be made. The government decided on 22 January that the new scales would be introduced on 1 September. A special INTO conference was called on 9 February. Further representations to the government a week later brought no result. Derrig said that the government had made its final offer and that an earlier date for the pay rise could not be fixed. Members were then balloted on the proposal. An explanatory letter, which went with the ballot papers, stated that if a majority favoured rejection, the Dublin teachers—who had already voted in favour of a strike the previous October—would be brought out. Derrig was informed of the result by letter on 11 March 1946, in which it was stated that 9,121 ballot papers had been issued, with 3,773 voting for acceptance and 4,749 against, giving a majority of 976 (599 eligible members did not vote). Derrig directed the secretary of the department to write a letter to the press, which appeared on 14 March, pointing out the fact that there were 10,750 national teachers on the government payroll and only 9,121 had been issued ballot papers. Of course, the answer was quite simple: there were a number of teaching members of religious orders who were not members of the INTO. Derrig's letter was unnecessarily provocative and halted any opportunity of stopping the strike set to begin on 20 March.

McQuaid was angry with the government. On the morning the strike began, the press published the text of a letter from the archbishop to T.J. O'Connell. It read in part:

> Your Organisation must have no doubt that the clerical managers
> of the city and the religious superiors have full sympathy with the
> ideal of a salary in keeping with the dignity and responsibility of
> your profession as teachers.

MacQuaid stressed his 'unremitting efforts' to get a settlement and
tried to calm fears about a wedge being driven between religious and
lay teachers. The archbishop pointed out that the religious could not
strike, nor could they prevent lay teachers from working if they
wished to do so.[44]

The letter placed the government in an awkward position. But on 5
April McQuaid wrote to O'Connell expressing the wish that the
children would return to school, 'pending a satisfactory settlement of
your difficulties'. On 6 April, O'Connell wrote to McQuaid stating
that his executive 'would be prepared to instruct the teachers to return
to work, without prejudice to their case, on condition that the case be
re-opened, and that Your Grace be accepted to act as mediator
between the Government and themselves.' That same day, McQuaid
replied to the into in the following terms: 'I am indeed prepared to
mediate, if I am accepted; but you will allow me to say, at this stage,
that the position of mediator would, in justice, require that I give to
both sides the most complete hearing.'[45] Ever mindful of the delicacy
of his position, McQuaid did not want to approach the government
personally lest he had 'even the appearance of wishing to bring any
pressure to bear upon the government'. He suggested the submission
of all the correspondence between O'Connell and himself to the
minister. That was done on 8 April and resulted in considerable
activity in the Department of Education. The reply was drafted a
number of times before being sent on 13 April. That made it a letter as
much to McQuaid as to O'Connell. Derrig's letter concluded: 'It
would, however, in the Government's view, be wrong to invite His
Grace to mediate in an issue which, so far as they [the government]
are concerned, has already been decided.'[46] Later that day Derrig
received one of the glacial replies for which McQuaid was well known:
'I am sensible of the pains you have taken to make clear to me the
considerations on which the Government declares that it has based its
decision not to invite the mediation of the Archbishop of Dublin.'[47]

The strike lasted until the autumn. It involved 140 schools, 1,200 teachers and 40,000 children in the Dublin area. The government was not disposed to give in and even Seán Lemass described the action of the teachers as a 'reckless and irresponsible step'. He said they were less concerned with the welfare of the teachers as a class 'than with undermining the authority and influence of the Government'.[48] It was unusual for Lemass to express himself in such an unconciliatory manner. His exasperation may have been a consequence of the fact that he was engaged in delicate negotiations for the establishment of a Labour Court during most of the strike. That Bill was finally signed by the President on 27 August 1946. This was achieved in the face of the persisting division in the leadership of the trade union movement, the continuation of the Wages Standstill Order and the teachers' strike.

Meanwhile, even greater bitterness had entered into the strike because an appeal had gone out to take children affected by the dispute into schools run by the religious. Patrick Caffrey was a striking teacher who was employed at the time in Little Denmark Street, Dublin. He recalls that the orders of brothers in the capital took in everybody, but certain orders of nuns were 'not too bad' and generally respected the INTO request not to accept any pupil that they would not ordinarily enrol. The strikers were supported by a levy imposed on other INTO members outside the capital. Times were tough, but strikers' families experienced no real hardship. As the new school year began in September, the INTO organised a series of meetings and demonstrations. On 10 September members of parents' associations and supporters of the strike held a meeting, attended by some 10,000 in Parnell Square. Pickets were placed on various schools. The strike looked as if it could drag on as the government continued its 'no surrender' policy.

Seán Moylan was Minister for Lands and a Fianna Fáil TD for North Cork. His brother was among the strikers. Moylan, who was to become Minister for Education in 1951, acted as a go-between, but de Valera continued to insist on unconditional surrender by the teachers: 'That', said Moylan, 'is something which I am not prepared to ask the teachers to accept.' As the strikers faced into the prospect of a long dispute, a decision was taken to make a dramatic protest during the All-Ireland football final in the last week of September. This was in the knowledge that the Taoiseach would be in attendance. According to one of the protesters, Patrick Caffrey, the strikers rolled up their banners tightly and stuck them down the legs of their trousers. They queued in a group at 10 o'clock that morning to get sideline tickets opposite the Hogan Stand. At halftime a signal was given and they unfurled their banners, climbed onto the pitch and protested directly across the field from where de Valera was sitting. Many of the 70,000 crowd were from the country where there was no strike in the schools. Popular reaction was muted, but the gardaí had been tipped off, according to Caffrey, and they moved in swiftly to take away the banners. Some younger gardaí then used the wooden supports to beat the teachers back into the crowd. Patrick Caffrey was struck on the shoulder as a garda waded in with one of the captured banners. There were no arrests and nobody was hurt, but the spectacle of respectable national teachers being forced to resort to such desperate tactics had an impact on the government. Seán Moylan put pressure on the cabinet to discuss the dispute at its meeting on 15 October. Under the pretext of firmness, it is possible to detect in the wording of the cabinet decision a softening of the government's position:

> The Government financial offer must be regarded as final except in so far as revision was provided for in the offer itself.
>
> With regard to discussion on other matters, there can be no commitments. The Minister for Education will, as has been stated, be ready to meet and discuss from time to time with the representatives of the teachers such other matters as the teachers may wish to raise.
>
> It was also decided that the Irish National Teachers' Organisation might be informed, if they raised the point, that it was understood that the manner in which the 'highly efficient' grading was determined was open to consideration by the Minister for Education.[49]

There is nothing in this which could not have been said at the beginning of the year.

Behind the scenes, McQuaid was again involved in conciliation moves and he wrote to O'Connell on 28 October 1946 to invite the teachers to return to work as soon as possible for the welfare of the children. That invitation, however, was not prejudicial to the 'natural rights of the Government and the Teachers, or to the just and equitable claims of the Teachers'.[50] The INTO agreed and returned to work. Editorial coverage in the *Irish Independent* (24 and 31 October) and in *The Irish Times* (27 September and 30 October) was very critical of the government. The Minister for Education insensitively sought to bring the new pay scales into operation for those teachers in Dublin who had *remained* at work during the strike. The cabinet wisely decided on 5 November that the new scale would be brought into operation for *all* from 31 October. There was also a question of paying a bonus to teachers who had remained at work throughout the strike; they numbered 316 nuns, 121 brothers, 52 lay women and 11 lay men. On average, they received £11. 14s.

Anti-Fianna Fáil sedition was soon being preached in the Teachers' Club in Dublin's Parnell Square. A young barrister from Cork and future Taoiseach, Jack Lynch, remembers overhearing discussions there before a Railway Cup final in March 1946 among teachers who felt that there was a need to found a new political organisation.

The improbable militants of 1946 reveal in conversation in the 1990s the legacy of deep-seated bitterness left by the strike. Many felt let down by their clerical teaching colleagues, but they were more forgiving of the nuns and clergy than they were of a government to which many members of the INTO had theretofore given their political allegiance.

SEÁN MACBRIDE AND CLANN NA POBLACHTA

On 10 May 1946, Seán MacCaughey, an ex-head of the IRA, died on hunger strike in Portlaoise prison.[51] Various political elements had come together to have him released. The failure to provide a constitutional 'republican' alternative to Fianna Fáil in the 1930s was an opportunity missed and that spirit gave rise to the desire to bring about a new consensus in Irish politics. It was decided to set up Clann na Poblachta at a meeting in Barry's hotel, Dublin, on 4 July 1946.[52] Seán MacBride, Con Lehane and Peadar Cowan were among those who attended the meeting. A public meeting was held in the Mansion House formally to launch the party. The speakers were Donal O'Donoghue, Fionán Breathnach, Con Lehane, Seán MacBride, Harry Diamond MP, Simon Donnelly and Peadar Cowan. Noel Hartnett and Maura Laverty were also on the platform. A UCD academic, Roger McHugh, presided.[53] MacBride emerged as party leader. He was the man who had been minuted at an IRA army convention in 1934 as saying that he had very little faith in the mass of the people,[54] but by 1947 MacBride was prepared to appeal to the very people in whom he had previously expressed lack of confidence.

The Minister for Health, Seán MacEntee, was never quite convinced that MacBride had severed his connections fully with his previous revolutionary associates. A detailed profile of MacBride can be found in MacEntee's papers.[55] It is noted that MacBride attended a meeting in Dublin on 24 September 1944, held for the purpose of reorganising the 'republican movement'. According to the Department of Justice source: 'Those who attended included many persons who were actively associated with the IRA and who at one time or another were leading activists in that organisation.'[56] MacBride was reported by the Department of Justice to have published on 31 May 1946 correspondence in the newspapers 'making an apologia for the I.R.A.'.[57] This same report relates how documents were captured by the police when they had arrested Charles Kerins for murder:

> Some of these documents, apparently from McAteer, Chief of Staff, and Steele, the Adjutant of the Northern Command of the IRA, to Kerins, who was Dep[uty] Chief of Staff, seemed to indicate that MacBride was in close touch with the organisation.[58]

A Department of Justice note named a number of Clann activists as all having had direct or indirect IRA connections in the past. The gardaí viewed the new political organisation with suspicion and kept a close eye on developments. The Taoiseach received a written complaint from members of the party following the holding of a meeting at the Royal Hotel, Bray, on 21 October 1946. Evidently members of the new party resented the police presence. In official notes, the Department of Justice admitted that gardaí were there. De Valera was told that they had been in the hotel in connection with the surveillance of a man suspected of petty larceny.[59] There is a basic contradiction between the two versions of events. It seems much more plausible that the gardaí were keeping certain 'subversives' under observation.

Meanwhile, concern over the activities of communists remained an abiding preoccupation of the authorities and it was feared that Clann na Poblachta had been infiltrated by the 'revolutionary left'. The weakened Labour Party, now divided into two antagonistic parties, had been penetrated by former members of the Communist Party of Ireland, according to G2 reports. Army intelligence reported as follows on 28 January 1944:

> There are good grounds, therefore, for concluding that the Communist Party, which has been given a new lease of life in Northern Ireland, has decided to pursue a policy of infiltration into the Labour party in the Twenty-Six Counties area and is availing of the cover which the name of the Party affords to pursue their activities amongst the Irish working classes. The fact that their nominees succeeded in the election (1943) is evidence of the success with which they are meeting in their new sphere of influence.[60]

Naturally, the activities of the Irish Friends of the Soviet Union were reported to G2, as were the meetings of the Communist Party of Ireland. Even Dr Erwin Schroedinger, senior professor of the School of Theoretical Physics at the Dublin Institute for Advanced Studies, Dublin, was the object of some suspicion in early 1946. G2 recorded the following: 'Little is known as to Schroedinger's views on current international politics but such indications as are available would point towards leftish and international views.'[61] There is a curious parallel between Fianna Fáil before coming to power in 1932 and Clann na Poblachta in 1946/47. Both parties once stood accused of being communistic, left-wing and fronts for the IRA. In the meantime, Fianna Fáil appeared to lose its anti-establishment radicalism and in 1947 Clann chiliasm contrasted with the neo-Spenglerianism of de Valera's government, where ministers appeared to be jaded by the unrelenting burden of office.

Clann na Poblachta acted as a catalyst for various disaffected groups. Its programme spoke of the need to introduce 'drastic reforms' to restore 'public morality' and confidence in democratic government. It wanted to eliminate political patronage, curb 'bureaucratic control' by officialdom and introduce sweeping reforms in social security: a basic minimum wage, state employment schemes in afforestation, housing, hydro-electrification and other construction work. Comprehensive social insurance was to be provided. The establishment of a National Monetary Authority was to equate currency and credit to the economic needs of full employment and full production. The means of production and distribution of commodities essential to the life of the people were to be organised and controlled so as to ensure a fair distribution. It was thus hoped to eliminate by such planning 'the wasteful and harmful system, whereby those who are unable to secure employment have to exist on doles and public charity, while essential work remains undone.' Clann na Poblachta proposed to end emigration and to make the country self-supporting through such schemes as the electrification of all rail transport; the creation of a deep-sea fishing fleet; and the planting of state forests. The slums were to be demolished and adequate housing was to be provided on the basis of a specified cubic capacity per head, while each dwelling was to have a kitchen and a bathroom. A very ambitious programme was also envisaged for rural society: provision of agricultural machinery on a cooperative basis; guaranteed prices for farm produce; the introduction of more social and educational recreation with the building of parish halls, libraries and sports fields.

At the cultural level, the Clann sought to remedy the 'alien, artificial and unchristian concepts of life' which were 'being constantly pumped into and absorbed by our people'. The party planned to create a national theatre and film industry; to produce films and books for educational purposes and for making Irish the spoken language of the people; to safeguard and extend the Gaeltacht areas; to create a council for the diffusion and encouragement of a knowledge of music and the arts, particularly in provincial towns and rural areas; the provision of free primary, secondary, technical and university education; to set up a council of education to coordinate all branches of education and to regulate admission to vocational and professional courses in accordance with the national need; to build additional schools and to modernise existing schools; and, finally, to raise the school-leaving age to sixteen and to provide continuation courses in agricultural and technical subjects. Moved by the millennarian desire of almost wishing to eliminate original sin from Irish society, the party's *ard fheis* was held at the end of October 1947. MacBride, Con Lehane, Peadar Cowan, Roger McHugh, Maura Laverty, Noel Hartnett, and many other prominent names were elected to the national executive. The *ard fheis* repudiated any suggestions that Clann na Poblachta had communist, fascist or unconstitutional tendencies. Indeed, whatever about the previous political and revolutionary affiliations of some of the more prominent members, the resolutions passed at the *ard fheis* confirmed that Clann na Poblachta was striving not to alarm the voters and it knew how to get across its message. The extensive use of an eight-minute film, entitled 'Our Country', illustrated the innovative electoral technique of Clann na Poblachta. The commentary by a founding member of the party, Noel Hartnett, summed up the message of Clann na Poblachta:

> Communism will not solve these problems. State control will not solve these problems. Only you the people can solve them. Instead of flag-waving, national records and personalities, what is needed is a policy based upon realities. Instead of recriminations and self-glorification based on past events, the need is for a vision, and planning for the future.

The problems referred to were emigration, bad housing, TB eradication and unemployment. The film showed slums, bare-footed children and urban squalor. It portrayed a grocer (played by Liam Ó Laoghaire) and depicted the shortage of essential goods and the luxuries displayed for the benefit of the few.[62] The novelty of such a technique may be partially lost on a video-sated generation.

The failure of the Irish Labour Party and of the Irish trade union movement to retain even the semblance of unity also contributed to the spread of Clann na Poblachta. James Larkin had died on 30 January 1947 at the height of yet another labour civil war. Thousands had lined the snow-covered streets of Dublin to pay their last respects as his coffin passed from Haddington Road to Glasnevin. Liam MacGabhann captured the mood of the day in *The Irish Press*:

> There were crowds at Jim Larkin's funeral—just as there were crowds in Jim Larkin's life. A half century of history marched through Dublin yesterday morning . . . they all came out, men in dungarees with overcoats buttoned up to the throats, marching erectly as he told them to march. It could have been a Citizen-army cum Irish-Volunteers parade, only for the slowness. The air of the city seemed to be muffled. And the men in the dungarees, and women grown old who have borne children since they struck

instinctively at the 400 bosses at Larkin's will, seemed to be there because they just had to be there.

The Taoiseach attended the requiem mass, which was celebrated by the archbishop of Dublin. Seán Lemass, James Ryan and Seán MacEntee were in the congregation, together with other ministers and the President, Seán T. O'Kelly. Seán O'Casey, who had known Larkin from the great lockout of 1913, eulogised the trade unionist's talents and achievements:

> Many were jealous of his great fight and of his influence on the working class, and many still are, but the life of this man, so great, unselfish, so apostolic, will live for ever in the hearts and minds of those who knew him, and in the minds of those who will hear of the mission to men, and of all he did to bring security and decency and honour to a class that never knew of these things until Jim Larkin came. There was a man sent from God whose name was Larkin. Jim Larkin is not dead, but is with us all, and will be with us all.[63]

O'Casey's prophetic note helps underline the fundamental chiliasm of Irish politics.

By contrast, Fianna Fáil was a party of government which had come to understand the limitations of the art of the possible. The unheroic daily grind of the routine administration of power did not excite political passions in the way that evocations of having to live up to the challenge of the 'dead generations' could do. The business of government, bureaucratic politics, administrative in-fighting and inch-by-inch progress continued at a pace which satisfied very few. The chief medical adviser in the Department of Health, James Deeny, commented on this period:

> There was so much opposition to everything Fianna Fáil did and so much of it, judged on purely technical grounds, was so unfair that one could forgive [them] for being tough. On the other hand Fianna Fáil, having tasted power, used it. If you belonged to any other party, you could reasonably feel that they were hard to stand.[64]

But that arrogance had not yet eclipsed the will to govern and reform. The challenge was to release the creative administrative energies for reform in the civil service so often stymied by the 'blockers' and reflex conservatives. In most cases, as Dr Deeny has pointed out, progress was made in the face of severe political, administrative and ecclesiastical opposition.

Dr Noël Browne, for example, has poignantly captured the prejudice, ignorance and basic lack of charity which characterised certain popular attitudes towards the scourge of tuberculosis:

> It is difficult to comprehend the sense of shocked disbelief with which one heard of a friend's misfortune in contracting tuberculosis. People faced not only personal isolation but also nearly inevitable residual physical disability or even death. . . . A bus conductor once told me that many passengers, in fear of their lives from tuberculosis, would hold their breath when passing Newcastle Sanatorium in case they caught the disease.[65]

Dr James Deeny had worked as a civil servant since 1944. His memoirs provide a valuable account of the intellectual and professional dynamism of the civil servants who made up the new Department of Health in January 1947. Health reform had suffered a major reverse in the middle of the previous year when Dr Con Ward, parliamentary secretary in the Department of Health and Local Government, was forced to resign over a matter concerning tax returns.[66] The minister in the department, Seán MacEntee, took over the portfolio until James Ryan was appointed the first Minister for Health and Social Welfare in January 1947.

The Health Bill was ready by August 1947. In essence this was, according to John Whyte, the Public Health Bill 1945, which had failed to get on the statute books because of Ward's sudden departure. It was very much a case of old wine in new bottles. The Bill was radical, wide-ranging and innovative. It was drafted by a remarkable group of far-sighted civil servants determined to modernise the Irish health service in two particularly contentious aspects—mother and child welfare and infectious diseases. The Bill gave the minister sweeping powers to detain people who were considered to be a probable source of infection. The Bill proposed the introduction of a free, non-means-tested scheme for mothers and for children up to the age of sixteen.

This was to be provided through the dispensaries, and full-time nurses were to be employed to help the doctors. Moreover, all school medical inspections were to be compulsory. There were many aspects of this Bill which did not appeal either to members of the medical profession or to the hierarchy. The state, according to John Whyte, was being given unprecedented powers of intrusion into the private lives of the citizen which touched upon the delicate matter of sexuality. An unsatisfactory situation was compounded further by the fact that there would be no free choice of doctor and that meant that non-National University of Ireland graduates might be treating Catholic mothers. Furthermore, there was the question of compulsion and state control. Taken together, these measures appeared to have been influenced by social welfare ideas associated with Sir William Beveridge and the British Labour government.

Were these the beginnings of the welfare state in Ireland? The Minister for Health, James Ryan, and his chief medical adviser, Dr Deeny, were most improbable social revolutionaries, but both men, together with the other senior civil servants in the Department of Health, realised the gravity of the situation and the magnitude of the task before them. Based on international trends in health care, the two Bills (1945 and 1947) were the result of wide study. The politicians and civil servants who drew up the legislation were pragmatists and were apparently more widely read in the rapidly developing field of post-war Catholic social thinking than was the Irish hierarchy. Social conservatism combined with the protection of vested interest to make confrontation practically inevitable between the Department of Health and Social Welfare on the one hand and the combined forces of the dominant sectors of the medical profession and the hierarchy on the other. A warning note had been struck when a Limerick doctor, James McPolin, informed Ryan on 9 July 1947 that the provisions of the Health Bill would injure the family:

If these reasons are sound it should appear that the family life will be attacked and as the Christian mind is still very robust in Ireland this mind will of its own nature present a stubborn resistance to the principles involved and hence it will be impossible to get the service to function in any kind of smooth manner.[67]

The doctor took exception to the idea of compulsory medical inspection. McPolin, in a letter to de Valera, told the Taoiseach that a group of Limerick doctors regarded the 'anti-family' sections of the bill as being due to 'inadvertence'. There was obvious nervousness in de Valera's office over the course of public debate on the Bill. In a letter to *The Irish Press* on 7 August 1947, James Dillon urged the President to consult the Council of State with a view to referring the Bill to the Supreme Court to test its constitutionality.

Anticipating constitutional and legal difficulties, Kevin Mangan, of the attorney general's office, did not think that the obligation to submit to medical inspection constituted an unjust attack on the life or person of the citizen. Neither did he see how the inalienable and imprescriptible right of the family could extend as far as to prevent medical inspection. He felt that the minister might be on more debatable ground when dealing with the articles on compulsory immunisation and isolation. Sterilisation and allied questions would be raised. But, overall, he did not think that the mother and child section ran in the teeth of any clear or express prohibition in the constitution.[68]

On 13 October 1947, de Valera received a letter from the hierarchy expressing objections to sections of the Health Bill. They were as follows:

(a) the alleged invasion of the rights of the family and of the church in regard to the medical education of mothers
(b) alleged violation of professional secrecy
(c) alleged violation of the rights of voluntary institutions.

De Valera showed no hurry in replying to the bishops. Following consultations with the attorney general and the Department of Health, de Valera replied to the hierarchy on 16 February 1948— two days before the fall of the government. Much time and pains had been taken over the reply.[69] (Dillon had initiated proceedings in regard to the constitutionality of the Act.) Therefore de Valera refrained, in the circumstances, from making any personal comment to the bishops, but sent a memorandum which had been supplied to him by the Department of Health:

Their Lordships may be assured that the Government, both in

their legislative proposals and in administration, have constantly in mind, not only the State's function as guardian of the common good, but also the respect which is due to the fundamental personal and family rights.

That was not language of confrontation. Facing the prospect of an imminent general election, de Valera did not want to provide church leaders with any excuse to be hostile.

ELECTORAL DEFEAT FOR FIANNA FÁIL

While de Valera was fending off a church-state crisis in the latter months of 1947, he had to face embarrassment over mainly unfounded allegations made regarding the comportment of leading members of Fianna Fáil over the sale of the Locke distillery, Kilbeggan, Co. Westmeath. Founded in the 1750s, the distillery was put up for sale in 1947 and the company secretary unsuccessfully sought to buy it. A number of other tenders were received and the Trans-World Trust, Lausanne, was successful. Among the people involved were a Swiss national, Georges Eindiguer, Horace Henry Smith (real name Alexander Maximoe, who had a British passport obtained under false pretences), and an Austrian national, Saschsell, who had been resident in Ireland since 1946. (There was even a mysterious woman called Dunnico in the exotic continental entourage.) An Irish businessman was also part of the consortium. The services of Senator William Quirke, of the auctioneers Stokes and Quirke, were employed and when, in the middle of September, a deposit of £75,000 had not been paid over on the purchase price of £305,000, the alarm was raised. Quirke informed the police of his suspicions. There was embarrassment for the government on two counts. First, the Department of Industry and Commerce had been consulted before the sale went through concerning the enlargement of the company's export quota. Secondly, when the police had already been called in to investigate the situation, it had been reported in the press that President Seán T. O'Kelly had entertained Eindiguer, Saschsell and others at Áras an Uachtaráin on 25 September. (The Áras visit was the subject of a stern exchange between McDunphy, the President's secretary, and the Department of the Taoiseach.) Eindiguer later left the country. Maximoe, who was wanted on criminal charges in England, was deported and escorted out of the country by two gardaí on the mailboat. He slipped away from his escort and was presumed drowned. Saschsell, who was alleged to have been—according to the report of the tribunal—'mixed up in a couple of very unsavoury transactions', was also sent out of Ireland.[70]

Oliver J. Flanagan raised the matter in the Dáil on 22, 29 and 30 October 1947. Under the protection of parliamentary privilege, he made a number of serious allegations involving ministerial collusion in the scandal. De Valera refused either to bury the issue or to brazen it out. By resolutions of the Dáil and the Seanad, he established a tribunal on 7 November 1947 to investigate the allegations. Judges Cahir Davitt, John O'Byrne and Kevin O'H. Haugh presided. They reported on 18 December after eighteen days of public hearings. The tribunal was severe in its assessment of Flanagan's evidence: 'We found him very uncandid and much disposed to answer questions unthinkingly and as if he were directing his replies elsewhere than to the Tribunal. On several occasions he contradicted himself and was disposed to shift his ground.'[71] But Flanagan did not suffer politically. Quite the reverse. He received 14,369 first preferences in the 1948 election.[72] Fianna Fáil was damaged by innuendo.

The Locke scandal served as a backdrop for the three by-elections which took place at the end of 1947—two of which were won by Clann na Poblachta. Bad weather, high emigration, shortages of all kinds, a prolongation of wartime gloom and a general dissatisfaction with Fianna Fáil combined to mobilise large sections of the public to support the new-look, new republican party. Seán MacBride fought a by-election in October in Dublin County, against Tommy Mullins (FF), a left-wing republican who was much more of a social radical than his Clann opponent.[73] Seán MacEntee's interventions may not have proved very helpful in the campaign. Missile-like accusations were levelled at MacBride concerning his IRA past and the crypto-communist nature of Clann na Poblachta.[74] MacEntee charged that MacBride had taken no part in the defence of the country during World War II. Neither had he 'once in public endeavoured to restrain them [the IRA] or utter a word of protest against their folly'. He had simply sat 'on the fence waiting to see what side would triumph in the end'.[75] In response, MacBride challenged de Valera to state whether MacEntee had been given instructions to carry on a campaign of 'vilification' against him? He rejected the charge that he had been pro-German during the war and pointed out that he had supported the policy of neutrality at every possible opportunity. The level of the exchanges can be gauged from the following MacBride rejoinder:

> I am not aware that Mr MacEntee performed any particular act of self-sacrifice or heroism since he took office. I am aware that his party provided him with a pension of £500 per year for life in 1938.

MacBride fought a clever campaign, emphasising the social issues.

> Seán MacBride is fighting your battles for a right to live in reasonable comfort in your own country; for a lower cost of living; for food subsidies and price controls; for increased old aged pensions; for free secondary education for your children; for decent housing; for proper social services; for municipally owned transport; for a *Christian state in reality, not merely in name.*[76]

The formula worked and he was returned to the Dáil. However, MacBride's election could be rationalised on the grounds that he was the son of a 1916 leader. The election of Clann na Poblachta's Paddy Kinane in Tipperary was potentially a much more serious blow to Fianna Fáil. By holding a seat in Waterford, Fianna Fáil regained some dignity and a little hope. But, even there, there was a solid loss of over 4,000 first preferences.

Fianna Fáil was divided over the wisdom of holding a general election in February 1948.[77] At least one TD did not believe that the party was prepared; Erskine Childers, whose father had been executed in 1922, wrote to his friend Seán MacEntee after the poll. He explained the reasons for defeat in the candid tone of one insider to another:

> Our TDs were careless, shockingly briefed and a very large number contented themselves with talking up Dev and down coalition. *This will not do for waverers.* . . . We underestimated the Clann. . . . We underestimated F.G.
>
>   There are 250,000 voters of age 21 to 25 who do not believe there is any substantial difference between us and F.G. They chose F.F. because of Dev and other personalities. There is in fact no policy difference save on the Irish Language.[78]

Childers also wrote to Tommy Mullins, general secretary of the party, on 10 February 1948:

There is no question the people are tired of some of the old faces and we may as well make up our minds that something will have to be done, regretfully perhaps, about members of the Party who have given great service in the past but who have become inarticulate between elections and whose personal prestige has been constantly declining.

Childers was shocked by many of the things that he saw in the Fianna Fáil organisation during the campaign. He attended meetings in 'appalling schools' where he was subject to criticism from parents:

I was amazed at the appearance, the clothes, the absence of cleanliness among many of our own Fianna Fáil supporters who were teachers and whom I met during the election; I was amazed too at the number who were obviously heavy drinkers.[79]

It was a bitter campaign, with the spectre of communism being raised yet again by MacEntee, who had a pamphlet published covering the various misdeeds of his opponents. It was rough-and-tumble politics.[80]

Clann na Poblachta fielded 93 candidates, a tactical error since it overextended its organisation and ran foul of MacEntee's recent constituency revisions. MacBride's party got ten seats. Fine Gael got 31, Labour 14 and National Labour five. Clann na Talmhan got seven and there were 12 independents. Fianna Fáil remained the largest overall party with 68 seats in a Dáil of 147. (It had lost eight seats.) That was quite a good performance, despite the fact that it had run such an uninspired campaign. Among the new deputies returned for a shrunken Fianna Fáil was the future Taoiseach, Jack Lynch. He was elected for Cork Borough with 5,594 votes. At another time, Fianna Fáil might have been able to depend upon the disunity and fragmented nature of the opposition to hold on to power. But that was not to be in February 1948.

5

The Inter-party Government, 1948–1951

É amon de Valera and Fianna Fáil lost power in 1948 after sixteen years in government. The former Master of the High Court and Fine Gael minister, Patrick Lindsay, recorded in his memoirs how he drove into Tuam and parked diagonally to the footpath in order to ask a garda if there was any news from Dublin. The reply was direct: 'At ten past five this afternoon, Mr John Aloysius Costello was elected Taoiseach of this country.' Lindsay invited the garda to have a drink: 'We'll have two' came the reply. When Lindsay inquired about parking his car properly, he was told firmly: 'Leave it where it is. We have freedom for the first time in sixteen years.' Five parties in the legislature formed an inter-party government.[1] Fine Gael was back in power as the largest party in a 'coalition' which included the Labour Party, the splinter group called National Labour (which was to reunite with the parent party in 1950), Clann na Talmhan, and Clann na Poblachta.[2] This was one of the most ideologically divided governments in the history of the state, united only by the unanimous wish to see Éamon de Valera and his party on the opposition benches and the desire to hold on to power for as long as possible. It very soon became faction-ridden. The ideological diversity of cabinet members was accentuated by the swift manifestation of personal animosities within, and between, parties.[3] The cabinet was a contrast of veterans and political neophytes. Richard Mulcahy had first become a cabinet minister in the early 1920s. By contrast, Dr Noël Browne was made a minister on his first day in the Dáil as an elected representative. It was a cabinet of talent, temperament and torpor.

John A. Costello was a compromise choice for Taoiseach: the civil war past of Mulcahy had been too much for reconstructed republicans like Seán MacBride to accept. Yet Costello did not have the administrative experience of the out-of-favour Mulcahy. He was a distinguished senior counsel who had served as attorney general in the government of William T. Cosgrave between 1925 and 1932. Between 1933 and 1948 he had continued his legal practice and had served as a deputy for Dublin South-East.[4] Costello had become Taoiseach without any ministerial experience—a decided disadvantage in a faction-ridden cabinet.

SEÁN MACBRIDE: COLD WARRIOR AND RIVAL TAOISEACH?

The new Minister for External Affairs, Seán MacBride—who was to become virtually a rival Taoiseach—wanted his country to play a major role in the international politics of the cold war. At 43, he was the leader of Clann na Poblachta. To the garrulous president of UCC, Alfred O'Rahilly, he was 'a promising young fellow'.[5] To an English journalist, he was 'smooth, not to say slick, in manner, an engaging and plausible talker'.[6] MacBride certainly entered Iveagh House with a most suspicious and untrusting attitude. He seemed to believe in the omnipresence of the British secret service.[7] According to one account, his first words to the secretary of the Department of External Affairs, Frederick Boland, on his arrival at Iveagh House were: 'Mr Boland, give me a list of all the British agents working in your department.'[8] The relationship went rapidly downhill from there and Boland suffered on for two years before becoming Irish ambassador in London.

Despite MacBride's revolutionary nationalist past, he was not left wing on cold war issues. For example, he told the US envoy extraordinary and minister plenipotentiary to Dublin, George Garrett, that 'if any country is attacked by Communists, we're in it'.[9] Frederick Boland also appeared to be concerned about the advance of communism. He told the assistant secretary of state for political affairs, Norman Armour, at a meeting in the State Department in October 1947, that 'he was much concerned with the general threat presented by Communist propaganda throughout the world, and that attempts were being made to get into Ireland even though his country had hitherto been pretty much immune from the disease.'[10]

Boland was not noted for his adherence to conspiracy theories, but it was a measure of the growing feelings of insecurity in Europe that a person as usually measured as the secretary of the Department of External Affairs was hinting at the possibility of the communist penetration of Ireland. It was not, therefore, a coincidence that the new Irish government at its first cabinet meeting sent a telegram to the Vatican desiring 'to repose at the feet of your Holiness the assurance of our filial loyalty and of our devotion to your August Person, as well as our firm resolve to be guided in all our work by the teaching of Christ, and to strive for the attainment of a social order in Ireland based on Christian principles.'[11]

The reasons for the dispatching of such a message were explained by a junior Irish diplomat, Denis R. McDonald, on 1 April 1948, to J. Graham Parsons, assistant at the us mission to the Vatican:

> No Irish Government could afford to be suspected of anti-clericalism or anything less than ardent Catholicism. Accordingly, when de Valera had been replaced by a coalition somewhat more liberal in complexion, it had been necessary, for political reasons, to demonstrate its devotion to the Holy See.[12]

In reality, there was little danger that the Vatican would have perceived the changeover as a threat to Catholicism in Ireland. The wording of the message was considered by some to have been inappropriate for a civil government; the secretary of the Department of the Taoiseach, Maurice Moynihan, did not feel that the civil power should 'repose at the feet' of the pope. But his objections were overruled.[13]

After only a few days in power, the government received word from Rome that there was a real danger of Italy falling under the influence of a communist/socialist alliance. Joseph Walshe, who had been Irish ambassador to the Vatican since 1946, wrote to Boland that what was going on in Italy was 'a fight for Western civilisation'. What were the consequences for Ireland? he asked. 'If Catholicism loses in Italy, we also shall have lost.' Between 21 and 25 February the Czech

Communist Party seized power in Prague. Walshe requested an audience with Pius xii to present the Irish government's message of loyalty.[14] The future Pope Paul vi, Giovanni Battista Montini, who worked in the secretariat of state, arranged the audience 'with unheard of promptitude'.[15] When the message had been delivered, Walshe told Pius XII that all the members of the government were praying for him at 'one of the gravest moments in the history of Christianity'. Moved by the message, according to the ambassador, the pope replied: 'Ireland is always faithful and I want her fidelity now.' Pius xii went on to speak of the 'imminent danger to the Church in Italy and in the whole of Western Europe'.[16] Walshe reassured the pope that the government and the people of Ireland were willing to do everything possible to serve him. The ambassador continued:

> I added specifically that the Government, as well as the people, would regard it as the greatest moment in our history if He deigned to make Ireland the home of the Holy See, for the period of persecution, if and when it came. For this offer, He expressed His deepest gratitude and went on to say, 'Ireland is the only place I could go to—only there would I have the atmosphere and the sense of security to rule the Church as Christ wants Me to rule it.'

Walshe described what happened next as the 'most unforgettable moment' of his life. The pope asked him 'almost sharply: "Yes, but what do you, as a follower of Christ, think I ought to do?"' The Irish ambassador advised the pope to stay. Pius xii replied: 'And that is what I think and that is what I intend to do. My post is Rome, and, if it be the Will of the Divine Master, I am ready to be martyred for him in Rome.'[17]

The gravity of Walshe's reports had the desired impact in Iveagh House. MacBride is likely to have discussed them with the Taoiseach. Costello was a close friend of Walshe: the ambassador was the godfather of one of the Taoiseach's daughters. An immediate meeting was arranged in Paris between MacBride and Walshe.

On 5 March 1948 Walshe wrote in 'great haste' to Boland enclosing an autographed letter addressed by the pope to the Taoiseach. Montini told Walshe that the pope had wanted to 'do something really special to show his appreciation' of the Taoiseach's 'filial and devoted message'.[18] Ireland was, according to Walshe, 'very much in the favour of the Holy See at the present time'. The country was 'above all of supreme importance as a Catholic bulwark in Europe at a time when the Holy See is so gravely perturbed about the Communist menace'. The ambassador felt that Ireland was not in any way divorced from the drama of Italian politics. 'The considerations are not political; they reach down to the very foundations of our civilisation. If Communism wins in Italy the centre of our civilisation will be so vitally affected that we cannot remain immune.'[19] After making contact with a US diplomat at the Vatican to gain support for his proposals, Walshe set out for Paris to meet Boland and the new minister. MacBride emerged from the meeting as anxious as the Irish ambassador to see the Italian left defeated. Walshe returned to Rome confident that he had been given a clear line of instruction by his minister to help the Christian Democrats win the election.

On his return to Dublin, MacBride took up the Italian question with the papal nuncio, Paschal Robinson, and with the archbishop of Dublin, John Charles McQuaid.[20] It appears that, at that point, government funding had been ruled out. The minister saw the nuncio on 23 or 24 March. Robinson, who was known for his good judgment in delicate diplomatic situations, favoured the minister making direct contact with the archbishops of Armagh and Dublin. MacBride spoke by phone to McQuaid[21] and later wrote both to McQuaid and to the archbishop of Armagh, John D'Alton.

The hierarchy made a public appeal for funds for Italy and the response was generous. In all, about £4,025 was sent to Walshe through the Department of External Affairs. The money was lodged to the embassy account and then transferred by the ambassador. By 5 May 1948, £57,036. 3s. 7d. had been sent to Italy via the nunciature in Dublin. The final Irish contribution came to over £60,000.[22] The Christian Democrats won the election, helped in a small way by the modest efforts of Irish Catholics.

Foreign policy continued to provide the best examples of decision-making skills more associated with the Marx Brothers than with government in a Western democracy. Costello declared Ireland a republic at a press conference in Ottawa on 7 September 1948. This followed an inspired leak in the *Sunday Independent* two days earlier. The Irish government's 'decision' to leave the Commonwealth has been the subject of considerable historical controversy. Was it possible for a Taoiseach simply to announce such a decision without a *formal decision* having been taken in government? It seems that that is exactly what happened and here I agree with the interpretation, based on available contemporary evidence, of Professor Ronan Fanning.[23] Professor Patrick Lynch, who was well placed to observe the situation, holds a diametrically opposed view.[24]

Boland recalled that he had drafted Costello's speech to the Canadian lawyers and that he had not put anything in the draft about the External Relations Act, 'nor was Seán MacBride anxious that I should'. Costello said after reading the draft text: 'It's fine but there's too much of the smell of the Empire about this.' Boland found that surprising since he had confined himself to Fine Gael policy. However, he felt that Costello was the head of an inter-party government and that forced him to do things that 'he really didn't believe in at all'. However, Boland felt that finally he had made the announcement in a 'burst of indiscretion' at the press conference. 'Back in Dublin there was nothing short of amazement', Boland commented. The phones rang in his office non-stop: 'All we could say is our Prime Minister has simply made an awful gaffe.'[25]

Costello was emphatic that his government had taken a decision on the repeal of the External Relations Act before his departure for Canada. Noël Browne, an irregular attender at cabinet meetings, denies that such a decision was ever taken before the event. He does, however, recall being summoned urgently to what he describes as a 'caucus meeting' of the cabinet soon after Costello's return to Dublin.[26] But the repeal of the External Relations Act was certainly news to the Department of External Affairs. MacBride was dining with Maffey in the Russell Hotel when he was informed of the announcement in Ottawa by a surprised secretary of the Department of External Affairs.[27] Boland was certainly taken completely by surprise. 'Jack Costello', he said, 'had about as much notion of diplomacy as I have of astrology.' Boland is equally interesting in his reflections on de Valera's reaction to the Costello *démarche*: the right thing had been done in the wrong way.

> You can safely say, if de Valera had remained in power, we would have remained in the Commonwealth, but all references to the Crown etc. would have been eliminated from the Act, although we would be prepared to acknowledge the King as head of the Commonwealth if others did it. That was Dev's idea all along.[28]

Boland recalled a meeting between de Valera and Churchill in 1953 at which he was present.

> Coming to the end of the lunch, Churchill said to de Valera: 'I want to put this question to you; if you had remained Head of the Irish Government, would you have taken the country out of the Commonwealth?' And Dev said, 'No', and, of course he was quite right because he had no objection ever to Ireland being a member of the Commonwealth. What he had an objection to was an Oath of Allegiance to the King as King of the Commonwealth, as India does today. But he told Churchill no, he wouldn't have done that. As a matter of fact, he had come to the conclusion that the Commonwealth was a very useful association for us, because they all—all the Commonwealth countries, particularly Canada, Australia, New Zealand—had a strong interest in Ireland, their interest in Ireland being this: they felt they could rely on the Irish to oppose any move to enlarge their role in the Commonwealth.[29]

The Republic of Ireland was formally inaugurated on Easter Monday 1949—the 32nd anniversary of the 1916 Rising—with much official fanfare but no great outpouring of popular enthusiasm. It was a hollow victory which led to a 'sense of renewed tension' between Dublin and London,[30] but the outcome could have been far worse for Anglo-Irish relations. It could not have been much worse for the future relationship between the two states on the island. The Labour government of Clement Attlee determined that Ireland would continue to enjoy Commonwealth preferences and that special citizenship rights were to be provided for British and Irish citizens. This benign attitude was due in part to the helpful intervention of the other Commonwealth countries with which Ireland had good relations.[31] But by the same token the Act resulted, as de Valera had appeared to understand in 1947, in further institutionalising partition. The Ireland Act of 1949 declared that 'the part of Ireland heretofore known as Éire ceased as from the eighteenth day of April 1949 to be part of His Majesty's dominions'. It gave a guarantee that 'in no event will Northern Ireland or any part thereof cease to be a part of His Majesty's dominions and of the United Kingdom without the consent of the parliament of Northern Ireland.'[32] This undesirable outcome from the point of view of Irish government policy was a perfect example of the triumph of the politics of muddle.

PARTITION AND NATO MEMBERSHIP

The partition question had made its ritual re-entry into Irish politics following de Valera's extended trip on losing office in 1948 to, among other countries, the United States, Australia and New Zealand. Ironically, he was also received in India by Lord and Lady Mountbatten, on the eve of independence; only a year before, that country had declared itself a republic and yet had remained a member of the Commonwealth. (The Indian premier, Pandit Nehru, visited Ireland in 1949.) Wherever he spoke, de Valera's repeated message was on the need to end partition. Perhaps the competitiveness between MacBride's Clann na Poblachta and de Valera's remobilising Fianna Fáil over partition may partially explain the reason why the Minister for External Affairs elevated that issue to centre stage when Ireland was invited to join NATO in early 1949.

Discussions on the establishment of the North Atlantic Treaty Organisation had been in progress since soon after the signing of the Brussels Pact on 17 March 1948.[33] The USA, Canada and Britain were the countries initially involved. It was decided that Ireland, Norway, Denmark, Iceland and Portugal should be kept informed of progress. There was some concern on the part of the British that the Irish government might attempt to link membership of NATO and the partition question. Their fears were soon realised. On 7 January 1949, the US minister in Dublin, George Garrett, gave an *aide-mémoire* to MacBride. It set out the objectives of the draft treaty and indicated that membership would be open to Ireland. The obligations would include a commitment to the idea of collective defence before and after an armed attack had occurred, 'by the provision of assistance commensurate with the resources and geographical location of each country'. But that would not necessarily involve a declaration of war in the event of an attack on another party: the treaty would not provide that any country automatically declare war, because the declaration of war in democratic countries was a parliamentary prerogative.[34]

Boland presents a very interesting account of the sequence of events within government which followed upon the receipt of the invitation to join NATO. MacBride's response, following consultation within his own party, was to take the line that the occasion offered

Ireland the 'great lever' to trade off Irish membership for a *démarche* on partition. He was convinced that the response would be positive. Boland did not feel that way. In fact, he thought 'it was rubbish'. It is not clear from Boland's later reflections whether the Washington embassy was instructed to take that line or to take soundings among the friends of Ireland in Congress. MacBride went to Paris for an Organisation for European Economic Cooperation meeting and, in his absence, Boland received a series of telegrams from Washington confirming his worst suspicions: 'Listen, you're making fools of yourselves' was Boland's recollection of the Irish-American reaction. Pending MacBride's return, he did not show the Washington telegrams to anyone. Boland speculated that the US envoy in Dublin had tipped off James Dillon about the response of the Irish Americans. (The Minister for Agriculture was radically opposed to MacBride's stance.) Boland did not think very much more about the matter:

> There was a cabinet meeting shortly after Seán MacBride came home, and the cabinet made it perfectly clear that they thought the people in America were right, that we were foolish to go on with this business of asking them to end partition as our price of going in. . . . Seán MacBride came from the cabinet meeting, and I remember he looked very sour-looking. He said to me: 'Have you been talking to James Dillon in my absence?' I said: 'No. We've had no discussions.' So Seán MacBride said to me: 'Well, he seems remarkably well-informed.' 'Well,' I said, 'I don't know but he did not hear it from me.'

This was a slight on Boland's professional standing and he refused to allow the matter to rest there. He requested to see the minister the same afternoon:

> You asked me there before lunch whether I'd been talking to James Dillon, and you seemed to think it curious that Dillon is so well-informed on the attitude of American Senators and Congressmen. What you implied was that I might have told him. Well, Minister, if you feel like that, my advice to you is, you need another head of your department.[35]

MacBride rejected this idea and Boland added: 'You must have confidence in the head of your department.'[36]

The consequent *aide-mémoire* was a victory for MacBride over many in government like Dillon who favoured participation in NATO. It was vintage old-guard nationalism, reminiscent of de Valera's objections to Article 10 of the League of Nations Covenant in the 1920s—objections which he managed to get over without any difficulty as time progressed and opportunity beckoned. MacBride, too, linked partition with the military obligations since 'six of her north-eastern counties are occupied by British forces against the will of the overwhelming majority of the Irish people.' It was argued, therefore, that in those circumstances, any military alliance which involved the British 'would be entirely repugnant and unacceptable to the Irish people'. Finally, the *aide-mémoire* invited participating nations to offer assistance and mediation to resolve the problem of partition.[37] This document was conceived by MacBride, who had a mind which continued to occupy a place in Plato's cave. The easily anticipated negative reply came without delay.

When the Irish ambassador to Washington, Seán Nunan, presented the *aide-mémoire* to the State Department on 9 February 1949, he stated that he was under instructions to impress upon the US administration that the reply was not to be regarded as closing the door and that the Irish government desired United States mediation in the problem of partition. John D. Hickerson, of the Office of European Affairs, told Nunan firmly that the Atlantic Pact was designed for security purposes and that it was not an appropriate means of settling problems of such long standing as the question of partition. Nunan was informed that the attitude of the United States would remain unchanged and that the decision of the Irish to leave the Commonwealth did not alter that position. Forlornly, Nunan again expressed the hope that the United States would mediate or investigate the situation. The ambassador was told that it was an issue for settlement between Britain and Ireland.[38]

At the fifteenth meeting of the Washington exploratory talks on security, on 4 March 1949, the Canadian ambassador to the United States, Hume Wrong, made the only passing reference to Ireland. He said that the Irish had made 'unacceptable conditions' for participation. There appeared to be full agreement on the matter and Ireland was not mentioned again until the meeting of the same group on 11 March.[39] Just before that meeting broke up, Dean Acheson, the US secretary of state, referred to the Irish *aide-mémoire* of 9 February 1949. He assumed that 'all agreed that the question should not be pursued further with Ireland'.[40] E.N. Van Kleffens, the Netherlands ambassador to the United States, wondered if it would not be advisable to take note of the Irish memorandum by conveying informally that the governments in the negotiations had regretfully come to the conclusion that, in view of the present point of view of the Irish government, Ireland's participation could not be successfully discussed. The American authorities agreed to undertake to make a communication of that nature.[41]

MacBride's posturing on NATO was as gauche as it was naïve. It introduced a note of crude horse-trading into high diplomacy. The two slighting references to Ireland at the meetings of ambassadors in Washington reflect the disdain of Acheson and his colleagues for such misplaced parish-pump opportunism. Just how high Ireland featured in the geopolitical calculations of Acheson can be gleaned from his memoirs where, in one of the two references he makes to the country in 798 pages, he said of events just after the outbreak of the Korean war in the summer of 1950:

In August Secretary of the Navy Francis P. Matthews in a speech in Boston called for preventive war. He was made Ambassador to Ireland. Then General Orville Anderson, Commandant of the Air War College, announced that the Air Force, equipped and ready, only awaited orders to drop its bombs on Moscow. He was retired.[42]

The NATO treaty was signed on 4 April 1949 in Washington by the USA, Canada, the five Brussels Pact countries, and also by Iceland, Norway, Denmark, Italy and Portugal. These countries were later joined in the alliance by Turkey and Greece. Ireland continued to remain outside. A second Irish *aide-mémoire*, dated 25 May 1949, attempted to reopen the issue of membership with Washington. The State Department firmly rejected the arguments of the Dublin government in a reply on 3 June.[43] The debacle over NATO may account for the circulation by the Government Information Bureau of a sycophantic profile of MacBride which appeared in the *Saturday Evening Post* on 23 April 1949. Seán Lemass took up the matter and there were exchanges in the

Dáil on two occasions.[44] The Taoiseach had finally to explain the situation and MacBride was forced to write a letter to de Valera on 12 May. The explanation was hardly convincing. MacBride claimed that he had, while abroad, instructed one of his officials to circulate one article, and that the profile article, which had arrived the same day, was circulated instead in error.[45] It had not taken very long for MacBride's prestige, admired if not feared in 1948, to wane irrevocably among civil servants and many cabinet ministers by the early summer of 1949.[46]

The Minister for Health, Noël Browne, was soon to become an implacable opponent of the party leader, MacBride. The relationship had once been quite close; Browne claimed that he had been knocked off his guard by 'the broken English but fluent French-speaking rabid Irish Republican with an aristocratic half-English background.'[47] Perhaps that might account in part for his early success in the cabinet of the inter-party government. The Clann leader, whatever Browne's later reservations, had political talent. MacBride helped outmanoeuvre the Department of Finance on the question of Marshall aid and gain control of the spending of most of it for his own department.[48] In May 1948, he led a delegation to Washington to try to persuade the Americans to give Dublin substantial grant aid. The task was a futile one, but the Irish made a spirited attempt to convince sceptical US officials of the virtues of the Irish case. Perhaps it might have helped the Irish case if the country had been confronted by a dangerous domestic pro-Moscow labour movement. That was demonstrably not the case.[49] Despite taking a decision not to accept a loan, the Irish government relented and by the time the fund closed in 1950, the country had received $128.2 m in loans and $18 m grant aid.[50]

MacBride had taken a keen personal interest in the course of European integration and had welcomed visitors to Dublin from the various groups pursuing that goal. Members of the European movement came to Dublin to speak and set up a branch. A member of the European federalist group had also visited the capital. MacBride sent a delegation to the Congress on European Union, held in The Hague in May 1948.[51] He was very supportive of the setting up of the Council of Europe in 1949 and differed from the British by wishing to have Spain and Portugal admitted as full members.[52] His contribution to the preliminary discussions on the Council of Europe saw him in a minority since he argued in favour of greater powers for the council itself.[53] He prided himself on being a federalist. But that may have been merely a fashionable conceit since he was usually intransigent on the question of the inviolability of sovereignty. Nevertheless, Ireland enjoyed a high reputation in European circles, thanks to the activities of its peripatetic French-speaking foreign minister.

THE NEW IRELAND: IMAGE AND REALITY

Other ministers in the inter-party government, including the Taoiseach, lacked MacBride's flair for self-publicity. But they were far from being untalented, as Noël Browne tends to argue in his memoirs.[54] In the main, the ministers were battle-scarred political veterans. If youth had been more strongly represented, the government might have been more innovative, but the administration proved far more experimental than might have been expected, given the presence of McGilligan, Mulcahy, MacEoin and others. Even the presence of the two rival Labour parties did not guarantee radicalism. But it is surprising how progressive economic ideas—which owed much to Keynes—came to the fore, thanks to civil servants like Patrick Lynch and Alexis Fitzgerald. In the memorable phrase of the former, Keynes had come to Kinnegad.[55] But only just and without much help or encouragement from the Department of Finance.

In a spirit of new-age optimism, the inter-party government undertook a large building programme of houses and hospitals, costing £120 million. To the horror of the Department of Finance, the decision was taken to borrow £6 million to fund the capital works programme. The Department of Finance, however, successfully halted the 'kick and rush' policy approach of some of the more inexperienced cabinet members. The establishment of the Industrial Development Authority (IDA)[56] was another of the government's innovative ideas, but it was muddle-headed in its execution. The functions of the IDA were refined in the course of the 1950s and served to attract foreign investment. The National Trust for Ireland, An Taisce, was set up in 1948 out of a concern for Irish heritage and the environment. Aer Lingus enjoyed mixed fortunes under the inter-party government.

The Minister for Agriculture, James Dillon, was an unlikely star-performer. He proved to be an effective reformer. Aware of the primitive state of the industry, he was receptive to good ideas, even from the opposition. He struck up a good working relationship with a Fianna Fáil backbencher, John Moher, who had made a study of the successful agricultural economies of Denmark and Holland. On one occasion, Moher put down a detailed question in the Dáil. When civil servants asked the minister how he wished to reply, Dillon responded: 'You can't argue with the facts.'[57] There was general agreement among the few experts on both sides of the house that Irish agriculture was in serious need of reform, but the conservatism and ignorance in the country tended to slow down progress. Moher recalled how the importation of a prize bull from Holland in the early 1950s had led to his denunciation from the altar in north Cork. He was not sure whether he was alleged to have sinned against the sixth or the ninth commandment. Evidently, there were moral objections to artificial insemination. It seems that it was also necessary to protect comely Irish cows from the evils of the world. Moher survived the 'scandal' and Irish cattle bloodlines were all the richer for this innovation.

Under the inter-party government, progress was made in the promotion of tourism. Standards were improved, hotels and guest houses graded and a general effort was made to improve hygiene. However, the decision to sell off the Fianna Fáil-acquired Aer Lingus Atlantic fleet was a retrograde step. The inter-party government did not usher in the millennium. The Irish economy remained weak and an exception to the post-war boom in Europe. Three years did not provide sufficient time to modernise.

Yet another innovation of the inter-party government was the establishment of the Irish News Agency (INA). This was as a result largely of the initiative of MacBride, who shared the old nationalist belief—expressed by Roger Casement in 1906—that Ireland's best interests were not protected by a hostile international press and news agency system. The thinking behind the establishment of the INA was confused. The object was to 'disseminate Irish news throughout the world in order that the Irish viewpoint may get much more publicity than has hitherto been possible through the medium of the existing news agencies.'[58] The existence of partition, the need to counter widespread, unfair anti-Irish propaganda in the press of the world, and the need to publicise the country as a location for industrial investment, were all advanced as reasons why the INA was being set up.[59] But it was not intended to be a propaganda machine. It was the intention to produce the news in an objective, truthful and accurate way. The agency was not going to be a mouthpiece for the government; it was going to concentrate on what was broadly described as news calculated to create an atmosphere of sympathetic interest towards Ireland: cultural and literary events, works of art and, when necessary, Ireland's viewpoint on political matters.[60] The Bill was signed by the President on 21 December 1949. The board of directors was appointed on 20 March 1950. Conor Cruise O'Brien, who was appointed managing director, visited the headquarters of a number of news agencies in London, Paris, Brussels and The Hague between 23 March and 4 April 1950.[61] He was told very delicately by the head of the Press Association in London that information coming from the INA would be regarded by journalists as being suspect.[62] Try as it might, the INA was perceived to be a government propaganda machine inside and outside the country. When, for example, controversy over the allocation of a sub-post office at Baltinglass, Co. Wicklow—which featured the untoward involvement of the Minister for Posts and Telegraphs and local TD, James Everett—was just over in early 1951, the INA was accurately accused of being a tool of government.[63] Cruise O'Brien minuted on 2 January 1951:

> We have learned, through M.J. MacManus, that Sweetman [editor] of the 'Irish Press' has drafted a leader attacking the Irish News Agency for allegedly slanting its coverage politically on the Baltinglass affair. This leader was to have appeared this morning but did not. It is possible that it was cancelled by someone higher up, but it is also possible that it is being kept as a rod in pickle.[64]

Everett had landed the government in deep trouble when he had transferred the running of the local sub-post office in Baltinglass to the publican and draper, Michael Farrell. Helen Cook, who had been running the business for a number of years on behalf of her sick aunt, had applied for the transfer of the sub-post office to her name. It had been in the Cook family for over eighty years and the application was seen as being merely routine. But to the surprise and anger of many locals, Farrell was awarded the sub-post office. This split the village, and a solid phalanx of locals formed an action committee to have the decision reversed.

The row became national news as a strong force of gardaí had to be drafted into Baltinglass to transfer the lines to Farrell's shop. Local feelings were strong and militants cut down telegraph poles. There were public meetings in the village. Paddy Cogan, an independent TD, took the lead for Miss Cook and was supported by the local clergy and many farmers. There was a spontaneous boycott of Farrell. A shop in the village which had a licence to sell stamps became a rival 'post office'. There were daily 'collections', and locals took turns to bring the mail to other post offices in neighbouring towns. Everett ran into a firestorm of protest. Finally, on 20 December 1950, Farrell precipitately resigned his post and the 'battle of Baltinglass' was over, only to be 'immortalised' by Sylvester Gaffney:

> *The job of sub-postmaster or mistress, as might be,*
> *Is not exactly one that leads to wealth and luxury;*
> *But Korea was a picnic and Tobruk was just a pup*
> *To the row the day the linesmen came to take the cable up.*

> *Now the case has gone to UNO, and we're waiting for the day*
> *When Truman, Attlee and MacBride will come along and say,*
> *'Get back behind your parallel, drop atom bombs and gas,*
> *And respect the boundaries and the laws of Sovereign Baltinglass.'*

The Irish Press, de Valera's newspaper, had followed the battle of Baltinglass with avid interest. Cruise O'Brien had good reason to believe that its editorial writers would embarrass the government as much as they could over Baltinglass.

The INA appears to have had very good intelligence about what was happening in *The Irish Press*. On one occasion, Dr Cruise O'Brien referred to the fact that he had heard that day, 25 January 1951, 'from our quisling in the Irish Press'.[65]

The INA was an arm of government publicity. When Fianna Fáil returned to power in 1951, the INA was dismantled and the publicity role handed over to the Department of External Affairs.

However the inter-party government was more successful as an innovator in other fields. Costello felt very strongly about the need to assist culture and the arts. MacBride appointed members to the first Cultural Relations Committee, which had been planned by the previous government. Among its more enduring achievements were the commissioning of three films by Liam O'Leary: 'W.B. Yeats—A Tribute' (1950), 'Ireland-Rome' (1950), about President Seán T. O'Kelly's visit, and 'Portrait of Dublin' (1952) which was suppressed by Frank Aiken after Fianna Fáil returned to power.

Dr Thomas Bodkin, who had first submitted a report on culture and the arts to the Irish government in 1922, was commissioned to write another report in which he castigated the running of the National Library, the National Museum and other institutions. His *Report on the Arts* was published by the Government Stationery Office in 1951. Costello steered an Arts Bill through the Dáil and it was signed by President Seán T. O'Kelly on 8 May 1951. However, the government changed before the Arts Council could be established. In opposition, Fianna Fáil was critical of the idea of setting up yet another advisory body (an Emigration Commission, a Prices Advisory Body and a Council of Education had already been established).[66] Back in office, in 1951, the idea held greater appeal.

The inter-party government's period in office coincided with the publication of a flurry of new books, poetry and magazines. In 1948 the following works appeared: *Tarry Flynn* by Patrick Kavanagh; *A Pillar of Cloud* by Francis Stuart; *The Game Cock and other stories* by Michael McLaverty, and Liam O'Flaherty's *Two Lovely Beasts*. The previous two years had seen the publication of Kate O'Brien's *That Lady*, Patrick Kavanagh's *A Soul for Sale* and Seán O'Faoláin's *The Irish*. In 1949 Máirtín Ó Cadhain published *Cré na Cille*, and Máirtín Ó Direáin, *Rogha Dánta*. Samuel Beckett's *Molloy* appeared in 1951.

Irish-language publications were strengthened by the establishment of *Feasta* in 1948. *Comhar* (1942) and *Inniu* (1943) were already highly regarded and widely read. The setting up of An Club Leabhar in 1948 provided a wider circulation for books in Irish. Seán Ó hÉigeartaigh's publishing venture, *Sairséal agus Dill* (1945), was a most welcome innovation. Two new religious magazines were established: *The Furrow* was set up in Maynooth in 1950 and *Doctrine and Life* was brought out by the Dominicans the following year. These were welcome additions to the Jesuits' *Studies*, the *Irish Monthly* and Maynooth's *Irish Ecclesiastical Record* and *Christus Rex* (1947). *The Bell* continued to make its vital contribution to Irish cultural and political life under the new post-war editorship of Peadar O'Donnell. Three literary journals, *Envoy*, *Poetry Ireland* and *Irish Writing* added to the debate. However, *The Leader*—under the editorship of T. Desmond Williams (and later with Patrick Lynch)—was by far the most provocative, best-informed and politically sharp of all the Irish publications.

In the visual arts, the Irish Exhibition of Living Art continued to have a strong and liberating impact. The establishment of the Wexford Opera Festival in October 1951 was an important development which quickly became a significant date in the calendar of international opera. The inter-party government had its defects, but its general benevolence towards the cultural world was refreshing and was appreciated by the artistic community.

IRELAND, MCCARTHYISM AND PREPARATIONS FOR WORLD WAR III

Despite the room provided for culture and creativity during this period, the Irish government remained very preoccupied by the advance of the cold war and by the necessity to make provision for the outbreak of a third world war. All left-wing activity was kept under close surveillance.

For example, the Irish Anti-War Crusade, or Peace Movement, was viewed by G2 as having being infiltrated by Communist Party activists. Although originally of Quaker origin, and in existence since 1938, the movement had developed to include 'two well-known Communists' by 1949, namely John de Courcy Ireland and Michael McInerney.[67] Both were men of the left undoubtedly, but their membership of the Communist Party remains unsubstantiated. Bryan, however, drafted notes on others who were involved on the left, including the Rev. H.J. Armstrong, Church of Ireland rector of Howth, who could not be described as a communist but fell 'within the category of "fellow-traveller"'. Others, such as Seán Nolan, Niall Gould, R.N. Tweedy, Paul O'Higgins, Denis Walsh and Joe O'Connor, had their various left-wing affiliations described in detail. Bryan concluded:

> It may be assumed that the Crusade, *per se*, is not Communistic but purely anti-war. There is little doubt that the leading Irish Communists would, and are, using the Crusade to further their own views and ends, particularly as regards their alleged peace campaign.[68]

Bryan also sought to ensure that no 'red' money came from abroad for the purposes of strengthening the voice of the Irish left. He discovered in January 1951 that money which he suspected had come from the United States for the use of communists was, in fact, 'a genuine business transaction'.[69] On 10 March 1952, Bryan commented upon the left-wing activities of the Trinity professor, Senator Joseph Johnston. His son, Roy, was described as being 'one of the most active young Communists in Ireland'. Only further research will determine whether he was accurate or wide of mark in his reports. There is little Bryan would not have known about the Irish left in the early 1950s.

While G2 continued to monitor the activities of Irish 'communists', a story broke in the press, after the coalition had come to power, involving the Russian crown jewels. When de Valera was in the United States in 1920, he loaned some money to a Soviet agent and was given jewels as security in return. The jewels were brought back to Ireland and handed over by Harry Boland (brother of Gerry Boland, who was murdered during the civil war) to Michael Collins. The jewels were then given to Mrs Boland for safe-keeping and when she died, they were returned to Maurice Moynihan, who deposited them in the safe in Government Buildings. When the inter-party government came to power in 1948, the packet was found in the safe and news immediately leaked to the press. The jewels were valued at £14,000 and plans were laid to put them up for public auction in London. Meanwhile, Frederick Boland had had enough of life in Iveagh House under the mercurial MacBride and, when the opportunity arose for him to replace John Dulanty in London, he took it, becoming ambassador to the Court of St James in 1950.[70] Moynihan called up Boland in London to tell him of the government's decision to auction the jewels. Boland replied that the Irish government was not free to sell them because the jewels were a pledge for a loan. He went to the Soviet ambassador and explained the situation, offering the jewels in return for the $25,000 which had been loaned to the Soviet agent. Six months later, the Soviet ambassador returned to say that details of the original transaction had been traced and his government was willing to place the said sum in any currency in any bank named by the Irish government. So ended the case of Ireland and the Russian crown jewels. So, too, ended Ireland's contact with the Soviet Union. In the cold war, Ireland was emphatically on the other side. That was very much how Washington viewed the Irish stance.

In September 1950, the State Department recommended that the current international situation made it desirable and appropriate for the National Security Council to re-examine Ireland's relationship with NATO and the Mutual Defence Assistance Program.[71] Dated 17 October 1950, the NSC document concluded:

> . . . it would be desirable to continue to maintain an attitude of readiness to welcome Ireland as a member of the North Atlantic Treaty Organization. However, it would be undesirable, and in all likelihood ruthless, for the United States again to take the initiative to encourage Ireland to enter NATO and it would be even more undesirable to extend military assistance to Ireland under a bilateral arrangement outside NATO.[72]

The document stated that the way was open for Ireland to seek admission to NATO at any time.

The National Security Council's analysis recognised that Ireland was strategically located and afforded valuable sites for air bases and naval and anti-submarine operations, supplementary to and in support of bases available in the British Isles and Northern Ireland. Ireland was a potential source of combat units in the event of war: 'Its unqualified adherence would be both logical and desirable, and would give further evidence of the solidarity of the free nations of the North Atlantic area.' President Truman approved this document on 3 November and directed its immediate implementation. It was reviewed by the NSC planning board in 1960, which considered that it did not need updating.

The rapid deterioration of the international situation in 1950 prompted the Irish government into a major review of the country's general state of preparation for the eventuality of a third world war. The first meeting of the Inter-Departmental Emergency Preparation Committee was held on 16 August 1950.[73] Originally comprising the secretaries of Finance, Defence, Justice, Industry and Commerce, Agriculture, External Affairs, Health and the Taoiseach, it was later expanded to include the secretaries of all the departments of state.

Addressing the first meeting, Costello spoke of the recent deterioration in the international situation. He wanted the secretaries to consider what steps should be taken in regard to essential supplies, civil defence, legislation and orders. Costello also wanted to set about providing reserve supplies of essential commodities, such as petrol, oil, coal and building materials, as a precaution against world shortages and price increases. The committee met thirteen times between August and early December. Civil defence preparations were reviewed and revised. The Department of Defence reserved vacancies in various relevant training courses in Britain. A land commission officer with experience of air raid precautions had been seconded to the Department of Defence and was to be sent to a rescue instructors' course in England. An Irish army officer had been nominated to do an administrative officers' course and other course places in Britain were to be filled. The assistant secretary of the Department of Posts and Telegraphs, J. Purcell, was to be controller of censorship, together with three other senior civil servants, who were to act as his staff.

The following commissioners were named to take over certain designated regions in the event of a breakdown of central government:

Region No.	Counties Comprised in Region	Regional Commissioner	Official Post
1.	Donegal, Sligo, Leitrim	L. Ó Muirthe	Assistant Secretary, Dept. of Education
2.	Mayo and Galway	P. O'Leary	Principal Officer, Dept. of Lands
3.	Clare, Limerick, Tipperary	W.A. Honohan	Deputy Assistant Secretary, Dept. of Social Welfare
4.	Cork and Kerry	John O'Donovan	Principal Officer, Dept. of Finance
5.	Waterford, Kilkenny, Carlow, Wexford	A. Kennan	Principal Officer, Dept. of Industry and Commerce
6.	Meath, Wicklow, Kildare	C.F. Dowling	Principal Officer, Dept. of Health
7.	Louth, Monaghan, Cavan	M.B. Lawless	Principal Officer, Dept. of Local Government
8.	Roscommon, Longford, Westmeath, Offaly, Laois	J. O' Callaghan	Assistant Secretary, Dept. of Justice

9.   Dublin   P.J. Daly   Assistant Secretary,
                                          Dept. of Local
                                          Government

The Taoiseach submitted a draft National Security Bill, based on the Emergency Powers Acts 1939 and 1942, and the General Elections (Emergency Provisions) Act 1943, to government on 12 September 1950. The Taoiseach, however, told Moynihan of the unease of a number of his cabinet colleagues on at least three occasions in September and October, over the possible effects of the various proposals for providing reserve stocks of commodities. This concern was tied up with a decision of the committee on 20 September to request the government to make direct approaches to the corresponding British departments with a view to securing information about British policy and plans for an emergency. It was similarly recommended that negotiations should be opened with the United States to procure stocks of essential commodities derived from dollar sources.

However, that decision was preceded by an interesting discussion within the committee, where it was stated that the relationship between Britain and Ireland had altered significantly between 1939 and 1950:

> It was pointed out that, when preparation was being made for the emergency that commenced in September, 1939, the relations that existed, notwithstanding Ireland's declared policy of neutrality, were of such a character that a very substantial amount of valuable information was procured as to the policy and plans of the British Government and it was found possible to make administrative arrangements which—although not in all cases fully observed by the British—proved, on the whole, of great advantage to this country in respect of supplies, foreign exchange, civil defence and other matters. For example, there was, at the time, a clear-cut understanding with the British Treasury that our reasonable requirements of foreign exchange would be supplied. No similar relations existed now, however, and in their absence, the preparation of precautionary measures in this country would be gravely impeded. . . . The restoration of contacts and relations between Irish and British Government Departments, similar to

those that existed in 1939, was, therefore, regarded by the committee as a matter requiring a most careful and urgent consideration.

It was decided to take up the matter with the Taoiseach. The committee also adverted to the possibility that the government might wish to consider securing from the British an agreement in principle to the exchange of information and the making of administrative arrangements to the advantage of both countries.[74] Notwithstanding the difficulties and the possible embarrassment, the government decided to accept those recommendations on 26 September: 1) the Irish ambassador was to be 'instructed' to make approaches to the British government to find out its emergency preparation plans; 2) that approach should not exclude the use of existing contacts between Irish and British government departments; and, 3) the Minister for External Affairs should open discussions with representatives of the government of the United States on the question of procuring stocks of essential commodities.[75]

This was a controversial and somewhat unwelcome decision. Naturally, the Department of External Affairs was sceptical about the practical value of such an initiative. Both Hugh McCann in Washington and Frederick Boland in London tried to deflect the government from taking immediate action. That was the substance of Iveagh House's position as represented by Brian Ó Gallchobhair at the seventeenth meeting of the committee on 19 March 1951.[76]

A delegation from the Industrial Development Authority visited the Board of Trade in London early in 1951 to discuss the acquisition of scarce materials. Boland sent a note on the outcome of the talks. This showed the ambassador's basic scepticism of the central policy idea:

Again, we will always be open to criticism here if we allow scarce materials to be used in Ireland for purposes which are prohibited here, and in the absence of some sort of official control in Dublin it is difficult to convince the British that we are able to prevent the use of scarce materials for 'frivolous' purposes.

Boland warned that, unless a national policy was developed, 'the British are going to treat us with great caution as they never know what is coming next and we shall gradually destroy our credit with them'.[77]

A few weeks later, MacBride was in the United States for Saint Patrick's day celebrations. A background note prepared in the State Department, in advance of the minister's arrival in Washington, confirmed that there was no change in US policy towards Ireland:

> The way for Ireland to get arms, therefore, would be to participate in the NATO. We are confirmed in this position by the fact that there is no guarantee that Ireland would be prepared to abandon its traditional policy of neutrality in the event of another war, even should we be willing to enter into a special defense relationship with that country.[78]

The director of the office of British Commonwealth and Northern European affairs, Raynor, saw MacBride on 13 March and was told about the struggle against communism, partition, and the need for military assistance. The Irish minister informed him that Ireland had formerly received 'a modest' supply of arms from the British, but she had not done so now for the past two years. He said that under present conditions Ireland was unable to defend itself, but that his people had the will to defend themselves against communist aggression. MacBride repeated his points to the White House assistant secretary, W. Averell Harriman. On the same day MacBride also met Dean Acheson. Perhaps this anxiety to win bilateral military assistance compelled the Irish minister to speak so militantly about the struggle against communism. He pressed for a dramatic declaration from Washington to capture the imagination of the free world and for 'something to which men could have faith'. This was, according to MacBride, 'especially important when one realised that fanatic believers in communism regarded communism practically as a religion'. At the time, Acheson simply said that he thought that it would be difficult to gain unanimity for such a text. However, a few years later Acheson referred to an unnamed 'gifted Irish Foreign Minister' in his *Power and Diplomacy* who had once urged him that it was his duty

> . . . to devise and state on one page, and in words which would set the world ablaze, the faith of free men. I pointed out to him that

the Irish temperament was far better suited to this high endeavor—though the requirement of brevity might be a hurdle—than my more mundane inheritance from the Scots lowlands, by way of Ulster, and the south of England. More than this, I offered him a quiet room and, for content and style, the Lord's Prayer, the Declaration of Independence, and the Gettysburg Address. But he had a luncheon engagement.

Accompanied by Acheson, MacBride met President Truman on 23 March and was reported as saying that Ireland wished very much to join the North Atlantic Treaty Organisation, but could not do so because of political difficulties. Truman simply replied that all the NATO nations had expressed the strong desire and hope that Ireland could and would join, but that the matter to which the minister referred (partition) was an issue between the two countries concerned. On the question of military assistance, MacBride said that in the event of a communist invasion, Ireland would be defenceless. Truman said that he would give the matter some thought, but he recalled the great strain being placed upon the United States by the urgent needs of allies who were more exposed than Ireland.[79] MacBride got nothing in the end. Upon his return to Ireland, he confronted a crisis which ultimately led to the downfall of the inter-party government.

MOTHER AND CHILD CRISIS

The archbishop of Dublin, John Charles McQuaid, enjoyed a very close personal relationship with the Taoiseach and other leading members of the government. MacBride had involved John Costello directly in the campaign to raise funds for the Italian Christian Democrats in 1948. MacBride had sought his help in the struggle to prevent an Italian nuncio replacing Paschal Robinson, who had died in 1948. This involved considerable interaction between Iveagh House and Drumcondra, the home of the archbishop of Dublin. McQuaid came to expect that he should be consulted in all government business which involved the Catholic Church. It was not an unreasonable assumption because ministers had shown excessive deference to the prelate. At least four inter-party ministers were members of the Knights of St Columbanus: the Tánaiste and Minister for Industry and Commerce, William Norton, Joseph Blowick, who was Minister for Lands, Mulcahy, Minister for Education, and finally the Minister for Justice, Seán MacEoin.[80] That, in itself, did not signify very much, but it helps underline the argument that the free enterprise mentality—so much a characteristic of the Irish business community and of the Knights—was represented in the cabinet. Most of the ministers shared an antipathy to increased powers being taken by the state, particularly in the matter of medicine and the health service in general.

Many Irish bishops continued to exhibit the same apprehension about the encroaching frontiers of the state as they had since 1922. Curtailing the influence of Trinity-educated doctors was a hidden objective. In the 1950s there was the added spectre of Beveridgeism and socialised medicine to concern the bishops and the doctors. Moreover, another Trinity graduate, Noël Browne, was Minister for Health and he did not appear to understand the new conventions governing relations between church and state which had evolved since the inter-party government had come to power—an intimate and deferential attitude, giving Archbishop McQuaid unsolicited but effective power of veto over government action in certain spheres: 'I am an Irishman second: I am a Catholic first', Costello was to tell the Dáil during the crisis. He was also to say in the same context: 'If the hierarchy give me any direction with regard to Catholic social teaching or Catholic moral teaching, I accept without qualification in all respects the teaching of the hierarchy and the church to which I belong.'[81]

Other ministers did not make so clear a profession of faith, but neither did Costello's formula provoke ministerial dissent. Notes on file by MacBride indicate that he felt it was politically impossible to ignore the views of the hierarchy. But he also felt that the ministers, who were all Catholics, could not disregard the views of the bishops. He qualified that stipulation somewhat by stating that due weight had also to be given to the heads of other religious denominations: 'In this case [the mother and child issue] we are dealing with the *considered views of the leaders of the Catholic Church to which the vast majority of our people belong; these views cannot be ignored*' (my emphasis).[82] This was hardly a formula which one would readily associate with a self-styled disciple of Wolfe Tone. Even Noël Browne was dutifully prepared to accept, as a minister in government, the decision of the hierarchy on matters of faith and morals.

The Department of Health, under its secretary, Pádraig Ó Cinnéide, proved to be a voice for dynamic and radical reform. The work of James Deeny has been referred to in chapter 4. Much was done to tackle the scourge of TB in the period of the inter-party government and Browne, who had contracted the disease earlier in life and as a child had seen his family devastated by tuberculosis, was a militant and effective reformer.[83] Browne spent three exhausting years in the Department of Health, where both he and his civil servants worked tirelessly to achieve reforms. The progress made in those years was as much a tribute to his civil servants as it was to himself. But his personal contribution was significant. His troubles really began when he tried to reactivate the controversial part of the Ryan Bill, referred to as the Mother and Child section, in 1950. This offered, without a means test, free but voluntary ante and post natal care for mothers, and for children up to the age of sixteen.[84]

Earlier in the crisis, on 10 October 1950, the secretary to the hierarchy, James Staunton, had written to Costello that the scheme was in direct opposition to the rights of the family and of the individual and was liable to 'very great abuse'. If adopted, the measures would 'constitute a ready-made instrument for future totalitarian aggression'. Staunton asserted, on behalf of the hierarchy, that 'the right to provide for health of children belongs to parents, not to the state'. The state had the right to intervene only in a subsidiary capacity, to supplement, not to supplant: '*It may help indigent or neglectful parents; it may not deprive 90 per cent of parents of their rights because of 10 per cent necessitous or negligent parents*' (my emphasis). It was not sound social policy, the letter stated, to impose a state medical service on the whole community on the pretext of relieving the necessitous 10 per cent from the so-called indignity of the means test.

Staunton also wrote that the right to provide for the physical education of children belonged to the family and not to the state since experience had shown that physical or health education was closely interwoven with important moral questions, on which the Catholic church had clear teaching:

Education in regard to motherhood includes instruction in regard to sex relations, chastity and marriage. The State has no competence to give instruction in such matters. We regard with the greatest apprehension the proposal to give to local medical officers the right to tell Catholic girls and women how they should behave in regard to this sphere of conduct at once so delicate and sacred.

Gynaecological care may be, and in some other countries is, interpreted to include provision for birth limitation and abortion. We have no guarantee that State officials will respect Catholic principles in regard to these matters. Doctors trained in instruction in which we have no confidence may be appointed as medical officers under the proposed service, and may give gynaecological care not in accordance with Catholic principles.

Staunton claimed also that the proposed scheme destroyed the confidential relationship between the patient and the doctor. It also meant, for the hierarchy, the elimination of private medical practitioners by a state-paid service.[85]

Browne was given this letter by the Taoiseach on 9 November, about a month after it had been delivered. The Department of Health prepared a detailed rejoinder which was forwarded to Costello. The Taoiseach chose not to send it immediately to the hierarchy.

There the matter rested until March 1951 when Browne sent a pamphlet explaining the mother and child scheme to the bishops. McQuaid wrote by return to Browne reiterating *as archbishop* 'each and every objection' that he had made when they had met on 10 October 1950. Browne claimed that he had been 'peremptorily ordered' to Drumcondra by the archbishop's secretary on that occasion.[86] In the first place, that was not the archbishop's style. He was, if anything, excessively polite and sensitive to the dictates of protocol. Furthermore, if Browne felt that he had been 'peremptorily ordered' to the palace of the archbishop, then why did he demean his office by going?

Browne and Costello corresponded following the receipt of the 8 March letter from the archbishop. The outcome was that Costello sent the original Department of Health memorandum to the hierarchy for a final appraisal of the scheme. The bishops gave 'long and careful consideration' to the memorandum at a meeting of the standing committee on 3 April and at the general meeting the next day. A detailed rejection of the scheme was prepared and approved. It was immediately forwarded to the government. The letter outlined the fundamental opposition of the hierarchy to the scheme. The bishops objected in principle to the state arrogating to itself the educational control 'in the very intimate matters of chastity, individual and conjugal'. There was outright opposition to control of aspects of the health service where 'the state must enter unduly and very intimately into the life of patients, both parents and children, and of doctors.' An objection was entered to the heavy taxation on the whole community necessary for such a scheme. There was a belief that the scheme would damage 'gravely the self-reliance of parents, whose family-wage or income would allow them duly to provide for themselves medical treatment for their dependants.'[87]

The episcopal response noted that 'no evidence has been supplied in the letter of the Taoiseach that the proposed Mother-and-Child Health Scheme advocated by the Minister for Health enjoys the support of the government.' The hierarchy had 'firm confidence' that it would yet be possible, 'with reflection and calm consultation', to provide a scheme respectful of the 'traditional life and spirit of our Christian people'.[88] It was significant that, in an official communication to government, the hierarchy felt bold enough to draw a distinction between the personal position of the Minister for Health and that of the remaining members of the government.

A few hours before the cabinet met to discuss the crisis on 6 April 1951, Browne did a prearranged radio broadcast in Irish and English to explain the scheme. This had a new poignancy because Browne had had time to read the hierarchy's reply, which had been presented to him by his private secretary just before he went on air. At the cabinet meeting, every minister was asked to speak on the issue; Browne did not have a single ally. Two days later he was called to a meeting of Clann na Poblachta where, in his words, he was subjected to a 'Kafkaesque-like trial process'.[89] On 10 April, he was forced to resign—ousted in a welter of publicity which involved, quite shockingly for the time, the publication in *The Irish Times* of all the confidential correspondence between Browne and his critics on the mother and child crisis.[90] Before leaving office, he ordered the destruction by his private secretary and another senior member of the Department of Health of all documents 'likely to be used or misused against us'.[91]

When the Dáil debated his resignation on 12 April, Browne sat on the opposition benches. De Valera, according to Browne, contributed little to the proceedings: 'We have heard enough', he muttered. Thus, said Browne, he and his party 'joined the political pygmies on the government benches'.[92]

Summing up what has been described—erroneously in my view— as a church-state crisis, the Irish-language magazine *Comhar* carried an editorial in which it was argued that, while the Taoiseach was entitled to listen to the bishops, 'it goes directly against the spirit and terms of the Constitution to say he [Taoiseach] was obliged to accept the views expressed by the bishops'. The editorial added: 'The worst aspect of the matter is the fact that the ordinary people believe that the bishops had no great case against the scheme.'

The *Comhar* leader said that the arguments put up by the doctors against the scheme 'seemed reasonable and quite innocent'. They were defending the independence of the doctors and they were opposing the 'socialisation of the profession'.

But the real reason, in the view of the leader writer, was as follows:

If the scheme did not involve a means test, most of the mothers of the country would take advantage of it; the state would pay for these cases and the Income Tax Commissioners would have the full amount of doctors' income. In short the doctors who would implement the scheme would have to pay their fair share of income tax for the first time ever. It is no wonder then that the doctors gathered up every group they could use to defeat the scheme.[93]

In retrospect, both church and state have cause to regret the manner in which the issues were handled. Many years later the then bishop of Ferns, Donal Herlihy, told me: 'we allowed ourselves to be used by the doctors, but it won't happen again'.[94]

The mother and child crisis brought the inter-party government to an abrupt end. Meanwhile, Fianna Fáil had had time to regroup. Three years in opposition had given the 'soldiers of destiny' time to rediscover that sense of urgency which Fianna Fáil had demonstrated in 1932. There were too many 'old soldiers' left on the front benches in 1951. Was de Valera at 69 the best choice to lead his party into the 1950s? The election which followed on 30 May had an indecisive outcome, but Fianna Fáil scraped back into power.[95]

6

The Politics of Drift, 1951–1959

B ack in Government Buildings again on 13 June 1951, de Valera presided over a minority government which depended upon the whim of certain independents to remain in office. Perhaps he might have contemplated again the idea of a snap election on a popular issue, to catch the opposition offguard. He had done that successfully in 1933, 1938 and again in 1944. But no such opportunity was to present itself. The 1950s were a time of economic depression.

De Valera did not opt for any radical departures in his new cabinet. The old faces remained. The Taoiseach, however, relinquished the External Affairs portfolio to Frank Aiken. The latter held that post, with the exception of the period of the second inter-party government in the mid-1950s, until his retirement in 1969. Against the advice of Seán Lemass, who became Tánaiste and Minister for Industry and Commerce, MacEntee was appointed Minister for Finance—a choice de Valera lived to regret. MacEntee's philosophical conservatism, when married to the Procrustean fiscal practices of some civil servants in Merrion Square, had a lethal political outcome for Fianna Fáil after the 1952 budget. However, de Valera showed some imagination when he appointed Seán Moylan as Minister for Education. Moylan was one of the very few Fianna Fáil ministers to have retained good relations with the INTO in 1946. His parents had been primary school teachers, as was his brother, who taught in Dublin and had been involved in the 1946 strike. The Conciliation and Arbitration Board awarded teachers long overdue salary increases. Moylan, who never went further than primary school himself, became one of the best ministers for education in the history of the state. He was certainly one of the best educated. Tom Derrig, living in the shadow of the entirely unnecessary teachers' strike of 1946, was given the Department for Lands. The talented Tom Walsh was made Minister for Agriculture. James Ryan, ever prudent and conciliatory, returned to Health and Social Welfare where the mother and child issue still remained to be resolved. A young Cork TD, Jack Lynch, was made parliamentary secretary to the government and to the Minister for Lands.[1] It must have been frustrating for a new generation of Fianna Fáil TDs to see so little movement at the top. Cabinet and parliamentary party meetings became even more protracted affairs, and consensus was usually achieved through a process of attrition—in the case of the parliamentary party each deputy being allowed to speak until de Valera chose the right psychological moment to put a motion. This was described by one Fianna Fáil backbencher as 'peace by exhaustion'.[2]

The lacklustre performance of Fianna Fáil at this time might also be partially explained by the poor health of Lemass, who was operated upon for gall-bladder trouble. Recuperating in hospital, he dutifully attempted to study the Irish language. But this did not prove to be a mystical experience and he quickly exchanged his grammar books for the drier work of his department. Back at his desk, Lemass accommodated himself to the existence of a revamped Industrial Development Authority, introduced the Restrictive Practices Act in the Dáil and revived the idea of a transatlantic air link with the US. (It was inaugurated in 1958.) Another state-sponsored body, An Foras Tionscail (the Underdeveloped Areas Board), was set up in 1952 to grant-aid the establishment of industry in the west and south-west. Foreign industry was encouraged through a generous export profits tax relief scheme introduced in 1957 and 1958. The Shannon Free Airport Development Company was set up in 1959 (a customs free area had been established at Shannon in 1947). The sea fisheries board, Bord Iascaigh Mhara, was set up in 1952 and the Agricultural Institute, An Foras Talúntais, was established in 1958. The Bovine

Tuberculosis Eradication Scheme was set up in 1954, with very indifferent results. It had cost the state £488m by the late 1980s. Bord Fáilte—the Irish Tourist Board—was instituted in 1955. An Tóstal (the gathering) was to be an annual event designed to attract the Irish overseas to return home for holidays. While the idea never quite lived up to expectations, it did provide some colour and excitement—occasionally spiced with controversy—in an otherwise depressed decade.

In the 1950s the Irish left their homeland in vast numbers. About 400,000 emigrated during that decade. Net emigration per annum between 1951 and 1956 was 39,353, or 9.2 per thousand of the population. That figure increased to 42,401 between 1956 and 1961. This was the highest rate since 'the exceptional period in the 1880s'.[3] Most dramatic of all was the haemorrhage from the west of Ireland. Between 1956 and 1961, the highest rates of net emigration per thousand average population were from Monaghan (26.5), Leitrim (22.7), Longford (20.8) and Mayo (20.3).[4] The profile remained much the same as in the 1930s when 68 per cent of male emigrants were agricultural labourers, while 64 per cent of female emigrants were domestics, hotel staff or servants.[5] Although the overwhelming part of emigration was from the countryside, there was also a steady stream from Dublin working-class areas, where the tradition of joining the British forces had not been broken. Economic recruitment remained the strongest motive. The vast majority went to the United Kingdom. The Continent was not a popular destination until the 1980s. While over 176,000 went to the United Kingdom between 1951 and 1956, only some 20,000 emigrated to the United States and Canada. The comparable figures for 1956–61 were 197,848 and 14,155 respectively. In the light of the experience in the 1980s, it is interesting to note that at no time in the 1950s—at the height of emigration—was the Irish quota filled for the United States. Another fact worth recording was that in 1961 some 398,000 in a population of 2,818,000 (14 per cent) were living outside the county of their birth. This was largely because of the growth of Dublin city and county. The sense of displacement experienced by many young country people, forced to come to the capital for work, could be almost as acute as that of their peers who had been driven to take the boat to Britain.

The poet Brendan Kennelly has captured the pathos of the annual 'scattering' of the Irish, particularly from the western seaboard, in a poem entitled 'Westland Row', the railway station in Dublin for the boat-train to England:

> Brown bag bulging with faded nothings;
>   A ticket for three pounds one and six
>   To Euston, London via Holyhead.
> Young faces limp, misunderstanding
> What the first gay promptings meant—
>   A pass into a brilliant wilderness,
>   A capital of hopeless promise.
> Well, mount the steps; lug the bag:
> Take your place. And out of all the crowd,
> Watch the girl in the wrinkled coat,
>   Her face half-grey.
> Her first time.[6]

In *An Irish Navvy*, Dónall Mac Amhlaigh displays his suppressed anger about his enforced return to England:

> I had a good short holiday and I shouldn't be unhappy. But after all, I envy the cattle lying on the green grass of Ireland. . . . But even the cattle are trundled across too, like the Paddies and Brigids of Ireland. Coming into Dún Laoire, I saw men in white clothes playing cricket and, somehow, I felt annoyed. A young man and his girl were walking by themselves down below us in the golden evening sunlight. It's well for you, my friend, that every day you arise can be spent round about this place. . . . Doesn't Dún Laoire look beautiful with the mountains behind it? The quay is lined with little sailing boats, and wooden rowing boats. The wealthy own them, those who can stay behind here. . . . I can sense the old feeling in my stomach that I get each time I leave Irish soil, but it won't last long. I'm getting used to it now. . . . We're a great people, surely.[7]

There is a burning sense of the injustice of enforced emigration in Mac Amhlaigh's prose.

However, while the official rhetoric of Irish politics favoured a rapid end to high emigration, Drs R.C. Geary and M.D. McCarthy, in their joint addendum to the *Commission on Emigration and other Population Problems 1948–1954*, were prepared to ask and answer the question: were people willing to make the sacrifices necessary to make an end to emigration? 'In our opinion the answer is "No" as the forced cessation of emigration would lead to heavy unemployment, a lowering of wage rates and a reduction of the average standard of living.'[8] Bishop Cornelius Lucey of Cork, in contrast, saw dangers in emigration, urbanisation and industrialisation. He favoured decentralisation and 'a more forthright declaration that Dublin is overgrown, that it is overgrown as the result of State action and that the basic remedy is to take away some of the State Departments from Dublin and locate them in the provinces.'[9] The bishop's ideas were not implemented—even when de Valera, the high priest of rural living, was in power. Emigration remained *a fact of life* for the Irish political elite.

But for the 'Paddies and Brigids' who remained at home there was little cheer and practically no prospect of joining the white-clad cricket-playing classes. The number of people in employment dropped by almost a quarter between 1946 and 1953 and real wages fell so that the average industrial worker earned less in 1958 than he/she had done in 1950.[10]

De Valera inherited a balance of payments deficit of £62 million in 1951 which the Department of Finance felt ought to be cleared. A rising star in the civil service, Ken Whitaker, drafted a memorandum in autumn 1951 which was ultimately adopted with minimum changes as departmental policy. Currency devaluation was ruled out. In the absence of Marshall aid and other funding, Whitaker argued that what was needed was:

. . . a realisation that if houses, electricity development, afforestation and all the other forms of capital expenditure are desired by the community, the desire should be expressed in the form of preferring these things to others—of turning over to the state some of the money now being spent on non-essential consumer goods so that the state can carry on with its capital programme without causing too much inflation.

The position would be corrected only if current and capital expenditure were curtailed and a greater proportion of it financed from taxation.[11] Seán MacEntee taxed beer, spirits, tobacco, petrol, oil and motor cars. At the same time, he removed food subsidies. In raising the price of the pint by a few pence, among the other measures, MacEntee blamed the recklessness of the inter-party government for the plight of the Irish economy. De Valera had spoken of the country living beyond its means.[12] The opposition accused the government of a destructively wrong approach to economic reform.[13] MacEntee countered with accusations of a coalition sell-out between 1948 and 1951 which had put the country in pawn.[14]

The budget debate spilled over into three by-election campaigns on 26 June 1952. The state of the parties, with Fianna Fáil still depending upon independents, was not altered. The governing party took two seats, in Mayo North and Waterford. Fine Gael won the seat in Limerick East. There were two by-elections on 18 June 1953 in Cork East and in Wicklow. Fine Gael took a seat from Labour in the former and won a seat from Fianna Fáil in the latter. A by-election in Galway South on 21 August 1953 was won by Fianna Fáil, while Fine Gael held its two seats in by-elections in Cork Borough and Louth on 3 March 1954. De Valera hung on to power until the spring of 1954.

CHURCH, STATE, CULTURE AND THE LAW

There was, despite the difficulties, at least one notable legislative achievement in this period. The Minister for Health, James Ryan, decided to broaden the scope of the mother and child provisions. He published a white paper in July 1952 and the proposals met with immediate criticism from a number of sources: right-wing Catholic groups, the Irish Medical Association (IMA) and the Catholic hierarchy. Maria Duce (under the leadership of Mary), founded by the Holy Ghost priest Denis Fahey, in 1945, mounted a campaign in the early 1950s to have article 44 of the constitution on religion replaced by a more suitably worded confessional formula. The Department of the Taoiseach had received hundreds of signatures on a printed form which had been given out by Maria Duce, but it had not unnerved the government. Neither was anyone in the Department of Health surprised to receive attention from *An Ríoghacht*, an Irish version of Catholic Action, over the proposed legislation on the mother and child scheme.[15] The Catholic hierarchy was mobilised by Archbishop McQuaid, who invited Ryan to call on him on 16 September 1952. The absence of a means test was the issue which

McQuaid raised and he indicated to Ryan that the minister was likely to run into trouble with the Bill.[16] At the meeting McQuaid did not alert the minister to the fears of the hierarchy. He simply signalled that he was chairman of a subcommittee of the national conference of bishops which had been set up after the October meeting to monitor the progress of the health legislation. The other members of the committee were Lucey of Cork, Browne of Galway and Staunton of Ferns. None of the four was noted for his moderation on the health issue.[17]

Ryan was hampered by the fact that de Valera was in Utrecht having an eye operation at the time of his meeting with McQuaid. Lemass, who was as sceptical of the views of the hierarchy as Ryan, took his place. Ryan saw McQuaid, Lucey and Browne on 6 October and learned that the bishops were prepared to accept the mother and child scheme if a means test was included. When Ryan had not replied to McQuaid by early November, McQuaid wrote to Lemass wondering why there had not been a response. The IMA had, in the meantime, come out against the scheme. Lemass and Ryan met the episcopal commission on 10 December while de Valera was still in Utrecht. Ryan agreed to introduce a means test for women in the upper income bracket where they would have to pay £1 per year for services.[18] Ryan introduced the Bill into the Dáil on 26 February, thinking that there was no longer any major disagreement between himself and the hierarchy.

However, when Ryan met the subcommittee on 23 March he discovered that it now opposed the Bill. The national conference of bishops met on 13 April 1953 and a letter condemning the Bill was sent to the national press (not including *The Irish Times*) for publication on 19 April. De Valera's official biographers record that this came as 'a complete surprise to de Valera'.[19] Ryan was equally nonplussed. De Valera, through the mediation of President O'Kelly, arranged to go with Ryan to see his former Blackrock College classmate, John D'Alton, in Drogheda where the cardinal was administering confirmation.

De Valera told D'Alton that the letter contained statements which were incorrect and said that he had been out of the country during the discussions and needed time to familiarise himself with the issues.[20] However, there was another consideration which may have carried even greater weight. De Valera had instructed the ambassador to the Vatican, Joseph Walshe, to test the soundness of the bishops' case in Rome. Walshe consulted Cardinal Michael Browne OP, a theological adviser to the pope. The opinion received was not very supportive of the Irish hierarchy's position. De Valera was in a position to tell D'Alton that the Irish episcopal statement was not based on the most up-to-date advice.[21] The government would be forced to state that in public if the letter appeared in print. Before de Valera left Drogheda, D'Alton had agreed to withdraw the letter and renew discussions between the hierarchy and the minister for health. Agreement was quickly reached between the parties. Ryan allowed a choice of doctor and hospital; no one would be obliged to accept treatment contrary to church teaching. There were adjustments on means testing, and medical inspections were not to take place in schools. The evidence points to a victory for the government.[22] The legislation completed all stages in the Dáil only three days before the 1954 general election. Little evidence can be found in this episode to confirm the 'Rome rule' thesis of Noël Browne. The idea that Ireland was a 'clerical republic' had also been argued by an American anti-Catholic author, Paul Blanshard, in 1954. He referred to the existence of an unofficial church-state alliance.[23] That was not the reality.

However, de Valera felt obliged to humour Archbishop McQuaid on occasion. For example, episcopal concern over 'evil literature' resurfaced in November 1953 while the Ryan Bill remained at a delicate stage of its development. The archbishop was concerned about 'the importation and circulation of newspapers and periodicals objectionable on moral grounds'. De Valera saw McQuaid on 19 November 1953 and directed the Minister for Justice, Gerry Boland, to ensure that 'every effort must be made to put an end to the sale of books of the kind in question'.[24] The Revenue Commissioners were consulted. It was decided that all consignments of paperback novels were to be carefully examined and 'where a consignment contains novels with titles, jacket-designs, or illustrations suggestive of indecent content, it is to be detained and a copy of each book forwarded immediately to the Censorship of Publications Board'. The gardaí were instructed to warn booksellers who displayed such books that they were liable for prosecution; but they were not to take proceedings until it was seen whether the warning was heeded or not.[25] McQuaid wrote later to thank de Valera for the measures taken 'to prevent the diffusion of evil books'. He intended so to inform the standing committee of the hierarchy.[26]

The Department of Justice reviewed the situation in March 1954 and recorded that in the intervening period 181 novels had been sent to the censorship board by customs officers; 165 of them had been prohibited. It had been decided that consignments of novels which were judged banned would not, as a matter of course, be returned to the consignors. The decision to give a warning to certain booksellers had not proved feasible since it had been found that the Act on which it was intended to rely (Dublin Police Act 1842) was insufficient to warrant such a step.[27] The Department of Justice seemed satisfied that the controls were working and the issue died down for a while. And work the controls did. Among the books still banned by the censor in 1954 were works by Léon Blum, Simone de Beauvoir, Noel Coward, Christopher Isherwood, Somerset Maugham, Kate O'Brien, Seán O'Faoláin, Frank O'Connor, Seán O'Casey, Liam O'Flaherty, Margaret Mead, Alberto Moravia, John Steinbeck, George Orwell and Jean-Paul Sartre. The censor took the wheat with the chaff.

Tony O'Malley, a young bank clerk and aspiring artist from Callan, Co. Kilkenny, described the post-Treaty generation of Irishmen as being filled with 'desperation and lust'. It is little wonder that Patrick Kavanagh, in his short-lived paper, *Kavanagh's Weekly*, spoke in his first editorial about the 'victory of mediocrity' in Ireland. In his final number, he raged against the spread of despair: 'There is nothing evil in communism that isn't rampant throughout Ireland today. Despair is on its way.' Yet Kavanagh believed, and continued to believe, that 'something is still possible in this country'—a country where the main state-run radio station was not noted for the spread of ideas.[28] He railed against provincialism and defended 'parochialism'. Kavanagh compared living in Ireland to being at a wake:

> Don't disturb the mourners with a thought. A wake is what is in progress in this country, a wake at which there is lashings of eating and drinking. The undertaker in his long, black cloak moves around on padded feet; he is the businessman of the country and his job is to be nice to everybody. Ideas are bad for trade.
>
> We came to the wake that had been going uproariously for at least thirty years and at the moment we are trying to get the family to remove the corpse—the corpse of 1916, the Gaelic language, the inferiority complex—so that the house may be free for the son to

bring in a wife. Will they take our advice or will the wake proceed to explosion point. . . .[29]

Kavanagh saw the country as being ruled by time-servers with no 'central passion'.[30] In the visual arts, the 1950s saw the rise of a number of great talents. Tony O'Malley developed his art of abstract painting while being posted on relief from one branch of the Munster and Leinster Bank to another. Heavily influenced by Braque, he recalls the less than positive reaction of his fellow lodgers to his early work and the need to keep secret his painting, lest an inquisitive landlady might complain about the smell of turpentine. When he gave presents of his early work to people, the drawing or painting was rarely hung on a wall; it was rather placed in a drawer for safe keeping, together with the mass and memorial cards. In the Irish countryside in the 1950s, the artist was not regarded as being entirely sane. Painting and painters—unlike hunting, shooting or sports—were treated with suspicion, Tony O'Malley remembered. But he ignored popular and professional prejudice, becoming a journeyman painter; at the same time he won a longstanding battle against TB, having to undergo multiple operations. His work gives the lie to the over-gloomy view of Ireland in the fifties. It showed the capacity of individuals to overcome in their art the petty prejudices of the decade. O'Malley was moved by the landscape and by the sculpture of Celtic Ireland:

My generation was reared on holy pictures, yet here were powerful, primordial images. In Jerpoint [Co. Kilkenny], the apostles are carved on a big stone. There is even a comic side to them, which I thought was good. There were no heavy, ornate trappings, just men doing a job: in the effigies women are lying down beside their lords and they are as powerful as their lords. I found it disturbing, attempting to reconcile these stark symbols with the awful sentimental images of the Belgian and Italian saints. Here were those craggy truths in stone and they disturbed me.

O'Malley was 'intoxicated' with the hills and the fields as 'an innocent in the countryside'. He saw landscape as symbol, like the Chinese, but his landladies from Monaghan to Kenmare were not likely either to appreciate or to approve of his approach. O'Malley had a personal and artistic courage which was shared by others of his generation; Seán O'Faoláin and Austin Clarke, joined by younger poets and writers, outflanked the mind of officialdom in the pages of *The Bell* (defunct in 1954) and *Envoy*. David Marcus worked to encourage poetry and the arts. *Dublin Opinion* and Flann O'Brien, in their respective styles, attacked the pompous and the ridiculous in Irish public life.

Irish society in the 1950s may have been authoritarian and restrictive, but there was a vibrant counter-culture to which many Irish writers, artists and thinkers contributed. The atmosphere of the times is captured very well in Anthony Cronin's *No Laughing Matter—The Life and Times of Flann O'Brien* and in his *Dead as Doornails*. Collections of short stories appeared by Benedict Kiely (1950), Frank O'Connor (1952), James Plunkett (1955), Liam O'Flaherty (1956), Seán O'Faoláin (1957) and Mary Lavin (1959). Mervyn Wall's *Leaves for the Burning* was published in 1952. Brian Moore brought out *The Lonely Passion of Judith Hearne* in 1955. Brendan Behan's *The Quare Fellow* was presented in 1956. Poetry collections by Richard Murphy and John Montague also appeared. Important works in Irish by the following also came out: Seán Ó Riordáin (1952), Máire Mhac an tSaoi and Seán Ó Tuama. Sections of the visual arts also showed the continued vitality of the 1940s. Michael Scott, a major talent in architecture, designed a new central bus station, Busáras, in a modern style which many northside Dubliners viewed with sympathy and benign amusement. It was a symbol of progress in a sea of economic stagnation. There was not much money around for architectural experimentation. But, despite the financial constraints, there were adventurous spirits in the 1950s like Carolyn Swift and Alan Simpson of the Pike Theatre who brought Samuel Beckett's *Waiting for Godot* to the Dublin stage in 1956. It ran for six months to full houses and then the production was taken on tour to county towns, where it met with popular success.

The temptation to treat 1950s' Irish Catholic culture as being monolithic cannot be sustained by even the most cursory review of the literature. The religious magazines, *Studies* and *The Furrow*, were sober and serious.[31] The *Irish Capuchin Annual* continued to make an important contribution to intellectual life in the country. *Christus Rex*, though never at the cutting edge of international sociological thought, was a forum for a 'new' discipline.

There is little evidence that the universities played as constructive a role in society as they might have done. Professor George O'Brien, the UCD economist, was urbane and articulate, while his disciple, James Meenan, enlivened economic debate in the country. The president of University College Cork, Alfred O'Rahilly, was a polemicist and a polymath who contributed to the commonweal, unlike many of his academic contemporaries, who appeared to doze through the decade. In contrast, some university students started to look outwards and sought to establish stronger intellectual links with Europe. The Irish Council of the European Movement, which had failed to take root in the late 1940s, was firmly established in Dublin in 1954.[32] Dónal O'Sullivan, Garret FitzGerald, Denis Corboy and Miriam Hederman O'Brien were among its early members. However, as has been stated earlier, the foreign policy preoccupations of the Irish government were fixed much more firmly on cold war concerns than on the political integration of Europe.

AIKEN, THE CIA AND THE DEFENCE OF IRELAND

The anxiety felt by the outgoing government in 1951 over the relative defencelessness of Ireland was transmitted to de Valera and his new Minister for External Affairs, Frank Aiken. The Taoiseach discussed Irish policy towards the US on 25 June 1951 with the *chargé d'affaires* in Dublin, Cloyce K. Huston: 'I know that many people say that I am a dictator or that my Government will be a dictatorship but I am not a dictator—not at all—far from it.' De Valera was aware of the general view that 'Ireland's unpreparedness [he did not mention the North Atlantic Pact] constituted a serious weakness in the defences of the democratic world.'[33]

Frank Aiken saw Douglas MacArthur, adviser on international affairs to Dwight Eisenhower, on 31 August 1951. He did not feel that there was any possibility of Ireland joining NATO or any other collective defence arrangement at that time, so ingrained was the tradition of neutrality and feeling over partition. On the other hand, Aiken argued that Ireland 'would resist communism more strongly than most European countries and therefore any assistance which was given it in strengthening its defensive posture would contribute indirectly but positively to overall defense of WE [Western Europe].' Aiken said it would be tragic for both the US and the UK to have Ireland as a defensive vacuum into which the Soviets could move following an attack on the West. In return for military supplies, he offered joint military staff talks, which would 'enable NATO planners to have knowledge of Ireland's defence plans so that there could be proper military coordination should aggression against Ireland occur'.[34] But he could not effect any change in US policy. The US embassy in Dublin believed that the US should maintain a friendly and understanding attitude, even if aid was impracticable.[35]

There followed an exchange of notes between Dublin and Washington on certain amendments that had to be made to existing bilateral Economic Cooperation Administration and the Mutual Defence Assistance agreements which followed the passage of the Mutual Security Act of 1951, but there was no substantive change in the US position.

It might have helped the Irish position somewhat if Dublin had been prepared to agree to re-establish direct links between G2 and the CIA in 1951. The director of the CIA, General Walter Bedell Smith, wrote to Colonel Bryan in August 1951 that it was intended to post a 'representative' to the American embassy in Dublin later that summer. He could be in contact with Bryan 'on a mutually profitable basis'. The Minister for Defence, Oscar Traynor, instructed Bryan to write that 'the present arrangements were more suitable to our circumstances' in view of the 'existing good relations with the Service attachés'.[36] There was no reluctance, evidently, to cooperate with the CIA at an inter-service level.

On 1 April 1952, Aiken met Eisenhower during an 'informal call' to SHAPE (Supreme Headquarters Allied Powers Europe), where he raised yet again the question of military supplies for Ireland. But he got the same reply from Eisenhower as he had received from MacArthur some months before. In July, the Irish embassy in Washington brought up with the State Department the question of Irish eligibility for military assistance. Little encouragement was given to the enquiry. The Irish government doggedly refused to take no for an answer. Further requests were made in early 1953.[37] The Inter-Departmental Emergency Preparation Committee continued its work during the Fianna Fáil period of government from 1951 to 1954. All emergency plans were completed shortly after the return of the second inter-party government in 1954.

The Tánaiste, Seán Lemass, went to the United States in September 1953 with a different set of priorities. While in Washington, he paid a courtesy call on the secretary of state, John Foster Dulles, and raised the status of Ireland's long-standing application for UN membership. Dulles outlined a number of possible ways to achieve membership, but did not offer hope for the early success of any of them. Afterwards, Lemass commented to a State Department official that it was the government's position to leave the application on file at the UN as it had done for several years.[38] Irish entry came finally in 1955 when Fianna Fáil was out of office.

COSTELLO RETURNS TO POWER

Devoid of a stable majority in the Dáil owing to losses in by-elections, there was little option for de Valera but to go to the country, which he did on 14 May 1954. An estimated one and a half million people turned out to vote, or over 75 per cent of the electorate. The theme of the Fianna Fáil campaign was political stability for the next five years.[39] Lemass argued that it was easy to know what the coalition was against, but never what they were for.[40] De Valera stressed the 'instability' of coalition government and argued that Fianna Fáil spoke with one voice. MacEntee talked of the bribery of the electorate by the opposition.[41]

When the votes were counted, Fianna Fáil were ten short of an overall majority with 65 seats. Fine Gael had 50 seats and Labour had gained four, bringing that party up to 19. Clann na Talmhan had five, Clann na Poblachta three and independents had five.[42] Costello was elected Taoiseach on 2 June by 79 votes to 66. Eight of the seats in the coalition cabinet went to Fine Gael, four to Labour and one to Clann na Talmhan. William Norton, described by Noël Browne as a person who 'distinguished himself in cabinet by a complete absence of ethical standards', was Tánaiste and Minister for Industry and Commerce. Fine Gael's T.F. O'Higgins was Minister for Health, and Gerry Sweetman, a new face, was an imaginative appointment to the Department of Finance. Liam Cosgrave was promoted to the External Affairs portfolio and James Dillon returned to Agriculture where he had performed so strongly earlier. It was an interesting mix of parties and personalities. But could the coalition live up to its various promises? 'F.G. PROMISES EVERYTHING' headlined the pro-Fianna Fáil *Irish Press*. The new government was pledged to reduce prices on butter and other essential foods, bring down taxes, raise old age pensions, increase pensions for the blind, widows and orphans, provide pensions for men at 65 and women at 60, increase maternity grants, introduce death benefits, expand the health services, build more houses and increase productivity.[43]

T.F. O'Higgins was immediately confronted by the opposition of the medical profession to the implementation of Ryan's Health Act. He was obliged to bring in a Bill on 7 July which permitted the staggering of services. This resulted in the postponement of specialist services for higher income groups until March 1956; the maternity and infant scheme, for the same group, was never finally implemented. This was a major concession to the medical lobby, as was the decision to set up a committee to advise on voluntary medical insurance. The establishing of the Voluntary Health Insurance (VHI) board, with a state priming grant of £13,000, was the outcome. This measure effectively put pay to 'socialised' medicine in Ireland and it was carried on by the incoming Fianna Fáil minister for health in 1957, Seán MacEntee.[44]

The new coalition—ever loyal to the precepts of the church— proved less compliant when the 'evil literature' problem arose. Costello filled two vacancies on the censorship board on 5 December 1956 with Robert Figgis (a Protestant) and Andrew F. Comyn. Professor John J. Piggott was elected chairman. The two appointments did not meet with the approval of either the archbishop of Dublin or the League of Decency. Neither was McQuaid pleased when he was informed that the Taoiseach was thinking at the end of 1956 of appointing Seán O'Faoláin as the new director of the Arts Council, which had been set up in 1951. The archbishop argued against the appointment at a meeting with Costello, but the Taoiseach remained firm. In a pained tone, McQuaid wrote on 24 December 1956 to Thomas Bodkin (one of the prime movers in the setting up of the Arts Council) regretting that it was not possible to have a director on whom the Catholic Church could rely: 'We shall stumble on, in the semi-gloom of minds that have never been disciplined from youth and that have not matured in the tranquillity of assured knowledge.' The Arts Council remained under the direction of O'Faoláin until 30 June 1959. Monsignor Pádraig de Brun, who might also have been regarded by the archbishop as having a mind which had not matured in the tranquillity of assured knowledge, took over on 1 November 1959.[45] One of the highlights of the latter's term in the Arts Council was the holding of an exhibition by Georges Rouault in Dublin as a form of apology to the family of a great artist for the humiliation he had suffered in Dublin in 1942. McQuaid proved to be too interventionist and had lost credibility as a consequence. Costello had good cause to rue the role that he had played in 1955 when McQuaid had attempted unsuccessfully to halt the playing of a soccer match between Ireland and Yugoslavia. The archbishop believed in the imposition of a sporting boycott on 'communist' countries. The Football Association of Ireland (FAI) had agreed to call off a match between the same sides in 1952. The association refused to do so again in 1955. The archbishop had his opposition communicated by phone to the FAI; the prelate had learned with regret that the match was taking place. He further regretted that the FAI had not had the courtesy to approach him for his views; he hoped the match would be cancelled.[46] There followed protests to the FAI from many Catholic organisations.[47] In view of the controversy, President O'Kelly consulted the Department of the Taoiseach and was told that 'it would be inadvisable for him to attend'.[48] The Number One Army Band was prevented from playing. The Irish team trainer withdrew his services.[49] The Radio Éireann commentator, Philip Greene, told the press that, in view of the opinions expressed by the archbishop, he would not be available to give a commentary on the game.[50] In the end, 22,000 spectators went to Dalymount to see the 'godless' Yugoslavs defeat the godfearing Irish by four goals to one. The former Shelbourne goalkeeper, president of the FAI and Fianna Fáil Minister for Defence (1951–54), Oscar Traynor, officially welcomed the teams.[51] The implicit government support given to the boycotting of the match was strange in view of the fact that the primary objective of the coalition, as stated in the agreed programme, was 'to restore the unity of Ireland and to safeguard Irish cultural tradition'.[52]

PARTITION AND *HIBERNIA IRREDENTA*

Irish policy towards partition remained, as it had in the days of Fianna Fáil, an exercise in rhetoric. Nothing was done to borrow from the approach in Europe which had led to the creation of the European Coal and Steel Community. The idea of functional integration did not appeal to politicians on either side of the House. The *Hibernia irredenta* mentality prevailed. In that vacuum, the initiative was seized yet again by the restructured IRA. A new campaign began on 12

December 1956 with an attack by 120 'volunteers' on ten different targets in Northern Ireland. 'Operation harvest' resulted in the deaths of six members of the Royal Ulster Constabulary (RUC) and eleven IRA 'volunteers', the introduction of internment in Northern Ireland and in the South and the mobilisation of 13,000 B-Specials.[53] The 'campaign' cost Stormont about £1m between 1956 and 1961 in payment for damages, £10m for increased police and military patrols and untold loss of capital investment. For many Catholics, the effect of the campaign was increased harassment and discrimination.

The deaths of Seán South and Feargal O'Hanlon, during an attack on an RUC barracks at Brookeborough, Co. Fermanagh in January 1957, demonstrated just how strong the mystique of self-styled 'republicanism' in the 1950s was south of the border. Both men enjoyed the status of popular martyrs and were viewed by many as being part of the purer, unsullied 'republican' tradition which was contrasted with politicians caught up in the materialist world of Yeats's 'greasy till'. Denis Donoghue captures that *mentalité* in his memoir, *Warrenpoint*:

> But the IRA thrives upon motives—nationality, Cathleen ni Houlihan, Mother Ireland—to which successive Irish governments, since de Valera came to power in 1932, have given mere lip service, keeping those motives notionally alive on the understanding that no one would act upon them. The rhetoric of Irish politics since 1932 has been a cynical exercise in bad faith.[54]

That was certainly a view held by Feargal O'Hanlon and Seán South. It led them to take up arms, which led in turn to their deaths, while the IRA campaign resulted in the deaths of others. If the size of their respective funerals was an indicator of support for their ideas, then the funeral pictures in *The Irish Press* speak for themselves. Thousands lined the streets of Dublin to pay their last respects as the remains of Seán South passed down O'Connell Street en route to his native Limerick.[55] Morbid curiosity may have brought many out onto the streets, but the crowds also reflected a clear ambivalence in Irish society towards the use of violence.[56]

THE CIA AND IRELAND

Washington had high hopes that the change of government in 1954 would bring about a better relationship between Washington and Dublin. The us ambassador, William H. Taft III, reported to Washington on 29 June 1954 that Cosgrave, the new minister, would be 'pleasant to work with in the future'.[57] Perhaps that was the reason why the CIA moved again to formalise the relationship between the two intelligence services in November 1954. They had been encouraged to do so by Taft on one of his trips to Washington in autumn 1954. Colonel R.J. Callanan had a visit from Daniel De Bardeleben, the CIA representative attached to the us embassy in London. He appreciated 'the circumstances which obliged the Irish authorities to withhold consent' from allowing a CIA agent to be assigned to the us embassy in Dublin in 1951. But the director of the CIA, Allen Dulles, was anxious to establish some measure of liaison between his representative in London and Irish military intelligence in order to get information about local communist subversive activities.

On 25 January 1955 the Department of Defence explained to the secretary of the Department of External Affairs that Callanan had suggested that the Americans write directly to Iveagh House about the matter:

We feel that, for many reasons, which I need not go into now, liaison with CIA would be to our advantage. We think, therefore, that an arrangement on the lines suggested should be approved. Furthermore we are of opinion that if the present proposal is not accepted the previous idea of appointing a CIA representative to the Dublin Embassy will be revived and we are anxious to avoid that happening if we possibly can.

'Minister agrees with D/Defence proposal' is minuted on the letter and dated 25 April 1955. Taft had delivered a letter from Dulles to Iveagh House on 21 March. It requested the 're-establishment of liaison between our respective intelligence services' and added:

In view of the danger which the free world faces from the forces of international communism and its front groups, it seems to me unfortunate that we have at present no mechanism for direct contact between representatives of our respective intelligence services. This thought is reinforced by my recollection of the excellent liaison which we enjoyed during World War II with your intelligence people. The long-term problem posed by communism today is certainly no less great.

Dulles suggested that if the Irish were receptive to the principle of liaison, it could be developed on a periodic basis by trips to Dublin 'which one of my representatives in Europe could make to confer with your intelligence officer'. The resulting exchange of ideas would lead to 'a most profitable association for us both'.[58] It was agreed that the CIA would make contact with Callanan to set up the liaison procedures. A former naval officer called Cram was nominated by De Bardeleben to act as intermediary. Irish approval was sent to Washington via Taft. The Irish ambassador, John Hearne, was so informed. Iveagh House wrote to Frederick Boland in London on 25 August asking him to nominate a member of his staff to handle messages from Callanan to De Bardeleben. Boland replied that his private secretary, Miss Collins, would do so, as she had done in the past for messages passing between Callanan and 'another governmental agency'. It was so arranged and the last file entry indicates that Callanan had sent five letters to the CIA by the autumn via that route.[59]

The clear and unequivocal nature of Irish support for the US policy of containment was emphasised when the Taoiseach toured America in March 1956. Speaking at Georgetown University on 16 March, he said Irish neutrality and the country's non-membership of NATO were the object of uninformed criticism:

In the battle of ideas we are firmly committed . . . our neutrality does not spring from indifference to the outcome [of a war]. And we hope to work with you in your Atlantic partnership and in the wider framework of UNO towards maintaining the peace.

Costello also addressed the House of Representatives on the objectives of Irish foreign policy: 'Communism, in our view, is a creed which confronts the established order of society with the most uncompromising challenge in history, a creed to which we are implacably opposed.'[60] Ireland was not neutral in the cold war.

RETURN OF FIANNA FÁIL

Reviewing the economic situation in January 1957, Costello spoke of the grave concern about the rise in unemployment and the lacklustre performance of the national economy.[61] The adverse trade balance for 1956 was £73.5 million.[62] Fianna Fáil tabled a vote of no confidence in the government at the end of January. Rather than face defeat in the Dáil, Costello sought a dissolution on 4 February and announced that polling day would be on 5 March 1957. In the seven by-elections held during the inter-party government's term, Fianna Fáil had whittled down the government majority, taking two seats from Fine Gael and one from Labour. Going into the election, if the seat left vacant by the death of Tom Derrig was excluded, Fianna Fáil had 67 seats, compared with 65 at the last general election. Fine Gael was reduced from 50 to 48, and the Labour Party had eighteen seats instead of nineteen.[63]

It was to be de Valera's last general election. Seán Lemass, the heir apparent, had produced a major policy document in mid-January. Its contents were a coded rejection of many of Fianna Fáil's sacred economic orthodoxies.[64] In a speech on free trade, he was more explicit: 'The general movement towards a more closely integrated European economy is likely to persist and, sooner or later, the country will have to decide its attitude to it.'[65] This speech was delivered a few weeks before the formal coming into being of the European Economic Community, of which Lemass was an admirer. De Valera also showed interest in the idea of greater European integration when he spoke on 11 February at Queen's University Belfast: 'The aim we should keep in front of us is a federation of states but until then we should do our best to make the United Nations as effective as possible.' [66] However, the Irish election was not fought on the issue of European integration. De Valera, at 75, conducted a vigorous valedictory campaign with brass bands, torchlight processions and monster meetings. Many Irish towns witnessed 'the chief's' last hurrah and his message was simple: coalitions were inherently unstable. They resulted in depression and unemployment and encouraged bargaining for places and power between irresponsible minority groups.[67]

At an eve of election rally, Lemass argued that the country could not afford to have 10 per cent unemployment.[68] Fortunately, he was spared the ignominy of knowing what was to happen in the 1980s and 1990s.

In a poll with 70.6 per cent turnout, Fianna Fáil was returned with a record 78 seats. An abstentionist Sinn Féin took four seats in the election: Monaghan, Kerry South, Longford-Westmeath and Sligo-Leitrim. Three of the seats were at the expense of Fianna Fáil and one was taken from an independent.[69] Seán MacBride failed to be re-elected for Clann na Poblachta, leaving the party with one seat. Fine Gael had 40, Labour 12, Clann na Talmhan three and independents nine.

Although Lemass was not yet leader of Fianna Fáil, he had a considerable say in the selection of the new cabinet members. Seán MacEntee did not return to Finance. He traded ministries with James Ryan—who had proved to have such a safe pair of hands in Health. Seán Moylan, who had lost his seat, was brought into the Senate and made Minister for Agriculture in May. Tragically for Irish agriculture, he died in November 1957, apparently only hours after handing in his resignation over a major policy disagreement.[70] (The veteran Paddy Smith took over the portfolio.) Oscar Traynor was Minister for Justice. There were a few new faces in the cabinet. Kevin Boland, the son of Gerry, was made Minister for Defence on his first day in the Dáil. It was believed at the time that Lemass had told de Valera that he would not serve in another cabinet with the older Boland. De Valera is supposed to have explained to Gerry that, much as he would have liked to have both in the cabinet, it was not appropriate to have a father and son with ministries.[71] Jack Lynch was named Minister for Education and the Gaeltacht. (He held the latter portfolio for only three months.)

The Donegal TD, Neil Blaney, was named Minister for Posts and Telegraphs. He moved to Local Government at the end of the year. Micheál Ó Moráin took over from Lynch as Minister for the Gaeltacht in June 1957. Erskine Childers, who was Minister for Post and Telegraphs between 1951 and 1954, took over the Lands portfolio. These were not the radical changes that Lemass would have wished; but it was a significant step in the direction of modernising Fianna Fáil. The new names were part of a younger generation, kept out of ministerial office by the political longevity of the party's founding fathers. However, it was one of the oldest cabinet ministers who attracted most publicity and controversy in those early months of the new government.

AIKEN AT THE UN

Ireland was admitted to the United Nations in 1955. Frederick Boland, appointed the first Irish head of mission, arrived in time to play an active part in the 1956 session which dealt with the Suez crisis and the revolution in Hungary. He also played an important role in the drafting of Irish policy principles, which Cosgrave announced to the Dáil in July 1956: 1) scrupulous fidelity to the obligations of the charter; 2) avoid becoming associated with particular blocs or groups as far as possible; and 3) do whatever the country could as a member of the United Nations to preserve the Christian civilisation of which Ireland was a part.

Dr Conor Cruise O'Brien, who was a member of the Irish mission staff, has pointed out the tensions inherent in trying to pursue a policy based on those three principles—a tension that was to manifest itself in the 1957 session.[72] Cruise O'Brien saw Aiken as seeking 'with considerable courage and pertinacity' to base his actions, from 1957 to 1961, on the principle that the country should 'try to maintain a position of independence, judging the various questions on which we have to adopt an attitude or cast a vote strictly on their merits, in a just and disinterested way'.[73]

The question of decolonisation, for example, commanded the attention of the Irish delegation throughout those years. Dr Cruise O'Brien spoke on the question of apartheid in the UN Special Political Committee in 1957. He said that the UN General Assembly should tell South Africa in plain language that it was maintaining an indefensible position in its policy of racial discrimination.[74] A strongly worded resolution was carried by the committee. The Irish stance provoked a strong response from a number of Irish people living in South Africa, most notably from an Irish emigrant, Scott-Hayward. He wrote to de Valera on 4 November, beginning 'My dear Chief' and argued: 'Could you visualise a population of twelve million primitive natives, enjoying equal rights and privileges with Ireland's three million whites? How long would Christianity exist under the power of the witch doctor?' While the draft reply from de Valera acknowledged Scott-Hayward's work on behalf of Irish unity, he said of apartheid: 'This is not only contrary to human dignity and a denial of basic human rights but also breeds innumerable offences against Christian charity and Christian justice.'[75]

However, de Valera and Aiken were reluctant to identify publicly with anti-apartheid pressure groups. The Taoiseach received a letter from the American Committee on Africa, signed by Martin Luther King, James A. Pike and Eleanor Roosevelt, on 15 August 1957. It requested him to sign a petition and join a day of world protest against apartheid. After careful consideration, de Valera declined to participate.[76] Such caution may have been a source of disappointment to young Irish diplomats, but it was a significant shift from the time in 1951 when it was considered appropriate for Aiken, together with Lemass and MacEntee, to give the South African high commissioner in London, A.L. Greyer, a private dinner at Dublin's Russell Hotel. Seán MacBride had been even friendlier to the South African government during his time as a minister. He returned a rifle, which had once belonged to a famous Boer scout, that had come into the possession of the Irish government.[77] By the 1960s Irish policy had become more forcefully anti-apartheid.

Besides taking a forward position on apartheid and decolonisation, Irish UN policy under Aiken was never reflexively pro-American. The minister's early independence from Washington was not viewed very favourably by Boland, who had formed a close working relationship with his US counterpart, Henry Cabot Lodge. Traditionally, Ireland had been counted as a safe vote in the 'automatic two-thirds'—that is the two-thirds majority required in the Assembly for a decision on any question of importance. In fact, the counsellor at the US embassy in Dublin, Arthur B. Emmons, had informed the State Department in August that the broad precepts enunciated by Cosgrave would continue to guide the Irish delegation at the twelfth session, 'for they are fundamental to Irish policy'. He also reported that Ireland would again support a resolution 'not to consider' proposals designed to replace the representative of the Republic of China in the General Assembly with a Chinese communist representative or otherwise to seat the Chinese communists.[78] But in 1957 Ireland decided to change its vote on China in favour of *discussion*.

Many years later Boland—who did not support the policy departure—explained that Aiken used to 'get these quirks'. Éamonn Kennedy, his second in command, was also opposed. Conor Cruise O'Brien and MacEntee favoured a shift in policy. Boland spoke of an unnamed bloody fool, not any of the above-mentioned, who said that Irish-Americans would not mind: 'Well, we brought down a ton of bricks', he recalled. The US envoy to the UN, Henry Cabot Lodge, had phoned the State Department on 23 September that 'the FM [Foreign Minister] of Ireland is going nuts'.[79] Washington immediately involved the highly politicised prelate Cardinal Francis Spellman of New York to lobby on behalf of the US. The secretary of state, John Foster Dulles, also tried to involve the Vatican. During an 'informal conversation' with the apostolic delegate to Washington on 26 September 1957, he mentioned US 'doubts concerning recent Irish proposals before the UN and an apparent new trend in Irish foreign policy'. The apostolic delegate promised to communicate those views immediately to the pope.[80]

The outcome of this initiative is not clear. Three days before that meeting and only an hour after the America delegation had been notified about how Ireland was going to vote, Spellman phoned the Irish consul-general in New York: 'Tell Aiken that if he votes for Red China, we'll raise the devil.'[81] Another phone call along the same lines was made by one of the cardinal's secretaries to the Irish permanent delegation. Boland commented that that tactic of involving the cardinal was 'an extreme mistake'. In his view there was no surer way to get Aiken to vote against the US position than to threaten him with a belt of a crozier.[82] When the US ambassador, Scott McLeod, saw both Aiken and de Valera on 2 October, the minister for external affairs was strong in his criticism of US tactics:

Mr Aiken stated he was very disappointed at the cavalier manner in which the US delegation operated when he sent Mr Boland to advise Mr Lodge of his intention to vote for full discussion of the Chinese representation issue. He stated he instructed Mr Boland to tell Mr Lodge that he, Aiken, was available for discussions of this subject. He said he went to some pains to make himself available in the corridors and elsewhere, and related that he actually approached Mr Lodge on one occasion to inquire about the President's health to give Mr Lodge an opportunity to open the question. He stated that, instead of discussing it with him, the department called Mr Hearne in and 'read him off' and on the same day asked Cardinal Spellman to intercede with Mr Aiken to get him to change his vote. He stated that this was not the way that friends discussed mutual differences of opinion, and that he resented the efforts to bring pressure to bear on him through the cardinal. I stated that I knew the Department had outlined its position to Ambassador Hearne, but I doubted very much if an approach had been made to the cardinal in this matter. He assured me that I was in error.[83]

The reaction was dramatic. Two Catholic papers in New York, *The Catholic Times* and the *Brooklyn Tablet*, attacked Ireland. Cardinal Cushing of Boston said: 'The encouragement given this diabolical regime by the Irish delegation at the UN shocked and saddened me and all the clergy and the faithful of the archdiocese of Boston.' It was only with extreme difficulty that Boland managed to persuade Spellman to restore good relations with de Valera.[84] To compound Washington's problem, Aiken also raised that autumn the question of US and Soviet troop reductions in Europe. He told the US ambassador, Scott McLeod, on 9 October 1957 that he had acted out of a fear that war was imminent:

> He thinks that there is a period of at most a few years, and possibly only a few months, before the Soviets will have the minimum capability with atomic weapons to undertake an attack on the United States. He states his proposal was put forward in the UN in an effort to stimulate the United States to take the initiative in the remaining time which it has to attempt to reach some kind of agreement with the Russians to relieve tensions and thereby bring about a wider area of the world which is subject to the regulation of international law.

In the same conversation, Aiken maintained that the 'current development of atomic weapons meant to reasonable men that efforts should be made to achieve the political unity which is necessary to avoid conflict.'[85] Aiken returned to Dublin, where he was forced to face the consequences of his 'draw-back' speech. The US embassy in Dublin had reported to Washington that the proposal would not be pursued by the Irish.[86] Iveagh House had been somewhat embarrassed by the queries it had received from the ambassadors of NATO countries resident in Dublin. Aiken met the relevant envoys and assuaged their anxieties. The Irish were in full retreat on the issue. Both Aiken and de Valera explained to the US ambassador that the proposal had been put forward without any expectation that the Russians would comply. Aiken said that if the Russians withdrew from her satellites in the East, those countries would quickly adopt pro-Western governments. De Valera confessed that he had no intimate knowledge of the military situation in Europe.[87] It appeared as if the Irish government was seeking to abandon that policy proposal as quickly as possible. These lessons were not lost on an Irish government or diplomatic service which rapidly abandoned the 'idealist' approach to foreign policy at the UN.

The IRA campaign continued after Fianna Fáil had returned to power. Internment was reintroduced and about 200 men were held at the Curragh, denying the 'movement' the use of many important 'volunteers'. The gardaí continued to track subversive activity. But there was some let up in cold war tension in Dublin towards the end of the 1950s. The 'godless' Czech soccer team came to Dublin on 5 April 1959 and was beaten by Ireland 2-0; the Minister for Justice, Oscar Traynor, again welcomed the players as president of the FAI.

CHURCH AND STATE

The vigilance of the moral majority in the 1950s was unrelenting. A serious problem recurred when An Tóstal's theatre committee, in 1958, decided to perform two plays, one, 'Bloomsday', a stage adaptation of James Joyce's *Ulysses*, and the other a world première of Seán O'Casey's *The Drums of Father Ned*. It had become known that Archbishop McQuaid did not approve of the selection, but he was not the only one involved in the campaign to stop the two plays being performed. Although the play had not been seen, one group wrote of O'Casey:

> This is the man who recently congratulated Russia on the 40th anniversary of its Revolution and ALL THAT HAS HAPPENED SINCE. All includes Communism, rejection of God and His Church, Torture and Imprisonment of Cardinals, Bishops, priests, nuns and other religious, etc.[88]

The archbishop mobilised opposition to the production of the two plays. He wrote to the Dublin Council of Trade Unions to explain why he had decided to withdraw permission for any religious ceremonies to inaugurate An Tóstal that year. (The organisers had asked the archbishop to open the festival with a votive mass.) The council decided to send a strong letter of protest to the Tóstal committee against the production of plays of an objectionable nature.[89] Changes were requested of O'Casey by the committee but the author decided to withdraw the play.[90] The Tóstal council then asked the theatre festival director to withdraw 'Bloomsday'. *The Irish Times* was outraged by such interference and suggested that the Tóstal committee should submit the programme for the festival the following year in advance to the archbishop. The paper drew the ire of Father Alfred O'Rahilly, who described it as representing the 'outlook of our Protestant, and also perhaps of our agnostic-liberal, fellow-citizens'. *The Irish Times* suffered from 'chronic episcopophagy. It has an obsessional disease of bishop-baiting', he wrote.[91]

On 30 January 1958, the standing committee of the hierarchy wrote to de Valera stating that it had under consideration the 'increase of evil publications' in Ireland and added 'there is widespread concern at the injury which can result to public and private morality' and 'general agreement on the necessity for effective defence of the public interest in the matter'. The bishops requested vigorous application of the law which already provided the police with ample powers. The bishops also recommended that the existing censorship board of five be increased to twenty, that a book be submitted to a group of three members and the decision be by a majority in each case, and that no members of the board had the right of veto.[92] The letter was an ill-judged attack on the integrity of the former Taoiseach and on the bona fides of two members of the censorship board appointed by him. The Minister for Justice, Oscar Traynor, struck a far from conciliatory note when he responded to an enquiry from 'the chief'. He acknowledged that the censorship board had met only three times in over fifteen months. He had been forced to sack the chairman and since then he had been flooded with protests:

This campaign was started off by a public statement by the archbishop of Dublin with reference to the 'foul books' that were on sale in the city and it was spearheaded by the Knights of Columbanus, an organisation in which the two other members of the Board who resigned with Professor Piggott are prominent and of which he himself is almost certainly a member. And I am sure that the campaign would never have even started at all but for the fact His Grace [McQuaid] was not consulted by the former Taoiseach or by me about recent appointments to the Board and was probably annoyed by the fact that I preferred to let Professor Piggott go . . . because he was not doing his duty rather than exceed my authority by removing my predecessor's two nominees who were doing theirs.

Traynor suggested that de Valera ought to 'spike the guns of this type of opposition and to rally the responsible members of the various parties in the Dáil to the support of the institutions of the State so that the hierarchy may be led to see at the outset that this Government and those which preceded it were carrying out their duties faithfully in accordance with the powers conferred on them.' Traynor suggested that de Valera meet Costello to work out a bipartisan approach, and that was done.[93] They met on 10 February 1958. The Department of Justice provided Traynor with a detailed memorandum which concluded that the law was not inadequate. Moreover, it was concluded that official statistics proved that there was no evidence of a decline in sexual morality. The memorandum was discussed at cabinet on 25 February 1958 and it was left to the Taoiseach and the minister for justice to draft a reply to the hierarchy in which all the bishops' suggestions were politely but firmly rejected.[94]

Life in the state for members of the minority churches could not have been easy at times. But there was a swift response by de Valera on at least one occasion when rank prejudice manifested itself. Fethard-on-Sea, a village in County Wexford, made international headlines in the summer of 1957. The wife of a local farmer disappeared from home with her two children, following a row over the religion in which the children were to be brought up. She was Church of Ireland and he was Catholic. Rumours spread that the woman had been induced to leave by Protestant friends. As a consequence, the businesses of local Protestants were boycotted and 'a statement by a Catholic bishop appeared to condone the boycott'.[95] De Valera repudiated the action in the strongest language. Speaking as the head of the government, he said:

I can only say, from what has appeared in public, that I regard this boycott as ill-conceived, ill-considered, and futile for the achievement of the purpose for which it seems to have been intended. . . .[96]

De Valera refused to pander to that pre-ecumenical spirit of provincial bigotry. His years in office had been marked by excellent working relations with the minority churches. As he prepared to step down from politics, de Valera's public contribution was recognised by churchmen from many denominations, who had good reason to respect the role he had played in impeding the growth of political Catholicism.

DE VALERA STEPS DOWN

De Valera resigned as Taoiseach on 17 June 1959 to become the Fianna Fáil candidate for the Presidency. Fine Gael put up Seán MacEoin. The election was held on 18 June. It was also decided to hold a referendum on the same day to pass the Third Amendment to the Constitution Bill, changing the proportional representation system of voting. The first-past-the-post system would have solved Fianna Fáil's electoral worries in the medium term, guaranteeing an overall majority unrivalled by the other political parties. It was a smart move and it almost worked, 453,322 voting for abolition of PR and 486,989 for retention.[97] By contrast, de Valera's presidential election victory was much more convincing: he had a majority of over 120,000.

When the Fianna Fáil parliamentary party met shortly afterwards, Seán Lemass emerged as the new leader. It was a foregone conclusion and the decision was taken without political bloodshed. Certain future party leaders might have had occasion to look back nostalgically at such an idyll of consensus.

De Valera did not leave politics a rich man. He was austere in his personal lifestyle and he expected high standards from members of his party. The 'get rich quick' brigade clambered on board the Fianna Fáil *Bountiful* mainly after his departure, and a mutinous crew some of them proved to be. Todd Andrews, a founder member of Fianna Fáil, speaks harshly in his autobiography of that general decline in standards:

> The decline started when some of his [de Valera] ministers could no longer afford to live on their incomes. Some of them met and associated with a class of people for whom frugality had no attraction. What Dev did not foresee, and would never have approved of, was the growth of a political generation whose rewards are fur coats, big cars, indoor swimming pools, vintage

wines and any other form of ostentation which fashion demands.[98]

De Valera certainly would not have approved of such developments. Land deals and financial scandals there may have been from the 1930s to the 1950s, but it was a time of relative innocence compared to what was to happen in the 1960s, 1970s and 1980s.[99]

Seán O'Faoláin once wrote that de Valera's concept of life was that of a 'dreary Eden'.[100] A dreary Eden may well have been a description of Ireland in 1959 with which many contemporaries would have agreed, but perhaps few would have appreciated the herculean administrative and political struggle necessary to make such a modest advance. Yet for the thousands forced to emigrate during the 1950s clasping only—in the words of Brendan Kennelly—'Brown bag bulging with faded nothings' that decade bore the raddle-mark of failure and despair.

7
Seán Lemass and the 'Rising Tide' of the 1960s

The 1960s have been called the best of decades.[1] There was a certain sense of spring in the air.[2] Lemass spoke of the rising tide lifting all boats; but that had to be achieved by looking with 'cold objectivity on the national assets and the national deficiencies so that we can plan properly together to exploit the one and remedy the other'. He warned that the nation

. . . just cannot afford any woolly thinking, any failure of leadership, any slipshod estimating of possibilities and problems, either in the Dáil, in the government, or in any of the organisations within the state to which important sections of our people look for their guidance.

Despite the obvious economic drawbacks imposed by the country's size, geographical location and island character, the Taoiseach felt that the handicaps could be overcome: 'All that is within our capacity.'[3] Lemass felt that technology could replace teleology. Prosperity would be achieved by the Irish through hard work, greater efficiency and entry 'into Europe'. This straightforward materialistic approach was almost heresy in Ireland—a belief in the attainment of worldly salvation through good works.

The 1960s were to be a time of both radical change and apparent radical change. A jumble of provincial and international images conjure up a decade of social ferment: the founding of RTÉ television in 1961 which produced, among other programmes, 'The Late Late Show'; popular music by groups like the Beatles; the home-grown variety, led by Brendan Bowyer and the Royal Showband, which required large dance-halls to hold the adoring crowds; the relaxation of cinema censorship which allowed the showing of, for example, 'Dr Zhivago' and 'The Graduate'; a new and more militant phase in the Irish women's movement; religious change stimulated by Vatican II and Catholic Church reform; the radical impact of free secondary education; student revolt in the universities; and the growth of the leisure industry, with holidays abroad in the sun. These were some of the images of a decade of optimism. Then, of course, there was the 'trouble' in Northern Ireland which finally insinuated its way into the politics of the South.

On the international stage, Ireland, Denmark, Norway and Britain failed to join the European Economic Community in 1962; there was the Cuban missile crisis of 1962, the cold war and the doctrine of Mutually Assured Destruction (MAD); the birth of the Common Agricultural Policy in 1963 was watched with envy from Ireland; the death of John F. Kennedy in November of the same year; violence and civil war in the Congo; the viciousness of the omnipresent Vietnam war and the growth of the protest movement; the Arab-Israeli 'six-day' war in June 1967; Soviet and Warsaw Pact forces invaded Czechoslovakia in 1968; and US astronauts landed on the moon in the summer of 1969. RTÉ news and television current affairs programmes made such events more proximate and helped remove a false sense of Ireland's remoteness from the maelstrom of world affairs, which had been a feature of the immediate post-war period. This was a decade which began with so much promise and ended, for various international and domestic reasons, in economic and political disarray.

Lemass had made a good start in directing the country along the lines of a planned economy. The First Programme for Economic Expansion, which covered the years 1958–63, bore some resemblance to the post-war ideas of Jean Monnet. In the words of Dr Ken

Whitaker, then secretary of the Department of Finance,

> . . . it was recognised that reliance on a shrinking home market offered no prospect of satisfying Ireland's employment aspirations, and that protectionism, both in agriculture and industry, would have to give way to active competitive participation in a free-trading world.

This new direction, according to the same source, transformed a spirit of 'disillusionment and despondency into hope and confidence.' Dr Whitaker argued that policy became 'more expansionary than was at first envisaged but this was an appropriate Keynesian response at a time when Irish costs were competitive and world trade was buoyant.'[4]

An instinctive Keynesian, Lemass would like to have made radical changes in his first cabinet. The emphasis, he decided for the moment, had to be on continuity. That was the main theme of the *Irish Press* coverage of his takeover.[5] Party members were in need of reassurance. Lemass gave it to them by appealing to the spirit of practical patriotism which was needed to strengthen the economic foundations of the state. He was also careful not to upset the Fianna Fáil hierarchy. Seán MacEntee became Tánaiste and Minister for Health and Social Welfare. Lemass would have preferred James Ryan as Tánaiste, but that would have given offence to the party faithful.[6] Frank Aiken remained in External Affairs, as did Oscar Traynor in Justice. The latter asked, due to ill-health, to be relieved of his post in 1961. He was a major loss. Ryan held the portfolio of Finance and was Lemass's closest colleague in the cabinet. Jack Lynch was given Industry and Commerce and Dr Patrick Hillery took over Education. Erskine Childers was Minister for Post and Telegraphs. Neil Blaney was made Minister for Local Government, and Lemass's son-in-law, Charles J. Haughey, was appointed parliamentary secretary to the Minister for Justice.

Lemass had erred on the side of caution in his selection of ministers. He now had, however, two future Taoisigh in his team. If Lemass did not have the mix of talent that he wanted in his cabinet, he had become Taoiseach at a time when the Irish economy was strengthening. The substantive intellectual battle over the movement of the country away from protectionism had been decided in favour of more open competition and a planned economy. It would be unfair to state that this was a little like reinventing the wheel, but the secretary of the Department of Finance, Whitaker, and Lemass and Ryan had gradually and painstakingly nursed politicians away from the false, womb-like security which economic protectionism had allegedly afforded Irish industry.[7] In 1959 the budget was balanced, according to Jim Ryan, for the first time in ten years. Naturally, the inter-party governments were blamed for the economic ills of the country.[8] Ryan reduced income tax by 6d., increased old age, blind and widows' pensions by 2s. 6d. a week, abolished some entertainment taxes, scaled down import levies on a wide range of goods, and increased state and military service pensions by 6 per cent.[9] If such an economic strategy was to continue, then Ireland had to modernise her economy and find new markets for her improved-quality products. To that end there had been imaginative developments in tourism and travel. Aer Lingus recorded an operating surplus of £500,000 in the half-year ending September 1961. Passenger traffic rose from 22,821 in 1960 to 35,344 in 1961. The transatlantic route was particularly successful.[10] A new industrial complex had been created in the Shannon customs-free area; customs restrictions were lifted on the importation of raw materials for the manufacture of goods in that area. The Shannon Free Airport Development Company (SFADCO) was set up in 1959.[11] Why the IDA could not have handled that particular region was a question whose answer also lay in the political rather than in the economic field.

NEUTRALITY, THE LEMASS DOCTRINE AND 1961 ELECTION

A new Anglo-Irish trade agreement was signed on 13 April 1960. The Irish protectionist position was becoming increasingly untenable in view of the development of the European Free Trade Association (EFTA) and the success of the European Economic Community. Debate on these matters was intense inside the civil service. Ultimately Ireland did not join EFTA. The government subscribed to the General Agreement on Tariffs and Trade (GATT) in December 1967. Ireland found that it could not postpone a decision on applying for membership of the EEC once it had been learned through diplomatic channels in April 1961 that Britain proposed to seek immediate entry. The government decided to send an *aide-mémoire* to the governments of the six member states, informing them of the Irish position.

Lemass told the Dáil, in July 1961, that Ireland would apply for membership of the EEC in the event of the British asking to join the Communities. Concern was expressed in the Dáil over the possible political and military implications of membership.[12] While Lemass was somewhat constrained in his answers in the Dáil, there was no doubt that he had little patience with the idea that Ireland should remain outside NATO. The following can be described as the 'Lemass doctrine'. He was quoted in *The New York Times* in June 1962 as saying:

> We recognise that a military commitment will be an inevitable consequence of our joining the Common Market and ultimately we would be prepared to yield even the technical label of our neutrality. We are prepared to go into this integrated Europe without any reservations as to how far this will take us in the field of foreign policy and defence.[13]

Following Ireland's formal application for membership on 31 July 1961, Dublin learned through diplomatic channels that there were reservations in Brussels about the country's economic and political suitability for membership.[14] Some of the member states— particularly Germany and the Benelux countries—were concerned about the implications of Irish neutrality for the EEC. The Council of Ministers met in Brussels from 25 to 27 September and agreed to open negotiations with the British and the Danes. The Irish were informed that there was need for further discussion. Another exchange of views with Dublin and the Council of Ministers was set for January 1962. Lemass failed to gain entry for Ireland in 1962 because of the intransigence of Charles de Gaulle.[15]

In the meantime, the government had to face a deteriorating political situation, widespread industrial unrest, a strike of power workers, and a crisis over the safety of Irish UN peace-keeping forces in the Congo. Ireland had responded to a UN request and had sent two battalions to the Congo in 1960 to participate in a peace-keeping mission where an attempt was being made to set up the mineral rich Katanga (now the province of Shaba) as an independent state. Conor Cruise O'Brien had been seconded from the Department of External Affairs by Dag Hammarskjold to act as UN representative in Elizabethville and in New York.[16] General Seán McKeown was appointed commander of UN forces in the Congo. This was to be the first of many UN peace-keeping missions. Nine Irish troops died in an ambush at Niemba on 8 November 1960.

Notwithstanding the difficulties, Lemass used the old de Valera ploy of taking advantage of a sense of crisis in the country to call a snap election for 4 October 1961. He made the announcement in the Dáil on 8 September and allowed the minimum time for campaigning. Lemass gave as his reason for doing this the application for membership of the Common Market.[17] *The Irish Times* regarded the campaign as being one of the dullest on record.[18]

Neither the gravity of the international situation nor the quest for membership of the EEC dominated the campaign speeches. One of the main issues was the question of compulsory Irish in the schools. The colourful leader of Fine Gael, James Dillon, stated the case eloquently for not making a pupil who had failed Irish fail the entire exam, even if he/she had passed the other subjects. This eminently sensible idea was described by a Fianna Fáil minister, Michael Hilliard, as 'an act of national treachery which brought Ireland back a century in the national advance'.[19]

Dillon was at pains to point out that Fine Gael was the party of free enterprise—a message at variance with the ideas for social reform articulated by the son of John A. Costello, Declan, who had been a TD since 1951. The Labour Party, under Brendan Corish, campaigned against the 'conservative' Fine Gael and Fianna Fáil parties. Opposition to coalition was restated and there was a call for an expansion of the public sector. Fianna Fáil ran on its economic record and on the EEC issue.

The feelings of many in the early 1960s was summed up by the writer Seán Dunne's father:

> 'Dev is the man,' my father said. It was de Valera's simple rural and nationalist vision that my father shared, but it was Lemass's pragmatism that he most admired. No matter how poor we might be, my father always believed it would be worse if Fianna Fáil was not in power. In this way, it seemed as if his world was a child born in the warm womb of Fianna Fáil and anyone who felt otherwise was an outsider.[20]

Yet, when the votes were counted, Dev's successor had suffered a serious rebuff from the electorate. He was denied an overall majority.

Fianna Fáil had 43.8 per cent of the vote and 70 seats, a loss of eight seats and a drop of 4.5 per cent of the vote. Fine Gael had done well, pushing up its percentage of the vote from 26.6 per cent in 1957 to 32 per cent in 1961. That gave the party a gain of seven seats. The Labour Party improved its share of the vote from 9.1 per cent in 1957 to 11.6 per cent; the gain in seats was to push the party's strength in the Dáil up from 12 to 16 (this included the Ceann Comhairle, who was returned automatically). Among the new faces in the Dáil on the Labour side were Steve Coughlan (East Limerick), a former member of Clann na Poblachta, and Michael Mullen, a leading member of the Irish Transport and General Workers' Union, the largest trade union in the country. Labour's Denis Larkin had lost his seat in Dublin North. Overall, the extra votes had been picked up by the Labour Party in Munster. The returns in Dublin had been disappointing.[21]

Fianna Fáil was three seats short of a majority. There were two Clann na Talmhan, two National Progressive Democrats and one Clann na Poblachta member.[22] (MacBride failed again to win a Dáil seat.) Lemass was returned to power by the votes of two independents, while three others abstained. That government survived until 1965 with the support of an independent. It might be said in retrospect that Lemass had to rely too quickly upon a younger generation of Fianna Fáil politicians who had not served a sufficient apprenticeship at the middle management, that is, the junior minister, level, but he did have real talent on the front bench. However, he had no women in his ministerial team, which showed that his progressive thinking was in need of further development.

Lemass was a good manager, but he was not a particularly good personnel manager. He lacked de Valera's infinite patience and father confessor skills, which kept backbenchers happy and feeling as if they were an important part of the team and not just lobby fodder. Lemass was too busy to baby-sit his party members.[23]

That made him enemies all too easily. Fianna Fáil was never the 'one, true church' which it was often depicted as being—a single river rushing towards the sea. An example of feelings of real hostility were expressed in a letter from Dr Con Ward to Seán MacEntee in 1962. The former was contemplating a political comeback. Regarded as one of the great losses to Fianna Fáil in Irish politics, Ward had been forced to resign from public life in 1946. He wrote that he had come into possession of a letter sent from 13 Upper Mount Street (Fianna Fáil headquarters) stating that his candidature would be opposed by the national executive. He told MacEntee: 'An Taoiseach was fully aware of the intrigue to which this letter put the finishing touch.' Ward claimed that he had 'uncovered the duplicity of Lemass to a degree that leaves no doubt as to his real standard of conduct'. He added:

> A former Taoiseach could truthfully have said that 'his standards were not high enough' for the position he occupies. It is hard to realise that you are Vice President of an organisation which has become so shockingly corrupt. I presume that you have to either play up, or give up. . . . My personal opinion is that the slick methods of which Lemass is now master will bring about his downfall and the Wards will shed no tears if and when his unworthy standards bring about his downfall as Taoiseach.[24]

Perhaps it might be unfair to conclude that, to have received such a letter, MacEntee must have shared some of Ward's antagonism towards Lemass. At least, Ward knew that MacEntee was disposed to be critical of the Taoiseach. These tensions were not known to many people. Fianna Fáil had a skill for keeping all major frictions and disagreements within the family.

Lemass was to visit Washington in 1963—just a few weeks before the assassination of President John F. Kennedy. He was strongly pro-Atlanticist in his thinking. He had had an opportunity to show Irish warmth towards the United States when the American president had made a triumphal visit to Ireland in June 1963. It was a time of political crisis for Lemass, with the government surviving defeat in the Dáil by one vote on the Finance Bill. Kennedy helped take people's minds off the mundane. The CIA, in a briefing document prepared for Kennedy before his visit, was told that Ireland was in a period of transition. This was, in the view of the CIA, due to two factors: the appearance of the post-revolution group of younger, more vigorous politicians and, secondly, the growing awareness that Ireland's destiny had to be realised within a larger European context. The 'repudiation of political extremism in the 1961 election', and the abandonment of the activities of the IRA, had made politics, 'always conservative, even more moderate in recent years'. All political parties, it was argued, adhered to the principles of non-military alignment except under EEC membership; abolition of the border between north and south;

and strong anti-communism.

The abandonment of Ireland's 'insular and parochial outlook' was due in great measure to the influence of Seán Lemass, according to a memorandum prepared for Kennedy by the CIA. In a profile of the Taoiseach, he was described as looking younger than his age:

> His managerial temperament has been described as the antithesis of de Valera's professional type. His ability and qualities of leadership are respected. Intelligent and shrewd, he is an efficient and hardworking administrator. While he has an engaging personality and friendly manner, he is said to be capable of great bitterness toward those who have offended him. According to some reports, he is not averse to using political patronage to get things done, and there were rumours that he was involved in black-market operations during World War II. He is an inveterate gambler and as a result has at times been involved in serious financial difficulties.

The suggestion that Lemass was personally involved in black-market operations during the war is preposterous.

At 81, de Valera was profiled as being a devout Roman Catholic who had always lived a disciplined and somewhat austere life: 'One of his strongest characteristics is the conviction of his own rightness; he appears unable to brook criticism of his judgment. Yet he has charm and personal magnetism, enjoys a joke, and finds great pleasure in his family.' Seán MacEntee's day-to-day political activities were said to 'resemble that of a ward heeler'. (This is defined in an American political dictionary as 'hack, hanger on, hangdog politician'.) His tendency to make ill-considered statements to score an immediate advantage had at times embarrassed his colleagues. The CIA stressed that MacEntee's political career had been marked by 'acrimonious controversy and by the use of caustic epithets for his opponents', things which had not endeared him to some of his associates.

The CIA reviewed Ireland's foreign policy position for the US president. Under Lemass, the country had shown a growing interest in participating in international affairs and in international organisations: 'While not in the least neutral to the ideological issues involved in the East-West struggle, Ireland pursues today an independent course in international affairs'. The CIA reminded

Kennedy that at the height of the Cuban missile crisis, 'the Irish were most cooperative with the United States Government and searched all Bloc air traffic transiting Shannon'. When the Irish had expressed a desire—sometime in 1963 presumably—to suspend the search, they had 'continued it at our request'.

The CIA saw Ireland as a very friendly, pro-American country which the US president could visit with little risk to his safety, except from overenthusiastic crowds:

> . . . the friendly and exuberant crowds who will wish to see and hear the President may create a security problem. The Irish look upon President Kennedy's visit as a triumphal homecoming for one of their own and as a great compliment being paid them by a world leader. The Irish police are relatively inexperienced in crowd control and the crowds will be far larger than any with which they have previously had to cope. The police may underestimate the problems involved and the manpower needed to protect the Presidential party from such overfriendliness.

The CIA got that right. Those summer days in 1963 were magical for Ireland.

Kennedy was profiled in *The Irish Press* as the *first citizen of the free world*; the same paper carried a main headline on 26 June, the day of his arrival: KENNEDY WELCOMED HOME.[25] When he visited distant relatives in County Wexford, *The Irish Press* used as its main headline: A DAY AMONG HIS OWN.

These were days of national celebration as Kennedy moved around the country drawing huge crowds. JFK personified the brash, self-image of the new Fianna Fáil: he was young and handsome; he was wealthy and almost self-made; he was a conservative social reformer who favoured free enterprise; but, above all, he was a successful Irish-American politician who had outmanoeuvered the WASP opposition in the United States and had made it to the White House. Kennedy was proof that the Irish were made of the 'right stuff'.[26] In his speeches, he brilliantly identified with his audiences and elevated the role of Ireland in world history in a manner long associated with the rhetoric of Irish-American ethnic politics. For example, Kennedy said on 28 June, while addressing a joint session of the Oireachtas:

All the world owes much to the little 'five feet high' nations. The greatest art of the world was the work of little nations. The most enduring literature of the world came from little nations. The heroic deeds that thrill humanity through generations were the deeds of little nations fighting for their freedom. And, oh, yes, the salvation of mankind came through a little nation.

Kennedy was surrounded by people everywhere he went. One of his aides records the anecdote of the nun who left her convent to see Kennedy on the pretext of buying a pair of shoes. When she went to a newspaper office to get a picture of the US president, the assistant commented about the visit: 'Isn't it great, sister?' She replied: 'Marvellous. Not a prayer said in four days.'

Kennedy, who was to be assassinated in Dallas on 22 November, caused great problems for his secret service men. He insisted on wading into the over friendly crowds in Dublin, Wexford, Cork, Galway and Limerick. He was genuinely touched and later wrote to de Valera that the visit had been 'one of the moving experiences of my life'.

After the visit, it was possible to believe that the Lemass tide would raise all boats.

RTÉ: AN AGENT OF SOCIAL CHANGE

The Kennedy visit made all the greater impact nationally because it was the first opportunity for the relatively newly established Irish television station, Radio Telefís Éireann, to show its skills. The coverage was exceptional. On New Year's Eve 1961, the new station had gone on the air. The President, Éamon de Valera, welcomed the new development which, on the one hand, could build up the character of a whole people but, on the other, could lead, through demoralisation, to decadence and dissolution. On the same opening night, Lemass spoke without any reference to any such fears. He stressed the central importance of television in opening out Ireland to the world.[27]

Michael Hilliard had brought the legislation through the Oireachtas. The Broadcasting Act, according to Brian Farrell, was 'clearly modelled on the Charter of the BBC'.[28] Muiris Mac Conghail, a former RTÉ senior executive, accepted that the Hilliard Act had been 'cast in the liberal vein'.[29] The popular presenter of 'This is Your Life,' Eamonn Andrews, was appointed chairperson of the RTÉ Authority. An American, Edward Roth, was the station's first director general.

The number of home-produced television programes in 1963 was 1,044 hours, compared with 1,178 imported hours. In 1964 it was 1,253 and 1,093 respectively. A range of important news, current affairs and chat shows, the most powerful being Gay Byrne's 'The Late, Late Show', were produced. Politicians were obliged to make the transfer to the world of the sound-bite and instant comment. This was not a world in which Lemass personally felt very comfortable. But the younger members of his cabinet were more televisual and adaptive; Jack Lynch, Charles Haughey, and Donogh O'Malley were among the new breed. There were 336,939 radio licences in the country in 1963 and 201,095 television licences. In 1964, there were 292,899 radio licences and 258,988 television licences.[30] By 1969 the figures were 160,888 and 432,735 respectively.[31] This was to rise to 781,795 television licences in 1989.[32] However, gone were the submissive radio days, and Irish television quickly established a reputation for independent news and current affairs coverage. The years between 1961 and 1966, marred by industrial unrest and strikes, may account for the barbed statement made by Seán Lemass on 12 October 1966 when he said that 'Radio Telefís Éireann was set up by legislation as an instrument of public policy, and as such is responsible to the government'. He stated that

> . . . the government have overall responsibility for its conduct, and especially the obligation to ensure that its programmes do not offend against the public interest or conflict with national policy as defined in legislation. To this extent the government rejected the view that Radio Telefís Éireann should be, either generally or in regard to its current affairs programmes, completely independent of government supervision.[33]

Looking back at those years as Taoiseach, Lemass was to regret bitterly Ireland's failed attempt to join the European Economic Community. So much had hinged upon the success of the Irish application. But the prevailing spirit of optimism in the early 1960s—marked by a buoyant economy and reverse emigration—masked temporarily such a major domestic and foreign policy setback. So much might have been different.

CULTURE AND LITERATURE IN A CHANGING WORLD

Yet so much was achieved in the cultural and artistic fields. The Irish

Film Finance Corporation was set up by the government in 1960 to help provide finance that would induce foreign film-makers to work in Ireland. Ardmore Film Studios had been opened in 1958. Córas Tráchtála (The Irish Export Board) set up the Kilkenny Design Workshop in 1963. The Council of Design was established in the same year and immediately called for the modernising of Irish cultural institutions. Light was allowed into the National Gallery at last when major renovations were carried out. The new Abbey Theatre, designed by Michael Scott, was opened in 1966. Cork got a new opera house a year later. Project 67, eventually becoming the Project Arts Centre, was also set up that year. The Arts Council, under Father Donal O'Sullivan, played an important role in such developments, but its early part in encouraging young Irish painters was not something it would wish to have recalled in too much detail. The Minister for Finance in 1967, Charles Haughey, displayed his patronage for the arts by raising the Arts Council's grant from £40,000 to £60,000.[34]

In the visual arts, the Rosc international art exhibition of 1967/68 was particularly important. Irish artists, inexplicably, were excluded from exhibiting. Robert Ballagh was among the relative newcomers to the art world. He quickly established himself as one of the leading young Irish artists of his generation.[35] Ballagh represented a group of independent artists who refused to bow to the conventions of many of the more settled members of the profession. John Behan, the sculptor, was another figure who represented that generation.[36] They were to benefit from a measure brought in by Charles Haughey in his 1969 budget which freed painters, sculptors, writers and composers who were living in Ireland from income tax on all earnings derived from creative work judged to be of cultural merit. By 1972, 338 artists had been granted tax exemptions. But what Behan and Ballagh wanted were 'more opportunities for the artist to use his talent'. 'It was a nice gesture', John Behan said.[37] Talent, and not mammon, was the real reason for the successes in the visual arts in Ireland in the 1960s and 1970s.[38]

There were a number of important figures in the field of music in the 1960s, but Seán Ó Riada was, for Louis Marcus, 'the outstanding artistic figure in the Ireland of the sixties'. He praised his flair and assurance, his discriminating regard for tradition, his ability to fuse the native and the international in a synthesis that promised real development. Marcus regarded Ó Riada as typifying 'those qualities of dynamism and national awakening for which Ireland so admired itself at that time'. He was an artist to whom 'the aged mind of Europe and its current *Zeitgeist* were . . . matters of urgent reality rather than intellectual curiosity.'[39] Ó Riada's music characterised all that was best in the Ireland of the 1960s. His work with Ceoltóirí Chualann and his influence on the musicians of a younger generation has been remembered with critical affection by his peers. Ó Riada gained a wide audience for his music through his work in radio and television. The soundtracks for the films 'Mise Éire' and 'Saoirse' were to evoke in a dramatic way the birth of the Irish state. The distinctive style of The Chieftains owed much to Ó Riada. Seán Ó Riada managed to concentrate so much artistic energy and achievement in his tragically short lifetime (1931–71); he developed a sense of excellence because, as Seán Mac Réamoinn has written, he 'knew what he was up against'.[40]

The world of theatre and literature was also well served in the 1960s. Brian Friel's *Philadelphia, Here I Come!* was produced for the first time in 1964. Its mordant, yet witty, exploration of the themes of emigration from rural Ireland and father-son relations drew wide audiences. Gar Private had the confidence to say about the father and the life that he was leaving:

> What the hell do you care about him. Screwballs! Skinflint! Skittery Face! You're free of him and his stinking bloody shop. And tomorrow morning, boy, when that little ole plane gets up into the skies, you'll stick your head out the window and spit down on the lot of them![41]

This summed up the impatience of a younger generation who actually had a choice about their future. John B. Keane's *The Field*, written the same year, treated of the destructive and jealous attachment to the land. That emotion took on a new meaning and context in the years of rapacious speculation and development of the 1960s; Peter Sheridan's film version of the play in the early 1990s brought the Kerry author deserved international acclaim. The main character, 'The Bull' McCabe, used words which had great significance for a contemporary Irish audience:

> I'm a fair man and I want nothing but what's mine! I won't be

wronged in my own village, in my own country by an imported landgrabber. The sweat I've lost won't be given for nothing. A total stranger has come and he wants to bury my sweat and blood in concrete. It's ag'in God an' man an' I was never the person to bow the head when trouble came and no man is goin' to do me out of my natural-born rights.[42]

Keane wrote sensitively in *Sive* (1959) about the plight of a young woman seeking her independence in the male-dominated world of arranged marriages. Ten years later another play, *Big Maggie*, continued his exploration of the 'human dilemmas that confront ordinary people in times of change'.[43]

By way of contrast, Aidan Higgins, in *Langrishe, Go Down* (1966), examined the theme of 'the big house' and genteel decay. James Plunkett, who had brought out a collection of short stories, *The Trusting and the Maimed*, in 1955, published *Strumpet City* in 1969. There he examined the struggle for trade union rights in the William Martin Murphy-dominated Dublin of 1913. His vivid depiction of working-class slums in the capital had relevance to the Ireland of the 1960s. Richard Power's *The Hungry Grass* revealed the inner world of an anguished Irish priest. John Broderick's *The Pilgrimage*, a novel that courageously raised the question of homosexuality, was banned in 1961. John McGahern published *The Barracks* in 1963 and *The Dark* in 1965. Poetry collections were published by Austin Clarke, John Montague, Patrick Kavanagh, Seamus Heaney, Thomas Kinsella, Richard Murphy, Seán Ó Tuama, Máirtín Ó Direáin, and Seán Ó Ríordáin.

But despite the advances in the arts, it was not a decade of unimpeded and inevitable progress. John McGahern's book, *The Dark*, was seized by customs in June 1965. It was a sensitive and evocative account of a boy's growth to adolescence which made reference to masturbation. In the pre-Roddy Doyle days of the mid-1960s, great offence was taken at the appearance of the word *fuck* on the first page of the novel. In October 1965 McGahern returned to his primary school teaching post in Clontarf, Dublin, only to be told that he had been dismissed by the clerical manager. No explanation was ever given to him for the action of his employers. The protagonist in McGahern's novel *The Leavetaking* faces a similar dilemma when he is told to resign by the headmaster as a consequence of his having married 'outside' the Catholic Church. The young teacher refuses to resign:

But how, *a mháistir*, can you stand before a class and teach Catechism?

'While living in sin?' I put it for him and he dumbly nodded his head back into his hands. 'That's no trouble, *a mháistir*. You know that as well as I do. All you need to teach is knowledge and skill. If I refused to teach it on a point of principle, then I'd have to resign, but I don't refuse. It's written down in black and white in the official—Notes for Teachers—on history that the cultivation of patriotism is more important than the truth. So when we teach history Britain is always the big black beast, Ireland is the poor daughter struggling while being raped, when most of us know it's a lot more complicated than that. And yet we teach it.'

Later in an interview, John McGahern recorded that it was his view that the archbishop of Dublin was directly responsible for his sacking: McQuaid had an 'absolute obsession with what he called impure books'. Despite being a year in arrears with his union dues, McGahern tried to get the INTO to take up his case. When John McGahern met the entire INTO executive, one unidentified male member said to him:

If it was just the banned book, then we might have been able to do something for you, though it would have been difficult. But with marrying this woman, you're an impossible case. . . . By the way, McGahern, what entered your head to go and marry a foreign woman when there's hundreds of thousands of Irish women going around with their tongues out for a husband.

This was a reference to the fact that the author had not married in a Catholic church. 'The whole thing that I really resented when I was young', he said in an interview many years after the event, 'was that you had to go into exile if you were an Irish writer, like Joyce and Beckett.' John McGahern felt that censorship was 'just a symptom of something that was much more dangerous and inhuman and, I would say, certainly fascistic in the real sense of the word'.[44]

However, the climate of tolerance improved for the arts about two years after the McGahern case. It must have precipitated the sense of urgency for legislative change. In fact, the Minister for Justice, Brian Lenihan, had begun to introduce wide-ranging changes as early as 1964. He replaced members of the appeal board in 1964 and nominated more liberal people. Certificates for limited viewing of certain films could be given under the new terms of reference. The age criteria were also introduced. In the past that approach had been rejected on the grounds that to say a film was for over eighteens would only have made it more attractive. The other age categories— twelves and fifteens—were impossible to police.

Under constant encouragement from people like the professor of English at Maynooth, Father Peter Connolly, and the TCD Senator Owen Sheehy Skeffington, Lenihan brought in legislation in 1967 to provide for the unbanning of books after twelve years. Brian Lenihan told the writer that this legislation was introduced against the strongest advice from Peter Berry, the secretary of the Department of Justice. The latter represented the mind-set of an earlier age and he was astonished when the legislation had a virtual trouble-free passage through the Dáil. The result was the release of 5,000 titles, and re-banning has since proved the exception.[45] James Joyce's *Ulysses* was not numbered in the above job lot. It was never, in fact, banned, but it was usually available only by special order in Irish bookshops in the early 1960s.[46]

Edna O'Brien was an author who was read widely by young people in Ireland in the 1960s. *The Country Girls* (1960), *The Lonely Girl* (1962), *Girls in their Married Bliss* (1963) and *August is a Wicked Month* (1965) were all censored. But that only encouraged their clandestine circulation. When a prominent Irish cleric stated in public that he liked the novels of Edna O'Brien, his provincial promptly received a handwritten letter from the archbishop of Dublin registering his opposition to the holding of such sentiments by a religious. The superior took no action other than to pass on a copy of McQuaid's script to the person in question.

Edna O'Brien had lived in London since 1959. In an interview she agreed that her books *The Country Girls* and *Girls in their Married Bliss* had disturbed people.

> I think so, yes. I think so because it was about the covert and the not-so-covert, rather foolish sexuality of two young girls. It was their romance and their sexuality because Baba was sex and Cait was romance. I admitted their sexuality, also unhappy married life—a young girl yearning and, indeed, eventually having sex with a much older married man.

In her writing she undermined the 'pedestal view' of women as being 'devoid of sexual desire, maternal, devout, attractive. Quite a handful!' Edna O'Brien showed 'two Irish girls full of yearnings and desire. Wicked!'[47] But to the generation which covertly read Edna O'Brien in places like boarding school dormitories, she provided proof that healthy Irish adolescents—male and female—were not deviants if they felt strong physical desire.

The cherished madonna image of Irish womanhood was behind the headlines which followed the innocent statement by a woman on 'The Late, Late Show' that she could not remember the colour of her nightdress on her honeymoon since she may not have been wearing one. The otherwise humanitarian Irish bishop, Dr Tom Ryan of Clonfert, phoned the television station 'in fairness to Christian morality' to protest at the item.[48] It is believed that he had been upset by the adverse reaction of his elderly housekeeper to the television item. This distinguished man ought to have known better. It was the age of instant communication. The following day, his remarks were the subject of unwanted lead headlines and the controversy rolled on and on. The actress Jayne Mansfield was also a victim of censorship in April 1967. The local parish priest, Monsignor Lane, opposed her appearance at the Mount Brandon Hotel, Tralee. He warned the men and women, the boys and girls of the town 'to dissociate themselves from this attempt to besmirch the name of our town for the sake of filthy gain'. Mansfield had her appearance cancelled. She countered by saying that she was the sole supporter of her five children and was a good Catholic.

Edna O'Brien had already explored the psyche, the libido and the desires of the Irish woman. That desire was stimulated, in a way which would have had an earlier generation of Irish bishops in cardiac arrest, by the popular music of the 1960s. The showband craze is another of the most enduring images of the energy and optimism of those years. The Beatles came to Dublin in 1963 and played to an adoring audience at the Adelphi cinema; imitation bands mushroomed in Ireland. The indigenous leisure industry gave the country Brendan Bowyer and the Royals, Joe Dolan and the Drifters, 'spit on me' Dickie Rock and the Miami Showband and many other idols who played to crowds of sometimes over three thousand in the newly constructed aircraft hanger-like ballrooms which mushroomed throughout the country in the early 1960s. In the boom time, which peaked in the mid-1960s, there were about 450 ballrooms of the new variety around the country. With the opening of Cloudland near Roosky, Co. Roscommon, Albert and Jim Reynolds went on to control an entertainment empire. (Albert Reynolds also went into the petfood business and into politics and succeeded equally well on both fronts.) There were soon other rival empires. Television coverage of the showband scene brought the images of mass hysteria in monochrome to many Irish homes. The Irish bishops could not have foreseen such a development in the 1930s when they successfully lobbied for the legislation which encouraged free enterprise to flourish in the leisure industry. The magazine *Spotlight* traced the movements of the 'stars', and an Irish top ten was first broadcast by radio on 2 October 1962.[49] Participation in the Eurovision song contest meant instant stardom. Whatever this phenomenon presaged, it was no longer the Ireland of the 1930s.

In social terms, what did this phenomenon reflect? Firstly, the showband craze offered young people, very often from deprived backgrounds, the illusive hope of moving from rags to riches. That happened in a few cases and the music industry had its survivors. But a majority of the musicians helped make profits for others. 'Bands were ripped off', according to the chaplain to the industry, Father Brian D'Arcy. Musicians worked incredibly long hours and travelled enormous distances to fulfil engagements. Most ultimately returned, if they were lucky, to the day job. Secondly, showbands proved to be a source of liberation for women. Eileen Reid, complete with wedding dress and beehive hairstyle, sang with the Cadets. Eileen Kelly, Tina and the trio, Maxi, Dick and Twink, provided a different type of role model for Irish women. They were competing and surviving in a 'man's world'. Irish women were no longer chaperoned to local parish dances. Thousands travelled long distances to the larger ballrooms. That was a source of liberation. Thirdly, there was little that was original in the showband music; it was formulaic and derivative. The more commercial side of the American country and western culture found its way into the remotest corners of the country. The showband industry was a metaphor and a model for the 'take-off' of Irish industry. The message was brash and clear—unfettered free enterprise was the path to modernisation.

THE CATHOLIC CHURCH: CONSERVATISM, CONTINUITY AND CHANGE

Paradoxically, the social teaching of the Catholic Church in the 1960s had begun to question seriously the free enterprise model of development which enjoyed so much favour in Lemass's Ireland. John XXIII (28 October 1958–3 June 1963) published his first social encyclical, *Mater et magistra*, on 15 May 1961 which called upon the richer nations to help the poorer. He emphasised the social obligations of property. The right to private possession of material goods was 'admittedly a natural one'. But the encyclical went on (43) that 'in the objective order established by God, the right to property cannot stand in the way of the axiomatic principles that "the goods which were created by God for all men should flow to all alike, according to the principles of justice and charity."' John XXIII reasserted the views of his predecessor on the use of material goods, that 'the right of every man to use these for his own sustenance is prior to every other economic right, even that of private property'. This point was developed by Pope Paul VI (1963–78) in his encyclical *Populorum Progressio* (26 March 1967): 'Private property does not constitute for anyone an absolute and unconditional right. . . .' (23)

Sections from *Populorum Progressio* were quoted in the Irish bishops' pastoral, *The Work of Justice*, in 1977. It was singularly ironic that a church which had thrown its ideological weight behind the movement to defeat social democracy and the extension of state power in key sectors of the economy up to the end of the 1950s now found it necessary to readjust its position significantly to bring Irish Catholic social teaching into line with papal teaching.

Cardinal William Conway, who had been appointed archbishop of Armagh in September 1963, affirmed in a speech in 1966 that the state should allow the maximum of freedom that was compatible with the common good. He felt that the application of that principle differed with the character of the society in question and noted that to reduce the state to the role it had played in the eighteenth century would produce chaos. But the experience in the interwar years in Europe had suggested to many people that there was a 'close connection between increased state control of the economy and totalitarianism'. While Cardinal Conway felt that it might be some time before 'we can fully measure the effect on human liberty and initiative of increasing central control . . . nevertheless, I think it is true to say that people understand this problem more clearly now than they did 20 years ago, and that some of the fears which were widely held at that time now appear to have been exaggerated.'[50] That may have been an indirect admission of failure of judgment on the part of the hierarchy in the mother and child crisis. However, it is certainly true that appointments to the hierarchy in the 1960s did not fear the state in the way that Archbishop McQuaid had done. Bishop Peter Birch of Ossory had set up social service centres in his diocese. A number of other members of the hierarchy laid stress on the new social teaching of the church.

Changes in the leadership of the Irish hierarchy provide only a partial explanation of what was happening in the Irish church in the 1960s. The Second Vatican Council (11 October 1962–8 December 1965) had a major impact on the way in which many members viewed the church, the relationship between clergy and laity, the question of religious freedom and church and state. The Irish hierarchy did not play a particularly innovative role at Vatican II. They could have drawn on a number of young theologians for expert advice, but they chose to play safe. Archbishop McQuaid took a predictably conservative line at the various sessions.[51] Returning from the Vatican Council in 1965, McQuaid told a congregation in Dublin's Pro-Cathedral that 'one could not but feel that the Holy Ghost had guided our deliberations'. He went on to assure those who might have been worried by 'much talk' of changes to come: 'Allow me to reassure you. No change will worry the tranquillity of your Christian lives. . . .'[52] This was quintessential McQuaid. It was not that he opposed change; the Holy Ghost had guided the decisions of the Council and the pope would instruct the members of the One True Church how to put the decisions into effect. Therefore, the tranquillity of the lives of Christians would not be disturbed in any way.

But that was not so. Churchmen and women had contributed to the new dialogue in Irish society. Magazines run by religious and diocesan clergy made an impact. *Studies, Herder Correspondence,*[53] *The Furrow* and *Doctrine and Life* were among the most influential. But the monthly *The Word* reached a wide popular audience and had an impact under its innovative founding editor, Brother Paul Hurley. *Christus Rex* and the *Irish Theological Quarterly* appealed to a limited audience, but all reflected a more open approach to the role of the Catholic Church in the modern world. Although vestiges of outmoded thinking towards other churches were in evidence, the ecumenical movement advanced significantly in the 1960s. The training of seminarians changed very much for the better. At the same time, the number of vocations dropped consistently from 1,375 in 1965 to 322 in 1989.[54] Vocations to orders of brothers had almost collapsed; 1980, the year following the papal visit, was an exception, with vocations up 20 per cent. But that was not sustained.

The problems created by falling vocations in the church in the 1960s were compounded by the number of clergy and nuns who were returning to the lay state. Figures are difficult to find for the 1960s, but the numbers were significant.

In response to the challenge of Vatican II, the Irish church modernised its structures to some extent. Commissions for Justice and Peace, the Laity, Emigrants and Liturgy were established. The Catholic Press and Information Office was set up. The Catholic Communications Institute of Ireland, under Father Joseph Dunn, was founded. 'Radharc' (Look) was to become one of RTÉ's longest running documentary programmes. It was directed by Joe Dunn, who was ably supported by Desmond Forristal, Tom Stack, Dermod McCarthy, Peter Lemass and Billy Fitzgerald. The priest programme-makers tackled a variety of topics, including the first film shot in an Irish prison, 'The Young Offender' (1963). 'Radharc' made films about devotional topics, but Joe Dunn laid emphasis on the social gospel, as in programmes like 'Honesty at the Fair' (1963), 'Down and Out in Dublin' (1964), 'The Boat Train to Euston' (1965) and 'Smuggling and Smugglers' (1965). The style of investigation was gentle, perhaps naïve by the standards of the 1990s, but it took courage to make such programmes. The archbishop of Dublin was supportive of the use of the new technology and gave the venture his cautious blessing and financial support. When the 'Radharc' team wished to travel to Africa to make a programme, Joe Dunn wrote to the archbishop on 2 April 1965 suggesting a number of reasons why the trip should be undertaken 'apart from the thrill of seeing real lions and tigers'. McQuaid replied on 5 April:

> I accept, in principle, the proposal of an African trip. You do not say who is to go. No tigers in Africa. And you may leave out the 'perhaps' in your suggestion that the trip could reasonably perhaps be made in the holidays.

'Radharc' went to Africa in 1965 and the team continued to travel and make films between the 1970s and 1990s.

The Conference of Major Religious Superiors also formed part of the Catholic infrastructure, together with the Irish Missionary Union. The setting up in 1973 of the Catholic development organisation, Trócaire, meaning mercy, helped heighten sensitivity in the country towards the Third World and place such issues as famine and other disasters on the domestic political agenda. At least 25 per cent of Trócaire's budget was spent on development education. The coordination of the workings of some of the above bodies was not so well worked out in practice. There was, however, an energy for reform and for responding to the changing pastoral needs of a church which was becoming increasingly urban.

Under Lemass, the government sought to keep a critical distance from the Catholic Church, but that was not always possible. However, he told Michael Mills in 1969, after he had retired from office, that he 'never had the slightest problem' with the Catholic Church as a pressure group. He could not recollect any occasion when the church had tried to influence him in a decision affecting government policy. Lemass recalled that members of the hierarchy had come to him once or twice to express concern, 'mainly in the context of the appointment of individuals in whom they had not much confidence, but never to the extent of pressing for a change.' When Lemass had been in doubt about the reaction of the church to the Adoption Bill (1964) and the Succession Bill (1965), he had gone along to discuss them with members of the hierarchy, 'but this was merely to clarify my own mind'.[55] Still, it was not quite as simple as that.

Cardinal Conway led the Irish church with caution and sensitivity in the context of the changing church-state relationship. The lessons of the 1950s were fresh in everyone's memory. The decision by the three major parties to set up an informal committee on the constitution would not have been viewed with apprehension by the hierarchy.[56] It recommended changes in article 3 which began 'Pending the re-integration of the national territory. . . .' Removing the irredentist sentiments, the proposed new wording read as follows: 'The Irish nation hereby proclaims its firm will that its territory be re-united in harmony and brotherly affection between all Irishmen.' Article 41.3 stated that 'no law shall be enacted providing for the grant of a dissolution of marriage'. The committee stated that 'it could be argued' that that was 'coercive'. It was 'unnecessarily harsh and rigid and could, in our view, be regarded as being at variance with the accepted principles of religious liberty as declared at the Vatican Council and elsewhere'. An alternative wording was proposed, in keeping with that thinking. Article 44 referred to the 'special position of the Catholic Church'. The committee felt that there was no doubt about the fact that 'these provisions give offence to non-Catholics and are a useful weapon in the hands of those who are anxious to emphasise the differences between North and South'. It was felt that the decisions of Vatican II had a bearing on the subject:

> It is clearly to be inferred from these documents, and the comments made on them by competent persons, that the Catholic Church does not seek any special recognition or privilege as compared with other religions and that her primary interest is to see that all citizens enjoy equal freedom in the practice of their religion whatever it may be.

There was general political consensus in favour of changing article 44 by the end of the 1960s. 'I personally would not shed a tear if the relevant sub-section of Article 44 were to disappear', Cardinal Conway said in September 1969. When the hierarchy met in Maynooth in October, a statement was issued afterwards agreeing 'that the recent statement by Cardinal Conway represented the bishops' views'.[57]

By late 1972 all-party agreement had been secured to amend the constitution and remove 'the special position' clause and the recognition of other 'churches' by name. The poll was just over 50 per cent. There was an 84 per cent majority in favour of change[58] (721,003 votes in favour and 133,430 against).[59] The outcome of both these referenda should not have been an occasion to draw conclusions about radical changes having taken place in Irish society. The original article 44 formula was simply an anomaly in post-Vatican II Ireland. *The Report of the Committee on the Constitution* had also concluded that article 41 on divorce ought to have been changed, but that would have required a Copernican change in the thinking of the Irish hierarchy and an acceptance of a North American model of church–state relations. If there was ever a favourable episcopal attitude towards changing the constitution in the 1960s and early 1970s, it had evaporated by the 1980s.

An alert government might have taken permanent warning from the united episcopal response to the publication of the encyclical *Humanae Vitae* (Of human life), with its strong reaffirmation of past papal condemnations of every form of artificial birth control. The text appeared in Irish newspapers on 30 July 1968. One leading Catholic gynaecologist in Dublin reacted obediently: 'The thing is settled; now that Rome has spoken that is the end of it. Now it is up to us to obey what the Pope has said.'[60] At a press conference in Dublin, Archbishop McQuaid said that the encyclical had affirmed the moral law with 'great firmness and immense compassion' and it was a reaffirmation that he very deeply welcomed. He was confident that it would find an immediate renewal of loyalty to the church by the priests and people in his care. These views were echoed by the bishop of Down and Connor, William Philbin, who felt that the event was not news; the church had simply restated the traditional position: 'Inherent in the conjugal act, there is the stipulation that nothing be done to destroy its unitive character between man and woman, and its procreative character.' He felt enormous sympathy for people in difficult positions, he said; the remedy was restraint 'and the grace of God will help people to be restrained at certain times'. Cardinal Conway and other members of the hierarchy also restated their acceptance of the papal ruling on birth control.[61] At the same press conference, the professor of moral and dogmatic theology and canon law at St Patrick's College, Maynooth, P.F. Cremin, suggested that, on the question of overpopulation, we had been talking about it for more than a hundred years—ever since the days of Malthus, in fact. And, while we were talking about it, a nuclear war might solve it overnight. 'It may sound melodramatic,' Dr Cremin said, 'but I know the Old Testament and the God of the Old Testament.'[62]

Yet there was anger at the decision and genuine distress among loyal Catholics who had used contraception in good faith. A UCC professor, Father James Good, reacted to press reports of what the encyclical contained on the night before it was published. He called the encyclical a 'major tragedy' and added: 'I have no doubt that the document will be rejected by the majority of Catholic theologians and by Catholic lay people.'[63] Many lay people were grateful to Father Good for his forthright comments. A Dublin gynaecologist, Karl Mullen, said that in his experience 40 per cent of married couples were practising methods of contraception other than rhythm, and that the safe period was only 60 to 70 per cent successful.[64] In 1967, according to an Irish Family Planning Association source, there were 12,000 women on the pill in Ireland. The demand for contraceptives in the capital was reflected in the establishment of the Irish Family Planning Association in 1969. This was followed by the setting up of Family Planning Services in 1974 and the Dublin Well Woman Centre in 1978. The Irish Women's Liberation Movement held a protest on 22 May 1971 against the law banning the importation of contraceptives. They went on a much publicised train trip to Belfast to purchase contraceptives and openly brought them in through Connolly station, Dublin. It pointed out the absurdity of the law which ultimately forced change on a reluctant Dáil Éireann by virtue of a court decision.

The publication of *Humanae Vitae* was a moment of silent crisis for many sexually active people in Ireland. The moral and psychological dilemmas that post-1968 Catholic society faced were captured very well by the English novelist David Lodge's *How Far Can You Go?* which was published in 1978.

In the 1960s it seems that many Irish people did not consider *Humanae Vitae* to be a resigning matter. They simply chose to ignore the official church teaching and use 'artificial means' of birth control. But, for some, it meant that their consciences forced them to leave the church. For others, loyalty to church teaching was of paramount importance. Whether this made for happy marriages or not remains to be documented.[65] But whatever the objective merits or defects of *Humanae Vitae*, the encyclical did challenge the laity to think for themselves and become, as a consequence, more independent of hierarchical structures. While there was strong evidence of clerical compassion and understanding on the question of birth control, the handling of the contraception controversy emphasised the transparent pastoral inadequacies of a male-dominated, celibate church.

HOUSING CRISIS AND DEVELOPMENT WITHOUT PLANNING

The question of birth control was not merely of academic importance to people living in overcrowded conditions in working-class Dublin. In the capital a points system was in operation for housing allocation. The more children a family had, the higher it was placed on the waiting list. There were 7,199 registered applications for housing accommodation on the corporation lists; of these 4,279 consisted of families of three people and under and 2,920 of families of four people and over. There was a concentration of effort to provide flats for many in the centre city. Plans were also in train to build on land to the north of the city, at Edenmore West where it was planned to build 4,000 dwellings on 550 acres and 60 houses at Raheny.[66] However, the city manager, T. O'Mahony, reported that in 1960/61 vacancies had provided 1,260 dwellings. The following year the figure was 856 dwellings and that would be reduced to 700 in 1962/63. The figures for the completion of new dwellings in those years were 277, 395 and 698 respectively. He recalled that since 1948/49, 18,158 new dwellings had been built under the Housing of the Working Classes Act, and 8,758 financed by way of loans under the Small Dwellings Acquisition Acts. A further 10,465 families had got new tenancies as a result of net vacancies. That made a total of 37,421 families rehoused during that period.

O'Mahony's recalling of the corporation's record could not mask the fact that there were only 1,035 dwellings under construction in 1962. There were over 9,000 applicants for housing, a majority of whom the city medical officer did not consider to be in immediate need of housing. The medical officer's estimate was that the effective waiting list was 4,018. That total included 1,036 families living in very overcrowded conditions as sub-tenants in corporation houses. The estimated number of dwellings needed to provide for the backlog was 3,000. The city manager felt that it could be provided in two and a half years.[67]

The housing report of the Dublin city council for 1963 records the death of four people killed when condemned houses collapsed in Bolton Street (2 June) and Fenian Street (11 June). The deaths resulted in many calls to the corporation from families concerned with the safety of their dwellings. At a special meeting of the Labour Party on 17 June 1963, Frank Cluskey TD put down a motion to cancel all bookings for the Mansion House round room and supper room in order to make them available for the housing of people who had been forced to evacuate dangerous buildings. The motion was withdrawn when it was agreed that the lord mayor and city manager would contact the Department of Defence, the Red Cross and school authorities with a view to obtaining emergency accommodation.[68]

A delegation of the Dublin corporation visited Paris, Copenhagen and Stockholm in 1964 to study housing projects at the suggestion of the Minister for Local Government, Neil Blaney. The intention was to examine industrialised building methods to speed up the building of corporation houses and flats. Upon their return, a meeting was held on 17 April 1964, at which it was agreed that an additional 1,000 dwellings a year for three years would be required to supplement the corporation's programme. It was also agreed that an additional 3,000 system-built houses could be provided for on a separate new site or sites.[69] Arising out of that continental visit, the minister gave the go-ahead for the building of 3,000 dwellings at Ballymun. Blaney, with the agreement of government, had nominated the National Building Agency to manage the contract. All materials to be used in the project were to be of Irish manufacture in so far as was practicable. Blaney proposed to have a contract negotiated as soon as possible with a consortium of building companies from Ireland, Britain and France.[70] He wrote to the city manager on 28 January 1965 detailing plans for the scheme. A special meeting of the Housing Committee was held the next day and it was agreed that the Minister for Local Government should authorise the National Building Agency Ltd to enter into a contract in the sum of £9,190,808 for the housing estate and £3,401,000 for certain desirable additions.[71]

Ballymun was opened in the late 1960s. The total number of units was 2,814. There were seven 15-storey blocks, nineteen 8-storey blocks and ten 4-storey blocks. In accordance with the terms of the Housing Act 1966, the corporation estimated that its accumulated housing need on 1 July 1967 was 8,518 and the prospective need up to 1971 was 11,040, a total of 19,558. By the end of the 1960s, building stretched out to Coolock/Kilmore on the north side and towards the Dublin mountains to the south of the city. Similar 'developments' had taken place in Cork, Limerick, Galway and other cities and towns. This approach to solving the housing question had a very high social and economic cost. It was short-term and short-sighted.

The capital city, unable to cope with the housing crisis, had been deformed by a boom in property speculation which replaced landmark buildings with ugly office blocks. The Theatre Royal, home of the Royalettes, Tommy Dando, Mickser Reid, Jimmy O'Dea, Noel Purcell and the best international stars, went under the wrecking ball in 1962.[72] The Capitol Cinema, known once as La Scala, where, ironically, Fianna Fáil had held its inaugural meeting in 1926, was also demolished and with it the neighbouring Palace Bar and Metropole cinema. The Queen's Theatre, Pearse Street, which had been home to the Abbey, was also torn down. Molesworth Street was gutted. The ESB, the national electricity company, pulled down 18-28 Lower Fitzwilliam Street to make way for a new office block in the face of the strongest opposition from the Georgian Society, Seán Keating, Micheál MacLiammóir and other members of the artistic community. An angry editorial writer in *The Irish Times* commented at the time: 'Venice indeed! How long would our demolition squads allow her to queen it in the Adriatic. And in Pisa, the Leaning Tower would have come down years ago. The authorities would have taken advice from experts that it was impossible to straighten it.'[73] Another landmark in vandalism was the destruction of 45 St Stephen's Green and part of Hume Street in 1970. An occupation of the site failed to save that part of the Irish heritage. In a speech on 11 March 1970, the Minister for Local Government, Kevin Boland, referred to the 'belted earls' who were supporting the six-month protest.

Dublin, in particular, had been defaced and deformed within a decade. Some of the ugliest buildings in Europe had been erected in what once had been an elegant city. All that had been in the name of *progress* and *development*. The past was not supposed to include Georgian Dublin or any other remnants of British culture. However, the 'modernisation' of Dublin had been good for some people. A number of new entrepreneurs had done very nicely out of the building boom and they had every reason to feel grateful. Fianna Fáil began to accept large donations and out of that was born Taca. The original idea was to bring together 500 large subscribers. The money would be invested for a year and then transferred into the Fianna Fáil election account. 'What Taca established,' Kevin Boland wrote,

was that the financial support of the entrepreneurial class was very substantial and had become vital and this was a very serious development indeed. The danger seen by a few in the early 1930s had materialised and it seemed to be only a matter of time until this financial dependence would manifest itself in the matter of policy to such an extent that the people would realise there had been a definite shift to the right in Fianna Fáil's political position.[74]

That shift was very evident as the decade progressed. Ordinary people witnessed a boom in property speculation while, at the same time, the housing crisis in the capital and in other Irish cities appeared to worsen. The spectacle of conspicuous consumption side by side with real poverty was a contradiction that could not be sustained. While poor people waited for ever on housing lists, the countryside faced 'horizon pollution' with the building of monuments to the bad taste of the *nouveau riche*. For the unhappy wife in Paul Durcan's poem, the new-found wealth of her haulier-husband was manifest in architectural kitsch:

> We live in a Georgian, Tudor, Classical Greek,
> Moorish, Spanish Hacienda, Regency Period,
> Ranch House, Three-Storey Bungalow
> On the edge of the edge of town:
> 'Poor Joe's Row'—
> The townspeople call it,
> But our real address is 'Ronald Reagan Hill'—
> That vulturous-looking man in the States.[75]

While the countryside was sprouting 'Georgian, Tudor, Classical Greek, Moorish, Spanish Hacienda, Regency Period, Ranch-House[s]', the state continued to fail to provide adequate housing and halting sites for the Travellers. The total number in that community was 6,591 in 1960, or 1,198 families (average size 5.5). Yet the *Report of the Travelling People Review Body* (1983) presented a poor rate of progress in providing halting sites and other facilities for this minority community. There was also evidence, from other sources, of considerable hostility towards the Travellers from elements in the settled community. Sections of Irish society were not noted for their openness or tolerance towards the poor, the disadvantaged and those who were simply different.

Out of a sense of social concern provoked by the contradictions between growing affluence and deepening poverty in Irish society, many members of the clergy became directly involved in the question of housing, much to the annoyance of a number of cabinet ministers. The Dublin Housing Action Committee had been formed. In University College Dublin, a history student, John Feeney, had founded *Logos*, a left-wing Christian group which was very active on the housing issue. A number of clergymen were also prominent. The Dominican, Father Fergal O'Connor, had set up Ally in the 1960s to provide homes for expectant single parents. Indirectly, that had brought to light certain anomalies in the allocation of public housing for single parents. His confrére, the prior of St Dominic's, Father Austin Flannery, had played an important role as editor of *Doctrine and Life*. He had also been a strong intellectual influence on prominent lay people. As the organiser of a television programme, 'Outlook', in the late 1960s, he had focused attention on the housing question. Father Michael Sweetman sj had, on one of these programmes, shared a platform with the veteran communist, Michael O'Riordan. For such transgressions, Father Flannery was attacked in 1968 for his 'abuse of privilege' by the Minister for Local Government, Kevin Boland, who also described him as being a 'so-called cleric'. The Minister for Finance, Charles Haughey, stated in the Dáil, in an aside, that Father Flannery was a 'gullible priest'. The Dominican ignored the Haughey aside and replied to Boland that he presumed the minister was not 'casting doubt on the validity of my ordination'. He presumed that Boland's remarks were 'merely a misuse of English'. Father Flannery said: 'My own intention and my sole intention as a Christian and as a priest is to speak on behalf of people who are in need.' The *Evening Herald* on 8 May carried the headline 'I DID NOT LIE'. This was Father Flannery's answer to the accusations that he was guilty of 'lies, falsehoods and deliberate distortions'. The episode helped gain considerable publicity for the poorly housed of the capital. This was an age of relative innocence. Following the appearance of Michael O'Riordan on the television programme, Father Flannery recalled how on every other occasion when one of his programmes was going out, a special branch detective was assigned to sit in the control box.[76] Politicians did not like the clergy to interfere in social issues. The more conventional type of priest who remained in the sacristy was preferred. Some of the clergy in the 1960s even talked of re-evaluating their role in education.

THE EDUCATIONAL REVOLUTION

The aspiration in the 1916 proclamation of 'cherish(ing) all the children of the nation equally' had become less a policy goal than a shibboleth in Irish politics. The OECD report, *Investment in Education*, was published in 1966. Professor Patrick Lynch had been appointed by

Patrick Hillery to conduct detailed research in the field of education. Some very disturbing findings emerged when pupil participation rates in schooling were studied. According to John Coolahan, the report analysed a cohort of 55,000 pupils and found the following:

> It was estimated that 17,500 of them left full-time education at primary level and 11,000 of these without having obtained the Primary School Certificate. Of the 37,500 who went to second level, 13,500, or 36 per cent, left without sitting for a junior post-primary certificate. The drop-out rate was most striking in the vocational sector where, from an entrance group of 16,000 to the two-year course, 7,000, or 44 per cent, left without having sat for the Group Certificate. . . . Of the approximate 10,000 who sat for the Leaving Certificate examination, only 2,000 entered university. The huge drop-out rates occurred at the transition from primary to post-primary and before sitting for the post-primary junior cycle examination.

The report also showed a marked association between social and economic status and participation in full-time education. Students aged 15 to 19 whose parents were farmers, professionals and senior employees were shown to have a four or five times greater chance of participating in post-primary education than those belonging to parents from a skilled, semi-skilled or unskilled working-class background. The students from the first group (children of farmers, professionals and senior employees) made up 85 per cent of university students.[77]

Father Liam Ryan, a member in the 1960s of the Sociology Department, University College Cork, showed just how far the country had yet to go when he wrote a study of early school-leavers in what was known as a 'tough spot', a large housing estate, ironically termed Parkland, in an Irish city. Aged between 14 and 16, the teenagers interviewed clearly showed that 'all the children of the nation' were not being cherished 'equally' fifty years after the 1916 Rising. The article also showed how little planning and help had been given to people moving for the first time into the corporation estates from either the inner city or from the countryside in the 1950s and 1960s. Before the credit unions were established, one resident explained:

The money-lenders were there in their thousands: well, thousands is a bit too many, but they were nearly there in their hundreds, and many still remain today. It was fierce. You could be short of money—I knew one woman who borrowed £5; until she paid back that £5 in one piece she had to pay £2 a month interest. She was paying for one and a half years and had paid back £30 before she cleared the debt.

Father Ryan's description of the ecology of poverty and deprivation is telling: 'Drink, family quarrels, bad management, sickness and unemployment, mental and physical difficulties, each one of these alone is sufficient to create endless problems for the families that experience them. When they are found in combination or all together, the resulting misery is unbelievable.' The only priority was to get a job as quickly as possible and to become a bread-winner. Few ever got to secondary school.

When asked about secondary school, one of the boys replied that if you were from Parkland you might just as well be in a football team for five years as be in secondary school: 'You just haven't a hope. A "black" has a better chance of getting a job in this city than a fellow from up here, although my brother says there are plenty of jobs if you go the right way about them.' Father Ryan concluded that Parkland, and places like it, were subversive of people's sense of dignity and self-worth. Such estates were the creation, partly of the people who lived there, but more directly of 'officialdom', 'with its policy that urban populations need only roads and houses'. Cities are for people, Father Ryan wrote, and 'people need playgrounds and swimming-pools, halls and community centres, and something to remind them that they are more important than motor cars or traffic lights or office blocks or supermarkets'. The 'Parklands' mushroomed because of a 'lack of vision in the past'.[78]

The writer Seán Dunne provides a very gentle and sensitive account of the life of a young boy growing up with his widowed father on a corporation estate in Waterford. It complements Liam Ryan's unremittingly grey image of 'Parkland'. What hope was there for the children of people who lived on the periphery of the town and on the periphery of society? They could be made to feel great shame and humiliation by their dependence upon the caprice of the agent of the state. There was the occasion when Dunne went with a woman, who was more his surrogate mother than housekeeper, to the dispensary in Lady Lane, Waterford, to see the doctor. When the doctor had finished examining the boy, Tessie asked him for 'one more thing'—bandages for her varicose veins. The doctor almost reduced her to tears with 'Your leg? What's wrong with your leg? You're supposed to get those bandages yourself. The appointment was made only for the young fellow. Are you on the same medical card?' In the end, he gave her the prescription for the bandages, but told her that it was the last time: 'There's nothing wrong with your leg that plenty of walking wouldn't cure and there's any amount of people who need bandages more urgently than you do.' As they walked from the room, a woman waiting outside asked in a whisper about the mood of the doctor: 'Like a fecking dog' came the reply as the woman put her eyes to heaven, blessed herself and said: 'Jesus, Mary and Joseph.' Outside Tessie told Sean: 'That fella's a dog. . . . A proper dog.'[79]

The capacity to humiliate was the prerogative of the professional classes. Much the same arrogance and condescension which the doctor exhibited towards Tessie went into the 'planning' and building of the urban sprawls in many Irish cities in the 1960s. Dublin's northside saw the wanton destruction of very beautiful countryside in the building of large estates. Old trees, which could have been used by the 'planners', were ruthlessly pulled down to make room for uniform housing. What would poorer people want with aesthetics? The idea of hearing birds sing and watch nature develop in an urban context was something which applied to the well-to-do suburb of Foxrock, in Dublin, and to Rochestown Road, in Cork, but was not for the people of Coolock (Dublin) or Gurranabraher (Cork). Delinquency was the only thing planned for in most large Irish urban areas in the 1960s.

However, in a limited number of cases, education provided the route to upward social mobility in the 1960s. As has been mentioned earlier, that decade witnessed a succession of young and talented ministers with responsibility for the Education portfolio. Jack Lynch, who was the minister from 1957 to 1959, handed over to Dr Patrick Hillery and the latter remained in that post until 1965. George Colley was minister for a year, but on 16 November 1966 Donogh O'Malley took the post, which he held until his death on 10 March 1968. The portfolio was then assumed by Brian Lenihan and held by him until after the 1969 general election. Lemass and his successor as Taoiseach, Jack Lynch, were both very committed to reforming and modernising the Irish educational system. The former had outlined his thinking on future Irish educational policy in the Dáil in 1959: 'The aim of government policy is to bring about a situation in which all children will continue their schooling until they are at least fifteen years of age.'[80]

Dr Patrick Hillery made a major policy speech on 20 May 1963. It contained an outline of many of the reforms which were introduced in the following decade. These included the extension of educational opportunity, the establishment of comprehensive schools and regional technical colleges, access by students of vocational schools to all public examinations and the promotion of higher technical education.

The first three comprehensive schools were opened in 1966. Of the 300,000 enrolled in full-time post-primary courses in 1980, over 25,000 were enrolled in comprehensive and community schools. Generous capitation grants for school building were also available in the early 1960s. The Local Authorities (Educational Scholarship, Amendment) Act of 1961 was improved and the state contributed to the scheme for the first time. Two-thirds of the scholarships went to second-level students and the remainder to university students. With state participation, the number of scholarships rose from 2,609 in 1960 to 9,614 in 1966. In the decade from 1963, total government expenditure on education rose from £25 million to £144 million, an increase from 3.4 per cent to 6.29 per cent of the GNP.[81] Lemass fully supported these developments.

The most dramatic development in the educational sector in the 1960s was when Donogh O'Malley announced the introduction of free post-primary education. The announcement, made on 11 September 1966, may have taken cabinet colleagues by surprise, but it is almost certain that the O'Malley speech was a ploy used often by Lemass to anticipate opposition and get a radical shift in policy approved by acclamation. This pre-empted interminable cabinet discussion and blocking tactics by the Department of Finance. Educational planning in the 1960s had been moving inexorably in that direction.[82] The main features of the new scheme were outlined in a number of important articles.[83]

The increase in participation at post-primary school level was as follows: 1957/1958, 96,056; 1962/1963, 121,394; 1966/1967, 148,883; 1967/1968, 118,557; in 1969/1970 the figure was 144,425, an increase of

10,834 over the previous year. By 1974, the number had reached 239,000 pupils at second level. Radical plans to change the structure of higher education in Ireland were introduced by Donogh O'Malley in April 1967. Running counter to the advice of the *Report of the Commission on Higher Education*, the minister proposed to merge TCD and UCD. On 6 July 1968 the government announced that the National University of Ireland would be dissolved and UCC and UCG would become independent universities. The plan, which came to nought, had at least the enduring virtue of provoking self-interested cerebral activity within the NUI system.

A number of other important decisions were taken around that time. St Patrick's College, Maynooth had opened its doors to lay students in 1966. The Catholic hierarchy removed the ban on Catholic students attending Trinity College in 1970. The Higher Education Authority (HEA) was set up in 1968 to deal with planning and finance in higher education; and the National Council for Educational Awards (NCEA) was established in 1972 with responsibility for the non-university third-level sector.

In 1968, UCD experienced a 'gentle revolution'. Demands ranged from the securing of better library facilities and less crowded classroom conditions to a wide-ranging debate on reasons for the continuation of social inequality in second- and third-level education. The following tables demonstrate the continuation of that inequality into the 1980s.

Social class differences in educational participation, 1960–61 and 1980–81

A: Social group participation rates in full-time education, by age

	1960/61		1980/81*
	14yrs	15–19 yrs	5–19 yrs
Farmers	69.4	27.7	45.7
Professional, employers, managers	73.6	46.5	76.4
Other non-manual†	63.4	28.0	50.1
Skilled manual	52.6	17.3	47.7
Semi/Unskilled manual	43.4	9.8	30.5
All	64.0	29.8	55.9

B: 1980/81 estimates. Percentage of entrants reaching second-level

	Leaving Certificate		Third-level	
	Boys	Girls	Boys	Girls
Upper non-manual	97	100	50	35
Lower non-manual	59	71	26	16
Skilled manual	32	74	10	11
Semi/Unskilled manual	16	41	4	7
All	50	69	21	16
Both sexes		59		19

Sources: *Investment in Education* 1965, Tables 6.27, 6.28, pp. 150–51; Breen 1984b, Table 2, p. 105.

*   Authors' estimates based on unpublished data from the 1971 and 1981 Censuses.

†   These figures combine groups C and D of the *Investment in Education* tables. The class categories in panel A are derived from the Census; in panel B they are based on the Hall Jones scale with farmers allocated according to Breen (1984c, p. 24).

Source: Richard Breen et al. (eds), *Understanding Contemporary Ireland: State, Class and Development in the Republic of Ireland* (Dublin: Gill and Macmillan, 1990), p. 132.

Breen and his colleagues draw three main conclusions from the literature. First, little headway had been made in lessening class disparities in education. Second, public expenditure on post-primary and third-level education is regressive; that is, the benefits of higher expenditure at third level go to pupils of better off families. Third, the introduction of free secondary education in 1967 was a 'blunt instrument'. Instead of reversing the disparities between the classes, it provided windfall gains to 'those parents of pupils who would have paid fees to send their children to secondary schools but who, under the scheme, receive this education free of charge.' (Breen et al., p.134.)

A study of the entrants to higher education in 1980, according to Professor Ó Buachalla, showed noticeable social and regional disparities in access and participation rates and a marked advantage in transfer rates to higher education enjoyed by students of the private fee-paying secondary schools:

Among the 1980 entrants, the children of the four upper social groups, representing 16 pc of the total population, constituted 46 pc of the entrants; skilled and semi-skilled workers represented 27 pc of the population, yet their children formed only 13.6 pc of the entrants.[84]

It would take a long time for all the children of the nation to be cherished equally.

WOMEN IN IRISH SOCIETY

The educational system was enabling women to look through and, in some cases, break through the 'glass ceiling' in the 1960s. The political parties certainly did not lead the way.[85] Examining the gender balance in successive Irish cabinets since the foundation of the state in 1922 reveals that not a single woman served as a minister or a junior minister until 1979. Maurice Manning points out that 'in the 57 years since Independence, 15 of the 26 counties have never once elected a woman TD, and in fact the Irish electorate has had very few women presented to it as candidates over the years.' He has recorded that, excluding the 24 successful Dáil candidates, there have been only 65 other women candidates over 19 general elections—and more than half of those had stood for small parties or as independents. Maurice Manning also shows that there was a total of six women elected to the Senate between 1922 and 1936. In the period from 1937 to 1977, 19 women had been elected to the Senate.[86] The record of women in local elections was quite poor. In 1934, according to Manning, 13 women were elected to 9 of the 27 councils: 10 were Fianna Fáil; 2 were Fine Gael and 1 was Labour. By 1977 there was no significant improvement in the record.[87]

Politics was not a very easy profession for women to break into in Ireland. There were six women TDs after the 1977 election. All came from political families. Eileen Desmond, who had been elected first to the Dáil in 1965, was the widow of the Labour TD, Dan Desmond, who had held a seat in Mid-Cork since 1948. Máire Geoghegan-Quinn was the daughter of the Fianna Fáil TD for Galway West, John Geoghegan. Upon his death she won his seat in a by-election in 1975. Both women were the first to hold ministerial office since the foundation of the state. Maire Geoghegan-Quinn was appointed Minister for the Gaeltacht in 1979. Eileen Desmond was made Minister for Health and

Social Welfare in 1981, becoming the first women to hold a senior ministerial post. Given the relative hostility towards the idea of women being allowed to play a role in Irish political life, it is hardly surprising that those elected to the Dáil in the later 1970s came from political families. Eileen Lemass (Fianna Fáil) was the widow of Noel Lemass, whose father had been Taoiseach. Síle de Valera was a scion of that distinguished Irish political family. Myra Barry was the daughter of the Fine Gael TD Dick Barry; she won a stunning victory at a by-election in Cork North-East in 1979. Brigid Hogan O'Higgins (Fine Gael), who was TD for Galway South from 1957 to 1969, was the daughter of the former Cumann na nGaedheal Minister for Agriculture, Patrick Hogan. Celia Lynch, who was also defeated in 1977, was the widow of the Fianna Fáil TD James Lynch; she had held a seat in Dublin since 1954. Joan Burke, who was a Fine Gael TD between 1964 and 1981, was the widow of James Burke. In the 1980s that pattern was to change completely. Women without any family connections in politics were elected to the Dáil, among them Mary Harney, Mary Flaherty and Alice Glenn. A dramatic breakthrough was made in the 1992 election when 20 women TDs were returned.

However, in the 1970s and 1980s women's issues were placed very much to the fore in Ireland. The civil rights movement in the United States and in Northern Ireland provided new role models and acted as a catalyst for the women's movement. The debate within the Catholic Church on the role of women had further underlined their second-class status in Irish society and pointed to the need to challenge the traditional teaching on birth control, married priesthood and women priests. The marriage bar in the teaching profession, in the public service and in local authorities and public health boards was an affront to the principles of natural justice. Sexism in the Irish educational system helped sustain many women's low self-image and too modest career expectations. Ireland lived in a time-warp on that particular question. Yet the trade union movement pressed for the Irish government to ratify Convention 100 of the International Labour Organisation, which provided for equal pay. The government faced the inevitable and conceded on 31 July 1973. The *Report of the Commission on the Status of Women 1972* gave substance to many of the criticisms of sexism and open discrimination against women which had been made vigorously from the latter part of the 1960s. Women journalists in *The Irish Press*, *The Irish Times* and other newspapers had helped raise issues and provoke debate. Various women's groups were founded in the late 1960s. The Irish Women's Liberation Movement was founded in 1970.[88] The issues raised were, in the main, pay equality, proper housing, availability of contraception, improved social welfare, access to justice, and greater educational opportunities.

The various groups had to work from a very low base. In 1971 working women in Ireland represented 27.3 per cent (287,867) of the Irish workforce of 1.1 million.[89] Bias against women participating in larger numbers in a labour force with high unemployment was quite consistent with the dominant image of the woman as housewife which had been manifest since the origins of the Irish state. In 1933 Éamon de Valera had told a meeting of the Fianna Fáil parliamentary party that it was necessary to have 'good labour conditions and that there should be no child labour and that as far as possible there should be less woman labour—that if doles were to be given it would be far more advantageous and less deteriorating to give the dole to women and to give all the work possible to men.'[90]

The same mind-set can be found in a 1953 Department of Education memorandum on the rules requiring women teachers to retire on marriage: 'the care and direction of a home, and the rearing of a family constitute a whole-time assignment sufficient to tax the strength and energy of the normal woman'. The usually enlightened Minister for Education, Seán Moylan, did not feel that a married woman could be expected to reach a high standard of efficiency in both spheres of her activity. The memorandum further stated: 'There is bound to be comment and a degree of unhealthy curiosity in mixed schools of boys and girls and even in schools for girls only, during the later months of pregnancy of married women teachers.' The Minister for Finance agreed that it was 'desirable in principle' for women teachers to retire on marriage.[91]

It would have been very difficult for a politician in the late 1960s to articulate such ideas in quite so frank a fashion.[92] Progress was very slow but consistent. The Council for the Status of Women was set up in 1973. The Anti-Discrimination (Pay) Act 1974 was a major advance. This established the right of men and women employed on like work by the same employer or an associated employer to equal pay. The Employment Equality Act was passed in 1977 and the Employment Equality Agency was set up in the same year. The Act prohibits discrimination on grounds of sex or marital status in recruitment for employment, in training, in conditions of employment or in the provision of opportunities for promotion. The Act also prohibits indirect discrimination. Progress was slow.

INDUSTRIAL UNREST, POLITICAL CONFLICT AND THE 1965 ELECTION

The economic 'take-off which Lemass had hoped for in the mid-1960s did not materialise as planned. The First Programme of Economic Expansion had covered the period 1959–1963. This was followed by a more ambitious plan in the Second Programme, covering the years 1964–1970. But so much of the programme was predicated upon Ireland's membership of the European Economic Community by 1970, that it had to be jettisoned and a Third Programme was launched in 1969 to cover the years to 1972.[93] Despite the fact that the planning did not work out, it was an important exercise in the rational management of national resources, which was radically affected by the country's failure to join the Common Market. Lemass's further efforts to build a consensus among the social partners, government, employers and trade unions, led to the establishment of the National Industrial and Economic Council (NIEC) in 1963. This exercise in neo-corporatism was well conceived, but the economic climate was not particularly conducive to success. However, Lemass took all the steps gradually to introduce the Irish economy to international competition. Ireland unilaterally reduced tariffs in January 1963 and January 1964 by 10 per cent each year. The Anglo-Irish Free Trade Area Agreement was negotiated in 1965 and came into effect in the middle of 1966. In the white paper *Closing the Gap* in 1963, Lemass showed that he was not afraid to court unpopularity. The introduction of turnover tax (two and a half per cent) in the 1963 budget illustrated that point.

Lemass faced growing industrial unrest in the early years of the 1960s. The proposed introduction of one-man buses in 1962 by the national transport authority, Córas Iompair Éireann (founded in 1945), resulted in strike action in May. The industrial action was called off following the successful mediation of a compromise by two priests. In April 1963 there was a further stoppage and a planned series of one-day stoppages for later in the year. The building industry was paralysed by industrial action in the summer of 1963.[94] In all, there were 60 disputes in 1962, 70 the following year and 87 in 1964. The number of people involved were 9,197, 16,067 and 25,245 respectively. The number of days lost were 104,024 in 1962, 233,617 in 1963 and 545,384 in 1964.[95]

Despite the industrial disputes and the residual row over turnover tax, Fianna Fáil continued to enjoy electoral success. This was due largely to the political ineptitude of Fine Gael, and, to a lesser extent, the Labour Party under the leadership of Brendan Corish. It was said somewhat cynically that the Fine Gael frontbench met more frequently in the Law Library than in Leinster House.[96] Many leading members of the party retained the mentality of an earlier generation—politicians by accident, members of the professions by social status, education and personal vocation. The youthful Garret FitzGerald, son of the Cumann na nGaedheal Minister for External Affairs, Desmond, found Fine Gael in the early 1960s to be conservative, clericalist and, to some extent, under the spell of Fianna Fáil's 'irredentist anti-partitionism'.[97] FitzGerald was persuaded that Fine Gael could deflect Ireland from falling under the 'materialist-nationalist axis emerging in the Government party'. Having taken certain soundings, he satisfied himself that he could make Fine Gael his type of party.

He found a kindred spirit in Declan Costello, the son of the former Taoiseach, John A. Costello. Although his father had proved to be very confessional in his thinking and his actions, the son was a Christian who had been heavily influenced by the radical shift in papal social teaching under John xxiii and Paul vi. He was the architect of the Fine Gael *Just Society* policy document, which marked an intellectual turning point in Irish politics. But the country failed to turn against the nationalist-materialist axis.

Costello was conscious of the fact that the Catholic Church in Ireland was 'the church of the vast majority of the people in this country and its voice is still listened to with respect'. It was not a besieged church, as was the case in Eastern Europe. Neither was it a minority church, as was the situation in continental Europe:

> It must, I suggest, use its great moral authority in the cause of social reform. It must act as a social conscience and speak out, not with a still quiet voice, but if necessary a large and strident one. If civil authority has failed to bring about social justice, it can, and I

suggest should, point out that failure. Where inaction is apparent, it can demand action, where injustices prevail it can demand justice. And this is called for, not merely to satisfy the demands of an abstract ideal, but as part of its pastoral function.

Costello suggested, for example, that priests should speak out on the housing shortage. He cited as an example the article of Father Peter Lemass in *The Furrow* (March 1969) in which the priest wrote of a young couple who were living with the wife's parents while waiting for a house. The talk is always about the future:

> 'Any word from the Corporation man? Did you call on the Housing Office today?'
> 'Just the usual; "your case is registered for consideration as a family of four persons. There are, however, applications on the waiting list from larger families".'
> Have more children and get a house! At present they are not really living; they are waiting to live, and while they wait, perhaps growing away from each other, getting used to separate habits. Maybe when at last the right letter comes from the Corporation, those separate habits will have become too ingrained, too set to alter.

Father Lemass wrote of the church's duty to insist urgently on the provision of housing as a human right:

> It is idle for either government or local authority to claim as an excuse 'If you want more houses, you will have to pay more rates, or higher taxes.' Where human rights are involved, such an argument is irrelevant.

He further argued that Irish society needed to recognise what the government seemed reluctant to acknowledge: that there was a housing emergency in the capital:

> In times of floods or earthquake we open schools, parish halls, and provide bedding and food for the homeless. It is not normally our duty to do this, but in time of an emergency it is. Isn't it then our duty to provide homes for the homeless, when we see the local authority failing to do this adequately?

Moved by such arguments, Declan Costello challenged politicians to act courageously. He recalled the statement of an unidentified figure in Irish public life who had said that he had not taken a certain course of action because he did not wish to get 'a belt of a crozier'. He did not think, however, that 'politicians should be deterred from political action in which they believe merely because it may invoke episcopal wrath.' But equally, Costello did not feel that churchmen should be deterred from criticising social conditions merely because they anticipated ministerial anger. 'Pusillanimity in clergy and lay people in their dealings one with the other is to be deplored', he said.[98] This plea for a creative critical tension between church and state brought thinking inside Fine Gael a considerable distance from the confessionalism of the mother and child crisis.

Garret FitzGerald, a polymath—economist, academic journalist, consultant, broadcaster and lay theologian—explained his political philosophy in an article in *Studies* in 1964:

> If we can successfully graft these liberal and socialist ideas, themselves largely Christian in their origin and inspiration, on to the particular form in which the Christian tradition displays itself in our country in this generation, we may succeed in developing an internally consistent philosophy of our own, appropriate to the needs of the time in which we live, and clearly superior to the excessive conservatism sometimes found in Catholic attitudes, as well as to the wishy-washy liberalism common in Britain, and the doctrinaire socialism of other countries.[99]

FitzGerald felt that the Catholic Church in Ireland had been ahead of other countries in relation to the religious article in the constitution, but he was critical of that Church's excessive emphasis on the rights of private property—'which no one in this all-too-bourgeois island challenges'.[100]

Both men, together with a younger element which had entered the party, worked on a range of documents in order to change policy. The *Just Society* document was substantially adopted by Fine Gael as its party platform in the April 1965 general election. Costello had presented the party hierarchy with an eight-point programme, which was revolutionary by the standards of Fine Gael. Among the proposals outlined, it called for economic planning, the creation of a

Department of Economic Affairs, direct government investment in industry, an emphasis on direct taxation and price controls. At the Fine Gael *ard fheis*, James Dillon was critical of 'young men in a hurry', and the powerful Gerard Sweetman was opposed to the eight-point platform. But Liam Cosgrave came to the rescue and a nine-point document was finally adopted.[101] Fine Gael was ready to fight a general election.

In February 1964, Fianna Fáil had won two crucial by-elections in Cork and Kildare. But the victory of Labour's Eileen Desmond in the Mid-Cork by-election in March 1965 was a major disappointment for Lemass. It was a seat which Fianna Fáil could have won, but large Fine Gael transfers to Desmond, whose husband had previously held the seat, ended the challenge of Flor Crowley on the third count.[102] This made the Dáil position of Fianna Fáil untenable and Lemass called an election for 7 April.[103] Lemass would not have been heartbroken to learn that one of the old guard, Dan Breen, was not going to stand again for the Dáil.[104] The Taoiseach ran hard on the record of the government, pointing to the better performance of the Irish economy in recent years and the good prospects for the future.

Fine Gael was better prepared than usual. Its programme was comprehensive and called for the establishment of a ministry of economic planning.[105] But it was difficult to observe any warmth for the platform in the speeches of the Fine Gael old guard.

Lemass again centred his campaign on the weakness of the political alternative. He told a meeting in Carlow on 24 March that the Labour leader, Brendan Corish, wanted to dictate the policy of the next government, but he would not have the choice: 'I have no intention of leading a "yo-yo" government to be jerked on a string held by Mr Corish.'[106] MacEntee, who was campaigning in his last general election, referred abusively in one speech to the two-headed giraffe of Fine Gael.[107] His contributions always enlivened and entertained, but they did not necessarily win votes for Fianna Fáil. It was announced during the campaign that a North-South tourist committee was to be set up to study practical ways of promoting the industry on both sides of the border.[108] But when the 'longest election count in the history of Irish politics' drew to a close on 13 April, it was clear that Lemass had not got his overall majority. Yet he had 72 seats and could still rely upon Joseph Sheridan, the Longford-Westmeath independent. Fianna Fáil scraped back into power.[109]

Dillon had come close to unseating Fianna Fáil. He paid the price of defeat, however, retiring from the leadership of the party immediately after Lemass had been elected Taoiseach. He was replaced by Liam Cosgrave, who had been in the Dáil since 1943 and had served as Minister for External Affairs during the inter-party government in the mid-1950s. Dillon had simply called Cosgrave into his office one day without warning, told him that he was retiring and that he (Cosgrave) was the new leader of Fine Gael. The swiftness of Cosgrave's appointment had taken many by surprise. Declan Costello was strongly positioned to bid for the leadership,[110] but the architect of the *Just Society* had been outmanoeuvred by Dillon and the conservative wing of the party. Fine Gael, therefore, remained a party with a nucleus of social Christian 'heretics' who succeeded, by virtue of their intellectual vitality and effervescence, in gaining positions of great influence in the 1970s and the leadership in the 1980s.

NORTHERN IRELAND AND NATIONALIST COMMEMORATIONS

Lemass was the first Taoiseach to approach Northern Ireland not so much as a 'problem', but as a neighbouring state requiring the development of friendly relations. In January 1965, he had travelled to Belfast to meet the Prime Minister of Northern Ireland, Terence O'Neill, at Stormont. The Taoiseach was accompanied by Dr T.K. Whitaker; the latter was to contribute much to North-South understanding through his activities in the 1980s and 1990s. Unprecedented and historic were the terms which both leaders used to describe the 40-minute exchange of views. The reality was more prosaic. Lemass and O'Neill simply discussed economic matters and attempted to isolate subjects of common interest. No political and constitutional issues were raised.[111] O'Neill made a return visit to Lemass in Dublin on 9 February. The views of the two leaders also coincided on that occasion. The outcome was considered a success and civil servants from Stormont and Dublin met subsequently to make practical recommendations.[112] Much could have come out of that initiative. It was a serious attempt to place North-South relations on a *functional* basis.

One practical outcome was the establishment of a five-person committee, in March 1965, to inquire into the possibility of establishing a 32-county electricity project.[113] Had that type of cooperation been attempted much earlier in the history of the two states, with less emphasis on the pyrotechnics of anti-partitionist rhetoric, the history of the relationship between Dublin, London and Belfast might perhaps have been quite different in the late 1960s. But no sooner had Lemass turned his capacious mind to this problem than the general election of 1965 intervened.

The year 1966 marked the fiftieth anniversary of the 1916 Rising. It was considered necessary to celebrate it with ritual and reverence, a sacred occasion redolent with religio-political symbolism. The nation would kneel as a mark of respect to honour the memory of what was chauvinistically phrased 'the men of 1916'. Schoolchildren would have the proclamation ever present before them in their classrooms. In fine, the most revered saints in the martyrology of Irish nationalism would be paid due obeisance.

There is nothing particularly unusual about the ritualised celebration of a nation's birth through force of arms. The United States does so; the Soviet Union used to do so on a grand scale, as did the French on the occasion of the bicentenary of their revolution in 1989. In Ireland in 1966 it was more a question of tone and timing. The previous year, the remains of Roger Casement, hanged in 1916, had been returned from Britain by the new Labour government and buried in Glasnevin. The tricolour-draped coffin was carried on an army gun carriage to the sound of muffled drums, with ten colonels acting as pall bearers, along the crowded streets of Dublin, while 600 soldiers, arms reversed, stood to attention. *The Irish Press* reported that he received a 'hero's salute from the silent thousands of his countrymen'.[114] The editorial spoke of the presence of the 'risen people' at the ceremony and commented that the work of Roger Casement was 'not yet complete'. There remained the question of unification: 'When that time comes—and come it will if we maintain the constancy that nurtured this great man—he will be truly at rest, with those others who throughout the generations have shared his vision and his faith.'[115] President de Valera said at the graveside: 'And as we stand here, each one of us will resolve that we shall do everything to work so that the people of that province and ourselves may be united in cooperation, that we will be all vying with each other in loving this land for which so many sacrifices have been made throughout the centuries.'[116]

Perhaps the nuance of de Valera's language was lost on many of his listeners. He did not speak of reunification but rather of cooperation, in keeping with Lemass's functional approach to Northern Ireland. However, once the 1916 celebrations got under way, the irredentism implicit in the phrase in the constitution 'pending the reintegration of the national territory' had again taken precedence. There was the opening of the Garden of Remembrance, a pageant in Croke Park, the television dramatisation of the Rising, and the thousands of small celebrations all over the country to honour what de Valera described as 'the seven brave men who, despite all the deterrents, made the decision to assert, once more, in arms our nation's right to sovereign independence'. He saw them as men who had been fully alive to their responsibilities, men of the fullest faith and love of country, unselfish and single-minded, and capable of sacrifices which inspired a 'national resurgence'. Time, de Valera said, had proven the 1916 leaders to be prophets.[117] One ominous manifestation of the physical force legacy was the blowing up in the capital of Nelson Pillar in Dublin's main thoroughfare on 7 March 1966. A visit to the country by Princess Margaret, sister of the British queen, in January had been accompanied by the blocking of roads and violent demonstrations.

Four points can be made regarding the 1916 commemoration celebrations. First, there is no necessary causal relationship between the tone of the events and the outbreak of violence in Northern Ireland a few years later. But what the celebrations did was to sensitise the Irish public and allow for a greater uncritical receptivity to the message of physical force nationalism. Secondly, the commemorations did illustrate the sharp contrast between promise and performance, ideal and achievement in the Irish state. The modern Irish state did not cherish 'all the children of the nation equally' in the mid-1960s—and the national performance was very poor by European standards. That helped generate a sense of social unrest. Thirdly, the commemorations provoked some reflection among Irish historians on the nature of Irish history and present-day events. It was little short of revolutionary to have professional Irish historians deal with such an allegedly polemical topic. At least, 1966 made respectable the writing of twentieth-century Irish history and initiated a scholarly debate which has continued with some vigour into the 1990s. Finally, the official 1916 commemorations implicitly celebrated the 'victory' and the 'vindication' of the Fianna Fáil political tradition.

Despite the 1916 'risen people' rhetoric, de Valera, at 84, was fortunate to win the presidential election which was held on 1 June 1966 by 558,861 votes to 548,144. His opponent was Thomas F. O'Higgins, a senior counsel in his late 40s from the social Christian wing of Fine Gael.[118] He campaigned vigorously around the country and presented a much more dynamic image than anything that Fianna Fáil could muster on behalf of de Valera. Certain speeches by Fianna Fáil ministers caused considerable annoyance to the electorate. The Minister for Lands and the Gaeltacht, Micheál Ó Moráin, described *The Irish Times* as 'the mistress of the Fine Gael party and mistresses can be both vicious and demanding'. O'Higgins replied, in a speech in the minister's home county of Mayo, that he did not know that *The Irish Times* was the mistress of Fine Gael. He did not know anything about the vicious demands of mistresses: 'On these questions I bow to the superior knowledge of Mr Moran.'[119] Garret FitzGerald has argued that the result of the 1966 presidential election strengthened the progressive wing of Fine Gael.[120]

Industrial unrest worsened.[121] Farmers were also on the march over farm prices and conditions. Two hundred men were on the road to Dublin on 13 October 1966.[122] Organised by the National Farmers' Association, the small groups were seen off by large numbers of supporters. Led by the president of the NFA, Rickard Deasy, the marchers were to meet in the capital. A mass meeting was held at Merrion Square on 19 October. As the crowd of 10,000 waited, Deasy went to the Department of Agriculture, only to be told by Charles Haughey's private secretary that the minister would not meet the NFA delegation. The farmers were invited to submit a memorandum to the minister. Deasy said that the pigeon holes in the department were blocked up to the ceiling with memoranda and added: 'We will remain here until the minister is available.' He then sat down on the steps in the rain with his fellow NFA members. 'We will stay here a bloody month if necessary', he told reporters. A short time later, William Bulfin from Offaly arrived to tell Deasy that he did not think the farmers could be contained. Word of the minister's refusal to meet the NFA had angered the crowd. Deasy explained that there was to be no violence and the crowd dispersed. A very ugly scene was narrowly avoided.

Later, a large force of gardaí remained on duty. They watched as Deasy and his supporters settled down for the night on the steps of the Department of Agriculture. On 20 October the group were still on the steps and Deasy told reporters that he was prepared to remain there 'until hell freezes over'. Good-humoured signs went up saying: Charlie's Checkpoint. Because of the cold winds, the protesters were given permission to erect a canvas shelter.[123] On 21 October farmers were reported to have attacked Haughey's car in Athlone. In another development, farmers who owned land in Dublin, Meath and Louth threatened to refuse to allow the Fingal and Ward Union Hunt from using their land because Mr Haughey was a member.[124] Haughey caused great anger and resentment when he referred to the NFA as a pipsqueak organisation. However, the minister was fully supported by Lemass in his tough stand against the NFA; the Taoiseach said that the government would not be bullied by what he called a small group of ambitious men who wanted the government to forego its responsibilities to agriculture.[125] In the end a softer line was taken and honour was saved on all sides, but what the 1966 NFA protest underlined was the anger in the farming community and the immediate need for new markets to be found for their produce in the European Economic Community.

LYNCH TAKES OVER

In October 1966 Lemass decided abruptly to retire from the position of Taoiseach.[126] It appears that his deteriorating health was not the main reason why he had decided to step down. He felt that it was time for the younger generation to take over. He was not going to make de Valera's mistake over again. Lemass had the news leaked to the *Irish Press* political correspondent, Michael Mills. The story was published but, surprisingly, it was flatly denied the following day by government sources. Mills persuaded the editor to hold off publishing a retraction. In the end, he was proved correct.[127]

The problem facing Fianna Fáil was that Lemass had not prepared an obvious successor. Different power blocs had developed in the party under him. Various candidates were to emerge to contest the leadership for the first time in the history of Fianna Fáil. In 1959 Lemass had taken over by right of apostolic succession. That was no longer a practical possibility. The old guard, MacEntee and Aiken, were too old. Aiken favoured the candidature of George Colley, who was en route to a meeting of finance ministers in Mexico when he received a telegram from Lemass stating his intention to retire. The Taoiseach left it up to Colley whether or not he wished to attend the meeting, but the minister returned post-haste to Dublin on unspecified 'urgent business'. Colley was considered to be a strong contender for the leadership. He represented an alliance between the old guard and the more technocratic wing of the party. But he had never been used by Lemass to 'trouble-shoot' in the party; he was never sent to the country to deal with difficult party problems, heal divisions and make peace between rival factions. He lacked credibility among the older backbenchers. Colley did not have a very strong base in the party. Much of his support for the leadership of Fianna Fáil was based on a negative factor—his backers did not regard him as an ideal leader, but they did not want Charles Haughey.

The son-in-law of Lemass, Haughey represented the new face of a Fianna Fáil party with a close affinity to the younger Irish business community, the people with the tailor-made clothes and the white cuffs. They had nothing in common with Seán Moylan's 'ass and cart' owners. Supported by Donogh O'Malley, another young man in a hurry, Haughey never found favour with the older guard like Aiken. He was regarded with deep suspicion and perceived as being a bit of an upstart and a whipper-snapper, with scant regard for propriety and party pieties.

The 'republican' element was represented by Neil Blaney, who had become a formidable figure in party circles in the 1960s. He was a border republican who had attempted to keep the 'phoenix flame' alive. The civil war and partition were not mere historical facts in his mind. Supported by Kevin Boland, a scion of another founding father, Blaney could have mustered strong support inside the ranks.

Very soon, Fianna Fáil was faced with the unprecedented reality of a contested leadership. A number of older backbenchers were alarmed about what was happening. A group of TDs went to Lemass to express concern about what a leadership battle would do to the party. It was essential, in their view, to maintain unity. Their proposal was to nominate the Corkman, Jack Lynch, as the unanimous choice for the succession. Lemass went for the idea. He was quick to see that it had its advantages. Whether Lynch would have been his first choice for the leadership is difficult to say, but he did have popular appeal and it was a way of preventing the different factions inside Fianna Fáil from engaging in a protracted and damaging power struggle. Moreover, Lynch had expressed no interest in the leadership. He had not sought to go forward as a candidate. In fact, the illness of his mother-in-law at the time had prevented him from even being passively interested in the job of Taoiseach.[128]

Lemass's pecking order for the leadership of Fianna Fáil was as follows: Jack Lynch, Patrick Hillery and finally George Colley. According to oral sources, Lemass had asked Lynch to stand earlier on, but he had refused. He later told Patrick Hillery that he was retiring and said to him simply: 'You could do it.' But Hillery was as emphatic as Lynch: he did not want to take the job. When it was evident that Colley was not acceptable to a large number of the parliamentary party, Lemass returned to Lynch, who reluctantly agreed to stand. The retiring Taoiseach secured the withdrawal of Blaney and Haughey. Colley refused to stand down and was defeated by 52 votes to 19.[129]

The Irish Press viewed the changeover as the end of a chapter in the history of the country. It was certainly the end of the reign by the remnant of Fianna Fáil's founding generation. Responsibility passed to a younger man in the person of Jack Lynch (49), who had an appealing personality, a mild manner, no trace of fanaticism, and a charism which could be converted into seats.[130] Although Lemass had endorsed his candidature, Lynch took office in a somewhat weak position. In fact, he was to hold the leadership of Fianna Fáil for thirteen years and demonstrate in that time that he was quite capable of dealing with mutiny.

Lemass could leave office with a sense of some satisfaction, but also with many regrets. He had not secured Irish membership of the European Community. That, he admitted, was his major disappointment as Taoiseach.[131] In the end, Lemass simply ran out of time. He had, according to a perceptive obituary in *The Irish Times* (he died in May 1971), 'come to power too late—he left power too early.'[132] His seven years in office were simply not long enough to see through the radical changes he had wanted to make. The decision-making structures of the Irish state required transformation. He succeeded in diagnosing what needed to be done and then ran out of time before he could set the country on a course to becoming a modern state. Lemass merely had time to make the mould of the new Ireland. He did not so much break as crack the old mould.[133] As a politician, Lemass was far less a 'gambler' than a taker of risks. This was shown in his choice of younger cabinet members. It was revealed by his visit to Belfast. It was demonstrated by the manner in which he attempted to turn Ireland towards Europe. It was exemplified by his radical attitude towards the need for educational reform.

Lemass has been described as the 'Managing Director of Ireland Inc.' and as the 'supreme pragmatist', with 'doctrinaire attitudes' holding 'no appeal for him in any field'.[134] But that is to diminish the influence of ideology on his political actions. Lemass had a very strong political philosophy. He knew what he wanted to achieve and he 'gave his country in the early '60s its best spell of administration in its modern history'.[135] Lemass knew that he was neither a de Valera nor a Kennedy and 'he never made the primary mistake of trying to do that', according to *The Irish Times*: 'He was his own man and did it in his own way'. That way was to avoid the politics of populism. His approach was based on the need to reform radically Irish economic and administrative structures. Beginning that long-postponed task as Taoiseach too late in 1959, Lemass entrusted its completion to a new generation of politicians. But a number were the prisoners of a past which Lemass had spent his public life trying successfully to transcend.

The Shifting Balance of Power: Jack Lynch and Liam Cosgrave, 1966–1977

Jack Lynch once described himself as having been a 'compromise candidate' for the leadership of Fianna Fáil. It was, according to the political editor of *The Irish Times*, Dick Walsh, a phrase he bitterly regretted using, and if it were taken to mean that he intended to relinquish control before too long, was completely misleading.'[1] Fianna Fáil required a populist, or an injection of the de Valera-factor, to win back an overall majority. Lynch was the person to provide that popular image, and provide it he did. One former Fianna Fáil minister described campaigning with Lynch as 'like walking into a town with Cú Chulainn'.[2] The new Taoiseach was crowned leader by the party at what *The Irish Press* described as 'the biggest and most impressive *ard fheis* in Irish political history'.[3] The party exuded a 'born-again' spirit.

In reality, Lynch had inherited an uneasy coalition of rival tendencies and factions. He had to balance the new and the old, the mohaired and the tweed-suited. Frank Aiken showed no willingness to retire and Lynch had little option but to reappoint him Tánaiste and

Minister for External Affairs. Charles Haughey took over from Lynch as Minister for Finance. Neil Blaney moved to Agriculture and Fisheries and Kevin Boland took over at Local Government. Childers, who was to be a close ally of Lynch's in the troubled times ahead, retained Transport and Power, but, in addition, he was given the portfolio of Posts and Telegraphs. Kevin Boland was put in charge of Local Government. Michael Hilliard became Minister for Defence and George Colley was Minister for Industry and Commerce. Seán Faulkner was Minister for Lands. Brian Lenihan retained the Justice portfolio but he was to move to Education on 27 March 1968 following the death of Donogh O'Malley. Micheál Moran (Micheál Ó Moráin) was moved at the same time from Lands and the Gaeltacht to Justice.

The dead minister's nephew, Desmond O'Malley, was chosen to stand for the vacancy in Limerick East on 22 May 1968. Neil Blaney was sent by headquarters to conduct the campaign. His style was somewhat out of tune with what the young O'Malley might have wanted. Roads were painted with signs stating 'Remember the 77'— a reference to those executed by the government during the civil war. The outcome of Limerick East and four other by-elections was to give the party a larger majority in the Dáil than at any time in the previous five years—73 seats to a combined opposition total of 71. Fine Gael had 46 seats, Labour 22 and independents 3. One independent continued to vote for the government, while another had not been in the house for a long time due to illness.[4] Lynch had delivered and Fianna Fáil had a good working majority.

In 1968 Lynch allowed himself to be persuaded to replace proportional representation with the British system straight vote. Two TCD academics, Basil Chubb and David Thornley, estimated that Fianna Fáil might win over ninety seats at the next general election if it were to be held under the British system.[5] A compromise proposal, favoured by Brian Lenihan and others in Fianna Fáil, was rejected. Both the Labour Party and Fine Gael opposed what was perceived as a move to institutionalise a Fianna Fáil majority. It was also evident that there was very little enthusiasm from sitting Fianna Fáil TDs for the change of electoral system.[6] It was a futile political exercise. Despite a protracted campaign, the arguments advanced in favour of change failed to convince. The elder statesmen of the party had to be encouraged to speak out on behalf of the government, so bad was the campaign going in the countryside. From the back benches Lemass argued vigorously for the introduction of the straight vote system.[7] Seán MacEntee, from his retirement, sent a letter to the press which showed that he had lost none of his flair for straight talking: 'Why do all the subversive elements in our society . . . urge us not to do this? Is it because experience elsewhere has shown that p.r. progresses from weak government, through civil disorder and chaos, to dictatorship.'[8] The opposition director of elections, Gerard Sweetman, described Fianna Fáil tactics as a double-cross.[9]

People were asked to vote on two questions: on the introduction of the straight vote system, and on the ratio of TDs to constituents. The *Irish Press* political correspondent, Michael Mills, was forced to ask during the canvassing: 'Is there any campaign on at all?' Driving through the country, there was not a poster or a car sticker in sight. 'Is it not all a great illusion?' he mused.[10] Blaney's magic was not working. None of the political parties could muster enthusiasm for their respective campaigns and there was considerable suspicion abroad about the motivation behind the referendum. There was a 65 per cent turnout and the government was roundly defeated. In the case of the 'straight-vote' proposal, the vote was 423,496 in favour and 657,898 against. Regarding the change of constituencies, the vote was 424,185 in favour and 656,503 against. Michael Mills correctly termed the result 'a shattering defeat' for Fianna Fáil. Both Fine Gael and Labour had good cause to feel relieved. FitzGerald and Jim Dooge, who was to be Minister for Foreign Affairs 1981–82, had calculated that Fianna Fáil would have got 80 seats out of 144 if the new system were to have been adopted.[11]

Conscious of the need to build an anti-Fianna Fáil coalition, FitzGerald has argued that Fine Gael made overtures to Brendan Halligan, general secretary of the Labour Party, in October 1967. Liam Cosgrave initiated contacts with Brendan Corish in January 1968. FitzGerald also met Corish and the matter was put to the Labour front bench. The reply came: 'nothing doing'. The idea of closer cooperation, and a possible merger between the two main opposition parties, was not as far-fetched as it might at first seem. Influential sections of the Fine Gael leadership had moved to the centre left; there were the original *Just Society* policies of 1965 and more recently the party had developed progressive policies on education, local government and the Irish language. FitzGerald felt that they represented 'a significant corpus of social democratic and reforming proposals'.[12] In May 1968, Michael O'Higgins had called for a 'united front' between the two parties in order to set up a coalition. He argued that Fianna Fáil had won six of the seven by-elections held since the 1965 general election, despite the fact that Fine Gael and Labour had received a majority of first preferences in five of them.[13] Ignoring the overture to fight the next election on the policies of the *Just Society*, Corish replied the following day that 'Fine Gael are a private enterprise party. We are socialists.' He explained that the country was 'at the end of an era' and Ireland was moving towards a 'two-party system of the left and the right'. He invited those who thought like the Labour Party to join forces with it and work for a Labour government.[14] Michael O'Leary, who was to join Fine Gael in 1982, described that party in 1967 as 'an alliance between the most reactionary elements of the countryside and a certain section of the professional classes of the towns'. Corish told delegates to the party's annual conference in 1969 that Fine Gael was no better than Fianna Fáil, wanting 'power for power's sake'. He felt that if, in the future, conference were to opt for coalition, he would accept the decision: 'But the party must appreciate that to me this is a matter of conscience and that in such an eventuality, my continued support for socialism will be from the back benches.'

But conscience is a flexible instrument in politics and Corish was to change his mind within twelve months. Despite the adverse social and industrial situation, a divided opposition meant that Fianna Fáil would be returned to power. A number of distinguished intellectuals added to Labour's appeal. Conor Cruise O'Brien returned from his teaching post in New York University and rejoined the party as a rank and file member. The political scientist and television current affairs presenter, David Thornley, declared his intention to seek a nomination. Justin Keating, also well known through his television appearances, was to be a Labour candidate. The celebration on 21 January 1969 of the 50th anniversary of the First Dáil provided an object lesson for the historically conscious of the vast difference between the revolutionary aspirations of the founders of the state and the political and social achievement of their successes. In November 1968, the government was forced to introduce a severe supplementary budget to meet additional government expenditure of £18.75 million. Stiff taxes were introduced to curb consumer spending.

Notwithstanding the financial difficulties, Lynch favoured an election in the summer of 1969. Charles Haughey introduced what was popularly perceived as being an 'election budget' on 7 April. *The Irish Press*'s front-page headline described it as being a 'Share and Care Alike' budget. It provided, according to Michael Mills, 'the most comprehensive social benefits ever provided for the weaker sections of the community'. A total of £12.5 million was provided in increased children's allowances. That meant an increase of 14s. 6d. per month for the second child and 13s. 6d. for the third child. The gains for Paddy Murphy, married with five children, buying a home and earning £30 per week were tabulated at 7 shillings by *The Irish Press*. In an interview with Michael Mills, Jack Lynch stated: 'We have never departed from our fundamental principles and policies.'[15]

Basil Chubb presciently saw the election as the 'temporarily delayed end of an era'.[16] The end of the era did not finally come until over 30 years later. However, both Fine Gael and Labour sought to break the political mould with no help from each other. 'Fine Gael into action; into government; into the seventies' read the slogan behind the main platform at the Fine Gael annual conference in May.[17] Cosgrave appeared confident that his party could form a government on its own. 'The seventies will be socialist' was the battle-cry of Labour. Chubb commented: 'The team colours are the same as usual, except that Labour has bright new red jerseys in place of the washed-out pink—though one or two of its backs don't seem to have got their new ones yet.'[18] Brendan Corish sought to achieve a forced merger of Fianna Fáil and Fine Gael. The Labour Party manifesto argued that the difference between the two civil war parties was in name only.[19] During the campaign Corish repeated that the Labour Party 'will not in any circumstances whatever enter a coalition'. Imprisoned by the isolationism of the Irish socialist tradition, the Labour Party sought through its new-found radicalism to atone for its past sins of conservatism. Labour tried to remain purer than pure. The party foolishly ran 100 candidates, many in constituencies where Labour had absolutely no hope of winning.

Sensing the need for a new campaign strategy, Fianna Fáil combined old-fashioned personalism and populism with a presidential-style national tour which was to become a feature of every other election. Charles Haughey was one of the people who planned Lynch's nationwide campaign trail.[20] The Fianna Fáil leader *met the people*: he did not merely address large gatherings but stopped off at hospitals, convents and county homes. Television was skilfully used, as were radio and photo opportunities. Lynch brought 'government to the people'.[21] The Taoiseach proved to be a competent and confident vote-getter. He was a natural and never forgot a face or a name; he was unassuming, affable, sincere and without any trace of personal arrogance. Lynch was the acceptable image. Foreign policy issues and the question of Northern Ireland did not play a major part in the campaign.[22] However, Fianna Fáil did not allow victory hinge on charism and all-Ireland medals. The party activists again showed a nuanced understanding of the intersecting boreens and townlands of Ireland. In the end, Fianna Fáil won a handsome majority—a gain of three seats, which brought the strength of the party to 75. Fine Gael also gained three seats and rose to 50, while Labour, the party most expecting the great leap forward, dropped from 22 to 18.

Fianna Fáil reacted triumphalistically to the victory. Kevin Boland wrote later in biblical fashion: 'Morale had never been higher; our enemies were confounded, a footstool under our feet and we were invincible again.'[23] Lynch picked his new team, leaving many of the ministers with the same portfolios.[24] It looked like a particularly strong cabinet and it ought to have been united under Jack Lynch. Within less than twelve months, however, the growing violence in Northern Ireland had exacerbated the personality conflicts within Fianna Fáil, accentuated ideological differences, and threatened the credibility of the Taoiseach as the country faced its most serious political crisis since 1922.

NORTHERN IRELAND AND THE ARMS TRIAL

By 1983 the Northern Ireland crisis had resulted in over 2,300 deaths of men, women and children (the death toll was over 3,000 by 1992). Those deaths, in an area with a population of one and a half million, are equivalent in proportionate terms to the killing of approximately 84,000 in Britain, 83,000 in France or 350,000 in the United States. In addition, over 24,000 people had been wounded and maimed. There had been over 43,000 recorded separate incidents of shootings, bombings and arson. In the North the prison population had risen from 686 in 1967 to about 2,500 in 1983. The lives of tens of thousands had been deeply affected. Thousands suffered from psychological stress because of the fear and tension generated by murder, bombing, intimidation and the impact of security measures. That was how the

New Ireland Forum report summed up the result of the violence since 1968.[25] A study undertaken for the New Ireland Forum—set up in 1983 by Dr Garret FitzGerald when he was Taoiseach—to consult on the manner in which lasting peace could be achieved in a new Ireland, calculated that the total cost of the violence to the exchequers of London and Dublin for the period 1969 to 1982 was 5,500 million punts and 1,100 million punts respectively. The indirect costs, in terms of lost output, to the economies of the North and the South could have been as high as 4,000 million punts and 1,200 million respectively.[26] In 1970, the tragedy which was already unfolding, ought to have alerted almost everyone to the dangers of thinking in the old physical force nationalist categories. But the cult of violence and respect for blood sacrifice was far too deeply entrenched.

The challenge to the constitutional tradition was felt acutely in 1969 and 1970 as the difficulties of the nationalist minority in Northern Ireland spilled across the border. Irish public opinion had been excited by the sight of refugees streaming south in August 1969. During the height of the crisis, there were over 3,000 people who had to be taken care of in the makeshift camps at Kilworth, Co. Cork, Gormanston, Co. Meath, Coolmooney, Co. Wicklow, Finner, Co. Donegal and in Kildare barracks. There was a generous response to appeals for clothing, food and blankets, but the refugees had to survive in less than ideal conditions.[27] That was a summer when the Lambeg drums—the symbol of Orangeism—presided over Northern Ireland 'like giant tumours'.[28] The Northern Ireland Civil Rights Association (NICRA), founded in February 1967, held a march in Dungannon on 24 March 1968 demanding one man, one vote. NICRA continued to escalate its strategy of civil disobedience. In January 1969, People's Democracy organised a student march from Belfast to Derry. It was attacked by loyalists in sight of partisan RUC men at Burntollet Bridge, near Derry. On 11 January 1969 there were disturbances following a nationalist protest in Newry, Co. Down. By August, Derry's Bogside was in a state of siege with serious disturbances on the streets exacerbated by police violence. Catholic areas of Belfast were under sectarian attack. The violence in Northern Ireland commanded daily international headlines as TV crews from major networks rushed to cover events.[29] A new generation of social democratic reformers, led by John Hume and Gerry Fitt, institutionalised that tradition in the Social Democratic and Labour

Party (SDLP) which was founded in 1970. The orthodox physical force nationalist tradition was perpetuated by Sinn Féin and its armed wing, the Irish Republican Army (IRA). The latter movement was revamped and reorganised in 1969, but within a year it had divided into two factions, Sinn Féin (Kevin Street) and Sinn Féin (Gardiner Place).[30] The two IRAs, in their macabre way, ensured that 'dying for Ireland' took on a new meaning in the 1970s and 1980s. Gunmen did not die for the people but—as Seumas Shields says in Seán O'Casey's *The Shadow of a Gunman*, 'its the people that are dyin' for the gunmen'.

The physical force nationalists of Sinn Féin and the IRA encountered an implacable opponent in John Hume, who never wavered in those years from adherence to a philosophy of non-violence. Born in Derry in 1937, he had been reared in a home where his father was one of the long-term unemployed. A beneficiary of the progressive British educational policy of the postwar years, Hume had studied History and French at St Patrick's College, Maynooth, where he also completed an MA on the social and economic history of Derry under the direction of Tomás Ó Fiaich. (The latter became archbishop of Armagh in 1977.) An ex-teacher, Hume first came to political prominence in the civil rights movement in Derry in 1968. He was also vice-president of the Derry Citizens' Action Committee 1968–69. He took a seat for Foyle from the nationalist leader, Edward McAteer, in the 1969 Stormont general election. Hume came to dominate Northern nationalist constitutional politics in the late 1970s and in the 1980s. He became a member of the European Parliament in 1979 and leader of the SDLP upon the resignation of Gerry Fitt later that year. A social democrat, Hume found himself very much at home in the ranks of the socialist group in the European Parliament. But he found it very difficult to bring the minority community of Northern Ireland along that Social Democratic path.

Hume's counterpart on the unionist side—different in almost every respect—was the Reverend Ian Richard Kyle Paisley. The leader of the Free Presbyterian Church, in the Ravenhill Road area of Belfast, he built his own Martyrs' Memorial Church. A forceful preacher, he turned his attention to politics in 1963. He was a street leader and an implacable opponent of reforming unionists like the Prime Minister of Northern Ireland, Terence O'Neill (1963–69). In 1970 Paisley was elected to both Stormont and Westminster. In 1979, he became a member of the European Parliament. In the 1960s, Paisley remained ambivalent in his attitude towards loyalist extremist groups.

Paramilitary loyalist 'defence associations', the forerunners of the Ulster Defence Association, founded in 1971 and finally banned in 1992, proliferated.

Decisive action by the British government in 1969, supported by a determined Northern government, might have saved the state from descending into Lebanon-like conflict. But years of benign neglect on the part of London, left the minority community in Northern Ireland in a very vulnerable position. The situation called for the deployment of the army on the streets in order to prevent all-out war in Belfast. In Dublin, Lynch withstood all calls to send the Irish army across the border or to send 'guns' to the North. It remained government policy, he said, to achieve unity by peaceful means.[31]

The Irish Minister for External Affairs, Patrick Hillery, worked hard at Iveagh House in August 1969 to prepare the text of a UN speech, together with Con Cremin and a young diplomat, Pádraic MacKernan. He travelled to New York to lobby members of the Security Council in favour of the Irish plea for a meeting to discuss the sending of a peace-keeping force to Northern Ireland. There were also crisis meetings in Westminster and at Stormont. The international press showed pictures of Belfast which resembled images of post-war Europe. British troops were ordered to take over security in the North as B-Specials were withdrawn from all areas. The UN Security Council met on 19 August.[32] However, as might have been expected, it adjourned its special meeting on Ireland without taking a vote on whether or not to discuss the Irish request for a peace-keeping mission.[33] Hillery was able to address the Security Council. He handled the brief, as *The Irish Times* commented in an editorial, without 'ranting or sunburstry'. It was an occasion for 'cool advocacy'.[34] Hillery sought a meeting with the UN Secretary General, U Thant. The minister left New York stating that the question had been left open. It was in that context that Jack Lynch issued a statement on 28 August, ruling out force as a solution and renewing his proposal for a federal Ireland. The Irish government had been denounced as 'green tones' by members of People's Democracy,[35] a left-wing civil rights group founded in Queen's University, Belfast in 1968. International diplomacy was not seen as a substitute for action, real action. That, of course, meant for some prominent people a resort to the use of arms. The Taoiseach had said when the August 1969 crisis first broke that the Irish government 'can no longer stand by and see innocent people injured and perhaps worse'. This was an example of the unintentional use of the traditional shadow language of anti-partitionism. That phrase was interpreted with licence by those of a deep shade of green inside Fianna Fáil. It fell to Lynch, Childers, Hillery, Lenihan, Colley and others to confront the 'sneaking regarders'.

Conor Cruise O'Brien has discussed perceptively the prevalence of an ambivalence towards political violence in the Fianna Fáil tradition, in an essay aptly entitled 'Shades of Republicanism':

> They like, on appropriate times and occasions, to see themselves as chosen ones, Soldiers of Destiny, Legion of the Rearguard, more Irish and better Irish than the rest of the people. This concept of a national elite stands in an uneasy relation to the similar image of itself held by the IRA. As true descendants of the Republican side in the Civil War the IRA has to look more plausible, *even to Fianna Fáil*, than Fianna Fáil does. This entails a sneaking respect for the IRA, the only category of the population not deemed to be less truly Irish than Fianna Fáil. 'The boys' might have to be disciplined from time to time, but your heart went out to them all the same. Especially when Fianna Fáil was out of office.[36]

Neil Blaney provided some evidence in an RTÉ radio interview that there had been hard words and plain speaking at the cabinet table in August before decisions on the North had been taken.[37] He was the most outspoken 'republican' in the Fianna Fáil cabinet. On the occasion of his twenty-first anniversary in the Dáil on 8 December 1969, he made a speech in Letterkenny, Co. Donegal, where he said that the Fianna Fáil party had never taken a decision 'to rule out the use of force if the circumstances in the Six Counties so demanded'. The Minister for Agriculture and Fisheries used a most incendiary form of language:

> If a situation were to arise in the Six Counties in which the people who do not subscribe to the Unionist régime were under sustained and murderous assault, then as the Taoiseach said on August 13th, we 'cannot stand idly [sic] by'.

He told his audience that much had been heard about the use of force but 'we should be clear where we stand here'. Blaney then cited Jack Lynch in the Dáil on 23 and 24 October as saying that 'the government in this part of Ireland has no intention of mounting an armed invasion of the Six Counties'. The minister quoted Liam Cosgrave as stating that 'the only way to achieve ultimate unity is by peaceful means and cooperation' while he said that Brendan Corish had told the Dáil that 'force is out'. Blaney continued:

> I believe, as do the vast majority, that the ideal way of ending partition is by peaceful means. But no-one has the right to assert that force is irrevocably out. No political party or group at any time is entitled to pre-determine the right of the Irish people to decide what course of action on this question may be justified in given circumstances.[38]

The speech was warmly welcomed by the Derry nationalist Eddie McAteer; he asked was it wrong for an Irish minister to say that the Irish government might intervene if Irish people on Irish soil were being attacked? He did say it was not yet time to write the full story, but added 'I can say that Neil Blaney was never far from our city in those fateful days of July and August.'[39]

In contrast, John Hume criticised Blaney and said that it was 'totally irresponsible to talk of the use of force in the present circumstances'. He said on RTÉ television: 'An extremist breeds an extremist.' He described the Blaney speech as hardline and maintained that it would have the effect of hardening the right wing of unionism. 'We must accept that there are 800,000 Protestants in the North who don't want a United Ireland', Hume said. The attitude of the republican movement for the past 50 years, he added, was to drive such people out by force. It was time to recognise the facts of life and to try to win over the minds of the people. The problem of partition, he said, would be settled only when the majority wanted it to be settled. The policy that he and those associated with him had been following had had more success over the last year or so than all the years of sabre-rattling, because opposition to the unionist regime was based on reason and logic, and not on emotion. John Hume said that the border was a sectarian border and to attempt to use force to break it down would lead not only to civil war, but to a religious war:

Economic cooperation, the encouragement of friendship and understanding, the development of Irish culture are the only means by which the problem can be solved. We have a common heritage and a common future.

Hume ended the interview by saying that it was 'not really Irish to be talking of shooting Protestant fellow-Irishmen'.[40]

Blaney's speech was a direct challenge to Jack Lynch's leadership, but government policy remained as Lynch had stated it at Tralee on 20 November. There was to be no resort to the use of force. In the Dáil, on 22 October, the Taoiseach said: 'We do not want to seek to impose our will on anyone by force.' He stated that Blaney accepted government policy on this matter. On 12 December, the press carried headlines that Blaney had rejected suggestions that there was a rift over Northern policy in the cabinet. But 'Bang Bang' Blaney, as the journalist John Healy called him in his 'Backbencher' column in *The Irish Times*, was not contrite. His commitment to party policy was equivocal.[41] On another occasion, Blaney rejected John Hume's criticisms: 'I do not regard John Hume as any Solomon in this matter of partition', he said. Asked if he would take the job of Taoiseach, he replied that Fianna Fáil had a fairly newly elected Taoiseach who was young, able and vigorous. Pressed on the matter, he said:

If there was a situation in which a Taoiseach was being sought for the party and that the party wished to consider me, well then, in all probability, I would have to consider very seriously the implications of that and leave it to the party's best judgment.[42]

Fianna Fáil held its *ard fheis* on the weekend of 16–18 January 1970, a week after the Sinn Féin split. Lynch took on Blaney and his supporters. He dared his opponents: if anyone wanted to change the government's policy on Northern Ireland, now was the time, and the *ard fheis* was the place to do it. He also asked that if people wanted the traditional Fianna Fáil policy to be pursued by the leader, they should say so at the *ard fheis*. There were shouts of 'We want Jack' from a majority of the 3,000 delegates: 'Whether we like it or not', Lynch said, we have to accept the fact that two-thirds of the one-and-a-half million people in the Six Counties wish to be associated with the United Kingdom:

The plain truth—the naked reality—is that we do not possess the capacity to impose a solution by force. Even if we had that capacity what would be the result if we decided to apply it? Do we want to adopt the role of an occupying conqueror over the one million or so Six-County citizens who at present support partition? Would we compel them to flee the country altogether or live under our domination, in constant opposition, feverishly nursing hatred and secretly plotting revenge. Thus, we would have worked ourselves into the role of overlord, a role that would necessitate the imposition by us on the subjugated new minority of the Six Counties, and the whole country, of some of the hateful tyrannical practices that we and the world so recently called an abomination. Is this the Ireland we want? Is this the kind of Irishmen we want to be? Is this the kind of unity that we want to achieve? The answer is surely clear.[43]

But was it? Blood sacrifice was a virus in Irish society.

Why did Lynch not sack Blaney in 1969? A number of reasons may be advanced. Blaney was the son of a founder member of Fianna Fáil; he was a powerful figure, with a strong following in the party. The Minister for Agriculture had built up his power base in Fianna Fáil as a result of being a good party organiser, a director of victorious by-elections and as somebody who kept faith with the 'republican' spirit of the founding fathers. In the volatile atmosphere of 1969, the sacking of Blaney might have divided the party, brought down the government and risked securing a victory for a leader who might have reversed the anti-force pledge of Jack Lynch. The apparent weakness of the Taoiseach may have been based on the calculation that a general election in 1970 could have threatened the stability of Irish democracy.

Yet the most likely explanation for Lynch's seeming inaction was that he knew that some elements in the party had always regarded him as an interim leader of Fianna Fáil. He was taken completely by surprise to learn that arms had reached the North with alleged help from the Republic. When exactly he knew what was happening is difficult to date precisely. The secretary of the Department of Justice, Peter Berry, was convinced that he had told Lynch on 17 October 1969 when the Taoiseach had come to visit him at Mount Carmel nursing home. Lynch disputed that contention. However, the Taoiseach was living in a Kafkaesque world from October 1969 until May 1970. There were times when he may have felt that he was confronted by a rival, parallel government. In the end, he did not know whom he could trust beyond the Attorney General Colm Condon, Patrick Hillery, Erskine Childers and a few others. Lynch could afford to take only a few other people into his confidence. His wife, Maureen, was always a rock of good sense and her alleged influence in political affairs had given rise to the quip 'petticoat power', a remark variously ascribed to disaffected members of Fianna Fáil.

The judgment of many of Lynch's ministers had been very poor on the Northern question in the summer of 1969. Was there not widespread ignorance inside Fianna Fáil about Northern Ireland? One former backbencher, John Moher, said that he could not recall Northern Ireland ever having been discussed at a parliamentary party meeting in the 1950s or 1960s.[44] The view that Lynch did not know about the moves to import arms in 1969 and 1970 has been greeted with incredulity, but the burden of evidence, based on the views of a confidential source, is that he did not know anything about what was going on. His minister for justice was in receipt of reports which provided beyond all doubt that there was a move to bring in arms for the North. Detailed and highly confidential reports were being sent to the Department of Justice from military intelligence and from the gardaí. But these reports were simply lying on the desk of the minister and were not being sent to the Taoiseach. Ó Moráin was ill and he was unable to do his job. While Lynch could excuse incompetence, he could not begin to comprehend that there was even the abstract possibility of the organised deception of the Taoiseach. That may again appear naïve in retrospect, but there was no precedent for a breach of faith on such a scale in the entire history of the state. Perhaps it was a measure of their arrogance that those allegedly involved with the plans to use government money to import arms mistakenly regarded Lynch as being soft-spoken, harmless and weak. That was a major miscalculation.[45]

On 5 May 1970, the Minister for Justice, Micheál Ó Moráin, was obliged to resign his cabinet position on the direction of Jack Lynch. He had been taken ill at a function in the Gresham Hotel on 22 April and removed to hospital.[46] The Minister for Agriculture, Neil Blaney, and the Minister for Finance, Charles Haughey, were dismissed from office two days later. The announcement came at 2.50 in the morning of 6 May, just in time for city editions of the papers.[47] The Minister for Local Government, Kevin Boland, resigned in sympathy with his colleagues, as also did Paudge Brennan, Blaney's parliamentary secretary.

There had been rumours of portentous political events for over a week, but even the wildest of rumours had not anticipated the 'earthquake', which Blaney had hinted at the previous week in the Dáil.[48] Liam Cosgrave had brought matters to a head on 5 May when he had pointedly asked Lynch how many ministerial resignations might be expected. The answer was evasive and Cosgrave had added: 'The smiles are very noticeable by their absence on the faces opposite.'[49] He had then gone to the Taoiseach with information that there was a move to import arms and that there was evidence of alleged high-level complicity.

Peter Barry, a former Fine Gael Minister for Foreign Affairs, is of the opinion that Lynch would not have acted had it not been for Cosgrave's intervention. The Taoiseach could not have acted if he was not aware of the facts. It seems bizarre that the leader of the opposition was the first to bring Lynch such sensitive news, but that was the reality. When made aware in this fashion, he had no alternative but to act as he did. Had the information come through normal channels, Lynch might have been tempted to conduct a cabinet reshuffle. He was denied that option by Cosgrave's dramatic intervention.

Lynch authorised immediate investigations, on foot of which he sought the resignations of both ministers. He said that he did so 'on the basis that I was convinced that not even the slightest suspicion should attach to any member of the Government in a matter of this nature.'[50] Cosgrave told the Dáil that he had been given information anonymously which alleged that there was a high-level attempt to import arms. There was mention of 'a document on official garda notepaper'. The plan, Cosgrave said, was to bring in £80,000 worth of arms under the pretence that the consignment was going to the Department of Defence. He called for the resignation of the government, as did the Labour Party leader, Brendan Corish. Senator John Kelly of Fine Gael felt that it was time for plain speaking and argued that a government 'from whose midst this appalling scandal has been dragged into the light of day has no right to claim the continued confidence of the people.'[51]

John Healy, the *Irish Times* columnist, wrote that Lynch and his party had taken a battering 'the like of which has not been seen in the House in this generation'.[52] Lynch reshuffled his cabinet on 9 May. Jerry Cronin went to Defence, replacing Jim Gibbons, who went to Agriculture and Fisheries. Gerard Collins was given Posts and Telegraphs and Robert Molloy took over Local Government. George Colley was given Finance and the Gaeltacht, and Desmond O'Malley took over the Department of Justice. Paddy Lalor was promoted to Minister for Industry and Commerce. Others remained in the same departments: Childers (Tánaiste and Health), Hillery (External Affairs), Joe Brennan (Labour and Social Welfare), Lenihan (Transport and Power), James Flanagan (Lands) and Pádraig Faulkner (Education).[53] As the final editions of the newspapers went to press on 9 May, the Dáil had gone through a marathon 21-hour debate. Lynch won by seven votes.[54] He had a *loyal* cabinet at last. Amid accusations and counter-accusations, Fianna Fáil managed to avoid losing power. Perhaps that was because the opposition was not anxious to face an election in such emotive circumstances. The country was in the midst of a cement strike, and a bank strike, which lasted from 30 March until 16 November.

Neil Blaney returned to a hero's welcome in Letterkenny.[55] Drama had been added to the sackings and resignations by virtue of the fact that Charles Haughey had been unable, for medical reasons, to present the budget to the Dáil on 22 April. He was in the Mater Nursing Home with a fractured skull, a broken eardrum and an injured clavicle. He had his solicitor, P.J. O'Connor, issue, on 25 May, a statement on his behalf. The sacked minister denied that he had 'at any time acted in breach of the trust reposed in me'. Compelled to refer to the circumstances which had brought to an end his membership of the government, Haughey stated that Lynch had requested his resignation 'on the grounds that he [the Taoiseach] was convinced that not even the slightest suspicion should attach to any member of the Government.' Haughey 'fully subscribed to that view'. He noted that the Taoiseach had received information 'of a nature which, in his opinion, cast some suspicion on me'. Not having had the opportunity to examine or test such information, he said that in the meantime 'I now categorically state that at no time have I taken part in any illegal importation or attempted importation of arms into this country.' Haughey 'fully accepted the Taoiseach's decision'. He believed that 'the unity of the Fianna Fáil party is of greater importance to the welfare of the nation than my political career'.[56]

By 10 May, Lynch had handed the papers on the alleged importation of arms to the Attorney General. Captain James Kelly, a former army intelligence officer, was arrested on 27 May. Albert Luykx, a Belgian who had lived in Ireland for over 20 years, was also arrested on the same day. Charles Haughey and Neil Blaney were both arrested the following day and charged with conspiracy to import arms and ammunition into the state. Kevin Boland accused Lynch of 'felon setting' and demanded a special conference of Fianna Fáil to remove him as parliamentary leader. On 4 June, Kevin Boland was expelled from the Fianna Fáil parliamentary party by secret ballot, 60 voting for the motion and 11 against; one ballot paper was left blank. On 22 June, the national executive of Fianna Fáil met and its general secretary, Kevin Boland, resigned.[57] Gerry Boland, a founding member—and still a vice-president and trustee of the party— resigned in solidarity with his son. (When he died in 1973, the family did not make any Fianna Fáil minister welcome at the funeral.)[58] Kevin Boland resigned his Dáil seat on 4 November. Blaney stayed in Fianna Fáil until 'the party left him' a year later. 'It isn't over yet', he commented in June 1970. The charges against Blaney were dropped by the Dublin District Court on 2 July and he was carried shoulder-high from the building. It wasn't over yet.

The remaining accused, together with the Belfast man, John Kelly, went on trial on 22 September, charged with conspiracy to import illegally, on different dates between 1 March and 24 April 1970, arms consisting of 500 pistols and approximately 180,000 rounds of ammunition. The trial judge, Mr Justice Andreas O'Keeffe, dismissed the jury on 29 September after certain exchanges. A new trial began before Mr Justice Seamus Henchy on 6 October and lasted fourteen days. Three of the four defendants admitted that they had attempted to import arms legally on the understanding that James Gibbons had sanctioned it. Haughey's defence was that he had no knowledge of the attempt to import arms and that he had played no part in the operation. In presenting the final case for the state, counsel said: 'For the purpose of establishing the case made by Mr Haughey in his defence, it is necessary, Gentlemen, to disbelieve the evidence of four other witnesses.' He was referring to Captain Kelly, Anthony Fagan (personal secretary to Mr Haughey in Finance), Peter Berry and Jim

Gibbons. In his summing up, Mr Justice Henchy said:

> I regret to say, Gentlemen, that it seems to me—and I think it will seem to you—in regard to the conversation which Mr Gibbons says took place in Mr Haughey's office on April 17th or April 20th, it either took place or it did not take place. Either Mr Gibbons, it seems to me, has concocted—invented as Counsel put it to him—this conversation or it happened in substance. Mr Haughey denies it, and he cannot see how his former colleague could say it is so. It is not like something said in the course of a conversation that could be misinterpreted. It seems to me, and you are free to dismiss my opinion, either Mr Gibbons concocted this and has come to court and perjured himself, or it happened. There does not seem to me to be any way of avoiding a total conflict on this issue between Mr Haughey and Mr Gibbons.[59]

The jury retired on 23 October. Tom MacIntyre described the scene when the jury returned a few hours later:

> A mob . . . owns Court No. 1 now, unmistakably, wait, Yes, the jury—and the court *rises* to the jury, a blind craven salute but no time to ponder it, the foreman, no-nonsense the cut of him, hands the verdicts to the clerk of court, pause, a silence now would split rock, and he reads, Not Guilty, Not Guilty, Not Guilty, Not—the place flies asunder to a brute roar, timber, bodies, spin of faces, that roar, it dips, renews itself—but a cleaner poetry, abruptly, through the fury, beyond it, where, on a span of wall between Bench and jury-box, the sealed windowless weeks are in procession through two open doors.[60]

Haughey emerged from the courthouse to cheers of 'We want Charlie' and 'Lynch must go'. Inside the nearby Four Courts Hotel, supporters of the four accused sang 'A Nation once again' and there were roars of 'We are Republican Fianna Fáil' and 'We are only starting'.[61] At a press conference, Haughey was reported as having called for the resignation of the Taoiseach: 'I think those who are responsible for this debacle have no alternative but to take the honourable course that is open to them.' Jack Lynch was in New York where he had addressed the 25th session of the General Assembly of the United Nations the day before the verdict was announced. He had spoken in moderate terms about Northern Ireland—the agreed policy of the Fianna Fáil party: 'I believe it to be the only realistic policy for the reunification of our country', he said. Haughey had said at his press conference that he did not think that the Taoiseach had represented Fianna Fáil policy as he had explained it at the United Nations. As regards the trial, he 'was never in any doubt that it was a *political trial*' (my emphasis). For good measure, Haughey had also attacked government financial policy when he expressed the view that he did not think that a mini-budget was required at the time.[62] Haughey had not waited very long to lay down a leadership challenge.

At a press conference in New York, Lynch said that 'no one can deny that there was this attempt to import arms illegally'. He made it clear that he was not going to put Gibbons out of the government. When asked to define republicanism, Lynch replied: 'Republicanism doesn't mean guns. It doesn't mean using guns. It is the state of a nation.'[63] Returning to Dublin on 26 October, Jack Lynch was met at the airport by the entire cabinet (with two exceptions, who were out of the country at the time), some fifty TDs and senators and by Frank Aiken, Seán MacEntee, Paddy Smith and Mick Hilliard. The *Irish Times* political correspondent, Michael McInerney, wrote that 'if anyone, after that display, wishes to say that they are better Republicans than Mr Lynch in Fianna Fáil, then they have a formidable task. . . . It was the Republic *par excellence*.'[64] If Lynch had an unmerited reputation for weakness, then his actions of the following days belied that mistaken notion. He won the parliamentary party meeting vote of confidence by 70 votes to three. This was followed by a meeting of the government on the following morning, 28 October. The press reported that Lynch was prepared to hold a general election before Christmas. The three dissident deputies had refused to pledge their support to the Taoiseach in the 'no-confidence' debate in the Dáil, scheduled to take place within two weeks. The government won the vote by 74 votes to 67, both Haughey and Blaney voting for Lynch. Boland resigned his seat in the Dáil and left Fianna Fáil to found Aontacht Éireann. Another Fianna Fáil TD, Seán Sherwin, resigned to join Boland's new party. Des Foley, a Fianna Fáil TD, attacked Lynch in the Dáil on 29 October 1970 and he resigned his seat on 4 November. Blaney and Paudge Brennan voted with the opposition in the no-confidence vote on James Gibbons on 10 November. Both were expelled from Fianna Fáil a week later.

The Dáil Committee of Public Accounts had been set up at the beginning of December 1970 to investigate the dispensing of the funds provided by the government for relief in Northern Ireland. It was a protracted affair and the committee's findings helped shed further light on the interstices of Irish politics. Sir John Peck, who was British ambassador in Dublin from 1970 until 1973, described Jack Lynch as being 'pure whipcord'.[65] Lynch's character was tested in the spring of 1971. The last hurrah for Blaney and Boland came at the Fianna Fáil *ard fheis* on 19–21 February at the RDS, Ballsbridge, where about 5,000 delegates gathered either to cheer or jeer Lynch. John Healy, in *The Irish Times*, captured the sometimes ugly mood of this gathering:

> 'Well—What did you think of the row?' 'What row? . . . I saw no row. There was no row. There never will be a row in Fianna Fáil. Never mind the papers. . . .' Of course it never happened. Kevin Boland was never incoherent with rage. Paddy Hillery, his face twisted in a rare display of the real Hillery temper, never told the faithful they had to choose between Kevin Boland and Fianna Fáil. The Taoiseach, Mr Jack Lynch, was never booed and no one chorused 'Union Jack, Union Jack' as he plodded manfully through his policy for Northern peace and integration. . . . I have not, since my days as a youngster and the Bolshie and Blueshirt rallies of my childhood, seen such naked passion exhibited publicly. . . .[66]

There was uproar as a delegate seized the microphone and there were scuffles between Boland and Lynch supporters. As Lynch began to speak, Boland was carried shoulder-high from the hall by chanting and cheering supporters. An RTE camera crew at the back of the hall were told to 'focus your . . . camera up the hall or elsewhere' as people covered their faces with programmes in case they might be filmed.[67] In the end, Lynch and his supporters won the day handsomely. Haughey, meanwhile, used his time in the 'sin-bin' of the back benches to build up his personal credibility within the party. It is quite misleading to conclude that when he would come to power in 1979, 'the forces of traditional irredentism' triumphed.[68] Lynch had won a decisive policy battle on Northern Ireland in 1970/71. Haughey would show no desire later to change that policy.

The activities of subversive organisations had increased in 1970. In April, a failed bank raid at Arran Quay, Dublin had resulted in the death of Garda Richard Fallon. The government had discussed the possibility of bringing in internment in the summer of 1970, but no decision had been taken.[69] The threat to introduce internment was made public by Jack Lynch. On 4 December 1970 it was claimed that 'a secret armed conspiracy exists in the country to kidnap one or more prominent persons. Connected with this conspiracy are plans to carry out armed bank robberies which the police believe may involve murders or attempted murders.' Detention centres were being prepared. Adverse public comment and a general air of disbelief did not deter the government. The Tánaiste, Erskine Childers, said in an interview on 4 January 1971 that 80 per cent of the public would support the introduction of internment. The government decision was based on information concerning the activities of extremists, and a warning was considered absolutely essential.[70] However, cabinet opinion in Dublin turned against internment.

In June 1970 the Conservative Party, under Edward Heath, had replaced Harold Wilson's Labour government. Reginald Maudling took over from James Callaghan as Home Secretary. The policy emphasis shifted to a reliance on military might. Between 3 and 5 July 1970 the director of military operations in the North, Sir Ian Freeland, sought to impose a curfew in the Lower Falls. The military conducted house-to-house searches and four people died in the ensuing violence. In Dublin, the Taoiseach phoned Hillery on 5 July to discuss what was to be done. Conscious that any action of his might compromise the government, Hillery said simply in reply: 'Leave this to me'. Lynch did not know what his foreign minister was planning.

Accompanied by a senior official from the Department of External Affairs, Éamon Gallagher, Hillery hired a car from Murrays and both men drove north together without an escort. No warning of their arrival was given to the RUC. Hillery walked down the Falls Road on 6 July 1970 and surveyed the damage for himself. It was a major propaganda coup which showed that the Dublin government was alive to the problems of the people in the North. The minister's unscheduled walk gained him international headlines and a frigid reaction from London.

Hillery paid a courtesy call on the British Foreign Secretary, Alec Douglas-Home, two days after his Belfast visit: 'I understand', wrote

Ambassador Peck, 'that the atmosphere was quite cordial, even friendly, but that in no sense could it be called constructive.' Hillery commented laughingly later 'that he had been summoned to the headmaster's study and given six of the best'.[71] He had told the British of the Irish government's fears that the harsh law-and-order policy was alienating the Catholic minority. He warned against military aggressiveness. Douglas-Home had called the visit 'a serious diplomatic discourtesy'.[72] Both Douglas-Home and Maudling remained unpersuaded by Hillery's arguments. Neither saw any reason to depart from their new policy of 'firm measures'.[73] In 1971 there were 17,262 house searches in the North; this had risen in 1973 to 75,000, or one-fifth of all houses in Northern Ireland. Dublin warned repeatedly against the use of such indiscriminate tactics.

On 9 August 1971 internment without trial was introduced in Northern Ireland without any prior consultations with Dublin. The move was all the more imprudent because the measure would have had to have been introduced simultaneously on both sides of the border in order to be effective. Ambassador Peck had called Lynch on 9 August, after the operation had got underway, only to be told that there was not the remotest possibility of internment being introduced in the South and that the consequences in the North would be catastrophic; for every man put behind the wire, a hundred more would volunteer, he said.[74] Ambassador Peck agreed later in his memoirs with those who regarded the introduction of internment as 'an appalling error'.

On 30 January 1972, 13 people were shot dead in Derry by soldiers of the First Parachute Regiment during a march organised by the Derry Civil Rights Association. Lynch described the killings as 'an unwarranted attack on unarmed civilians'. Civil rights leaders referred to it as 'another Sharpeville', where South African police had shot dead 67 during a peaceful demonstration against the 'pass laws' in 1960. On 2 February various organised groups in Dublin, including a strong trade union contingent, marched to the British embassy in Merrion Square. Some sections of the crowd chanted 'Burn, Burn, Burn' as a prearranged plan by the Provisional IRA was put into action and the building was fire-bombed. Gardaí looked on helplessly as uniformed PIRA members took over traffic duty and 'crowd control'.[75] That episode helped cure many Irish people of their ambivalence about militant 'republicanism'. They were revolted by the wanton burning of the embassy. But others took the lesson of 'Bloody Sunday' to mean that the IRA had a mandate to kill, murder and maim. The Official IRA had murdered the Unionist senator John Barnhill near Strabane, in December. They had also burned the home of the Stormont Speaker, Ivan Neill. On 22 February 1972, the Official IRA was responsible for the bombing of a parachute regiment's headquarters at Aldershot, Hampshire, in which seven people were killed—five of them women who worked in the canteen.[76] The Officials narrowly failed to assassinate the Unionist MP John Taylor on 25 February in Armagh. He was hit by six bullets in the attack.

The Provisional IRA was ruthless in its attacks. Among the worst was the explosion of a bomb in a crowded restaurant, the Abercorn, in Belfast on 4 March 1972. The no-warning attack left two women dead and 136 injured. The victims were mainly women and children who were taking a rest from shopping. One woman, who was out to buy her wedding dress, lost an arm and an eye. Two sisters each lost both their legs.

On 6 October 1972 gardaí closed down the Kevin Street office of Provisional Sinn Féin. A bomb exploded at Connolly Station, Dublin, on 28 October and four hotels in the capital were fire-bombed. The Sinn Féin *ard fheis* showed that the Provisionals were exhibiting no signs of moderation. Seán MacStiofáin, the leader of the Provisional IRA, was arrested on 19 November. He was charged under the Offences against the State Act two days later. He went on a hunger and thirst strike. Sentenced on 25 November, he shouted as he was leaving the court: 'I will be dead in six days. Live with that.' Protests grew and the foreign press assembled in Dublin. John Charles McQuaid and his successor, Father Dermot Ryan, visited MacStiofáin in hospital. The Labour TD David Thornley also paid him a call. Demonstrators marched on the Mater Hospital where MacStiofáin was held and, in the confusion, an effort was made by IRA men disguised as priests to snatch him from the hospital. He was moved to the Curragh where he gave up his hunger strike after 58 days, on 16 January 1973.

The Special Criminal Court had been reintroduced by the Minister for Justice, Desmond O'Malley, in May 1972. (This had been first instituted in 1939 to deal with subversion in a war setting.) It allowed for the setting up of juryless courts, presided over by army officers sitting as judges. In 1972, the court had civil judges. This was a serious intrusion into the civil liberties of the citizen, but it was deemed to be warranted by the crisis. On 22 November, Lynch had introduced an Offences against the State (Amendment) Bill into the Dáil. This permitted the conviction of a suspect solely on the testimony of a senior police officer that he believed that the person was a member of an illegal organisation. There was strong opposition to the Bill from members of the Labour and Fine Gael parties. Ironically, it was believed at the time that many members of the opposition supported the legislation, but, for political reasons, it was decided to oppose. There was the suggestion that the issue was being used to loosen Cosgrave's hold on Fine Gael so as to prepare the way for an early takeover by Garret FitzGerald.[77] Patrick Cooney, who was to become Minister for Justice in the coalition government of 1973, said that the likes of the Bill 'can only be found on the statute books of South Africa'. He also argued that there was a limit to the 'measures a democracy is entitled to adopt in order to protect itself'.[78] The government looked as if it would lose the vote by 71 to 70 on 1 December. Cosgrave had made a strong law and order speech in the Dáil two days previously, but the government had refused to accept any opposition amendment.

As the country waited for the news that a general election was to be held, the debate continued on Friday evening, 1 December, in Leinster House. The course of events was changed when two bombs exploded in Dublin, one outside Liberty Hall and a second in Sackville Place, killing two people and injuring 127. Within an hour of the blasts, Fine Gael announced that it had withdrawn its amendment and had agreed to abstain. Lynch won the vote by 69 votes to 22. The Bill went through the Senate on 2 December and was signed into law by President de Valera that night. Some members of the Fianna Fáil cabinet, among them Brian Lenihan, favoured going to the country.[79] Tactically, Lynch had the advantage over a radically divided opposition. There were, however, pressing issues to be dealt with by the government. Not the least of these was the need to put prominent members of the IRA behind bars. There were immediate arrests. It was reported that about 120 were listed for rounding up by the gardaí. Ruairí O'Bradaigh, the president of Sinn Féin (Kevin Street), was arrested on 29 December and later sentenced to six months in prison for membership of the IRA.

A bomb had exploded in the main street of Belturbet, Co. Cavan, on 28 December, killing a teenage boy and a girl. Violence was now a factor in the life of the Irish state and continued to have a deleterious effect on the performance of the Irish economy.

IRELAND GOES INTO THE EEC; FIANNA FÁIL LOSES POWER

The spillover of the Northern troubles into domestic Irish politics was not sufficient to deflect the government from pursuing vigorously Irish membership of the European Economic Community. Fianna Fáil and Fine Gael supported entry, while the Labour Party, the trade union movement and a variety of nationalist groups, including both Sinn Féins, opposed EC membership. One slogan on the 'No' side invoked the Northern internees as an authority for opposition: 'The boys in Long Kesh say vote no'. But when the result of the referendum was announced on 11 May 1972, the five-to-one majority in favour of entry surprised even the optimists on the 'Yes' side. In a 71 per cent turnout, 1,041,891 voted in favour and 211,891 against—a majority of almost 830,000. That represented an 83 per cent 'Yes' vote and a mere 17 per cent for the 'No' side. There was a clear 'Yes' majority in each of the 42 constituencies. The lowest majority in favour was 73 per cent—in Dublin South-West.[80]

Later that year Ireland joined the British and the Danes at the Paris summit where 1980 was set as the date by which European unity was to be achieved. Jack Lynch put forward the name of Dr Patrick Hillery for the post of European Commissioner. He was given the Social Affairs portfolio and served with distinction in Brussels from 1973 until 1976. Brian Lenihan took over as Minister for Foreign Affairs. The departure of Hillery to Brussels deprived Lynch of one of his closest advisers. His counsel in the early months of 1973, when Lynch was deciding upon the timing of a general election, may have been sorely missed.

On 5 February 1973, Jack Lynch announced to a surprised chamber that the 19th Dáil was being dissolved and that a general election would take place on 28 February. He gave three reasons for his decision. First, his party was in a minority situation in the Dáil. That had led to great uncertainty and he felt that strong leadership was required to carry through the government programme. He needed a clear mandate. The Northern situation was another factor. The general election would be over before a plebiscite was held in Northern Ireland on 8 March. (Northern Ireland voters were asked to decide whether they wished to remain part of the United Kingdom.

The SDLP and nationalist organisations discouraged people from voting. There was less than a 60 per cent turnout, 591,820 voting for and 6,463 against.) Finally, Lynch did not wish to see a presidential and a general election held on the same day in June. There were other factors which encouraged the Taoiseach to go for a spring election. It would be held before the Electoral Amendment Bill had been introduced in the Dáil. The election would also take place about five weeks before 140,000 new voters, aged between 18 and 21, would be entitled to vote.

Fianna Fáil had been in power for sixteen consecutive years and, according to Brian Lenihan, 'the people were tired of us'. A Fine Gael/Labour 'People's Coalition' was forecast immediately by the political correspondents. This was not going to be a repeat of 1969.[81] On 7 February 1973 the papers reported that the opposition leaders had agreed on the 'basics' of coalition.[82]

Both parties signed a fourteen-point programme which declared that the national coalition would aim to transform Ireland into a 'modern progressive society based on social justice'.[83] This was not so much a programme as a string of platitudes pledging peace, social and economic reform, civil rights, ending all discrimination against women, strict price control and voluntary wage control, removal of value-added tax from food, industrial democracy, social reform, the abolition of rates and the removal of the differential rents system.[84] Under the heading, 'Status of women', the programme promised: 'Legislation will be introduced to end all forms of existing discrimination against women.'

The Irish Times's 'Women First' page picked an all-woman cabinet. The choice for Taoiseach was Mary Bourke (Robinson) because 'more than any other Irishwoman in public life today she had made her mark as an intelligent, independent, courageous and determined politician'. The assessment continued:

Not quite four years ago, Mary Bourke was an unknown barrister from Ballina, a pretty young thing with a first class degree from Trinity College, Dublin, and a brilliant academic record from Trinity through Harvard University. Her election to the Senate surprised everyone, including herself. She could easily have settled in for a pleasant four years in the Leinster House debating club, at a comfortable bonus of £1,500 a year in salary. But Ireland's youngest senator has instead stirred up a steady whirlwind. . . . In a little over three years, she has made more impact on Irish life than virtually anyone in Dáil Éireann, male or female, and she would no doubt prove as formidable and daring in the position of critical leadership.

Others mentioned for high office were Seán MacEntee's daughter, Máire Mhac an tSaoi (Tánaiste and Minister for External Affairs), and Thekla Beere (Minister for Industry, Transport and Power). There was no shortage of candidates or talent.[85] The point of the article was that no woman had served in a full cabinet position since Countess Markievicz had been appointed Minister for Labour in 1919. An article in *The Irish Times*, on 7 February, had posed a list of questions women were to ask canvassers for candidates in the election concerning equal pay, equal opportunities, the right to serve on a jury, free legal aid, support for single parents and access to contraception. This was an election where women's issues were very much on the political agenda. It was also an election where there was *an alternative* to Fianna Fáil.

The campaign took place in terrible weather conditions. Fianna Fáil found itself on the defensive from the outset. The national coalition promised to better the government record on a range of matters. The proposal to introduce a capital gains tax surfaced early in the campaign and the opposition parties committed themselves to its introduction.[86] But even that did not frighten the electorate. Fianna Fáil perceived that it was in deep trouble. There was a complete change of electoral tactics on 22 February. Jack Lynch promised to increase social welfare and children's allowances, abolish rates on houses by 1 April 1974, and provide a pound of butter at 8 pence monthly to each family on social welfare. This was described by the coalition as a volte-face and an election bribe.[87] *The Irish Times*, in an editorial, commented that the Fianna Fáil campaign 'seems to be going to pieces'. The new election package was seen as 'panic measures'. The editorial writer felt that the calibre of the Lynch cabinet had been 'now mercilessly exposed to the television cameras'. It was felt that the Taoiseach's 'drawing power would have to be absolutely phenomenal to counter the incompetence shown by many of his lieutenants on the same medium'. There was also the charge that Lynch's constructive line on Northern Ireland was not echoed by the party in its 'scramble for votes'.[88]

Amid charge and counter-charge, 1,400,000 voters went to the polls on 28 February. The turnout was over 76 per cent. The PR system was worked well by the coalition. Fianna Fáil got 46.2 per cent of the vote, compared to 45.6 in 1969, and still lost. Two of the sacked ministers, Neil Blaney and Charles Haughey, headed their respective polls with 8,368 and 12,901 votes respectively.[89] Lynch lost the election, but his party had been beaten only by the 'bounce of the ball' in a number of marginals. The state of the parties was as follows: Fianna Fáil 69, Fine Gael 54, Labour 19 and others 2. That gave the national coalition 73 seats against 69 for Fianna Fáil. The two independents were Neil Blaney and Joseph Sheridan.

THE RISE AND FALL OF THE NATIONAL COALITION

The new government was announced on 15 March. Cosgrave had been elected Taoiseach the day before. There were no real surprises in the new team. There were, however, surprises over the allocation of portfolios. Declan Costello, who had re-entered politics, was made Attorney General. This was a major disappointment since it deprived the country of the opportunity to witness one of the most innovative social reformers at work in a ministry like Health and Social Welfare, Labour or Education. Garret FitzGerald, who had been shadow spokesman on Finance, was made Minister for Foreign Affairs; Richie Ryan was given Finance and was to have earned (undeservedly) by the end of his term in office the names 'Red Richie' or 'Richie Ruin'. Patrick Cooney was made Minister for Justice, Richard Burke was given the Education portfolio and Paddy Donegan was put in charge of Defence. The Labour deputies were given the following: Corish was Tánaiste and Minister for Health and Social Welfare; James Tully was Minister for Local Government; Michael O'Leary was Minister for Labour; Justin Keating was Minister for Industry and Commerce; and Conor Cruise O'Brien was Minister for Posts and Telegraphs.[90] It was a government of all the talents, and tensions.

Ostensibly, the old order was changing. The resignation of two figures from Irish public life in the early 1970s reinforced that perception. On 4 January 1972, John Charles McQuaid retired as archbishop of Dublin after spending over 30 years in the post; he died on 7 April 1973. Éamon de Valera retired from the presidency in June 1973; he died on 29 August 1975. Both men had been close friends in the 1930s. They were representative of a culture of service which had been a feature of the political life of the young state. In the 1970s, both men had lost their relevance. But the culture of service, upon which both had built their public lives, was an ever-diminishing influence in a state which had come to revere the philosophy of radical individualism. Conor Cruise O'Brien has stated that de Valera's greatest achievement, paradoxically, was

> . . . the consolidation of the Irish Free State ('what is now the Republic') into a stable, working democracy. That could not have been done without a certain amount of controlled obfuscation and he was (among other things) a master obfuscator. But in the post-de Valera Fianna Fáil, both the obfuscation and the contradictions it was designed to mask got fatally out of control, endangering the democracy that de Valera stabilised.[91]

It was the first time that Fianna Fáil had had to fight a presidential campaign as an opposition. They had a good candidate in Erskine Childers, a man who had been unwavering in his support of Lynch's position on the North. Tom O'Higgins, the opposition candidate, had lost the 1966 election to de Valera by only 10,717 votes. In 1973 he lost to Childers by 48,096 votes. A member of the Church of Ireland, Childers went to Áras an Uachtaráin with ambitious plans. He sought to make the presidency more open to the people and he threw himself into a round of visits, speech-making and travelling. On 16 November 1974, he delivered a lecture on drug abuse to the Royal College of Physicians. Shortly after completing his speech, he suffered a heart attack and died in the early hours of the morning.

Childers had little time to achieve his goals. The idea of an activist President may not have appealed to the national coalition. His successor, Cearbhall Ó Dálaigh, was an agreed candidate. His inauguration took place on 19 December 1974. He was to be treated shamefully on occasions by the coalition government. Matters reached a head in September 1976 when he referred an Emergency Powers Bill to the Supreme Court to test its constitutionality. The Bill permitted, among other things, the detention for seven days of people suspected of offences under the Offences against the State Act. On 15 October 1976, the Supreme Court found it to be constitutional and the President signed it the same day.[92] An editorial in *The Irish Times* pointed out that the ruling had explicitly preserved the detained person's right to communicate and to have access to legal and medical advice.[93] The accident-prone Minister for Defence, Patrick Donegan, made critical remarks about the President while addressing a function on 18 October at Columb Barracks, Mullingar. He used the most unlikely, but probably sanitised, phrase, 'a thundering disgrace' to describe the President in front of senior ranking army officers. The *Irish Times* leader writer felt that he would have to resign. The question was asked: 'are his views shared by other members of the Government—above all, are they shared by the Taoiseach?'[94] Inexplicably, Cosgrave did not sack Donegan. Instead, the minister sought a meeting with the President to tender an apology. Ó Dálaigh was not available to receive him. In the Dáil, on 21 October, five votes decided that Donegan should not resign. Cosgrave made it clear that a written apology had been sent to the Áras. The Taoiseach said: 'He made what I regard and what he himself regards as a serious comment on what the President did in a personally disrespectful way and he immediately announced his intention to apologise for it.' The Fine Gael TD and constitutional lawyer, John Kelly, sought to make a distinction between the incumbent and the office itself. He felt that it was 'bottomless absurdity' to claim that the Donegan comment was an attack on a state institution.[95]

Ó Dálaigh's resignation from the presidency was published in the press on 23 October. From his home in County Wicklow, he issued a statement stating that it was his only way to assert publicly his personal integrity and 'to protect the dignity and independence of the Presidency as an institution'. While Jack Lynch insisted that the resignation had parallels with the uncertain state of the country back in 1926 when Fianna Fáil was first founded, the parliamentary secretary to the Taoiseach, John Kelly, persisted in representing events as 'the worst outbreak of hysterical humbug' that he could remember. Kelly accepted that Donegan's annoyance was misplaced and its expression could not have been more unfortunate, but he regarded the idea that criticism of the President, as such, was a blow to the constitution as 'a piece of pious bunk which I believe those guilty of it will come to look back on with embarrassment'. The origins of the 'totempole' conception of the presidency lay 'in our malignant Paddyism, our instinct to look over our shoulder at what the English do, or did, and our abject acceptance that a convention good enough for the Queen of England is more than good enough for us.' Kelly disliked the several straight importations from Britain which had come to form part of the conventions surrounding the presidency; a gift of a sturgeon (the 'royal' fish), the requirement that the President send £50 gifts to centenarians and 'I suppose we should only be thankful that we are not expected to celebrate a bogus birthday for him as well.' Kelly preferred Ireland to use France or the United States as models.[96]

However, Ó Dálaigh—who had always been as a judge a strong defender of personal liberties—may have had good cause for concern. There had been a spate of bank robberies, kidnappings and a campaign of growing intimidation throughout the country. There were rumours about a so-called 'heavy gang' working inside the gardaí. No matter how serious the threat to the security of the state, no government was ever permitted to take shortcuts with the administration of justice. The circumstances, for example, surrounding the arrest of Nicky Kelly and his subsequent prosecution in connection with the March 1976 Cork-Dublin mail-train robbery remained a matter of public concern into the early 1990s when pressure grew to grant Kelly a presidential pardon.[97] It was finally given in 1992.

The presidential succession was more easily resolved than was the healing of the national coalition's self-inflicted wound. The Taoiseach spoke to Jack Lynch about finding an agreed candidate. Patrick Hillery, who had just come to the end of his term as EC Commissioner, was approached by Lynch and asked whether he would like to take on the office. Hillery, who did not have any ambitions in that direction, felt that he could not turn it down once he had been asked. He might have been considered at 53 the natural heir to the leadership of Fianna Fáil, but once he had agreed to take the position, he in effect excluded himself from politics for all time. He may not have realised that at the time, but it would have been unthinkable for him to resign the presidency to contest the Fianna Fáil leadership. It would have been a most serious blow to the status of the office of the President if two incumbents had resigned the post in succession. There was nothing particularly Machiavellian in Cosgrave's ploy. He simply wanted to dampen down as quickly as possible the ill-feeling towards the government which had been provoked by the Donegan affair. Dr Patrick Hillery was inaugurated as President on 3 December 1976. He was to hold that position for the next fourteen years.

The Donegan affair marked a low point in the term of the national coalition. The government of all the talents had begun with so much hope and optimism. It was a ragged and dispirited group by the time Ó Dálaigh resigned. What were the forces which brought this about? A substantial part of the explanation for the deterioration of the national coalition rested in the rapid decline in the international economic climate. Justin Keating describes the impact on the Irish economy of the first oil crisis at the end of 1973 as like 'falling over a cliff'.[98] Ireland imported over 70 per cent of its primary energy requirements. The crisis raised the price of oil by about ten times the 1972 rate. At the same time, election promises had to be kept. Local authority rates were cut, death duties abolished and social welfare benefits and services were extended.[100] The convention of balancing public expenditure had been abandoned by George Colley in 1972. The coalition continued that practice, but the Minister for Finance began to cut back in the years 1976 and 1977 and 'had the policy been continued in 1978–9, then the public finances would have been largely restored to order before the world economy turned down again in 1980'. That is the view of Kieran Kennedy and his team of economists.[101]

Efforts were made in difficult circumstances to sustain economic growth and social reform, but divisions within government prevented the introduction of many radical measures. A wealth tax was introduced, only to be repealed by Fianna Fáil in 1978. The actual yield was as follows: 1975, £3,672,411; 1976, £6,488,613; and 1977, £5,806,067. Arrears were paid up to 1984, netting over £4m for the Revenue Commissioners.[102]

The Minister for Foreign Affairs, Dr Garret FitzGerald, was an outstanding member of that government. He enjoyed a very good working relationship with Keating. Under FitzGerald's direction, Iveagh House underwent a major expansion, and the Irish diplomatic network was extended to include Moscow. At another level, FitzGerald sought to initiate discussion on the question of pluralism in Irish society. However, the redirection of society along that path was vigorously opposed by Cosgrave and the more conservative members of the cabinet. A Bill was introduced in 1974—necessitated by the McGee judgment in 1973—to provide for the unrestricted importation of contraceptives. Mrs Mary McGee was the wife of a fisherman. Born in 1944 and married in 1968, she lived in a mobile home with her husband and their four children. The family income was about £20 a week. During each of her pregnancies, she had suffered serious complications. Another pregnancy, according to her doctor, might have resulted in paralysis or death. The couple decided to use an artificial method of contraceptive. Her doctor issued her with a prescription for spermicidal jelly which was neither manufactured nor sold in Ireland. Mrs McGee, therefore, was obliged to import it from England. The Irish customs seized her parcel, acting under the Criminal Law Amendment Act. In the absence of new legislation, the couple sought to take the matter to the courts with the financial help of the Irish Family Planning Association. Mary McGee's action was dismissed in the High Court, but was upheld upon appeal to the Supreme Court. The decision legalised the importation of contraceptives for married couples. It was up to the legislature to react. But when it came before the Dáil, the Taoiseach, Liam Cosgrave, the Minister for Education, Richard Burke, and five other Fine Gael TDs voted against their own government's Bill. The measure was defeated and legislation on contraception was not enacted for a further four years.

Dr Conor Cruise O'Brien displayed strong moral courage throughout this period, consistent with his reputation at other times in his various careers. He was an outspoken critic of the IRA and an unrelenting exposer of ambivalences in the Irish psyche. His 1976 Broadcasting Amendment Act was widely criticised by journalists because of the ban it placed on the interviewing of subversives; but it was necessary in the context of the time and the years have demonstrated the wisdom of its wording.

With such talent at its disposal, how was it possible for media commentators to contemplate the demise of the coalition? Fianna Fáil won two important by-elections in March 1975 in Galway North-East and Galway West. Lynch failed to win another by-election later that year in Mayo West. Fianna Fáil could only look on with apprehension as the Minister for Local Government, Jim Tully, sought to redraw the constituency boundaries with the same attention to detail as Kevin Boland had lavished on that task. This reversal of Boland's gerrymander became known as the 'Tullymander'. However, not everyone in the Labour Party was very happy with the redrawn constituencies. Tully did no favour to his Labour colleague, Justin Keating, who subsequently lost his seat, as did Conor Cruise O'Brien in the next general election. It was called on 16 June 1977. That was nine months earlier than was legally necessary.[103]

It was a major miscalculation, provoked to some extent by the arrogant assumption that the coalition could not lose. Many respected political commentators continued to believe right up to the end that the national coalition would win. 'Coalition set to take election,' read the headline in *The Irish Times* on 16 June over a story by the highly experienced Dick Walsh. However, a resurgent Fianna Fáil had prepared carefully for the contest. A policy committee had produced a manifesto entitled *Action Plan for National Reconstruction*. A number of extravagant promises were added to the document before publication. Fianna Fáil set an 80,000 job creation target between 1977 and 1980. Lynch said that any government in Ireland which allowed the unemployment figure to rise above 100,000 deserved to be rejected by the electorate.[104] Fianna Fáil gave a promise to cut taxes by about £160m. There were pledges to abolish rates on private dwellings and road tax on cars up to 16 horse power. There were to be increases in personal tax allowances and a reduction in the social welfare stamp for low-wage earners. This was a 'pork barrel' election. It was Christmas in June for mainly the Irish middle classes. This interpretation of the 1977 election has been firmly rejected by Jack Lynch, who maintains that the Fianna Fáil programme was progressive and of benefit to all sectors of the community.[105] The promises certainly appealed to the voters, many of whom felt badly let down by the coalition. Fianna Fáil had 84 seats and a twenty-seat majority over all other parties. Fine Gael fell from 53 to 43 seats and Labour from 20 to 17.[106] Mary Robinson, who was to be elected President of Ireland in 1990, was among the defeated Labour candidates. The day belonged to Jack Lynch and a triumphant Fianna Fáil.

Charles Haughey and the Poverty of Populism

J ack Lynch returned to power with his invincible majority and his personal prestige restored. His majority proved yet again that Fianna Fáil was the party of 'the people'. Many of the same faces were appointed to cabinet, but the pack was reshuffled somewhat. George Colley was Tánaiste and Minister of Finance and the Public Service. His arch rival, Charles Haughey, was brought back into the cabinet as Minister for Health and Social Welfare. Michael O'Kennedy was made Minister for Foreign Affairs and Gerard Collins was given Justice. Desmond O'Malley, another Haughey rival, was made Minister for Industry, Commerce and Energy. John Wilson was given the Education portfolio and Martin O'Donoghue was Minister for Economic Planning and Development. Jim Gibbons returned to Agriculture and Brian Lenihan was appointed to Fisheries. Anthony Hederman was made Attorney General.

There were 106,000 unemployed in 1977 and the figure dropped to 90,000 in 1979.[1] Industrial strategy was geared towards the creation of full employment. Expansionism was back in vogue after the hair-shirt days of the national coalition. The government gambled on growth. If it were merely a question of short odds, then the failure that was to follow might have been defensible, but the strategy was profligate and prodigal. The government's foreign borrowing behaviour mirrored in the lifestyle of a private citizen would have prompted him to seek help from gamblers' anonymous. The national debt was £4,220m in 1977. The following year it rose to £5,167m and it went to £6,540m in 1979. In 1980, the figure was £7,896m and £10,196m in 1981.[2] The younger generation were the losers as a government rolled the dice and forfeited the family silver.

LOCAL GOVERNMENT AND THE MAKING OF THE DEMOCRATIC DEFICIT

The redeeming of another electoral promise was to have an even more subversive effect on the structure of Irish democracy. The removal of domestic rates following the Fianna Fáil electoral victory was an attractive prospect for middle-class householders. Notwithstanding the promise by Fianna Fáil to make good the loss from central funding until 1982, de-rating led to the gradual impoverishment of local authorities. In 1976 the state bore about 40 per cent of local expenditure. The following year rates brought in £107.4m or 34 per cent of local authority income. But in 1978 that dropped to £81.6m or 21 per cent of income. In 1979 the comparable figures were £89.7m or 21 per cent. That has to be compared to the state grant of £145.7m (46 per cent), £228.9m (50 per cent) and £266.4m (61 per cent) in the years 1977 to 1979 respectively.[3]

The Cork city manager commented in his estimate of expenses for 1992 that the government grants in compensation for the loss of domestic rates had fallen short of the amounts that would have been collectable, had the domestic rates liability remained in position. He said that it had been £1.3m in 1983 and had risen to £14m in 1991. The total cumulative loss for Cork city since 1983 was close to £60m.

The establishment in April 1971 of the eight health boards was short-sighted and a waste (and they in turn would be replaced by a central Health Service Executive in 2004). This further diverted money from the local authorities, where state funding in the first part of the 1970s fell by about 10 per cent as a consequence. The health board idea was poorly conceived. There was a need to centralise the recruitment and monitoring of consultancy work at a *national* level. It did not help in this facet of specialised medicine to divide up the country into eight regions. Other aspects of medicine, however, might have been much better left in the control of local authorities. It made no sense whatsoever to have a dispensary doctor under a regional authority in Cork when it would have been much more efficient to deal with Tralee, only thirty miles away.[4] Richard Haslam recorded the remark of a former Minister for Health about the health boards: 'how do you unscramble an egg'?[5]

Membership of the European Community worked in many continental countries to reinforce and strengthen regional and local democracy—Spain, Germany and Italy being three of the most obvious cases. But in Ireland, central government took it upon itself to act as national broker with Brussels. Local initiative was positively and actively discouraged. Only government departments and their respective ministers were permitted by the government to mediate professionally with the EC. The political party in power filtered EC funds through the central system. Various interest groups, notably the Irish Farmers' Association (IFA) and the Confederation of Irish Industries (CII) saw the advantage of maintaining a professional lobby in Brussels. Unlike the experience of many European regions, local authorities in Ireland did not see fit to follow suit. Neither were they encouraged to do so by the Department of Finance or the Department of the Environment. For example, a letter sent to all county managers on 29 July 1988 stipulated that the Committee of Ministers and Departmental Secretaries on the European Community Internal Market and Structural Funds, which was chaired by the Taoiseach, had decided that all contact with Brussels had to be reported to the relevant government departments in Dublin:

> . . . in the circumstances you would arrange to have any such contacts on or after 1st August notified to the Department— addressed to 'Secretary, Department of the Environment, Planning Administration Section, Hawkins House, Dublin 2' and marked for the attention of Mr Liam Johnston. *The notification should give the names of the relevant community officers contacted, the names of local authority officers and/or members involved and a very brief indication of the outcome of any such contacts.* (my emphasis)[6]

This communication, however well-intentioned and harmless in intent, was received with some irritation by the city and county managers and by the local authorities. The regions and local government felt not merely a sense of loss of power. There was a feeling of helplessness, engendered by a falsely induced sense of dependence upon the professionalism of the national administration in the capital.[7] Tom Barrington, the leading exponent of devolved government in Ireland, has argued that 'we now have by far the most centralised state in Western and Middle Europe'. In his view, that meant 'we are 50 per cent more centralised than the European norm, and three times as centralised as the leading European local democracy, Denmark'. Ireland had the fewest number of local authorities, a very restricted number of local public representatives, and an extremely restricted range of local discretion. Barrington commented in 1992 that a recent figure of appointed representatives on the boards of state-sponsored bodies gave a total of some 2,200, which contrasted with some 1,500 locally elected representatives.[8] However, the democratic deficit did not result in any outbreak of local revolts against central government. People simply remained complacently disempowered.

MORALITY, CHURCH AND STATE

Opposition to government in the 1970s and 1980s came from another quarter. There was a danger in the late 1970s that the state would find growing opposition from the Catholic Church for its relative failure in social policy and in its attitude towards the poor of the Third World. The work of the development organisation, Trócaire, sensitised many of the bishops and obliged prelates to see the links between poverty at home and in the Third World. The traditional hostility of the Catholic Church to liberal capitalism was manifest in the hierarchy's joint pastoral, *The Work of Justice*, which was published in 1977. There was a strong attack on the problem of unemployment and on the prevalence of poverty in society. The number of poor was estimated at 20 per cent of the population. There was a demand for redistribution of wealth from the better-off section of society to the poorer groups. The need for job creation to take precedence over economic planning was emphasised.[9] The hierarchy wanted to see a more compassionate society created in Ireland. The joint pastoral could be read as an episcopal judgment on the most significant failure of the modern Irish state. The Maynooth sociologist Liam Ryan argued that the hierarchy ought to adopt the *conscience of society* model in dealing with church-state matters.[10]

But, while it was relatively easy to win support for a position in moral theology which had become the norm since Vatican II, it was quite a different matter to eliminate the residual majoritarianism, which had been the basis of the traditional teaching of the Irish Catholic Church since the foundation of the state. Here the hierarchy simply failed to develop a coherent pastoral response which would take into account the radical shifts in Irish society. This was very much in evidence in the matter of sexual morality. The hierarchy had published *Human Life is Sacred* in 1975. While there was little vocal, public demand for the legalisation of abortion in the 1970s and early 1980s, there were a significant numbers of Irish women taking the boat/train or flying to London to terminate unwanted pregnancies. In the late 1980s, the figure was put at between 2,000 and 3,000 a year. That did not appear to be an issue where there was a demand for legislation, but the non-availability of divorce was of more widespread concern. The high incidence of marital breakdown was a matter which touched the lives of a growing number of people in Ireland in the 1970s. The constitutional ban on divorce required modification to cope with the social changes in Ireland. But this was an issue of great importance, as events in the 1980s were to prove. The extension of the nullity laws was one of the ways that bishops thought that the matter could be handled in the late 1970s. While divorce meant the dissolving of a *valid* marriage, a decree of nullity from the Catholic church meant that *no valid* marriage had existed. The Irish courts had recognised a nullity jurisdiction, despite the fact that a person who had received a dispensation from the church and had remarried was living in a bigamous union. This had created numerous anomalies over succession rights.

An important piece of church reform had been carried out by Cardinal Conway during the early 1970s. The Catholic hierarchy had revised the marriage tribunal structure throughout the country. This work was built upon by his successor, Monsignor Tomás Ó Fiaich, who was ordained archbishop of Armagh on 2 October 1977. He was made a cardinal on 30 June 1979. Ó Fiaich, a strong nationalist and Irish language enthusiast, sustained Conway's Northern policy. He usually proved to be far less preoccupied about matters of sexual morality than many of his fellow bishops. Credit for the revision of the marriage tribunal structures must go to his predecessor, but Ó Fiaich made sure that the reforms worked. Originally, a tribunal existed for each of the dioceses. That remains the situation in Britain. But in 1976 the number in Ireland was reduced to four—based in

Dublin, Cork, Galway and Armagh. The country was divided geographically. The four areas did not coincide with the archdioceses. Official Catholic Church statistics show that there were 779 applications for nullity decrees in 1976 for the whole of Ireland. There were 111 judgments, of which 79 decrees of nullity were given. However, in about 75 per cent of cases, according to official sources, there is a prohibition, called a *vetitum* (veto), on one or both of the partners from marrying again. The comparable figures for 1977 were 885 applications, 139 judgments and 104 decrees of nullity. In 1978 the numbers were 778, 154 and 91. There were 620 applications in 1979, 108 judgments and 75 decrees of nullity. The figures for 1980 to 1984 are as follows:

	Applications	Judgments	Decrees of Nullity
1980	694	152	76
1981	674	125	73
1982	650	134	83
1983	713	180	94
1984	686	133	118[11]

Nevertheless, this process dealt with only a fraction of marital breakdown cases. But divorce was not an issue which most politicians in the 1970s were willing to tackle. Strong opposition could be expected from the hierarchy. The bishop of Ardagh and Clonmacnois, Dr Cahal Daly, had refused to accept that the Northern situation should be used as a pretext for pressing constitutional change in the Irish Republic. He was adamant that the question of divorce should be debated strictly on its merits, without any reference to political considerations. The issue was too grave and its implications for family life, for the welfare of children, for the quality of life and of society, too serious, for it to be made the coinage of political trading. Bishop Daly had made those remarks in a speech in which he had regarded, in his personal capacity, the two sections of article 44 on religion in the constitution as a 'complete irrelevance, an irritant, and a distraction from other important matters'.[12] The introduction of divorce was an issue for politicians to face in the 1980s and 1990s.

In the late 1970s, trying to legislate on the matter of contraception rather than divorce was where politicians concentrated great energy. There was a renewed effort to try to bring the law into line with the ruling in the Mary McGee case. It would be generally agreed that the

1973 coalition government had handled the contraception question with considerable clumsiness. It was still illegal, under the Criminal Law Amendment Act of 1935, to import or sell contraceptives in 1977. The 'pill' was available on prescription. It was estimated in 1978 by a committee of the Irish Medical Association that 48,000 Irishwomen were using the 'pill'. Other methods of family planning could be obtained through a network of clinics. In 1979 there were five in Dublin and one each in Cork, Limerick, Galway, Bray and Navan.[13] There was a widespread demand for the services on offer: the Irish Family Planning Association saw about 30,000 people in 1976 and over 53,000 in 1978. There was strong evidence in opinion polls that attitudes had changed radically towards the availability and sale of contraceptives during the 1970s. A poll in 1971 had found that 63 per cent of the respondents were opposed to the sale of contraceptives; only 34 per cent were in favour.[14] But in 1977, an opinion poll found that 43 per cent favoured the legalisation of contraceptives for married couples, 21 per cent favoured legalisation for all adults, and only 23 per cent were opposed to legalisation.[15]

The Catholic bishops maintained their opposition to the legalisation of contraception. Traditionally, the bishops had taken a straight majoritarian line. John Charles McQuaid had told his flock in a pastoral letter in 1971 that any contraceptive act was always wrong in itself. Therefore, to speak of a right to contraception on the part of the individual, 'be he Christian or non-Christian or atheist, or on the part of a minority or of a majority, is to speak of a right that cannot even exist'. The archbishop said that the public consequences of immorality that must follow upon legalisation for 'our whole society are only too clearly seen in other countries'.[16] He regarded the legalisation of contraception as 'a curse upon the country'. Referring to the linking of the reunification of Ireland with the enactment of contraceptive laws in the Irish Republic, McQuaid said: 'One must know little of the Northern people if one can fail to realise the indignant ridicule with which good Northern people would treat such an argument.'[17]

The official episcopal statement on contraception in 1973 contained the following line: 'There are many things which the Catholic Church holds to be morally wrong and no one has ever suggested, least of all the Church herself, that they should be prohibited by the State.'[18] The argument had been shifted from an assertion of majority Catholic rights to a defence of the common good. Notwithstanding the shift in emphasis in the statement of the bishops, Cardinal Conway in December 1973 clearly believed that such legalisation in the Republic would bring about a change for the worse in the quality of life; such a change, he said, had taken place in the North. Neither did he think that it would be possible to restrict the use of contraceptives to married couples. Their use would spread, he said, to young people and it would affect marital fidelity and mean a general extension of promiscuity. That had been the experience in other countries: 'The young have high moral standards but we should not make the environment for moral living more difficult for them.' There were indications that the position in Northern Ireland had had the effects the bishops talked about, he continued. Conway stressed his concern for young people and for society as a whole. He rejected the idea that the legalisation of contraception was an issue in relation to the question on Northern Ireland 'but I think it would be utterly unrealistic to think that the attitudes of the average Unionist towards a united Ireland would be changed in the slightest degree if the law in the Republic were changed.'[19] There had been no substantial change in the attitude of the hierarchy since that time. In 1978, the Catholic hierarchy issued another statement on contraception which followed along the same lines as the earlier formulation, where emphasis was laid upon the effects of a change in the law on society as a whole.[20]

It fell to the Minister for Health, Charles Haughey, in 1977 to introduce new legislation on contraception. Although there was a pressing social need to move quickly on this matter, Haughey responded on the trot rather than at a gallop. The minister made sure that the Catholic bishops and about 18 other interested bodies were consulted. The Church of Ireland, when approached, approved of the giving of family planning advice by the health authorities, expressed concern about abortifacients, and favoured the sale of contraceptives.[21] At the end of 1978, the Bill was published. It was a great disappointment to those who felt that Haughey was a liberal on social issues. Contraceptives were to be sold through chemist shops on a doctor's prescription. That prescription could be given by a doctor, if he or she were satisfied that the person was seeking the contraceptives, bona fide, for family planning purposes or for adequate medical reasons and in appropriate circumstances.[22] Purchase was not confined to married couples, but that was only because it was difficult to define a married couple. Some couples, for example, may have been married in the eyes of the church but not in the eyes of the state. In reality, the Bill was designed to confine access to contraceptives to married couples. Ireland became the only country in Western Europe where condoms were a prescription item.

A vociferous debate developed on the proposed measures. Was Haughey simply showing his own latent conservatism by pursuing such a course? Many thought that that was the case. Was Haughey displaying his skills as a practitioner of the art of the possible? Ideally, he might have liked to go further, but did he feel that conservative forces in the Oireachtas might vote down the Bill? Only access to official archives will provide definitive answers, but there was another variable that might have encouraged him to act with caution. As a contender for the leadership of Fianna Fáil in the relatively near future, Haughey had no intention of unnecessarily alienating support in the party. It is likely that his own conservatism on this question was reinforced by his desire to maximise his chances to become the next leader of Fianna Fáil. The wording of the Health (Family Planning) Bill 1978 was a logical consequence of his career trajectory.

The Dáil debate that followed was emotional and acrimonious. John Kelly argued that the legislation was superfluous; all that was needed was the removal of section 17 of the Criminal Law Amendment Act 1935. Haughey interpreted that as leading to a situation where 'artificial contraception would be universally available without limitation or control to every person in our community'.[23] Oliver J. Flanagan of Fine Gael was opposed to the Bill: changing the law, he said, could not make the use of contraceptives morally right. What was wrong remained wrong regardless of what the state said: 'The Church, with its experience of 2,000 years, tells us that artificial contraception is morally wrong.'[24] His colleague, Jim O'Keeffe, in a long reflective contribution, suggested that contraception was a question of private morality and that couples should be guided by their own conscience.[25] Barry Desmond, for the Labour Party, said that the Bill could not be acceptable for 'anybody who has concern for human rights or for women as persons'. He wanted to know from the minister how many of the 18 organisations that he said he had consulted when framing the legislation represented young women: 'How many represented unprivileged women, women living in overcrowded homes, in bad homes or women suffering the tensions of having to share those housing conditions with in-laws?'[26]

Desmond described Haughey's approach as 'a legislative crawl'.[27]
Haughey saw it as a 'sensible, middle-of-the-road type of solution
to a serious and complex situation'.[28] In framing the legislation, he
explained to the Dáil, he had sought to tread the middle ground. He
was faced with the necessity to make artificial contraceptives available
'to married persons or for family planning purposes'. On the other
hand, he did not, nor could he accept, 'the situation where artificial
contraceptives would be made freely available to everybody without
any limitation of any kind.'[29] The Labour Party opposed the Bill on
the grounds that it did not go far enough. Fine Gael was given a free
vote. The only minor tremor in the Dáil when the vote was taken was
the defection of the Minister for Agriculture, Jim Gibbons. A bitter
rival of Haughey's since the 'arms trial' of 1970, Gibbons refused to
support the Bill on grounds of conscience, but it passed into law with
a safe majority in July 1979. Haughey could claim a victory because
the passage of such a measure had eluded legislators since 1971. There
was no church-state crisis. It was an Irish solution to an Irish problem
which, by design or on purpose, had not done Haughey's leadership
ambitions any damage. Neither did the fact that the Irish economy
was running into great difficulties. The white paper, *National
Development 1977–1980*, was foredoomed. It was a case of the
Hibernian miracle, as Joseph Lee has termed it, that never was.[30]

Meanwhile the tragedy of Northern Ireland was underlined by a
report on 18 January 1978 from the European Court of Human Rights
in Strasbourg which held that interrogation techniques used on
internees in 1971 did not amount to torture, but had been 'inhuman
and degrading' treatment. The case had been taken by the Irish
government. Amnesty International published its report in June 1978
on the alleged ill-treatment of people in Castlereagh RUC
interrogation centre. It claimed that the physical and mental
maltreatment of suspects was still taking place.[31] Lynch had retained
a law and order policy in relation to the activities of subversives in the
Irish Republic. However, he had investigations carried out into the
activities of certain sections of the gardaí under the national coalition.
Section 31 of the Broadcasting Act remained. There was no amnesty
for 'republican' prisoners. Lynch's government suffered some
embarrassment when an effort was made to sack the Garda
Commissioner, Edmund Garvey. In March 1979 the Supreme Court
upheld a High Court decision that Garvey's dismissal on 19 January

1978 was null and void. He was awarded damages and costs. Garvey resigned on 15 April 1979.

Lynch enjoyed one major diplomatic success on Northern Ireland. Jimmy Carter, the US president, on 30 August 1977 recognised that the Irish government had a role to play in any settlement and committed his administration to support a system of government achieved by peaceful means that would be acceptable to both sections of the community in the North.[32] The voice of Washington was not welcomed by London.

The Provisional IRA demonstrated that it was still as ruthless as ever when on 17 February 1978 they fire-bombed the La Mon restaurant, in Comber, Co. Down at a cost of sixteen lives. The standing committee of the bishops said on 25 February that the overwhelming majority of Irish people wanted the campaign of violence to end immediately in Northern Ireland. But the Provisional IRA responded with more violence. On 14 November they admitted causing extensive damage to Armagh city and setting off firebombs and explosives in 13 other towns and villages. They promised that they were preparing for a prolonged war. Earlier in the month they had carried out bombing attacks in Belfast, Armagh, Dungannon, Enniskillen, Cookstown and Castlederg. On 30 March 1979, the Irish National Liberation Association (INLA) killed the Conservative spokesman on Northern Ireland, Airey Neave, when a bomb was exploded under his car as he drove from the House of Commons underground car park. (In September 1977, Seamus Costello—the founder of the political wing of the INLA, the Irish Republican Socialist Party—had been shot dead in Dublin.) There was little sign of a breakthrough during the time of James Callaghan's Labour government, from 1976 until 1979. The Northern Secretary at the time, Roy Mason, was certainly one of the most maladroit people to have held that post since the suspension of Stormont. Callaghan tended to concentrate on economic rather than on political advance in Northern Ireland. He did increase the number of seats for Northern Ireland at Westminster. Ironically, the votes of MPs from the North were decisive in Callaghan's defeat in the Commons on 28 March 1979 by 311 to 310.[33] Margaret Thatcher and the Conservative Party were returned to power on 3 May. She promised in her first speech to the Commons to pursue a tough security policy with no amnesty for convicted terrorists.

JACK LYNCH RESIGNS

In June 1979 Fianna Fáil faced with foreboding the first direct elections to the European Parliament. Local elections were to be held on the same day. A world oil crisis had radically reduced the availability of petrol to the public.[34] Ration books might have been introduced had it not been for the fact that the country had been without a postal service for the previous five months. The summer weather had temporarily reduced the pressure on demand, but rationing appeared unavoidable in the autumn. Some candidates were reduced to using bicycles to campaign in the city areas. FitzGerald, leading Fine Gael in his first electoral campaign since being appointed leader, accused Lynch of a 'weak-kneed' approach to the business of government where he had refused to dismiss incompetent ministers and seek new talent within his party.[35]

Fianna Fáil was confronted by hostility from many quarters. There was outrage in the farming community over the imposition of a two per cent levy on farmers' turnover.[36] Lynch received a very rough reception in his native Cork where striking postal workers thumped his car and called for the resignation of the Minister for Posts and Telegraphs, Pádraig Faulkner.[37] To make matters worse, Fianna Fáil had predicted that the party would win eight Euro-seats out of fifteen in the 7 June poll. The outcome was a major setback for Lynch. Fianna Fáil's share of the vote dropped by almost 16 per cent from the record level of the previous general election. The party failed completely in its ambition to take eight of the Euro-seats.[38] It won five seats, getting 34.68 per cent of the vote, compared to 50.63 per cent in 1977. In Munster, Fianna Fáil lost a seat to the farmers' candidate, T.J. Maher. Neil Blaney was elected in Connacht/Ulster. Labour won four seats and Fine Gael got four. In Northern Ireland, John Hume (SDLP), Ian Paisley (Democratic Unionist) and John Taylor (Official Unionist) were also elected to the European Parliament.

The abolition of domestic rates had saved Fianna Fáil from humiliation in the local government elections. Nevertheless, the results clearly reflected growing disillusionment with the government. Electricity charges had increased by 20 per cent on 1 June. The national understanding on wages had collapsed and the government appeared to be set for a clash with the unions over an attempt to impose a new 7 per cent wage limit.[39] Charles Haughey was the person to benefit most from Lynch's discomfort. He showed scant respect for many of his cabinet colleagues. Shortly before the Euro elections, he had revealed that he was having talks with one of the postal strike union leaders. That was at a time when the government was trying to maintain a firm line on pay increases. Breaking ranks was against the rules. Haughey was ostracised by his cabinet colleagues.[40]

The postmortem at the parliamentary party failed to allay the fears of many TDs. The election setback could have been explained by a combination of mid-term disenchantment with the government, hostility over the postal strike and the imposition of an agricultural levy. Five TDs stayed behind after the meeting and discussed the idea of a change of leadership. They were Albert Reynolds, Thomas McEllistrim, Jack Fahey, Seán Doherty and Mark Killilea. Two Fianna Fáil senators, Flor Crowley and Bernard McGlinchey, later joined the 'heave' against Lynch, as did the junior minister in the Department of Finance, Ray MacSharry.[41] A caucus of the main anti-Lynch people met on 5 July. There were about 20 TDs in attendance. One source named the outspoken Kildare TD, Charles McCreevy, as having been there. The Mayo TD Pádraig Flynn also attended.[42] In the following weeks, overtures were made to recruit other TDs.[43]

Lynch was on holiday in Portugal on 27 August 1979 when the Provisional IRA murdered Earl Mountbatten by blowing up his boat off Mullaghmore, Co. Sligo. The earl's grandson, and a boatboy, were also killed outright. Lord and Lady Brabourne were seriously injured; she died of her injuries later. That same day, the IRA killed 18 British soldiers in two bomb blasts at Narrow Water Castle, between Newry and Warrenpoint, Co. Down.[44] Lynch attended the funeral of Mountbatten in London where he had discussions with the British prime minister, Margaret Thatcher. A radical security review and greater cross-border cooperation were discussed. On 9 September 1979 Síle de Valera, a grand-daughter of 'the chief', used the occasion of a Liam Lynch commemoration ceremony indirectly to challenge the Taoiseach's leadership.[45]

However, the visit by Pope John Paul II to Ireland from 29 September to 1 October, was a welcome intermission for Lynch from the daily grind of party factionalism. Over 2.5 million people attended the seven venues of the itinerary. The visit was originally intended to include Northern Ireland, where an ecumenical service of reconciliation was planned for St Patrick's Cathedral, Armagh. It was intended to bring the victims of violence together from all denominations. But the Mountbatten killings, together with the death of the British soldiers near Warrenpoint, forced a last-minute and very reluctant cancellation by the Holy See. The pope did say mass in the archdiocese of Armagh, near Drogheda, where he appealed to all men and women engaged in violence: 'On my knees I beg you to turn away from the path of violence and to return to the ways of peace .... Further violence in Ireland will only drag down to ruin the land you claim to love and the values you claim to cherish.' Pope John Paul II also spoke at Limerick, where he reasserted traditional Catholic family values. In some respects, the Limerick speech should be seen as a formal rejection of FitzGerald's pluralist model which had been explained to the Holy See's secretary of state, Cardinal Casaroli, in the mid-1970s—evidence that the pope had carefully read the Irish file.

At the popular level, the visit gave a strong boost to Catholic morale. The euphoria of the Eucharistic Congress had been recreated to some extent at least, in 1979. But the situation in the country was quite different—and was the expression of fervour more cultural than religious? The pope's visit exacerbated a tendency towards triumphalism in certain Catholic circles. That, in turn, bred an assertiveness, even an arrogance, among lay elements determined to return the country to the pristine purity of 1932. A troubled and traumatic decade for church and state followed.

The struggle for the leadership of Fianna Fáil continued behind the scenes. Other things being equal, Dr Patrick Hillery would have been Lynch's choice as his successor. That was an open secret at the time of Ó Dalaigh's death, but Dr Hillery had definitely rejected a return to Irish politics when he had become President. However, it seemed plausible in certain circles that Hillery might have been actively considering the idea of contesting the leadership when it became vacant; if Hillery's reputation could be damaged irrevocably, he would be forced to retire as President, and Lynch would be obliged to stand for the presidency as the Fianna Fáil candidate. What took place then was not so much a conspiracy to unseat Lynch, as a haphazard attempt to employ *whatever means were deemed necessary* to change the leadership of Fianna Fáil. Some believe that this was one of the most Machiavellian and sinister episodes in modern Irish political life. Rumour and innuendo were employed in an attempt to undermine the reputation and character of the leading citizen of the state with a view to forcing his resignation. Whispers of a scandal began during the papal visit. Dr Hillery stated in an interview many years later that he and his wife had become the victims of a 'structured rumour' concerning the state of their marriage. So strong did the scandalmongering become that on one particular night the main RTÉ television current affairs programme was on standby and the studio ready for immediate use. The rumour was that Dr Hillery would announce his resignation around 9.00 pm. One phone call to Dr Hillery's secretary, Mícheál Ó hOdhrain, who was relaxing at home on the evening in question, killed the rumour dead.[46]

Jack Lynch was particularly concerned and he sought to act in defence of the President. A maladroit decision was taken to call in the editors of the national newspapers and RTÉ. The President agreed to meet them. The editors in turn 'passed the buck' to the political correspondents, who found the assignment distasteful and embarrassing; but once the senior pressmen had been compelled to undertake the assignment at the Áras, they had no alternative but to ask the hard questions. The President's situation was complicated when a broadcast journalist left early to meet a deadline without being present for the end of the conference. Confusion reigned in Dublin newsrooms as editors wrestled with what was on and what was off the record. The story that was finally printed in the press went beyond recording the simple statement that the President was not going to resign.[47]

The calling of the press conference brought the political correspondents into uncharted waters. A strong tradition in Irish political journalism was being undermined; the private life of a President was not a subject of journalistic comment. For example, Seán T. O'Kelly's weakness for whiskey was well known during his two terms of office, but nobody ever reported that the President was 'under the weather' on occasions at the end of an official function. In general, too, Irish journalists left politicians to lead their private lives in peace. Broken marriages and extra marital affairs were known about but were not the subject of reportage.[48] The Hillery episode was a classic case of the 'we know it isn't true, but let's hear him deny it' school of 'dirty tricks' politics. It was a new and most unwelcome departure.

Jack Lynch was very much aware of the dissatisfaction with his leadership within the party. He knew the people who were involved in the 'heave' against him. One of his supporters had accidentally gone into one of the meetings of the anti-Lynch caucus. The TD was observant enough to note the identity of every other deputy in the room and reported his findings to Lynch. The Taoiseach was not easily frightened and his personality did not allow him to walk away from a struggle. Moreover, Ireland held the presidency of the European Community in the latter part of 1979; it was not an opportune time to step down from the leadership. Still, the political tide was running against him. The poor showing of Fianna Fáil in the local elections and in the European elections was compounded by the loss of two by-elections in Cork to Fine Gael. Lynch was scheduled to leave for the United States on 7 November. Before going, he made the decision that he would retire at the end of the year when Ireland had successfully completed the presidency of the EC. In his absence, the anti-Lynch campaign gathered momentum. During his US trip the Taoiseach showed signs of the constant strain under which he was working. He ran into particular difficulty over an earlier denial at a Fianna Fáil parliamentary party meeting that he had agreed while on a visit to the British prime minister, Margaret Thatcher, in the wake of the Mountbatten killings, to permit a five kilometre overflight of Irish territory by helicopters when British security forces were in 'hot pursuit'. Permission had first to be given by a senior Irish army officer. However, such a perfectly sensible arrangement—which was not discontinued by Lynch's successor—excited passions among Fianna Fáil backwoodsmen and women. The question has never been satisfactorily resolved as to whether this commitment ever received cabinet approval. It is probable that it did not. The arrangement with the British was confirmed by Lynch at a press conference in Washington. A Fianna Fáil backbencher, Bill Loughnane, had recently gone so far as to call the Taoiseach a liar. Lynch immediately charged George Colley with the task of expelling the backbencher. But Major Vivion de Valera TD, among many others, was opposed to the move and Lynch failed to get his way.

In such an atavistic atmosphere, Lynch allowed himself upon his return to be a willing party to one of the worst miscalculations in recent Irish political history. George Colley went to see Lynch to discuss the situation. Neither man wanted Haughey to succeed to the leadership of Fianna Fáil, but the campaign to have him elected was getting stronger. Lynch allowed himself to be persuaded that Colley could win a vote for the leadership in the parliamentary party. Timing was of the essence. A sudden, shock resignation by Lynch would give Colley the advantage of surprise. That tactic was based on a series of miscalculations. First, it was assumed that certain members of the front bench would be automatically loyal to the Lynch/Colley camp. Secondly, it was believed that the anti-Haughey feeling was still strong enough among TDs to guarantee automatic support for Colley. It was also wrongly believed that Haughey's 1970 humiliation had put an end to his prospects of becoming Taoiseach. Thirdly, it was assumed that the Haughey camp was not yet fully prepared.

Lynch resigned as Taoiseach and leader of Fianna Fáil on 5 December 1979, having been assured by at least one numerate member of the party that the sums had been done and that Colley had the necessary 42 votes to win.[49] However, a Martyn Turner cartoon in *The Irish Times* more faithfully captured the real mood inside Fianna Fáil: it showed Lynch addressing Fianna Fáil TDs as follows—'If you could stop canvassing for a moment, I would like to unexpectedly announce my resignation.'[50] The race had been on for months—some would say since 1970. The political correspondents in the Leinster House pressroom had, in their quieter moments, competed with each other to keep an accurate tally of the loyalty of Fianna Fáil TDs. One well-known journalist who was shown a list of Colley supporters said that, to his certain knowledge, a number of the names were committed to Haughey. For example, Michael O'Kennedy, believed to have been a safe Colley vote, took the other side. Charles Haughey won the contest by 44 votes to 38.

It is too early to try to make any definitive judgments on the position of Jack Lynch in the history of the state. John Healy wrote of the two kinds of politician—the innovator and creative leader, like Seán Lemass, who challenges a political community to accomplish great things; and the defender, who sees his role as an upholder of the status quo: 'Jack Lynch was a full back seeing no one scored off him; Lemass the dashing full forward always seeking to score goals.' Healy identified Lynch's toughness, his determination and his opposition to 'verbal republicanism'.[51]

There has been a tendency to attribute the divisions within Fianna Fáil to Jack Lynch's weakness of leadership. That is a fundamental mistake. The ideological divisions and personality conflicts within Fianna Fáil pre-dated Lynch. He had to contain that conflict and bring about a new consensus within his party.[52] He nearly achieved that objective, but his main contribution was the defeat of the serious threat to Irish democracy which had been precipitated by the Northern crisis. His unalterable commitment to the preservation of the democratic institutions of state halted the first attempt at the 'privatisation' of official government business. He was required to play the 'full back' by force of circumstance. In relation to the internal affairs of Fianna Fáil, Lynch was engaged in a policy of containment rather than consensus. Perhaps he lacked sufficient political ruthlessness to finish off his opponents. In the circumstances, containment was as much as he could have hoped to achieve.

CHARLES HAUGHEY TAKES THE REINS

The changeover of leadership was not smooth. Colley made a speech at Baldoyle, Co. Dublin on 20 December 1979 where he said: 'I did not promise loyalty to the Taoiseach.'[53] Haughey called Colley in and exacted a qualified loyalty pledge from him. The Tánaiste gave Haughey loyalty as *Taoiseach*, but not as *leader of Fianna Fáil*. An uneasy truce prevailed. If leading members of Fianna Fáil found it difficult to swallow the idea of Haughey being leader of the party, opposition parties were hostile in the extreme. For six hours in the Dáil on 11 December leading members of the opposition questioned Haughey's suitability for the job of Taoiseach. Fine Gael's John Kelly declared him 'totally unfit' for that office. What he disliked most about Haughey was his relentless publicity and the remorseless self-advertising; he did not like Haughey's concern with his image. De Valera, in his view, did not have that. Neither did Lemass. Kelly hated the back-slapping, the currying of favour and the polished veneer. When it slipped, he said, something very ugly appeared in view.[54] Garret FitzGerald said that he did not speak with any degree of pleasure in opposing Haughey. The leader of Fine Gael, who had been at UCD with Haughey, said that an overweening ambition was attributed to him which was not so much a desire to serve but rather a wish to dominate, indeed to own the state. Despite his recognised political skills, FitzGerald said that Haughey came 'with a flawed pedigree'. Haughey, according to FitzGerald, preferred to maintain 'an indecent ambiguity' over his attitude to the IRA.[55] This was a tough speech, but the use of the term 'flawed pedigree' was injudicious and only won sympathy for Haughey.

The Labour leader, Frank Cluskey, attacked Haughey for helping to bring about an unjust society. As Taoiseach, he said, he would only reinforce the structure of injustice; he belonged to a breed of people dominated by the principle that the end justified the means. Cluskey claimed that such people set out to acquire personal wealth, influence and political power. They were the ambitious, ruthless young men of the middle and late '60s who were responsible for land speculation and jerry-built houses. Dr Noël Browne said that Haughey was 'one of two politicians in Irish life of whom I have always been afraid in his use of power'. He was a cross between Richard Nixon and Dr Salazar, the Portuguese dictator. Browne questioned whether Haughey would be prepared to hand over power if he was defeated in the House.[56]

'The Boss', as Charles Haughey was to become known, was elected Taoiseach by 82 votes to 62; shortly after he came to power, Seán MacEntee gave an interview in which he said pointedly: 'All my sins are public.' He contrasted, by implication, the party of de Valera with Fianna Fáil in the 1970s when national aims became subordinate to personal ends. In the past, they had called for sacrifice, but there was today the problem of 'how to tax and be loved'. MacEntee added disapprovingly: 'Parties and Governments now have to try to please everyone. Parties have to compete for votes with promises rather than policies. Personalities are more important than policies. We are becoming a nation of "mé féiners".'[57]

Robust and radical individualism was the cornerstone of Haughey's new political style. He was part of the Irish *nouveau riche*. He could not have been more of a contrast to any of his predecessors who had occupied the leadership of Fianna Fáil. MacEntee and Aiken neither liked nor trusted him. Joseph Lee has seen him as having had much in common with David Lloyd George.[58] The comparison with the US president, Richard Nixon, who was forced to leave office in 1974 in order to avoid impeachment, may be equally appropriate. 'You would argue that [Nixon] is not a moral leader,' Henry Kissinger once told a vocal critic of the US president, the novelist Norman Mailer, '. . . but perhaps you go along with me that he has political genius.' Mailer replied, 'Absolutely.' Both Nixon and Haughey had suffered a sustained humiliation at the hands of their political rivals. Both men fought their way back to power. Finally, both took full advantage of wielding that power to smite their enemies and reward their loyal followers.[59]

Something of a political outcast, Haughey had allowed feelings of resentment and mistrust to burnish his political character and distort his judgment. He built a loyal entourage around himself during his time in the wilderness in the 1970s, for four years of which Fianna Fáil was out of power, and from that circle of camp followers he tried to build his base in the party. Haughey had a rather restricted pool of talent to draw upon for his ministerial team. It was not enough, Napoleon once observed, that he should have good generals; he wanted them to be lucky generals also. Haughey was not particularly lucky in his choice of a number of his generals.

Upon assuming office, Haughey kept Colley as Tánaiste but sacked four ministers: Jim Gibbons (Agriculture), Martin O'Donoghue (Economic Planning and Development), Denis Gallagher (Gaeltacht) and Bobby Molloy (Defence). Those promoted to the cabinet included a woman, Máire Geoghegan-Quinn (Gaeltacht), Michael Woods (Health and Social Welfare), Patrick Power (Fisheries and Forestry), Ray MacSharry (Agriculture) and Albert Reynolds (Posts and Telegraphs). Michael O'Kennedy, one of Haughey's crucial swing votes, was given Finance. Colley went from Finance to Tourism and Transport. He was expected to move within a short time to the new Department of Energy. Desmond O'Malley, Colley's chief backer, retained Industry, Commerce and Energy. Gerry Collins remained in Justice and Brian Lenihan got Foreign Affairs.[60] Haughey dropped four ministers of state and named ten new ones. Lee has commented that Haughey made 'indulgent appointments even by the relaxed standards of political indebtedness'.[61] The new government was not so much a ministry of all-the-talents as a ministry of all-the-loyalists.

The acrimony between Haughey and his predecessor was palpable. Lynch made public the fact that he had only made one request to the Taoiseach following his resignation, asking that Martin O'Donoghue be made EC Commissioner in January when Dick Burke's term was up. Patronage went to the loyal and dedicated: Michael O'Kennedy received that prize. Gene Fitzgerald went from the Department of Labour to Finance, an appointment which caused raised eyebrows in the civil service.

Haughey's first government lasted about a year and a half. It was not a particularly easy time to be in office. It has been argued that three factors, which had changed the economic climate after 1978, were beginning to hit the Irish economy:

Firstly, the transition phase was now ended during which Ireland had benefited more than the generality of EEC farmers as Irish prices were adjusted to EEC levels. Secondly, entry into the European Monetary System (EMS) in 1979 largely deprived Ireland of the so-called 'green pound' devaluations, which were granted when the Irish pound depreciated along with sterling. . . . Thirdly, and most serious of all for Ireland from a long-term viewpoint, the squeeze on the Community budget arising from growing food surpluses brought increasing pressure to limit production both by cutting prices to producers and by imposing levies on surplus production.[62]

On 9 January 1980, Charles Haughey went on television to address the country about the state of the economy. The emphasis was on the need for fiscal rectitude: 'In our present economic situation, it is madness to think that we can keep on looking for more money for less work. . . .' (Ironically, as revelations in the 1990s showed, Haughey was living beyond his own personal means at the time.) The Taoiseach asked for a universal commitment to industrial peace.[63] The budget was framed against the background of PAYE marches and demands for radical reform of the taxation system. Yielding to public pressure, but with a desire to postpone having to do anything immediately about reform, the Commission on Taxation, under the chairmanship of Dr Miriam Hederman O'Brien, was set up in March. That decision had also been made necessary as a consequence of the case of Francis and Mary Murphy. A married couple, they had claimed in the High Court that special provisions of the Income Tax Act pertaining to married persons were repugnant to the constitution. On 12 October 1979 the court ruled that sections of the 1967 Act were unconstitutional. Henceforth married couples had the right to be assessed for tax separately. The Commission issued five reports, but more attention might have been paid to its recommendations.

Haughey could not afford to sound too much like the new British prime minister, Margaret Thatcher. His budgetary strategy was marked by the 'good intention' to close the gap between budgetary projections and actual results. The following table shows just how unsuccessful the exercise was:

Current Deficit (£ million)			Excess of actual
Year	Budget	projection	over projection
1979	289	522	233 (81 per cent)
1980	347	547	200 (58 per cent)
1981	495	802	307 (62 per cent)
1982	679	988	309 (46 per cent)[64]

Haughey's style of leadership was not to let individual ministers get on with their work. His approach was interventionist and intrusive. The Department of the Taoiseach grew rapidly in size to take into account its new role as shadow to a number of key ministries, including Foreign Affairs. Haughey took a personal interest in negotiating the second national understanding—and a new national wage agreement was signed in autumn 1980. But this was not done before Aer Lingus craft workers caused holiday traffic chaos by striking. They agreed to return to work on 3 July after 34 days on strike. Inflation had reached 20 per cent by mid-May 1980. An increase in ministerial salaries was postponed in June.

A £50 million subsidised interest scheme for firms in crisis was announced in the early summer. The Taoiseach said on 25 June that at least 25,000 new manufacturing jobs would be created that year and job approvals under the IDA were expected to be about 30,000.[65] The jobs, sadly, did not materialise. Haughey simply lacked the will to govern strategically. He had a comfortable majority, with a maximum of two-and-a-half years to run in government. Hard decisions that were likely to cost votes were simply not taken. The decision to fund Knock airport provides a very good case-study of the process of 'privatising' government decision-making which went on under Haughey. Knock, an international Marian shrine, was visited by Pope John Paul II in 1979. The parish priest of the area, Monsignor James Horan, was a 'building' priest. He had constructed a basilica on the original church site. His ambition was to build an international airport near the town capable of taking transatlantic jets. Haughey agreed to the funding of the project, against the express recommendation of the Department of Finance and the Department of Transport. A comment on the memorandum for government said of the request: 'This is irregular.' A senior Finance official had written beside it: 'It is outrageous.'[66] This was to cost the state an initial £13 million. Haughey's lame comment on the file was that he thought that he was giving funding for the building of a grass airstrip. My criticism is not so much of the decision itself as of the manner in which the decision was taken.[67] The settlement of a teachers' pay dispute and a strike of Talbot car workers were also cases where Haughey's managerial style and impatience with his ministerial subordinates resulted in the privatising of government decision-making.

During the first Haughey government, the new Taoiseach had to confront a deteriorating situation in Northern Ireland and a most difficult time in Anglo-Irish relations. The human cost of Northern-related violence was demonstrated yet again on 7 July 1980 when Detective Garda John Morley and Garda Henry Byrne were shot dead near Ballaghadereen, Co. Roscommon, while trying to apprehend bank robbers, who got away with £35,000. The same day, the Criminal Law Jurisdiction Act 1976 was used for the first time when three men from County Monaghan were charged with murdering a UDR man in Northern Ireland. In an unprecedented midnight sitting of the Special Criminal Court, a man was charged on 9 July with the murder of one of the gardaí shot in County Roscommon. Paradoxically for some, Haughey held firmly to the substance of Lynch's line on Northern Ireland. Haughey condemned the US-based pro-IRA fund-raising organisation, Noraid, on 27 July for providing 'support for the campaign of violence' in Northern Ireland.

Haughey had met the British prime minister, Margaret Thatcher, at Downing Street on 21 May 1980. This was the occasion when Haughey presented Thatcher with an Irish Georgian silver teapot. The communiqué spoke of the two leaders' mutual desire to 'develop new and closer political cooperation between their Governments'. It was agreed to hold regular meetings on a continuing basis, accompanied by other ministers when appropriate. While agreeing with Thatcher that any change in the constitutional status of Northern Ireland would come about only with the consent of a majority of the people of Northern Ireland, Haughey reaffirmed that it 'is the wish of the Irish Government to secure the unity of Ireland by agreement and in peace'. Finally, the communiqué stated that both leaders agreed 'on the importance they attached to the unique relationship between the peoples of the United Kingdom of Great Britain and Northern Ireland and of the Republic and on the need to further this relationship in the interest of peace and reconciliation.' There was a final reference to the satisfaction of both leaders with the efforts being made, both separately and in cooperation, in the field of security.[68] Haughey elaborated on the communiqué at a press conference after the meeting. He was very positive about the progress. In a later interview on BBC's 'Panorama', Haughey called Thatcher 'a practical politician'. It was difficult to envisage higher praise from so supreme a pragmatist. In the same interview, he was asked about his role in 1969/70:

> As far as I'm concerned I did, at any time of my public and political life, what I thought was right and honourable and in the best interests of this country and people of this country and I have no regrets. All these matters have been dealt with before— ten years ago—in the courts and in other ways. I believe they are history and should be left to history.[69]

Síle de Valera again broke Fianna Fáil ranks to criticise the policies of Thatcher. She made reference to the intensification of the protests in support of the restoration of 'special category status' in Northern prisons. This had been conceded in 1972 and withdrawn for new prisoners after March 1976. That dissatisfaction ultimately resulted in the 'dirty protest', where prisoners smeared their cells with their own excrement, refused to clean them or wear prison clothes. That had been going on for over four years. Cardinal Ó Fiaich was among those who spoke very vigorously in support of concessions before it was too late. After a visit to the H-Blocks in the Maze prison in August 1980, he stated:

> One would hardly allow an animal to remain in such conditions, let alone a human being. The nearest approach to it that I have seen was the spectacle of hundreds of homeless people living in the sewer pipes in the slums of Calcutta. The stench and filth in some of the cells, with the remains of rotten food and human excreta scattered around the walls, was almost unbearable. In two of them I was unable to speak for fear of vomiting.[70]

The protest moved into a new phase when seven 'republican' prisoners refused to take breakfast on 27 October and threatened to fast 'to death'. A month later, on 25 November, Haughey told the Dáil that a solution would be possible if some adjustment could be made in the prison rules or in the interpretation of their application. The Irish government conveyed its concern to the British government and its anxiety about the possible consequences.[71] During a break in the Luxembourg European Council on 1–2 December, Haughey and Thatcher had a brief opportunity to discuss the hunger strikes. Haughey said afterwards: 'Our entire efforts are directed to bringing forward some solutions which will make sure that no lives are lost, directly as a result of an escalation of violence.'[72]

An Anglo-Irish summit was held at Dublin Castle on 8 December 1980. Thatcher was accompanied by the Foreign Secretary, Lord Carrington, Humphrey Atkins, the Northern Ireland Secretary of State, and the Chancellor of the Exchequer, Sir Geoffrey Howe. Haughey was flanked by Lenihan and O'Kennedy. A communiqué stressed that the economic, social and political interests of the peoples of the United Kingdom of Great Britain and Northern Ireland and the Republic were inextricably linked, 'but the full development of these links has been put under strain by division and dissent in Northern Ireland'. The best prospect of attaining the objectives of peace, reconciliation and stability 'was the further development of the unique relationship between the two countries'. Both leaders promised to devote their next meeting in London to 'special consideration of the totality of relationships within these islands'.[73]

Few would disagree that the conference had been successful. But in his anxiety to communicate its importance, at a subsequent press conference and at an off-the-record briefing for Irish political correspondents, Haughey's sure touch deserted him. He over-sold the significance of the meeting by conveying the impression that Anglo-Irish relations could be 'in the middle of an historic breakthrough'. He set no limits to the institutions that might be agreed. Lord Carrington had recently helped negotiate the independence of Zimbabwe. Haughey called him 'a statesman of the finest calibre'. In Belfast, loyalists were even more convinced that the British were going to do a deal with Dublin behind their backs. Consequently, that stayed the hand of the British in dealing with 'republican' prisoners who were still on hunger strike.[74]

Atkins submitted a document to the H-Block prisoners. Cardinal Ó Fiaich appealed for a halt to the protest. The hunger strikes were called off on 18 December. About 20 January 1981, prisoners agreed to move to clean cells in the H-Block. They washed, shaved and had haircuts. But when their relatives arrived with clothes, the prison authorities refused to pass them on. A riot ensued and the decision was taken to go back on hunger strike. However, it was decided to stagger the start of the hunger strike. On 1 March Bobby Sands, a 27-year-old from Belfast, began. He was joined by Francis Hughes from south Derry on 15 March. Ten were to die before the hunger strike was called off on 3 October 1981, confident that they were following in a hallowed tradition. Paul Durcan captured the barrenness of that 'republican' world in the lines:

> In a public house, darkly-lit, a patriotic (sic)
> Versifier whines into my face: 'You must take one side
> Or the other, or you're but a fucking romantic . . . .'[75]

Sinn Féin decided to put Sands's name forward as a candidate to fill the seat at Westminster left vacant by the death of Frank Maguire, an independent republican Westminster MP for Fermanagh-South Tyrone. The SDLP declined to put forward a candidate and Sands won on 9 April by 1,446 votes from the Official Unionist, Harry West. Some 30,000 had voted for Sands. There was some hope that concessions would be made which would save the lives of the hunger strikers. Pope John Paul II sent his secretary, John Magee (now bishop of Cloyne), to the North. Sands was presented with a silver crucifix. It is not known what was said at the meeting, but it appears likely that Magee, a Newryman, was in touch with many Northern bishops who were aware of the tragedy in the making and the likely consequences for Northern Ireland. Haughey sent Síle de Valera to visit Sands on 20 April. She was accompanied by John O'Connell and Neil Blaney. On 23 April Haughey met members of Sands's family. He died on 5 May on the 66th day of his hunger strike. Thousands attended the funeral, which attracted international media attention. A guard of honour, clad in black, flanked the coffin, which was led by pipe and drum band. There were the final rites in the impoverished liturgy of physical force nationalism. Sands's death brought ugly scenes to the streets of Dublin, Belfast and Derry. There were demonstrations outside Government Buildings in Dublin. Businesses in most Irish towns were intimidated into closing down for the funeral. Francis Hughes died on 12 May after 59 days on hunger strike. There were further demonstrations in Dublin. Haughey met the sister of Patsy O'Hara on 19 May; he and another hunger striker, Raymond McCreesh, died two days later.

The Taoiseach had tried to get the British to see their way to bringing an end to the hunger strikes. He had said at a dinner in Cork, on 8 May 1981, that he had taken every step open to him that appeared likely to be effective in resolving the situation since the beginning of the hunger strikes. He would continue to work towards that objective: 'There is no human problem which cannot yield to a humanitarian and practical solution. I believe that reasonable people everywhere not alone in these islands, but around the world, now wish to see such a solution.'[76] Haughey made a similar speech on 12 May, following the death of Hughes.

The deterioration in Anglo-Irish relations, from the December summit to the succession of hunger strikes, has got to be seen against the background of the impending general election in the Irish Republic. Haughey had hoped to get a new mandate shortly after the holding of the Fianna Fáil *ard fheis* on 15 February 1981. But the *ard fheis* was postponed because of a fire on 14 February in the Stardust ballroom, in the north Dublin suburb of Artane, which claimed the lives of 48 young people and left 128 seriously injured. It was in the Taoiseach's own constituency and close to where he had been raised. He visited the scene of the disaster, declared a special day of mourning, and immediately proceeded to set up a tribunal of inquiry. The Dáil was adjourned on 17 February as a mark of respect. Haughey was profoundly upset by the disaster. A panel of solicitors was appointed by the government to act on behalf of the victims free of charge. Two years later the tribunal reported and found that the fire probably had been set deliberately. The survivors went through further suffering while attempting to acquire a modicum of compensation. The youth of northside Dublin, in the picturesque words of Roddy Doyle's character Jimmy Rabbitte, in *The Commitments*, 'the blacks of Ireland'.[77] A park was opened to commemorate the victims of the fire in Coolock, Dublin on 19 September 1993. In a speech on 3 April 1981, the Taoiseach speculated that the historians of the future might well describe the twentieth century as the century in which youth came decisively and unmistakably into its own: 'Our responsibility to our young people is simply to secure their future here at home. We want them to be able to find fulfilment and achievement in their own country in a way which no other generation before them has been able to do.' He ended on a euphoric note: 'To the young people of Ireland I say, your future is in Ireland and Ireland's future rests with you.'[78] But that was not how the 1980s worked out for many Irish youths. Between 1981 and April 1986 about 72,000 people emigrated. The figures were particularly high for people in the 25–39 age-group.[79] By the late 1980s emigration rates had reached the heights of the 1950s, and by the early 1990s there were over 300,000 people unemployed.

GARRET FITZGERALD AND A COALITION INTERLUDE

Haughey's address to the *ard fheis* on 11 April 1981 was a rallying cry to the party. He did not call an election until 21 May and then went for the shortest campaign permitted under the constitution. Polling day was 11 June. There were 9 H-block candidates in the field. (Two were elected, causing the loss of vital Fianna Fáil seats.) Fianna Fáil ran on its record in government and on its policy document 'Programme for the 80s'. Fine Gael's manifesto promised large cuts in income tax and other benefits for individual groups. The Labour Party, under Frank Cluskey, was more social democratic in its policy objectives.

There was no overt coalition strategy, but opposition parties agreed to give Fianna Fáil candidates the lowest preferences on the ballot. Fine Gael argued that it could get a sufficient number of seats to form a single-party government. Fianna Fáil countered that Haughey was the only option. A number of low blows were thrown in the campaign as Fianna Fáil began to discover that the political current might be running against the party. A minister of state, Tom McEllistrim, tried to panic his constituents by saying that Frank Cluskey might become Minister for Agriculture in a coalition government; 'Vote for a Coalition and they will move in and take your land', he warned.[80] Fianna Fáil won 78 seats out of 166, compared with 84 out of 148 in 1977. Fine Gael got 65. Labour took 15 seats; its vote fell from 11.6 to 9.9 per cent. Four deputies lost their seats, including the party leader, Frank Cluskey, Ruairí Quinn and John Horgan.[81] Mary Robinson, who had stood for the Labour Party in Dublin West, had again not been elected. She felt that working-class people 'did not respond with any degree of political awareness of their critical position and seemed to have no perception of the degree of social change necessary to alter their predicament'.[82] Gallagher estimates that Fine Gael-Labour transfers had deprived Fianna Fáil of five seats.

FitzGerald, who became the new Taoiseach, had helped increase his party's vote from 30.5 to 36.5, while Fianna Fáil fell from 50.6 to 45.3. The coalition had won the vote in the Dáil by 82 to 78 with the support of independents. John O'Connell became Ceann Comhairle. Jim Kemmy, a Limerick socialist, voted with the coalition. Noël Browne and Joe Sherlock (Workers' Party) voted against Haughey for Taoiseach and then abstained when FitzGerald's name was put forward.[83] Michael O'Leary, the newly elected leader of the Labour Party, was made Tánaiste and Minister for Industry and Energy. However, the country's fourth coalition lasted only eight months. It found that the economy was in an even more critical state than had been anticipated. FitzGerald returned from the Áras to tell the Dáil: 'In the couple of hours since I was appointed Taoiseach . . . even in that brief time I have learned something of the scale of the damage done.' The new Minister for Finance, John Bruton, introduced a supplementary budget on 21 July 1981. It imposed an embargo on public service recruitment and on new special pay increases. It raised the VAT rate from 10 per cent to 15 per cent. Excise duties were increased and a bank levy of £5m was imposed. Haughey attacked the new economic policies as being rooted in 'monetarism'—'a harsh, uncaring economic policy. It puts books before people.' He also told the Dáil on the same occasion that monetarism took 'no account of the social degradation, of the waste of human talent and potential, of the hardship and misery that unemployment involves'. Haughey predicted that the new deflationary polices would put people out of jobs and would have 'disastrous implications for employment, particularly for youth employment'.[84]

In the midst of the economic crisis, FitzGerald sought to reawaken the call for constitutional reform which had been silent since the late 1960s. FitzGerald, interviewed on RTÉ radio on 27 September 1981, said: 'What I want to do, if I may, is to take a phrase from somebody [Brian Lenihan] the other night on television: I want to lead a crusade, a republican crusade, to make this a genuine republic.' He added: 'If I were a Northern Protestant today, I cannot see how I could be attracted to getting involved with a state that is itself sectarian— not in the acutely sectarian way that Northern Ireland was . . . [but] the fact is our laws and our Constitution, our practices, our attitudes, reflect those of a majority ethos and are not acceptable to Protestants in Northern Ireland.'[85] To Haughey and Fianna Fáil, the 'constitutional crusade' was manna from heaven. It provided an opportunity to shift the debate to terrain where Haughey was much more sure-footed; FitzGerald could be portrayed as having launched an attack on the very integrity of the Irish state. Within two days of the broadcast, Haughey had attacked the Taoiseach for 'the goldmine of propaganda' that he had handed to the enemies of unity, who would use it 'relentlessly and remorselessly from here on in'. Haughey had chosen the unveiling of the de Valera memorial at Ennis, on 11 October, to deliver a speech on 'Éamon de Valera and the colonial mentality' which was a direct reply to the constitutional crusade. He spoke of 'our accusers'. Then Haughey adopted the novel tactic of conducting a dialogue with Éamon de Valera (he had died in 1975) as to what he would want contemporary Ireland to be:

It is helpful for us at this time to contemplate what Éamon de Valera would say to us were he amongst us here today in Ennis. He set no limit to the march of the Irish nation. He sought an Ireland, unified and free, which would in its constitution and its laws respect and accommodate the diverse traditions that exist in this island and he would urge us to continue to work for that objective.

He would urge us to create a just, compassionate, and tolerant society. He would glory in the fact that we have an increasing population consisting largely of a new generation of educated, talented young people and he would urge us to give them the encouragement, the support and leadership they need, to achieve their full potential. He would urge us also to have a special care of the less well off and the weaker sections of our community; to make their welfare our deep and abiding concern and to see that they are fully protected from the hazards of life and the harsh effects of economic forces.[86]

Haughey had been allowed the latitude to mobilise large sections of traditional Irish society to the standard of Fianna Fáil in defence of nationalism and Catholicism: 'I cannot see our state as sectarian', he said on 7 January 1982.[87] In his memoirs, FitzGerald wrote that his own constitutional crusade was 'stillborn', but he added that it represented 'a time-bomb ticking away at the heart of the narrow and exclusive form of Catholic nationalism to which Fianna Fáil traditionally ties its fortunes.'[88]

Meanwhile the hunger strike campaign continued. The Irish government supported moves by the Irish Commission for Justice and Peace to try to end the protest. The British were mistaken if they thought that FitzGerald would be less difficult on the question of the hunger strikes than Haughey had been. In order to exert greater pressure, FitzGerald had written to President Ronald Reagan, who conveyed—according to the Irish ambassador—the concern of the Speaker of the House, Tip O'Neill, and Senator Ted Kennedy to Margaret Thatcher. In July 1981 the H-Blocks committee organised a march to the British embassy in Dublin. Over 2,000 gardaí were on duty. They faced demonstrators armed with stones and pick-axe handles. A delegation was let through to hand in a letter of protest, but they had to be removed by the gardaí after they had forced their way into the embassy. Over 100 gardaí were injured as the protesters aimed missiles at legs unprotected by the short shields. Baton charges broke up the demonstration, but protesters did damage on their way back to the city centre. The government ensured that future marches to the British embassy did not result in injury to people or damage to property. FitzGerald had met members of the families of the hunger strikers. He had refused to take the radical course that they urged upon him, but there had been twenty-five exchanges between Dublin and London at prime ministerial or ministerial levels within six weeks. In the end, FitzGerald felt that nothing further could be done.[89] Four more hunger strikers died in the first three weeks of August. A courageous mother took her unconscious hunger-striking son off the fast in early September. The macabre exercise finally ended on 3 October 1981 after 217 days.

The hunger strikes overshadowed coalition politics and tended to detract from the credit which ought to have gone to FitzGerald for his handling of EC and domestic politics. A number of important decisions were taken by the coalition: the Youth Employment Agency was established, a Combat Poverty Agency was set up, and a revision of the grant scheme for third-level education was completed. An effort was made to overhaul the Dáil committee system. FitzGerald proposed the setting up of four new committees: women's rights; marital breakdown; youth affairs; and development cooperation. In mid-January 1982, Haughey agreed to the establishment of all but the committee on marital breakdown. FitzGerald had too little time in the end to make an impact.

An attempt to impose VAT on children's clothing and footwear in the budget of 27 January brought the coalition tumbling down. Jim Kemmy, the independent Limerick deputy, voted against John Bruton's budget and the government fell by 82 votes to 81. As FitzGerald watched the Fianna Fáil whip carry the vote down, he *experienced a moment of total exhilaration* [my emphasis]: '*This was it. We were going into battle on a budget that we could defend with conviction and enthusiasm.*'⁹⁰ Haughey had other ideas. After a meeting of the Fianna Fáil front bench immediately after the government had lost the vote, Haughey issued a statement: 'It is a matter for the President to consider the situation which has arisen now that the Taoiseach has ceased to retain the support of the majority in Dáil Éireann. I am available for consultation by the President should he so wish.'⁹¹ This was a reference to the power of the President under the constitution not to grant a dissolution of the Dáil. If that were to happen, Haughey would take power without any election.

While FitzGerald was waiting to go to Áras an Uachtaráin, a number of phone calls were made to the residence by Fianna Fáil front benchers in an effort to speak to President Hillery. The President was not available to take the calls. FitzGerald was delayed going to the Áras because the President's secretary had to be present; he happened to be at the theatre that evening. FitzGerald was later with the President for three-quarters of an hour.⁹²

I have been in a position to ascertain from highly placed sources that the record of the logged telephone calls has been preserved and that it will be possible to write a detailed account of the controversial events of that evening from primary sources. An interim judgment must take into account the impropriety of the efforts made by senior politicians to approach the President of Ireland on the question of the dissolution. That was exclusively a matter for the President. To risk even being perceived as attempting to exert pressure was demeaning of his office, but to have had at least six telephone calls placed to the Áras that evening revealed among those responsible little or no respect for the institutions of the state. The general disregard for state institutions was to be demonstrated in a much more public fashion within a few months.

HAUGHEY AND THE GUBU GOVERNMENT

The election which followed was fought out in vigorous fashion. FitzGerald's party increased its share of the vote, but lost two seats. Fianna Fáil increased its number of seats from 78 to 81. Labour held on to 15 seats and there were seven other deputies, including three from the Workers' Party. Haughey was to be Taoiseach again.

But he had first to beat off growing dissatisfaction inside Fianna Fáil. The Kildare TD, Charles McCreevy, had backed Haughey for the leadership, but throughout 1981 he had become disillusioned with a party which seemed to be 'against everything and for nothing'. In January 1982, Haughey successfully sought his expulsion from the parliamentary party—a move which was openly opposed by members of the shadow cabinet. On 25 February the Fianna Fáil parliamentary party met. Haughey, in order to still rumours about his unpopularity, had put down a motion for his own re-election. Desmond O'Malley decided that he would stand for the leadership of the party. Jack Lynch issued a statement supporting O'Malley's decision and Haughey was forced to face the challenge 'head on'. In the days before the vote, the Haughey camp had done a very strong canvass of O'Malley's backers and the challenger's support had buckled.[93] At the parliamentary party meeting, one of O'Malley's supporters—according to Bruce Arnold—Martin O'Donoghue, called for unity behind Charles Haughey. O'Malley had no alternative but to withdraw his name.

Neither Haughey nor FitzGerald had given up the idea of becoming the next Taoiseach. The courtship of the independents began. Tony Gregory, an independent TD for Dublin's inner city, met both sides. He secured from Haughey a £50m deal for what was effectively his constituency in return for his support. It was an example of 'pork barrel' politics on a grand scale. Neil Blaney was already regarded as a secure vote. John O'Connell was to be made Ceann Comhairle. Jim Kemmy was a lost vote to Fianna Fáil. That left the three Workers' Party TDs: Joe Sherlock, Proinsias de Rossa and Paddy Gallagher. They decided to support Haughey, but when the division bell went for the crucial vote on 9 March 1982, they found themselves outside the chamber. Led by a Fianna Fáil senator, the three burst into the press gallery, scrambled across to the distinguished visitors' gallery and jumped into the chamber. Thus three Marxists helped secure Haughey's return to power in the 23rd

Dáil. (As a result of this episode, the press gallery doors are now always closed during a division.) The new cabinet brought fresh blood to the front benches. Ray MacSharry was made Tánaiste and Minister for Finance. Paddy Power, from Kildare, was given Defence and was to become internationally known during the Falkland Islands crisis, and Seán Doherty, from Roscommon, was made Minister for Justice. He was to draw more headlines than any previous politician with that portfolio. Desmond O'Malley was given Industry, Commerce and Tourism. Gerard Collins became Minister for Foreign Affairs, Martin O'Donoghue got Education and Raphael Burke was given the Environment portfolio. Brian Lenihan was given Agriculture, Michael Woods got Health and Social Welfare, Pádraig Flynn, the Gaeltacht; Albert Reynolds, Industry and Energy; Gene Fitzgerald, Labour and the Public Service; and John Wilson got Transport, Posts and Telegraphs. This was as much a coalition as had made up the previous government. There were the diehard loyalists and the dissidents, but could Haughey successfully preserve Jack Lynch's policy of containment?

One of Haughey's first duties as Taoiseach was to visit Washington. President Reagan had invited FitzGerald to meet him in March 1982. Ambassador Seán Donlon had worked hard to secure the invitation. Haughey presented Reagan with a map of the Slieve Bloom mountains, which was the territory of the O'Regans. The White House occasion was a glittering public success. It was a good start to a new Haughey administration, but there was no dramatic diplomatic breakthrough. Reagan disclaimed any direct American role in the Northern Ireland question.

Haughey returned to Dublin where the new Dáil met on 23 March. The government survived by the casting vote of the Ceann Comhairle, but fortune then presented the Taoiseach with an opportunity to increase his majority. The decision by Michael O'Kennedy to return from Brussels, where he had not been happy as Commissioner, provided an opening for Haughey to gain another vital vote. The nomination of an EC Commissioner was the most important piece of political patronage open to a Taoiseach. By right, it always went to a loyal party retainer, but on this occasion Haughey decided to offer the post to Richard Burke, who had been left to languish on the back benches by FitzGerald since returning to Dublin from Brussels. After a little soul-searching, Burke agreed to take the job and was excoriated at a Fine Gael parliamentary party meeting for his decision. Burke resigned from Fine Gael, but felt that his erstwhile party could hold the seat in the by-election. Haughey thought that Fianna Fáil had a fighting chance of taking the seat.[94] The Taoiseach would have pulled off a master 'stroke' if the high-risk strategy paid off. As Burke set out for Brussels, Haughey had at least solved his short-term Dáil problems.

MacSharry brought in the budget on 5 May 1982; it included provision to cover the Gregory deal for Dublin's inner city, an extra £4m for prisons and £2m to begin Cork's deepwater harbour. VAT was removed from books. The budget deficit was to be reduced from £715m to £679m.[95] FitzGerald later described the budget as an 'unstable edifice—which largely collapsed during the course of the year'.[96] The budget provisions precipitated, in part, a renewal of the PAYE revolt. The minority Fianna Fáil government was in difficulties from the very outset. For example, Haughey had to face the personal embarrassment of seeing his election agent and close friend charged with personation. He got off, but the incident was 'ridiculed publicly . . . and it set the tone for the new administration'.[97] This government, above all others, was about possession politics.

On 2 April the Argentinian military junta invaded Las Malvinas, or the Falkland Islands. This ushered in one of the worst phases in Anglo-Irish relations since the outbreak of the economic war in 1932. Despite his use of the nationalist card, Haughey lost the Dublin West by-election on 25 May; Liam Skelly was returned for Fine Gael, easily defeating Haughey's sister-in-law, Eileen Lemass. It was a bitter personal blow to Haughey, who had needlessly given away a plum piece of patronage to Dick Burke for no return at all. A second by-election took place, in Galway East, in July. Fianna Fáil held the seat comfortably, but with a 5 per cent drop in its vote.[98]

Haughey got little rest that summer. He was embroiled with the unions over the decision to defer payment of a 5 per cent final phase of the national agreement. Machiavelli has written that a politician needs *fortuna* or luck. Haughey did not have any that August. On the 13th, Malcolm Edward MacArthur was arrested in the flat of the Attorney General, Patrick Connolly, and charged with the murder three weeks earlier of Nurse Bridie Gargan in the Phoenix Park. The Attorney General, who was away on holidays, returned from New

York and resigned, despite his total innocence in the episode. He was a man of honour. Haughey, acting in the place of the Minister for Justice, Seán Doherty, who was on holiday, described the episode as Grotesque, Unbelievable, Bizarre and Unprecedented. Conor Cruise O'Brien wrote of the GUBU factor, and this was to remain the popular name for Haughey's short-lived 1982 administration.

But Haughey's bad luck did not end there. In late September, Seán Doherty was embroiled in a controversy over a case in which his brother-in-law, who was a garda, was cleared of an assault charge. It was discovered that a leading prosecution witness from the North had been unable to attend court at Dowra, Co. Cavan, because he had been detained en route by the RUC. This became known as the 'Dowra affair'. However, Doherty made headlines in other ways also as Joyce and Murtagh argue in their book, *The Boss*. [99] John Waters has written a sympathetic portrait of Doherty, arguing that the 'media line' about the then Minister for Justice was 'that his was the politics of the stroke, the fix, the parish pump, of graft, crookery and whatever you're having yourself; he was the archetypal rural redneck, corrupted by power'. Waters continues:

> The legends of his infamy had long since blurred and merged, so that truth and legend had become as one. He was the man, they said, who had tried to have a Garda sergeant disciplined for doing his duty; he had been involved in a late-night car crash in Kerry in the company of a blonde pop singer to whom he was not related; he had tapped the telephones of two of the country's leading journalists, and had involved the most senior officers in the country's police force in the bugging of a conversation between party colleagues. [100]

Whatever about Doherty's hero-status in Castlerea, he will not be remembered as the best Minister for Justice that the state has produced since independence. Only the initiated would have been able to realise that there were times when Doherty 'was fighting his demonic public image by sending it up'. [101] However one wishes to simplify the Dublin/Roscommon divide, Doherty still represented an unacceptable face of Fianna Fáil for many people, no matter how many layers there were to his *persona*. As Minister for Justice, he authorised a tap on the phones of two prominent journalists, Bruce

Arnold and Geraldine Kennedy. This was part of an effort to stop information being leaked to the press. Doherty claimed almost ten years later that he had been asked by cabinet to stop the leaks on their deliberations.[102] Doherty further claimed that he had actually handed the transcripts to Charles Haughey in his office. The Taoiseach, it was claimed, had taken them without comment. Three other members of that cabinet disputed Doherty's recollections; they were Ray MacSharry, John Wilson and Des O'Malley. Wilson, who was Minister for Posts and Telegraphs, denied that he had ever authorised that a 'tap' be put on the phones of the two journalists. Another member of that cabinet, Albert Reynolds, recalled that the question of leaks from the cabinet had been discussed. The issue ultimately helped bring down Haughey in February 1992. Doherty did not say that he had been authorised to tap phones. He said that he had been asked to stop the leaks. He judged that tapping phones was the correct course of action and he was not discouraged in thinking that that was what Haughey had in mind. *The Cork Examiner* led with a story on 16 January 1992 that Haughey and two senior ministers saw the transcripts of the conversations from taps placed on the phones of the two journalists in 1982. In the case which the two journalists and Mavis Arnold took against the state, Justice Hamilton ruled in the High Court on 12 January 1987 that 'the tapping of the plaintiffs' telephones had been deliberate, conscious and unjustifiable and was an actionable infringement of their constitutional rights.' He also found that 'the damage suffered by them had been aggravated by the fact that the tapping had been done by an organ of state which was constitutionally obliged to defend their rights.'[103] Arnold and Kennedy were awarded £20,000 each and Mavis Arnold was awarded £10,000. The phone tapping was an abuse of power and it was as unacceptable in Roscommon as it was in Dublin or in any other part of the state. Doherty 'took the rap' for performing as a loyal minister in the twilight world of GUBU. But a decade later Haughey took 'the fall'.

A number of Fianna Fáil front- and backbenchers had occasion to become disturbed about the drift of political events in 1982. At a cabinet meeting on 5 October, Des O'Malley and Martin O'Donoghue expressed reservations about the leadership of Haughey and resigned. Haughey said on radio that he would meet the challenge head on. He was of the opinion that the dissidents were a small minority; he preferred a roll-call vote to a secret ballot. The dissidents would have to 'stand up and be counted' and go the full distance. 'Go dance on somebody else's grave', Haughey told his opponents. The party meeting on 6 October lasted for 12 hours. Haughey won by 58 to 22. Safe for the time being, the Taoiseach launched the policy document 'The Way Forward' in mid-October. It was an election manifesto designed to correct the drift in party fortunes. After the launch of the document, an incident occurred that was to be a source of additional scandal when it was revealed the following year. The former Minister for Education, Martin O'Donoghue, had a meeting in the office of the Minister for Finance. At the request of the Minister for Justice, the assistant commissioner of the Garda Síochána, Joe Ainsworth, had provided MacSharry with a recorder to tape his conversation with O'Donoghue.[104]

On 1 November Haughey turned his attention to Northern Ireland where Sinn Féin had captured 10 per cent of the vote, and five seats, in the Assembly elections. He responded to a motion at a recent Sinn Féin *ard fheis* to ensure that all their candidates were to 'be unambivalent in support of the armed struggle'. Three RUC men had been blown up by a landmine near Dungannon on 27 October. Clearly and unambiguously, Haughey said:

> Contrary to what may be claimed, no organisation has an electoral mandate North or South to pursue a campaign of violence. The people of this part of Ireland have consistently and overwhelmingly rejected the pursuit of political ends by violent means, as indeed have the great majority of the Northern community. . . . In a democracy there is room for many political parties, but there can be only one lawful authority.[105]

Meanwhile, Haughey faced a bitter two-day debate in the Dáil on a Fine Gael no confidence motion. The death of Bill Loughnane TD on 18 October weakened Fianna Fáil. James Gibbons, Haughey's old political enemy, suffered a heart attack. The three Workers' Party deputies had belatedly seen the light and were determined to oppose Fianna Fáil in the next session. When the vote was taken on 4 November, the government was defeated by 82 votes to 80. Polling day was set for 24 November.

This was a testing campaign for Dick Spring, elected leader of the

Labour Party on 1 November 1982 following the defection of Michael O'Leary to Fine Gael.[106] The new leader of the Labour Party was a TCD graduate, a barrister and recent Irish rugby international. He was the son of the former Labour Party TD from Tralee, Co. Kerry, Dan Spring, who had been first elected to the Dáil during World War II. His son was made Minister of State in the Department of Justice on his first day in Leinster House on 30 June 1981. He survived a terrible car crash on 15 December that year which left him with very severe back injuries. In the internal struggle over coalition in the Labour Party during the autumn of 1982, Spring was very firmly on the side of his party leader, Michael O'Leary, during the crucial annual conference in Galway that October; Michael D. Higgins led the anti-coalition camp and Spring was on the losing side. But following the sudden resignation of O'Leary from the leadership and from the party, Spring emerged as a compromise candidate between Michael D. Higgins and Barry Desmond. He was 32.

Fianna Fáil went into the campaign with the opinion polls recording a 7 per cent drop in support for the party. FitzGerald was preferred as Taoiseach by 51 per cent, to 31 per cent for Haughey and 18 per cent undecided. The Labour Party maintained an open mind on coalition. This meant that it was possible to work out local arrangements on transfers.

Fine Gael ran on a more restrained programme than previously. An end to political interference with the gardaí was pledged. The party promised pay restraint in the public sector, a family income supplement for low paid workers, increased payments for private patients in hospitals and the establishment of a National Development Corporation.[107] But other issues also insinuated their way into the campaign. The uncertainty of the political situation provided an opportunity for an anti-abortion lobby, calling itself the Pro-Life Amendment Campaign (PLAC), to play off one side against the other. Fearing a shift of a block of orthodox Catholic votes, both Fianna Fáil and Fine Gael proved to be much more malleable than might otherwise have been the case. FitzGerald recalls with reference to his first administration:

I told the PLAC that I had instructed the Attorney General to advise me about the best way of giving constitutional protection to the life of the child and that during the course of the next Dáil I would take such steps as might be necessary to provide this constitutional protection. Charles Haughey went one better by promising an amendment during 1982.

FitzGerald wanted, as he told the Fine Gael annual conference in October, to have an amendment as an integral part of a general constitutional review.[108] While that may have been how the leader of Fine Gael wished to pursue the matter, PLAC had unnerved many Fine Gael supporters as its members lobbied with an intensity that was to become a feature of the brokerage politics of the 1980s. Fianna Fáil produced a text two days before the election. It read: 'The State acknowledges the right to life of the unborn and, with due regard to the equal right to life of the mother, guarantees in its laws to respect and, as far as practicable, by its laws to defend and vindicate that right.' In good faith, FitzGerald accepted that wording at the time, only to change his mind shortly after returning to power. The 'abortion question' formed part of the sub-text of the election campaign, as also did a certain paranoia about British interference in Irish politics.[109]

The campaign reached a level of high farce when FitzGerald's innocent lunch with the Duke of Norfolk was converted into a major conspiracy. It was alleged that the duke had been a former head of British military intelligence.[110] But what was happening to the government of the country while the parties were preparing and fighting two elections in 1982? It was drifting towards economic and civic bankruptcy.

THE SECOND FITZGERALD COALITION 1982–87
Fine Gael won 70 seats and Labour 16. Fianna Fáil had taken 75 seats, the Workers' Party two and there were three independents. The Labour Party, under Dick Spring, decided to join a coalition with Fine Gael. When the Dáil reconvened on 26 November FitzGerald was elected Taoiseach; Spring was made Tánaiste. Haughey was condemned to the opposition benches for nearly five years. His loss of the election precipitated another serious move to have him dethroned as leader. His great rival, George Colley, had died on 17 September 1983.

On 20 January 1983, the Garda Commissioner, Patrick McLaughlin, and the deputy commissioner, Joseph Ainsworth, submitted their resignations to the government to take effect on 1 February. This bombshell followed the discovery by the Minister for Justice, Michael Noonan, that the phones of two journalists had been tapped. Haughey denied all knowledge of the tappings. A committee of enquiry was set up by Fianna Fáil and it cleared Haughey. Meanwhile, there were strong rumours on 26 January that the leader of Fianna Fáil was about to resign. *The Irish Press*, the next day, published Haughey's political obituary. It was true that Haughey had contemplated resignation. He had even worked on the draft of a statement to that effect, but as the media reported with growing certitude that Haughey's resignation was imminent, support for the beleaguered Fianna Fáil leader grew. RTÉ was not going to hound him out of office, party loyalists vowed. As journalists waited outside Leinster House, Haughey was relaxing at a concert in a centre city theatre. The appearance of the obituary in *The Irish Press* helped turn the tide in his favour. Haughey supporters rallied outside Fianna Fáil headquarters on 31 January where a former junior minister, Niall Andrews, accused the media of executing Charles Haughey just like the dead heroes of the past.[111] On 2 February 1983, 40 deputies signed a petition for the holding of a party meeting. The following day, a 40-year-old Donegal TD, Clem Coughlan, was killed in a car crash on his way to Dublin. A former Haughey supporter, he had reached the conclusion that it was time for a change of leadership. When the parliamentary party met, Jim Tunney, the chairman, immediately adjourned the meeting. Confusion reigned as he hurriedly left the room, uttering the words, 'go dti an tseachtain seo chugainn' (until next week). Many TDs were unaware that the meeting was actually over. On 4 February, Ben Briscoe and George Colley put down a motion for the parliamentary party: 'That Fianna Fáil members of Dáil Éireann request the resignation of Mr Charles J. Haughey as party leader now.' Forty-one deputies signed a petition for the holding of a special meeting of the parliamentary party on the day after Clem Coughlan's funeral, but the request was not granted and it was finally set for 7 February. That gave Haughey and his supporters a weekend to put 'some backbone' into the party. In a radio interview, he explained that he had refused to resign because he thought that the majority of the parliamentary party was behind him: 'Politics are my life. I fight battles, I try and move things forward, do what I can, achieve progress, achieve reforms, achieve improvements, look after the old people, look after the disadvantaged.'[112]

Ray MacSharry, who had taped a conversation with Senator O'Donoghue, resigned from the front bench, together with Seán Doherty, who also lost the party whip. O'Donoghue lost the whip for his opposition to the leader. Haughey proved himself to be the Houdini of Irish politics yet again on 7 February. He won a vote to continue as leader of Fianna Fáil by 40 to 33. It was a virtuoso performance. Haughey had, like Richard Nixon, made one of the greatest comebacks since Lazarus.[113]

The Fine Gael/Labour coalition which came into office on 14 December 1982 made an historic contribution to greater understanding on the island; together with John Hume, the leader of the SDLP, FitzGerald conceived the idea of establishing a New Ireland Forum.[114] This examined in a radical way the future development of all the people of the island. All constitutional parties were invited to attend. The first session of the forum was held in Dublin Castle on 30 May 1983; the president of University College Galway, Colm Ó hEocha, was in the chair. There were 28 private sessions, 13 public sessions and 56 meetings of the steering group. A total of 317 written submissions were received from Ireland and abroad. A Forum delegation visited Northern Ireland on 26 and 27 September 1983 and held discussions in London on 23 and 24 January 1984 with groups from all the major parties. Important reports, some of which have already been referred to, were commissioned by the Forum.[115] The radical or traditional nature of the contents of the final report are a matter of historical dispute.[116]

But there is no doubting the historical significance of the Anglo-Irish Agreement which was signed on 15 November 1985, at Hillsborough Castle, by Garret FitzGerald and Margaret Thatcher. This provided the framework in which both Dublin and London might structure the handling of the long-term problems of Northern Ireland.[117] Very warmly welcomed internationally, the agreement encountered vigorous opposition from Northern loyalists, who felt that the pass had been sold by London. In Dublin the agreement was seen as a major diplomatic triumph, but there were influential dissenting voices. Mary Robinson, who was to become President of Ireland in 1990, resigned from the Labour Party over the agreement. Conor Cruise O'Brien was another strong and determined opponent of the agreement, fearful of its negative impact on loyalists. But the Irish Foreign Minister, Peter Barry, had no such reservations and worked very hard to ensure that the agreement was implemented without delay. The Maryfield secretariat was established, outside Belfast, and functioned with British and Irish staff despite intimidation from strident members of the unionist community. The agreement's architecture remained firmly in place in the 1990s.

Meanwhile the findings of the New Ireland Forum had given FitzGerald a new intellectual authority for the radical revision of the constitution:

> It is clear that a new Ireland will require a new constitution which will ensure that the needs of all traditions are fully met. Society in Ireland as a whole comprises a wider diversity of cultural and political traditions than exists in the South, and the constitution and laws of a new Ireland must accommodate these social and political realities.[118]

However, legislators in the 1980s faced the task of having to amend the laws and to take into account the changing nature of Irish society. Peter Barry made a speech on church-state relations in September 1985 at Iveagh House during a luncheon in honour of the cardinal secretary of state, Agostino Casaroli. Barry spoke of the intimate relationship between the Catholic Church and government since the foundation of the state: 'Nevertheless, in retrospect, it has been argued—most notably by the Catholic Bishops at the Public Session of the New Ireland Forum on 9 February 1984—that the alliance of Church and state was harmful for both parties.' The minister spoke of instances of misunderstanding between church and state in the 1970s and early 1980s. It was of little or no benefit to either the church or the state when they were seen to be at loggerheads, he said, but that was the price that had to be paid for a relationship based on equality and mutual respect. While the minister asserted the right of all church leaders to alert the consciences of their followers to what they perceive to be the moral consequences of any proposed legislation, he affirmed the right of members of the houses of the Oireachtas to legislate in accordance with their conscience, in what they consider to be the best interests of the Irish people.

That speech was delivered between the holding, in 1983 and 1986, of two referenda which demonstrated the ineptitude and, in some cases, the deviousness of Irish political leadership and the radical conservatism of the Irish electorate. The Haughey formula on abortion became article 40.3.3 of the constitution, following a referendum on 7 September 1983. The campaign proved to be one of the most vitriolic and divisive in the history of the state. The exchanges had echoes of the passion and the vindictiveness of post-Treaty Ireland in 1922.[119] FitzGerald found himself in a most invidious position. The Attorney General, Peter Sutherland, had prepared for government a memorandum of over 100 pages which cautioned against the acceptance of the Haughey formula. Its ambiguity was a matter of concern to Sutherland, who laid out before government a number of possible undesirable interpretations. Nevertheless, FitzGerald felt obliged to allow the formula to stand, but he reversed his original position and urged against voting for the Haughey wording. The Taoiseach warned on 3 September 1983: 'If, therefore, we adopt this amendment, we could be opening up the possibility that we are all trying to close off: the introduction of abortion.'[120] But the then archbishop of Dublin, Dermot Ryan, took a diametrically opposite point of view: 'A 'yes' vote on Wednesday will . . . block any attempt to legalise abortion in the country.'[121] The original mistake was for Dr FitzGerald to have accepted so readily the Fianna Fáil wording. Writing in 1992, he expressed regret about what happened at that time:

> For my part I was seriously at fault in accepting without adequate consideration or legal advice—however much in good faith— the proposed wording when it was put forward by Fianna Fáil in early November, 1982. The fact that, given the scale of the Fine Gael and Labour defections in the eventual Dáil division on the issue, the amendment would clearly have been put through the Dáil by Fianna Fáil in opposition, even if I had rejected it from the outset, is a poor excuse for my error of judgment.

Dr FitzGerald was also very critical of the Catholic hierarchy's refusal to allow the Taoiseach the opportunity to explain to the bishops face-to-face the legal defects that had emerged 'and to have insisted on discussing the proposed change in the amendment with us through an intermediary, with all the dangers of confusion inherent in such indirect contact.' He felt that the bishops were also wrong to have 'set themselves up as authorities on constitutional law superior to the Government's constitutional advisers, as they did in their pro-amendment statement on August 22nd, 1983'.[122] The Labour Party ministers had refused to support the Haughey formula from the very outset. There had been considerable discussion inside government and, in the end, the coalition had produced an alternative formula: 'Nothing in this Constitutiion shall be invoked to invalidate or to deprive of force or effect a provision of the law on the grounds that it prohibits abortion.' That wording was, according to Dr FitzGerald, endorsed as being preferable to the main churches other than the Catholic Church,[123] but the people ultimately voted on the original Haughey formula.

The eighth amendment to the constitution was passed by 66.9 per cent (841,233) in favour to 33.1 per cent (416,136) against. The turnout was 54.6 per cent.[124] A High Court ruling in February 1988 held that it was unlawful for clinics in Ireland to provide counselling services for women on abortion in Britain or elsewhere. The Supreme Court ruled in 1989 in favour of spuc seeking an injunction restraining the publication of the phone numbers and addresses of British abortion clinics in student welfare clinics. But that did not resolve the problem of abortion in Ireland. The following statistics have been given for women with Irish addresses having abortions in Britain:

1980	3,320
1981	3,603
1982	3,653
1983	3,677
1984	3,946
1985	3,888
1986	3,918
1987	3,673
1988	3,839
1989	3,721
1990	4,064
Total	41,302

The Oireachtas failed to introduce legislation to deal with this question after 1983. A Supreme Court justice, Niall McCarthy, said in the course of his judgment in 1992:

> In the context of the eight years that have passed since the amendment was adopted, and the two years since Grogan's case,

the failure by the legislature to enact the appropriate legislation is no longer just unfortunate; it is inexcusable. What are pregnant women to do? What are the medical profession to do?. . . . The amendment, born of public disquiet, historically divisive of our people, guaranteeing in its laws to respect and by its law to defend the right to life of the unborn, remains bare of legislative direction.[125]

These remarks were part of a Supreme Court judgment delivered on 5 March 1992 in the case of a pregnant 14-year-old alleged rape victim who had been prevented by injunction from returning to England for an abortion. The Supreme Court overturned the High Court ruling by a four-to-one margin and accepted that abortion was legal in limited cases where there was a real danger that the pregnant woman was liable to commit suicide. The eighth amendment had—as Peter Sutherland had advised the government in 1983—opened the way for limited legalised abortion in Ireland. A referendum on 25 November 1992 removed the ambiguity concerning the right to provide information and the right to travel. But the electorate, for diverse reasons, rejected the wording of the final part of the amendment:

It shall be unlawful to terminate the life of an unborn unless such termination is necessary to save the life, as distinct from the health, of the mother where there is an illness or disorder of the mother giving rise to a real and substantial risk to her life, not being a risk of self-destruction.

This was defeated by 65.4 per cent to 34.6 per cent, leaving the legislature with a major dilemma.

The tragic 'X case' was the indirect result of a failure of government—so much a feature of public life in Ireland during the 1980s and early 1990s. The lack of success of the coalition government's effort to amend the constitution on divorce on 26 June 1986 was yet another example of a failure of the Oireachtas to tackle the serious question of marital breakdown in Ireland until 1995.[126] Even if allowance is made for the role of organised lobbies and the influence of the 'pulpit', leaders of the coalition had to accept some responsibility for the reckless manner in which the government entered a referendum campaign on divorce without adequate preparation or detailed study of the implications. The coalition picked the time, yet appeared to be on the defensive from the outset. Answers to basic questions on property rights and social welfare entitlements had not been anticipated and prepared in advance. The behaviour of Fianna Fáil provides another explanation for the failure of the divorce referendum of 1986. Opinion polls had showed a majority in favour of removing the constitutional ban, but there was very little possibility of success without the support of the major political parties. Fianna Fáil did not remain neutral. Party members supported the anti-divorce campaign.

The Fine Gael/Labour coalition of 1982–87 had resulted in a productive partnership, but it was a partnership that had its ideological tensions and personal pressures. The Labour Party remained very much the junior partner, yet the good personal relationship between FitzGerald and Spring helped to smooth over many difficult problems. The ideological divisions were most evident in the run-up to the 1984 budget. No good working personal relationship was capable of masking the clashes between Labour and Fine Gael ministers which occurred over different policy priorities. For example, the Minister for Trade, Commerce and Tourism, Frank Cluskey, clashed with cabinet colleagues over a plan to refinance the Dublin Gas company at a cost of about £126 million. He opposed giving such enormous state finances to a private company. When he was out-voted in the cabinet, he resigned in December 1983. The other Labour ministers remained in government until 20 January 1987. There were deep divisions over the proposed budgetary measures proposed by FitzGerald. There was also considerable unease within the wider Labour Party over the content of the EC's Single European Act, which sought to deepen the process of integration. In opposition to proposed spending cuts, Spring led the Labour ministers out of government. FitzGerald called a general election for 18 February 1987. It was a bad election for Labour and for Dick Spring in particular. He managed to retain his seat in North Kerry by only four votes.

THE END OF THE HAUGHEY ERA

Charles Haughey returned to office in 1987, failing to gain an overall majority for the fourth successive time. But electoral success remained a form of self-imposed failure in the eyes of those in Fianna Fáil who continued to believe that a charismatic leader could channel the loyalty of the electorate into a Lynch-style 1977 victory. Moreover, Haughey had failed to retain consensus inside the party. His predecessors had all had to deal with division and dissension within the ranks. Lynch, in particular, had retained Fianna Fáil unity through very difficult times. But in 1985 Haughey caused a split in the party. His hostility to the Anglo-Irish Agreement provoked a Fianna Fáil backbencher, Mary Harney, to vote with the government. She was promptly expelled and, a few days before Christmas, Desmond O'Malley and Mary Harney founded the Progressive Democrats. Two other Fianna Fáil TDs, Bobby Molloy from Galway and Pearse Wyse from Cork, joined the PDs and the party's ratings moved up in the polls. At its first election outing in 1987, the PDs gained fourteen seats and deprived Fianna Fáil of both an overall majority and the talents of Bobby Molloy and Mary Harney—two excellent administrators. Haughey had to rely upon the casting vote of the Ceann Comhairle to remain in power. That was a humiliation for a leader who saw himself more as a chief than as a chairman. He lacked Lynch's talent to deliver a majority and he now also lacked his predecessor's ability to contain dissent within the family.

Ray MacSharry was made Minister for Finance in the new government. Albert Reynolds was appointed Minister for Industry and Commerce; he took over the finance portfolio when MacSharry was made an EC Commissioner in November 1988. Brian Lenihan was Tánaiste and Minister for Foreign Affairs. His sister, Mary O'Rourke, became Minister for Education. Gerard Collins was appointed Minister for Justice and Pádraig Flynn Minister for the Environment. Ray Burke was given charge of the Department of Industry and Commerce. What was new in that government was Haughey's determination to stop the drift towards greater economic dislocation which confronted the nation. MacSharry and his successor, Albert Reynolds, pursued a strong policy of retrenchment.

The government was assisted in this domain by the strategy of the new Fine Gael leader, Alan Dukes. He had taken over the leadership in March 1987 following the surprise resignation of Garret FitzGerald. Dukes was recruited from the same wing of the party as his predecessor. An economist by profession, Dukes had worked for a number of years at the European Commission in Brussels. His 'Tallaght strategy' was based on the principle that it was not simply the job of an opposition to be negative. Dukes refused to engage in the blood sport of politics for its own sake. He resisted the temptation to cannibalise the government, to the frustration of a number of his colleagues. Fine Gael voted with the government on 42 occasions during the legislative year 1988 and only 12 times against.[127] Haughey, who had been ambivalent in his attitude towards the Single European Act, was obliged in government to take the lead to ensure that a majority was secured for the measure in the 1987 referendum.[128] The new-look Fianna Fáil had a resolve and a determination to take hard, politically unpopular decisions. Yet the 'Haughey factor' continued to operate against the political interests of Fianna Fáil. There were rumours about business interests involved in efforts to defraud the European Community. Barry Desmond of the Labour Party was accused of national sabotage in the Dáil by Haughey when he raised the matter in March 1989. Political insiders were speculating about the possibility of a major financial scandal and of conflict between senior civil servants and government ministers over what constituted policy based on a cabinet decision. The alleged privatisation of government decision-making was a growing cause for concern since more and more government business was allegedly done by word of mouth without attention to due procedures. So much now depended upon the individual probity of senior civil servants who found themselves more and more often in an administrative no-man's land. The state was fortunate to have been served at the time by officials who might not have been in a position to prevent or pre-empt partisan policy adventurism. But, at the very least, all exchanges and conversations could be documented for the record.

Despite the fact that he was not in any immediate danger of losing office, Haughey remained haunted by his own self-imposed sense of failure. He had not emulated the success of Jack Lynch in 1977. It may have been pride or vanity which allowed him to remain convinced that he could deliver an overall majority for his party. The failure to realise that such a prospect was elusive led to one of the most egregious mistakes of his political career—comparable only to George Colley's miscalculation of 1979. Sound political judgment deserted him in 1989. Against the advice of senior government ministers, Haughey allowed himself be trapped into calling an unnecessary general election. The outcome was traumatic for his party and directly contributed to his departure from the leadership of Fianna Fáil in controversial circumstances on 11 February 1992.

Haughey was forced to enter into a coalition with his opponent, Desmond O'Malley, whom he had forced out of Fianna Fáil in February 1985. There was a religious fervour attached to being a member of what was somewhat arrogantly referred to as 'the party'— the 'one true church' of Irish political orthodoxy. Departure was not so much a defection as an act of apostasy, casting a person into exterior darkness.

The bitterness between the leadership of the two parties was palpable. O'Malley and Mary Harney had set up the PDS on 21 December 1985 to break 'the mould of Irish politics' and give the voters 'a new and real alternative' to what was termed the civil war parties. There was a pledge to build a 'New Republic' and a call to transform Irish politics. Both Harney and O'Malley knew the reality of Haughey's Fianna Fáil from the inside. They had shown a moral courage as party dissidents which has yet to be documented. Robert Molloy and Pearse Wyse had also left the womb of Fianna Fáil. Máirin Quill, first elected for the PDS in 1987, had unsuccessfully contested two elections for Fianna Fáil in Cork in 1977 and 1981. A doughty fighter, she was another apostate in the eyes of the Fianna Fáil faithful. She was not a talent any professional party would lightly have allowed defect. Finally, there was Peadar Clohessy (Limerick East), who had first been elected to the Dáil in June 1981 for Fianna Fáil. He had lost his seat in the February 1982 election. A founder member of the Progressive Democrats, he won a seat in the Dáil in 1987.

Following the general election of 1989, the sweet irony was that those six former Fianna Fáil TDS stood between Haughey and an overall majority. The PDS had lost eight seats, but O'Malley and his depleted band held the balance of power. Fianna Fáil had dropped from 81 to 77 seats. Fine Gael had increased its strength from 51 to 55 under the leadership of Alan Dukes.[129] Labour moved from 12 to 15 TDS and the Workers' Party from four to seven. There were six independents. Haughey had been unlucky. Fianna Fáil had secured the same percentage of the votes as in 1987, 44.1 per cent, but had lost vital seats.

There was much invocation of 'core values' as Haughey and his colleagues wrestled with the prospect of bringing the party into a coalition for the first time in its history. The dilemma was made all the more acute because 'the party' was contemplating the prospect of having to share power with 'apostates'. The cynic might well argue that

Fianna Fáil wrestled with its conscience and Fianna Fáil won. But Haughey made his most enduring contribution to the future of Fianna Fáil by opting for coalition; he broke the party's taboo of single-party government or nothing. The PDS were offered two full ministries, a junior ministry and a number of seats in the Senate. O'Malley went back in cabinet as Minister for Industry and Commerce. Molloy became Minister for Energy and Mary Harney was appointed junior minister for the Environment. A number of Fianna Fáil ministers held onto the same portfolios. However, Brian Lenihan, while still Tánaiste, was shifted to Defence. Gerard Collins moved to Foreign Affairs, Ray Burke was given Justice and Séamus Brennan was put in charge of Tourism and Transport. There may not have been much love lost between O'Malley and Haughey, but the competition between the two parties in coalition resulted in an improvement in the quality of government performance.

While the idea of coalition continued to rankle with rank and file members of Fianna Fáil, worse was to follow in 1990 when Brian Lenihan unexpectedly lost the presidential election to the Labour Party candidate, Mary Robinson. The Fianna Fáil candidate's campaign had been dogged by bad luck and suggestions that he had been economical with the truth. Lenihan, who had had a successful liver transplant, may not have been robust enough physically to take on a demanding countrywide campaign, yet his health held up. It was the contradictions and confusion over his different accounts over what happened on the night of the dissolution of the Dáil in January 1982 which led to the total unravelling of his bid for the presidency. To make matters worse, Haughey sacked Lenihan from the cabinet in response to an ultimatum from the PDS while the campaign was nearing its end.

Despite his self-created difficulties, Lenihan had fought a dignified campaign.[130] The same could not be said of a number of his supporters. Fianna Fáil had spent a large sum of money towards the end of the battle trying to adopt 'red scare' tactics to damage Mary Robinson. 'Is the left right for the Park?' read press advertisements, and voters were exhorted to opt for Fianna Fáil if 'you want to stop radical socialists taking over the Presidency'.[131] That was a strategy of despair. It lacked credibility and accentuated, if anything, the growing weakness of Lenihan's candidature. Robinson had campaigned very hard and was known in the countryside as a moderate. It was difficult to smear her. Fianna Fáil might have remembered with profit at the time the aphorism of Seán Lemass—mud thrown is ground lost. During the last critical days of campaigning, lack of discipline produced two significant 'own-goals' for Fianna Fáil. A deputy from Wexford, John Browne, was reported in the *Wexford People* as having said at a meeting about Mary Robinson: 'She's the biggest hypocrite in the campaign. She's pro-divorce, pro-contraception, and pro-abortion. Is she going to have an abortion referral clinic in Áras an Uachtaráin? That's what I'd like to know.'[132] It is difficult to calculate precisely how many votes Pádraig Flynn lost Brian Lenihan by his radio outburst on the Saturday before the election. Speaking from RTÉ's Castlebar studio in a panel discussion, he said:

> She was pretty well constructed in this campaign by her handlers, the Labour Party and the Workers' Party. Of course, it doesn't always suit if you get labelled a socialist, because that's a very narrow focus in this country—so she has to try and have it both ways. She has to have new clothes and her new look and her new hairdo and she has the new interest in family, being a mother and all that kind of thing. But none of us, you know, none of us who knew Mary Robinson very well in previous incarnations ever heard her claiming to be a great wife and mother. Mary Robinson reconstructs herself to fit the fashion of the time, so we have this thing about you can be substituted [sic] at will, whether it's the pro-socialist thing, or pro-contraception, or pro-abortion— whatever it is. But at least we should know. Mary Robinson is a socialist; she says it and has admitted it previously. Now she may have changed her mind, and if she has changed her mind, so be it. But at least she should tell us that she has changed her mind, and not be misleading us.[133]

Flynn was gracious enough later to admit his lapse and apologise. On 9 November 1990 Mary Robinson was elected President of Ireland by a majority of 86,557 votes. She had secured 817,830 votes to Lenihan's 731,273. Her election had truly 'rocked the system'.

Alan Dukes was the first to pay for Robinson's victory with his own head. He had chosen to ignore the advice of a number of prominent Fine Gael frontbenchers who favoured giving support to the candidature of Mary Robinson. In the end, the poor showing of the

Fine Gael candidate, Austin Currie, had crystallised revolt in that party. At a time in Irish politics when the election of Mary Robinson had signified the possibility of radical change, Alan Dukes, the social democrat, was ditched for John Bruton, the technocrat. There is little sentiment in Irish politics, but changing leaders in that fashion was a serious strategic mistake for Fine Gael since it removed from its front bench the youthful Dukes, who alone in his party had the ability to subject Haughey's reeling Fianna Fáil to the death of a thousand cuts.[134] However, the sacking of Dukes did not simply reveal dissatisfaction with the performance of an inexperienced leader. It reflected the profound unease that a powerful section of the party felt with being taken along a social democratic path, while many of the front bench and party backers were conservative Christian democrats, if not Catholic integralists in one or two cases. Fine Gael was much more comfortable using the language of the technocrats. In making that radical philosophical shift, it tried to weaken the hold of the philosophy of Garret FitzGerald. But in so doing, it generously left a vacuum in Irish politics which a more tactically shrewd Fianna Fáil might have been in a position to fill in the 1990s as it discovered the politically lucrative side of a liberal agenda. Fianna Fáil's role as protector of Catholic sexual morality would last only for as long as it was seen to deliver votes and marginal seats. A reverse strategy in the 1990s was more likely to recapture the citadel of Dublin for the Party of Reality.

The Taoiseach enjoyed the glamour and the high profile of the Irish presidency of the European Community from January to June 1990—a presidency that was being described as 'historic' by members of the cabinet before it had even begun. It cost the country about £12m to host. It was well planned and well carried through. Haughey won the admiration of many civil servants for his ability to master the diverse briefs and chair with great efficiency crucial meetings—particularly the two European Councils which were held in Dublin.

But the halo effect did not last very long and the country faced a deepening financial crisis in 1991. There were serious differences of opinion between Haughey and the Minister for Finance, Albert Reynolds, over economic strategy. There was embarrassment for the government when the Irish Family Planning Association was prosecuted in the Circuit Court for selling condoms at a stall in the Virgin megastore. Richard Branson, the owner of the store, was on hand to point out what he thought of the ruling. On appeal to the Circuit Court on 26 February 1991 the fine was doubled. The condom issue was discussed at cabinet on 12 March and Haughey found that he was backed by only two ministers when it was proposed to reduce the age for buying condoms from eighteen to sixteen. A number of ministers were adamant in their opposition, Michael O'Kennedy and John Wilson among them.[135] Meanwhile, unrest within Fianna Fáil grew. For a time it looked as if there was going to be a different policy in the various health boards as central government contemplated devolving power in an effort to avoid having to make a decision.

But questions of sexual morality were swiftly reduced to a secondary place when a series of scandals shook public confidence in sectors of the Irish business world. On 13 May 1991 ITV's 'World in Action' transmitted a programme on the Goodman meat empire. The reverberations were still being felt in Irish politics at the end of 1993. A report by High Court inspectors into Greencore in March 1992 was highly critical of the management of Siúicre Éireann.[136] There was much public discussion about the existence of a politically favoured 'golden triangle' in the Irish business world.

The local elections in May 1991 saw the Fianna Fáil vote slip to 37.8 per cent.[137] That meant that Haughey had little chance of securing the elusive overall majority for the party in the next general election, but that was only the beginning of his difficulties. The backroom men of Fianna Fáil felt that it was time for the messiah, who had failed on every occasion to deliver an overall majority, to step down.

Conflict within Fianna Fáil forced Haughey to sack Albert Reynolds and Pádraig Flynn at the end of 1991. After all, the party was structured as the 'one true church'; pluralism was not tolerated. Máire Geoghegan-Quinn, Michael Smith and Noel Treacy also lost junior ministries about the same time. It looked as if the 'survivor' of Irish politics had done it again. Haughey had beaten off the opposition inside the party once more. He told an interviewer on 22 September 1991: 'Some of these Chinese leaders go on 'til they are eighty or ninety—but I think that's probably a bit long.'

However, his decision to appoint Dr James McDaid as Minister for Defence and Noel Davern as Minister for Education baffled and infuriated some of his most loyal supporters. A number of loyal junior ministers and promising backbench TDs felt that they had been passed over. There was a sensation in the Dáil when Dr McDaid declined to accept the Defence portfolio. The opposition had brought into the House a copy of a newspaper with a front-page picture of McDaid in a crowd outside the Four Courts following the release of James Pius Clarke, who had won his case against being extradited to Northern Ireland.[138] Vincent Brady was then given the Defence portfolio. Haughey must have hoped that 1992 would bring better luck, but that was not to be. Seán Doherty, the Cathaoirleach of the Seanad, stated on a late night TV programme that when he was Minister for Justice in 1982,

> there was a decision taken in cabinet that the leaking of matters from cabinet must be stopped. I, as Minister for Justice, had a direct responsibility for doing that—I did that. I do feel that I was let down by the fact that people knew what I was doing.

This was a reference to the 'tapping' of the phones of two journalists. At a press conference on 21 January 1992, Doherty claimed that Haughey had been fully aware in 1982 that the phones of two journalists were being tapped. He claimed that he had handed the transcripts directly to Haughey. The Taoiseach flatly denied Doherty's statement, but he was forced to resign on 11 February 1992. He was replaced by Albert Reynolds as Taoiseach a few weeks later. Pádraig Flynn was made Minister for Justice and there were ministerial positions for the other dissidents. The country and western wing of Fianna Fáil (a phrase attributed to Haughey) now held the reins of power.

THE HAUGHEY LEGACY

In *The Prince*, Machiavelli wrote of the qualities necessary to become a successful ruler: 'a prince is successful when he fits his mode of proceeding to the times, and is unsuccessful when his mode of proceeding is no longer in tune with them.' Niccolo continues, in his *vade mecum* of power politics, to provide an abundance of advice for the aspiring leader:

> . . . the first estimate of his [the Prince's] intelligence will be based upon the character of the men he keeps about him. If they are capable and loyal, he will be reputed wise, for he will have demonstrated that he knows how to recognise their ability and

keep them loyal to him. If they are otherwise, he will be judged unfavourably, for the first mistake a ruler can make lies in the selection of his ministers.

Machiavelli wrote that ministerial minds were of three kinds: one is capable of thinking for itself; another is able to understand the thinking of others; and a third can neither think for itself nor understand the thinking of others. Haughey, out of loyalty to his faithful friends and out of fear of producing a serious rival, relied too heavily on Machiavelli's third division, with disastrous results for the country and dire consequences for Fianna Fáil.

At one level, Haughey has been unfairly judged by the standards of his three predecessors. Times had changed and politics in Ireland had changed. Haughey was not de Valera, and yet Fianna Fáil sought to encourage him to play the role of charismatic leader. In reality, he was 'the boss', a political fixer and a good ward politician. Perhaps his own vanity also contributed to the attempt to package and market the 'boss' as a born-again de Valera. Under Haughey, Fianna Fáil refused to grow up and he refused to allow the party to grow up. He was too much of a centraliser and too much of a leader who wished to keep all the power in his own hands. His opponents will assert that he had created the situation through his own inept and self-willed leadership-style. Another leader might have managed to hold the party together for a little while longer. But the dynamics of Irish politics had presaged the end of Fianna Fáil dominance. The Lynch landslide in 1977 had been an aberration. Yet for the party it remained the litmus test of political success. Haughey had 'failed' again and again. It was the ultimate heresy when he was forced to bring the PDS into coalition in 1989. Pursuit of an overall majority by Fianna Fáil in the 1980s had become as futile as the quest for the philosopher's stone. Haughey will be regarded as the leader who could neither maintain Fianna Fáil's unity nor its overall majority. The former was very much his own fault because he lacked Lynch's ability to contain dissent. The latter he could have done very little about, but single-party government remained his personal objective.

Haughey had the misfortune to belong to a party which demanded a heroic profile of its leaders and a worldly capacity to win power. He also had the great misfortune to inherit an antiquated administrative structure. The houses of the Oireachtas remained fossilised in the decision-making structures of a Westminster before Irish independence. Public administration was largely unreformed and choked by excessive centralisation. Haughey could have become an administrative reformer of great significance, going down in history as the person who modernised the Irish state. That did not happen. Haughey must have felt like the British racing driver Stirling Moss in a Model T Ford. He simply became frustrated and tried to do too much himself.

The most severe criticism that can be levelled against Charles Haughey is that he became the first Taoiseach in the history of the state to attempt to privatise the running of government. Ireland has been noted for its closed system of administration, but, at least, that system of government was mediated by a career civil service rooted in a tradition and a culture of public service. Did Charles Haughey, and some of his government ministers, try to skip a loop in the vital chain of administrative and political decision-making?

Charles Haughey was, in conclusion, one of the most talented Fianna Fáil politicians ever to hold a senior ministry in an Irish government. His was less a personal failure than the victim of Fianna Fáil populism. Haughey was encouraged to bring that populism to its logical conclusion. It may be judged that, towards the end, he had an insight which forced him to face political reality and form a coalition in order to stay in power. Haughey was an impressive performer when he took charge of a meeting. His real administrative worth was displayed during the Irish presidency of the EC in 1990. He dazzled senior civil servants with his planning and chairmanship skills. Had he performed at that level throughout his terms as Taoiseach, the country might have moved forward rapidly. That simply did not happen. The government of the country suffered because Fianna Fáil in the 1980s was in a state of incipient, and sometimes outright, civil war.

The growing public cynicism with Irish politics in the late 1980s was reflected in Dermot Bolger's novel *The Journey Home* (published in 1990). It treats of a country devoid of civic virtue and almost without hope. Bolger's Ireland is dominated by men like Justin Plunkett, a grandson of one of the country's revolutionary nationalist heroes, who had done very nicely for himself—property developer, moneylender and junior government minister. Hano, an alienated figure on the periphery of the Irish landscape, pictures that pillar of the community as he moves through a bar, slapping the shoulders of those who would have disappeared by the following Friday. Perhaps he was just carrying on his father's work: clearing the country of debris, propelling it towards its destiny as a pleasure ground for the rich, a necklace of golf courses encircling the city, a modest number of natives left for service industries.[139]

Seán Dunne's poem 'Throwing the Beads' has a relevance with which a majority of Irish families in the last decade of the twentieth century could readily identify.

> A mother at Shannon, waving to her son
> Setting out from North Kerry, flung
> A rosary beads out to the tarmac
> Suddenly as a lifebelt hurled from a pier.
> *Don't forget to say your prayers in Boston.*[140]

Amid the scandals and the political crises of the late 1980s and early 1990s, it would be relatively easy to speak of the victory in Ireland of radical individualism and corporate greed. But there were competing value systems which challenged that philosophy. There were lay and clerical voices which stood against the drift towards the creation of an even more highly stratified society. They provided examples of the triumph of decency over administrative inefficiency, corruption and greed. The creative impulse was reflected in Irish literature, music and the visual arts. A generosity of spirit was evident in Ireland when confronted by the challenge of the Third World. Sections of the public service reflected a sense of administrative excellence. There was a basic generosity among young people and a sense of common decency which refused to allow corruption, dishonesty and deception become the norm. Many examples could be cited of the struggle for basic justice by individuals and groups. It is important to conclude by showing how standards of decency may sometimes prevail. Here is a good example of what is meant.

Mary Hanrahan owned a sizeable model farm at Ballycurkeen, Carrick-on-Suir, Co. Tipperary. She was a grand-niece of the nineteenth-century owner, John Mandeville. She was also related to the Young Irelander and Fenian, John O'Mahony.[141] Born in Newcastle West, Co. Limerick in 1920, she had moved to the farm in the late 1930s and took it over when her uncle died in 1940.[142] The war years were a difficult time for farming, with the emphasis on compulsory tillage. Mary Hanrahan was innovative and purchased a tractor which she had to drive from Kanturk to Ballycurkeen—a journey that took two days at that time.[143] She was the sole manager of the farm before marrying John Hanrahan in 1942. They had four children. The 265-acre holding was particularly well managed and the family enjoyed a reputation as model farmers. But things began to go inexplicably wrong in the late 1970s. At this stage, the farm was being managed by her son, John. Cattle began to get sick and people living on the farm experienced bad health. The Hanrahans had little doubt as to the cause of the trouble. Emissions from the nearby chemical plant of Merck, Sharp and Dohme were considered responsible. The family sought to solve the problem first by consulting the factory, but, without finding redress, the Hanrahans felt obliged to go to law.

What followed was a legal battle lasting for five years which showed in the end the inadequacy of local and national administrative structures to provide for the protection of the environment. The High Court found against the Hanrahans in August 1985. The creditors closed in and the family was deserted by many in the area. The farm was put on the market, but it was a forced sale and no reasonable bid was made. However, farm equipment and furniture were auctioned off. The family doctor advised that the family should move out for health reasons. Mary Hanrahan chose to remain on the farm with her sister. There were sick animals which needed to be looked after and they could not be left alone at night. She had six good guard dogs and she kept a loaded shotgun in her bedroom at night. 'I was always a good shot', she said. The painters had been called in to seal up the windows. The doors were insulated with masking tape. Walking up the fields one day, Mary Hanrahan said that she knew exactly how Robinson Crusoe must have felt.[144]

She recollected how she had drawn upon the inspiration of her ancestor John O'Mahony to keep going. Mary Hanrahan was sustained by a deep faith: 'When you are in desperate, dire trouble, you don't say ordinary prayers. You just kneel down and start talking as I am talking to you.' She believed in the Communion of Saints and asked Mandeville and O'Mahony to intercede on the family's behalf. There is gentle irony in the idea of an excommunicated Fenian, whose body was not allowed in the 1860s to lie in state in any Dublin church, being asked to intercede at a time of deep family crisis. There were bad times, but, Mary Hanrahan said, 'I was not the sort of person who would collapse and cry. The day we lost the case, defeat didn't really come into it. I did not stop to analyse how much trouble we were in. We just got on with it. . . . And if the worst came to the worst and we lost the farm, you can always start again. Nobody starves nowadays.'

She never missed a day in court. Mary Hanrahan was in the witness box for two days: 'If you are telling the truth, you have no problems. You don't have to worry about contradicting yourself. I simply pointed the finger.' She found that there were many people who stood by them in their worst hour: solicitors, senior counsel, experts from Trinity College, vets and agricultural advisers, and the occasional neighbour. A notice of appeal was lodged with the Supreme Court on 12 November 1985. The appeal came up two years later and the case ran for thirteen days. It took the three judges seven months to arrive at a verdict and on 5 July 1988, the court held Merck, Sharp and Dohme liable for damages to the Hanrahans for offensive smells, for injury to John Hanrahan's health, and for the cattle ailments in so far as they were caused by factory emissions.[145] The battle was over and the Hanrahans ought to take credit for teaching the country an indispensable lesson about the protection of the environment. Speaking about learning the ten commandments during her schooldays, Mary Hanrahan said that in one's dealings with other people there was right and wrong. But referring to present-day Ireland, she said that there was a large grey area opening up between right and wrong for many people and it appeared to be getting wider. 'You just can't make yourself rich at the cost of anyone else', she said. By the end of the 1980s and the early 1990s, many wealthy and powerful people in Ireland had added, she said, an eleventh commandment: 'Thou shalt not be found out.' In relation to the case which took up so many years of her life, the descendant of O'Mahony and Mandeville said firmly: 'You have to stand up and be counted.'[146] That was what happened in 1992.

Albert Reynolds, who replaced Haughey as Taoiseach, took an early opportunity to reassure the Fianna Fáil faithful that his objective was single-party government. He termed the PDs' presence in government a 'temporary little arrangement'. When in doubt, leave out, was how a new minister referred to O'Malley's party in power. Fianna Fáil's search for the philosopher's stone was still on in mid-1992 as the 'country and western' wing of that party went for single-party rule. Cabinet meetings were bruising affairs. But the PDS refused to continue in government following Reynolds's appearance at the Beef Tribunal, during the course of which he had spoken harshly about his fellow minister, Desmond O'Malley. The election that followed was as unnecessary as it was unwanted by the public. It simply underlined the ineptitude of government at a time of unprecedented national economic crisis. Furthermore, there was growing popular outrage at the separation of the well-being of the economy from the well-being of the people. The 'fundamentals' were deemed to be sound, while the unemployment figures rose above 300,000.

The general election was conducted in a spirit of recrimination and mud-slinging. Fianna Fáil was in disarray. Their campaign was organised with all the finesse of the 1961 Bay of Pigs landing in Cuba, which has gone down in history as the 'perfect planning failure'. Saatchi and Saatchi, Margaret Thatcher's favoured advertising agency, had the job of packaging and marketing Fianna Fáil; 'We can make it happen' was its patronising campaign slogan. Things went badly wrong for Fianna Fáil as the party's canvassers encountered unprecedented hostility on the doorsteps.

A few days before people went to the polls, an anti-Labour advertising blitz was carried out. Voters were warned that a victory for Labour would result in higher taxes, further borrowing and a running down of the economy. Dick Spring described such negative campaigning as the politics of the gutter. He advised his followers to vote left. That meant voting for Proinsias de Rossa's Democratic Left—a recently formed breakaway from the hardline, pro-Moscow, Marxist Workers' Party. John Bruton, the leader of Fine Gael, saw himself as the next Taoiseach at the head of a rainbow coalition which would include Labour and the PDS. While such an arrangement suited both Fine Gael and the PDS, it did not please Labour. Spring had not been consulted before Bruton had made his intentions public, and the perceived presumptuousness of Fine Gael offended Labour. Spring stunned many with a suggestion early in the campaign that there was no reason why he should not be considered for the top position in government. The idea brought guffaws from Fianna Fáil, but the smile was on the other side of their faces after polling day on 25 November. Labour won 33 seats—an increase of 17. The PDS went from 6 to 10. Fianna Fáil dropped from 77 to 68. Fine Gael went from 55 down to 45 and the Democratic Left from 6 to 4. The Greens retained a single seat and independents held the remaining five places. If the outcome was traumatic for Fianna Fáil, it was an unqualified disaster for Fine Gael. Political pundits predicted that Dick Spring would let history repeat itself and join an anti-Fianna Fáil rainbow coalition with Fine Gael and the PDS. Instead, he spent nearly two weeks after the election talking to the Democratic Left. Reflexively and imprudently, Fine Gael and the PDS ruled out the formation of a government which involved the Democratic Left. But that was not Labour's plan; its intention was to absorb, rather than to include the Democratic Left in government. Fine Gael, whose very recovery as a party depended upon getting into power, bungled the courtship of Labour. The Fine Gael bridegroom waited at the altar without ever having made a formal proposal. Spring, after a perfunctory discussion with Bruton, sought a partner in government elsewhere. Fianna Fáil had ruled nothing out during the interval since returning to government was the only way to avert civil war in the party and to stage a political comeback. Talks were set in train between the two parties and were brought to a successful conclusion in January 1993. A Labour/Fianna Fáil coalition was formed with Albert Reynolds as Taoiseach; he followed the revolutionary tactic of simply being himself. Reynolds was not concerned about charisma or image-making and he did not seek to resurrect the role of an Éamon de Valera or Jack Lynch. The new Taoiseach shared Seán Lemass's impatience with the theology of high church Fianna Fáil. He worked well with the Tánaiste, Dick Spring. On a positive note, both Reynolds and Spring shared the urgent determination to end violence in Northern Ireland. That was a policy goal and not a pious aspiration; it was the key to achieving other central policy goals. The Downing Street Declaration of December 1993 was the outcome. Inspired by the witness of Senator Gordon Wilson, who lost his daughter in the 1987 Enniskillen Remembrance Day bombing, people hoped against hope that lasting peace could and would be finally achieved.

Alexis de Tocqueville argues that

> . . . time does not halt its progress for peoples any more than for men; both men and peoples are daily advancing into an unknown future, and when we think that they are stationary, that is because we do not see their movements. Men may be walking and seem

stationary to those who are running.[147]

With a woman President and 20 women elected to the 27th Dáil, the 1990s was a decade when *mná na hÉireann*, who had, to quote Mary Robinson, 'felt themselves outside history', would be 'written back into history'.[148] It would be more correct to argue that their role in the development of the state would at last receive due recognition in the history texts, 'finding a voice where they found a vision'—to use the words of the poet Eavan Boland. But it was only a dawn of sorts—a somewhat false one at that.

Ireland in the New Century

Few academics of any discipline could have predicted the dramatic political, economic, social, cultural and religious changes of the middle and late 1990s on the island of Ireland. The emergence of stable coalition governments displaced the fractious arrangements of the earlier part of the decade. The turnaround in the economy, and in particular the sharp, unprecedented growth in employment in the latter 1990s, helped to raise all boats capable of floating in the first place. Domestic economic reforms and favourable global economic conditions, including a low interest rate regime comparable to the post-war golden era, aided in the birth of the so-called 'Celtic Tiger', as did the injection of significant capital sums from Brussels in the form of EU structural funds. Peace broke out in Northern Ireland to the surprise of many who had been conditioned to feel that the thirty-year-old era of violence was endemic and beyond resolution. That surprising and ever-fragile turnaround further helped the economy to flourish in both parts of the island.

But rapid economic transformation helped expose inadequacies in the Irish state. The modernising influence of membership of the EU demanded deep changes in the civic culture and in national political and administrative structures. Suddenly, the Irish state was obliged to confront a series of scandals that caused huge embarrassment to Irish banking. The government confronted challenges to the inadequacies of previous administrations in relation to the management of industrial schools and child sexual abuse in state-funded institutions. There were also serious questions to answer regarding the management of the national blood transfusion service and the treatment of haemophiliacs. There was a scandal over charging families for the care of the elderly without statutory authority. There followed a scandal that could involve the state in the payment of billions of euro in compensation to elderly residents in nursing homes who had their pension entitlements put towards the cost of their residential care; this was done without statutory authority and it was known to be the case since 1976.

Tribunals of inquiry proliferated as high-level politicians Charles Haughey and Raphael Burke were pilloried for being in receipt of funds undeclared to the Revenue Commissioners. Liam Lawlor and Michael Lowry also became household names through their appearance before tribunals. The actor Joe Taylor did a brilliant job nightly on Vincent Browne's radio show re-enacting their testimony with a cruelly accurate realism. An ugly aspect of Irish public life was portrayed to an incredulous public.

The Garda Síochána, a most professional and dedicated body of men and women who had served the state with great loyalty in very difficult times, did not escape opprobrium in the investigation of their activities in Donegal. The second report of the Morris Tribunal, set up in 2002 to investigate complaints against gardaí in Donegal, was published on 1 June 2005. The findings were very damaging, accusing members of the force of 'gross negligence' and 'shocking conduct.' Words like 'bizarre,' 'disturbing' and 'shocking' were also used in Mr Justice Frederick Morris's report. The repercussions of the findings on the force were likely to be profound.

Moreover, the Catholic Church was significantly undermined by a series of scandals involving the conduct of clergy who were very prominent in the public eye. The Bishop of Galway, Eamon Casey, and a well-known Dublin priest with his own radio show, Fr Michael Cleary, were exposed in the media for having had a child in the case of the former and children in the case of the latter. The private lives of both men were splashed over the front pages of international newspapers.

Serious allegations were also made against state-funded and religious-run orphanages and industrial schools. Many of those charges stretched back for decades. Individual members of the diocesan clergy and male and female religious orders were accused of excessive use of corporal punishment and, in a small but disturbing number of cases, of child sexual abuse. It was not uncommon in the first years of the twenty-first century to witness on television news reports of the jailing of brothers and priests for crimes against children in their classrooms and in their care. The repeated high-level mishandling of the official church response to such crimes further shocked an already demoralised once-loyal laity. The congregations in Irish churches might have diminished anyway during the 1990s. But by the early twenty-first century the level of defection was unprecedented.

The paradox of economic advancement and institutional crisis was a defining characteristic of the latter part of the twentieth century. Arrested modernity characterised the operations of aspects of the civil service, the relationship between the civil service and cabinet government and the relationship between government administration and the private sector. Part of the problem was that the country had suddenly been overtaken by rapid economic growth for which it was not prepared. Handling the problems of affluence was not a challenge any Irish government had had to face since the foundations of the state. Moreover, the fruits of this rapid economic growth were not evenly shared. Disparities were accentuated within society.

Unlike post-war Britain, Ireland had no asset-stripped protectorates or colonies from which to receive immigrants to support the economic boom. Yet record numbers of refugees sought asylum in the closing decade of the twentieth century—in total almost 60,000 between 1992 and 2003[1]—posing the challenge of a humane response from society in general. The non-national constituent of Irish society grew also in the form of foreign workers: by 2003 an unprecedented 47,000 were legally established in employment here. The economic turnaround was, therefore, markedly different from the prosperity of the 1960s, as not only was involuntary emigration from Ireland stemmed, but immigration was required to meet the employment demands of the Irish economy. Factual and anecdotal evidence suggests that in managing the asylum process and in fair dealing with foreign workers, Ireland has not exactly distinguished itself.

CHANGING THE POLITICAL CONFIGURATION

As was pointed out in the last chapter, the leader of the Labour Party, Dick Spring, surprised many by entering a coalition led by Albert Reynolds following the 1992 general election, as the aim of many Labour voters had been to get Fianna Fáil out of government. The architect of the agreement was Fianna Fáil's Bertie Ahern, who had entered Dáil Éireann in 1977. He was a skilled negotiator and an able unifier. Ahern's talent for political adroitness made him in the eyes of many of his colleagues leadership material despite being a Haughey loyalist. He had patience and sound judgement, and, some would argue, vision.

The 'historic compromise' between Fianna Fáil and Labour served different purposes. Labour viewed the step as having broken the mould in Irish politics. There were senior Labour TDs naïve enough to believe that Fianna Fáil could be returned to its radical social roots of the 1930s. Labour appeared to be under the impression in 1992 that, with thirty-three seats, it could be the tail that wagged the dog. Fianna Fáil saw the arrangement as a temporary means to retain power. They were resilient and accustomed to being in power. The previous coalition, that 'temporary arrangement', in the words of Albert Reynolds, between the Progressive Democrats and Fianna Fáil, had ended in tears, but the outcome had been more painful for the former than the latter.

Despite the fact that Labour secured major ministerial portfolios, such as Foreign Affairs, its leaders were very much mistaken if they thought the 1992 election result would launch the party on the road to a historic political breakthrough. A tax amnesty in 1993—in the eyes of some a tax dodgers' charter—provoked a highly negative reaction among many of those who had voted for Labour, and this slowed down the onward march of the party. Fianna Fáil pressed for an amnesty; it was popular amongst a sector of its followers. Labour ministers, feeling the deep knife-cuts of fiscal retrenchment, felt that their departments would not suffer as badly once the windfall in undeclared tax had been collected. Many of its voters were incandescent that Labour ministers sat complicit in cabinet while the Revenue Commissioners were thwarted from being able to collect millions of pounds in undeclared earnings. Wealthy people who owed, in some cases, millions of pounds in taxes were allowed to settle on favourable terms. That decision was characteristic of a weak state; while it would be going too far to say a corrupt state, the amnesty had a corrupting and corrosive influence on the relationship between those in power and the ordinary, decent members of the electorate who were compliant taxpayers. The electorate remembered that tax amnesty well into the new century, as evidence crystallised of widespread fraud perpetrated by well-heeled citizens over payment of taxes.

Apart from achieving significant progress towards peace in Northern Ireland, the Fianna Fáil–Labour coalition was more a historical blunder than a historic compromise. Labour failed to sup with a long spoon when in partnership with Fianna Fáil, and paid the electoral price.

On 17 November 1994, Albert Reynolds resigned as Taoiseach amid controversy over the appointment of the Attorney General, Harry Whelehan, as President of the High Court. The latter had been criticised for his handling of Fr Brendan Smyth's extradition from Northern Ireland on charges of child sexual abuse.[2] Whelehan also resigned as President of the High Court. The coalition government fell from office. However, for the first time in the history of the Irish state, the fall of a government was not followed by a general election.

Protracted discussions took place between the new leader of Fianna Fáil, Bertie Ahern, and Labour about the formation of a new coalition. This seemed the most likely outcome, and Ahern was poised to be the new Taoiseach. However, contrary to general expectations, Dick Spring chose to lead his party into government with a 'rainbow' coalition of Fine Gael and the Democratic Left. John Bruton, the leader of Fine Gael, became Taoiseach and Spring continued to hold the Foreign Affairs portfolio and the position of Tánaiste. This proved to be a relatively effective partnership. Under its stewardship, the economic fortunes of the country continued to improve. Those advances were not sufficient, however, to dissuade the electorate from turning to Fianna Fáil in a general election on 6 June 1997. Fianna Fáil won seventy-seven seats, an increase of nine on their 1992 tally; Fine Gael got fifty-four (also up nine seats), Labour got seventeen (down sixteen seats) and the Progressive Democrats got four (down six seats). After much negotiation, Fianna Fáil and the Progressive Democrats formed a new coalition government, with Bertie Ahern as

Taoiseach and Progressive Democrat leader Mary Harney as Tánaiste. The new government, however, was dependent on four Independent TDs for support in the Dáil.

Despite the significant ideological and personality differences between the two parties, the Fianna Fáil–Progressive Democrat coalition held firm until the general election of 17 May 2002. There were times when the Tánaiste, Mary Harney, and the Fianna Fáil Minister for Finance, Charlie McCreevy, appeared to have more in common on policy issues than the latter had with his own party. A noteworthy development was the appointment on 7 July 1999 of Michael McDowell as Attorney General. That position had become vacant upon the nomination of David Byrne as European Commissioner to succeed Pádraig Flynn.

On 5 November 1997, Dick Spring stepped down as leader of the Labour Party, to be replaced by Ruairí Quinn. The latter had seen his party humiliatingly diminished in a general election where Labour was made to pay for its decision to enter government with Fianna Fáil. Aware that social democracy in Ireland would not make progress with a divided left, Quinn entered into merger talks with Democratic Left. The fusion of the two parties greatly strengthened the performance of the Labour Party in the Dáil. On the other hand, it created major tensions in constituencies where members of both parties had bitterly opposed each other, particularly over conflicting policy on Northern Ireland.

Change was also on the horizon in the 1997 presidential election. President Mary Robinson, so much the symbol of the 'new' Ireland, resigned shortly before the end of her term to take up an appointment as United Nations High Commissioner for Human Rights on 12 September 1997. According to traditional political logic, Albert Reynolds ought to have been the Fianna Fáil candidate for the presidency. Brian Lenihan had lost that election for Fianna Fáil in 1990 for the first time in the history of the office of President. Determined to win in 1997, Bertie Ahern was fortunate enough to persuade a talented academic, Professor Mary McAleese, to stand as the Fianna Fáil nominee. However wise the choice, it meant having to ensure that Albert Reynolds did not get the party nomination. When the parliamentary party came to decide the matter, Ahern could afford to vote personally for Reynolds as he was confident that he had already secured a majority of votes for his preferred candidate. Mary

McAleese got the nomination. Ahern revealed to Fianna Fáil his qualities as a premier league politician. It was a demonstration and a warning of his capabilities.

Mary McAleese went on to win the presidential election by a handsome margin. She served with distinction in that office. Her first term was not in any way overshadowed by the success of her immediate predecessor. President McAleese quickly demonstrated her own unique style. She proved to be an independent, critical voice unafraid to take a stance that would prove that she was a risk taker for peace and reconciliation. Both the President and her husband, Martin, worked in a highly imaginative way to build bridges with the unionist and loyalist communities in Northern Ireland. She came to symbolise something much deeper about the 'new' Ireland than what was conveyed in the shallow cliché: the 'Celtic Tiger'. At the end of her first term, the two major opposition parties correctly judged that her re-election was unstoppable. The Labour Party agonised over whether or not to run Michael D. Higgins, a very popular and much respected life-long standard-bearer of the left. Pragmatism won out. Mary McAleese was returned unopposed in 2004 for a second term, and she continued in her self-assured way to work to empower the different sectors of Irish society on the island.

The change in Ireland's economic circumstances was mirrored by an apparent change in attitudes towards Europe. On 7 June 2001 the electorate voted to reject the Treaty of Nice in a referendum. Fifteen countries had negotiated the treaty over a ten-month period seeking to set out the arrangements for a union of twenty-seven member states, in preparation for the forthcoming enlargement of the EU. Fears of threats to Ireland's influence in Europe, of diminished national self-determination and of the erosion of Irish neutrality drove the 'No' campaign. Only 35 per cent of eligible voters took part in the referendum. It was a matter of great surprise that 54 per cent voted no. An editorial in *The Irish Times*, entitled 'Defeat for Complacency', argued: 'This is a decisive result, which must be accepted and respected by the government and the campaign protagonists. It is also a regrettable one, both in substance and in terms of democratic procedure.'[3]

In terms of democratic procedure, the debate on the future of Europe simply did not take place. The Fianna Fáil–Progressive Democrat government's 'Yes' campaign was more of a public relations exercise than an organised political campaign. The party loyalists simply did not turn out. Moreover, the yes side was thwarted from the outset by divisions within the coalition. In September 2000 the Tánaiste, Mary Harney, had accused her EU partners of being 'wedded to an outmoded philosophy of high taxation and heavy regulation which condemns millions of their people to unemployment'.[4] The Tánaiste and the Minister for Arts, Heritage, Gaeltacht and the Islands, Síle de Valera (a granddaughter of Éamon de Valera), preferred to downplay the European influence on Ireland and emphasise the strong links between Ireland and the US.

By the end of the referendum campaign, the Minister for Finance, Charlie McCreevy, had openly broken with the Taoiseach on Ireland's future attitude towards the EU. He had defied the EU's budgetary policy guidelines earlier in the year. A formal reprimand from the European Commission and Council of Ministers left him unrepentant. 'I hope everyone wears the green jersey on this and stands together to defend our economic success', Harney said in defence of her friend and ministerial colleague on national radio.[5]

All the major political parties supported Nice in June 2001, but the mismanaged campaign and the government's failure to gauge the mood of the electorate resulted in an embarrassing, unprecedented revolt against Europe. Humiliated at home and abroad, the government announced the establishment of a Forum on Europe to stimulate informed debate on an increasingly vexatious topic. Another referendum was held on 19 October 2002 and, much to the relief of the Irish and European political establishments, a higher turnout of over 49 per cent saw a reversal of the first result: almost 63 per cent of the poll voted in favour of the measure. Ireland was back in the camp of 'good' Europeans.

In the general election of 17 May 2002, the coalition was returned to office, with Ahern again as Taoiseach. He almost secured an overall majority for Fianna Fáil, a feat not achieved by any party in Ireland since the landslide Fianna Fáil victory in 1977. Fianna Fáil won eighty-one seats, while the Progressive Democrats doubled their representation to eight seats, allowing the coalition to dispense with the need for Independent support. Fine Gael were the major losers, dropping from fifty-four to thirty-one seats and losing many high-profile names in the process. Charlie McCreevy quipped, with some truth, that the electorate had voted the opposition out of office.

Smaller parties also gained, with Sinn Féin quintupling its representation to five seats, and the Green Party trebled its representation to six. In addition, three more Independents were elected, bringing their total to fourteen.

In 2004, Ireland took over the presidency of the EU and quickly demonstrated the strength of its convictions for advancing the cause of European integration. Having inherited the thorny issue of a draft European constitution, which the Italian presidency had kicked to touch, the Irish presidency succeeded admirably in securing consensus among the twenty-five member states for a draft constitution by June 2004. This was a formidable performance, illustrating a mastery of the European diplomatic circuit necessary to square the numerous circles of respective national interests within the ambit of the practical and the possible.

Much of the credit for the successes in Europe was due to the personal stewardship of the Taoiseach, Bertie Ahern. His highly effective negotiating and interpersonal skills were employed with considerable success, again mirroring the popularity he had with the Irish electorate. But Ahern could only watch on helplessly as France voted against the ratification of the constitution at the end of May 2005 and the Netherlands followed suit a few days later. The consequences for the future of Europe would be profound and profoundly depressing for those who supported the deepening of European integration. If Ahern's brokerage of support for the constitution was not in ruins in early June 2005, it appeared impossible to stop other countries following the example of the French and the Dutch. There was support for the constitution among the political leadership in the European Union. But there was a growing suspicion of it at a popular level, reflecting in a cruel and challenging way the prevalence of the democratic deficit in the EU. What way would Ireland vote in a referendum on the constitution? In summer 2005, the answer to that question remained very problematical.

The war which began in Iraq on 19 March 2003 proved to be a further challenge for the Irish presidency of the EU. Tensions between Paris/Berlin and London/Washington ran very high and threatened to damage EU–US relations. Ahern was placed in the unenviable position of having to speak on behalf of an EU radically divided over the US unilateralism that had brought about war in Iraq without a covering

UN Security Council resolution. The failure to secure a UN mandate called the legality of the venture into question. The Italians, the Spaniards and the British actively supported President George W. Bush, while the Germans and the French led international opposition to the war. Ahern, as the leader of a small nation state, managed to ward off a formal rift among the members of the EU.

At the same time, Ahern sought to preserve his party's traditional support for a policy of neutrality. While not sending any Irish troops to the war zone, Ahern interpreted neutrality as not necessitating the revoking of permission for the US to use Irish airspace and Shannon Airport as a refuelling stop. He held that line despite the domestic unpopularity of the war reflected in a number of anti-war marches and an attack on a US plane on the ground at Shannon which was carried out by peace activists.

In spite of Ahern's successes in foreign policy, the Irish electorate were not slow to hold Fianna Fáil to account over its failure to deliver on its sometimes rash electoral promises made in 2002. Charlie McCreevy's insistence in advance of the election that there would be 'no cuts, secret or otherwise' grated with an electorate who after the election almost immediately perceived a range of cutbacks in the public services, many of which had been planned before the election. Fianna Fáil spokespersons tried to explain that there were in fact no cutbacks, simply reductions in the level of increases in public spending. The public did their own arithmetic and, at the first opportunity, voted with their feet.

Fianna Fáil faced the electorate on 11 June 2004 in local and European elections and lost badly. Mark Brennock of *The Irish Times* summarised the salient details: 'support slumped to 32 per cent, its lowest ever in a local election, down seven points from the 1999 local polls and nine from the 2002 general election'.[6] Fianna Fáil also lost two of its European Parliament seats, leaving it with one less than Fine Gael, who managed its vote to secure a seemingly impossible five seats. Notably, Sinn Féin gained one seat in the North and in the Republic in the European Parliament.

There was some comfort for the government in the passage on the same day of the referendum to restrict the right to citizenship by removing the automatic right to citizenship from Irish-born children of non-national parents. It was a controversial proposal and earned the government robust criticism in the campaign. The criticism, involving accusations of racism, was unfounded.

The law provides that a person may be an Irish citizen by virtue of birth, descent, marriage or naturalisation. It is also possible to be awarded honorary citizenship but that is rare.[7] In the referendum voters were asked if they wished to add the following new wording to Article 9 of the constitution:

> 2. 1° Notwithstanding any other provision of this Constitution, a person born in the island of Ireland, which includes its islands and seas, who does not have, at the time of the birth of that person, at least one parent who is an Irish citizen or entitled to be an Irish citizen is not entitled to Irish citizenship or nationality, unless provided for by law.
>
> 2° This section shall not apply to persons born before the date of the enactment of this section.

What would this mean? Put simply, before the referendum everyone born in Ireland was entitled to be an Irish citizen; that entitlement was provided for by the constitution and by law. If the referendum was passed, people born in Ireland would have a constitutional right to Irish citizenship only if, at the time of their birth, one of their parents was an Irish citizen or was entitled to be an Irish citizen.

In the event, the referendum was passed by 79 per cent to 21 per cent. Commenting on the three polls conducted on 11 June 2004 (European and local elections and citizenship referendum), *The Irish Times* said:

> The people have spoken in the highest poll in years and they had much to say. They passed the controversial citizenship referendum overwhelmingly. They inflicted a damaging mid-term blow to Fianna Fáil and its seven-year coalition with the Progressive Democrats. They changed the balance of power within the alternative government with the resurgence in Fine Gael. They gave Sinn Féin a significant breakthrough. And they probably laid the groundwork for national politics for the next decade.[8]

The editorial continued: 'the Minister for Justice, Mr McDowell, correctly tapped into the public mood on citizenship. The strategy to hold the referendum alongside the local elections probably led to the exceptional increase in turnout. It is also conceivable those extra 10 per cent or so voted against the Government.'

Not surprisingly the post-mortem within Fianna Fáil demanded a scapegoat and a strategy for future electoral success. Surprisingly quickly, the party appeared to deliver both. The highly controversial—but, it must be said, equally highly competent—Charlie McCreevy was ditched. He was eased out of office to a high-profile European Commissionership. It is called a golden parachute. Fianna Fáil then went in search of its soul. Fr Seán Healy of the Conference of Religious of Ireland (CORI) was invited to guide Fianna Fáil back on the path to a caring society, lecturing to the party at a summer retreat, ironically, in a luxury spa hotel at Inchydoney, outside Clonakilty in west Cork. Before 2004 had ended Fianna Fáil had begun reinventing itself, just as the Taoiseach remembered too that all along he was in fact a socialist! At the time of writing, this transformation of Fianna Fáil appears to be in progress on the back of a benign budget from the new Minister for Finance, Brian Cowen, in December 2004. Fianna Fáil is improving in the opinion polls again. The Soldiers of Destiny are destined to march to the left. Whether this will be more spin than substance remains an open question. Ironically, it may well be a McCreevy legacy—the ludicrously generous Special Savings Incentive Accounts that were introduced to persuade consumers to save and therefore not to overheat the economy, the incentive being a 25 per cent bonus from the exchequer—that injects the crucial 'feel good' factor into the economy and the electorate at the time of the next general election in 2006 or 2007. That remains to be seen.

ECONOMIC TRANSFORMATION

The transformation of the Irish economy from the doom and gloom of the 1980s to the roaring tiger of the 1990s was phenomenal by any standard. In 1993, Irish gross domestic product growth was about 2 per cent, in line with previous years. Unemployment stood at about 15 per cent, about the average it had been for the previous decade, while forced emigration ensured it was not even higher. Interest rates were high: the Central Bank short-term facility was 13 per cent in February 1993, gradually easing to 7 per cent by the end of the year.[9] New car registrations in 1993 slumped by over 10 per cent on the previous year to almost 61,000.[10] But the signs of change were already present. It must be remembered that Ireland had been going through a painful restructuring of its national finances since 1987, in an attempt to redeem the fiscal irresponsibility of the previous decades. The country, moreover, was about to see the benefits of substantial capital transfers of about IR£7 billion from Brussels, successfully negotiated by Albert Reynolds as Taoiseach, combined with a favourable international climate for investment. In addition, the combination of gradually declining but still relatively high interest rates and a new fiscal regime delivered low inflation, an essential ingredient in buying industrial relations stability as trades unions accepted a social partnership approach that combined low wage increases with tax cuts.

By April 1994, the government's economic think-tank, the Economic and Social Research Institute, in its *Medium Term Review 1994–2000*, felt particularly upbeat about the prospects for the economy. In particular, if the policy mix was balanced properly it felt Ireland could reach its potential annual growth rate of 5 per cent and, unlike the recent 'jobless growth', it would also deliver jobs.[11] When economic growth doubled to almost 6 per cent in 1995 other commentators felt Ireland was indeed a competitor-successor of the high-performing Pacific-rim 'tiger economies' of the early 1990s. The 'Celtic Tiger' was duly born. And the jobs were delivered too, with the unemployment rate falling annually to reach a record low of under 4 per cent in 2002. Having stabilised at just over 4 per cent since then, it is still remarkably low, about half the EU average in 2004.

The Irish economy is a small open economy, heavily dependent on the traded sector. Part of the recent success has been in the clustering of specific industries, such as the information and communications technology sector and the chemical and biotechnology sectors. This has seen substantial direct investment— bolstered by traditional IDA Ireland financial supports—by leading global players in these industries. Intel and IBM have substantial manufacturing plants in Ireland, in addition to the latter's traditional and growing services sector. Dell Computers has its Europe, Middle East and Africa operations based in Limerick and Dublin. Similarly, Microsoft located its European headquarters in Dublin. On the chemical side, major employers such as Pfizer, Glaxo-Smithkline and Shering Plough have long had operations in Ireland. In recent years significant new investments by leading names such as Bristol Myers Squibb and Wyeth have added to these players. Ireland has also been successful at attracting various call centres and shared service centres that provide multilingual customer and technical support and a range of back-office operations for American and European companies wishing to outsource aspects of their business. While they provided much-needed employment in the 1990s, such operations also limited scope to add value or move up the value chain.

The success stories have not been entirely driven by foreign direct investment. Some Irish entrepreneurial start-ups rode the technology tiger with varying success. Baltimore Technologies, now worthless but once the darling of the high-tech security sector, demonstrated that Irish people had the capacity to play at a global level. True, nobody—or very few—foresaw the dot.com bust of March 2001. Other home-grown success stories on the international stage were Iona Technologies and Élan Corporation. Both rode the crest of the market, but later experienced pressures in the marketplace and major setbacks.

Still riding high is Ryanair, the improbable airline that the national carrier, Aer Lingus, initially refused to take seriously as a threat.[12] Under the irrepressible and straight-talking Michael O'Leary, the airline delivered the goods, and briefly in 2004 was the largest airline in Europe, measured by market capitalisation. The low-cost no-frills Ryanair model would eventually form an essential part of a survival plan for Aer Lingus, whose chief executive, William Walsh, showed remarkable tenacity in turning the ailing company around and back to profit in 2002 after a troubled period. He left the company in early 2005 and shortly after was appointed chief executive of British Airways.

The roar of the 'Celtic Tiger' could be heard on the ground too amid the surge in new car registrations in the 1990s. As can be seen from the table below, the surge peaked in the scramble for the magical millennium number plate.

New car registrations 1993–2003[13]

1993	1994	1995	1996	1997	1998	1999	2000	2001	2002	2003
60,792	77,773	82,730	109,333	125,818	138,538	170,322	225,269	160,908	150,485	142,992

Interestingly, in the breakdown of types of cars, one sees traditional European elite brands such as BMW and Mercedes-Benz as the favoured vehicles of the *noveau riche*.[14] Also, the increased presence of jeeps and four-wheel drives, especially in urban areas where they have little functionality other than allowing their owners to look down on other drivers, bears testimony to the growing affluence of many Irish people and their susceptibility to absorb trendiness.

The combined effect of all this success was, apart from the creation of an unprecedented number of jobs, to boost Ireland's exports and grow the economy at an average of about 7 per cent per annum between 1994 and 2003. Exchequer returns grew, and the government was favoured with the delightful challenge of having to dispose of budget surpluses. By the turn of the century, Ireland achieved what had seemed like an impossible dream and exceeded average EU per capita income; this was an extraordinary feat given that Ireland's per capita income was about 60 per cent of the EEC average at the time of joining in 1973.

The gains, however, have been spread unevenly. This is a message that comes naturally to bodies such as CORI. But it is well substantiated in the literature too, with commentators such as Peadar Kirby pinpointing the fault-lines of Ireland's wealth distribution, and indeed challenging the very foundations on which recent Irish development has been built.[15]

This view contrasts with the November 2004 assessment by the Economist Intelligence Unit that, considering a broad range of criteria, Ireland offered the best quality of life among 111 countries surveyed.[16] No doubt, for those who are in a position to benefit from low interest rates, under which they might own a second or third home, relatively moderate taxation rates and low capital gains tax rates, the Economist Intelligence Unit's findings ring true.

But for those enjoying none of the above, and deprived of a whole lot more, Ireland could be the most miserable country in the world. One such area that seemed tainted with misery was the general health services. Throughout the 1990s, the health services sector struggled to repair the damage inflicted by severe cutbacks in the 1980s. Hospital closures then reduced capacity, and as the population grew in the 1990s, and the economy expanded, people's expectations naturally grew commensurately. Expectations of an improved basic health service were not delivered upon. Although expenditure on health increased dramatically in this period, much of it was of a recurrent nature which did not deliver sufficient expansion in capacity to meet basic needs. The acute shortage of beds in hospitals resulted in wholesale bottlenecks, clogging of the corridors, and a demeaning of patients forced to wait on trolleys. General practitioners who are denied access to hospital beds for routine referral cases are forced to refer their patients to Accident and Emergency (A&E) wards, where they wait until bed places are freed up. Other patients with minor ailments compound the congestion by presenting themselves at A&E because the financial cost is cheaper than a visit to their local general practitioner. In the short term an increase in the cost of A&E services will act as a deterrent, but will not solve the fundamental problems of affordable or accessible health services. Fundamental reform of Ireland's health service is long overdue. In 2004–5 the government sought to deliver this reform by abolishing the regional health boards and replacing them with a single national agency, known as the Health Service Executive, which was charged with responsibility for the delivery of all health and personal social services. How successful this will be in practice remains to be seen.

Clearly seen, however, is the positive potential of the ban on smoking in the workplace that was introduced in March 2004. The Minister for Health, Micheál Martin, resolved early in his tenure to bring about a smoke-free society. He then set about delivering on this measure, steering the legislation through the Dáil and steadying the nerves of many in his own party who often appeared ready to capitulate to the Irish Hospitality Federation's intensive lobbying against the ban. In this, Martin set an example for the rest of the EU member states in bringing forward ground-breaking, progressive health legislation.

The professionalism with which Martin and his officials delivered the smoking ban was in marked contrast to the bumbling manner in which, it appears, a succession of Health ministers and their officials handled the issue of the illegal deduction of pension entitlements from patients in long-stay public nursing homes.

There had been a parallel case in the mid-1990s. Without any statutory authority to support their action, health boards had been attempting to means test all the members of a family collectively when assessing what would be given by way of maintenance to an elderly bed-ridden parent or other family member. The Ombudsman,

Kevin Murphy, investigated the practice following the receipt of various complaints. He discovered that the health boards were acting without any legal basis and put a stop to the practice. Undisclosed compensation was paid to families so abused. The pension entitlements issue points to an even greater scandal. Since 1976 successive governments had illegally applied the pensions of patients in long-stay public nursing homes towards the cost of their residential care. Then, in late 2004 the government hurriedly attempted to apply retrospective legitimacy to their actions in the form of the Health Amendment (NO. 2) Bill 2004.[17] President Mary McAleese invoked her right to have the Council of State deliberate on the constitutionality of the measure, and the proposed legislation was duly referred to the Supreme Court.[18] On 24 January 2005 the Supreme Court heard the case and delivered a highly embarrassing judgment on 16 February. The court held that constitutional rights to private property had been infringed in the form of the illegal charges.[19] The financial implications were so enormous that the court indicated the government could disallow cases that were statute-barred, or older than six years. The final cost had not been determined at the time of writing, with suggestions varying from €2 billion to €3 billion, affecting anything between two and three hundred thousand pensioners, many of them deceased. The reaction of the Minister for Health and Tánaiste, Mary Harney, pointed to even more disturbing revelations. She greeted the judgment with the claim that the health boards and departmental officials had been guilty of 'systemic maladministration' in handling the matter over twenty-eight years.[20] In putting forward the legislation the previous December, Harney had then maintained that the health boards had acted in good faith. However, revelations arising from the preparation of the case for the Supreme Court prompted this change of mind, though the same revelations were not sufficient to persuade her to abandon the legislation. The outcome and level of public disservice generated by the whole affair (which is still a matter of official investigation at the time of writing) reinforced public disquiet.

SOCIAL CHANGE

As the Irish economy experienced dramatic buoyancy in the 1990s, society also underwent far-reaching change. The emerging Ireland at the end of the century seemed radically different, having undergone fundamental constitutional change. On 24 November 1995, the second divorce referendum removed the constitutional ban on divorce in the South. The Fifteenth Amendment of the Constitution (No. 2) Bill 1995 provided for divorce if satisfied 'at the date of the institution of the proceedings, the spouses have lived apart from one another for a period of, or periods amounting to, at least four years during the previous five years'. The outcome could not have been much closer: on a turnout of 62.2 per cent, a total of 818,842 voted for the proposal, and 809,728 against.[21]

The Catholic Church had vigorously opposed this change, but many lay Catholics reluctantly took the view that divorce was a social necessity if the issues of marriage breakdown and inheritance were to be addressed. Yet, surprisingly, the uptake of divorce as reflected below has not been as dramatic as predictions suggested.

Divorce, judicial separation and nullity 1997–2003[22]

	Divorces granted	*Judicial separations*	*Nullity*
1997	93	1,431	3
1998	1,408	920	23
1999	2,315	967	34
2000	2,710	998	47
2001	2,817	1,018	59
2002	2,571	940	40
2003	2,710	998	47

The troubled and divisive issue of abortion still awaited legislation in 2005. The table below gives the annual figures for the number of women giving Irish addresses who had abortions in Britain during the period 1991–2001. Between 1980 and 2003, at least 111,456 Irish women had abortions in Britain.[23]

Irish women travelling to Britain for abortion 1991–2001

Year	*1991*	*1992*	*1993*	*1994*	*1995*	*1996*	*1997*	*1998*	*1999*	*2000*	*2001*
No.	4,154	4,254	4,402	4,590	4,532	4,894	5,340	5,891	6,226	6,391	6,673

On 25 November 1992, simultaneous with the general election, three referenda were held in relation to the issue of abortion: on the right to travel, the right to information and—the most controversial aspect—the substantive issue of abortion:

> It shall be unlawful to terminate the life of an unborn unless such termination is necessary to save the life, as distinct from the health, of the mother where there is an illness or disorder of the mother giving rise to a real and substantial risk to her life, not being a risk of self-destruction.[24]

Voters accepted the first two proposals and rejected the third. In 2000 an all-party committee in the Oireachtas studied the issue, and its findings were reported later that year to government. There was no easy answer. Abortion continues to divide Irish opinion and any future debate is likely to be every bit as acrimonious as was the case in the referenda of 1983 and 1992.

Irish people became less divided on the issue of women's role in society. While governments promoted gender equality, women remained unequally represented in the Oireachtas, and male appointees still dominated top civil service jobs. But change was occurring, and women were increasingly represented in the higher level positions. The Department of Foreign Affairs had the best record in this regard: here, women were more strongly represented at all levels than they were in other departments, and women were appointed as ambassadors to a number of postings, including Austria, France, China, Argentina and the United Nations.

Further evidence of change was the election of two female presidents of Ireland in the 1990s (and the re-election, unopposed, of Mary McAleese in 2004). Building on the success of President Mary Robinson's tenure, the race to succeed her was between four women and one man—suggesting a change of mindset among the major political parties and a belated acknowledgement of women's capabilities. However, despite the successes of the Robinson and McAleese presidencies, there was still a major imbalance in Oireachtas membership in 2005. Government had seen rising female participation in senior cabinet posts, not least in the office of Tánaiste, which was occupied by the Progressive Democrats leader, Mary Harney, from 1997 to the time of writing in 2005. Economic expansion since the mid-1990s created opportunities for entrepreneurial women to shine, but a combination of the 'old school tie' and 'rugby and golf-club culture' ensured many competent women still laboured under the glass ceiling. There was little prospect of a breakthrough. The Catholic Church remained probably the most recalcitrant of Irish institutions regarding gender equality. The Church of Ireland permitted the ordination of women priests in the 1990s—an issue that continued to divide that church. But the innately conservative majority of the Irish Catholic hierarchy, on instructions from the Holy See, remained impenetrable on the question of the ordination of women.

The Irish Catholic Church, despite the influence of many dynamic female religious, remained a redoubt of patriarchal attitudes. But the combined strength of laywomen and nuns, supported by many males, had also served as a strong lobby for change. Since most of those who regularly attended mass and received the sacraments in Ireland were women, the failure of the leadership of the Catholic Church to listen and learn had cost the institution dearly. There was new hope of greater understanding of that historical problem following the appointment of Diarmuid Martin as coadjutor Archbishop of Dublin in 2003.

Organised networks of women have grown in stature, in part owing to the referenda on abortion and divorce in the 1980s and 1990s. The 'women's vote' has become an important force that political parties ignore at their peril. In the field of education, women attend universities and third-level colleges in increasing numbers, often forming the majority in arts and other faculties. However, although universities are obliged by new legislation to introduce greater gender equality, the number of women professors and senior lecturers in Irish third-level colleges remains pathetically small. Women have made more of an impact in the upper echelons of the trade union movement than in any other Irish institution. The professions, such as medicine and law, have made some advances in recent years. But the numbers of women judges and consultants, although growing, are quire small. Irish women are, in contrast, very well represented in the arts, both as artists and in management.

ASYLUM SEEKERS, ECONOMIC MIGRANTS AND GUEST WORKERS

As women departed from their traditional roles, prejudice and poor prospects dogged the newest members of Irish society: the asylum seekers and refugees. The growing economy made Ireland an attractive destination for those from more disadvantaged areas in Europe and Africa. Immigration to Ireland had been minimal in the twentieth century, limited to small numbers of displaced people—from Jews fleeing Russian pogroms in the early part of the century to the post-World War II period when first Poles, then Hungarians in 1956, Chileans in 1973, Vietnamese in 1979 and Bosnians in the 1990s abandoned their communist-dominated or war-ridden countries for a more peaceful life in Ireland.

Since 1991, however, people of more than a hundred different nationalities have applied for refuge in Ireland.[25] The table below shows the number of applications for asylum in Ireland during the period 1992–2003.

Applications for asylum 1992–2003[26]

Year	1992	1993	1994	1995	1996	1997	1998	1999	2000	2001	2002	2003
No.	39	91	362	424	1,179	3,883	4,626	7,724	10,938	10,325	11,634	7,900

The unconfirmed figures for asylum applications for 2004 showed a further sharp drop to 4,766, continuing the downward trend established in 2003. Nigerians accounted for 1,776 (37.3 per cent) of those claims, while Romanians made 286 (6 per cent) applications.[27]

The Irish government adopted a range of measures to seek to deal with this issue. In 2000, it signed an agreement with Nigeria to help deport unsuccessful asylum seekers. Only about one out of ten Nigerian asylum seekers have succeeded in gaining refugee status. The government also tightened security at Irish ports and airports. In November 2000, and at the behest of the Irish government, new document controls were introduced by Irish Ferries staff at Cherbourg. These controls were aimed at preventing asylum seekers with false or inadequate documentation from boarding at Cherbourg.[28] The Minister for Justice, John O'Donoghue, told the Dáil in February 2001 that people who might have been trying to enter Ireland to seek asylum had been turned back at Cherbourg due to the new controls. He also said that such people could claim asylum in France or the state through which they entered EU territory. These Cherbourg measures drew strong criticism from spokespersons for church organisations, who viewed them as the 'pre-emptive exclusion' of asylum seekers. There were fears that the tightening up of regulations might push more and more asylum seekers into the arms of unscrupulous traffickers.

However stringent the entry measures, the refugees still arrive. Successful and pending applicants have added an unprecedented multicultural aspect to Irish society. These refugees, together with the tens of thousands of migrant workers who are encouraged to come to work in the booming economy under the work permit system (as illustrated in the table below), present Ireland with the challenge of adapting its relatively homogeneous society to the reality of multiculturalism. One aspect of this challenge is addressing the undercurrents that fuel fears of outsiders or foreigners, which are always susceptible to political exploitation. Such undercurrents were probably best seen in the various misleading allegations in the run-up to the citizenship referendum in June 2004, in which (as has been seen) an overwhelming majority of 4:1 voted in favour of abolishing the automatic right to Irish citizenship of every person born on the island of Ireland. What are the implications of this vote for those who seek to achieve greater tolerance in Irish society?

Work permits issued 1999–2003[29]

Year	New permits	Renewals	Group permits	Total
1999	4,328	1,653	269	6,250
2000	15,434	2,271	301	18,006
2001	29,594	6,485	357	36,436
2002	23,326	16,562	433	40,321
2003	21,965	25,039	547	47,551

CORRUPTION: LOW STANDARDS IN SOME HIGH PLACES

In February 2002 the Department of the Taoiseach placed a useful explanation of the subtle but important distinctions between a tribunal of inquiry and a parliamentary inquiry on its website. Given what is about to unfold in the following pages, it is as well to recall these in detail.

The main difference between a Parliamentary Inquiry (non statutory) and a Tribunal of Inquiry is that non statutory inquiries are not vested with the powers, privileges and rights of the High Court; Tribunals of Inquiry are. Tribunals are established by resolution of the Houses of the Oireachtas to enquire into matters of urgent public importance. It is not a function of Tribunals to administer justice, their work is solely inquisitorial. Tribunals are obliged to report their findings to the Oireachtas. They have the power to enforce the attendance and examination of witnesses and the production of documents relevant to the work in hand. Tribunals can consist of one or more people, a lay person, or non lawyer may be the Sole member of a Tribunal. Tribunals can sit with or without Assessors (experts in the subject concerning the Tribunal). Assessors are not Tribunal members. Sittings are usually public but can, at the Tribunal's discretion, be held privately.[30]

As outlined in the table below, a total of twenty-one tribunals of inquiry were established in Ireland between the foundation of the state and 1990.[31] Many of these were set up in response to tragedies or disasters. Except for two instances— the Ward affair in 1946 and the controversy surrounding the sale of Locke's Distillery in 1947—the Irish public were not exposed to any tribunals involving allegations of corruption or scandal among public representatives or public servants.

Year	Tribunal of inquiry
1925	Retail prices of articles in general consumption
1926	Ports and harbours
1928	Shooting of Timothy Coughlan
1929	Whether cereal mixture was in the national interest
1930	Marketing of butter
1933	Pig production
1934	Grading etc. of fruit and vegetables
1935	Town tenants
1936	Pearse Street Fire
1938	Public transport
1943	Fire at St Joseph's Orphanage, Cavan
1943	Dealings in Great Southern Railway stocks

1946	Allegations concerning Parliamentary Secretary
1947	Disposal of Locke's Distillery
1957	Cross-channel freight rates
1967	Death of Liam O'Mahony in Garda custody
1969	Television programme on illegal moneylending
1975	Allegations against the Minister for Local Government
1979	Whiddy Island Disaster
1981	Fire at Stardust Club, Artane
1984	The 'Kerry Babies' Case

This period of relative innocence was rudely interrupted by events in the 1990s as a decade (and more) of investigations shattered that innocence and public credibility in many of the pillars of the establishment. Starting with an investigation into the beef industry in Ireland in 1991—the fallout from which would help to bring down a government in 1994—the whole fabric of Irish society came under investigation: the church, the health services, the financial services. The table below lists most of the more serious investigations. Most disturbing was the succession of findings that pointed to systemic abuse of children in state-run institutions; incompetence and cover-ups in the health services; and complicity in avoiding taxation among certain financial institutions.

Year	Inquiries, investigations and reports
1991	Beef processing industry
1996	Hepatitis C scandal
1997	McCracken Inquiry into alleged payments by Dunnes Stores
1997	Moriarty Tribunal investigating Dunnes payments to Haughey and Lowry
1997	Flood/Mahon Inquiry to investigate planning irregularities in Dublin
1998	Evasion of Revenue Obligations: Special Savings Accounts
1999	Tribunal of Inquiry into HIV and Hepatitis C
1999	Laffoy Commission investigating clerical sexual abuse

2000	Parliamentary Inquiry into DIRT (first report)
2001	Parliamentary Inquiry into DIRT (final report)
2002	Morris Tribunal (investigating alleged corruption in Donegal gardaí)
2002	The Barr Inquiry into the shooting dead of John Carthy at Abbeylara
2002	Report of the inspectors appointed to enquire into the affairs of Ansbacher (Cayman) Limited
2004	Report of investigations into the affairs of National Irish Bank Financial Services Limited

This culture of scandal and corruption pervaded public life in the 1990s, yet most people viewed with disbelief, if not stupefaction, the revelations that emerged about the governance of the Irish state. In 1994, the Finance Bill permitted Irish tax exiles to spend six months in the country each year while retaining their non-residence status. The same year the shocked citizen read about a 'passports for sale' scheme, about which the populace, until then, had been told nothing. A foreigner making a million-pound investment in the country was entitled, under this official scheme, to apply for an Irish passport. In one case, a passport was granted to a Saudi Masri family who had invested in a pet-food firm. The scheme was legal but many feared that beneficiaries may be unworthy. The full list of recipients has yet to be analysed. The policy had serious consequences for the international status of an Irish passport. It also had multilateral implications because the holder of an Irish passport was also a citizen of the EU, with all the residency rights that that bestowed in each of the member states.

Ironically, it was the EU—at least in the minds of many people—that prompted the start of investigations in the early 1990s, with requirements regarding higher standards of accountability and transparency than appeared to apply in the Irish beef industry. In May 1991, the Oireachtas established a tribunal of inquiry into the beef-processing industry. The terms of reference of the 'Beef Tribunal' were to inquire into allegations regarding illegal activities, fraud and malpractice raised in Dáil Éireann and referred to in an ITV television documentary broadcast on 13 May 1991. By the time the chairman of the tribunal, Mr Justice Liam Hamilton, reported on 29 July 1994, the country had been given an insight into the rather bizarre operations of the industry and into its relationship with the Departments of Agriculture and Industry and Commerce. The report also cast light on government decisions in relation to the beef industry. Fintan O'Toole, journalist and keen follower of the proceedings, summarised the findings as follows:

> There had been, for three years, a sustained and intense relationship between a government and a company . . . In the course of that relationship the government broke the law and asked few questions of the company . . . The company was, at the same time, abusing public funds on a large scale and contriving to cheat the public of taxes . . . The public still faced potential liabilities of up to £200 million, liabilities which it had unknowingly incurred without any benefit in order to help a private company in Ireland and a violent dictator in Iraq.[32]

The founder of the Progressive Democrats, Desmond O'Malley, must take much of the credit for bringing these serious matters to public attention.

When the next tribunal was established, it was in a position to act with greater freedom. The McCracken Tribunal was set up by the rainbow coalition under Fine Gael leader John Bruton in early 1997 to investigate alleged payments by supermarket millionaire Ben Dunne to Charles Haughey and to the former Fine Gael minister Michael Lowry. Mr Justice Brian McCracken of the High Court presided over hearings that produced sensational testimony. Ben Dunne was centre stage. His evidence was extraordinary. On one occasion, it emerged, Dunne dropped in on Haughey in 1991 on his way from playing golf. It was about a week after Haughey had seen off a vote of no confidence in his leadership within the Fianna Fáil party. Sensing that the Taoiseach was depressed, Ben Dunne said, he took out of his pocket three bank drafts to the value of £210,000. No name had been inserted on the drafts. Dunne said, 'Look, that is something for yourself.' Haughey allegedly replied, 'Thank you, big fellow.' The McCracken report, published on 15 July 1997, concluded: 'It is quite unacceptable that a member of Dáil Éireann, and in particular a cabinet minister and Taoiseach, should be supported in his personal lifestyle by gifts made to him personally. It is particularly unacceptable that such gifts should emanate from prominent businessmen.'³³ McCracken referred the papers to the Director of Public Prosecutions. The tribunal findings were a devastating blow for Haughey, but worse was to follow in the form of follow-up investigations led by Mr Justice Michael Moriarty.

The Moriarty Tribunal was established in September 1997 to investigate payments to Charles Haughey and Michael Lowry. It was also charged with investigating whether any political decision made by either of those men while in office might have benefited a person or a company making a payment. Moriarty also investigated Ansbacher deposits (offshore accounts), and the long-awaited report on this issue appeared in July 2002. The response of the Tánaiste, Mary Harney, to its publication was instructive:

> The report raises issues at the heart of our democracy. A state that does not collect taxes, through lack of will or authority, or as a result of a degeneration of its political culture, is a failed state. There has been a great deal of discussion, some of it quite ill-informed, about the State's exercise of sovereignty in the international arena. The exercise of sovereignty within the State, however, occurs prior to that. One of the first sovereign acts of a democratic state is to raise taxes to allow it to function. This is why the events and the systematic failures set out in the Ansbacher report are vital matters for this House and for citizens who believe in a functioning democratic society. The systematic and planned denial of taxes to the State was a denial of its sovereignty. It was a subversion, one could say, of citizens' votes, of their equality before the law and of their right to live in a fair society. It undermined the ability of the State to provide vital public services and it cost us all dearly.³⁴

In May 2000, Moriarty estimated that Haughey had been in receipt of £8.6 million from leading businessmen between 1979 and 1996. The revelations continued; matters are still unfinished at the time of writing.

Lawyers argue over costs and the state continues to pick up the tab. In moving the Commissions of Investigation Bill (2003) in March 2004, Minister for Justice Michael McDowell outlined the costs of these tribunals:

It is estimated that between 1997 and October 2003 the accumulated cost to the State of tribunals and other major inquiries was more than €100 million. That figure does not include third party costs. Many of the tribunals and inquiries are ongoing. The approximate annual cost of these ongoing tribunals and inquiries is some €47 million. The accumulated cost overhang in respect of third parties could run to hundreds of millions of euros.[35]

Almost coincidental with the start of Moriarty was the establishment of a tribunal of inquiry into certain aspects of the planning process under Mr Justice Feargus Flood in October 1997. In July 1995 an unusual notice had appeared in two Irish national newspapers. Posted by a Newry-based firm of solicitors on behalf of an anonymous client, it offered a reward of £10,000 to 'persons providing information leading to the conviction of persons involved in corruption in connection with the planning process'.[36] It was followed in 1996 by a series of general allegations by *Sunday Business Post* journalist Frank Connolly about a politician receiving payments. Then in July 1997 both Connolly and the *Sunday Tribune* named the politician concerned: it was Raphael Burke, who had just been appointed Minister for Foreign Affairs that June amid some controversy. On 8 August 1997 *The Irish Times* published the following edited statement issued by Burke:

> During the last two years I have been the target of a vicious campaign of rumour and innuendo. Since my appointment as Minister for Foreign Affairs this campaign has intensified. The stories which have appeared in the media in recent weeks are, as one prominent journalist acknowledged in a letter to me last week, 'the culmination of a lengthy series of smears' about me.

Burke resigned as minister and TD on 7 October, just as the Flood Tribunal was being established. The Flood (later Mahon) Tribunal was tasked with investigating the planning background of 726 acres in north County Dublin. Raphael Burke was alleged to have received a payment of £80,000 from Joseph Murphy Structural Engineering. Burke admitted getting £30,000. The terms of reference of the tribunal were extended in June 1998 following a disclosure that another £30,000 had been paid to Burke by Rennicks Manufacturing Ltd.

Flood was also given the power to investigate all illegal payments to politicians in the context of the planning process. In April 2000, two builders testified to giving donations to Burke and Fianna Fáil over a fifteen-year period but did not know how the money had been divided between them. Burke proved an unco-operative witness but was ultimately exposed. In January 2005 he was sentenced to six months' imprisonment without appeal. In his interim report in September 2002, Flood found, amongst other things, that Burke had been in receipt of corrupt payments, and the pattern was deep: the purchase of Burke's home (Briargate) in 1973, for instance, was not 'a normal commercial transaction'. In the opinion of the tribunal, 'the transfer of Briargate to Mr Burke amounted to a corrupt payment to him from Mr Tom Brennan and his associates'.[37]

In 2003, another man intimately acquainted with the Flood proceedings, the former Dublin City Assistant Manager, George Redmond, was sentenced to one year's imprisonment, a sentence he subsequently successfully appealed.

The Fianna Fáil Dublin West TD Liam Lawlor also appeared before Flood. He resigned from the Fianna Fáil parliamentary party in June 2000. He was fined and imprisoned for one week on 17 January 2001 for failure to comply with the tribunal. Lawlor again faced the wrath of Flood for non-compliance, getting another week in Mountjoy on 8 August 2001. He remained a member of Dáil Éireann when sentenced to a twenty-eight-day stretch in February 2002, again for non-compliance, and decided not to contest the general election later that summer. In the face of Lawlor's treatment others took fright.

Frank Dunlop, a public relations consultant and former Fianna Fáil press officer, caused a sensation when he told the Flood Tribunal that in 1991 he had given £112,000 to fifteen Dublin city councillors before they voted on a controversial planning application for a major shopping centre. He claimed that he had made payments of £180,000 to thirty-eight politicians on behalf of a property developer. At the time of writing, legal battles continue over the basic truth and over costs as outlined in the fourth interim report of the Planning Tribunal in June 2004. This report, prepared by Mr Justice Flood's successor as chairman of the tribunal, Mr Justice Alan Mahon, also sought legislation and a modification of the terms of reference of the inquiry.[38]

The Ansbacher revelations were not a mere aberration, the result of allowing a corrupt individual to run a bank on behalf of a corrupt politician. Far from it; if anything, Ansbacher seemed to represent an elite version of all the general corruption in Irish financial services. DIRT evasion was rampant in Ireland from its inception in the mid-1980s until the Comptroller and Auditor General alerted officials to what many must have already known: that the banks had used the discretion afforded them under a modification of the original DIRT proposals to facilitate wholesale tax evasion. A subsequent investigation by the Dáil Public Accounts Committee yielded a windfall for the exchequer. As a result of the original DIRT 'look-back' audit of thirty-seven financial institutions completed in October 2000, a total of €220 million was collected in tax, interest and penalties for the years of assessment 1986–99.[39] The Revenue Commissioners set a deadline of 15 November 2001 for voluntary disclosure by individuals: 3,675 bogus account holders paid up to the tune of €227 million on 8,380 accounts. In February 2002, Revenue began investigations of non-disclosed accounts: that October 30,000 individuals received enquiry letters, and a further 90,000 were due to be issued.[40] Estimates vary as to what the final sum will be, inclusive of interest and penalties, but it will probably be more than €1 billion.

The initial disclosures regarding DIRT evasion provoked a defensive response from those charged with regulating the banks during this period. In August 1999, at the opening session of the Public Accounts Committee investigation, former Central Bank Governor Maurice Doyle explained that the culture of the time was not to rock the boat for fear it would cause a flight of capital out of the country, with the risk of severely damaging the economy.[41] Doyle suggested the politicians were fully aware of the evasion: in truth, they were not the only ones. Apparently, the culture of the time was against taking any action, just as the growing culture within financial circles was one of greed and complicity.

Inspectors began investigating the affairs of National Irish Bank on 30 March 1998; by 15 June they had widened the investigation to include the bank's financial services division.[42] The findings, published in the inspectors' report in July 2004, were as damning of an institution as they could be. The inspectors found that bogus non-resident accounts were opened and maintained to evade tax; fictitiously named accounts were opened in branches to facilitate concealment of monies from the Revenue Commissioners; Clerical Medical Insurance policies were promoted as a secure investment for funds concealed from Revenue; and there was improper charging of interest and fees to customers.[43] The inspectors noted, however, that the 'problem of DIRT evasion was an industry-wide phenomenon'. The operational environment was deemed to be so target-driven as to be conducive to fostering such malpractice. The inspectors concluded that 'responsibility for the improper practices rests with the senior management' at the time covered by the investigations and indicated that they had not received the full co-operation from the bank.[44] The financial services regulator reported by the end of 2004 that all of the personnel named in the report as deemed unfit to serve in financial services had left the industry. The most high-profile case was that of a former middle-ranking official at the National Irish Bank, Beverly Flynn, who took a libel action against RTÉ reporters for allegations made about her work activities. The Fianna Fáil TD lost the case and subsequently lost the Supreme Court appeal. As a consequence, she lost the Fianna Fáil whip, but retained her seat in Mayo, which she had won while the legal proceedings were in progress. Those proceedings unearthed a culture of dishonesty mirrored in the inspectors' investigations.

Such a culture was not exclusive to National Irish Bank. An investigation into AIB, completed by the Irish Financial Services Regulatory Authority (IFSRA) on 7 December 2004, found that €34.2 million was owed to customers arising from systemic overcharging on foreign exchange transactions from 1996 to 2004.[45] The investigation, which resulted from an anonymous tip-off on 20 April 2004, two weeks before RTÉ broke the story publicly, revealed that 'certain staff and management within certain areas of AIB appear to have been aware of the fact that AIB were charging over the amount notified to the Regulator'. AIB had failed to inform the regulator, despite numerous opportunities; moreover, the bank was found to have inadequate procedures for reporting up the line, and also faced many other criticisms.[46] A second aspect of the AIB investigation concerned the activities of one of its subsidiaries, AIB Investment Managers, and a former client, a British Virgin Island investment company named Faldor Ltd. This had been under investigation since September 2003 after the managing director of the AIB subsidiary informed the regulators of a scheme that involved artificial share deals and which appeared to have tax implications for the designated beneficiaries—senior executives of AIB. It is unnecessary to dwell on the details; suffice to note the succinct remarks of the IFSRA report: 'Overall, the conclusion of the Financial Services Regulator is that in certain parts of AIB, there were ineffective standards of governance and a culture that led to unacceptable behaviour and practices in the late 1980s and 1990s.'[47]

Public confidence in central government, in local government, in the health boards and in the banks had been shaken by revelations and by crisis. In searching for stability and integrity, surely the citizen—in a sea of doubt about the pillars of society—could at least turn to the Catholic Church for reassurance and petrine-like probity? That did not prove to be the case.

CATHOLIC CHURCH FACES MAJOR DIFFICULTIES

From the early 1990s the Catholic Church in Ireland faced a succession of difficulties, including revelations concerning prominent clergy fathering children, scandals concerning sexual abuse by a small number of clerics, and allegations concerning sexual and physical abuse in state institutions run by religious orders. The mismanagement of the initial response from the hierarchy and religious orders to the allegations turned these events into a crisis of credibility for the Catholic Church, leading to public outrage and a series of investigations. The Catholic Church bore the brunt of the backlash, with few critics pondering the role of the state, which had ultimate responsibility for many of the institutions in these matters. The initiative taken in 1999 by the Taoiseach, Bertie Ahern, in making an unequivocal apology on behalf of the state to the victims of abuse contrasted with the procrastination and seemingly reluctant manner with which church authorities addressed the issue. These ghosts of the past compounded the difficulties of the Catholic Church at the end of the twentieth century. Falling vocations and an ageing religious corps, combined with falling mass attendance and weakening religious observance, suggested that the Catholic Church in Ireland was facing into uncharted waters.

The scandals began with the resignation of the Bishop of Galway, Eamon Casey, in May 1992 on instructions from Rome, following press reports that he was the father of a child who was then in his early teens. Casey was among the best known of the Irish bishops, noted for his strong stance on issues of human rights, poverty and development in the Third World. Another celebrity, a priest of the Dublin archdiocese, Fr Michael Cleary, had two children by his housekeeper. Cleary had his own radio programme, was well known around the country as a singer and performer, and had been on the podium in Knock in 1979, together with Bishop Casey, to welcome Pope John Paul II. Both were known as stout defenders of papal teaching on priestly celibacy. The contradiction between theological posture and practice, rather than their personal actions in private, was what shocked the laity most and caused scandal and adverse comment.

Although those two cases caused hurt and wounded clerical credibility, the damage done by them to lay confidence in the clergy and hierarchy was minimal compared with the succession of revelations throughout the 1990s regarding the involvement of a small number of clergy and religious in child sexual abuse. Between 1983 and 2000, eighteen diocesan priests were convicted of such abuse in Irish courts; a further three Irish diocesan priests were convicted abroad, and two former diocesan priests were also convicted. During the same period, ten religious order priests, nine religious order brothers and a number of former religious order brothers were also convicted. During this period there was a total of forty convictions for clerical child sexual abuse in the Republic of Ireland and eight in Northern Ireland.[48] Figures for the archdiocese of Dublin released in March 2003 indicated that allegations of abuse had been made against thirty-five priests who had served in the archdiocese over the previous fifty years; some 107 victims had approached the diocese about this matter; the archdiocese had paid compensation in twenty-nine cases involving allegations against diocesan priests, while thirty more cases were continuing.[49]

One case in particular—that of Fr Brendan Smyth—exposed the inadequacy of the church authorities' response to clerical child sexual abuse. It demonstrated the complete absence of protocols and procedures and revealed the extent to which church authorities sought to resolve matters 'in house'. Smyth, a member of the Norbertine Order, abused children from the early 1960s. In 1968 he was sent back to Ireland in disgrace from the diocese of Providence, Rhode Island, where he had abused young children.[50] He worked in Belfast in the 1980s where he abused the children of at least one family. Arrested in 1991 in Northern Ireland on charges of paedophilia, he was released on bail and returned to his monastery in the South, refusing to return to Belfast to stand trial. The RUC issued warrants for his extradition in 1993. The Irish government took no action. When this came to light in 1994, it became a matter of high politics. The Labour Party, critical of its Fianna Fáil partners in coalition, resigned from office and the government fell. In April 1997, Fr Smyth was found guilty in a Dublin court on seventy-four charges of indecent and sexual assault; he died in jail later that year. In 1995, the journalist Chris Moore published a study of the Smyth case entitled *Betrayal of Trust*. Fr Kevin Hegarty, in his foreword to the book, stated: 'If the church listens humbly to what the scandals have revealed about its structures, this time of tragedy and pain can also be a time of redemption . . . The less defensive the church is about its failures, the more open it is about its need to learn, the more able it will be to proclaim the Good News.'[51] The Smyth tragedy was a case study for ecclesiastical authorities on how *not* to handle current and future cases of clerical child sexual abuse.

Serious allegations were also made against state-funded and religious-run orphanages and industrial schools. Many of the allegations related to events going back to the 1940s and 1950s. Two television programmes set the framework for public discussion in this area.

Dear Daughter, broadcast on RTÉ on 28 February 1996, was the autobiography of Christine Buckley, who told the story of her time in St Vincent's Industrial School, Goldenbridge, Dublin, run by the Sisters of Mercy. Her account was an indictment of the manner in which the school allegedly operated. The programme was part documentary and part drama, reconstructing the painful experiences of the narrator in a most forceful form. Unfortunately, the response to the broadcasting of *Dear Daughter* was almost exclusively popular rather than academic or scholarly. There was, of course, a necessity for both kinds of reaction, and the work of Harry Ferguson in particular sought to provide an academic counterpoise to the popular, not to say populist, tone of much of the commentary at the time.[52] But Ferguson's work, no less than earlier studies by Joseph Robins in 1980 and Jane Barnes in 1989, was overshadowed in the public debate that followed transmission of *Dear Daughter*.[53]

The second television programme was a three-part documentary entitled *States of Fear* which was screened by RTÉ in April and May

1999. Made by Mary Raftery, a senior producer and director with RTÉ, the series explored in shocking detail the industrial school system in Ireland. The broadcasting of *States of Fear* produced an unprecedented public response, ranging from shock and disbelief to anger bordering on fury. Kilometres of newspaper columns and many hours of broadcasting time, on both radio and television, were devoted to the issues raised in the screenings. It would not be an exaggeration to say that there was a palpable sense of anger in the air, aimed generally at the Catholic Church and more particularly at the male and female religious orders under whose care most of the children had been detained in industrial schools.[54]

Mary Raftery followed up the screening of *States of Fear* with the publication, in co-operation with Eoin O'Sullivan of Trinity College Dublin, of a valuable book entitled *Suffer the Little Children: The Inside Story of Ireland's Industrial Schools*.[55] The book is an important contribution to our understanding of the culture, ethos and history of the Irish industrial school system in the twentieth century. It is all the more important because it was written with full access to many of the relevant records on the subject held in the Department of Education and Science. *Suffer the Little Children* offers one reconstruction of Ireland's 'best kept secret'.

Having said this, however, the publishers' contention that the book is a 'definitive history of industrial schools in Ireland' is rather far-fetched, since there are some inherent weaknesses in it. Firstly, the book emerged from the television series and, perhaps in part due to these origins, the structure of the book is conceptually weak; it might, for instance, have been more appropriate to divide the project into two books—the first based on transcripts of the testimonies of those who suffered abuse in industrial schools and the second consisting of a historical analysis of the industrial school scheme in general. A second weakness, which is particularly surprising since the authors had access to the relevant files in the Department of Education and Science, is the fact that the first three chapters providing the historical background to industrial schools in Ireland are academically weak; polemical in tone, they lapse all too easily into generalisation. Another weakness of *Suffer the Little Children* is what may be called 'presentism'—judging the past by the standards of the present and projecting contemporary ways of thought backwards in time. The past can be fairly judged only on the basis of its own norms and culture. Unfortunately, the authors of this book all too easily succumb to the temptations of 'presentism'. Finally, and perhaps most fatal in the context of a claim to be a definitive history, the book is based on an analysis of only a portion of the historical record. Through no fault of their own, the authors were not in a position to examine the records of the religious-run institutions themselves since these records were not made available to them on legal advice. Therefore, although the book is excellent in terms of unearthing the facts and of disabusing us of many of the myths associated with the industrial school system, its analysis of how and why this system developed as it did is inadequate, leaving some important questions and avenues largely unexplored.

However, the TV journalists involved had performed a great public service. The most shocking revelations to emerge related to the sexual abuse of children. It was contended that this abuse was widespread, was constant and spanned a number of decades. There is no need here to give a verbatim account of the personal testimonies of the abused: suffice it to say that the term 'sexual abuse' fails to convey the physical and emotional pain suffered, and the feelings of degradation and worthlessness and the lasting psychological damage endured as a result. The past must be unmasked. The injustices suffered by children in the care of the state must be addressed. There is no escaping the burdens of the recent past. The television documentaries need to be supplemented by informed debate rooted in scholarship.

These observations also apply to understanding another facet of the Irish state's 'child care' system. At different stages, the Sisters of Mercy and the Good Shepherd Sisters ran ten Magdalene asylums. As the name suggests, those homes were for unmarried mothers and/or 'fallen women'. The taboo associated with sex outside of marriage, and the stigma of illegitimacy, meant that young single pregnant girls were often taken away to religious-run institutions in order to have their babies. When they had given birth, the girls remained with their babies for a few months. They were then transferred to the Magdalene home, which was often situated a few hundred yards from the orphanage where their children lived. Usually the children were given up for adoption or put into foster care. These institutions are the subject of a study by Frances Finnegan entitled *Do Penance or Perish.*[56]

The general debate on these areas at the beginning of the twenty-first century is characterised by outrage and incomprehension. How could it have happened? The answer will require a very painful examination of the public's complicity in the running of such institutions. There were many innocent victims of the harshness of such institutions. But there were also willing collaborators in all levels of official life. There were the bystanders. It may be very painful to accept the fact that industrial schools and Magdalene laundries were convenient institutions in which to lock away many of the darker secrets of a not-so-perfect Christian Ireland. Girls made pregnant through rape and incest may have found their way to such homes while the perpetrators of these crimes went free.

What insight is there into the religious personnel who ran these institutions on the state's behalf? Teresita Durkan, a former member of the Sisters of Mercy, was sent to the twenty-three-strong Goldenbridge community in 1959 but she was not assigned to the industrial school which was the focus of the TV programme *Dear Daughter*. Nevertheless, her pen-portrait of the manager of Goldenbridge industrial school and the central authority figure in *Dear Daughter*, Sister Xavieria (like herself a Mayo woman), is revealing.[57] Durkan reflects on the lack of resources available in those times: Xavieria 'didn't have to do it all by herself, of course. But funding and staffing were so meagre, personnel so poorly paid, training for child-care work in Ireland unknown or just acquired on the job, psychological and other support services and structures as yet hardly on the horizon.'[58] Durkan portrays a person working under extreme professional stress in a world close in years to 2005 but a universe away in terms of what has happened in the intervening years regarding the development of the profession of child care and the provision of support and training for those working in the profession. Here were children with special needs—emotional and educational—and the state did nothing to provide for those special needs. Teresita Durkan's reflections are painfully honest: 'Looking back, I know that it's possible to live within the same small world—a community, a convent, a work-compound, a neighbourhood, even a very poor hill in Valparaíso—and to settle for the invisible boundaries that separate such places. I have, in my time, avoided what made me uncomfortable, especially the things that brought me face-to-face with my own passivity and inadequacy.'[59]

The historian must confront those 'invisible boundaries' in the context, as pointed out by Harry Ferguson, that many of the children who were admitted to industrial schools in Ireland were placed there for their own safety. Some—the number has yet to be determined—had already been the victims of abuse.[60] Ferguson concludes:

> It is vital to the creation of a just society that the issues raised by *States of Fear* are resolved by ensuring that the survivors receive justice and healing. The voices of those who were involved in child care need to be heard, too. It is also crucial that we learn from the scandal and critique, and develop Raftery and O'Sullivan's work . . . The more we are able to understand the complexities of perception and trust and power-relations in the past the less likely we will be to repeat such tragic system failures today.[61]

RESPONSES AND RESPONSIBILITIES

Between the Fr Brendan Smyth case and the resignation of Bishop Brendan Comiskey in 2002, the Catholic Church in Ireland had to confront growing criticism of its handling of clerical child sexual abuse cases over a span of nearly a decade. The hierarchy set up an advisory committee on child sexual abuse issues on 27 April 1994, under Bishop Laurence Forristal of Ossory. It had a broad remit including advising on an appropriate response by the church to allegations of child sexual abuse and identifying guidelines and procedures. A wide process of consultation with various parties took place, including 'listening days' in January and February 1995 with organisations in the statutory and voluntary sectors involved in child protection and welfare. The advisory committee heard the views of religious superiors, and the Irish Bishops' Conference was briefed on a regular basis. The guidelines were published in 1996 in *Child Sexual Abuse: Framework for a Church Response*, which came to be known as the Green Book. In 2005, it was revealed that the twenty-six dioceses had complied with a key recommendation—the setting up of a support resource.[62]

On 1 April 2002, the Archbishop of Armagh, Seán Brady, and the Cardinal Archbishop of Dublin, Desmond Connell, issued a press statement stating that 'the sexual abuse of children by priests is an especially grave and repugnant evil. To all victims of such abuse, to their families and to their parish communities, we again offer our profound apologies.'[63] This statement followed the resignation of Bishop Brendan Comiskey of Ferns earlier the same day as a consequence of his handling of the case of Fr Seán Fortune, a priest who committed suicide while facing child sexual abuse charges. The bishop said that he had found Fortune 'impossible to deal with'; he had confronted him regularly, removed him from his ministry, sought professional advice in several quarters, tried compassion and firmness, but never succeeded in managing a satisfactory outcome. Comiskey admitted that he 'should have adopted a more informed and more concerted approach to any dealings with him and for this I ask forgiveness'.[64] The setting up of a judicial inquiry into the handling of child sexual abuse matters in the Diocese of Ferns was still being discussed by government in summer 2005. On 27 June 2002, it was announced that Judge Gillian Hussey would chair a new and fully independent church commission on child sexual abuse. Established jointly by the Irish Bishops' Conference, the Conference of Religious of Ireland (cori) and the Irish Missionary Union (imu), its remit was to establish 'the truth about the extent of child sexual abuse within the Catholic Church in Ireland, and the response of Church authorities to complaints of such abuse'.[65]

Cardinal Desmond Connell came under pressure and issued two statements outlining his responses since becoming Archbishop of Dublin in 1988 to allegations of child sexual abuse against members of his clergy. He explained how he had provided resources for priests who had offended in the form of professional advice and residential care in treatment centres. He had removed priests from pastoral ministry and introduced disciplinary measures, including dismissal from the clerical state. He had ordered an examination of the diocesan archives for the past fifty years. The names of seventeen priests against whom allegations had been made had been handed over to the police. His archdiocese had followed the 1996 guidelines.[66]

However, an rté *Prime Time* investigation, in October 2002, into the handling by the cardinal of allegations of clerical child sexual abuse raised further questions. Amid demands for his resignation, on 23 October 2002, he issued another statement outlining the record of his archdiocese. There was growing criticism of the Hussey commission. Cardinal Connell felt obliged to defend it. But the commission was stood down in December 2002. This followed an announcement by the Minister for Justice, Equality and Law Reform,

Michael McDowell, that the government, at its meeting on 2 December, had approved a proposal from him for the preparation of a scheme for a new statutory-based mechanism for investigating into matters of significant and urgent public importance. The proposed legislation was informed in the first instance, he said, by the public concern expressed following the RTÉ *Prime Time* programme as well as by the minister's consultations with victims' organisations, representatives of the Catholic hierarchy and other interested parties.[67]

On 30 December 2002, two abuse victims, Marie Collins and Ken Reilly, met Cardinal Connell to discuss a number of issues connected with clerical child sexual abuse. As a follow-up to that meeting, Collins and Reilly met with a number of church representatives and other groups and expressed serious concerns about what they saw as the archdiocese's inadequate pastoral support for victims. These concerns, they pointed out, applied particularly in the case of those who had recently reported for the first time that they had been abused. Collins and Reilly stressed that, irrespective of when the abuse may have taken place, victims felt particularly vulnerable at the time when they first reported it. Seeking to address this criticism, Cardinal Connell committed resources to provide a support network.[68] A follow-up meeting in July 2004 with Connell's successor, Archbishop Diarmuid Martin, reported progress.[69]

In June 2003, the Irish Bishops' Conference, CORI and the IMU established a Working Group on Child Protection to develop a comprehensive and integrated child protection policy. It was chaired by Maureen Lynott and had representatives from a number of bodies as well as two survivors of clerical sexual abuse. The group concluded its work in September 2004, and in January 2005 it produced its final document, *Our Children, Our Church*, which sets out a comprehensive and integrated child protection policy for the Irish Catholic Church.

The Fianna Fáil–Progressive Democrat government first discussed the need for a formal response to the needs of victims of childhood abuse in March 1998. A subcommittee of the cabinet was established in December 1998. The Minister for Education and Science, Micheál Martin, was named as chair. It included the Tánaiste, Mary Harney, and had eight members in total. The subcommittee made a number of important recommendations that were accepted by cabinet. These included commitments to amend the provisions in the Child Care Act 1991 relating to residential centres for children with physical and mental disabilities; to introduce legislation to cover the compiling of a register of sex offenders; to make fully operational the Social Services Inspectorate in the Department of Health and Children; and to modernise facilities and services for young offenders.

On 11 May 1999, the Taoiseach, Bertie Ahern, made an unprecedented public statement: 'On behalf of the State and of all citizens of the State, the Government wishes to make a sincere and long overdue apology to the victims of childhood abuse for our collective failure to intervene, to detect their pain, to come to their rescue.' Ahern quoted from the short preface to the 1970 Kennedy Report on industrial schools, which states 'All children need love, care and security.' He continued: 'Too many of our children were denied this love, care and security. Abuse ruined their childhoods and has been an ever present part of their adult lives, reminding them of a time when they were helpless. I want to say to them that we believe that they were gravely wronged, and that we must do all we can now to overcome the lasting effects of their ordeals.'[70] Ahern also indicated that the cabinet that same day had endorsed the setting up of an inquiry, later provided for under the Commission to Inquire into Childhood Abuse Act, passed by the Oireachtas in 2000. A High Court judge, Mary Laffoy, was appointed to chair the commission. Religious orders that had once been responsible for the running of reformatories and industrial schools could be called to give testimony before this commission. There was also provision for religious orders to provide a written report on the history of the institutions for which they had responsibility.

The government and eighteen religious orders signed an indemnity on 5 June 2002. The religious orders agreed to pay €128 million (€78.5 million of this in land) to the Statutory Redress Scheme, which was set up under the Residential Institutions Redress Act 2002 'to assist the recovery of persons who as children were resident in certain institutions and who suffered or who have suffered injuries that are consistent with abuse while so resident'.[71] The deed was not to be construed as an admission of liability by either party with regard to any alleged injury suffered by any applicant. 'Any payment made under the scheme would be without admission of liability or responsibility for any alleged acts of abuse and no liability or responsibility was or would be apportioned between the said parties or any other person arising out of any sums paid from the special account under the scheme.'[72] The indemnity limiting the eighteen religious orders' liability to €128 million was quickly seen as having been far too generous on the part of the state, whose ultimate liability remained uncertain and could potentially run into billions of euro in compensation for survivors of abuse.

A Stewartship Trust was set up in 1996 by the Catholic bishops to take responsibility for paying compensation to victims of clerical child sex abuse. The four archbishops act as trustees. Each of the twenty-six dioceses was required to make a contribution to the fund. For example, in 2004 the Diocese of Ferns gave €123,270 and the Diocese of Killala contributed €60,809. In March 2005, Achonry, Ardagh and Clonmacnoise, Meath, Kildare and Leighlin, Cashel and Emly, Ossory, Cloyne and two other dioceses had yet to disclose the amount they contributed to the trust.[73] A statement issued by the hierarchy in early 2005 outlined the exposure of the church to retrospective claims:

In 1995 serious legal issues arose between the Bishops of each diocese and Church & General [insurance company] regarding the entitlement of dioceses to indemnity, in respect of civil claims for damages arising from clerical child sexual abuse, under the policies of insurance then in place. . . .

These issues were resolved in 1996 on terms which included the payment of a single sum of €4.3m for division among the dioceses. Rather than apportion it, the Bishops decided to place this sum in a trust fund which they established: 'The Stewardship Trust'. The Trust is empowered to provide financial assistance to Bishops towards the cost of legal liabilities arising from abuse claims. The Trust also funds child protection and other victim response initiatives undertaken at national level by the Bishops' Conference. . . .

Since the establishment of the Stewardship Trust in 1996, 143 claims against 36 priests who had worked in dioceses in Ireland have been settled at a cost to the Stewardship Trust of €8.78m. The claim costs in 2003 amounted to €1.9m and in 2004 were €2.9m.

Most of these cases occurred prior to 1996 and thus are not covered by any existing insurance policy. Since the total sums agreed in 1996 and 1999 are nearing depletion, new resources need to be provided. Accordingly, the Bishops decided that the operation of the Stewardship Trust requires review, and this process is being undertaken by the Trustees.[74]

No matter how generous the diocesan contributions may prove to be, the total sum may not be nearly enough to meet the large number of compensation demands already registered. Selling off some of the assets of the dioceses is the only alternative.

TAKING STOCK: THE CATHOLIC CHURCH IN THE NEW CENTURY

While public attention was focused on scandal and controversy, the Catholic Church in Ireland faced the critical challenge and the growing strain of fulfilling its basic pastoral and institutional needs in a rapidly changing environment. A 1999 survey estimated that the total number of Catholic religious in Ireland was 10,975.[75] The diocesan clergy, charged with running most of the parishes in the country, experienced the same downward trend in recruitment as did religious orders in Ireland. The age profile was also very high, most diocesan clergy being over fifty-five. That meant the virtual abandonment of the idea of retirement in the larger dioceses as bishops struggled to keep churches open. There was an inevitable cut in the number of weekday and Sunday masses. In the cities, churches were closed at certain times during the day as there was a danger of vandalism and theft. That would have been unthinkable in the Ireland of earlier decades. In rural dioceses, a shortage of priests meant that it was no longer possible to keep clergy resident in certain parishes. The amalgamation of parishes was unavoidable, and even the merging of smaller dioceses is now a possibility.

The declining number of religious meant a radical reduction in their traditional and central role in secondary education. The era of religious personnel having their salaries reinvested in the running of their schools is virtually over. Lay teachers are now obliged to take over many of the duties traditionally undertaken by religious, such as supervision outside of class hours. The major male teaching orders, such as the Holy Ghost Fathers, the Jesuits, the Vincentians, the Marists and the Christian Brothers, together their female counterparts, have already put in place systems for the continuation of the Catholic educational tradition within new legal frameworks. While the religious orders themselves may no longer be present, their schools will continue to operate and will continue to uphold the traditions and spiritual ideas of their founding religious orders. This will mean entrusting lay people, whether under deeds of trust or as a company, with the running of these schools. The same challenge confronts the voluntary hospitals traditionally run by religious orders such as the Sisters of Charity, Sisters of Mercy and Bon Secours Sisters. The implications of this trend for the Catholic Church and Irish society are enormous. The hidden subsidies and economic transfers provided by the social capital of church personnel, particularly in the education and health fields, are fast coming to an end. The state will have to face the consequences of this radical change in the coming years.

The Catholic Church experienced a falling-off in attendance at weekly mass and participation in the sacraments during the 1990s. During the second half of the twentieth century Ireland maintained very high mass attendance figures relative to other 'Catholic' countries such as Italy, Spain, Portugal and Belgium. By the late 1990s, those figures had collapsed and religious observance in Ireland looked very much like that in other European countries. What was most notable in Ireland was the speed of the collapse. There was strong evidence of a great disillusionment, despondency and lack of trust in the leadership of the Catholic Church. Priests, once invested with great trust by the laity, were struggling to regain credibility. Many lay people were discerning; they recognised the idealism and the unselfishness of large numbers of clergy and religious. But mistrust of the institution itself was palpable.

The place of religion in the lives of Irish people ought not to be measured exclusively by the health of the institutional church. In the summer of 2001, the relics of Saint Thérèse of Lisieux were taken in solemn procession around Ireland, North and South. The popular response was overwhelming. Tens of thousands of people—young and old—came out to participate in all-night vigils and to line the streets respectfully as the procession passed through scores of towns. The phenomenon of the warm response to the relics of Saint Thérèse is replicated in the high turnout at the annual pilgrimage to Croagh Patrick, regular pilgrimages to Lough Derg and the packed cathedral during the annual Galway Novena of Prayers. Other novenas are also well attended in Dublin, Cork, Dundalk, Drogheda and other towns around the country.

How does an observer read the significance of such phenomena at a time of unprecedented crisis in the institutional church? Perhaps they symbolise the strong attachment to religious values in a country where the clerical church has lost prestige and esteem. They may also point to a general desire to seek reassurance from great figures and symbols at a time of uncertainty and turmoil. This kind of devotion does not signal a revival of the traditional church or a reversal of the most profound secularisation of Irish society. But what it may show is that there is a base on which new Catholic structures can be built in the new century.

The twentieth century in Ireland was the Catholic Century. No institution was more powerful in shaping the lives of most of the people living on the island. That is now in the past. The 1990s brought to public attention the negative legacy of an institution that had helped mould and shape the consciousness of generations of Irish people. There is, however, a need for balance. In striking that balance future historians will look not only to the negative legacy but also to the tremendous contribution of priests, brothers and nuns to the development of Ireland's education, health and social services. Irish men and women in missionary orders also did extraordinary work in providing education, health care and pastoral ministry for people in many countries in Africa, Asia, Latin America, the Caribbean, the United States, Canada, Australia and New Zealand.

This work did not go unappreciated. When Pope John Paul II came to Ireland in September 1979, he expressed his gratitude for the work of the Irish church at home and abroad. He remained a strong supporter of Irish Catholicism, and intended to make a return visit in 2005 which would include a visit to Northern Ireland. His death on 2 April 2005 ended the hopes of the Irish hierarchy and the Irish people in this regard. But welcome as his return would have been, the historical reality must be faced: even Pope John Paul's charisma would not have been able to reverse the slide towards secularisation in contemporary Ireland.

THE SEARCH FOR PEACE IN NORTHERN IRELAND

While few would have predicted in the late 1980s the extent of the crisis in Irish Catholicism, there were also many who looked deterministically at the violence in Northern Ireland and, shrugging their shoulders, concluded: it was ever and will always be thus. For the Irish state the hidden cost of that violence between 1969 and the late 1990s has yet to be calculated. The localisation of the violence, for the most part, in Northern Ireland itself may mislead the observer. The Irish state was a casualty of that violence. International investment was frightened away by uncertainty about the future of the island as a whole. The tourist industry suffered greatly for over twenty years. The Irish state was obliged to invest heavily in security and in measures to contain and defeat the activities of the IRA within its jurisdiction. There was a need to devote large sums of money and personnel to the struggle against subversives: border security, the protection of banks, the staffing of prisons, the provision of additional protection for senior politicians and members of the judiciary.

Reviewing the time spent on the Northern question by taoisigh and ministers in their respective departments and in cabinet may reveal the true extent of the opportunity cost of violence in Northern Ireland on the life of the Irish state. Few areas of policy consistently absorbed so much of the government's time as the emerging peace process in Northern Ireland. Anglo-Irish relations, a central foreign policy interest, were often disrupted and dislocated by division and discord over British policy in Northern Ireland. Northern Ireland issues took up the time of senior Irish diplomats abroad, time that could otherwise have been spent promoting the cultural and economic well-being of Ireland.

In the early 1990s, the leader of the SDLP, John Hume, initiated a dialogue with the leader of Sinn Féin, Gerry Adams, believing that Adams, together with other leading republican figures, favoured an end to the 'armed struggle'. Peace was the object of those discussions. Sceptics in the Southern media, most notably the *Sunday Independent*, sneered at Hume's efforts and denigrated others who became involved in the process. These included the courageous Senator Gordon Wilson, whose daughter Marie had been a victim of the IRA bombing in Enniskillen, Co. Fermanagh, in which eleven people were killed and sixty-three injured on Remembrance Sunday, 8 November 1987. Many will remember his emotion-charged words after he had been taken from the rubble alive: 'I have lost my daughter and we shall miss her, but I bear no ill will. I bear no grudge. Dirty sort of talk is not going to bring her back to life. She was a great wee lassie.'[76] Those words stand out for their magnanimity in nearly thirty years of violence. He went further. On 7 April 1993 Gordon Wilson met with representatives of the IRA to try to persuade them to stop their military campaign. His endeavours ultimately yielded fruit.

By 1993, three political leaders shared a view that the end-game was in sight in Northern Ireland. The prize was lasting peace not military victory. The Taoiseach, Albert Reynolds, the British Prime Minister, John Major, and the US President, Bill Clinton, moved beyond the strategy of containment that had previously prevailed. They collectively came to be persuaded that peace was a realisable goal. Those who did the persuading included senior civil servants in Dublin and London, diplomats in both the Irish and British foreign services and the ubiquitous John Hume, who was responsible for the idea which launched the important Forum for Peace and Reconciliation in Dublin in 1994.

John Major shared with one of his remote predecessors, David Lloyd George, an instinct that what had not been won by military means might be achieved through indirect talks, discussions and negotiations. Peter Brooke, Northern Ireland Secretary between 1989 and 1992, also shared that view. His successor, Sir Patrick Mayhew, who was to remain Northern Ireland Secretary until 1997, equivocated between hopefulness of a breakthrough and lapses into more arcane policy methods.

Bill Clinton was unique among US presidents, being the first to devote so much of his personal time and energy to finding a way forward in the resolution of Anglo-Irish problems. Senator George Mitchell, who became his close adviser in this area, wrote: 'He was the first American president to visit Northern Ireland while in office, the first to make ending the conflict there a high priority for the US government.'[77] Clinton's interest in Ireland dated back to his time as a Rhodes scholar at Oxford University in the late 1960s. When campaigning for the Democratic nomination for President in 1992, Clinton was accused of opportunism, as he had given priority to the Anglo-Irish issue. He told an influential audience in New York that, if elected to the White House, he would appoint a special peace envoy for Northern Ireland and grant Gerry Adams a visa to enter the United States.[78] The latter suggestion was highly contentious and a source of friction between Washington and London. Clinton did not act upon that promise immediately.

Despite work behind the scenes, the Northern situation showed little promise of a peaceful resolution at the time. In October 1993 an IRA bomb killed ten people and injured fifty-seven in a fish-and-chip shop on the Shankill Road, Belfast. In retaliation two members of the Ulster Freedom Fighters went on the rampage in a bar in Greysteel, Co. Derry, shooting dead seven people.[79] Talks, discussions and talks about talks continued amid this violence. There were unsuccessful inter-party talks in Northern Ireland, Irish government contacts with republicans, British government contacts with Sinn Féin, and the ongoing Hume–Adams talks. The latter showed promise, with a joint statement on 25 September 1993 reporting considerable progress on the creation of a peace process.

On 15 December 1993, John Major and Albert Reynolds issued a joint declaration on Northern Ireland. The significance of the Downing Street Declaration, as it became known, has been summarised thus:

> The [Downing Street Declaration], whose terms were negotiated not simply with nationalists and republicans but with unionists and loyalists, marked a decisive shift in the analysis of the conflict and in the political approach to it. It located the roots of the conflict in a historical process on the island of Ireland which primarily affected the people of Ireland . . . it reaffirmed the British government's lack of 'selfish strategic or economic interest' in Northern Ireland and its intent to promote agreement on the island . . . it affirmed a (revised) notion of national self-determination . . . which was conjoined with an Irish acceptance of the need for consent of all significant groups to a constitutional settlement . . . and it pledged change in both parts of the island . . . in an attempt to undo the causes of conflict . . .[80]

Here was a possible way forward. But there had been many historical 'turning points' before where Northern Ireland had failed to turn.

Clinton provided the impetus. On the advice of John Hume and the Irish government, he offered Gerry Adams a forty-eight-hour visa to visit the United States. Clinton explained the reason for his decision in his memoirs: the National Security Council 'determined that we should grant the visa, because it would boost Adams's leverage within Sinn Féin and the IRA, while increasing American influence with him.

That was important, because unless the IRA renounced violence and Sinn Féin became a part of the peace process, the Irish problem could not be resolved.'[81] Hume supported the timing of the visit for January 1994.[82] During Adams's visit, President Clinton, National Security Council and White House staff, as well as Irish-American interest groups and political heavyweights such as Ted Kennedy on Capitol Hill, all impressed on him the importance of the republican movement abandoning the use of political violence.

With the assistance of further US support, an IRA ceasefire was brought into effect from midnight on 31 August 1994. On 13 October the Combined Loyalist Military Command (covering the Ulster Defence Association, the Ulster Freedom Fighters, the Ulster Volunteer Force and the Red Hand Commando) also called a ceasefire. The ceasefires provided the opportunity for both the British and Irish governments to enter into direct dialogue with Sinn Féin and the two loyalist parties with paramilitary links, the Progressive Unionist Party and the Ulster Democratic Party.

The Irish government set up the Forum for Peace and Reconciliation in an effort to facilitate talks between the different traditions on the island. It held its first meeting in Dublin Castle on 28 October 1994. Boycotted by unionists, it was attended by almost all the other major political parties on the island with the exception of Democratic Left. The forum helped to extend further the dialogue between rival groups on the island while it also commissioned a number of useful studies.[83]

Adams was given an unlimited visa to enter the US in September 1994, allowing him to travel throughout the country. His supporters may have attempted to show him as a latter-day Éamon de Valera as he moved triumphantly around. However, despite the outward bravado and shows of triumphalism, Adams kept to the central message that the time had come to trade the armed struggle for the political process.

In February 1995, the British and Irish governments published *Frameworks for the Future* (popularly known as the 'Framework Documents') in an effort to sketch proposals for a constitutional and institutional settlement. The British Prime Minister, John Major, and the Taoiseach, John Bruton, sought to describe how an honourable accommodation might be reached without prejudice to the differing traditions in Northern Ireland. The Framework Documents also applied the principles of the Downing Street Declaration by outlining proposals for constitutional change on both sides of the border, together with plans for new political structures within Northern Ireland, between North and South, and between Britain and the Republic of Ireland. There was a further commitment in the area of mutual respect for human rights and a pledge to submit the outcome of talks with the parties to referenda in both the North and the South.

Adams was invited to participate in talks in Washington with government representatives. Sinn Féin was permitted to fund-raise in the United States, and Clinton invited Adams to the White House for celebrations on St Patrick's Day 1995. Two days before, the President was photographed shaking hands with the Sinn Féin leader.[84] On 29 March the British government announced that it was prepared to hold an exploratory dialogue with Sinn Féin.

When Major visited Washington in April, Clinton praised the courage of the British for having opened discussions with Sinn Féin. He also regenerated Anglo-American relations, bruised by the radical divergences in policy over Northern Ireland. But the British continued to insist that the IRA would have to decommission weapons before Sinn Féin would be allowed to participate in all-party talks. In June, while the IRA ceasefire continued to hold, Sinn Féin announced that they were no longer prepared to meet with British officials. Unionists resisted attempts to normalise relations with Sinn Féin. Adams raised unionist ire in August 1995 when he told a Belfast rally: 'They [the IRA] haven't gone away, you know.'[85]

It had been a bad summer in Northern Ireland. The marching season had been filled with particular menace. Portadown in County Armagh became the epicentre of street conflict. Orange marchers and nationalists confronted each other near the Catholic estates on the Garvaghy Road. The Rev. Ian Paisley of the Democratic Unionist Party and David Trimble of the Ulster Unionist Party marched together with their followers down the road and held hands aloft in triumph at the end, to the great delight of their followers. Catholic residents were obliged to stand by, humiliated, as they witnessed an act of Orange triumphalism. When the leader of the Ulster Unionist Party, James Molyneaux, resigned at the end of August 1995, Trimble was elected as his successor. His bravado on the Garvaghy Road had not done his popularity and standing in unionist circles any harm.

Meanwhile, the White House sustained the momentum created by the ceasefires. On 9 January 1995, seven days after he had retired as senator for Maine, George Mitchell was appointed special adviser to the President and to the Secretary of State on economic initiatives in Ireland. He made his first visit to Northern Ireland a month later and was struck by the symbolism of the so-called Peace Line—a 30-foot-high wall, topped in some places with barbed wire, which separated the Catholic Falls area from the Protestant Shankill area of Belfast, cutting through streets. 'It is one of the most depressing structures I've ever seen. To call it the Peace Line is a huge irony,' he wrote.[86]

In the years that followed few people did more than George Mitchell to dismantle the divisions between communities in Northern Ireland. As he listened to people in Belfast discuss their problems, he became aware that he 'could just as well be in New York, Detroit, Johannesburg, Manila, or any other big city in the world'. He was told that there was a strong correlation between unemployment and violence and that, without jobs in the inner cities, there would never be a durable peace. While he recognised that the dispute in Northern Ireland was 'not purely or even primarily economic in origin and nature', he saw that it was necessary to address the issue of jobs and prosperity.[87]

A tangible sign of us willingness to give economic support to the peace process was the organisation of a major trade and investment conference in Washington in May, which attracted hundreds of us and Northern Ireland business people as well as major political leaders.

With determined efforts being made by the Irish and us governments to sustain the IRA ceasefire, Clinton visited Ireland and Britain between 29 November and 1 December 1995. After talks in London with John Major and an address to the Houses of Parliament, on 30 November President Clinton flew to Belfast for his first Irish trip. It was, he recalled, 'the beginning of two of the best days of my presidency'. In Belfast he spoke with evident conviction to employees and guests at the Mackie Metal Plant about being proud to support Northern Ireland. 'Irish Protestant and Irish Catholic together have added to America's strength. From our battle for independence down to the present day, the Irish have not only fought in our wars; they have built our nation, and we owe you a very great debt.' He warned that there would be those who would oppose the peace process: 'The greatest struggle you face is between those who, deep down inside, are inclined to be peacemakers, and those who, deep down inside, cannot yet embrace the cause of peace. Between those who are in the ship of peace and those who are trying to sink it, old habits die hard.'[88] Clinton assured his audience that the United States would stand with those who took risks for peace, in Northern Ireland and around the world. The US President then attended a civic reception in front of Belfast City Hall, followed by a concert there at which local musician Van Morrison sang to the tens of thousands who had gathered: 'There will be days like this.' Hope and history seemed well on course to rhyme, as Seamus Heaney, a Derryman who had just won the 1995 Nobel Prize for Literature, wrote in his poem 'Doubletake'.

Clinton persuaded George Mitchell to chair the newly established three-person International Body on Arms. The British government remained very nervous about the initiative but agreed to support it, nominating the recently retired Chief of the Canadian Defence Forces, General John de Chastelain, to the new body. The Irish government proposed the former Prime Minister of Finland, Harri Hokeri, to sit on the body. Its report was published in January 1996 and urged all parties in peace negotiations to commit themselves to six principles underpinning democracy and non-violence. These 'Mitchell Principles' included the total and verifiable decommissioning of all paramilitary weapons. The Mitchell report proposed that the parties should consider a proposal whereby decommissioning might occur during negotiations.[89]

There was little time for celebration. The IRA had other ideas. At 7.01 p.m. on Friday, 9 February 1996, the IRA ended its ceasefire by exploding a massive bomb at Canary Wharf in London's Docklands. Weighing about 1,000 pounds, it was concealed within a specially designed compartment in a lorry. Two local workers died and over a hundred were injured in the blast, which caused widespread and hugely expensive damage to the financial services sector. The IRA, in a statement, demanded 'an inclusive negotiated settlement' and accused the British government of 'bad faith' and the unionists of 'squandering this unprecedented opportunity to resolve the conflict'.[90]

On 15 June, a one-and-a-half-ton bomb in a van destroyed Manchester city centre. There was further violence on Portadown's Garvaghy Road during the summer months. In October, the IRA exploded two bombs inside British army barracks in Northern Ireland.

Mitchell and his two colleagues continued with the task of attempting to secure progress through inclusive talks. But movement was slow. Dependent upon unionist votes to sustain its majority in the House of Commons, the Conservative government dragged its feet on Northern Ireland. Elections to a forum in Northern Ireland in May 1996 saw Sinn Féin take 15.5 per cent of the vote, a very strong performance given that the party had stated that it would not take its seats. The talks continued, but little progress could be made without the presence of Sinn Féin. In 1997, the IRA caused disruption on British motorways by phoning bomb threats to the police. The same tactic prevented the Aintree Grand National from being run in April.

The victory of the Labour Party in the British general election in May 1997 helped to shift the alignment of political forces in Northern Ireland. As Tony Blair's party won by a landslide, unionist MPS no longer held the balance of power in the House of Commons. The new Northern Ireland Secretary, Mo Mowlam, laid less emphasis on decommissioning than her Conservative predecessors, she energised the process with a refreshing candour matched by none of her predecessors or successors, and her personal commitment and political adroitness helped lay the foundation for radical change.

Yet the violence continued. In June, the IRA killed two policemen in Lurgan, Co. Armagh. Twenty-one people died in sectarian attacks in 1997. Loyalists were responsible for thirteen of those deaths. Portadown's Garvaghy Road was again the scene of violence during the marching season as the Orange parade was forced through this nationalist area with the help of the police and the British army.

In the light of the continuing violence, it came as a major surprise when the IRA announced a resumption of its ceasefire on 20 July 1997. Sinn Féin was admitted to the peace talks on 9 September. The British Prime Minister, on a visit to Belfast, enraged many unionists by shaking hands with Gerry Adams. Blair later repeated the handshake inside 10 Downing Street.

On 12 January 1998, the two governments published propositions on 'heads of agreement'. This was the result of a round of intensive negotiations between Dublin and London, between Belfast and Dublin, and within Northern Ireland that had begun on 24 September 1997. Under the Taoiseach, Bertie Ahern, the Irish negotiating team included the Minister for Foreign Affairs, David Andrews, and the Progressive Democrat Minister of State at the Department of Foreign

Affairs, Liz O'Donnell. The chairman of the talks, George Mitchell, set a deadline of midnight on 9 April 1998 for completion of the agreement. There were frenetic last-minute discussions involving Tony Blair, Bertie Ahern and the leaders of the Northern parties. And of course President Clinton was involved. He recalled that Good Friday 1998 'was one of the happiest days of my presidency. Seventeen hours past the deadline for a decision, all parties in Northern Ireland agreed to a plan to end thirty years of sectarian violence. I had been up most of the night before, trying to help George Mitchell close the deal. Besides George, I talked to Bertie Ahern, and to Tony Blair, David Trimble, and Gerry Adams twice, before going to bed at 2.30am. At five, George woke me with a request to call Adams again to seal the deal.'[91] A new British–Irish agreement was signed, with both governments pledging that they would give effect to its provisions.

In referenda on 22 May 1998, the people of Ireland, North and South, endorsed the agreement. For the first time since 1918, all the people on the island voted together to decide their political future.[92] In the South, the electorate also voted to amend Articles 2 and 3 of the constitution. This was an act of faith in the peace process.

The Good Friday Agreement (also known as the Belfast Agreement) was divided into eleven sections. It began with a declaration of support and commitment to a range of principles, including non-violence and partnership, equality and mutual respect. The governments set out their shared views on constitutional issues, based on the principles of consent and self-determination as set down in the Downing Street Declaration of 1993. This was followed by provisions for the setting up of a new assembly in Northern Ireland, a North–South council and a British–Irish council. New and enhanced provisions with regard to rights and equality of opportunity formed the next section, followed by a commitment by all parties to work in good faith and to use any influence they had to achieve decommissioning of weapons within two years of approval of the agreement. Under the heading of security, there was provision for the normalisation of security arrangements and practices. A programme for the rapid release of prisoners was outlined, and the final section discussed the agreement's validation and review.

Elections to the new Northern Ireland Assembly took place on 25 June 1998. When the body met on 1 July, David Trimble was elected First Minister Designate and Séamus Mallon of the SDLP was elected

Deputy First Minister designate. When, following election in September, the Assembly Executive was formed on 2 December 1999, Sinn Féin held two ministries. The political and administrative talent now on display simply underscored the squandered years since the introduction of direct rule in the early 1970s. The gun, the bomb and the bullet had deprived generations in Northern Ireland of an opportunity to participate in the normal business of government. The violence had had a negative impact on the economic and social development of the island as a whole since the 1960s.

In the year of the Good Friday Agreement—1998—fifty-five people died in violence in Northern Ireland. Three Catholic brothers, aged between eight and ten, died on 12 July when loyalists petrol-bombed their home in a predominantly Protestant area of Ballymoney, Co. Antrim. On 15 August—a traditional Catholic holiday—twenty-eight people were killed in a car-bomb blast in Omagh, Co. Tyrone. The attack also claimed another victim, who died a few days later. A republican splinter group, the Real IRA, had placed a 500-pound bomb in a parked car in a crowded shopping street on a sunny summer Saturday. It was one of the worst outrages of the Troubles.

A fortnight after the explosion, President Clinton, accompanied by his wife Hillary and daughter Chelsea, joined Tony Blair and his wife Cherie on a visit to Omagh to meet about seven hundred of the injured and their relatives. A plaque was unveiled which read: 'In remembrance of the men, women and children who died in the terrorist bombing, August 15, 1998. May their memory serve to foster peace and reconciliation.'[93] President Clinton returned to Ireland in September that year. In Dublin, Bertie Ahern told him that while many people had been involved in the peace process, 'it would not have been possible without you'. On 13 December 2000 Clinton spoke to an audience of over eight thousand people in Belfast. He said: 'I believe in the peace you are building. I believe there can be no turning back.'[94]

However, without turning back, going forward proved difficult. The Northern Executive was suspended on a number of occasions, largely arising from unionist difficulties with Sinn Féin's inability to deliver on decommissioning of weaponry. The Executive performed remarkably well in the circumstances, perhaps better than it objectively ought to have given the pervasive climate of suspicion that hung over it. However, in mid-October 2002 it was again suspended after unionists refused to share power following a police raid on Sinn Féin's offices within Stormont amid allegations of a spy ring. It proved too difficult to restart and the suspension remained throughout 2003 in the hope that elections to the Northern Ireland Assembly planned for November of that year would resolve difficulties. The elections did not solve the problem, however, as the main beneficiaries were the DUP and Sinn Féin, who became the largest and second largest parties in Northern Ireland, respectively.

The prospect of at last becoming First Minister of Northern Ireland did not usher Ian Paisley to the negotiating table with undue haste. In fact as the election results were announced, and the political configuration of Northern Ireland was transformed, it became clear that Paisley would bide his time, determined to push as far as possible for his electoral pledge of a renegotiation of the Good Friday Agreement. These efforts neared fruition towards the end of 2004: the IRA resolved to go further on decommissioning, and the DUP appeared ready to enter a power-sharing arrangement with Sinn Féin. At the eleventh hour, however, negotiations bogged down over the method of verification of decommissioning. Sinn Féin were outraged at what they termed the DUP's triumphal insistence that there be a published photograph of the act of decommissioning.

The unfolding public row was then subsumed in the fallout from the robbery of the head office of the Northern Bank in Belfast on 20 December 2004. A record £26 million (approximately €38 million) was stolen in a daring, meticulously planned raid, which the Chief Constable of the Police Service of Northern Ireland, Hugh Orde, attributed to the IRA in a report on the robbery in January 2005. The Taoiseach, Bertie Ahern, was particularly strident in his criticisms, accusing the Sinn Féin leadership of having foreknowledge of the robbery while negotiating on a Northern settlement. He was also critical of what he termed the manner in which Sinn Féin appeared to be able to adjust paramilitary activity to suit stages of the negotiations. At the same time, Ahern was not prepared to impose sanctions on that party, and he urged that similar restraint be exercised in London and Washington. Sinn Féin leaders Martin McGuinness and Gerry Adams denied the allegations of collusion, and denied the IRA had carried out the operation. However, such assurances seemed unconvincing to the public, who in February were further assured of the IRA's culpability by the Independent

Monitoring Commission. The peace process was indeed in a perilous state and no one—not the experienced negotiators on all sides nor the public North and South—needed a menacing intervention from the IRA to tell them the situation was serious.

Worse was to follow for Sinn Féin. On 30 January 2005, Robert McCartney, a thirty-three-year-old father of two, was stabbed to death with a kitchen knife outside a public house in Belfast's Short Strand. His companion was also stabbed and was fortunate to escape with his life. Those responsible wiped the crime scene clean of incriminating evidence. The gang warned the other customers in the bar to forget what they had seen. The intimidators were believed to be members of the IRA. They were known to the partner and the five sisters of the victim. 'The struggle in terms of what it was 10 years ago is over', Robert McCartney's sister Catherine said. 'We are now dealing with criminal gangs who use the cloak of romanticism around the IRA to murder people and walk away from it.' This was a reference to the organised racketeering and money-laundering in which the IRA are involved.[95]

Within the space of a few weeks, Robert McCartney's partner and five sisters had mounted an extraordinary campaign to confront the Sinn Féin leadership. A public meeting was held in the Short Strand where Sinn Féin were told to name and shame those who were involved in the killing. The McCartney family travelled to Dublin to meet Bertie Ahern and government ministers. They attended the Sinn Féin *ard fheis* in Dublin but refused to be assuaged by the blandishments of Gerry Adams. They held their ground in Belfast, confronting the local IRA and demanding that the culprits be turned over to the police. Within a matter of weeks, they displayed to people on the island that there was no need to fear the IRA. In a sense, they were like the Mothers of the Plaza de Mayo in Buenos Aires who defied the military junta in Argentina from the late 1970s. While Gerry Adams was outside the White House on St Patrick's Day 2005, the McCartney family were inside being received by President George W. Bush. Paula McCartney was asked afterwards by a CBS news reporter whether she was afraid of the IRA: 'Absolutely not afraid, no', she replied. 'I think they should be the ones to be afraid now.'[96] Returning from the United States, Gemma McCartney was reported as saying: 'I've got a degree in modern history and I can see parallels between these IRA thugs and the Nazis.'[97]

The impact of the McCartneys' message on the status of Sinn Féin in the United States, the source of much of its funding, will be calculated by another generation of historians. But it was significant that Senators Ted Kennedy, Hillary Clinton and John McCain were among the sponsors of a bipartisan motion of condemnation of the McCartney killing. That action, and the freezing out of Gerry Adams during his visit to the US for St Patrick's Day, together with the coast-to-coast negative publicity, reflect a waning in confidence in the US about the constitutional and democratic bona fides of Sinn Féin.

The early years of the twenty-first century might prove to be a watershed in the history of Northern Ireland. Robert McCartney's partner and sisters may yet come to be seen as having helped secure the unshackling of people in Northern nationalist communities from the rule of vigilantism and gangsterism. McCartney's murder and the fallout from it may be the catalyst that finally breaks Sinn Féin from the IRA. But those republican bonds run very deep, and it is not quite clear in these early years of the new century whether the gunmen run Sinn Féin or vice versa. It is too early to tell whether, like de Valera and Fianna Fáil in the 1920s, Adams will finally break with the IRA and the violent, revolutionary republican tradition in Irish nationalism.

IRELAND IN THE NEW CENTURY: PROBLEMS AND PROSPECTS

The search for economic, social and political stability and independence has been a central theme in Irish history since 1922. Against great adversity, the William T. Cosgrave, Éamon de Valera and John A. Costello governments revolutionised the relationship between Ireland and Britain and achieved a strengthening of the democratic institutions of the state. They remained solid and steadfast through civil war, years of subversive activity, World War II and the cold war. That generation of politicians sought to deal with both the 'enemy within' and threats from outside which were at their most dangerous during World War II.

But that nationalist leadership also sought to protect Ireland from the 'contamination' of outside cultural and ideological influences. They were reinforced in their policies by the strength of a Catholic Church favouring the idea of an island sheltered from the evils of the world, the flesh and the devil. Sporting organisations like the GAA bolstered fears about the danger of playing 'foreign' games. The result of all these influences was the establishment of a very hierarchical and patriarchal society where the elites were of the pompous view that the citizen needed to be protected and shielded.

The fundamental political struggle in Ireland since the 1960s has been very much a struggle by the citizen to achieve a sovereignty of action, responsibility over all facets of his/her life, and vindication of the right to know. However, the Irish government—schooled in the ways of a former British administration and reinforced by four decades of paternalistic independent government—showed great reluctance to concede the basic right of the citizen to know and to share in the governance of the state. Keeping citizens in the dark was a prerequisite of official administrative practice.

Irish political, religious, business and administrative elites acted in many cases as if they knew best. The consequence was a shared culture of closed government throughout different sectors of Irish life: in banking, the civil service, the professions, politics, the church and educational institutions at all levels. There were very strong forces operating against open government. The level of secrecy in Irish society was very highly developed. Closed structures did not lend themselves to accountability. Therefore, despite the positive and reforming experience of membership of the EU, political leaders like Charles Haughey refused to modernise and open up government and Irish society to greater public scrutiny. Structures and mentality combined to foster clientelism, croneyism, gombeenism and corruption into the 1990s.

By 2005, support for closed government might have been expected to have been confined to a museum of Irish folk ways. But the scandals and, in some cases, corruption in areas such as the health boards, financial institutions, planning process and politics pointed to an even greater threat to the rights of the citizen. The political class in the time of Cosgrave and de Valera were paternalistic and thought that they knew best; they believed that they were acting on behalf of citizens who needed to be sheltered. Paternalistic it may have been, but they firmly believed that they were acting in the public good or public interest. They may have been, and often were, mistaken in their actions. But they acted out of a genuine patriotism. In the last two decades of the twentieth century, the phrases 'the common good' and 'the public interest' were less frequently heard on the lips of political leaders in Ireland. There was a decided lack of patriotism or respect for the rule of law within sectors of Irish society with power, money and influence.

However, the voice of reform was also to be found within Irish politics and the public service. Tribunals of inquiry were set up to investigate many facets of Irish society. There was a significant, and some may have thought irreversible, breakthrough in the removal of the administrative Chinese wall between citizens and government and the agencies of government. One symbol of that refreshing movement towards reform was the success of the Labour Party Minister for State at the Department of the Taoiseach, Eithne Fitzgerald, in steering a radical piece of legislation through the snipe-grass of a divided senior civil service. The Freedom of Information Act became law on 21 April 1997 and came into force on 21 April 1998. It obliged government departments, health boards, local authorities and a range of other statutory agencies to publish information on their activities and to make personal information available to citizens. It also established a number of statutory rights: a legal right for each person to access information held by public bodies and government departments; a legal right for each person to have official information relating to himself/herself amended where it is incomplete, incorrect or misleading; a legal right to obtain reasons for decisions affecting himself/herself.[98] The Act, according to Maeve McDonagh, marked a departure from the traditional approach to disclosure of official documents by ensuring that the provision of access to official records was no longer at the discretion of the holder of those records and that there was no requirement that an individual seeking access to records under the Act should have to establish any particular interest or reason for obtaining access to the records sought.[99]

Between 1997 and early 2003, the legislation proved very successful, initiating a radical redefinition of the relationship between the citizen and government. In 2002 alone, there were 17,000 requests for disclosure under the Freedom of Information Act, over two-thirds of which came from the general public.[100] The working of the Act was a shock to the Irish body politic. Another democracy might have sought to build on these foundations and to strengthen provisions for wider disclosure. But in Ireland, the political and civil service elites reverted to radical conservatism. The Freedom of Information (Amendment) Act 2003 severely restricted the scope and operation of the legislation. Categories of records were removed from its ambit; charges for requests for information were increased; definitions covering exemptions were widened; dates for disclosure were extended; and secretaries general of government departments were given wide-ranging powers to restrict access to documents.[101]

The Freedom of Information (Amendment) Act 2003 revealed the strength of conservatism among very powerful elements within the government and civil service elites in Irish society and demonstrated the resilience of the advocates of the model of closed government. The much-spoken-about 'abuses' of the Freedom of Information Act, if they were abuses, were a small price to pay for transparency in the government and administration of a country tainted in the latter part of the twentieth century by corrupt practices and lack of accountability.

The neo-liberal economic model was the chosen path for the new Irish economy. There was a radical and definitive break from the neo-corporatist Seán Lemass model of the 1960s. As an axiom of economic faith, the new ideology required the selling off of state assets. The privatisation of Telecom Éireann was a very good example of what a state ought not to do: just as the technology was being invented to bring about a communications revolution, a decision was taken to sell to the private sector. Unfortunately there is no shortage of examples of the madness of the new ideology. The space beside the railway tracks was given over to phone companies for the laying of fibre optic cables. Car parks at railway stations were leased out to private companies. Garda telephone communications masts were let to the private sector for use in their mobile telephone operations. Electronic voting machines were purchased at vast expense and never used – and then their storage provided windfall profits for the private sector.

The implementation of policy based on this neo-liberal economic philosophy required the rapid construction of a national road infrastructure. Little thought was given to the modernising of the antiquated Irish rail system. Engines and rolling stock introduced on the Cork–Dublin line in the early 1980s were still in use in 2005. Travel by rail between the country's two major cities took up to three hours, while the same journey on the continent would take no more than an hour and a half. And despite the monumentally expensive improvements to the road networks, many cities and large towns in the country daily suffered virtual gridlock as commuters battled through traffic to work. People going to work travelled distances comparable to people living in the suburbs of the great US cities. The suburbs of Dublin stretched out to what was once virgin countryside on the northside: Malahide, Skerries, Balbriggan, Drogheda and Dundalk. From the south, daily commuters to Dublin were coming from as far as Gorey and Carlow. Once-beautiful towns within an eighty-mile radius of Dublin had become replicas of the ugly suburbs around the capital. There appeared to be little willingness to learn from the past. Dublin itself proved to be an exception to that general trend. Public housing in the inner city was designed to much higher specifications than in the past. Moreover, the tower blocks in Ballymun—once a shining symbol of brash modernity in the 1960s—were by 2005 demolished and replaced by houses in which human beings could live without the trauma of lifts that never worked and heating that went unregulated.

The imperatives of rapid road transport set in train a major struggle between those supporting 'progress' and groups of concerned citizens interested in preserving Irish heritage. What happened when a road was routed through a listed historical site? The road was generally built at the cost of irreparable loss to heritage and history. Since 1990, according to research undertaken by David Edwards, 10 per cent of recorded monuments in the country have disappeared. That is over three thousand monuments. The list of types of monuments lost forever makes for depressing reading: raths/hill forts, ring forts, fulachta fiadh/kitchen middens, megalithic tombs, Bronze Age burial mounds, castle ruins, bawn walls, medieval and post-medieval graveyards, souterains, standing stones, wells.[102] Carrickmines in south County Dublin is a good case in point. Plans for the building of the M50 motorway were routed through the site of an 800-year-old castle and surrounds. Despite obtaining a Supreme Court ruling in February 2003 which recognised the late medieval frontier fortress as a national monument, those who campaigned to have the excavation extended and the site preserved were ultimately defeated by the combined might of Dún Laoghaire–Rathdown County Council, the National Roads Authority and the Fianna Fáil Minister for the Environment, Heritage and Local Government, Martin Cullen. And so, despite years of struggle to stop the destruction of the site, the development went ahead and the road was built, much to the satisfaction, it must be said, of frustrated motorists travelling into the capital from the south. It was part of a pattern of development and a metaphor for modern Ireland in which heritage continually lost out to 'progress'.

The privatised world in which young Irish people grew up and earned a living was also riddled with pressures. The volatility of economic life called for great flexibility and mobility. The community and social safety mechanisms of a pre-modern society were no longer in place. It was easy to change jobs. But it was also easy to fall from employment to unemployment and to homelessness. Focus Ireland estimated that the number of homeless in Ireland increased from 1,500 in 1989 to almost 5,600 in 2002. In the same period, the number of households waiting on housing lists increased from just under 20,000 to almost 48,500.[103]

In 1999, there were 455 suicides recorded in Ireland. By 2001, the number rose to 519, before dropping back to 444 in 2003. Confronted with this alarming situation, the health authorities commissioned a national study on suicide. Published in 2001, it found a number of worrying trends in relation to the population generally and young males particularly.[104] It found that almost five times more men died from suicide than women, and that suicide is the principal cause of death for men aged 15–35 years.[105] Alcohol and unemployment, particularly long-term unemployment, were factors associated with young male suicide. While no relationship with the Celtic Tiger was cited in the report, one could read between the lines. The implications were obvious: as Irish society becomes more competitive and more work oriented and moves at an ever faster pace, the pressures on young males in particular become more unbearable.

Alcohol abuse among the young is widespread in Ireland in the early twenty-first century, particularly on national holidays, at sporting and music events, and in university towns throughout the country. The abuse of alcohol may partially explain the high incidence of another regrettable feature of contemporary Ireland: sexual violence against women. Extraordinary work has been done by the Rape Crisis Centres around the country to provide support and counselling for victims of sexual assault and sexual abuse. The true scale of violence of this kind is difficult to calculate, since the actual number of incidents is much higher than those reported to the authorities and the number of cases taken to court by the Director of Public Prosecutions is small relative to the incidents reported. Nevertheless, a telephone survey in 2002 did provide some indication of the extent of sexual abuse in Ireland. Some 3,118 randomly selected Irish adults took part in the survey, representing a 71 per cent participation rate of those invited.[106] The survey found that 42 per cent of women reported some form of sexual abuse or assault in their lifetime, with the most serious form of abuse, penetrative abuse, being experienced by 10 per cent of women. Almost one-third of women and a quarter of men reported some level of sexual abuse in childhood. Of those disclosing abuse, over one-quarter of women and one-fifth of men were abused by different perpetrators as both children and adults (i.e. 'revictimised'). Most perpetrators of child sexual abuse (89 per cent) were men acting alone. One-quarter of perpetrators of sexual violence against women as adults were intimate partners or ex-partners; in the case of abused men the figure was 1.4 per cent. The report found that alcohol was involved in almost half of the cases of adult sexual assault. Reluctance to disclose details of sexual abuse was one of the most worrying features of the report.

Was the situation any better in the past? It is difficult to answer that question with precision. But the more the files are examined on the history of the Irish state, the more it becomes clear that Cosgrave and de Valera's Ireland was no idyll. There was widespread sexual abuse, but much of it went unreported and concealed. There was a hypocrisy in traditional Ireland towards many abuses such as rape, incest, child sexual abuse and pregnancy out of wedlock. But there was also a sense of community, albeit sometimes a very oppressive kind of community, in urban and rural Ireland. That sense of community, that collective culture, has been seriously weakened by the anonymity of much of contemporary Ireland. There are two specific episodes from the last two decades of the twentieth century which serve as a reminder of the weakness of civic culture in Ireland. Both involve women and both showed up the absence of safeguards in Irish society.

Ann Lovett was a fifteen-year-old schoolgirl who died alone on a winter evening in January 1984 giving birth near a statue of Our Lady, in Granard, Co. Longford. Paula Meehan, in her poem 'The Statue of the Virgin at Granard Speaks', captures something of that great tragedy. The statue is the narrator:

It can be bitter here at times like this,
November wind sweeping across the border.
Its seeds of ice would cut you to the quick.

The whole town tucked up safe and dreaming,
even wild things gone to earth, and I
stuck up here in this grotto, without as much as
star or planet to ease my vigil. ...

But on this All Soul's Night there is
no respite from the keening of the wind.
I would not be amazed if every corpse came risen
from the graveyard to join in exaltation with the gale,
a cacophony of bone imploring sky for judgement
and release from being the conscience of the town.

On a night like this I remember the child
who came with fifteen summers to her name,
and she lay down alone at my feet
without midwife or doctor or friend to hold her hand
and she pushed her secret out into the night,
far from the town tucked up in little scandals,
bargains struck, words broken, prayers, promises,
and though she cried out to me in extremis
I did not move,
I didn't lift a finger to help her,
I didn't intercede with heaven,
nor whisper the charmed word in God's ear.[107]

The second case involves Brigid McCole, a mother of twelve from
Donegal who was one of over a thousand women found to have been
infected with the hepatitis c virus resulting from being given
contaminated Anti-D, a product administered to certain women in
childbirth. She died in October 1996 after a protracted legal battle for
compensation with the Department of Health. Her death led to a
tribunal of inquiry into the controversy. Hundreds of haemophiliacs
were also infected with both hepatitis c and HIV from products they
used to help their blood to clot. According to the journalist Fergal
Bowers, about ninety people have died arising from the scandal. The
state paid out hundreds of millions of euro in compensation on
behalf of the taxpayer. All ministers and civil servants should use the
files of the Department of Health in relation to these scandals as a case
study in training on how not to treat a citizen of this state.[108]

There are many challenges confronting the Irish state in the years ahead, not least the achievement of a permanent peace in Northern Ireland. There is the need to achieve basic respect for citizens and those from abroad living and working in this country. There is the requirement to strengthen tolerance and to eradicate the toxins of racism. There is the requirement to do better for the elderly who have served the state in their working lifetime and who ought to be protected from illegal acts by agents of that state. There is the imperative to improve the educational system and to provide wider social access to all levels of education. There is the need to cultivate a culture of honesty and of probity in all sectors of Irish public and private life. Ireland has a long road to travel before acceptable standards are achieved in these and other areas.

For this author, one personality stands out at the beginning of the twenty-first century as an exemplar of the independent citizen in Ireland. He is not a politician or a public figure but a painter. Tony O'Malley, who died aged eighty-nine on 22 January 2002, was a self-taught painter who was influenced by his sense of place and by a deep love of the history, heritage and environment of his native Callan in County Kilkenny and of the island as a whole. Contracting tuberculosis as a young man, he suffered the indignity of being committed to a sanatorium. There he saw the Minister for Health, Noël Browne, help to restore the dignity of the human being. Seeing patients lying on old, unsanitary horsehair mattresses, Browne instructed officials to get them proper bedding. O'Malley never forgot that episode. Leaving the safe world of the bank where he worked as a clerk, he eschewed authority and hierarchy and, for the rest of his life, maintained an independence of action and of thought free from the constraints of political correctness and false social respect. His life as an artist was a struggle to achieve his own style and artistic expression. Ignoring the constraints of the academy, he developed his own abstract style that could be lyrical or dark. He explored the richness of his own interior life in his many 'inscapes' and he celebrated nature and its exuberance in work inspired by the landscapes of Ireland, Spain, southern England and the Caribbean. He refused to be told how or what to paint. His ideas were his own. His work and his example as a citizen of an independent republic endure as a beacon in a culture that increasingly tolerates, if not actually promotes, the despoliation of heritage and the environment in the name of a false modernity.

The main street in the capital city—O'Connell Street—features many fine monuments. A statue to Daniel O'Connell stands at the Liffey end, one to Charles Stewart Parnell dominates the opposite Rotunda end, and one in honour of James Larkin lies in between. All three men were personalities of great importance in the recent history of the island. The latest addition to these monuments, erected to commemorate the millennium, is the 'spire'. Opinions vary on the 'spire'. While it has its admirers, there are many who regard it as being out of proportion with its surroundings, out of sympathy with the location and simply out of place. A symbol of post-modernity, if it is anything, its very lack of meaning has a meaning in a society that is in large measure post-colonial, post-nationalist and post-Christian. But there is also a new vitality, honesty and openness in Irish life. Irish society is characterised by a very healthy clash of ideas where authority is challenged and accountability is demanded. Liberation from the authoritarianism of both church and state has taken many decades to achieve. The current clash of ideas and values is a healthy feature of a more open society.

In 1904 Horace Plunkett published *Ireland in the New Century*. He wrote: 'We have been too long a prey to that deep delusion, which, because the ills of the country we love were in past days largely caused from without, bids us look to the same source for their cure.' He argued that 'Ireland must be re-created from within. The main work must be done in Ireland, and the centre of interest must be Ireland.' Plunkett felt that 'when Irishmen realise this truth, the splendid human power of their country, so much of which now runs daily or disastrously to waste, will be utilised; and we may then look with confidence for the foundation of a fabric of Irish prosperity, framed in constructive thought, and laid enduringly in human character'.[109] That is a statement of classic Irish liberalism. It was hopeful, but not wildly optimistic, at a time when Ireland was part of the United Kingdom and without the immediate prospect of home rule. A century later, Plunkett's admonitions and optimism remain relevant.

Notwithstanding the many difficulties and challenges, the establishment of the Irish state was not 'a cod', to use the description of Michael Moran, the central character in John McGahern's novel *Amongst Women*. This is no mean republic. Ireland is independent and sovereign, a respected member of the European Union and of the

United Nations. At home, a precarious peace continues to hold in Northern Ireland. Both parts of the island enjoy economic prosperity. But the scars of that violence are both visible and invisible. Many who survived the car bombs and sectarian attacks over the thirty years of violence await retribution and justice or a simple explanation as in the case, for example, of those who escaped with their lives in the Dublin and Monaghan bombs on 17 May 1974. If they never learn who did it, the survivors and the relatives of the dead need to know the *why* from those who ought to know.

What remains today is the need to build a strong civic culture that is linked with movements in Europe steeped in the traditions of humanism and social inclusiveness. That may give renewed energy to those wishing to challenge the building of Irish society on pick-and-mix post-modernism and economic neo-liberalism with its strong anti-statist bias. The rejection of the European Constitution in referenda by the French and Dutch in mid-2005 reinforced the retreat from greater and deeper integration by two founder members of the Union. That ought to have been a major source of concern for a small country like Ireland with so much of its prosperity bound up in the continued stability in Europe and in the deepening of the integration process.

Notes

Introduction to the First Edition (pp. xvii–xxi)

1. Archbishop Lombard in Brian Friel's play *Making History* (Faber and Faber, London, 1989), pp. 15–16.
2. This article was published six years later. See Francis Shaw, 'The Canon of Irish History—A Challenge', *Studies*, VOL. LXI, NO. 242 (Summer 1972), p. 117.
3. See Máirín Ní Dhonnchadha and Theo Dorgan (eds), *Revising the Rising* (Field Day, Derry, 1991).
4. See, in particular, the work of Conor Cruise O'Brien, *States of Ireland* (Hutchinson, London, 1972).
5. *The Irish Review*, NO. 1 (1986), p. 5.
6. *The Irish Review*, NO. 12 (Spring/Summer 1992), pp. 1–12.
7. See Brendan Bradshaw, 'Nationalism and Historical Scholarship in Modern Ireland', *Irish Historical Studies*, VOL. XXVI, NO. 104, 1988–9, pp. 329–51 and by the same author: 'Revisionism Revised', *The Aisling*, August 1992, pp. 63–70. For a general discussion on revisionism, see Luke Gibbon, 'Challenging the Canon: Revisionism and Cultural Criticism', in Seamus Deane (ed.), *The Field Day Anthology of Irish Writing* (Field Day, Derry, 1991), VOL. III, pp. 561–680.

Introduction to the Second Edition (pp. xxiii–xxvii)

1. *http//www.entemp.ie/press/2000/210700.htm*

Chapter 1: A War without Victors: Cumann na nGaedheal and the Conservative Revolution (pp. 1–64)

1. Ruth Dudley Edwards, *An Atlas of Irish History* 2nd ed. (Methuen, London and New York, 1986), p. 255.
2. MacRory to Amigo, 28 September 1920, Amigo Papers, Southwark Diocesan Archives, London; quoted in Mary Harris, 'The Catholic Church and the Foundation of the Northern Irish State 1912–1930', Cambridge PhD, 1991.
3. Graham Walker, *The Politics of Frustration: Harry Midgley and the Failure of Labour in Northern Ireland* (Manchester University Press, Manchester, 1985),

p. 21: 'Votes were cast amidst much intimidation and violence. Personation . . . was predictably rife.'

4. *Northern Ireland Parliamentary Debates, House of Commons*, VOL. 1, 19–22 June 1921.

5. *Irish Catholic Directory*, 1922, p. 552: quoted in Harris, 'The Catholic Church and the Foundation of the Northern Irish State 1912–1930', p. 106. Harris also quotes the bishop of Dromore, Mulhern, writing in July 1921 that he was 'actually on the run'. He added: 'apart from personal reasons, the effects of an attack upon the Bishop would be endless in disastrous consequences around here'. Mulhern to John Hagan, 18 July 1921, John Hagan papers, Irish College, Rome. See Harris, p. 106.

6. *Dáil Éireann (Private Sessions)*, 14 December 1921, pp. 110–11.

7. *Dáil Éireann (Private Sessions)*, 6 January 1922, p. 283.

8. *Dáil Éireann (Private Sessions)*, 14 December 1921, p. 139.

9. This phrase is taken from Geoffrey Prager, *Building Democracy in Ireland: Political Order and Cultural Integration in a Newly Independent Nation* (Cambridge University Press, Cambridge, 1986), p. 91.

10. De Valera to John Hagan, 13 January 1922 (John Hagan papers).

11. T. Desmond Williams, 'From the Treaty to the Civil War', in T. Desmond Williams (ed.), *The Irish Struggle 1916–1926* (Routledge and Kegan Paul, London, 1966), pp. 127–28.

12. Nicholas Mansergh, *The Unresolved Question: The Anglo-Irish Settlement and its Undoing 1912–1982* (Yale University Press, New Haven and London, 1991), p. 208.

13. *Dáil Éireann (Private Sessions)*, 17 December 1921, pp. 242–43.

14. Michael Hopkinson, *Green against Green: The Irish Civil War* (Gill & Macmillan, Dublin, 1988), p. 67.

15. C.S. Andrews, *Dublin Made Me* (Mercier Press, Dublin and Cork, 1979), pp. 219–308.

16. *Irish Independent*, 18 March 1922.

17. Maurice Moynihan (ed.), *Speeches and Statements by Éamon de Valera 1917–1973* (Gill & Macmillan, Dublin, 1980), p. 98 ff.

18. I have used a chronology drawn up by Colonel J.J. O'Connell in 1936 for some of the details in this section. s9180, Department of the Taoiseach, National Archives, Dublin.

19. J. Dunsmore Clarkson, *Labour and Nationalism in Ireland* (Columbia University Press, New York, 1925), p. 456. This strategy is criticised in Emmet O'Connor, *Syndicalism in Ireland 1917–1923* (Cork University Press, Cork, 1988), p. 150 ff.

20. Emmet O'Connor, *Syndicalism in Ireland*, p. 151.

21. James Anthony Gaughan, *Thomas Johnson: 1872–1963: First Leader of the Labour Party in Dáil Éireann* (Kingdom Books, Dublin, 1980), pp. 212–93.

22. J.J. Lee, *Ireland 1912–1985: Politics and Society* (Cambridge University Press, Cambridge, 1989), p. 59.

23. Mansergh, *The Unresolved Question*, p. 209ff; see also Brian Farrell, 'The Drafting of the Irish Free State Constitution', in three parts, *The Irish Jurist*, VOL. 5 (1970), pp. 115–40; VOL. 6 (1970), pp. 343–55; and *The Irish Jurist*, new series, VOL. 7 (1971), pp. 111–35.

24. Tim Pat Coogan, *Michael Collins A Biography* (Arrow, London, 1991), pp. 373–74.

25. Intercepted letter from P. Osborough to prisoner in the North, 24 June 1922, s3827, Department of the Taoiseach, National Archives, Dublin.

26. 'Chronological statement of outstanding events in 1922, prior and immediately subsequent to the attack on the Four Courts on 28 June 1922', s1322, Department of the Taoiseach, National Archives, Dublin.

27. Diarmuid O'Hegarty to Lloyd George (draft letter), 23 June 1922, s1322, Department of the Taoiseach, National Archives, Dublin.

28. s1322, Department of the Taoiseach, National Archives, Dublin.

29. Sheila Lawlor, *Britain and Ireland 1914–1923* (Gill & Macmillan, Dublin, 1983), p. 192, quoting 'most secret' appendix to conclusions of conference of ministers in the secretary to the cabinet, Sir Maurice Hankey's, hand, 24 June 1922, CAB 21/255 (11 a.m.).

30. ibid.

31. Coogan, *Michael Collins*, p. 331.

32. Provisional Government Decision (P.G. 37), 27 June 1922, s1350, Department of the Taoiseach, National Archives, Dublin.

33. Coogan, *Michael Collins*, p. 395 ff.

34. For a good account of the civil war from the government standpoint, see Niall C. Harrington, *An Episode of the Civil War: Kerry Landing, August 1922* (Anvil Books, Dublin, 1992), p. 28 ff.

35. Moynihan, (ed.), *Speeches and Statements by Éamon de Valera*, p. 107.

36. Lord Longford and Thomas P. O'Neill, *Éamon de Valera* (Arrow Books, London, 1970), p. 197.

37. León Ó Broin (ed.), *In Great Haste: The Letters of Michael Collins and Kitty Kiernan* (Gill & Macmillan, Dublin, 1983), p. 210.

38. Coogan, *Michael Collins*, pp. 387–88.

39. Interview with Kathleen McKenna Napoli, Rome, 1979.

40. Terence de Vere White, *Kevin O'Higgins* (Methuen, London, 1948), pp. 119–20.

41. Conor Brady, *Guardians of the Peace* (Gill & Macmillan, Dublin, 1974), p. 33.
42. Niall C. Harrington, *Kerry Landing, August 1922* (Anvil Books, Dublin, 1992), p. 141.
43. ibid.
44. ibid., p. 147 ff.
45. Interview with T. Desmond Williams: two brothers of the two dead men, Gerry Boland and Seán Lemass, became Fianna Fáil ministers.
46. Interview with Con Cremin: Seán Lemass gave that view to the then secretary of the Department of Foreign Affairs when they were on an official visit to Africa in the early 1960s.
47 Seán T. O'Kelly to Hagan, 26 August 1922 (John Hagan papers, Irish College, Rome). O'Kelly was jailed following a raid on his home, from which Free State troops removed practically all his private correspondence.
48. O'Kelly to Hagan, 26 August 1922 (Hagan papers).
49. Mulcahy to Hagan, 11 September 1922 (Hagan papers).
50. Maryann Gialanella Valiulis, *Portrait of a Revolutionary: General Richard Mulcahy and the Foundation of the Irish State* (Irish Academic Press, Dublin, 1992), p. 175.
51. De Valera to Mrs Ryan, 21 September 1922 (Hagan papers).
52. Thomas O'Doherty to Hagan, 11 November 1922 (Hagan papers).
53. Dermot Keogh, *The Vatican, the Bishops and Irish Politics 1919–1939* (Cambridge University Press, Cambridge, 1986), p. 96.
54. Moynihan (ed.), *Speeches and Statements by Éamon de Valera*, p. 108.
55. *Dáil Éireann Debates*, 28 November 1922.
56. Patrick O'Donnell to Hagan, 25 November 1922 (Hagan papers).
57. Cahir Davitt Memoir, unpublished manuscript in possession of Father Thomas Davitt CM, Vincentian Community, 44 Stillorgan Park, Blackrock, Co. Dublin, p. 51.
58. Cahir Davitt Memoir, p. 51.
59. Keogh, *The Vatican, the Bishops and Irish Politics 1919–1939*, p. 98.
60. ibid., p. 97.
61. Cahir Davitt Memoir, pp. 58–59.
62. ibid., pp. 75–76.
63. Keogh, *The Vatican, the Bishops and Irish Politics 1919–1939*, p. 99.
64. Andrews, *Dublin Made Me*, pp. 243–44.
65. Hagan to Mrs Ryan, 26 December 1923, Jim Ryan papers, P88/92, Archives Department, UCD.
66. Hopkinson, *Green against Green*, p. 273. This outstanding account of the civil war has drawn together the data quoted above. However, there is no

comprehensive account available on the financial effects of the civil war on Irish society.

67. ibid., p. 273, quoting Ronan Fanning, *Independent Ireland* (Helicon, Dublin, 1983), p. 39.

68. Hopkinson, *Green against Green*, p. 273. For an account of the performance of the Irish army during the war, see John P. Duggan, *A History of the Irish Army* (Gill & Macmillan, Dublin, 1991).

69. This is the view of Hopkinson, *Green against Green*, p. 273.

70. Longford and O'Neill, *Éamon de Valera*, p. 229.

71. The Vice-President was the Minister for Home Affairs, Kevin O'Higgins, Ernest Blythe held the Finance portfolio and Desmond FitzGerald was made Minister for External Affairs. Education was held by MacNeill until 24 November 1925 when John Marcus O'Sullivan took it over, Industry and Commerce by Patrick McGilligan. Defence was Mulcahy's responsibility until 19 March 1924; that portfolio was to provide Cumann na nGaedheal with its stiffest post-civil war challenge. There were also four ministers not members of the executive council: Paddy Hogan, Agriculture; F. Lynch, Fisheries; James Burke, Local Government; and James J. Walshe, Posts and Telegraph.

72. Brady, *Guardians of the Peace*, p. 72 ff.

73. ibid., p. 103.

74. Mulcahy was also commander-in-chief (August 1922–August 1923). See Valiulis, *Portrait of a Revolutionary*, p. 111 ff.

75. ibid., p. 219.

76. Maurice Moynihan memorandum on conversation with Costello, 22 December 1948, s3678D, Department of the Taoiseach, National Archives, Dublin.

77. s3578D, Department of the Taoiseach, National Archives, Dublin.

78. Moynihan memorandum, 22 December 1948, s3678D, Department of the Taoiseach, National Archives, Dublin.

79. Mulcahy memorandum, 19 March 1924, s3678, Department of the Taoiseach, National Archives, Dublin.

80. I am grateful to Father Gearóid Ó Súilleabháin for background information on the role of his father in putting down the mutiny.

81. Maryann Gialanella Valiulis, *Almost a Rebellion: The Army Mutiny of 1924* (Tower Books, Cork, 1985), p. 113.

82. See Kevin Boyle, 'The Tallents Report on the Craig-Collins Pact of 30 March 1922', *The Irish Jurist*, VOL. 12, NO. 1 (1977), pp. 148–86.

83. For details on this episode, see J.B. Cunningham, 'The Struggle for the Belleek-Pettigo Salient 1922', in *Donegal Annual*, 1982, pp. 38–59.

84. Mary Harris, 'The Catholic Church and the Foundation of the Northern Irish State 1912–1930', p. 135.

85. M Ó C [Michael Collins] to Duggan, 4 May 1922, P4/377, Kennedy Papers, University College Dublin Archives.

86. Provisional government meeting, 1 August 1922, Blythe Papers, P24/70, University College Dublin Archives.

87. Memorandum from Acting Minister of Home Affairs, 9 August 1922, P24/70, Blythe Papers, University College Dublin Archives.

88. Text taken from Arthur Mitchell and Pádraig Ó Snodaigh (eds), *Irish Political Documents 1916–1949* (Irish Academic Press, Dublin, 1985), pp. 118–19.

89. Brief for the Counsel of the Irish Free State, Boundary Bureau papers, Box 7, National Archives, Dublin.

90. *Irish Independent*, 4 February 1922.

91. Harris, 'The Catholic Church and the Foundation of the Northern Irish State 1912–1930', p. 168.

92. Some of O'Shiel's information may have come from Raymond Burke, a Devlinite who had been in contact with both Churchill in the Colonial Office and members of the Northern government and had written to the provisional government regarding the possibility of release of the political prisoners. See R. Burke to A. McCann, 21 August 1922, S5750/1, National Archives, Dublin.

93. Deputation to the Provisional Government, 11 October 1922, S11209, National Archives, Dublin.

94. Harris, 'The Catholic Church and the Foundation of the Northern Irish State 1912–1930', p. 169.

95. Final Report of the North-East Boundary Bureau, S4743, National Archives, Dublin.

96. The North-East and the Coming British Elections, S8892, National Archives, Dublin.

97. E.M. Stephens papers, MS 4240, TCD.

98. O'Shiel to each member of the Executive Council, S2027, National Archives, Dublin.

99. ibid.

100. Michael Laffan, *The Partition of Ireland, 1911–1925* (Dundalgan Press, Dundalk, 1983), p. 99.

101. Executive Council Minutes, 12 August 1924, S4743, National Archives, Dublin.

102. O'Shiel memorandum to each minister, May 1923, S2027, National Archives, Dublin.

103. Geoffrey Hand, [Introduction] *Report of the Irish Boundary Commission* (Irish University Press, Shannon, 1969), p. ix.

104. ibid., p. 8.

105. ibid., p. 11.

106. ibid., p. 12.

107. Harris, 'The Catholic Church and the Foundation of the Northern Irish State 1912–1930', p. 107.

108. E.M. Stephens papers, MS 4240, TCD.

109. Harris, 'The Catholic Church and the Foundation of the Northern Irish State 1912–1930', p. 195.

110. Hand, *Report of the Irish Boundary Commission*, p. 146.

111. Text of Agreement in D. McArdle, *The Irish Republic*, pp. 977–78.

112. Keith Middlemass (ed.), *Tom Jones Whitehall Diary* (Oxford University Press, London, 1969), p. 245.

113. *Dáil Debates* 1925, VOL. 13, col. 1303.

114. *Dáil Debates* 1925, VOL. 13, cols 1305–7.

115. See Harris, 'The Catholic Church and the Foundation of the Northern Irish State 1912–1930', p. 204.

116. See Michael O'Neill, '70 Years ago—Saint Columban's Society', *The Far East*, January 1988, p. 3. I am also grateful to Father O'Neill for showing me part of his manuscript on the history of his order. See also Edmund M. Hogan, *The Irish Missionary Movement: A Historical Survey, 1830–1980* (Gill & Macmillan, Dublin, 1992). Church of Ireland and other religious missionary movements also flourished during this period.

117. *Irish Catholic Directory*, 1927, p. 581.

118. ibid., p. 583.

119. Quoted in J.H. Whyte, *Church and State in Modern Ireland 1923–1979*, 2nd ed. (Gill & Macmillan, Dublin, 1984), p. 25.

120. *Irish Catholic Directory*, 1926, p. 597.

121. ibid., p. 597.

122. Not every Irish bishop shared the preoccupations of the majority with the evils of dancing. One bishop used to organise a dance after the end of the harvest on his farm outside Cavan town. The fiddle player was a priest on the staff of St Patrick's College. This piece of information was given to me by Bishop Francis MacKiernan of Kilmore, December 1991.

123. David Thomson, *Woodbrook* (Barrie & Jenkins, London, 1975), pp. 84–85.

124. Keogh, *The Vatican, the Bishops and Irish Politics 1919–1939*, p. 129.

125. Michael Adams, *Censorship: The Irish Experience* (University of Alabama Press, Alabama, 1968), p. 48.

126. James Meenan, *George O'Brien: A Biographical Memoir* (Gill & Macmillan, Dublin, 1980), pp. 120–22.

127. ibid., pp. 117–18.

128. Padraic O'Farrell, *The Burning of Brinsley MacNamara* (Lilliput Press, Dublin, 1990).

129. Séamus Deane, *A Short History of Irish Literature* (Hutchinson, London, 1986), p. 187.

130. ibid., p. 206.

131. Mainie Jellett exhibition guide, Irish Museum of Modern Art, 1992, p. 1.

132. See Bruce Arnold, *Mainie Jellett and the Modern Movement in Ireland* (Yale University Press, New Haven and London, 1991) and S.B. Kennedy, *Irish Art and Modernism 1880–1950* (Institute of Irish Studies, Belfast, 1991).

133. Kennedy, *Irish Art and Modernism*, p. 40.

134. Seán Rothery, *Ireland and the New Architecture 1900–1940* (Lilliput Press, Dublin, 1991), p. 90 ff.

135. Tom Garvin covers this theme in a very original manner in his book *Nationalist Revolutionaries in Ireland 1858–1928* (Clarendon Press, Oxford, 1987).

136. Brian P. Kennedy, *Dreams and Responsibilities: The State and the Arts in Independent Ireland* (Arts Council, Dublin, 1990), p. 6 ff.

137. Séamas Ó Buachalla, *Education Policy in Twentieth-Century Ireland* (Wolfhound Press, Dublin, 1988), pp. 60–61.

138. ibid., pp. 61–62.

139. ibid., p. 64.

140. s8970, Department of the Taoiseach, National Archives, Dublin.

141. W.F. Mandle, *The Gaelic Athletic Association and Irish Nationalist Politics 1884–1924* (Gill & Macmillan, Dublin, 1987), p. 211.

142. Marcus de Búrca, *The GAA: A History* (Cumann Lúthchleas Gael, Dublin, 1980), p. 208 ff.

143. For the best analysis of the industrial development of early modern Ireland, see Mary E. Daly, *Industrial Development and Irish National Identity 1922–1939* (Gill & Macmillan, Dublin, 1992); see also Brian Girvin's book review in the *Economic and Social Review*, VOL. 24, NO. 4 (July 1993), pp. 401–04.

144. *Saorstat Éireann Official Handbook* (The Talbot Press, Dublin, 1932), p. 305.

145. *Saorstat Éireann Official Handbook*, see pp. 13, 152 and 160.

146. Maurice Manning and Moore McDowell, *Electricity Supply in Ireland: The History of the ESB* (Gill & Macmillan, Dublin, 1984), p. 77.

147. Rex Cathcart, 'Broadcasting—The Early Decades' in Brian Farrell (ed.), *Communications and Community in Ireland* (Mercier Press, Dublin, 1984), p. 40 ff.

148. Patrick Lynch, 'The Social Revolution that never was', in T. Desmond Williams

(ed.), *The Irish Struggle 1916–1926* (Routledge and Kegan Paul, London, 1966), p. 53.

149. *Report of the Commission of Inquiry into the Civil Service 1932–1935* (Stationery Office, Dublin), VOL. 1, paragraphs 8 and 12, quoted in Ronan Fanning, *The Irish Department of Finance 1922–1958* (Institute of Public Administration, Dublin, 1978), p. 175; also quoted in Seán Dooney, *The Irish Civil Service* (Institute of Public Administration, Dublin, 1976), p. 1.

150. Frederick W. Powell, *The Politics of Irish Social Policy 1600–1990* (Edwin Mellen Press, New York, 1992), p. 186.

151. Manning and McDowell, *History of the ESB*, p. 17.

152. Kieran A. Kennedy, Thomas Giblin and Deirdre McHugh, *The Economic Development of Ireland in the Twentieth Century* (Routledge, London, 1988), pp. 38–39.

153. ibid., p. 39.

154. Ronan Fanning, *The Irish Department of Finance*, p. 110, quoting James Meenan, *The Irish Economy since 1922* (Liverpool University Press, Liverpool, 1970), p. 129.

155. ibid., p. 111.

156. This was in response to a criticism of the Coiste Gnótha of Cumann na nGaedheal. Its secretary, Séamus Dolan, had written to Blythe pointing out the volume of criticism that had been received over the old age pensions' decisions. Ernest Blythe Papers, P24/453, Archives Department, UCD; quoted in Micheál Martin, 'The Formation and Evolution of the Irish Party Political System, with particular emphasis on the Cork City Borough Constituency, 1918–1932', MA thesis, UCC, 1988, p. 139 ff.

157. A memorandum from the Attorney General's office, 17 December 1924, was sent to the President's office 'regarding the legal powers of the Civil Service Commission to exclude women from Civil Service examinations.' The matter had arisen when the minister for finance had written a memorandum on the admission of women to the open competitive examination for junior executive posts. S. Ua Broin told the establishment officer, Boland, that he was of the opinion that the Civil Service Commissioners had no power to exclude women from the examination of junior executive; s4195, Department of the Taoiseach, National Archives, Dublin.

158. Clare Eager, 'Splitting Images—Women and the Irish Civil Service', in *Seirbhís Phoiblí*, VOL. 12, NO. 1 (April 1991), pp. 15–23.

159. T.J. O'Connell, *100 Years of Progress: The Story of the Irish National Teachers' Organisation 1868–1968* (INTO, Dublin, 1969), p. 280 ff.

160. R.M. Fox, *Louie Bennett: Her Life and Times* (Talbot Press, Dublin, n.d.) and

Anon., *Ten Dublin Women* (Women's Commemoration and Celebration Committee, Dublin, 1991).

161. Dermot Keogh, *The Rise of the Irish Working Class: The Dublin Trade Union Movement and Labour Leadership 1890–1914* (Appletree Press, Belfast, 1982), p. 87 ff.

162. William O'Brien, *Forth the Banners Go* (Three Candles Press, Dublin, 1969).

163. See Charles McCarthy, *Trade Unions in Ireland 1894–1960* (Institute of Public Administration, Dublin, 1977), p. 54.

164. The background to this labour civil war can be found in the William O'Brien papers and in the Tom Johnson papers, National Library, Dublin. See also Emmet Larkin, *James Larkin: Irish Labour Leader 1876–1947* (Mentor, London, 1968); Anon., *Fifty Years of Liberty Hall* (Three Candles, Dublin, 1959); Anon., *The Attempt to Smash the Irish Transport and General Workers' Union* (ITGWU, Dublin, 1924) and J. Dunsmore Clarkson, *Labour and Nationalism in Ireland* (Columbia University Press, New York, 1925). John Coolahan, *Irish Education: Its History and Structure* (Institute of Public Administration, Dublin, 1981), pp. 165–66.

165. Liam De Róiste Diaries, Book 52, 18 November 1924; quoted in Micheál Martin, 'The Formation and Evolution of the Irish Party Political System, with particular emphasis on the Cork City Borough Constituency, 1918–1932', MA thesis, UCC, p. 145.

166. Martin, 'Irish Party Political System', p. 144; Martin argues that Cumann na nGaedheal lacked even a basic local party structure in the Cork city area.

167. *The Story of Fianna Fáil—First Phase* (Fianna Fáil publication, Dublin, 1960), p. 9.

168. *An Phoblacht*, 6 June 1927.

169. ibid., 5 February 1925.

170. Interview Seán MacBride, March 1977.

171. Hagan memorandum, 31 May 1925 (Hagan papers).

172. Longford and O'Neill, *Éamon de Valera*, p. 243.

173. Moynihan (ed.), *Speeches and Statements by Éamon de Valera*, pp. 126–30.

174. Sinéad de Valera to Hagan, 25 April 1926 (Hagan papers).

175. *The Story of Fianna Fáil*, p. 11.

176. Fianna Fáil handbill (Hagan papers) circa 1926.

177. Seán Lemass to Dermot Keogh, 21 April 1970.

178. *Irish Independent*, 4 June 1927.

179. *Leinster Leader* and *The Western People*, 4 June 1927.

180. I am grateful to Dr Mary Harris for this reference.

181. *Nation*, 18 June 1927.

182. *Leader*, 9 July 1927.

183. Gerry Boland said that many of the signatures were taken directly from names in the telephone book. Interview with author.

184. Gearóid Ó Súilleabháin, who had resigned from the army following the army mutiny, successfully contested the by-election caused by the assassination of Kevin O'Higgins, on behalf of Cumann na nGaedheal. Interview with his son, Father Gearóid Ó Súilleabháin.

185. *Dáil Debates*, 12 July 1927, VOL. XX, col. 757.

186. Moynihan (ed.), *Speeches and Statements by Éamon de Valera*, p. 149.

187. Tom Johnson papers, MS 15706, National Library, Dublin; I used this memorandum for the first time in 1970 when I submitted a minor thesis on Fianna Fáil and the two 1927 elections. See Department of History, UCD.

188. Terence de Vere White, *Kevin O'Higgins*, p. 227, puts forward the view that Cosgrave sought to force the anti-Treatyites into the Dáil. That view was shared by the contemporary sources. See *Round Table*, NO. 69 (1927), p. 140.

189. Two members of Fianna Fáil, Dan Breen and Paddy Belton, had both gone into the Dáil earlier in the year.

190. Tim Pat Coogan, *Ireland since the Rising*, p. 65.

191. Tim Pat Coogan told me in a letter, 10 April 1970, that the late Ned Lawlor of the *Irish Independent* had been told by Robert Smyllie of *The Irish Times* that he had been one of the drinking companions of the unfortunate Jinks. Smyllie had been raised in Sligo.

192. Countess Markievicz had died in Dublin on 15 July in a public ward of Sir Patrick Duns Hospital. There was also a second by-election pending.

193. James Anthony Gaughan, *Thomas Johnson*, p. 321 ff.

194. Mansergh, *The Unresolved Question*, p. 191.

195. David W. Harkness, *The Restless Dominion: The Irish Free State and the British Commonwealth of Nations 1921–1931* (Macmillan, London, 1969), p. 57; Michael MacWhite was named as Irish representative.

196. Dermot Keogh, 'Profile of Joseph Walshe, Secretary, Department of Foreign Affairs, 1922–46', *Irish Studies in International Affairs*, VOL. 3, NO. 2 (Autumn 1990), pp. 59–80.

197. Harkness, *The Restless Dominion*, pp. 81–134.

198. ibid., pp. 65–66.

199. Conor Cruise O'Brien, 'Ireland in International Affairs', in Owen Dudley Edwards (ed.), *Conor Cruise O'Brien Introduces Ireland* (André Deutsch, London, 1969), pp. 107–10.

200. Born in Coleraine, Co. Derry on 12 April 1889, he was the son of a relatively prosperous businessman who had been MP for South Fermanagh from 1892 to

1895. His father had taken the anti-Parnell side in the 1890s. Educated at Clongowes Wood College and UCD, he was called to the bar and lectured in law at his *alma mater* while playing a role in Sinn Féin politics. See David Harkness, 'Patrick McGilligan: Man of Commonwealth' in *The Journal of Imperial and Commonwealth History* VOL. VIII, NO. 1 (October 1979), pp. 117–35 and see also Harkness, *The Restless Dominion*, p. 135 ff.

201.Mansergh, *The Unresolved Question*, p. 271.

202.Department of the Taoiseach, s2011, National Archives, Dublin and see also Keogh, *Ireland and Europe 1919–1989* (Hibernian University Press, Cork and Dublin, 1989), Chapter 1.

203.Dermot Keogh, *Ireland and Europe 1919–1989*, pp. 29–33.

204.Harkness, *The Restless Dominion*, pp. 140–41; see also Desmond FitzGerald papers. This collection is now housed in the Archives Department, UCD.

205.Harkness, *The Restless Dominion*, p. 141.

206.See copy of letter from McGilligan to the Secretary of State for Dominion Affairs, 17 July 1930, s6051, Department of the Taoiseach, National Archives, Dublin.

207.Mansergh, *The Unresolved Question*, p. 274.

208.Quoted in Mansergh, *The Unresolved Question*, p. 274.

209.Department of Justice, Summary of Events from January 1931 to March 1932, p. 1, s9472, Department of the Taoiseach, National Archives, Dublin.

210. Summary of Events 1931–1932, p. 2.

211. ibid., p. 1.

212. ibid., p. 2.

213. ibid., p. 3.

214. O'Duffy memorandum, s5864B, Department of the Taoiseach, National Archives, Dublin; quoted in Keogh, 'De Valera, the Catholic Church and the "Red Scare", 1931–1932', in J.P. O'Carroll and John A. Murphy (eds), *De Valera and his Times* (Cork University Press, Cork, 1983), p. 136.

215. Summary of Events 1931–1932, p. 8.

216. ibid., pp. 8–9.

217. ibid., p. 3.

218. Keogh, 'De Valera, the Catholic Church and the "Red Scare" 1931–1932,' p. 138.

219. ibid., p. 141 ff.

220.Whyte, *Church and State 1923–1979*, pp. 37–43.

221. *Catholic Bulletin*, VOL. 21, NO. 1 (1931), p. 10.

222. *Catholic Bulletin*, VOL. 21, NO. 2 (1931), p. 143.

223. Keogh, *The Vatican, the Bishops and Irish Politics 1919–1939* (Cambridge University Press, Cambridge, 1986), p. 175.

224.ibid., p. 177.

225.ibid., pp. 167–68.

226.Fanning, *The Irish Department of Finance 1922–1958*, pp. 210–15; *The Cork Examiner*, 6–11 November 1931.

227.See *The Irish Press*, 27 January to 7 February 1932.

228.Summary of Events 1931–1932, p. 3.

229.See Michael O'Toole, *More Kicks than Pence: A Life in Irish Journalism* (Poolbeg Press, Dublin, 1992), pp. 56–72.

230.Keogh, *The Vatican, the Bishops and Irish Politics 1919–1939*, p. 182, and interviews with T. Desmond Williams, March 1977.

231. *Irish Independent*, 30 January 1932.

232. This was published by Cumann na nGaedheal, 5 Parnell Street, Dublin, 1932; de Valera had a copy, but it is not clear whether he had it during the actual election campaign. It is probable that he did. See pp. 118–119 and 158.

233. Keogh, 'De Valera, the Catholic Church and the "Red Scare" in J.P. O'Carroll and John A. Murphy (eds), *De Valera and his Times* (Cork University Press, Cork, 1983), pp. 149–50.

234. *The Irish Press*, 5 February 1932.

235. *The Irish Press*, 8 February 1932.

236.Cosgrave challenged de Valera over his role in the Treaty negotiations. He went over old ground, but did not allow himself to be sidetracked from the economic issues. *The Irish Press*, 8 February 1932.

237. *The Irish Press*, 2 January 1932.

238. *The Irish Press*, 17 February 1932.

239.Joseph Lee, *Ireland 1912–1985: Politics and Society* (Cambridge, Cambridge University Press, 1989), p. 170.

240.Gaughan, *Tom Johnson*, p. 339.

241.Thomas J. O'Connell had lost his seat.

242.Gaughan, *Tom Johnson*, pp. 341–42.

243.Summary of Events 1931–1932, p. 3.

244.*The Irish Press*, 26 February 1932.

245.*The Irish Press*, 27 February 1932.

246. ibid.

247.*Catholic Bulletin*, VOL. XXII, NO. 4 (April 1932) pp. 255–56.

248.*Round Table*, NO. 86 (March 1932), p. 367.

249.T. Desmond Williams's profile of William T. Cosgrave, *The Irish Times*, 1956; cutting supplied to me by the author.

Chapter 2: De Valera and Fianna Fáil in Power, 1932–1939 (pp. 65–109)

1. This was related to me by the late John Moher, Fianna Fáil TD for North Cork.

2. *The Irish Press*, 20 February 1932.

3. Quoted by David Harkness in 'The Unionist Reactions: Bitterness and Hostility', in *The Irish Times* supplement '50 years of Fianna Fáil', 26 May 1976.

4. Quoted in *Round Table*, NO. 89 (December 1932), p. 126.

5. Frank Aiken told me that he was aware of the plotting, particularly among reserve officers, against Fianna Fáil. *The Irish Press* claimed on 26 February that two Cumann na nGaedheal ministers were rumoured to have been plotting against de Valera coming to power. Cosgrave described such rumours as 'grotesquely untrue' and explicable only 'by a disordered imagination or a guilty political conscience'. *Round Table*, NO. 87 (June 1932).

6. Michael Mills's profile of Seán Lemass, 'Fighting the World Slump of the Thirties: Rise and Decline of the Blueshirts,' *The Irish Press*, 24 January 1969.

7. *Round Table*, NO. 87 (1932), pp. 501–02.

8. MacEntee to de Valera, 18 March 1932, MacEntee papers, P67/94, Archives Department, UCD. All the above is based on this document.

9. Based on information given to me by the late Professor T. Desmond Williams. H.P. Boland, head of establishments, Department of Finance, had been one of the officers who, together with J.J. McElligott of Finance, had called a meeting of all the senior civil servants and counselled that the transfer of power should take place without incident. In other words, the civil service was to adopt a professional approach to the change of government and regard it as a normal part of the democratic process. Many civil servants, who had spent ten years working with Cumann na nGaedheal ministers, may not have felt very enthusiastic about working with men who had been the leaders of the 'irregulars' during the civil war.

10. Dermot Keogh, *Ireland and Europe 1919–1989* (Hibernian University Press, Cork and Dublin, 1989), p. 36.

11. Charles Alphand to the Quai d'Orsay, 5 April 1932, French consular reports, Quai d'Orsay; copy of original document kindly supplied by my postgraduate student, Robert Patterson. I am grateful to my friend Professor Matthew McNamara, for his translation from the French.

12. Alphand to the Quai d'Orsay, Irish Consular files, Quai d'Orsay, 5 March 1932.

13. Alphand to the Quai d'Orsay, Irish Consular files, Quai d'Orsay 4 March 1932.

14. Paul Canning, *British Policy towards Ireland 1921–1944* (Clarendon Press, Oxford, 1985), p. 125.

15. Nicholas Mansergh, *The Unresolved Question: The Anglo-Irish Settlement and its Undoing 1912–1972* (Yale University Press, New Haven and London, 1991), p. 282.

16. Deirdre McMahon, *Republicans and Imperialists: Anglo-Irish Relations in the 1930s* (Yale University Press, New Haven and London, 1984), pp. 58–59.

17. *Round Table*, NO. 90 (March 1933), p. 291.

18. The most comprehensive accounts of the governor general's difficulties can be found in Brendan Sexton, *Ireland and the Crown 1922–1936: The Governor Generalship of the Irish Free State* (Irish Academic Press, Dublin, 1989).

19. Perhaps the memoirs of Todd Andrews are the best source of the mildly anti-clerical side of Fianna Fáil. See *Man of No Property: An Autobiography*, VOL. II (Mercier Press, Dublin, 1982), pp. 235–36 and the earlier volume, *Dublin Made Me*; Andrews records that one of de Valera's close associates was a follower of Madame Blavatsky. See *Man of No Property*, p. 236. A number of older Fianna Fáil members, Gerry Boland and Tommy Mullins in particular, did not disguise in interviews their impatience with the Catholic hierarchy and senior clergy.

20. Ronan Fanning, *Independent Ireland* (Helicon, Dublin, 1983), p. 129.

21. C.S. Andrews, *Man of No Property: An Autobiography*, VOL. II (Mercier Press, Dublin, 1982), p. 236.

22. *Irish Independent*, 14 April 1931.

23. *The Irish Press*, 20 June 1932; another editorial, 23 June, was actually entitled 'Resurrection'.

24. In a book by Father Augustine, O.F.M. cap., *Ireland's Loyalty to the Mass* (Sands, London, 1933), there is a good illustration of this symbiosis of religion and politics. Referring to the spirit of those who 'clustered round the Mass-rock', he argued that it still existed: 'It walks abroad in this land of ours in which religion and national ideals have ever been blended, in which Faith and Fatherland, and not Fatherland and Faith, was always, is still, and, please God, ever will be the glorious rallying cry', pp. 218–19.

25. This committee was set up by the Minister for Justice, James Fitzgerald-Kenney, on 17 June 1930 under the chairmanship of William Corrigan K.C. The secretary was Christopher Smith of the Department of Justice. The members of the committee were: John J. Hannon S.J., Dean H.B. Kennedy, Francis J. Morrin, James Power and V. O'Carroll. See Department of the Taoiseach, S5998, National Archives, Dublin.

26. Evidence was taken from a wide range of people and organisations. Representatives of trade unions, the Catholic Church, the Legion of Mary Magdalen Asylums, Saor an Leanbh, the gardaí and the courts gave testimony. See report, pp. 43–44.

27. Corrigan report, pp. 9–10; it is not clear whether the offensive reference to unmarried mothers was first contained in the Local Government report, p. 113.

28. Corrigan report, pp. 12–13.
29. S.A. Roche memorandum to de Valera, 13 November 1933, s5998, Department of the Taoiseach, National Archives, Dublin.
30. Dermot Keogh, *The Vatican, the Bishops and Irish Politics 1919–1939* (Cambridge University Press, Cambridge, 1986), pp. 206–07.
31. John Whyte, *Church and State in Modern Ireland 1923–1979* (Gill & Macmillan, Dublin, 1984), p. 50.
32. Flann O'Brien, 'The Dance Hall', *The Bell*, VOL. 1, NO. 5 (February 1941), p. 52.
33. Brian Friel, *Dancing at Lughnasa* (Faber and Faber, London, 1990), pp. 38–42.
34. Seán O'Faoláin, editorial/review of M.J. MacManus, *Éamon de Valera* (Talbot Press, Dublin, 1945) in *The Bell*, VOL. 10, NO. 1 (April 1945), pp. 1–18; see also Seán O'Faoláin, *The Life Story of Éamon de Valera* (Talbot Press, Dublin and Cork, 1933) and *De Valera: A New Biography* (Penguin, London, 1939).
35. Mary Daly, 'An Irish-Ireland for Business?', *Irish Historical Studies*, VOL. XXIV (November 1984), p. 255.
36. ibid., p. 272.
37. James Anthony Gaughan, *Thomas Johnson: 1872–1963: First Leader of the Labour Party in Dáil Éireann* (Kingdom Books, Dublin, 1980), p. 342.
38. See McMahon, *Republicans and Imperialists*, chapter 5.
39. *Round Table*, NO. 89 (December 1932), p. 141.
40. *Round Table*, NO. 90 (March 1933), p. 267.
41. McMahon, *Republicans and Imperialists*, pp. 106–07.
42. He made very few changes in his cabinet. Geoghegan retired and P.J. Ruttledge took over as Minister for Justice. The Department of Lands and Fisheries went to J. Connolly. Frank Aiken and Gerry Boland succeeded each other in that position in 1936.
43. James Bowyer Bell, *The Secret Army: History of the Irish Republican Army 1916–79* (Academy Press, Dublin, 1979), p. 132.
44. Tim Pat Coogan, *The IRA* (Pall Mall Press, London, 1980), p. 77.
45. Bowyer Bell, *The Secret Army*, p. 139.
46. General Army Convention, minute book, 17 March 1934, MacEntee papers, P67/525, Archives Department, UCD; a letter in this book, addressed to Seán Russell, may indicate that the minutes were seized when he was arrested in 1936.
47. *Republican Congress*, 12 January 1935.
48. Maurice Manning, *The Blueshirts* (Gill & Macmillan, Dublin, 1970), p. 77 ff.
49. Report of Signor Nicola Pascazio, who was on mission to Ireland in February and March 1934, entitled *La Rivoluzione d'Irlanda* (Rome, 1934); see Ministro della Cultura Popolare, Busta 364, folio 142, Archivio Centrale dello Stato, L'Eur, Roma.

50. Quoted in confidential notes on events from 1 January 1931 to 31 December 1940; prepared by the Department of Justice. The copy consulted had the name of S.A. Roche, secretary of the Department of Justice, written on it. MacEntee papers, P67/534, Archives Department, UCD.

51. Interview with Frank Aiken, 1977.

52. Michael Mills, 'Seán Lemass looks back', *The Irish Press*, 24 January 1969.

53. Dillon to MacDermot, 25 September 1934, Frank McDermot papers, MS 1065/2/4, National Archives, Dublin. Dillon believed that what O'Duffy had actually said was much worse.

54. Manning, *Blueshirts* p. 121.

55. ibid., p. 125.

56. Department of Justice notes on events from 1 January 1931 to 31 December 1940, p. 103, MacEntee papers, P67/534, Archives Department, UCD.

57. MacDermot to O'Duffy, 9 July 1934, MacDermot papers, MS 1065/3/1, National Archives, Dublin.

58. The government had introduced a Bill in 1933 to establish adult suffrage to replace a poll limited to rated occupier, but it was rejected by the Senate.

59. Dillon to MacDermot, 25 September 1934, MacDermot papers, MS 1065/2/4, National Archives, Dublin.

60. *Round Table*, NO. 97 (December 1934), pp. 158–59.

61. Dillon to MacDermot, 25 September 1934, MacDermot papers, MS 1065/2/4, National Archives, Dublin.

62. Tierney to MacDermot, 4 October 1934, MacDermot papers, MS 1065/4/5, National Archives, Dublin.

63. Tierney to MacDermot, 27 September 1934, MacDermot papers, MS 1065/4/5, National Archives, Dublin.

64. Anon (ed.), *Peace and War: Speeches by Mr de Valera on International Affairs* (M.H. Gill, Dublin, 1944), p. 46.

65. ibid., p. 56.

66. *Dáil Debates*, VOL. LIX, col. 531, 6 November 1935.

67. *Dáil Debates*, VOL. LIX, col. 522, 6 November 1935.

68. *Round Table*, no. 101 (December 1935), pp. 132–33.

69. *Irish Independent*, 4 October 1935.

70. *The Irish Times*, 5 October 1935.

71. See *The Irish Press* and *The Irish Times*, 7 and 8 October 1935.

72. Frank MacDermot papers, MS 1065/14/5, National Archives, Dublin.

73. *Round Table*, NO. 101 (December 1935), p. 135.

74. Joseph Lee, *Ireland 1912–1985: Politics and Society* (Cambridge University Press, Cambridge, 1989), p. 187.

75. Kieran A. Kennedy, Thomas Giblin and Deirdre McHugh, *The Economic Development of Ireland in the Twentieth Century* (Routledge, London, 1988), pp. 47–48.
76. Paul Canning, *British Policy towards Ireland 1921–1944* (Clarendon Press, Oxford, 1985), p. 159.
77. Kennedy et al., *The Economic Development of Ireland*, p. 46.
78. Lee, *Ireland 1912–1985*, p. 192.
79. Kennedy et al., *The Economic Development of Ireland*, p. 44.
80. *The Irish Press*, 29 April 1937.
81. *The Irish Press*, 20 January 1937.
82. *The Irish Press*, 27 January 1937: speech by Seán T. O'Kelly reviewing progress of government.
83. Lee, *Ireland 1912–1985*, p. 193.
84. *The Irish Press*, 29 January 1934.
85. Séamas Ó Buachalla, *Education Policy in Twentieth-Century Ireland* (Wolfhound Press, Dublin, 1988), p. 65.
86 Séamus Murphy, *Stone Mad* (Routledge and Kegan Paul, London, 1982), p. 209.
87. John Coolahan, *Irish Education: Its History and Structure* (Institute of Public Administration, Dublin, 1981), p. 42.
88. Patrick Kavanagh, *The Green Fool* (Martin, Brian and O'Keeffe, London, 1971), pp. 144–58.
89. Anne O'Dowd, *Spalpeens and Tattie Hokers: History and Folklore of the Irish Migratory Agricultural Worker in Ireland and Britain* (Irish Academic Press, Dublin, 1981), p. 198.
90. *The Irish Press*, 17 September 1937.
91. *The Irish Press*, 18 September 1937.
92. Diarmuid Breathnach, *Almanag Éireannach* (Oifig an tSoláthair, Baile Átha Cliath, 1981), p. 94.
93. *The Irish Press*, 21 September 1937.
94. J.P. Whelehan, 'Ten Coffins,' *The Capuchin Annual*, 9 (1938), pp. 201–03.
95. O'Dowd, *Spalpeens and Tattie Hokers*, p. 198.
96. For background to the development of radio in Ireland, see Brian Farrell (ed.), *Communications and Community in Ireland* (Mercier Press, Dublin, 1984).
97. *Irish Independent*, 22 February 1936.
98. See *Irish Christian Front* (pamphlet, Dublin, 1936), National Library of Ireland collection. See also *Irish Independent* for the last week in August 1936.
99. *Round Table*, NO. 107 (June 1937), p. 596 and NO. 105 (December 1936), p. 163.

100. Eoin O'Duffy, *Crusade in Spain* (Browne & Nolan, Dublin, 1938), p.11 ff.

101. *Irish Independent*, 17 October 1936.

102. Keogh, *Ireland and Europe 1919–1989*, p. 77 ff.

103. On the origins and development of the liberal journal, *Ireland Today*, see Brian P. Kennedy, 'Ireland To-day: A Brave Irish Periodical', *Linen Hall Review*, VOL. 5, NO. 4, pp. 18–19. The right wing of Fianna Fáil party, as personified by Seán MacEntee and Seán T. O'Kelly, favoured recognition of Franco. The less powerful left wing of Fianna Fáil, represented by Tommy Mullins, sought to give active support to the government of the Spanish republic. A stormy parliamentary party meeting, on 19 November 1936, saw the minute book record that it was decided 'after a lengthy discussion' that 'no action need be taken in this matter [recognition of the Irish Christian Front] by the Fianna Fáil Party.' Fianna Fáil parliamentary party minutes book, 19 November 1936, Fianna Fáil Headquarters, Upper Mount Street, Dublin.

104. Keogh, *Ireland and Europe 1919–1989*, p. 67.

105. ibid., p. 83 ff; see also *Dáil Debates*, VOL. 64, 27 November 1936 and VOL. 65, 18 February 1937.

106. ibid., pp. 67–68.

107. Journal of Alexander J. McCabe [uncatalogued], National Library of Ireland.

108. See *Irish Independent* and *The Irish Press*, 22 June 1937.

109. For background to the history of those who fought on the republican side in Spain, see Michael O'Riordan, *The Connolly Column: The Story of the Irishmen who fought for the Spanish Republic 1936–1939* (New Books, Dublin, 1979) and Seán Cronin, *Frank Ryan: The Search for the Republic* (Repsol Press, Dublin, 1980).

110. See Dermot Keogh, 'The Irish Constitutional Revolution: An Analysis of the Making of the Constitution' in Frank Litton (ed.), *The Constitution of Ireland 1937–1987, Administration* (special issue), VOL. 35, NO. 4 (1988), p. 11.

111. Keogh, 'The Irish Constitutional Revolution', p. 32 ff. The president of Blackrock College, John Charles McQuaid, gave de Valera considerable help with the drafting of the constitution.

112. From de Valera's account of his contact with the churches (de Valera papers), Gort Mhuire, Killiney, Co. Dublin.

113. *The Irish Press*, 16 June 1937.

114. *The Irish Press*, 1 July 1937.

115. *The Irish Press*, 21 June 1937.

116. *The Irish Press*, 30 June 1937.

117. *The Irish Press*, 8 July 1937; following the acceptance of the new constitution, the title President of the Executive Council was changed to Taoiseach (Prime

Minister) and the Executive Council was called the cabinet. The office of President was created, replacing that of governor general.

118. *Report of the Commission on the Second House of the Oireachtas*, 1 October 1936; quoted in Thomas Garvin, *The Irish Senate* (Institute of Public Administration, Dublin, 1969), p. 15.

119. MacEntee papers, P67/186, Archives Department, UCD.

120. Author's interview with Seán MacEntee, March 1977.

121. Mansergh, *The Unresolved Question*, p. 302 and Canning, *British Policy towards Ireland*, p. 176.

122. Mansergh, *The Unresolved Question*, pp. 303–04.

123. Canning, *British Policy towards Ireland*, pp. 218–19.

124. *The Irish Press*, 1 June 1938.

125. *The Irish Press*, 8 June 1938.

126. *The Irish Press*, 10 June 1938.

127. *The Irish Press*, 8 June 1938.

128. Lemass to MacEntee, 7 May 1938, MacEntee papers, P67/360, Archives Department, UCD.

129. *The Irish Press*, 22 June 1938.

130. *The Irish Press*, 27 June 1938.

Chapter 3: In Time of War: Neutral Ireland, 1939–1945 (pp. 110–160)

1. *Evening Echo*, 4 September 1939.

2. Patrick Kavanagh, *Collected Poems* (MacGibbon and Kee, London, 1968), p. 136.

3. Walshe to John Hearne, Ottawa, 1 January 1941, quoted in Keogh, *Ireland and Europe 1919–1989*, p. 119.

4. John P. Duggan, *A History of the Irish Army* (Gill & Macmillan, Dublin, 1991), p. 180.

5. Comdt Peter Young, 'The Way We Were', *An Cosantóir*, VOL. 49, NO. 9 (September 1989), pp. 35–36.

6. Duggan, *Irish Army*, p. 183.

7. Lt Cdr Daire Brunicardi, 'The Marine Service', *An Cosantóir*, VOL. 49, NO. 9 (September 1989), pp. 23–26.

8. Capt. T. KcKenna, 'Thank God We're Surrounded by Water', *An Cosantóir*, VOL. 33, NO. 4 (April 1973), p. 108.

9. For a detailed account, see A.P. (Tony) Kearns, 'The Air Corps 1939–1945', *An Cosantóir*, VOL. 49, NO. 9 (September 1989), pp. 13–19.

10. Maurice Moynihan (ed.), *Speeches and Statements by Éamon de Valera 1917–1973* (Gill & Macmillan, Dublin, 1980), pp. 416–17.

11. Brian Farrell, *Chairman or Chief: The Role of Taoiseach in Irish Government*

(Gill & Macmillan, Dublin, 1971), p. 97.

12. This thesis has been persuasively argued by Trevor Salmon, *Unneutral Ireland: An Ambivalent and Unique Security Policy* (Clarendon Press, Oxford, 1989), pp. 120–54.

13. Tim Pat Coogan, *The IRA* (Pall Mall Press, London, 1980), pp. 139–40. The report on the raid went before cabinet on 23 February. It approved the dismissal of one captain, the placing of two colonels on half-pay for a year and their case was to be reviewed after that; a commandant and a second lieutenant were given the option to retire or face enforced retirement for misconduct or inefficiency, four senior officers were censured, paraded and admonished, while two corporals and a private faced court martial. Cabinet Minutes, 23 February 1940, G.C./147; see also S11646, Department of the Taoiseach, National Archives, Dublin. On 28 December 1941, the IRA successfully raided the military magazines at Inniscarra, Co. Cork, and got away with explosives, detonators and cable. Department of Justice, *Notes on IRA activities 1941–1947*, p. 32, MacEntee papers, P6/550, Archives Department, UCD.

14. Author's interview with Gerry Boland, 1970.

15. Enno Stephan, *Spies in Ireland* (Stackpole, Harrisburg, Pennsylvania, 1969), pp. 28–33.

16. See file on German broadcasts to Ireland, 205/108, Department of External Affairs, National Archives, Dublin.

17. See memorandum, 29 September 1954, Secretary's files, A34, Department of Foreign Affairs, National Archives, Dublin.

18. PENAPA, January 1941 (copy in military archives, Cathal Brugha Barracks, Dublin). The reference was kindly supplied to me by Dónal Ó Drisceoil.

19. Robert Fisk, *In Time of War: Ireland, Ulster and the Price of Neutrality 1939–45* (André Deutsch, London, 1983), p. 373.

20. There was also evidence of anti-semitism in at least one Gaelic League pamphlet published in 1942. It read: 'We cannot allow film-making to remain in the hands of the Jews, the external enemies of Christianity.' Conor Cruise O'Brien, Seán O'Faoláin special issue, *Cork Review*, 1991, p. 95.

21. Department of Justice, *Notes on IRA activities 1941–1947* (copy no. 4, issued to the Minister for Local Government), p. 37, Seán MacEntee papers, P67/550, Archives Department, UCD. The party put up three candidates in the 1943 election in Cork City (1,419 votes out of 39,232 valid votes); Dublin City N.W. (the party leader got 697 out of 46,752 votes); Louth (585 out of 39,649 votes) and Waterford (926 out of 39,649). Seven candidates were put forward by the party in the general election of 1944. Each failed to secure any substantial

portion of the quota and all lost their deposits. The party got 647 votes in Cork City, 795 in Dublin City and 607 in Dublin County.

22. Moynihan (ed.), *Speeches and Statements by Éamon de Valera*, pp. 435–36.

23. León Ó Broin, *Just Like Yesterday* (Gill & Macmillan, Dublin, no date), p. 136.

24. Malcolm MacDonald, *Titans and Others* (Collins, London, 1972), pp. 84–85; See also Keogh, *Ireland and Europe 1919–1989*, pp. 130–37 and Paul Canning, *British Policy towards Ireland 1921–1944* (Clarendon Press, Oxford, 1985), p. 278 ff.

25. Department of the Taoiseach, s14213, National Archives, Dublin.

26. Unmarked secretary's file, Department of External Affairs, quoted in Keogh, *Ireland and Europe 1919–1989*, p. 142.

27. Author's interview with Maurice Moynihan.

28. Keogh, *Ireland and Europe 1919–1989*, pp. 165–72.

29. See *Leader*, January, February, March and April 1953, and in a revised form in *The Irish Press*, June and July 1953.

30. Boland to Seán Nunan, 3 March 1954, s15469A, Department of the Taoiseach, National Archives, Dublin.

31. This report was written at the time a libel case was being prepared against Professor Williams. The Foreign Office was prepared to release the documents in question if requested by the court in Dublin to do so. In a conversation with Williams in 1948, Boland recalled what he said he had found in the German Foreign Office archives on Kerney. But the contents did not seem to accord with the four documents selected by the British Foreign Office as being relevant to the Williams case. The legal officer of the Foreign Office expressed the opinion that the papers on the file did not, in his view, justify the criticisms of Kerney which had been made by Williams. Boland was allowed to read the documents. He came to the same conclusion as the Foreign Office legal adviser. There remains the possibility that Williams saw other documents in the German Foreign Office.

32. Historians ought to be highly suspicious of basing judgments on *Abwehr* documents; Clissman and Veesenmayer had to demonstrate to their superiors that the visit to Madrid was not a total waste of time.

33. Veesenmayer report to his superiors, quoted in Boland to Nunan, 23 March 1954, s15469A, Department of the Taoiseach, National Archives, Dublin. Kerney returned to Dublin again in 1943 where he was seen by de Valera: 'The then secretary', wrote Boland, 'told me that the Taoiseach had spoken to Kerney very seriously indeed.' Kerney, who had reported before returning about the setting up of a neutral bloc of Catholic powers, was told to report to the Spanish government, the initiators of the idea, that Ireland was not interested.

But the real reason for bringing Kerney back, according to Boland, was to 'talk to him seriously about the need for extreme care and prudence in security matters, particularly in view of the prospect of a second front being opened.'

34. Keogh, *Ireland and Europe 1919–1989*, p. 136.

35. Maffey to Cranborne, 23 December 1940, Prem 3/128/09013, PRO, London.

36. Cranborne to War Cabinet, 3 December 1940, Prem. 3/128/09013, PRO, London.

37. Gray to Eleanor Roosevelt, 10 February 1941, Roosevelt papers, PSF (diplomatic), box 56, Franklin D. Roosevelt Library, Hyde Park, New York.

38. Gray to Roosevelt, 30 November 1940, Roosevelt Papers, PSF (diplomatic), box 56, Roosevelt Library, Hyde Park, New York; Gray also sent a copy of the memorandum to Sumner Welles. Dillon made an unauthorised speech on neutrality at the annual party conference at the end of 1940. Although the speech was greeted with applause, he was forced to leave the party.

39. I am grateful to Larry McDonald, Military Intelligence Section, National Archives, Washington for helping me to track down a number of oss reports relevant to Ireland. He also put me in contact with Mr Quigley.

40. Gray to Sumner Welles, 7 March 1941, RG 59, 841D.00/1306, National Archives, Washington.

41. Department of State memorandum, 18 March 1941, RG 59, 841D.24/57, National Archives, Washington.

42. Sumner Welles minutes, 19 March 1941, RG 59, 841D.24/57, National Archives, Washington.

43. State Department memorandum, 2 April 1941, RG 59, 841D.24/59 National Archives, Washington.

44. Interview with Frank Aiken, 1977.

45. For a detailed account of the visit, see Joseph L. Rosenberg, 'The 1941 Mission of Frank Aiken to the United States: An American Perspective', *Irish Historical Studies*, VOL. XXII, NO. 86 (September 1980), pp. 162–77.

46. Moynihan (ed.), *Speeches and Statements by Éamon de Valera*, p. 462.

47. ibid., p. 464.

48. There is a mistaken view that the United States was prepared to invade Ireland from the North in 1942. This was really part of a contingency arrangement to support the Irish army in its efforts to repel a German land invasion. This subject is discussed in Adrian Higgins, 'The day we almost invaded Ireland— Was there a secret World War II plan to send GIs into Neutral Ireland?', *The Washington Post*, 15 March 1992.

49. These figures have been compiled from the detailed lists prepared by G2; Secretary's files A26, Department of Foreign Affairs, National Archives, Dublin.

50. The legal officer in the Department of External Affairs, Michael Rynne, prepared a memorandum on this matter on 30 November 1942. It urged flexibility and creativity in interpreting international law; Secretary's files, A26, Department of External Affairs, National Archives, Dublin.

51. Walshe minutes, 10 May 1943, Secretary's files, A26, Department of External Affairs, National Archives, Dublin.

52. Memorandum to cabinet, September 1940, B42633 1, Military Archives, Dublin; I am grateful to Mervyn O'Driscoll for supplying me with references on the treatment of German refugees.

53. *Report of the Commission on Emigration and other Population Problems, 1948–1951* (Dublin, 1956), p. 128; the report makes the point that these figures are not that accurate because more than one card could be issued to a person, and there was no guarantee that a person to whom a card had been issued would have left the country.

54. The cited source 'Reminiscence of an Irish Diplomat: Frederick H. Boland, Ambassador to London, Permanent Representative at the United Nations and President of the General Assembly 1960', was compiled by Mella Boland (Crowley). It is based on a series of extended conversations with her father during the latter years of his life. The manuscript is at an early stage in the editing process. The page sequence has not been standardised; hence it has been impossible to cite individual pages. This document is referred to as 'Boland manuscript' throughout the text. I am grateful to Dr Boland's wife, Frances (Kelly) Boland, for the help that she has given me in the researching of this book. I also sorted a small but important collection of personal papers left by Dr Boland which are now housed in Trinity College, Dublin.

55. Department of Defence memorandum for government, 20 June 1945, Secretary's files, P81, Department of Foreign Affairs, National Archives, Dublin.

56. Moynihan (ed.), *Speeches and Statements by Éamon de Valera*, p. 458.

57. Joseph T. Carroll, *Ireland in the War Years* (David and Charles, Newton Abbot, 1975).

58. Note from Department of Finance, 4 September 1941 to ESB, Department of External Affairs, 416/1, National Archives, Dublin.

59. Department of Foreign Affairs, file 416/1, National Archives, Dublin.

60. Department of Foreign Affairs, file 221/145A, National Archives, Dublin.

61. Boland manuscript.

62. See Taoiseach's Department, S1 1586A, quoted in Fisk, *In Time of War*, pp. 484–85.

63. ibid.

64. Boland manuscript.

65. J.H. Whyte, *Church and State in Modern Ireland 1923–1979*, 2nd edition (Gill & Macmillan, Dublin, 1984), pp. 93–94.

66. Boland manuscript.

67. I am grateful to my postgraduate student Dónal Ó Drisceoil, who has completed a doctoral thesis on Irish censorship during World War II, for the help given in the preparation of this section; see his *Censorship in Ireland, 1939–45: Neutrality, Politics and Society* (CUP, Cork, 1996).

68. Boland manuscript.

69. Bryan sent Walshe a letter on 23 August 1943, together with a transcript of a conversation concerning the number of airmen who had come down in Ireland. The figure of 73 was given in a return call.

70. MacRory to Gray (copy), 20 October 1941, PSF (dip), box 56, Franklin D. Roosevelt Library, Hyde Park, New York.

71. He was responsible for the winding up of the initiative by the founder of the Legion of Mary, Frank Duff, of the Pillar of Cloud society. This was an attempt to establish a Christian-Jewish dialogue in Dublin at a time when the Jewish community was facing up to the fact of the systematic genocide of the Jews of Europe. See León Ó Broin, *Just Like Yesterday* (Gill & Macmillan, Dublin, n.d.), pp. 147–48.

72. Department of Justice memorandum, 24 September 1945, S11007A, National Archives, Dublin.

73. S.A. Roche to Moynihan, 25 September 1946, S11007/1B, Department of the Taoiseach, National Archives, Dublin.

74. This letter was drafted by Joseph Walshe of the Department of External Affairs; Briscoe may have been present to help with the drafting.

75. Bowen to Foreign Office, 9 November 1940, British Cabinet Papers, Prem. 4/53/6, PRO, London.

76. *Dáil Debates*, VOL. 91, cols 569–72, 9 July 1943; quoted in Fisk, *In Time of War*, p. 372 and Carroll, *Ireland in the War Years*, p. 137.

77. J. Smyth, leas-runaidhe, Longford County Council, to the secretary to the government, 6 August 1943, Department of the Taoiseach, S13310A, National Archives, Dublin.

78. This letter, dated 18 June 1943, was addressed Rathgar, Dublin. S13320A, Department of the Taoiseach, National Archives, Dublin.

79. Keogh, *Ireland and Europe 1919–1989*, pp. 177–78.

80. Finbarr O'Shea, 'Government and Trade Unions in Ireland 1939–1946: The Formation of Labour Legislation', MA thesis, UCC, 1988, p. 40; see his essay in Dermot Keogh and Mervyn O'Driscoll, *Ireland in World War Two: Diplomacy*

and Survival (Mercier Press, Cork, 2004).

81. ibid., pp. 40–42.

82. ibid., p. 43; see also cabinet minutes G.C. 2/154, 8 March 1940; and see S11616, Department of the Taoiseach, National Archives, Dublin.

83. ibid., p. 52.

84. ibid., pp. 208–11.

85. Fergus A. D'Arcy and Ken Hannigan (eds), *Workers in Union: Documents and Commentaries on the History of Labour* (National Archives, Dublin, 1988), p. 201.

86. O'Shea, 'Government and Trade Unions', p. 138.

87. For details, see Cabinet minutes, G.2/351, SPO S11725B. The Department of Finance memorandum to government, 26 February 1942, is on the same file. O'Shea, 'Government and Trade Unions', p. 247.

88. Maurice Moynihan (ed.), *Speeches and Statements by Éamon de Valera 1917–1973* (Gill & Macmillan, Dublin, 1980), p. 466.

89. Máirtín Ó Direáin, *Dánta 1939–1979* (An Clochomar, Baile Átha Cliath, 1980). I am grateful to Dr Mary Harris for giving me this reference and for translating the poem.

90. Moynihan (ed.), *Speeches and Statements by Éamon de Valera*, p. 466; Mr Moynihan told me in an interview that de Valera had not said 'comely' but 'happy' maidens. De Valera had read through the text just before the broadcast and made the change, which can be heard on the broadcast.

91. Thomas McCarthy, *Seven Winters in Paris* (Anvil Press, London, 1989), p. 41.

92. Bernard Share, *The Emergency: Neutral Ireland 1939–45* (Gill & Macmillan, Dublin, 1978), p. 77.

93. An editorial in *The Irish Press*, on 24 May 1943, attacked Patrick McGilligan for a speech that he had made at Carlow lamenting the hardship caused by the scarcity of potatoes in Dublin. The criticism was made that when McGilligan was in government in 1929 he was not 'wont to be tender-hearted'.

94. See *The Irish Press* for the first two weeks in June 1943 when the coalition idea was attacked vigorously. See also de Valera's speech under the headline 'Coalition project is dead' which ran beside a front-page cartoon showing Lemass administering medicine to one of the Fine Gael TDs, *The Irish Press*, 12 June 1943.

95. *The Irish Press*, 31 January 1943.

96. *The Irish Press*, 5 June 1943. MacEntee was particularly vigorous in another 'anti-Labour' speech where he attacked the veteran Jim Larkin and a supine Labour leadership that had allowed itself to be influenced by him. That was more than many of the other ministers could take.

97. Lemass to MacEntee, 10 June 1943, MacEntee papers, P67/363, Archives Department, UCD.

98. MacEntee to Lemass, 10 June 1943, MacEntee papers, P67/363, Archives Department, UCD.

99. *The Irish Press*, 10 June 1943; the editorial of that day was entitled sarcastically 'Humpty Dumpty'.

100. MacEntee to de Valera, 28 June 1943, MacEntee papers, P67/366, Archives Department, UCD.

101. See O'Shea, 'Government and Trade Unions' pp. 124–46. See also, as cited in Lee, *Ireland 1912–1985*, p. 241, Charles McCarthy, *The Decade of Upheaval*, p. 259; see also Arthur Mitchell, 'William O'Brien, 1881–1968 and the Irish Labour Movement', *Studies*, VOL. 60, NO. 239 (Winter 1971), pp. 311–31.

102. *The Irish Press*, 11 May 1944.

103. Breandán Ó hEithir, *The Begrudger's Guide to Irish Politics* (Poolbeg Press, Dublin, 1986), p. 108.

104. *The Irish Press*, 11 and 12 May 1944.

105. *The Irish Press*, 15 May 1944.

106. *The Irish Press*, 20 May 1944.

107. *The Irish Press*, 2 June 1944.

108. *The Irish Press*, 10 June 1944.

109. Terence Brown, *Ireland: A Social and Cultural History 1922–1979* (Fontana, London, 1981), p. 151; see also new edition covering to 2002 (Harper Perennial, London, 2004).

110. Quoted in Frank O'Connor's introduction to the 1964 edition of *The Tailor and Ansty* (Mercier Press, Cork and Dublin, 1990), p. 5; this theme was taken up more systematically in William Reich, *The Mass Psychology of Fascism* (Penguin, London, 1975).

111. O'Connor, introduction to *The Tailor and Ansty*, p. 168.

112. See *Seanad Debates*, VOL. 27, NOS 1, 2 and 3. The debates took place at the end of November and on 2, 3, 9 and 10 December 1942.

113. See special issue on Seán O'Faoláin of *The Cork Review*, 1991 for a comprehensive background to his life and times.

114. Translation: 'That's the sort of stuff that Máire is praising. *Amour courtois* says one person; idealised adultery says another. But the doctor of divinity Aodh Mac Aingil understood the matter better; "Dirty poems that lead to lust," he says.' Letter to the editor, *Comhar*, Bealtaine 1945, reprinted in *Comhar 1942–1982*, pp. 26–27; I am grateful to Dr Mary Harris for helping with this reference. The author of the original article, Máire Mhac an tSaoi, confirmed that the letter was a send-up.

115. S.B. Kennedy, *Irish Art and Modernism 1880–1950* (Institute of Irish Studies, Belfast, 1991), p. 115 ff.

116. Bruce Arnold, *Mainie Jellett and the Modern Movement in Ireland* (Yale University Press, London and New Haven, 1991), p. 193.

117. Unfortunately, I had researched and written the above piece before I had an opportunity to benefit from reading Arnold's treatment of the Rouault affair, see *Mainie Jellett*, pp. 187–92.

118. The advisory members and six others represented expert opinion in the arts. They were: Dr George Furlong, Director of the National Gallery; Seán Keating RHA; John Maher; Dermod O'Brien RHA; Sarah Purser RHA (the friends had been formed largely due to her efforts); and Lucius O'Callaghan RHA. A majority of the committee voted in favour of rejection. Sarah Purser was not at the meeting and later indirectly expressed her disapproval of what had been decided at the meeting.

119. Quoted in Myles na gCopaleen's 'Cruiskeen Lawn', *The Irish Times*, 10 October 1942.

120. *The Irish Times*, 10 October 1942 and *Irish Independent*, 12 October 1942; the curator of the Municipal Gallery, Kelly, had been interviewed about the painting in the *Irish Independent*, 9 October 1942. He attempted to stay clear of the controversy, but he did suggest that it was not fair to describe the picture as an oil painting. Curran pointed out in his letter that nobody had made that claim about the painting, which had been executed in mixed media.

121. *Catholic Herald*, 16 October 1942.

122. Quoted in letter by Curran, *The Irish Times*, 8 October 1942.

123. *The Irish Times*, 8 October 1942.

124. *The Catholic Herald*, 16 October 1942.

125. *The Irish Times*, 8 October 1942.

126. For Curran's defence, see his letter to *The Irish Times*, 8 October 1942; Curran may have been helped in his researching of this subject by his daughter, a distinguished art critic, who had studied painting in Paris in the 1930s. Professor Ó Briain was replying *(Leader*, 2 January 1943) to an attack by L.S. Gogan *(Leader*, 19 December 1942 and 9 January 1943) on Rouault.

127. *The Catholic Herald*, 16 October 1942.

128. *The Irish Times*, 28 November 1942.

129. *The Irish Times*, 10 October 1942; Keating replied to the columnist, stating that it was the *Irish Times* editorial staff who had phoned his home asking for his opinion. He said that it was absurd that he had ever suggested that people could not form their own opinion; *The Irish Times*, 12 October 1942.

130. Text of Leen speech which was kindly supplied to them by Father Enda Waters

cssp. It is entitled: 'À propos of Rouault's Picture. "Christ and the Soldier". It is dated November 1942 and is one of four versions in his notes.

131. A second Leen text entitled 'Rouault and Tradition' was kindly sent to me by Father Enda Waters; Leen papers, Holy Ghost Fathers archives, Kimmage, Dublin.

132. ibid.

133. *Irish Catholic Directory*, 1945, pp. 674–75.

134. Interview with Mrs Frances Boland, 1992.

135. *Irish Catholic Directory*, 1945, p. 675; McQuaid outlined his thinking on Catholic education in two works: *Higher Education for Catholics* and *Catholic Education: Its Functions and Scope*, quoted in Pat Buckley, 'The Primate's Primal Truths', supplement with *Fortnight*, 297, pp. 11–12; see also John Feeney, *John Charles McQuaid: The Man and the Mask* (Mercier Press, Dublin, 1974), pp. 20–21.

136. Dulanty to Walshe, 14 April 1944 (contains typed version of the Molony letter). Secretary's files, P84, Department of Foreign Affairs, National Archives, Dublin.

137. *Report of Commission on Vocational Organisation 1943*, Appendix 1, p. 498: the commission normally held meetings of two days' duration at intervals of two or three weeks, holding a morning and afternoon session each day. H.P. Boland, who had been a committee member, was prevented from playing a very active role because of his prolonged illness.

138. Michael Browne, *Bulwark of Freedom: Vocational Organisation—Democracy in Action* (Catholic Truth Society Pamphlet, Dublin, 1945), p. 15.

139. *Report of Commission on Vocational Organisation 1943*, p. 527; this entry was pointed out to me with some irritation by Maurice Moynihan.

140. Joseph Lee, 'Aspects of Corporatist Thought in Ireland: The Commission on Vocational Organisations 1939–43', in Art Cosgrove and Donal McCartney (eds), *Studies in Irish History presented to R. Dudley Edwards* (University College Dublin, 1979), pp. 339–40; see also Don O'Leary, *Vocationalism and Social Catholicism in Twentieth Century Ireland* (Irish Academic Press, Dublin, 2000).

141. See Dermot Keogh, 'Ireland, the Vatican and Catholic Europe, 1919–1939', PhD EUI, Florence 1980, p. 523, quoting Department of the Taoiseach, S13552.

142. *Seanad Debates*, VOL. 29, col. 1323, 21 February 1945.

143. *Irish Independent*, 31 October 1944.

144. *The Irish Press*, 8 March 1945.

145. ibid.

146. *The Irish Press*, 23 March 1945.

147. Relations between Browne and the government deteriorated. De Valera wrote to Browne on 2 May 1945, indicating the need for a number of the most minor editorial changes in the report; he referred to the publication of evidence. On 19 May, Browne replied in a most intemperate manner. The former secretary to the commission, P. O'Toole, was interviewed by a member of the Taoiseach's office on 25 May 1945 and his recollections were in substantial disagreement with those views stated by Browne in his letter to de Valera. The Taoiseach sent a letter to the bishop which was a firm rebuttal of the many points that he had made. De Valera stated that he had given instructions to proceed with the reprinting of the report and inclusion of the editorial changes. Browne was left to smart over the refusal of the government to accept any of the report's ideas. All his efforts and energies as chairman had been for nothing.

148. J.H. Whyte, *Church and State*, p. 101.

149. ibid., p. 110.

150. James Deeny, *To Cure and To Care: Memoirs of a Chief Medical Officer* (Glendale Press, Dublin, 1989), p. 106.

151. ibid., p. 112.

152. Sir William Beveridge had reported to the British government in 1942. His report was to form the basis for the reform of the British health service and favour the introduction of socialised medicine which the post-war Labour government acted upon with alacrity.

153. Department of Local Government and Public Health memorandum, 16 March 1943 (circulated to cabinet on 18 March), s13053, Department of the Taoiseach, National Archives, Dublin.

154. Lee, *Ireland 1912–1985*, p. 277 ff.

155. Seán MacEntee's observations on a memorandum from the Irish Tourist Board, entitled 'Towards an Irish Recreational Policy'. Department of the Taoiseach, s13087A, National Archives, Dublin.

156. Cabinet minutes, 14 December 1945, G.C.4/127: Tourist Traffic Act 1939, National Archives, Dublin.

157. Department of Industry and Commerce memorandum, 27 November 1945, Department of the Taoiseach, s13087A, National Archives, Dublin.

158. Department of External Affairs minutes, probably written by Joseph Walshe, 15 December 1943, Secretary's files, A25, National Archives, Dublin.

159. Maffey to Walshe, 22 December 1943, Secretary's files, A25, Department of Foreign Affairs, National Archives, Dublin.

160. RG 59, 841.01/301, National Archives, Washington.

161. State Department memorandum, 28 February 1944, RG 59, 841/01/301, National

Archives, Washington.

162. State Department telegram to US embassy, London, 1 April 1944, RG 59, 841.01/325B, and Memorandum for Admiral Leahy, 31 March 1944, RG 59, 841D.01/325A, National Archives, Washington.

163. This compromise was communicated by Walshe to the Americans in mid-April. Gray telegram, 14 April 1944, RG 59,841D.01/332, National Archives, Washington.

164. Gray to State Department, 6 May 1944, RG 59, 842.01/355, National Archives, Washington.

165. For the text of de Valera's appeal to the belligerent powers, 24 March 1944, see Moynihan (ed.), *Speeches and Statements by Éamon de Valera*, pp. 469–70; see also chapter III in my forthcoming *Ireland and the Vatican, 1922–1960* (Cork University Press, Cork, 1994).

166. Keogh, *Ireland and Europe 1919–1989*, pp. 183–91.

167. Boland to Murphy, Secretary's files, A72, 16 August 1945, National Archives, Dublin.

168. Stuart had been born in Queensland, Australia, but moved at an early age to County Antrim where he was brought up. Boland minuted that his claim to Irish citizenship was based on the birth of one of his parents in one or other of the Northern counties.

169. Geoffrey Elborn, *Francis Stuart: A Life* (Raven Arts Press, Dublin, 1990); David O'Donoghue, *Hitler's Irish Voices—The Story of German radio's wartime Irish service* (Beyond the Pale, Dublin, 1998) and Mark M. Hull, *Irish Secrets: Geerman espionage in Ireland, 1939–45* (Irish Academic Press, Dublin, 2003) See also Carolle J. Carter, *The Shamrock and the Swastika: German Espionage in Ireland in World War II* (Pacific Books, Palo Alto, California, 1977), pp. 109–111. See also Mervyn O'Driscoll, *Ireland, Germany and the Nazis: politics and diplomacy, 1919–1939* (Four Courts Press, Dublin, 2004)

170. Unsigned Department of External Affairs memorandum, 1 October 1947, Department of Foreign Affairs, Secretary's files, P 17, National Archives, Dublin.

171. ibid., see also MacWhite to Secretary, 25 August 1941: MacWhite's source for this information was the Swedish ambassador to the Quirinale. Secretary's files, P 17, National Archives, Dublin.

172. Bryan to Walshe, 12 December 1945, Department of Foreign Affairs, Secretary's files, p 17, National Archives, Dublin.

173. See Charles Bewley, *Herman Göring & the Third Reich* (Devin-Adair, USA, 1952).

174. Walshe minutes on conversation with Maffey, 25 July 1945, Department of

Foreign Affairs, Secretary's files, P 17, National Archives, Dublin; at this point, Walshe was attempting to play down Bewley's importance or relevance. But, nevertheless, Walshe did not deny Bewley's pro-Nazi past. He, more than most, knew most of what there was to be known about the man.

175. Unsigned Department of External Affairs memorandum, 1 October 1947, Department of Foreign Affairs, Secretary's files, P 17, National Archives, Dublin.

176. Walshe minutes, 25 July 1945, Department of Foreign Affairs, Secretary's files, P 17, National Archives, Dublin.

177. Warnock minute, 17 December 1954, Department of Foreign Affairs, Secretary's files, p. 17, National Archives, Dublin. Bewley continued to live in Italy and died in Rome, in his bed, in 1969.

178. Two verses of this poem, quoted in full here, are cited in Terence Brown, *Ireland: A Social and Cultural History 1922–1979* (Fontana, London, 1981).

Chapter 4: Seán MacBride and the Rise of Clann na Poblachta (pp. 161–189)

1. See Boland manuscript.

2. Interview with Cornelius Cremin, Toosist, Co. Kerry. Cremin was abroad at the time and would have heard about the background to the incident upon his return to Dublin on holiday; see also Niall Keogh, Con Cremin and Irish Foreign Policy 1935–1958, PhD dissertation, UCC, 2003.

3. Quoted in Lord Longford and Thomas P. O'Neill, *Éamon de Valera* (Arrow Books, London, 1970), p. 411; he also made the point that Hempel had behaved correctly towards Ireland during the war and that his comportment was in marked contrast to that of the US envoy, David Gray.

4. Boland manuscript. Hempel, as has been pointed out earlier, was never a Nazi sympathiser.

5. The State Department said that the calls of de Valera and McDunphy *[sic]* were 'most unfortunate even though greater courtesies were shown at time of President Roosevelt's death, namely the adjournment of Dáil and resolutions of condolence passed by Dáil and Seanad.' An extended critique of the episode can be found in Dermot Keogh, Éamon de Valera and Hitler', *Irish Studies in International Affairs*, VOL. 3, NO. 1 (Autumn 1989), pp. 69–92; see also my *Ireland and Europe 1919–1989*, pp. 191–96.

6. In a Department of Justice confidential publication, *Notes on IRA Activities 1941–1947*, a section dealing with the de Valera visit is entitled 'Death of Herr Hitler', p. 81. This had to have been published at least two years after the visit. Why the undue deference to 'Herr' Hitler in a confidential Department of Justice publication is a mystery. See Seán MacEntee papers, P67/550 (copy no.

5—issued to the Minister for Local Government), UCD Archives.

7. See Department of Justice, *Notes of IRA Activities, 1941–1947*, p. 81, (Seán MacEntee papers). The Italian envoy to Dublin, Count Vitaliano Confalonieri, reported to Rome that some of the demonstrators wore swastika badges and a few Nazi flags were flown. (Report 10 May 1945, telegram number 364/100, Political, File, Ireland and Italy, 1945, Italian Department of Foreign Affairs, Rome); this may have been a reference to members of a small ultra-nationalist group called Ailtirí na hAiseirighe, which had been set up in March 1942 and which adopted a corporatist philosophy.

8. Dermot Keogh, 'Éamon de Valera and Hitler: An Analysis of International Reaction to the Visit to the German Minister, May 1945', *Irish Studies in International Affairs*, VOL. 3, NO. 1 (Autumn 1989), pp. 69–92.

9. *The Times* (London), 14 May 1945.

10. *The Irish Times*, 2 October 1946.

11. Maffey memorandum to Dominions Office, 21 May 1945, DO 35, 1229, X/MO2134, PRO, Kew.

12. See Dermot Keogh 'Anglo-Irish Relations, 1945–1948', paper presented to the EUI, Florence, 1978, pp. 11–13.

13. Eric Machtig to Maffey, 18 July 1945, DO 35 1229. WX110/3, PRO, London.

14. Sir John Maffey's annual report for 1945–1946, FO 371/54722, W8736, PRO, London.

15. F.S.L. Lyons, *Ireland since the Famine* (Weidenfeld and Nicolson, London, 1971), p. 551.

16. *The Irish Times*, 21 May 1945.

17. *The Irish Times*, 12 May 1945.

18. *Dáil Debates*, VOL. 101, cols 2128–2181, 19 June 1946.

19. Patrick McCartan was a northerner who had been a Dáil Éireann envoy in the United States between 1919 and 1921; see Patrick McCartan, *With de Valera in America* (FitzPatrick Limited, Dublin, 1932).

20. *The Irish Times*, 13 June 1945.

21. *The Irish Times*, 12 June 1945.

22. *The Irish Times*, 11 June 1945.

23. *The Irish Times*, 4 June and 14 June 1945.

24 *Results of Presidential Elections and Referenda 1937–1984* (Department of the Environment, Dublin, 1984), pp. 10–12.

25. These two anecdotes were told to me respectively by Father John Lee, OFM, and Mr Paddy Mulligan, former captain of the Irish rugby team.

26. *The Irish Times*, 18 and 19 June 1945. O'Kelly's departure from the cabinet resulted in a reshuffle. The Minister for Industry and Commerce and the

Minister for Supplies, Seán Lemass, became Tánaiste, and the former Minister
for the Coordination of Defensive Measures, Frank Aiken, became Minister for
Finance.

27. *The Irish Times*, 18 June 1945; Fine Gael won one seat, and Labour, which was
the biggest party in the old corporation, lost two seats. The green corporatist
party, Ailtirí na hAiseirighe, polled 3,180. Independents, overall, polled 18,841.

28. *Dáil Debates*, VOL. 101, cols 2129–2181, 19 June 1946.

29. Finbarr O'Shea, 'Government and Trade Unions in Ireland 1939–1946: The
Formation of Labour Legislation', MA thesis, UCC, 1988, p. 157.

30. Ronan Fanning, *The Irish Department of Finance 1922–1958* (Institute of Public
Administration, Dublin, 1978), p. 344.

31. *The Irish Press*, 8 October 1947.

32. James Staunton, joint secretary to the National Conference of Bishops, to de
Valera, 13 October 1947, Department of the Taoiseach, S15398, National
Archives, Dublin.

33. Quoted in letter from Maurice Moynihan to the secretary of the Department
of Industry and Commerce, 10 October 1947 (letter was marked urgent),
Department of the Taoiseach, S15398, National Archives, Dublin.

34. De Valera to Staunton, 16 February 1948, Department of the Taoiseach, S15398,
National Archives, Dublin.

35. Paradoxically, the Department of Justice was quite well disposed to the idea of
Ireland becoming a refuge for leading members of the European right. See
Keogh, *Ireland and Europe 1919–1989*, chapter 7.

36. Séamas Ó Buachalla, *Education Policy in Twentieth-Century Ireland*
(Wolfhound Press, Dublin, 1988), p. 95.

37. The exclamation of Pyrrhus after the battle of Asculum in Apulia.

38. *The Irish Press*, 7 September 1946, filed on Department of the Taoiseach,
S10236D, National Archives, Dublin.

39. De Valera to Patrick O'Carroll, Holy Ghost Missionary College, Kimmage,
Dublin, 16 April 1946, Department of the Taoiseach, S10236C, National
Archives, Dublin; Father O'Carroll had written to de Valera on 7 April offering
to act as a 'go-between', but his offer was declined. The significance of this will
be discussed later.

40. Michéal Ó Slatarra, Ballymoreen, Littleton, Thurles, to de Valera, 14 April 1946,
Department of the Taoiseach, S10236C, National Archives, Dublin.

41. Riobard Ó Caoimh, Borris in Ossory, Co. Laois, to de Valera, 20 June 1945,
Department of the Taoiseach, S10236B, National Archives, Dublin.

42. T. J. O'Connell, *100 Years of Progress: The Story of the Irish National Teachers'
Organisation 1868–1968* (INTO, Dublin, 1969), p. 210.

43. ibid., p. 214.

44. ibid., pp. 218–19.

45. McQuaid to O'Connell, 6 April 1946, Department of the Taoiseach, s10236c, National Archives, Dublin.

46. See text and drafts, Department of the Taoiseach, s10236 c and d, National Archives, Dublin.

47. McQuaid to Tom Derrig, 13 April 1946, Department of the Taoiseach, 10236d.

48. Quoted in O'Connell, *100 Years of Progress*, p. 224.

49. Cabinet Minutes, item 4, 15 October 1946, g.c. s/198.

50. *The Irish Press*, 30 October 1946.

51. D.R. O'Connor Lysaght, *The Republic of Ireland* (Mercier Press, Cork, 1970), p. 160.

52. A statement appeared in the press signed by Fionán Breathnach, Thomas Burke, Peadar Cowan, Úna Bean Austin de Staic, Simon Donnelly, Michael Ferguson, Michael Fitzpatrick, Seán Fitzpatrick, James Hannigan, Noel Hartnett, Michael Kelly, James J. Killeen, Con Lehane, Seán MacBride, Seán MacGiobúin, Patrick J. Moclair, Maoilseachlainn Ó Cuinn, Donal O'Donoghue, Pádraig O'Donoghue, Michael A. O'Kelly and Pádraig Ó Nuallin. The signatories constituted themselves as the provisional executive. See *Irish Independent*, 5 July 1946.

53. Undated note on Clann na Poblachta, probably compiled by the Department of Justice. Seán MacEntee papers, p67/543, Archives Department, ucd.

54. ira general army convention (handwritten minute book), 17 March 1934. Séan MacEntee papers, p67/525, Archives Department, ucd.

55. See *Notes on ira Activities 1941–1947* (Department of Justice confidential publication), [Copy no. 5, issued to the Minister of Local Government], Appendix ix, p. 158 ff. Seán MacEntee papers, p67/550; see also p67/539 for a profile of MacBride.

56. MacEntee papers, p67/539, Archives Department, ucd.

57. MacEntee papers, p67/542, Archives Department, ucd.

58. MacEntee papers, p67/542, Archives Department, ucd.

59. *Notes on ira Activities 1941–1947* (Department of Justice), p. 98; MacEntee papers, p67/550, Archives Department, ucd.

60. g2 report, 28 January 1944, secretary's files d/fa, a55/1.

61. g2 memorandum, 7 March 1946, secretary's files d/fa, a55/1.

62. Publicity blurb for the picture. Seán MacEntee papers, p67/379, Archives Department, ucd.

63. *The Irish Press*, 30 and 31 January; see also *The Irish Times*, 31 January 1947 for description of the funeral.

64. James Deeny, *To Cure and To Care: Memoirs of a Chief Medical Officer* (Glendale Press, Dublin, 1989), p. 155.

65. Noël Browne, *Against the Tide* (Gill & Macmillan, Dublin, 1986), p. 71.

66. Ruth Barrington, *Healthy Medicine and Politics in Ireland 1900–1970* (Institute of Public Administration, Dublin, 1987), pp. 174–75.

67. McPolin to Ryan, 9 July 1947, Department of the Taoiseach, s14227, National Archives, Dublin; see also files s13444A-E.

68. Kevin Mangan to John Garvin (Department of Health), 24 June 1947, Department of the Taoiseach, s14337, National Archives, Dublin.

69. Draft of letter, with final changes made in Maurice Moynihan's hand. The latter had written on the top: 'Provisionally approved by the Taoiseach, subject to the amendments indicated in red ink. 11.2.48.' s14227, Department of the Taoiseach, National Archives, Dublin.

70. Department of the Taoiseach, s14153C, National Archives, Dublin.

71. Locke *Tribunal Report* (Stationery Office, Dublin, 1947), p. 5; also quoted in Lee, *Ireland 1912–1985*, p. 297; one of the judges, Cahir Davitt, took exception to the remarks of the Minister for Finance in the Inter-party government, who commented in the Dáil that the tribunal judges had been wrong in their findings in respect of Flanagan. This was rejected by Davitt in a letter to the Taoiseach, John A. Costello, on 21 October 1949: 'The effect of this unpleasant business upon my mind is to leave me with an acute personal distaste for any further extra-judicial assignments,' he wrote, adding: 'I in common with my colleagues did at the time and still do bitterly resent these remarks made as they were by a responsible Minister.' See Department of the Taoiseach, s15153C.

72. Joseph Lee, *Ireland 1912–1985: Politics and Society* (Cambridge University Press, Cambridge, 1989), p. 297.

73. Tommy Mullins was a War of Independence and civil war veteran. He was a founder member of Fianna Fáil and a man who took a strong interest in left-wing politics. I interviewed Mullins a number of times. His papers, a rather disappointing collection which does not include his more important material, can be found in the Archives Department, UCD.

74. See Seán MacEntee papers, in particular, P67/372, 373, 542, 543 and 539, Archives Department, UCD.

75. *The Irish Times*, 16 October 1947.

76. Text of MacBride election leaflet in MacEntee papers, P67/542, Archives Department, UCD.

77. Lord Longford and Thomas P. O'Neill, *Éamon de Valera* (Arrow Books, London, 1970), p. 430.

78. Childers to Tommy Mullins, undated but probably sent around 10 February

1948. MacEntee papers, P67/299, Archives Department, UCD.

79. Childers to Tommy Mullins, 10 February 1948, P67/299, MacEntee papers, Archives Department, UCD.

80. John A. Murphy, "Put them out!" Parties and Elections, 1948–1969', John J. Lee (ed.), *Ireland 1945–70* (Gill & Macmillan, Dublin, 1979), pp. 1–15. See also Tom Garvin, *The Evolution of Irish Nationalist Politics* (Gill & Macmillan, Dublin, 1972), pp. 174–77; and Joseph Lee, *Ireland 1912–1985: Politics and Society* (Cambridge University Press, Cambridge, 1989), p. 299 ff.

Chapter 5: The Inter-party Government, 1948–1951 (pp. 190–219)

1. For background, see Ronan Fanning, *Independent Ireland* (Helicon, Dublin, 1983), pp. 164–65 and John A. Murphy, *Ireland in the Twentieth Century* (Gill & Macmillan, Dublin, 1975), pp. 120–23.

2. There were thirteen ministers and five parties.

3. The vindictiveness of the atmosphere which ultimately came to prevail in the cabinet can be found in the highly subjective but very readable account in Browne's *Against the Tide*, a book which has sold over 75,000 copies in Ireland.

4. See American legation report for a extensive profile of Costello, 15 July 1948, Dublin, Security Segregated Records, Box 16, 800–Ireland, RG 84, NARA, Washington.

5. Comment by Alfred O'Rahilly, recorded by D.A.L., 30 January 1948, Dublin, Security Segregated Records, 800–Irish Politics, RG 84, NARA, Washington.

6. *The Observer* (London), 18 January 1948.

7. That point is demonstrated very well by Seán Cronin in his book *Washington's Irish Policy, 1916–1986* (Anvil Press, Dublin, 1987), pp. 196–97, 256–68. Cronin argues that 'MacBride's conspirational upbringing made him suspicious of the close links between the Irish bureaucracy and the British, particularly in the Department of Finance' (p. 196). The secretary of the Department of Finance, J.J. McElligott, had, in fact, taken part in the 1916 Rising, but he was probably suspicious of MacBride because of both his 'unorthodox' economic theories and his revolutionary past. The head of army intelligence, Colonel Dan Bryan, was never wholly at ease with the idea of MacBride being in government. That negative feeling was reciprocated; MacBride felt that Bryan was too close to British military intelligence.

8. Told to the late Professor T. Desmond Williams by Frederick Boland; personal interview with Williams. The number of diplomats of all ranks working at Iveagh House at the time was not more than fifteen.

9. Garrett to Secretary of State, 9 September 1948, Dublin, Security Segregated Records, Box 16, 800–Ireland, 1948 (Ireland Act), RG 84, NARA. Garrett became minister to Dublin on 10 April 1947. He was given the rank of ambassador in 1950.

10. He also mentioned as further possible evidence of communist propaganda the fact that one of the theatres in Dublin had produced 'Winter Set' in which Paulette Goddard and Burgess Meredith had appeared. Boland felt that the theatre in question was in no position to produce such a play with that cast at their own expense and 'he felt sure that some interested group must have been responsible for supplying the necessary funds'. Norman Armour minute of conversation with Frederick Boland entitled 'Communist Trend in Ireland,' 24 October 1947, Dublin, Confidential Files, 841D. 00B/10–2447, RG 59, NARA.

11. Quoted in John Whyte, *Church and State in Modern Ireland 1923–1979* (Gill & Macmillan, Dublin, 1984), p. 184.

12. J. Graham Parsons to Washington, 1 April 1948, Myron Taylor Collection, Box 19, RG 59, NARA, Washington.

13. Interview with Maurice Moynihan. A distinguished civil servant and active member of the Legion of Mary (an Irish variant of Catholic Action), Moynihan had served in the Department of the Taoiseach under de Valera.

14. See Walshe letter, Secretary's Files, P140, D/FA, National Archives, Dublin.

15. Walshe to Boland, 25 February 1948 (Secret and confidential), D/FA P140, Secretary's file, National Archives, Dublin.

16. Walshe to Boland, 25 February 1948, D/FA P140, Secretary's files, National Archives, Dublin.

17. In the early weeks of 1948, there had been some speculation about the pope having to move from Rome if the Left took over.

18. Walshe to Boland, 5 March 1948, P256, P12/2a, National Archives, Dublin.

19. Walshe to Boland, 5 March 1948, P256 and P12/2a, National Archives, Dublin.

20. Leo T. McCauley minute, 23 March 1948, D/FA, P140, Secretary's file, Iveagh House, Dublin. (The reference was to Walshe's telegrams nos 21, 22, 23, which contained the text of Gedda's telegrams to the United States.)

21. The late Professor T. Desmond Williams told me that it was on this occasion that Boland was most unfavourably impressed with MacBride, who spoke with great deference to the archbishop on the phone. But once he had put down the receiver, he was dismissive of the prelate to the point of being contemptuous.

22. D/FA, P140, Secretary's files, National Archives, Dublin.

23. Fanning, *Independent Ireland*, pp. 172–80.

24. Patrick Lynch, who was Costello's private secretary, accompanied him on his

trip to Canada. See also Patrick Lynch and James Meenan (eds), *Essays in Memory of Alexis Fitzgerald* (Gill & Macmillan, Dublin, 1987), pp. 35–62.

25. Boland manuscript.

26. Noël Browne, *Against the Tide* (Gill & Macmillan, Dublin, 1986), pp. 129–31.

27. Reminiscence of Lord Rugby (Sir John Maffey), *The Irish Times*, 10 July 1962; this was also confirmed to me by Boland, who said that MacBride was 'amazed'.

28. Boland manuscript.

29. Boland manuscript; de Valera had lunch with Churchill at Downing Street in 1953. The topics of discussion at the lunch, referred to in de Valera's official biography, were the North and the return of Roger Casement's body. See Longford and O'Neill, pp. 442–43. There appears to have been no reference in the records to the meeting quoted by both authors or any mention of the events of 1949.

30. *FRUS*, 1950, VOL. III, p. 1494, Policy statement prepared in the State Department, 15 August 1950, 611.40A/8–1550.

31. F.S.L. Lyons, *Ireland since the Famine* (Weidenfeld and Nicolson, London, 1971), pp. 559–63.

32. Murphy, *Ireland in the Twentieth Century*, p. 127; since this section was written, Ian McCabe's *A Diplomatic History of Ireland 1948–1949* (Irish Academic Press, Dublin, 1991) has been published.

33. The signatories were Britain, France and the Benelux countries. Article 4 read: 'If any of the high contracting parties should be the object of an armed attack in Europe, the other high contracting parties will, in accordance with the provisions of article 51 of the Charter of the United Nations, afford the party so attacked all the military and other aid and assistance in their power.'

34. Denis J. Maher, *The Tortuous Path: The Course of Ireland's Entry into the EEC 1948–73* (Institute of Public Administration, Dublin, 1986), pp. 17–18.

35. Boland manuscript; the poet Eavan Boland recalls that her father may have tendered his resignation on that occasion.

36. Boland manuscript.

37. Maher, *The Tortuous Path*, pp. 17–18.

38. *FRUS*, 1949, VOL. VI, p. 90.

39. *FRUS*, 1949, VOL. VI, p. 154.

40. *FRUS*, 1949, VOL. IV, p. 192.

41. *FRUS*, 1949, VOL. IV, p. 192.

42. Dean Acheson, *Present at the Creation* (Norton, New York, 1987), p. 479.

43. Maher, *The Tortuous Path*, p. 19.

44. See *Dáil Debates*, VOL. 115, cols 927–932 and VOL. 115, cols 1256–1261, 17 May 1945.

45. Department of the Taoiseach, s14532, National Archives, Dublin.

46. Joseph Lee, *Ireland 1912–1985: Politics and Society* (Cambridge University Press, Cambridge, 1989), p. 306.

47. Browne, *Against the Tide*, pp. 95–96.

48. Dermot Keogh, *Ireland and Europe 1919–1989* (Hibernian University Press, Cork and Dublin, 1989), pp. 219–20.

49. See documents from National Archives Washington; see also Department of the Taoiseach, s14106a–c, National Archives, Dublin. See also Lee, *Ireland 1912–1985*, p. 304 ff and Fanning, *Finance*, p. 418 ff.

50. I am grateful to Patricia Dromey for the information on which this section is based. Ms Dromey is working on a doctoral thesis on Ireland and Marshall aid; see Bernadette Whelan, *Ireland and the Marshall Plan 1947–1957* (Four Courts Press, Dublin, 2000).

51. Keogh, *Ireland and Europe 1919–1989*, pp. 219–20.

52. *The Irish Times*, 4 May 1949.

53. Department of the Taoiseach, s14455, National Archives, Dublin.

54. Browne, *Against the Tide*, p. 189 ff.

55. Patrick Lynch, 'The Irish Economy since the War, 1946–1951,' in Kevin B. Nowlan and T. Desmond Williams (eds), *Ireland in the War Years and After* (Gill & Macmillan, Dublin, 1969), pp. 185–200.

56. For background on the ida, see Lee, *Ireland, 1912–1985*, p. 310 ff; Brian Farrell, *Séan Lemass*, pp. 82–83 and Fanning, *Independent Ireland*, p. 193.

57. Interview with the late John Moher.

58. *Dáil Debates*, vol. cxvii, col. 757, 12 July 1949.

59. *Dáil Debates*, vol. cxvi, col. 1245,23 June 1949.

60. See *Dáil Debates*, vol. cxvii, col. 762, 13 July 1949 and *Seanad Debates*, 30 November 1949, col. 182; and 7 December 1949, col. 367.

61. Unsigned memorandum on Irish News Agency, Department of Foreign Affairs, ina series, folder 62, National Archives, Dublin.

62. Conor Cruise O'Brien report, undated, Department of Foreign Affairs, ina series, folder 62, National Archives, Dublin.

63. There are a series of minutes by Conor Cruise O'Brien on this Baltinglass affair. See Department of Foreign Affairs, ina series, folder 34, National Archives, Dublin.

64. This attack was based on a story which appeared in the *Gaelic American* on 16 December. Dr Cruise O'Brien wrote: 'This story is ours all right. The head on it is the Gaelic American's own. There was, of course, no intention of political slanting. I have been through our Baltinglass coverage and we need not hesitate to place it before the Oireachtas, if necessary.' Department of Foreign Affairs, ina series, folder 34, National Archives, Dublin.

65. Department of Foreign Affairs, INA series, folder 34, National Archives, Dublin.

66. Brian P. Kennedy, *Dreams and Responsibilities: The State and the Arts in Independent Ireland* (Arts Council, Dublin, 1990), p. 77 ff.

67. Dan Bryan memorandum, November 1950, Department of Foreign Affairs, Secretary's files, A55 1, National Archives, Dublin. De Courcy-Ireland was described as being 'one of the leading Irish Communists'. He was, according to Bryan, an 'able and well qualified writer of Communist opinion under several classes'. McInerney, a journalist and later the political correspondent of *The Irish Times*, was described as being a member of the Irish Workers' League.

68. Bryan Memorandum, November 1950, Department of Foreign Affairs, Secretary's files, A55 1, National Archives, Dublin.

69. Bryan to Seán Nunan, secretary of the Department of External Affairs, 18 January 1951, Department of Foreign Affairs, Secretary's files, A55 1, National Archives, Dublin.

70. Frederick Boland's wife told me that her late husband had taken the London job because he could no longer stand MacBride. His predecessor, Joseph Walshe, had been secretary of External Affairs from 1922 until 1946. Boland was a mere four years in the post. The vacancy became available when Dulanty, who had reached the age of 70, failed to win cabinet approval for an extension. Boland commented about MacBride's reasons for offering him the post: 'I could never really work out whether my going to London was due to Seán MacBride's desire to get rid of me or to Jack Costello's feeling that they should have in London someone they could rely on not to intrigue. I never knew exactly.' Boland manuscript.

71. *FRUS*, 1950, VOL. III, memorandum by the US Secretary of Defense to the executive secretary of the NSC, s/s-NSC files: Lot 63 D 351: NSC 83 Series, p. 1476.

72. NSC 83, 17 October 1950, *FRUS*, 1950, VOL. III, pp. 1478–1481.

73. There are a number of boxes of files on the work of this committee. See Department of the Taoiseach, S14939, S14880A, B, C. See also files S14885, S14889, S15906, S15907, S15910, S15911, S15912, S15913, and S15915. The relevant Department of Foreign Affairs files are closed to researchers, but the Iveagh House memoranda are available on the files from the Taoiseach's office.

74. Moynihan draft minutes of meeting, 21 September 1950, Department of the Taoiseach S14939, National Archives, Dublin.

75. Moynihan memorandum, 27 November 1950, Department of the Taoiseach, S14939, National Archives, Dublin.

76. Iveagh House had already heard from Washington. Hugh McCann had written a long letter on 7 October 1950 requesting clarification of his instructions. He

made the point that priority was sought by NATO members. McCann to secretary, 7 October 1950, Department of the Taoiseach, s14909, National Archives, Dublin.

77. Boland to Seán Nunan, 1 March 1951, Department of the Taoiseach, s14909, National Archives, Dublin.

78. Memorandum and enclosure by the assistant secretary of state for European Affairs, George W. Perkins, drafted by a member of British Commonwealth and Northern European Affairs section, 12 March 1951, RG 59, 740A 13/3–1251, *FRUS*, 1951, VOL. VI (Part I), p. 514 ff.

79. *FRUS*, 1951, VOL. VI, Part I, p. 521.

80. Evelyn Bolster, *The Knights of Saint Columbanus* (Gill & Macmillan, Dublin, 1979), pp. 95–99; see also Éamonn C. McKee, 'Church-State Relations and the Development of Irish Health Policy', *Irish Historical Studies*, VOL. XXV, NO. 98 (November 1986), pp. 176–77; for Fianna Fáil and the Knights of Columbanus, see Bolster, chapter 2.

81. Fanning, *Independent Ireland*, p. 185.

82. MacBride memorandum, circulated after 6 April 1951 cabinet meeting, which he attempted to have inserted as part of the official record. Although that was not permitted, it is fortunate that the document has survived since it shows MacBride's confessional thinking on the issue. Department of the Taoiseach, s14997C, National Archives, Dublin. Also quoted in Fanning, *Independent Ireland*, p. 186.

83. Browne, *Against the Tide*, chapters 1, 2 and 7. See also Barrington, *Health, Medicine and Politics in Ireland*, pp. 197–260 and Deeny, *To Cure and To Care*, p. 150 ff. Browne writes movingly about the scourge of TB and about the devastation it caused in Ireland.

84. Whyte, *Church and State 1923–1979*, chapters VII and XII, plus appendix B; Barrington, *Health, Medicine and Politics*, chapter 9; Deeny, *To Cure and To Care*, chapter 8; Fanning, *Independent Ireland*, pp. 181–87.

85. Staunton to Costello, 10 October 1950, Whyte, *Church and State 1923–1979*, pp. 424–45.

86. Browne, *Against the Tide*, p. 157.

87. Whyte, *Church and State 1923–1979*, pp. 447–48.

88. ibid., pp. 447–48.

89. Browne, *Against the Tide*, pp. 178–79; Browne also claimed that he learned at the meeting that MacBride had had him followed by the Special Branch.

90. This was later published in Whyte, *Church and State 1923–1979*, appendix B, pp. 399–428.

91. Browne, *Against the Tide*, p. 186; there is an implication that the two civil

servants started to destroy official documents of their own volition. This seems most unlikely without ministerial approval.

92. Browne, *Against the Tide*, p. 188.

93. 'Cás an Dochtúra de Brún', editorial in *Comhar*, VOL. 10, NO. 5 (May 1951); I am grateful to Dr Mary Harris, University of North London, for giving me this reference in translation.

94. Donal Herlihy interview, Rome, 1979; Herlihy was in an excellent position to judge the events of 1951 from his vantage point as rector of the Irish College in Rome.

95. Farrell, *Seán Lemass*, p. 84 and Farrell, *Chairman or Chief*, p. 56.

Chapter 6: The Politics of Drift, 1951–1959 (pp. 220–249)

1. For general historical background, see Joseph Lee, *Ireland 1912–1985: Politics and Society* (Cambridge University Press, Cambridge, 1989), pp. 321–22; see also Brian Farrell, *Seán Lemass* (Gill & Macmillan, Dublin, 1983), p. 85.

2. John Moher interview.

3. James Meenan, *The Irish Economy since 1922* (Liverpool University Press, Liverpool, 1970), p. 204 ff.

4. Meenan, *The Irish Economy since 1922*, quoting *Census of Population, 1961, vol. VII.*

5. Meenan, *The Irish Economy since 1922*, quoting *Report of the Commission on Emigration and Other Population Problems*, para. 272.

6. Quoted in Terence Brown, *Ireland: A Social and Cultural History 1922–1979* (Fontana, London, 1981), pp. 237–38.

7. Dónall Mac Amhlaigh, *An Irish Navvy* (Routledge and Kegan Paul, London, 1964) (translated by Valentin Iremonger from *Dialann Deoraí*), p. 182.

8. *Commission on Emigration and Other Population Problems*, p. 335; the population of Dublin in 1951 was 522,183 and Dún Laoghaire was 47,920. Cork had 74,567 inhabitants, Limerick 50,820 and Galway 21,316.

9. ibid.

10. Mary E. Daly, *Social and Economic History of Ireland since 1800* (The Educational Company, Dublin, 1981), p. 163.

11. Quoted in Éamonn C. McKee, 'From Precepts to Praxis: Irish Governments and Economic Policy, 1939–1952', PHD, University College, Dublin, 1987.

12. *The Irish Press*, 24 March 1952.

13. Mulcahy in the Dail, *The Irish Times*, 23 April 1952.

14. *The Irish Press*, 22 May 1952.

15. John Whyte, *Church and State in Modern Ireland 1923–1979* (Gill & Macmillan, Dublin, 1984), p. 280.

16. Ruth Barrington, *Health, Medicine and Politics in Ireland 1900–1970* (Institute of Public Administration, Dublin, 1987), p. 247.

17. Department of the Taoiseach, s13444J, National Archives, Dublin, and Barrington, *Health, Medicine and Politics in Ireland*, p. 247.

18. ibid.

19. Lord Longford and Thomas P. O'Neill, *Éamon de Valera* (Arrow Books, London, 1970), p. 442.

20. Departmental minute, 18 April 1953, s13444J, National Archives, Dublin. See also Barrington, *Health, Medicine and Politics in Ireland*, pp. 239–40 and Whyte, *Church and State*, p. 285 ff.

21. Confidential source. I have found no supporting evidence for this hypothesis in the archives of the Department of Foreign Affairs. However, if Walshe wrote to de Valera on this matter, he would have used 'back channels', and material might be found in the de Valera papers.

22. Barrington, *Healthy Medicine and Politics in Ireland*, p. 241.

23. Paul Blanshard, *The Irish and Catholic Power* (Derek Verschoyle, London, 1954), p. 67 ff.

24. Department of Taoiseach, s2321 A, National Archives, Dublin.

25. Department of Justice minute, unsigned, 14 December 1953, Department of the Taoiseach, s2321 A, National Archives, Dublin.

26. McQuaid to de Valera, 29 December 1953, Department of the Taoiseach, s2321 A, National Archives, Dublin.

27. Department of Justice, unsigned minute, 25 March 1954, Department of the Taoiseach, s2321 A, National Archives, Dublin.

28. *Kavanagh's Weekly*, VOL. 1, NO. 13 (final number), quoted in Peter Kavanagh (ed.), *Patrick Kavanagh*, p. 137.

29. *Kavanagh's Weekly*, VOL. 1, NO. 5, cited in Kavanagh (ed.), *Patrick Kavanagh, Man and Poet* (Goldsmith Press, Newbridge, 1987), p. 129.

30. *Kavanagh's Weekly*, VOL. 1, NO. 1, Kavanagh (ed.), *Kavanagh*, p. 124.

31. *Studies* was the forum for Patrick Lynch's important article, 'The Economist and Public Policy', VOL. XLII (Autumn 1953), pp. 241–74.

32. Miriam Hederman O'Brien, *The Road to Europe: Irish Attitudes 1948–61* (Institute of Public Administration, Dublin, 1983), p. 47.

33. Huston to Secretary of State, 28 June 1951, RG 59, 740A.00/6–2871, FRUS, 1951, VOL. IV (Part 1), pp. 524–27.

34. US ambassador in France, David K. Bruce to Secretary of State, 31 August 1951, RG 59, 740A.5/8, ERUS, 1951, VOL. IV (Part 1), pp. 527–28.

35. Huston to Secretary of State, 21 September 1951, 740A.5/9–2151, FRUS, 1951, VOL. IV (Part 1), p. 533.

36. See Ronan Fanning, 'The Dublin Link', *Sunday Independent*, 6 January 1991; see also Lt. Gen. Peadar McMahon to Seán Nunan, secretary of External Affairs, 25 January 1955, Department of Foreign Affairs, Secretary's files, A60/A, National Archives, Dublin.

37. See *FRUS*, 1952–1954, VOL. VI (Part 2), p. 1558 ff; the Mutual Security Agreement between Ireland and the United States was finally signed on 17 June 1954, just two weeks after the inter-party government had been returned to power. It came into force on 15 February 1955.

38. *FRUS*, 1952–1954, VOL. VI (Part 2), pp. 1561–62.

39. See Seán Lemass speech, *The Irish Press*, 13 May 1954.

40. Editorial in *The Irish Press*, 15 May 1954.

41. *The Irish Press*, 17 and 18 May 1954.

42. *The Irish Press*, 21 May 1954.

43. *The Irish Press*, 1 June 1954.

44. Barrington, *Health, Medicine and Politics in Ireland*, pp. 245–47.

45. Undated minute, Department of the Taoiseach, S2321B, National Archives, Dublin; for background to the appointment of O'Faoláin to the Arts Council, see Brian P. Kennedy, *Dreams and Responsibilities*, pp. 117–18.

46. The archbishop's views had been given to the FAI in a phone message between Father O'Regan and J. Wickham. The former had asked whether it was the policy of the FAI to bring in representatives of a country which had persecuted Cardinal Stepinac. *Irish Independent*, 17 October 1955.

47. Knights of Columbanus, An Ríoghacht and the Catholic Association of International Relations all protested. *Irish Independent*, 17 October 1955.

48. Moynihan minute, 19 October 1955, Department of the Taoiseach, S10657C, National Archives, Dublin, 1949; O'Kelly had attended the Ireland-Sweden game in Dublin in 1949. On that occasion one Swedish newspaper commented sarcastically, noting the warm manner in which he greeted each Irish player, that since all the players lived outside Ireland, the President was glad to see them again. William Warnock, Irish Legation, Stockholm, to Iveagh House, 24 November 1949, Department of the Taoiseach, S14650A, National Archives, Dublin.

49. *The Irish Times*, 19 October 1955.

50. *Irish Independent*, 17 October 1955.

51. Traynor had been Minister for Defence in the previous Fianna Fáil government. He was to become Minister for Justice in 1957.

52. *The Irish Press*, 1 June 1954.

53. See Henry Patterson, *The Politics of Illusion: Republicanism and Socialism in Modern Ireland* (Hutchinson, London, 1989), pp. 80–81; see also Tim Pat Coogan, *The IRA* (Pall Mall Press, London, 1980), pp. 309–44 and James

Bowyer Bell, *The Secret Army: History of the Irish Republican Army 1916–79* (Academy Press, Dublin, 1979), pp. 289–326.

54. Denis Donoghue, *Warrenpoint* (Jonathan Cape, London, 1991), pp. 162–63.

55. *The Irish Press*, 1–10 January 1957.

56. This theme has been explored most extensively by Conor Cruise O'Brien. See, in particular, 'Shades of Republicanism', in Conor Cruise O'Brien, *Herod: Reflections on Political Violence* (Hutchinson, London, 1978). More recently, the same author has analysed the concept of nationalism in *God Land: Reflections on Religion and Nationalism* (Harvard University Press, Cambridge, 1988).

57. Taft to State Department, 29 June 1954. RG 59, 740A, 00/6–2954, *FRUS*, 1952–1954, VOL. 2 (Part 2), p. 1563.

58. Allen Dulles to Cosgrave, 26 February 1955, Department of Foreign Affairs, Secretary's files, A60/1, National Archives, Dublin.

59. Department of Foreign Affairs, Secretary's files, A60/1, National Archives, Dublin.

60. Department of the Taoiseach, S13570C, National Archives, Dublin.

61. *The Irish Press*, 25 January 1957.

62. *The Irish Press*, 12 March 1957; the adverse trade balance for 1950 was £87 million, £123 million for 1951, £70.5 million in 1952, £68.5 million in 1953, £64.5 million in 1954 and £94 million in 1955.

63. *The Irish Press*, 5 February 1957; Clann na Poblachta still had three seats, Clann na Talmhan had five and there were five independents.

64. *The Irish Press*, 18 January 1957; see also Farrell, *Seán Lemass*, p. 93.

65. *The Irish Press*, 15 February 1957.

66. *The Irish Press*, 12 February 1957.

67. De Valera, quoted in *The Irish Press*, 21 February 1957.

68. *The Irish Press*, 5 March 1957.

69. *The Irish Press*, 8 March 1957.

70. This was told to me by his close friend, John Moher. Apparently, his resignation was never made public.

71. John Moher is again my source.

72. Cruise O'Brien, 'Ireland in International Affairs', in Owen Dudley Edwards (ed.), *Conor Cruise O'Brien Introduces Ireland* (André Deutsch, London, 1969), pp. 104–34; see also his memoir *My Life and Themes* (Poolbeg Press, Dublin, 1998).

73. Cruise O'Brien quotes from the three principles, outlined in 1956 by Liam Cosgrave, on which Irish foreign policy was based. See *Dáil Debates*, VOL. CLIX, cols 127–226, 3–4 June 1956.

74. *The Irish Times*, 2 November 1957.

75. Draft letter, undated, but probably mid-November 1957, Department of the Taoiseach, s1115a, National Archives, Dublin.

76. Draft letter of reply sent by Iveagh House to de Valera, dated 6 September, Department of the Taoiseach, s11115a, National Archives, Dublin.

77. See Department of the Taoiseach, s15153, National Archives, Dublin. I am grateful to Mr Maurice Moynihan for the information concerning the return of the rifle to the South African government during the time of the first inter-party government.

78. rg56, 320/8–1657, National Archives, Washington; see also Cruise O'Brien, *To Katanga and Back: A un Case History* (Simon and Schuster, New York, 1962), p. 22.

79. Papers of John Foster Dulles, Telephone calls series; Box no. 7, a67–28, Dwight D. Eisenhower Library; reference found by Maurice Fitzgerald.

80. rg59, 320/9–2457, National Archives, Washington.

81. Cruise O'Brien, *To Katanga and Back*, p. 23.

82. Boland manuscript.

83. McLeod minute of meeting, 2 October 1957, rg 59, 320/10–1057.

84. Boland manuscript; Boland continued to play a distinguished role at the un until he retired in November 1963 to become chancellor of Trinity College, Dublin. Boland was president of the 4th committee in 1957. He also presided at the fifteenth assembly of the un during the course of which Khrushchev and Hammarskjöld exchanged views.

85. Minute of McLeod meeting with Aiken, 9 October 1957, rg 59, 320–10–1057, National Archives, Washington.

86. Report by Arthur B. Emmons iii, 17 October 1957, rg 59, 320/10–1757, National Archives, Washington.

87. McLeod memorandum, 2 October 1957, rg 59,320/10–1057, National Archives, Washington.

88. Copy of letter to An Tóstal theatre festival, 11 December 1957. Department of the Taoiseach, s15297c, National Archives, Dublin.

89. *The Irish Press*, 12 February 1958.

90. *The Irish Press*, 12 February 1958.

91. *The Standard*, 28 February 1958.

92. The bishop of Raphoe, William MacNeely, and the bishop of Achonry, James Ferguson, to de Valera, 30 January 1958, s2321b, National Archives, Dublin.

93. Oscar Traynor to de Valera, 4 February 1958, Department of the Taoiseach, s2321b, National Archives, Dublin; Professor Piggott, Professor Christopher O'Reilly and Dermot O'Flynn resigned on 14 September 1957 and were replaced by Judge Charles Conroy, chairman, F.T. O'Reilly and Emma Bodkin.

94. Draft of letter from de Valera to Bishop MacNeely, circa 6 March 1958, Department of the Taoiseach, s2321B, National Archives, Dublin.
95. Maurice Moynihan's introductory note (115), *Speeches and Statements by Éamon de Valera*, p. 580.
96. The wife and children ultimately returned home; see s16247, Department of the Taoiseach, National Archives, Dublin.
97. *The Irish Press*, 20 June 1959.
98. C.S. Andrews, *Man of No Property* (Mercier Press, Dublin, 1982), p. 235.
99. For a polished and elegant review of de Valera's career, see Lee, *Ireland 1912–1985*, pp. 330–41.
100. Seán O'Faoláin, *De Valera—A New Biography* (Penguin, London, 1939), p. 180.

Chapter 7: Seán Lemass and the 'Rising Tide' of the 1960s (pp. 250–302)

1. Fergal Tobin, *The Best of Decades: Ireland in the 1960s* (Gill & Macmillan, Dublin, 1984).
2. Cardinal William Conway, who replaced Cardinal D'Alton as archbishop of Armagh in 1963, spoke of a 'certain sense of spring in the air through the Church as a whole and, if I mistake not, in Ireland also.' Quoted in Tobin, *The Best of Decades*, p. 77.
3. Brian Farrell, *Seán Lemass* (Gill & Macmillan, Dublin, 1983), pp. 120–21.
4. T.K. Whitaker, *Interests* (Institute of Public Administration, Dublin, 1983), pp. 90–91.
5. Profile of Lemass in *The Irish Press*, 24 June 1959.
6. Farrell, *Chairman or Chief*, p. 60.
7. Denis J. Maher, *The Tortuous Path: The Course of Ireland's Entry into the EEC 1948–73* (Institute of Public Administration, Dublin, 1986), p. 98 ff.
8. *The Irish Press*, 29 April 1959.
9. *The Irish Press*, 16 April 1959.
10. *The Irish Press*, 9 October 1961.
11. Maher, *The Tortuous Path*, p. 87.
12. *Dáil Debates*, 12 April 1961, VOL. 188, cols 169–170 and 16 May 1961, cols 295 ff.
13. See also *The New York Times*, 18 July 1962, quoted in Maher, *The Tortuous Path*, p. 152.
14. Ireland had accredited a representative to the EEC in the summer of 1959. Department of the Taoiseach, s16671A, National Archives, Dublin.
15. Joseph T. Carroll, 'General de Gaulle and Ireland's EEC Application,' in Pierre Joannon (ed.), *De Gaulle and Ireland* (Institute of Public Administration, Dublin, 1991), pp. 81–97.

16. Conor Cruise O'Brien, *To Katanga and Back: A UN Case History* (Simon and Schuster, New York, 1962), p. 44 ff. He gives two reasons for his being chosen: one that he was Irish and the second that Hammarskjöld had read and liked his book *Maria Cross*. The latter reason is confirmed by Boland in his memoirs. He mentions the name of another Irish diplomat who had been considered, but states that the determining factor for the UN secretary general was the fact that he liked *Maria Cross*: see Boland manuscript.

17. *The Irish Press*, 9 September 1961.

18. *The Irish Times*, 27 September 1961; quoted in Michael Gallagher, *The Irish Labour Party in Transition 1957–82* (Manchester University Press, Manchester, 1982), p. 46.

19. *The Irish Times*, 26 September 1961; quoted in Gallagher, *The Irish Labour Party in Transition*, p. 47.

20. Seán Dunne, *In My Father's House* (Anna Livia Press, Dublin, 1991), p. 75.

21. Gallagher, *The Irish Labour Party in Transition*, p. 48 and Appendix 1.

22. *The Irish Press*, 11 and 12 October 1961. In this round, Lemass was freer to name his own cabinet. MacEntee (Health), Aiken (External Affairs), Ryan (Finance) and Smith (Agriculture) were retained by him. However, Smith resigned Agriculture in 1964 and the talented and ambitious Charles Haughey, son-in-law of Lemass, was switched from the portfolio of Justice to fill the vacancy. A newcomer, Brian Lenihan, moved up from the position of parliamentary secretary to the Minister for Justice. Hillery, Lynch and Blaney held onto the same ministries: Education, Industry and Commerce and Local Government respectively. Boland was made Minister for Social Welfare and Gerald Bartley took over Defence. At the junior level, Lemass brought in George Colley to Lands and Donogh O'Malley to Finance.

23. Interview with John Moher and other members of Fianna Fáil.

24. MacEntee papers, P67/328, Archives Department, UCD, Dublin.

25. *The Irish Press*, 26 and 27 June 1963; the CIA report was found by my MA student Maurice FitzGerald.

26. See editorial in *The Irish Press*, 29 June 1963.

27. Tobin, *The Best of Decades*, pp. 60–61.

28. Farrell, *Lemass*, p. 112; see also S14996, Department of the Taoiseach, National Archives, Dublin.

29. Muiris Mac Conghail, 'The Creation of RTÉ and the Impact of Television', in Brian Farrell (ed.), *Communication and Community in Ireland* (Mercier Press, Dublin and Cork, 1984), pp. 66–67.

30. *Statistical Abstract of Ireland*, 1965, pp. 317–18.

31. *Statistical Abstract of Ireland*, 1970/71, p. 334.

32. *Statistical Abstract of Ireland*, 1990, p. 324.
33. Quoted in Mac Conghail, 'The Creation of RTÉ', p. 69.
34. Many of the facts in this section have been taken from Brian P. Kennedy, *Dreams and Responsibilities: The State and the Arts in Independent Ireland* (Arts Council, Dublin, 1990), p. 137 ff.
35. See Ciaran Carty, *Robert Ballagh* (Magill, Dublin, 1986).
36. Kennedy, *Dreams and Responsibilities*, p. 165.
37. ibid.
38. See the following books on the visual arts: Bruce Arnold, *A Concise History of Irish Art* (Thames and Hudson, London, 1989); Kenneth McConkey, *A Free Spirit: Irish Art 1860–1960* (Antique Collectors Club, London, 1990); and S.B. Kennedy, *Irish Art and Modernism 1880–1950* (Institute of Irish Studies, Belfast, 1991).
39. Seán MacRéamoinn, 'An tÉadach is an Duine,' in Bernard Harris and Grattan Freyer (eds), *Integrating Tradition: The Achievements of Seán Ó Riada* (Irish Humanities Center, Ballina, 1981), p. 9.
40. Seán Mac Reamoinn, 'An tÉadach is an Duine', in Harris and Freyer (eds), *Integrating Tradition*, p. 9.
41. Gar O'Donnell (private) in 'Philadelphia here I come!'. See Brian Friel, *Selected Plays* (Faber and Faber, London, 1984), p. 33.
42. John B. Keane, *Three Plays* (Mercier Press, Cork and Dublin, 1990), p. 7.
43. Fintan O'Toole, 'Introduction', in *Three Plays* by John B. Keane (Mercier Press, Cork and Dublin, 1990), p. 7.
44. Interview with John McGahern in Julia Carlson (ed.), *Banned in Ireland: Censorship and the Irish Writer* (Routledge, London, 1990), pp. 53–68. See also John McGahern, *The Leavetaking* (Faber and Faber, London, 1974), for an account of a teacher in a similar situation.
45. John Whyte, *Church and State in Modern Ireland 1923–1979*, pp. 343–44; interview with Brian Lenihan.
46. The writer Seán Dunne gave me this valuable piece of information.
47 Edna O'Brien interview, in Julie Carlson (ed.), *Banned in Ireland: Censorship and the Irish Writer*, pp. 71–79.
48. Tobin, *The Best of Decades*, p. 140.
49. See, in particular, chapters 1, 10 and 25 in Vincent Power, *Send 'em Home Sweatin': The Showbands' Story* (Kilnadore Press, Dublin, 1990); I am also grateful to the author for his help researching the showband scene.
50. John Whyte, *Church and State in Modern Ireland 1923–1979* (Gill & Macmillan, Dublin, 1984), p. 335.
51. Xavier Rynne, *Letters from Vatican City* (Faber and Faber, London, 1963), p. 108.

52. John Feeney, *John Charles McQuaid: The Man and the Mask* (Mercier Press, Dublin, 1974), p. 55.

53. A number of the essays relating to Ireland which appeared in *Herder Correspondence* can be found in Desmond Fennell (ed.), *The Changing Face of Catholic Ireland* (Geoffrey Chapman, London, 1968).

54. See John Weafer, 'Vocations: A Review of National and International Trends', *The Furrow*, VOL. 39, NO. 8 (August 1988), p. 505. See also Weafer, 'Change and Continuity in Irish Religion, 1974–1984', *Doctrine and Life*, VOL. 36, NO. 10 (December 1986), pp. 507–17; Weafer, 'Listening to the Young Church', *The Furrow*, VOL. 42, NO. 1 (January 1991), pp. 18–27; and Weafer, 'The Irish Laity: Some Findings of the 1984 National Survey', *Doctrine and Life*, VOL. 36, NO. 5 (May-June 1986), pp. 247–53.

55. The above remarks are based on Michael Mills's interview with Lemass in *The Irish Press*, 27 January 1969.

56. George Colley was chairman. The following people served: David Andrews, Don Davern, Senator James Dooge, Seán Dunne, Denis Jones, Robert Molloy, T.F. O'Higgins, Senator Michael O'Kennedy, Senator Eoin Ryan, Gerard Sweetman and James Tully. In November 1966, Seán Lemass, who had stepped down from the leadership of Fianna Fáil, joined the committee in place of Davern.

57. Whyte, *Church and State 1923–1979*, p. 350.

58. ibid., p. 389.

59. On the same day, Irish voters approved the reduction of the voting age in general and presidential elections and referenda from 21 to 18 (724,836 for and 131,514 against). Department of the Environment, *Results of Presidential Elections and Referenda 1937–1984*, pp. 33–35.

60. *The Irish Times*, 30 July 1968.

61. *The Irish Times*, 5 August 1968.

62. *The Irish Press*, 30 July 1968.

63. *The Irish Times*, 30 July 1968.

64. *The Irish Times*, 1 August 1968.

65. See Peter Lennon, 'Sex and the Irish', *The Irish Times*, 31 October 1966; this article is a vigorous attack on 'a failure' of education in Ireland. Lennon emphasised the receptivity of Irish society to outside influences and attacked an educational system which was 'supervised by clerical authority'. That system failed to provide adequate sex education, he argued.

66. Reports and printed documents of the Corporation of Dublin, January-December 1961, no. 109, pp. 406–10; see also report *Housing—Progress and Prospects* (Government Publications, Dublin, 1964) which laid the basis for

many of the developments in the 1960s and 1970s.

67. Reports and printed documents of the Corporation of Dublin, January-December 1962, no. 132, pp. 462–84.

68. Minutes of the Dublin City Council (special meeting), 17 June 1963, pp. 126–30, Dublin Corporation Archives.

69 Report, no. 62, 1964, pp. 269–74.

70. Minutes of the Dublin City Council, 11 January 1965, pp. 20–22 and 77–79.

71. Reports and printed documents of the Corporation of Dublin, January-December 1965, no. 2, pp. 2–4, 53–61 and 351–67.

72. Frank McDonald, *The Destruction of Dublin* (Gill & Macmillan, Dublin, 1985), p. 40.

73. Quote in McDonald, *The Destruction of Dublin*, p. 20.

74. Kevin Boland, *The Rise and Decline of Fianna Fáil* (Mercier Press, Cork, 1982), p. 101.

75. Paul Durcan, 'The Haulier's Wife meets Jesus on the Road near Moone', in *The Berlin Wall Café* (Blackstaff Press, Belfast, 1985), p. 4.

76. Interview with Father Austin Flannery, November 1991; for further details see *The Irish Press*, *Evening Press*, *Irish Independent*, *Evening Herald* and *The Irish Times* for 3–9 May. See *Washington Post*, 21 September 1968. See also *Nusight*, June 1968, and article by Peter Lemass 'Housing', *The Furrow*, VOL. 20, NO. 3 (March 1969), pp. 116–27. Dermot Bolger has edited an important collection of essays which captures the sense of displacement of the migrants in the new Dublin suburbs: *Invisible Dublin* (Raven Arts Press, Dublin, 1991).

77. John Coolahan, *Irish Education: Its History and Structure* (Institute of Public Administration, Dublin, 1981), pp. 165–66.

78. Liam Ryan, 'Social Dynamite: A Study of Early School-Leavers', *Christus Rex*, VOL. XXI, NO. 1 (January 1967), pp. 7–44; this was one of the most important sociological articles written during the 1960s. It is to be regretted that its findings seemed to make no difference to public planning in the 1970s and 1980s. The 'official mind' in many Irish urban centres—town planners, architects and local government officials—consigned people to live in bad surroundings; it was good enough for the lower orders. I am certain no architect ever lived in the kind of houses designed for the estates of urban Ireland.

79. Dunne, *In My Father's House*, pp. 78–81.

80. Séamas Ó Buachalla, *Education Policy in Twentieth-Century Ireland* (Wolfhound Press, Dublin, 1988), p. 73.

81. Ó Buachalla, *Education Policy in Twentieth-Century Ireland*, pp. 74–75 and Coolahan, *Irish Education*, pp. 193–94.

82. *The Irish Times*, 12 September 1966.

83. Cited in Seán O'Connor, 'Post-Primary Education: Now and in the Future', *Studies*, VOL. LVII, NO. 227 (Autumn 1968), p. 234.

84. Ó Buachalla, *Education Policy in Twentieth-Century Ireland*, p. 76.

85. Maurice Manning, 'Women in Irish National and Local Politics 1922–77' in Margaret MacCurtain and Donnacha Ó Corráin (eds), *Women in Irish Society: The Historical Dimension* (Arlen House, Dublin, 1978), p. 94.

86. ibid., pp. 94–95.

87. ibid., p. 97.

88. Yvonne Fitzsimons, 'The Origins of the Contemporary Women's Movement in Ireland: A Comparative Perspective'. Paper presented to the Political Studies Association of Ireland, 19–20 October 1990, p. 8.

89. Eunice McCarthy, 'Women and Works in Ireland', in MacCurtain and Ó Corráin (eds), *Women in Irish Society*, p. 104.

90. Fianna Fáil parliamentary party minutes, 19 August 1933, Fianna Fáil Archives, Upper Mount Street, Dublin.

91. Department of Education memorandum for cabinet, 14 February 1953 and Department of Finance memorandum 19 February 1953. I am grateful to Dr Mary Harris for a copy of the cited documents. Department of the Taoiseach, s6369A, National Archives, Dublin.

92. For future literature on this topic, see the Annual Reports of the Employment pamphlet, *Code of Practice—Equality of Opportunity in Employment 1990* and reports by John Blackwell, *Women in the Labour Force* (Employment Equality Agency, Dublin, 1986). See also second report by the same author, July 1989 and supplement, January 1990.

93. Kennedy, Giblin and McHugh, *The Economic Development of Ireland in the Twentieth Century*, pp. 66–68.

94. Charles McCarthy, *The Decade of Upheaval: Irish Trade Unions in the Nineteen Sixties* (Institute of Public Administration, Dublin, 1973), chapters 1–4.

95. *Statistical Abstract of Ireland, 1965* (Dublin: Institute of Public Administration, 1973), p. 236.

96. Tobin, *The Best of Decades*, p. 133.

97. Garret FitzGerald, *All in a Life: An Autobiography* (Gill & Macmillan, Dublin, 1992), p. 67.

98. Declan Costello, 'The Priest and Public Affairs', *Christus Rex*, VOL. XXIII, NO. 4 (October 1969), pp. 293–98.

99. Garret FitzGerald, *Studies*, VOL. LII, NO. 212 (Winter 1964), p. 340; Dr FitzGerald refers to this article in *All in a Life*, p. 65.

100. FitzGerald, *All in a Life*, p. 65.

101. Tobin, *The Best of Decades*, p. 133.

102. *The Irish Press*, 12 April 1965.

103. *The Irish Press*, 13 April 1965.

104. *The Irish Press*, 19 March 1965.

105. Garret FitzGerald, *All in a Life*, p. 65.

106. *The Irish Press*, 25 March 1965.

107. *The Irish Press* 20 March 1965.

108. *The Irish Press*, 3 April 1965.

109. Ryan retired and was replaced in Finance by Jack Lynch. George Colley took over Education, and Paddy Hillery went to the new Department of Labour. Seán Flanagan was brought in as Minister for Health and Donogh O'Malley as Minister for Education. Brian Lenihan was the new Minister for Justice. His father had also won a vital seat for Fianna Fáil in the election by a final margin of 13 votes.

110. FitzGerald, *All in a Life*, p. 70.

111. *The Irish Press*, 15 January 1965.

112. *The Irish Press*, 10 February 1965.

113. *The Irish Press*, 11 March 1965.

114. *The Irish Press*, 1 March 1965.

115. *The Irish Press*, 2 March 1965.

116. Maurice Moynihan (ed.), *Speeches and Statements by Éamon de Valera 1917–1973* (Gill & Macmillan, Dublin, 1980), p. 604.

117. Maurice Moynihan (ed.), *Speeches and Statements*, pp. 605–06; for a fresh look at the historiography of 1916, see Mairín Ní Dhonnchadha and Theo Dorgan (eds), *Revising the Rising* (Field Day, Derry, 1991).

118. Department of the Environment, *Results of Presidential Elections and Referenda, 1937–1984*, p. 15.

119. Tobin, *The Best of Decades*, pp. 142–43.

120. FitzGerald, *All in a Life*, p. 76.

121. Statistical Abstract of Ireland.

122. *The Irish Times*, 14 October 1966.

123. *The Irish Times*, 21 October 1966.

124. *The Irish Times*, 22 October 1966.

125. *The Irish Times*, 27 October 1966.

126. *The Irish Press*, 2 November 1966. According to Brian Lenihan, Lemass had been suffering from phlebitis and his doctor had advised him that he should think of slowing down. But he had ignored that advice until, shortly before his shock announcement, he was forced to leave a public function when he began to feel ill.

127. *The Irish Press*, 1 November 1966; Michael Mills must have been absolutely sure of his source. His reputation was such that he would not have gone into print without being certain that he was on safe ground.

128. I have built this account of the leadership struggle against Fianna Fáil on a number of interviews with party members and journalists who wrote on political affairs in the 1960s.

129. *The Irish Press*, 10 November 1966.

130. *The Irish Press*, 9 November 1966.

131. Miriam Hederman O'Brien, 'Fifty Years of Active Service—A tribute to Seán Lemass', *The Irish Press*, 9 November 1966; see also interview in *The Word*, January and February 1966 and interview with Michael Mills in *The Irish Press*, 18 January 1969.

132. *The Irish Times*, 12 May 1971.

133. ibid.

134. ibid.

135. ibid.

Chapter 8: The Shifting Balance of Power: Jack Lynch and Liam Cosgrave, 1966–1977 (pp. 303–336)

1. Dick Walsh, *The Party: Inside Fianna Fáil* (Gill & Macmillan, Dublin, 1986), p. 95.

2. Confidential source.

3. *The Irish Press*, 23 November 1966.

4. *The Irish Press*, 9 December 1966.

5. Michael Gallagher, *The Irish Labour Party in Transition, 1957–82* (Manchester University Press, Manchester, 1982), p. 75.

6. Interviews with Fianna Fáil activists.

7. *The Irish Press*, 14 October 1968.

8. *The Irish Press*, 13 October 1968.

9. *The Irish Press*, 16 October 1968.

10. *The Irish Press*, 4 October 1968.

11. Garret FitzGerald, *All in a Life* (Gill & Macmillan, Dublin, 1992), pp. 77–78.

12. FitzGerald, *All in a Life*, pp. 78–80.

13. Gallagher, *The Irish Labour Party in Transition*, p. 170.

14. ibid., p. 170.

15. Michael Mills, interview with Jack Lynch, *The Irish Press*, 17 June 1969.

16. *The Irish Press*, 17 May 1969.

17. *The Irish Press*, 19 May 1969.

18. *The Irish Press*, 17 May 1969.

19. Gallagher, *The Irish Labour Party in Transition*, p. 173.

20. Dick Walsh, *The Party*, p. 95.

21. Michael Mills interview with Jack Lynch, *The Irish Press*, 17 June 1969.

22. Joe Carroll, 'Hardly any mention of foreign policy', *The Irish Press*, 16 June 1969.

23. Dick Walsh, *The Party*, p. 95. There were, however, a number of people of talent elected to the opposition benches. Garret FitzGerald had succeeded John A. Costello in Dublin South-East. Conor Cruise O'Brien, Justin Keating and David Thornley were elected for Labour.

24. Micheál Ó Moráin was given Justice, Neil Blaney Agriculture and Fisheries, Kevin Boland Local Government and Social Welfare. Patrick Lalor was given Posts and Telegraphs, Pádraig Faulkner Education, George Colley Industry and Commerce and the Gaeltacht, Brian Lenihan Transport and Power, Charles Haughey Finance, Joseph Brennan Labour, Seán Flanagan Lands, Jim Gibbons Defence, and Colm Condon was made Attorney General. Erskine Childers was appointed Tánaiste and Minister for Health. Patrick Hillery went to Iveagh House as Minister for External Affairs.

25. *New Ireland Forum Report*, p. 15.

26. *New Ireland Forum Report*, pp. 15–16; see also special study for *New Ireland Forum: The Cost of Violence arising from the Northern Ireland Crisis since 1969.*

27. I am grateful to members of the Red Cross and of the Irish army who helped me to research the background to the refugee situation in 1969 and 1970.

28. That phrase was used by Seamus Heaney in his collection, *North* (Faber and Faber, London, 1975), p. 68.

29. Paul Arthur and Keith Jeffery, *Northern Ireland since 1968* (Basil Blackwell, Oxford, 1988), pp. 33–61.

30. For background, see Henry Patterson, *The Politics of Illusion: Republicanism and Socialism in Modern Ireland* (Hutchinson, London, 1989).

31. *The Irish Times*, 29 August 1969.

32. *The Irish Times*, 18 August 1969.

33. *The Irish Times*, 21 August 1969.

34. *The Irish Times*, 21 August 1969.

35. See editorial in *The Irish Times*, 22 August 1969.

36. Conor Cruise O'Brien, *Herod: Reflections on Political Violence* (Hutchinson, London, 1978), p. 137.

37. *The Irish Times*, 15 December 1969.

38. *The Irish Times*, 9 December 1969.

39. *The Irish Times*, 12 December 1969.

40. *The Irish Times*, 10 December 1969.

41. *The Irish Times*, 12 December 1969; for Backbencher column, see *The Irish Times*, 13 December 1969.

42. *The Irish Times*,15 December 1969.

43. *The Irish Times*, 19 January 1970.

44. Interview with John Moher.

45. This theory was developed for me by Liam Moher, *The Cork Examiner*, who had it first expounded when he was with his father, the ex-Fianna Fáil TD, John Moher, in the house of Father Bobby Dineen—who had played on the same Cork team as Lynch and knew him well.

46. Walsh, *The Party*, p. 109.

47. Bruce Arnold, *What Kind of Country: Modern Irish Politics 1968–1983* (Jonathan Cape, London, 1984), p. 65.

48. Article by Dick Walsh in *The Irish Times*, 6 May 1970.

49. *The Irish Times*, 6 May 1970.

50. Arnold, *What Kind of Country*, p. 66.

51. *The Irish Times*, 8 May 1970.

52. *The Irish Times*, 7 January 1970.

53. *The Irish Times*, 9 May 1970.

54. *The Irish Times*, 11 May 1970.

55. *The Irish Times*, 9 May 1970.

56. Quoted in Tom MacIntrye, *Through the Bridewell Gate: A Diary of the Dublin Arms Trial* (Faber and Faber, London, 1971), p. 214. Other accounts of the Arms Trial can be found in *Magill*, May, June and July 1980: see also Kevin Boland, *'We Won't Stand (idly) By'* (Kelly Kane, Dublin, 1972) and by the same author, *The Rise and Decline of Fianna Fáil* (Mercier Press, Dublin, 1982). See also James Kelly, *Orders from the Captain* (The author, Dublin, 1971) and T. Ryle Dwyer, *Charlie: The Political Biography of Charles J. Haughey* (Gill & Macmillan, Dublin, 1987).

57. Arnold, *What Kind of Country*, p. 71.

58. See Tom MacIntrye, *Through the Bridewell Gate*, p. 205 and Arnold, *What Kind of Country*, p. 75, footnote 59; see also coverage in *The Irish Times* and *The Irish Press*, 24 October 1970.

59. ibid.

60. Tom MacIntrye, *Through the Bridewell Gate*, pp. 207–08.

61. *The Irish Times*, 24 October 1970.

62. *The Irish Times*, 24 October 1970.

63. *The Irish Times*, 26 October 1970.

64. *The Irish Times*, 27 October 1970.

65. John Peck, *Dublin from Downing Street* (Gill & Macmillan, Dublin, 1978), p. 111.

66. *The Irish Times*, 22 February 1971.

67. *The Irish Times*, 22 February 1971.

68. Clare O'Halloran, *Partition and the Limits of Irish Nationalism* (Gill & Macmillan, Dublin, 1987), p. 188.

69. See 'Diaries of Peter Berry', 5 July 1970, *Magill*, June 1980.

70. *The Irish Times*, 4 January 1971.

71. John Peck, *Dublin from Downing Street*, p. 111.

72. W.D. Flackes and Sidney Elliot, *Northern Ireland: A Political Directory*, 3rd ed. (Blackstaff Press, Belfast, 1989), p. 68.

73. *Sunday Times Insight Team*, Ulster, p. 224.

74. John Peck, *Dublin from Downing Street*, pp. 128–29.

75. I was a member of the National Union of Journalists group which set out for the embassy. The march was manipulated to descend into a riot by the IRA. The trade union movement was not sufficiently disciplined to demand the withdrawal of its members once the attack took place on the embassy building. The windows were first smashed by a man with a hammer. He had to climb over the railings and avoid falling into the basement before smashing the glass to enable the fire-bombers to throw their Molotov cocktails through the broken glass frames. There was nothing spontaneous about the direction which the march took. The demonstration was used by the IRA.

76. Flackes, *Northern Ireland*, p. 99.

77. Interviews with politicians; I was working as a journalist in *The Irish Press* at the time.

78. Derek Dunne and Gene Kerrigan, *Round up the Usual Suspects: Nicky Kelly and the Cosgrave Coalition* (Magill, Dublin, 1984), p. 75.

79. Two referenda were held on 7 December 1972. The first (article 16) lowered the minimum voting age from twenty-one to eighteen. There were 724,839 in favour and 131,514 against. The second (article 44) removed the reference from the constitution to the 'special position of the Roman Catholic Church' and recognised other denominations. The vote in favour was 721,003; 133,430 were against. The poll was the lowest in any referendum since the adoption of the 1937 constitution.

80. *The Irish Times*, 12 May 1972.

81. See lead story by Michael McInerney, *The Irish Times*, 6 February 1973.

82. *The Irish Times*, 7 February 1973.

83. Gallagher, *The Irish Labour Party in Transition*, p. 118.

84. See Michael McInerney story, *The Irish Times*, 8 February 1973.

85. *The Irish Times*, 14 February 1973.

86. *The Irish Times*, 15 February 1973.

87. *The Irish Times*, 23 February 1973.
88. *The Irish Times*, 23 February 1973.
89. *The Irish Times*, 2 March 1973.
90. *The Irish Times*, 14 and 15 March 1973.
91. Conor Cruise O'Brien, 'Mystique, Politique and de Valera', *The Observer*, 17 October 1982.
92. *The Irish Times*, 16 October 1976.
93. *The Irish Times*, 16 October 1976.
94. *The Irish Times*, 19 October 1976; Cosgrave and Donegan were at school together in Castleknock College.
95. *The Irish Times*, 22 October 1976.
96. *The Irish Times*, 25 October 1976.
97. See Joe Joyce and Peter Murtagh, *Blind Justice* (Poolbeg Press, Dublin, 1984); see also Dunne and Kerrigan, *Round up the Usual Suspects*.
98. Interview in Glenties, Co. Donegal, August 1990.
99. Kieran A. Kennedy, Thomas Giblin and Deirdre McHugh, *The Economic Development of Ireland in the Twentieth Century* (Routledge, London, 1988), pp. 75–76.
100. ibid., p. 76.
101. ibid., p. 77.
102. See the work of Cedric Sandford and Oliver Morrissey, *The Irish Wealth Tax: A Case Study in Economics and Politics* (ESRI, Dublin, 1985).
103. Gallagher, *The Irish Labour Party in Transition*, p. 216.
104. Arnold, *What Kind of Country*, p. 130.
105. Justin Keating, Conor Cruise O'Brien, Brendan Halligan and David Thornley lost their seats. The last two even lost their deposits. Two new Labour TDs were elected in Dublin, John Horgan and Ruairí Quinn. Gallagher, *The Irish Labour Party in Transition*, p. 217.

Chapter 9: Charles Haughey and the Poverty of Populism (pp. 337–399)

1. J.J. Lee, *Ireland 1912–1985: Politics and Society* (Cambridge University Press, Cambridge, 1989), p. 488.
2. Figures kindly supplied to me by the Department of Finance.
3. Desmond Roche, *Local Government in Ireland* (Institute of Public Administration, Dublin, 1982), pp. 148–50.
4. For a background article on the demise of local government, see Richard B. Haslam and Neil Collins, 'Local Government Finance in the Republic of Ireland—The Aftermath of Rates Abolition', in Ronan Padison and Stephen

Bailey (eds), *Local Government Finance: International Perspectives* (Routledge, London, 1988).

5. I am grateful to Richard B. Haslam, former county manager of Limerick and a colleague at UCC, for pointing out this comment to me.

6. Department of the Environment to each city and county manager (copies to assistant managers) 29 July 1988 [copy kindly given to me by Richard Haslam].

7. For an interesting treatment of the centralisation theme, see Lee, 'Centralisation and Community' in Lee (ed.), *Ireland 1945–70*, pp. 84–102.

8. See Tom J. Barrington, 'The Civic Deficit in Ireland'. Paper read to Daniel O'Connell summer school, 25 October 1992. T.J. Barrington was chairman of a group of experts who advised in the drafting of Local Government Reorganisation and Reform (Stationery Office, Dublin, 1991).

9. See *The Work of Justice, Irish Bishop's Pastoral 1977*, produced as a pamphlet.

10. Liam Ryan, 'Church and Politics: The Last Twenty-Five Years', *The Furrow*, vol. 30, no. 1 (January 1979), pp. 3–18.

11. Information supplied by Jim Cantwell of the Catholic Press and Information Office. The reason for such a high percentage of nullity decrees which contain a prohibition on marriage has to do with the fact that the cause of the nullity is judged to be serious enough to put at risk the validity of a future marriage. The vetitum may be lifted by the local bishop only if he is satisfied, after investigation, of the person's fitness for marriage in all essential respects. The purpose of the vetitum is 'to prevent the sacrament of marriage being brought into disrepute and to protect the genuine interest of any future spouse', according to the official handout from the Catholic Press and Information Office.

12. *Irish Catholic Directory*, 1973, pp. 655–66.

13. John Whyte, *Church and State in Modern Ireland 1923–1979* (Gill & Macmillan, Dublin, 1984), pp. 403–06.

14. *This Week*, 25 June 1971, p. 13, quoted in Whyte, *Church and State*, p. 404.

15. *Magill* (1, 3) December 1977, p. 27, quoted in Whyte, *Church and State*, p. 405.

16. Quoted in Whyte, *Church and State*, pp. 405–06.

17. *Irish Catholic Directory*, 1972, quoting McQuaid on 28 March 1971, p. 730.

18. See the statement of the hierarchy in the national press, 26 November 1973; also quoted in Whyte, *Church and State*, pp. 406–07.

19. *Irish Catholic Directory*, 1975, quoting Conway, 3 December 1973, p. 658.

20. *The Irish Times*, 5 April 1978.

21. Martin Mansergh (ed.), *The Spirit of the Nation: The Speeches of Charles J. Haughey* (Mercier Press, Cork and Dublin, 1986), p. 282.

22. Whyte, *Church and State*, p. 415.

23. Mansergh (ed.), *The Spirit of the Nation*, p. 261; Haughey's reply to the second stage, 25 April 1979, *Dáil Debates*, VOL. 313, cols 1477 ff.

24. *Dáil Debates*, VOL. 313, col. 1261, 5 April 1979.

25. *Dáil Debates*, VOL. 313, cols 1283–6, 25 April 1979.

26. *Dáil Debates*, VOL. 313, cols 1294–5, 5 April 1979.

27. *Dáil Debates*, VOL. 313, col. 1196, 25 April 1979.

28. *Dáil Debates*, VOL. 315, col. 1090, 26 June 1979.

29. *Dáil Debates*, VOL. 315. cols 1088–9, 26 June 1979.

30. Lee, *Ireland 1912–1985*, p. 491.

31. See newspaper reports 14 June 1978.

32. Jim O'Donnell (ed.) *Ireland—The Past Twenty Years* (Institute of Public Administration, Dublin, 1986), p. 75.

33. Eight unionists voted with the Conservatives, and two Official Unionists, Harold McCusker and John Carson, voted with Labour. The SDLP's Gerry Fitt and the independent, Frank Maguire, abstained. See Flackes, *Northern Ireland*, p. 10.

34. *The Irish Times*, 1 June 1979.

35. *The Irish Times*, 2 June 1979.

36. Bruce Arnold, *What Kind of Country: Modern Irish Politics 1968–1983* (Jonathan Cape, London, 1984), p. 135.

37. *The Irish Times*, 2 June 1979.

38. *The Irish Times*, 12 June 1979.

39. *The Irish Times*, 13 June 1979.

40. Joe Joyce and Peter Murtagh, *The Boss: Charles J. Haughey in Government* (Poolbeg Press, Dublin, 1983), p. 91.

41. Arnold, *What Kind of Country*, p. 137.

42. Joyce and Murtagh, *The Boss*, p. 91.

43. Arnold, *What Kind of Country*, p. 138.

44. Patrick Bishop and Eamonn Mallie, *The Provisional IRA* (Heinemann, London, 1987), pp. 249–50.

45. Lee, *Ireland 1912–1985*, p. 497.

46. I was working in the RTÉ newsroom at the time and ran foul of a senior newsroom executive when, as a mere reporter, I dared to question the veracity of the story which they had on tablets of stone. It was a matter of some journalistic satisfaction to have been in a position to help knock down the story that night.

47. A question by one of the journalists about an alleged trip which the President was supposed to have made to the Isle of Wight without the permission of the government was deemed by the Áras to be particularly sinister. The

speculation at the time was, had a hostile source in the cabinet helped plant such a question.

48. See Renagh Holohan's 'Divorce in the Dáil', *The Irish Times*, 18 January 1992. A number of TDs spoke to her about the fact that they had remarried. They were Senator Maurice Manning (Fine Gael), Charlie McCreevy (Fianna Fáil), Ben Briscoe (Fianna Fáil) and Ruairí Quinn (Labour Party).

49. Interview with Brian Lenihan and other members of Fianna Fáil.

50. *The Irish Times*, 6 December 1979.

51. *The Irish Times*, 6 December 1979.

52. In an interesting evaluation of Lynch's legacy, Lee quotes Senator Professor John A. Murphy on the question of achieving consensus. Lee argues that the attainment of consensus was, in the circumstances, an important contribution to Irish politics. Lee, *Ireland 1912–1985*, pp. 497–98 ff.

53. *The Irish Press*, 20 December 1979.

54. Donal Foley, 'New Taoiseach bitterly criticised in Dáil debate', *The Irish Times*, 12 December 1979.

55. *The Irish Times*, 12 December 1979; in his memoirs, Garret FitzGerald sets that particular speech in context. See *All in a Life*, pp. 341–42.

56. *The Irish Times*, 12 December 1979.

57. Michael McInerney, Seán MacEntee, 'All my sins are public', 13 December 1979.

58. Lee, *Ireland 1912–1985*, p. 499.

59. Quoted in Walter LaFeber, *The American Age* (Norton, New York, 1989), p. 619.

60. *The Irish Times*, 12 December 1979.

61. Lee, *Ireland 1912–1985*, p. 500.

62. Kennedy et al. (eds), *The Economic Development of Ireland in the Twentieth Century*, pp. 83–88.

63. Mansergh (ed.), *The Spirit of the Nation*, p. 325.

64. Whitaker, *Interests*, p. 112.

65. Mansergh (ed.), *The Spirit of the Nation*, p. 377.

66. Arnold, *What Kind of Country*, p. 167.

67. Knock airport provides a very important service to the north-west seaboard of Ireland. It has ruled out for many people from Mayo and neighbouring counties the necessity of having to make a long car, bus or train trip to and from Shannon or Dublin. In the long term, Knock will prove to be moderately successful as internal air travel in the country is developed. It is likely, however, to remain a burden on the central exchequer.

68. Mansergh (ed.), *The Spirit of the Nation*, p. 362.

69. Mansergh, *The Spirit of the Nation*, p. 363; the Arms Trial period was very much part of the contemporary Irish politics. *Magill* published three issues on

that topic in May, June and July 1980.

70. Patrick Bishop and Eamonn Mallie, *The Provisional IRA* (Heinemann, London, 1987), p. 281.
71. Mansergh (ed.), *The Spirit of the Nation*, p. 405.
72. ibid., p. 404.
73. ibid., p. 406; the leaders pledged themselves to work on a range of studies.
74. For the best treatment of the hunger strike during this period, see Pádraig O'Malley, *Biting at the Grave: The Irish Hunger Strikes and the Politics of Despair* (Blackstaff Press, Belfast, 1990). See also Tim Pat Coogan, *On the Blanket: The H-Block Story* (Ward River Press, Dublin, 1980).
75. Paul Durcan, 'In Memory: The Miami Showband: Massacred 31 July 1975' in Edna Longley (ed.) *The Selected Paul Durcan* (Blackstaff Press, Belfast, 1982), p. 93.
76. Mansergh (ed.), *The Spirit of the Nation*, pp. 489–90.
77. Roddy Doyle, *The Commitments* (Minerva, Dublin, 1991) p. 30ff: 'Fuck off a minute.—Soul is the rhythm o' the people', Jimmy said again.—'The Labour Party doesn't have soul. Fianna fuckin' Fáil doesn't have soul. The Workers' Party ain't got soul. The Irish people—no. The Dublin people—fuck the rest o' them.—The people o' Dublin, our people, remember need soul. We've got soul.'
78. Mansergh (ed.), *The Spirit of the Nation*, pp. 456–60.
79. Terry Corcoran, 'Tracking Emigration flows' in Joe Mulholland and Dermot Keogh (eds), *Emigration, Employment and Enterprise* (Hibernian University Press, Cork and Dublin, 1989), pp. 29–30.
80. The above description of the party manifestos and campaign is based on Gallagher, *The Irish Labour Party in Transition*, pp. 237–38.
81. See Lee, *Ireland 1912–1985*, p. 506 and Gallagher, *The Irish Labour Party in Transition*, pp. 240–41.
82. Quoted in Gallagher, *The Irish Labour Party in Transition*, p. 242.
83. ibid., p. 247.
84. Mansergh (ed.), *The Spirit of the Nation*, pp. 511–13.
85. Garret FitzGerald, *All in a Life*, p. 378.
86. Mansergh (ed.), *The Spirit of the Nation*, p. 524.
87. ibid., p. 572.
88. Raymond Smith, *Garret: The Enigma* (Aherlow Publishers, Dublin, 1985), p. 24.
89. ibid., p. 375.
90. ibid., p. 397.
91. Raymond Smith, *Garret: The Enigma*, p. 24.

92. FitzGerald, *All in a Life*, p. 398; this incident was to become a major issue of contention in the presidential election of 1900. Brian Lenihan, *For the Record* (Blackwater Press, Dublin, 1991).

93. Arnold, *What Kind of Country*, pp. 181–82. Also oral sources; see also Smith, *Garret: The Enigma*, p. 22 ff.

94. FitzGerald, *All in a Life*, p. 406.

95. Mansergh, *The Spirit of the Nation*, p. 616.

96. FitzGerald, *All in a Life*, pp. 406–07.

97. Joyce and Murtagh, *The Boss*, p. 104.

98. Arnold, *What Kind of Country*, p. 189.

99. See p. 126 ff.

100.John Waters, *Jiving at the Crossroads* (Blackstaff Press, Belfast, 1991), p. 157.

101. ibid., p. 169.

102. *The Irish Times*, 16 January 1992; interview with Doherty.

103. Geraldine Kennedy, Bruce Arnold and Mavis Arnold, *Plaintiffs* v. *Ireland and The Attorney General, Defendants* [1984 NO. 5011P], 12 January 1987, *The Irish Reports*, 1987, p. 587 ff.

104.Shane Kenny, *Go Dance on Somebody Else's Grave* (Kilnadore Press, Dublin, 1990), pp. 14–15.

105. Mansergh, *The Spirit of the Nation*, p. 708.

106.O'Leary had failed to secure an endorsement for coalition at the annual conference of the Labour Party in Galway on 23 October. The decision taken was to hold a post-election delegate conference to decide the matter. On 28 October, O'Leary resigned; five days later he joined Fine Gael.

107. FitzGerald, *All in a Life*, p. 418.

108.ibid., pp. 416–17.

109.Mansergh, *The Spirit of the Nation*, p. 713.

110. ibid., p. 709.

111. Kenny, *Go Dance on Somebody Else's Grave*, p. 17.

112 Mansergh, *The Spirit of the Nation*, p. 725.

113. This comment was attributed to Seán Duignan, former RTÉ journalist.

114. Interviews with Garret FitzGerald and John Hume on the origins of the New Ireland Forum.

115. These included such studies as *The Cost of Violence* arising from the Northern Ireland crisis since 1969; *The Economic Consequence of the Division of Ireland since 1920*; and *A Comprehensive Description of the Economic Structure and Situation, North and South*. There were studies on the impact of integrated economic policy and on the legal system.

116. Clare O'Halloran, *Partition and the Limits of Irish Nationalism* (Gill &

Macmillan, Dublin, 1987), pp. 195–210; the former stresses the continuity in
the thinking in the report with traditional Irish nationalism. See p. 195 ff.
Garret FitzGerald provides a personal account in *All in a Life*, p. 460 ff; see
also Lee, *Ireland 1912–1985*, pp. 680–81.

117. See Anthony Kenny, *The Road to Hillsborough: The Shaping of the Anglo-Irish
Agreement* (Pergamon Press, Oxford, 1987); Tom Hadden and Kevin Boyle,
The Anglo-Irish Agreement: Commentary Text and Official Review (Edwin
Higel Ltd, London, 1989) and FitzGerald, *All in a Life*, p. 494 ff.

118. *New Ireland Forum Report*, 23 May 1984, p. 23.

119. Tom Hesketh, *The Second Partitioning of Ireland: The Abortion Referendum of
1983* (Brandsma Books, Dublin, 1990), pp. 300–63.

120. Quoted in Gerald Barry, 'A Constitutional Nightmare', *Sunday Tribune*, 8
March 1992.

121. Quoted by Gerald Barry, *Sunday Tribune*, 8 March 1992.

122. Garret FitzGerald, 'Damage of 1983 amendment will not be easily undone', *The
Irish Times*, 22 February 1992.

123. In the division of the Dáil, Fine Gael and Labour split three ways, with eight
Fine Gael and four Labour deputies voting for the Fianna Fáil formula. The
coalition government's alternative formula read: 'Nothing in this Constitution
shall be invoked to invalidate or to deprive of force or effect a provision of the
law on grounds that it prohibits abortion.'

124. Hesketh, *The Second Partitioning of Ireland*, p. 364.

125. *The Irish Times*, 6 March 1992.

126. However, it was not all defeat for the coalition government. Before leaving
office in 1987, Garret FitzGerald had brought in an Adoption Act which
provided for the adoption of children born in wedlock who had been
abandoned by their parents. The Status of Children Act was also successfully
brought through the Oireachtas in the 1980s.

127. T. Ryle Dwyer, *Haughey's Thirty Years of Controversy* (Mercier Press, Cork,
1992), p. 134.

128. Dermot Keogh, *Ireland and Europe 1919–1989* (Hibernian University Press,
Cork and Dublin, 1989).

129. Stephen Collins, *The Haughey File* (O'Brien Press, Dublin, 1992), pp. 121–22;
Alan Dukes won the leadership, John Bruton is believed to have come second
and Peter Barry third.

130. Brian Lenihan, *For the Record* (Blackwater Press, Dublin, 1991), pp. 183–94.

131. Fergus Finlay, *Mary Robinson, A President with a Purpose* (O'Brien Press,
Dublin, 1990), pp. 120–21.

132. ibid., p. 129.

133. ibid., pp. 135–36.

134. Stephen Collins uses this apt phrase as the title of a chapter in *The Haughey File*, p. 196.

135. ibid., p. 203.

136. *The Irish Times*, 4 March 1992.

137. Collins, *The Haughey File*, p. 207.

138. ibid., p. 224.

139. Dermot Bolger, *The Journey Home* (Viking, London, 1990), p. 80.

140. Reproduced in Mulholland and Keogh (eds), *Emigration, Employment and Enterprise*, p. 15.

141. Mary Hanrahan, whose maiden name was Quaid, recalled her happy childhood growing up in County Limerick, where many of her closest friends were Protestants. She played tennis and hockey and enjoyed horse-riding. Her mother died when she was seven and she remembered that a Protestant neighbour looked after the family and took them to the funeral; she was almost certain that the same woman gave out the Rosary. She felt that religious differences between people did not matter, but said that it was hard when a Protestant friend died and she was prevented from going to the funeral by the laws of the Catholic Church. Interview, 3 February 1992.

142. Interview with Mary Hanrahan; see also the excellent book by Jerry O'Callaghan, *The Red Book: The Hanrahan Case against Merck, Sharp and Dohme* (Poolbeg, Dublin, 1992).

143. O'Callaghan, *The Red Book*, p. 3.

144. Interview with Mary Hanrahan.

145. O'Callaghan, *The Red Book*, p. 196.

146. Interview with Mary Hanrahan. I interviewed Mrs Hanrahan in a room in her home where she kept the trunk in which the belongings of the Fenian John O'Mahony were brought back to Ireland in the 1860s.

147. Alexis de Tocqueville, *Democracy in America* (Doubleday, New York, 1969), vol. 1, part 2, chapter 2, pp. 174–75.

148. See Mary Robinson's first address to the people of Ireland as their elected first citizen. See Finlay, *Mary Robinson*, p. 159.

Chapter 10: Ireland in the New Century (pp. 400–467)

1. Office of Refugee Applications Commissioner (ORAC) website statistics [cited 11-01-2005] <*http://www.orac.ie/PDF/PDF%20Stats/Annual%20Statistics/Annual%20Report%202003.pdf*>

2. The Fr Brendan Smyth case is discussed in greater detail later in this chapter.
3. *The Irish Times*, 9 June 2001.
4. *The Irish Times*, 20 September 2000.
5. *Morning Ireland*, RTÉ Radio One, 12 February 2001.
6. *The Irish Times*, 14 June 2004.
7. Referendum Commission, *Background Information on the Citizenship Referendum*, Refendum Commission website [cited 30-04-2005] <*http://www.supportdynamics.com/refcom/refcomwebsite.nsf/(WebFiles)/3A2FAB6C6295 812380256E9900468BE9/$FILE/citizenship%20booklet%20English.pdf*>
8. 'The people had much to say', editorial, *The Irish Times*, 14 June 2004.
9. Central Statistics Office, *Economic Series, 1996* (Stationery Office, Dublin, 1997), p. 52, p. 47.
10. Statistics gleaned from Central Statistics Office, *Statistical Abstract 1997* (Stationery Office, Dublin, 1998), p. 311, Central Statistics Office, *Statistical Yearbook of Ireland 2004*, p. 318, at CSO website [cited 30-04-2005]<*http://www.cso.ie/releasespublications/documents/statisticalyearbook/2004/statisticalyea rbook2004.pdf*>; and Economic and Social Research Institute, *Irish Economy Overview*, at ESRI website [cited 20-09-2004] <*http://www.esri.ie/content.cfm?t=Irish%20Economy&mId=4*>
11. Sara Cantillon, John Curtis and John FitzGerald, *The Medium-Term Review 1994–2000* (Economic and Social Research Institute, Dublin, April 1994), Chapter 4, 'The Central Forecast'.
12. See Siobhán Creaton, *Ryanair: How a Small Irish Airline Conquered Europe* (Aurum, London, 2004).
13. Central Statistics Office, *Statistical Abstract 1997*, p. 311, *Statistical Yearbook of Ireland 2004*, p. 318.
14. The increase is best reflected in the almost doubling of registrations of both vehicles between 1998 and 2003, two years in which overall registrations were almost the same.
15. See Peadar Kirby, *The Celtic Tiger in Distress: Growth with Inequality in Ireland* (Palgrave, London, 2002).
16. See report by Liam Reid and summary by Dan O'Brien, senior European editor at the Economist Intelligence Unit, in *The Irish Times*, 17 November 2004.
17. For greater detail on the unravelling of this fiasco for the government, see reports and statements posted on the Ombudsman's website, in particular *An Investigation by the Ombudsman of Complaints Regarding Payment of Nursing Home Subventions by Health Boards* (2001) and press statement entitled 'Nursing Home Charges', 20 December 2004.

18. See reports by Martin Wall and Carl O'Brien, *The Irish Times*, 16 December 2004 and following days.

19. See *The Irish Times*, 17 February 2005, for extensive coverage of the judgment and reaction to the case. The court, it should be noted, found that the prospective charges did not infringe rights, but that the government would have to bring forward fresh legislation to effect them.

20. ibid.

21. Department of the Environment and Local Government, *Reifirinn in Éirinn, 1937–1999* (Dublin, 2000), pp. 42–44.

22. *Courts Service Annual Report 2002*, p. 94, at Courts Service website [cited 26-04-2005] <*http://www.courts.ie/courts.ie/Library3.nsf/f0e0a24268c0a3da80256da 500428fb8/2e2eced5958c881980256da6003a28de?OpenDocument*> and *Courts Service Annual Report 2003*, p. 115, at Courts Service website [cited 26-04-2005] <*http://www.courts.ie/Courts.ie/library3.nsf/(WebFiles)/275EAE48CFFA2B578025 6F3400481E57/$FILE/Annual%20Report%202003.pdf*>

23. This does not include Irish women who travelled to Britain to have an abortion and gave a British address, so the real number may be substantially greater. See <*http://www. ifpa.ie/abortion/iabst.html*>

24. Department of the Environment and Local Government, *Reifirinn in Éirinn, 1937–1999*, p. 36.

25. Paul Cullen, *Refugees and Asylum-Seekers in Ireland* (Cork University Press, Cork, 2000), p. 17.

26. ORAC website statistics [cited 11-01-2005] <*http://www.orac.ie/PDF/PDF%20 Stats/Annual%20Statistics/Annual%20Report%202003.pdf*>

27. *Monthly Reports, December 2004*, table 5, p. 6. ORAC website [cited 25-04-2005] <*http://www.orac.ie/pdf/PDFStats/Monthly%20Statistics/2004/December_ORAC _Monthly_Statistics.pdf*>. Also, see Cullen, *Refugees and Asylum-Seekers in Ireland*, p. 17, for statistics on previous years. In 1998, for example, 40 per cent of applicants came from Nigeria and 22 per cent from Romania, with Algeria, Libya, Angola and Congo together making up 15 per cent. In 1999, Romania headed the list with 1,678 applications, followed by Nigeria with 1,155, then Poland (459), Kenya (219), Algeria (206), Moldova (197), Congo/Zaire (175), Slovakia (141), Angola (125) and Russia (113).

28. *The Irish Times*, 11 June 2001.

29. Department of Enterprise, Trade and Employment website statistics [cited 12-01-2005] <*http://www.entemp.ie/labour/workpermits/statistics.htm#byyear*>

30. Department of the Taoiseach website statement regarding tribunals of inquiry, 13 February 2002 [cited 20-09-2004] <*http://www.taoiseach.gov.ie/index.asp? locID=235&docID =403&COMMAND=PRINTER*>

31. ibid.

32. Fintan O'Toole, *Meanwhile Back at the Ranch: The Politics of Irish Beef* (Vintage, London, 1995), pp. 281–82.

33. *Report of the Tribunal of Inquiry (Dunnes Payments) 1997* (Stationery Office, Dublin, 1997), p. 73.

34. *Dáil Debates*, VOL. 553, col. 1880, 11 July 2002.

35. *Dáil Debates*, VOL. 581, col. 922, 4 March 2004.

36. Quoted in *The Second Interim Report of the Tribunal of Inquiry into Certain Planning Matters and Payments* (Stationery Office, Dublin, September 2002), p. 2.

37. ibid., pp. 138–39.

38. *The Fourth Interim Report of the Tribunal of Inquiry into Certain Planning Matters and Payments,* pp. 16ff [cited 25-04-05] <*http://www.planning tribunal.ie/images/SITECONTENT_286.pdf*>

39. *2002 Annual Report of the Comptroller and Auditor General and Appropriation Accounts*, VOL. 1 (Stationery Office, Dublin, 2003), p. 9.

40. ibid.

41. *Irish Examiner*, 1 September 1999.

42. *Report of Investigations into the Affairs of National Irish Bank Limited and National Irish Bank Financial Services Limited by High Court Inspectors Mr Justice Blayney and Mr Tom Grace* (Government of Ireland, CD ROM, 23 July 2004), p. i.

43. ibid.

44. ibid., pp. ii–iii.

45. Irish Financial Services Regulatory Authority (IFSRA), *Investigations in AIB Group on Foreign Exchange and Other Charging Issues and Deal Allocation and Associated Issues*, p. 25 [cited 30-01-2005] <*http://www.ifsra.ie/ data/news_files/ AIBReport.pdf*>

46. ibid., pp. 8–9.

47. ibid., p. 15. The AIB revelations on foreign currency irregularities were particularly ironic, given that in 2002 the activities of a rogue trader at another AIB subsidiary, Allfirst, based in Baltimore, USA, cost the bank almost $700 million. An inhouse AIB investigation by the former Comptroller of the US Currency, Eugene Ludwig, found those losses dated back to about 1997. Professor Edward Cahill, head of the Accountancy Department at University College Cork, had already interpreted such trends. He suggested that the 'isomorphic nature of the bank's internal governance structures, as influenced by their environment, was clear. The rational-actor model of accounting and its surveillance systems was rejected by the evidence.' See Edward Cahill, 'The

Legitimisation of Tax Evasion and the Governance of Banks: An Explanation', ESRI seminar paper, 11 April 2002.

48. I am grateful to the Religious Affairs Correspondent of *The Irish Times*, Patsy McGarry, for providing me with these figures.

49. My thanks to Fr Damien McNiece for a copy of the press release containing this information, 14 March 2003; see *<http://www.cps.dublindiocese.ie/ article_ 20.shtml>*

50. See Chris Moore, *Betrayal of Trust: The Fr Brendan Smyth Affair and the Catholic Church* (Marino Books, Dublin, 1995), p. 205.

51. Ibid., p. 13. This scandal was also the subject of a TV documentary made in Belfast for the UTV *Counterpoint* programme.

52. See Harry Ferguson, 'Protecting Irish Children in Time: Child Abuse as a Social Problem and the Development of the Child Protection System in the Republic of Ireland', in Harry Ferguson and Tony McNamara (eds.), *Protecting Irish Children: Investigation, Protection and Welfare*, special edition of *Administration*, VOL. 44, NO. 2 (Summer 1996), pp. 5–36; see also Harry Ferguson, 'Learning from the Past: Child Abuse and Institutional Care in Historical Perspective', in National Conference of Priests of Ireland (ed.), *Child Abuse in Institutional Care: Learning from the Past and Hoping for the Future* (Papers from a Public Conference held in Kilkenny, 3 April 2000), pp. 22–40, and Harry Ferguson, 'Child Abuse Inquiries and the Report of the Kilkenny Incest Investigation: A Critical Analysis', *Administration*, VOL. 41, NO. 4 (Winter 1993–94), pp. 385–410.

53. Joseph Robins, *The Lost Children: A Study of Charity Children in Ireland 1700–1900* (Institute of Public Administration, Dublin, 1980); Jane Barnes, *Irish Industrial Schools 1868–1908* (Irish Academic Press, Dublin, 1989). An earlier contribution to the literature on this subject was a pamphlet published in 1966 by the London branch of Tuairim and entitled *Some of our Children: A Report on the Residential Care of the Deprived Child in Ireland*.

54. Two books published in 1998 and 1999 respectively provided further personal testimony on life in Irish industrial schools: see Susan McKay, *Sophia's Story* (Gill and Macmillan, Dublin, 1998), and Bernadette Fahy, *The Freedom of Angels: Surviving Goldenbridge Orphanage* (O'Brien Press, Dublin, 1999).

55. Mary Raftery and Eoin O'Sullivan, *Suffer the Little Children: The Inside Story of Ireland's Industrial Schools* (New Island, Dublin, 1999).

56. Frances Finnegan, *Do Penance or Perish: A Study of Magdalene Asylums in Ireland* (Congrave Press, Piltown, Kilkenny, 2001). Peter Mullan has made a feature film on the topic entitled *The Magdalene Sisters*. It is claimed that some 30,000 Irish women worked in the Magdalene laundries.

57. Teresita Durkan, *Goldenbridge: A View from Valparaíso* (Veritas, Dublin, 1997), pp. 76–78.
58. ibid., pp. 77–78; Durkan spells the name as 'Xaveria'.
59. ibid., p. 30.
60. Harry Ferguson, 'States of Fear, Child Abuse, and Irish Society', *Doctrine and Life*, VOL. 50, NO. 1 (January 2000), pp. 20–30. Ferguson writes (p. 30): 'As well as the profound injustices done to the children of the poor and their parents, the fact that some children who entered the industrial schools had been abused at home and the role that the community played in tolerating such actions need to be part of our collective memory. The same must be said of the fact that some children welcomed the opportunity to leave home for a place of safety—and found it in the schools. That some children who were abused at home experienced further abuse within the care system only adds to the tragedy.'
61. ibid., p. 30.
62. Information supplied by Child Protection Office Maynooth, June 2005.
63. Press release, 1 April 2002, Catholic Communications Office [cited 20-09-2004] *<http://www.catholiccommunications.ie/Pressrel/1-april-2002.html>*
64. Press release, Diocese of Ferns, 1 April 2002.
65. Press release, 27 June 2002, Catholic Communications Office [cited 20-09-2004] *<http://www.catholiccommunications.ie/Pressrel/27-june-2002.html>*
66. Press release, Archdiocese of Dublin, Cardinal Connell's letter on child sexual abuse, 5 October 2002 [cited 30-04-2005], *http://www.cps.dublindiocese.ie/article_13.shtml*; Cardinal Connell's statement on 12 October following Prime Time programme, *<http://www.cps.dublindiocese.ie/article_15.shtml>* Response to Prime Time Programme, Press Release 18 October 2002, *<http://www.cps.dublindiocese.ie/article_14.shtml >*
67. Department of Justice Press Release of Statement by Minister, 3 December 2002 [cited 30-04-2005] *<http://www.justice.ie/80256E01003A02CF/vWeb/PCJUSQ5ZYJH7-en>*
68. Joint Statement from Marie Collins, Ken Reilly, Cardinal Connell and Bishop Eamonn Walsh, 30 December 2002, Archdiocese of Dublin Press release [cited 30-04-2005] *<http://www.cps.dublindiocese.ie/article_19.shtml>*
69. Press release, Archdiocese of Dublin, 14 July 2004 [cited 30-04-2005] *<http://www.cps.dublindiocese.ie/article_108.shtml>*
70. Speech by An Taoiseach, Mr Bertie Ahern, TD, announcing Government Measures Relating to Childhood Abuse on Tuesday 11 May 1999, copy supplied by Press Office, Taoiseach's Department.
71. Quoting from the Indemnity, paragraph A; copy supplied to me by the

Department of Education and Science. Figures are quoted from Mark Hennessy, 'Dáil Committee investigates abuse claim deal', *The Irish Times*, 1 February 2003.

72. Quoting from the Indemnity, paragraph F.

73. Patsy McGarry, 'Nine dioceses yet to indicate sex abuse trust contributions', *The Irish Times*, 29 March 2005.

74. Excerpts from press release, Catholic hierarchy, 16 March 2005: see *<http:// www.catholic communications.ie/Pressrel/16-march-2005.html>*

75. Michael J. Breen (ed.), *A Fire in the Forest: Religious Life in Ireland* (Veritas, Dublin, 2001). The survey was conducted by John A. Weafer.

76. Many records exist. See for example the BBC website of the Troubles [cited 30-04-2005] *<http://www.bbc.co.uk/history/war/troubles/agreement/ennibomb .shtml>*

77. Senator George Mitchell, *Making Peace: The Inside Story of the Making of the Good Friday Agreement* (Heinemann, London, 1999), p. 26.

78. Andrew J. Wilson, *Irish America and the Ulster Conflict 1968–1995* (Blackstaff Press, Belfast, 1995), p. 293.

79. David McKittrick, Seamus Kelters, Brian Feeney and Chris Thornton, *Lost Lives: The Stories of the Men, Women and Children Who Died as a Result of the Northern Troubles* (Mainstream, Edinburgh and London, 1999), p. 1336. Nine people died immediately in the Shankill Road bomb blast and a tenth died later.

80. Joseph Ruane and Jennifer Todd (eds.), *After the Good Friday Agreement: Analysing Political Change in Northern Ireland* (University College Dublin Press, Dublin, 1999), pp. 6–7.

81. Bill Clinton, *My Life* (Hutchinson, London, 2004), p. 580.

82. Interview with John Hume, University College Cork, 1995.

83. I was commissioned by the forum to make a study of the role of the Catholic Church in the development of the Irish state. See *Building Trust in Ireland: Studies Commissioned by the Forum for Peace and Reconciliation* (Blackstaff Press, Belfast, 1996), pp. 89–213.

84. Wilson, *Irish America and the Ulster Conflict*, pp. 298–99.

85. Reported in *The Irish Times*, 14 August 1995.

86. Mitchell, *Making Peace*, pp. 10–11.

87. ibid., pp 10–12.

88. Clinton, *My Life*, p. 686, and *The Irish Times*, 2 December 1995.

89. Mitchell, *Making Peace*, pp. 33ff.

90. See 'IRA hints more attacks may follow'. Report by Mark Brennock, *The Irish Times*, 16 February 1996.

91. Clinton, *My Life*, p. 784.

92. Department of Foreign Affairs information leaflet, *Northern Ireland Peace Process: The Making of the Good Friday Agreement of 1998* (Dublin, 1998).

93. See *The Irish Times*, 4 September 1998.

94. Cited in The Irish Times On-line reports [cited 30-04-2005] <*http://www.ireland. com/special/clinton/news/story36.htm*>

95. Jodie Ginsberg, 17 March 2005, Reuters <*http://xtramsn.co.nz/news/0,,11965-4203944,00.html*> According to the same source, Police Service of Northern Ireland figures showed there were about 300 punishment beatings carried out by the IRA in 2003–4 and 179 in the ten months to January 2005, while in 1993, the year before the first ceasefire, there were 126.

96. <*http://www.cbsnews.com/stories/2005/03/16/eveningnews/main681058.shtml*>

97. With its usual high regard for accuracy, the *Sunday Independent* turned that into its lead headline: 'McCartneys call SF/IRA "Nazi thugs"'. See *Sunday Independent*, 20 March 2005.

98. Freedom of Information, Government of Ireland website: <*http://www.oasis. gov.ie/ government_in_ireland/government_and_politics_at_national_level/ offices_of_state/freedom_of_information.html*>

99. Maeve McDonagh, 'Freedom of Information and the Public Interest', University College Cork Law Department website <*http://www.ucc.ie/ucc/ depts/law/foi/conference*>

100. Maeve McDonagh, 'Freedom of Information in Ireland: Five Years On', posted 22 September 2003 <*http://www.freedominfo.org/reports/ireland/ireland.pdf*>

101. For further details see ibid.

102. Interview with Dr David Edwards, Department of History, University College Cork, April 2005.

103. See Focus Ireland website statistics <*http://www.focusireland.ie/htm/housing_ homelessness/facts_figures/statistics.htm*>

104. *Suicide in Ireland: A National Study, 2001* [cited 25-01-2005] <*http://www. nehb.ie/nehb/publications/reports/suicideinirl.pdf*>

105. ibid., p. 64.

106. Breda Allen, *Sexual Abuse and Violence in Ireland*, Executive Summary <*http://www.drcc.ie/ about_us/savi.html*>. All information in this paragraph is taken from this report. I am grateful to Breda Allen for making a copy of this summary available to me before it was added to the official website.

107. Paula Meehan, 'The Statue of the Virgin at Granard Speaks,' in *The Man Who Was Marked By Winter* (The Gallery Press, Oldcastle, Co. Meath, 1991).

108. See article by the editor of irishhealth.com, Fergal Bowers, posted 21 February 2004 <*http://www.irishhealth.com/?level=4&id=5643.*>

109. Horace Plunkett, *Ireland in the New Century* (John Murray, London, 1904), p. 291.

Bibliography to the First Edition

Primary Sources

IRELAND

National Library of Ireland
Frank Gallagher papers
Harry Kernoff papers
Tom Johnson papers
Shane Leslie paper
Art Ó Briain papers
William O'Brien papers

Archives Department, University College Dublin
Ernest Blythe papers
Dan Bryan papers
Desmond FitzGerald papers
Hugh Kennedy papers
Seán MacEntee papers
Mary MacSwiney papers
Patrick McGilligan papers
Richard Mulcahy papers
Diarmuid Ó hÉigeartaigh papers
James Ryan papers

Dublin Archdiocesan Archives
Edward Byrne papers
Michael Curran papers
William Walsh papers

Armagh Archdiocesan Archives
Michael Logue papers
Joseph MacRory papers
Patrick O'Donnell papers

Franciscan Archives, Killiney
Éamon de Valera papers relating to the 1937 constitution

Jesuit Archives, Dublin
Edward Cahill papers
Minutes of Jesuit committee on the framing of the 1937 constitution

National Archives, Dublin
Dáil Éireann papers
George Gavan Duffy papers
Frank MacDermot papers

Department of the Taoiseach
Irish Executive Council Minutes
Irish Cabinet Minutes
Cabinet S files

Department of Foreign Affairs
Secretary's files
Confidential Diplomatic Reports from Berlin, Bonn, Paris, Vichy, Madrid, Rome,
    Lisbon, London, Buenos Aires, Washington, New York, Chicago and San
    Francisco
General Registry files

Department of Justice
H files
(See also files on Blueshirts and on subversive organisations)

Department of Labour
Files relevant to the introduction of trade union legislation and the setting up of
    the Labour Court

Military Archives, Cathal Brugha Barracks, Dublin
Department of Defence files
Files relating to censorship during World War II (Department for the
    Coordination of Defensive Measures)

Trinity College, Dublin
Frederick H. Boland papers

Unpublished Memoirs
Con Cremin memoirs, in the possession of his family.
Cahir Davitt memoirs, in the possession of his son, Father Thomas Davitt, CM,
    Vincentian Community, 44 Stillorgan Park, Blackrock, Co. Dublin.

Frederick H. Boland manuscript; an unpublished typescript based on interviews with his daughter, Mella Boland (Crowley). This was kindly loaned to me by Mrs Frances Boland.

Correspondence
Two letters to the author from Seán Lemass

ENGLAND

Public Record Office, London
Dominions Office
Foreign Office series, FO371
Home Office
Prime Minister's Office (PREM)

UNITED STATES OF AMERICA

National Archives, Washington DC
State Department, RG 59
General Records, Ireland
Confidential reports, Ireland
Military Records, Ireland
OSS reports (London) relating to Ireland
Myron Taylor papers

Cornell University, Ithaca, New York
Myron Taylor papers

US *Presidential libraries*
Franklin D. Roosevelt Library, Hyde Park, New York: general files relevant to Ireland
Reports of David Gray
Harry Truman Library, Independence, Missouri
Graham T. Parsons oral history
General files relevant to Ireland

ITALY

Irish College, Rome
Michael Curran papers
John Hagan papers
Tobias Kirby papers
Michael O'Riordan papers

Italian Foreign Ministry, Rome
Diplomatic reports (Ireland)

Italian Government Archives, Rome
General files on Ireland in the 1930s

FRANCE

Irish College Paris
General college papers
Patrick Boyle papers

French Foreign Ministry
Consular Reports (Dublin) 1924–1938

INTERVIEWS

Frank Aiken
Peter Barry
Frederick Boland
Gerry Boland
John Bruton
Con Cremin
Alan Dukes
Garret FitzGerald
Mary Hanrahan
Miriam Hederman O'Brien
Patrick Hillery
Justin Keating
Brian Lenihan
Jack Lynch
Patrick Lynch
Máire Mhac an tSaoi
Seán MacBride
Michael Mills
John Moher
Maurice Moynihan
Tommy Mullins
Conor Cruise O'Brien
Tomás Ó Fiaich
Tony O'Malley
T. Desmond Williams

Secondary Sources

Acheson, Dean, *Present at the Creation: My Years in the State Department* (Norton, New York, 1987).

—*Power of Diplomacy* (Harvard University Press, Cambridge, 1958).

Adams, Michael, *Censorship: The Irish Experience* (University of Alabama Press, Alabama, 1968).

Akenson, Donald Harman, *Between Two Revolutions: Islandmagee ,Co. Antrim, 1798–1920* (Archon Books, Connecticut, 1979).

Ambrose, Stephen E., *Nixon: The Triumph of a Politician 1962–1972* (Simon and Schuster, New York, 1989).

Andrews, C.S., *Dublin Made Me: An Autobiography*, VOL. I (Mercier Press, Dublin and Cork, 1979).

—*Man of No Property: An Autobiography*, VOL. II (Mercier Press, Dublin, 1982).

Anon., *Fifty Years of Liberty Hall* (Three Candles, Dublin, 1959).

Arnold, Bruce, *What Kind of Country: Modern Irish Politics 1968–1983* (Jonathan Cape, London, 1984).

—*A Concise History of Irish Art* (Thames and Hudson, London, 1989).

—*Mainie Jellett and the Modern Movement in Ireland* (Yale University Press, London and New Haven, 1991).

Arthur, Paul and Keith Jeffery, *Northern Ireland since 1968* (Basil Blackwell, Oxford, 1988).

Aughey, Arthur, *Under Siege: Ulster Unionism and the Anglo-Irish Agreement* (Blackstaff Press, Belfast, 1989).

Augustine, Fr. O.F.M. cap., *Ireland's Loyalty to the Mass* (Sands, London, 1933).

Barrington, Ruth, *Healthy Medicine and Politics in Ireland 1900–1970* (Institute of Public Administration, Dublin, 1987).

Barrington, T.J. and T. Walsh, *Towards a New Democracy* (Dublin, 1983).

Bartlett, Thomas, Chris Curtin, Riana O'Dwyer, Gearóid Ó Tuathaigh, *Irish Studies: A General Introduction* (Gill & Macmillan, Dublin, 1988).

Batley, Richard and Gerry Stoker, *Local Government in Europe: Trends and Development* (Macmillan, London, 1991).

Bell, James Bowyer, *The Secret Army: History of the Irish Republican Army 1916–79* (Academy Press, Dublin, 1979).

Bew, Paul, Peter Gibbon and Henry Patterson, *The State in Northern Ireland 1921–1972: Political Forces and Social Classes* (Manchester University Press, Manchester, 1979).

Bew, Paul, Ellen Hazelkorn and Henry Patterson, *The Dynamics of Irish Politics* (Lawrence and Wishart, London, 1989).

Bew, Paul and Henry Patterson, *Seán Lemass and the Making of Modern Ireland, 1945–66* (Gill & Macmillan, Dublin, 1982).

—*The British State and the Ulster Crisis from Wilson to Thatcher* (Verso, London, 1985).

Bielenberg, Andy, 'The Locke Family and the Distillery Industry in Kilbeggan', *History/Ireland*, VOL. I, NO. 2 (Summer 1993), pp. 46–50.

—*Locke's Distillery: A History* (Lilliput Press, Dublin, 1993).

Birch, P., 'Poverty and the Church' in Stanislaus Kennedy (ed.,) *One Million Poor? The Challenge of Irish Inequality* (Turoe Press, Dublin, 1981).

Blackwell, John, *Women in the Labour Force* (Employment Equality Agency, Dublin, 1986).

Bishop, Patrick and Eamonn Mallie, *The Provisional IRA* (Heinemann, London, 1987).

Blanshard, Paul, *The Irish and Catholic Power—an American interpretation* (Derek Verschoyle, London, 1954).

Boland, Kevin, *Up Dev* (Dublin, n.d.).

—'*We Won't Stand (idly) By*' (Kelly Kane, Dublin, 1972).

—*The Rise and Decline of Fianna Fáil* (Mercier Press, Cork, 1982).

Bolger, Dermot, *The Journey Home* (Viking, London, 1990).

—*Invisible Dublin: A Journey through Dublin's Suburbs* (Raven Arts Press, Dublin, 1991).

—(ed.), *Letters from the New Island* (Raven Arts Press, Dublin, 1991).

Bolster, Evelyn, *The Knights of Saint Columbanus* (Gill & Macmillan, Dublin, 1979).

Bowman, John, *De Valera and the Ulster Question, 1917–73* (Clarendon Press, Oxford, 1982).

Boyce, D. George, *Ireland 1828–1923: From Ascendancy to Democracy* (Blackwell, Oxford, 1992).

Bradley, Dan, *Irish Struggle 1900–1976* (Athol Books, Belfast, 1986).

Brady, Conor, *Guardians of the Peace* (Gill & Macmillan, Dublin, 1974).

Breathnach, Diarmuid, *Almanag Éireannach* (Oifig an tSoláthair, Baile Átha Cliath, 1981).

Breen, Richard, Damien F. Hannan, David B. Rottman and Christopher T. Whelan (eds), *Understanding Contemporary Ireland: State, Class and Development in the Republic of Ireland* (Gill & Macmillan, Dublin, 1990).

Brown, Terence, *Ireland: A Social and Cultural History 1922–1979* (Fontana, London, 1981).

Browne, Michael, *Bulwark of Freedom: Vocational Organisation—Democracy in Action* (Catholic Truth Society Pamphlet, Dublin, 1945).

Browne, Noël, *Against the Tide* (Gill & Macmillan, Dublin, 1986).

Bruce, Steve, *God Save Ulster: The Religion and the Politics of Paisleyism* (Oxford University Press, Oxford, 1986).

Brunicardi, Lt Cdr Daire, 'The Marine Service', *An Cosantóir*, VOL. 49, NO. 9 (September 1989), pp. 23–26.

Buckley, Patrick, 'The Primate's Primal Truths', supplement with *Fortnight*, 297, pp. 11–12.

Cairns, Ed, *Caught in Crossfire: Children and the Northern Ireland Conflict* (Appletree Press, Belfast, 1987).

Canning, Paul, *British Policy towards Ireland 1921–1941* (Clarendon Press, Oxford, 1985).

Carlson, Julia (ed.), *Banned in Ireland: Censorship and the Irish Writer* (Routledge, London, 1990).

Carroll, Joseph T., *Ireland in the War Years* (David and Charles, Newton Abbot, 1975).

—'General de Gaulle and Ireland's EEC Application' in Pierre Joannon (ed.), *De Gaulle and Ireland* (Institute of Public Administration, Dublin, 1991), pp. 81–97.

Carter, Carolle J., *The Shamrock and the Swastika: German Espionage in Ireland in World War II* (Pacific Books, Palo Alto, California, 1977).

Carty, Ciaran, *Robert Ballagh* (Magill, Dublin, 1986).

Casey, Michael, *What Are We At? Ministry and Priesthood for the Third Millennium* (Columba Press, Dublin, 1992).

Cathcart, Rex, 'Broadcasting—The Early Decades', in Brian Farrell (ed.), *Communications and Community in Ireland* (Mercier Press, Dublin, 1984), 39–50.

Chubb, Basil, *The Government and Politics of Ireland*, 3rd ed. (Longman, London, 1992).

—*The Politics of the Irish Constitution* (Institute of Public Administration, Dublin, 1991).

Clarke, Liam, *Broadening the Battlefield: The H-Blocks and the Rise of Sinn Féin* (Gill & Macmillan, Dublin, 1987).

Clarkson, J. Dunsmore, *Labour and Nationalism in Ireland* (Columbia University Press, New York, 1925).

Collins, Stephen, *The Haughey File* (O'Brien Press, Dublin, 1992).

Connolly, P. (ed.), *Literature and the Changing Ireland* (Colin Smythe, Gerrard's Cross, Bucks., 1982).

Coogan, Tim Pat, *The IRA* (Pall Mall Press, London, 1980).

—*Ireland since the Rising* (Pall Mall Press, London, 1966).

—*On the Blanket: The H-Block Story* (Ward River Press, Dublin, 1980).

—*Michael Collins: A Biography* (Arrow, London, 1991).

Coolahan, John, *Irish Education: Its History and Structure* (Institute of Public Administration, Dublin, 1981).

Corcoran, Terry, 'Tracking Emigration Flows,' in Joe Mulholland and Dermot Keogh (eds), *Emigration, Employment and Enterprise* (Hibernian University Press, Cork and Dublin, 1989), pp. 29–33.

Corish, Patrick J., *The Irish Catholic Experience: A Historical Survey* (Dublin, Gill & Macmillan, 1985).

Cosgrove, Art and Donal McCartney (eds), *Studies in Irish History presented to R. Dudley Edwards* (University College Dublin, 1979).

Costello, Declan, 'The Priest and Public Affairs', *Christus Rex*, VOL. XXIII, NO. 4 (October 1969), pp. 293–98.

Cronin, Anthony, *An Irish Eye* (Brandon, Dingle, 1985).

Cronin, Seán, *Frank Ryan: The Search for the Republic* (Repsol Press, Dublin, 1980).

—*Irish Nationalism: A History of its Roots and Ideology* (Academy Press, Dublin, 1980).

—*Washington's Irish Policy, 1916–1986* (Anvil Press, Dublin, 1987).

Cross, Eric, *The Tailor and Ansty* (Mercier Press, Cork, 1990).

Curtin, Chris and Thomas M. Wilson, *Ireland from Below: Social Change and Local Communities* (Galway University Press, Galway, 1988).

Daly, Mary E., *Social and Economic History of Ireland since 1800* (The Educational Company, Dublin, 1981).

—'An Irish Ireland for Business?: The Control of the Manufacturers Acts, 1932 and 1934', *Irish Historical Studies*, VOL. XXIV (November 1984), pp. 246–72.

—*Industrial Development and Irish National Identity 1922–1939* (Gill & Macmillan, Dublin, 1992).

D'Arcy, Fergus A. and Ken Hannigan (eds), *Workers in Union: Documents and Commentaries on the History of Labour* (National Archives, Dublin, 1988).

de Búrca, Marcus, *The GAA: A History* (Cumann Lúthchleas Gael, Dublin, 1980).

de Vere White, Terence, *Kevin O'Higgins* (Methuen, London, 1948).

Deane, Séamus, *A Short History of Irish Literature* (Hutchinson, London, 1986).

—, Seamus Heaney, Richard Kearney, Declan Kiberd, Tom Paulin, *Ireland's Field Day* (University of Notre Dame Press, Notre Dame, 1986).

Deeny, James, *To Cure and To Care: Memoirs of a Chief Medical Officer* (Glendale Press, Dublin, 1989).

Donoghue, Denis, *Warrenpoint* (Jonathan Cape, London, 1991).

Dooney, Seán, *The Irish Civil Service* (Institute of Public Administration, Dublin, 1976).

Dooney, Seán and John O'Toole, *The Irish Government Today* (Gill & Macmillan, Dublin, 1992).

Doyle, Roddy, *The Commitments* (Minerva, London, 1991).

Dudley Edwards, Owen (ed.), *Conor Cruise O'Brien Introduces Ireland* (McGraw-Hill, New York, 1969).

Dudley Edwards, Ruth, *An Atlas of Irish History*, 2nd ed. (Methuen, London and New York, 1986).

Duggan, John P., *Neutral Ireland and the Third Reich* (Lilliput Press, Dublin, 1989).

—*A History of the Irish Army* (Gill & Macmillan, Dublin, 1991).

Dunn, Derek and Gene Kerrigan, *Round up the Usual Suspects: Nicky Kelly and the Cosgrave Coalition* (Magill, Dublin, 1984).

Dunne, Joseph, *No Tigers in Africa: Recollections and Reflections on Twenty Five Years of Radharc* (Columba Press, Dublin, 1986).

Dunne, Seán, *In My Father's House* (Anna Livia Press, Dublin, 1991).

Durcan, Paul, *The Berlin Wall Café* (Blackstaff Press, Belfast, 1990).

Dwyer, T. Ryle, *Irish Neutrality and the USA 1939–47* (Gill & Macmillan, Dublin, 1977).

— *Éamon de Valera* (Gill & Macmillan, Dublin, 1980).

— *Michael Collins and the Treaty: His differences with de Valera* (Mercier Press, Dublin, 1981).

—*Charlie: The Political Biography of Charles J. Haughey* (Gill & Macmillan, Dublin, 1987).

—*Haughey's Thirty Years of Controversy* (Mercier Press, Cork, 1992).

Dyrness, William A., *Rouault: A Vision of Suffering and Salvation* (William B. Eerdmans, Grand Rapids, Michigan, 1971).

Eager, Clare, 'Splitting Images—Women and the Irish Civil Service', *Seirbhís Phoiblí*, VOL. 12, NO. 1 (April 1991), pp. 15–23.

Earl, Lawrence, *The Battle of Baltinglass* (George Harrap, London, 1952).

Elborn, Geoffrey, *Francis Stuart: A Life* (Raven Arts Press, Dublin, 1990).

English, Richard and Cormac O'Malley (eds), *Prisoners: The Civil War Letters of Ernie O'Malley* (Poolbeg, Dublin, 1991).

Falconer, Alan, Enda McDonagh and Seán MacReamoinn (eds), *Freedom to Hope: The Catholic Church in Ireland Twenty Years after Vatican II* (Columbia Press, Dublin, 1985).

Fanning, Ronan, *The Irish Department of Finance 1922–1958* (Institute of Public Administration, Dublin, 1978).

—*Independent Ireland* (Helicon, Dublin, 1983).

—'Neutral Ireland?', *An Cosantóir*, VOL. 49, NO. 9 (September 1989), pp. 45–48.

—'The Dublin Link', *Sunday Independent*, 6 January 1991.

Farrell, Brian, *Chairman or Chief: The Role of Taoiseach in Irish Government* (Gill & Macmillan, Dublin, 1971).

—(ed.), *Communications and Community in Ireland* (Mercier Press, Dublin, 1984).

—*Seán Lemass* (Gill & Macmillan, Dublin, 1983).

Farrell, Michael, *Northern Ireland, The Orange State* (Pluto Press, London, 1980).

Feeney, John, *John Charles McQuaid: The Man and the Mask* (Mercier Press, Dublin, 1974).

Fennell, Desmond (ed.), *The Changing Face of Catholic Ireland* (Geoffrey Chapman, London, 1968).

Finlay, Fergus, *Mary Robinson: A President with a Purpose* (O'Brien Press, Dublin, 1990).

Fisk, Robert, *In Time of War: Ireland, Ulster and the Price of Neutrality 1939–45* (André Deutsch, London, 1983).

FitzGerald, Garret, *Planning in Ireland* (Institute of Public Administration, Dublin, London, 1968).

—*All in a Life: An Autobiography* (Gill & Macmillan, Dublin, 1992).

—'Damage of 1983 amendment will not be easily undone', *The Irish Times,* 22 February 1992.

Flackes, W.D. and Sidney Elliot, *Northern Ireland. A Political Directory* (3rd ed.), (Blackstaff Press, Belfast, 1989).

Fogarty, Michael, Liam Ryan and Joseph Lee, *Irish Values and Attitudes: The Irish Report of the European Values System Study* (Dominican Publications, Dublin, 1984).

Foster, Roy, *Modern Ireland 1600–1972* (Allen Lane, London, 1988).

—*The Oxford Illustrated History of Ireland* (Oxford University Press, London, 1989).

Fox, R.M., *Louie Bennett: Her Life and Times* (Talbot Press, Dublin, n.d.).

Friel, Brian, *Selected Plays* (Faber and Faber, London, 1984).

Gallagher, Michael, *The Irish Labour Party in Transition 1957–82* (Manchester University Press, Manchester, 1982).

—*Political Parties in the Republic of Ireland* (Gill & Macmillan, Dublin, 1985).

Garvin, Thomas, *The Irish Senate* (Institute of Public Administration, Dublin, 1969).

—*The Evolution of Irish Nationalist Politics* (Gill & Macmillan, Dublin, 1972).

—*Nationalist Revolutionaries in Ireland 1858–1928* (Clarendon Press, Oxford, 1987).

Gaughan, James Anthony, *Thomas Johnson: 1872–1963: First Leader of the Labour Party in Dáil Éireann* (Kingdom Books, Dublin, 1980).

Girvin, Brian, 'National Identity and Conflict in Northern Ireland', in Brian Girvin and Roland Sturm (eds), *Politics and Society in Contemporary Ireland* (Gower, London, 1986), pp. 105–34.

—*Between Two Worlds: Politics and Economy in Independent Ireland* (Gill & Macmillan, Dublin, 1989).

Hadden, Tom and Kevin Boyle, *The Anglo-Irish Agreement: Commentary, Text and Official Review* (Edwin Higel Ltd, London, 1989).

Hand, Geoffrey, [Introduction] *Report of the Irish Boundary Commission* (Irish University Press, Shannon, 1969).

Harkness, D. W., *The Restless Dominion: The Irish Free State and the British Commonwealth of Nations 1921–1931* (Macmillan, London, 1969).

—'Patrick McGilligan: Man of Commonwealth', *The Journal of Imperial and Commonwealth History*, VOL. VIII, NO. 1 (October 1979), pp. 117–35.

— *Northern Ireland since 1920* (Helicon, Dublin, 1983).

Harrington, Niall C., *An Episode of the Civil War: Kerry Landing, August 1922* (Anvil Books, Dublin, 1992).

Harris, Bernard and Grattan Freyer (eds), *Integrating Tradition: The Achievements of Seán Ó Riada* (Irish Humanities Center, Ballina, 1981).

Harris, Mary, 'The Catholic Church and the Foundation of the Northern Irish State 1912–1930', Cambridge PhD, 1991.

—*The Catholic Church and the Foundation of the Northern Irish State 1912–1930* (Cork University Press, Cork, 1993).

Heaney, Seamus, *North* (Faber and Faber, London, 1975).

Hederman O'Brien, Miriam, *The Road to Europe: Irish Attitudes 1948–61* (Institute of Public Administration, Dublin, 1983).

Hesketh, Tom, *The Second Partitioning of Ireland: The Abortion Referendum of 1983* (Brandsma Books, Dublin, 1990).

Hindley, Redge, *The Death of the Irish Language* (Routledge, London, 1990).

Hopkinson, Michael, *Green against Green: The Irish Civil War* (Gill & Macmillan, Dublin, 1988).

Hoppen, K. Theodore, *Ireland since 1800: Conflict and Conformity* (Longman, London, 1989).

Horan, James, *Memoirs, 1911–1988* (Brandon Press, Dingle, 1992).

Hussey, Gemma, *At the Cutting Edge: Cabinet Diaries 1982–1987* (Gill & Macmillan, Dublin, 1990).

—*Ireland Today: Anatomy of a Changing State* (Townhouse; Viking, Dublin and London, 1993).

Joannon, Pierre, *De Gaulle and Ireland* (Institute of Public Administration, Dublin, 1991).

Joyce, Joe and Peter Murtagh, *The Boss: Charles J. Haughey in Government* (Poolbeg Press, Dublin, 1983).

Kavanagh, Patrick, *Collected Poems* (MacGibbon and Kee, London, 1968).

—*The Green Fool* (Martin, Brian and O'Keeffe, London, 1971).

Kavanagh, Peter (ed.), *Patrick Kavanagh: Man and Poet* (Goldsmith Press, Newbridge, 1987).

Keane, John B., *Three Plays* (Mercier Press, Cork and Dublin, 1990).

Kearns, A.P. (Tony), 'The Air Corps 1939–1945', *An Cosantóir*, VOL. 49, NO. 9 (September 1989), pp. 13–19.

Keatinge, P., *The Formulation of Irish Foreign Policy* (Institute of Public Administration, Dublin, 1973).

—*A Place among the Nations: Issues of Irish Foreign Policy* (Institute of Public Administration, Dublin, 1978).

—*Ireland and EC Membership Evaluated* (Pinter, London, 1991).

Kee, Robert, *The Green Flag: A History of Irish Nationalism* (Weidenfeld and Nicolson, London, 1972).

—'Neutrality as a form of warfare', *Sunday Times*, 15 May 1983.

Kelly, Ann, *Cultural Policy in Ireland* (UNESIS, Paris, 1989).

Kelly, James, *Orders from the Captain* (The author, Dublin, 1971).

Kennedy, Brian P., *Dreams and Responsibilities: The State and the Arts in Independent Ireland* (Arts Council, Dublin, 1990).

—'Ireland To-day: A Brave Irish Periodical', *Linen Hall Review*, VOL. 5, NO. 4, pp. 18–19.

Kennedy, Kieran A., Thomas Giblin and Deirdre McHugh, *The Economic Development of Ireland in the Twentieth Century* (Routledge, London, 1988).

Kennedy, S.B., *Irish Art and Modernism 1880–1950* (Institute of Irish Studies, Belfast, 1991).

Kenny, Anthony, *The Road to Hillsborough: The Shaping of the Anglo-Irish Agreement* (Pergamon Press, Oxford, 1986).

Kenny, Shane, *Go Dance on Somebody Else's Grave* (Kilnadore Press, Dublin, 1990).

Keogh, Dermot, *The Rise of the Irish Working Class: The Dublin Trade Union Movement and Labour Leadership 1890–1914* (Appletree Press, Belfast, 1982).

—*Ireland and Europe 1919–1989* (Hibernian University Press, Cork and Dublin, 1989).

—*The Vatican, the Bishops and Irish Politics 1919–1939* (Cambridge University Press, Cambridge, 1986).

—'Mannix, de Valera and Irish Nationalism', in John O'Brien and Pauric Travers (eds), *The Irish Emigrant Experience in Australia* (Poolbeg Press, Dublin, 1991), pp. 196–225.

—'Ireland, de Gaulle and World War II', in Pierre Joannon (ed.), *De Gaulle and Ireland* (Institute of Public Administration, Dublin, 1991), pp. 23–52.

—'Irish Department of Foreign Affairs' in Zara Steiner (ed.), *The Times Survey of Foreign Ministries of the World* (Times Books, London, 1982), pp. 276–96.

—'De Valera, the Catholic Church and the "Red Scare" 1931–1932', in J.P. O'Carroll and John A. Murphy (eds), *De Valera and His Times* (Cork University Press, Cork, 1983), pp. 134–59.

—'William Martin Murphy, Dublin Financier (1844–1919)', in *Dictionary of Business Biography* (London, 1986), pp. 389–94.

— 'Jewish Refugees and Irish Government Policy in the 1930s and 1940s', in Proceedings of Conference—*Remembering for the Future*, Oxford, July 1988 (Pergamon Press, Oxford, 1988). Conference Preprint, VOL. 1, pp. 395–403.

—'The Irish Constitutional Revolution: An Analysis of the Making of the Constitution' in Frank Litton (ed.), *The Constitution of Ireland 1937–1987*, *Administration*, Dublin, VOL. 35, NO. 4. (1988), pp. 4–84.

—'Church and State in Europe' in Adrian Hastings (ed.), *Directory of Vatican II after 25 years* (SCM Press, London, 1990), pp. 289–303.

—'Church, State and Society', in Brian Farrell (ed.), *De Valera—his constitution and ours* (Gill & Macmillan, Dublin, 1988), pp. 103–22.

—'Catholicism and the Formation of the Modern Irish state', in *Irishness in a Changing Society*, edited by The Princess Grace Irish Library (Barnes and Noble Books, Totowa, New Jersey, 1989), pp. 152–77.

—'Ireland, Vichy and de Valera, de Gaulle', in Bernard Tricot (ed.), *Charles de Gaulle* (Institute of Charles de Gaulle, Paris, 1991), p. 20.

— 'Ireland and the Single European Act', in Clive Church and Dermot Keogh (eds), *The Single European Act: A Transnational Study* (Canterbury Consortium, Cork, 1990).

— 'Argentina and the Falklands (Malvinas): The Irish Connection', in Alastair Hennessy and John King (eds), *The Land that England Lost: Argentina and Britain, a Special Relationship* (British Academic Press, London, 1992), pp. 123–42.

—'Origins of Irish Diplomacy in Europe, 1919–1921', *Etudes Irlandaises*, 1983, NO. 7–Nouvelle Serie, December 1982, pp. 145–64.

— 'Eamon de Valera', *Historia 16*, Año VII, NO. 79 (1983), pp. 101–12.

— 'Irlanda: La Era del Nacionalismo Revolucionario', *Siglo XX (Historia Universal)*, NO. 7 (1983), pp. 65–78.

—'Mannix, de Valera and Irish Nationalism' (Part 1) *Australasian Catholic Record*, VOL. IXV, NO. 2 (April 1988), pp. 159–73.

— 'Mannix, de Valera and Irish Nationalism' (Part 2) *Australasian Catholic Record*, VOL. IXV, NO. 3 (July 1988), pp. 343–57.

—'Éamon de Valera and Hitler: An Analysis of International Reaction to the Visit to the German Minister, May 1945', *Irish Studies in International Affairs*, VOL. 3, NO. 1 (Autumn 1989), pp. 69–92.

— 'The Treaty Split and the Paris-Irish Race Convention', *Etudes Irlandaises*, NO. 12 (December 1987), pp. 165–70.

— 'The Jesuits, and the 1937 Constitution', *Studies*, VOL. 78, NO. 309 (Spring 1989), pp. 82–95.

— 'Profile of Joseph Walshe, Secretary, Department of Foreign Affairs 1922–46, *Irish Studies in International Affairs*, VOL. 3, NO. 2 (Autumn 1990), pp. 59–80.

—'Democracy gone Dotty: Seán O'Faoláin and the Professorship of English at University College Cork', *The Cork Review*—Seán O'Faoláin special issue (Triskel Arts Centre, Cork, 1991), pp. 29–33.

— 'Ireland, the Vatican and the Cold War: The Case of Italy, 1948', in *Journal of Modern History*, VOL. 34, NO. 4 (1991), pp. 931–52.

—'Ireland, the Vatican and the Cold War', *Irish Studies in International Affairs*, VOL. 3, NO. 3 (1991), pp. 67–114.

—'Ireland and the Cold War—the Case of Italy in 1948', West European Programme, NO. 10, Woodrow Wilson Center, Smithsonian Institution, Washington DC, 1992.

—'L'Irlande et de Gaulle', *Espoir, revue de l'Institut Charles de Gaulle*, NO. 80 (mars 1992), pp. 65–74.

—*Ireland and the Challenge of European Intergration* (Irish Association for European Studies—Hibernian University Press, Cork and Dublin, 1989).

—[with Joe Mulholland] *Emigration, Employment and Enterprise* (Patrick MacGill Summer School, Hibernian University Press, Cork and Dublin, 1989). (Introduction by Senator Edward Kennedy.)

—[with Mike Haltzell] *Northern Ireland and the Politics of Reconciliation* (Cambridge University Press, New York, 1993).

—[with Joe Mulholland] *Education in Ireland: For What and for Whom* (Hibernian University Press, Cork and Dublin, 1990).

—*Beyond the Cold War—Europe and the Super Powers in the 1990s* (Hibernian University Press, Cork and Dublin, 1990).

—Clive H. Church and Dermot Keogh (eds), *The Single European Act: A Transnational Study* (Canterbury Consortium, Cork, 1991).

Kiely, Benedict, *Drink to the Bird: A Memoir* (Minerva, London, 1992).

LaFeber, Walter, *America, Russia and the Cold War, 1945–1992*, 7th ed. (McGraw-Hill, New York, 1993).

Laffan, Michael, *The Partition of Ireland, 1911–1925* (Dundalgan Press, Dundalk, 1983).

Larkin, Emmet, *James Larkin: Irish Labour Leader 1876–1947* (Mentor, London, 1968).

Laurent, Eric and Seán MacBride, *L'exigence de la Liberté* (Amnesty International, Stock, 1981).

Lawlor, Sheila, *Britain and Ireland 1914–1923* (Gill & Macmillan, Dublin, 1983).

Lee, J.J., 'Aspects of Corporatist Thought in Ireland: The Commission on Vocational Organisations, 1939–43' in Art Cosgrove and Donal McCartney (eds), *Studies in Irish History presented to R. Dudley Edwards* (University College Dublin, 1979), pp. 324–46.

—(ed.), *Ireland 1945–70* (Gill & Macmillan, Dublin, 1979).

—'Seán Lemass' in J.J. Lee (ed.), *Ireland 1945–70* (Gill & Macmillan, Dublin, 1979).

—*Ireland: Towards a Sense of Place* (Cork University Press, Cork, 1985).

—*Ireland 1912–1985: Politics and Society* (Cambridge University Press, Cambridge, 1989).

Lemass, Peter, 'Housing', *The Furrow*, VOL. 20, NO. 3 (March 1969), pp. 116–27.

Lenihan, Brian, *For the Record* (Blackwater Press, Dublin, 1991).

Levine, June, *Sisters: The Personal Story of a Feminist* (Ward River Press, Dublin, 1982).

Lindsay, Patrick, *Memories* (Blackwater Press, Dublin, 1992).

Litton, Frank (ed.), *The Constitution of Ireland 1937–1987, Administration* (special issue), VOL. 35, NO. 4 (1988).

Longford, Lord and Thomas P. O'Neill, *Éamon de Valera* (Arrow Books, London, 1970).

Lynch, Patrick, 'The Irish Economy since the War, 1946–1951' in Kevin B. Nowlan and T. Desmond Williams (eds), *Ireland in the War Years and After* (Gill & Macmillan, Dublin, 1969), pp. 185–200.

—'The Economist and Public Policy', *Studies*, VOL. XLII (Autumn 1953), pp. 241–74.

Lynch, Patrick and James Meenan (eds), *Essays in Memory of Alexis Fitzgerald* (Gill & Macmillan, Dublin, 1987).

Lyons, F.S.L., *Ireland since the Famine* (Weidenfeld and Nicolson, London, 1971).

Mac Amhlaigh, Dónall, *An Irish Navvy* (Routledge and Kegan Paul, London, 1964) (translated by Valentin Iremonger from *Dialann Deoraí*).

McArdle, D., *The Irish Republic* (Gollancz, London, 1937).

McCabe, Ian, *A Diplomatic History of Ireland 1948–1949: The Republic, the Commonwealth and NATO* (Irish Academic Press, Dublin, 1991).

McCarthy, Charles, *The Decade of Upheaval: Irish Trade Unions in the Nineteen Sixties* (Institute of Public Administration, Dublin, 1973).

—*Trade Unions in Ireland 1894–1960* (Institute of Public Administration, Dublin, 1977).

McCarthy, Eunice, 'Women and Work in Ireland', in Margaret MacCurtain and Donncha Ó Corráin (eds), *Women in Irish Society: The Historical Dimension* (Arlen House, Dublin, 1978), pp. 104–17.

McCarthy, Thomas, *Seven Winters in Paris* (Anvil Press, London, 1989).

Mac Conghail, Muiris, 'The Creation of RTÉ and the Impact of Television', in Brian Farrell (ed.), *Communication and Community in Ireland* (Mercier Press, Dublin and Cork, 1984), pp. 64–74.

McConkey, Kenneth, *A Free Spirit: Irish Art 1860–1960* (Antique Collectors Club, London, 1990).

MacCurtain, Margaret and Donncha Ó Corráin (eds), *Women in Irish Society: The Historical Dimension* (Arlen House, Dublin, 1978).

MacDonagh, Oliver, *States of Mind, A Study of Anglo-Irish Conflict, 1780–1980* (George Allen & Unwin, London, 1983).

McDonald, Frank, *The Destruction of Dublin* (Gill & Macmillan, Dublin, 1985).

MacDonald, Malcolm, *Titans and Others* (Collins, London, 1972).

McElroy, Gerald, *The Catholic Church and Northern Ireland Crisis, 1968–1986* (Gill & Macmillan, Dublin, 1991).

MacEoin, Gary, *Memoirs and Memories* (Twenty-third Publications, Mystic, Connecticut, 1986).

McGahern, John, *The Leavetaking* (Faber and Faber, London, 1974).

—*Amongst Women* (Faber and Faber, London, 1990).

MacIntyre, Tom, *Through the Bridewell Gate: A Diary of the Dublin Arms Trial* (Faber and Faber, London, 1971).

McKee, Éamonn C, 'Church-State Relations and the Development of Irish Health Policy: The Mother-and-Child Scheme, 1944–53', *Irish Historical Studies*, VOL. XXV, NO. 98 (November 1986), pp. 159–94.

—'From Precepts to Praxis: Irish Governments and Economic Policy, 1939–1952', PHD, University College, Dublin, 1987.

McKenna, Captain T., 'Thank God We're Surrounded by Water', *An Cosantóir*, VOL. 33, NO. 4 (April 1973), pp. 103–23.

McMahon, Deirdre, *Republicans and Imperialists: Anglo-Irish Relations in the 1930s* (Yale University Press, New Haven and London, 1984).

MacManus, M.J., *Éamon de Valera* (Talbot Press, Dublin, 1945).

McQuaid, John Charles, *Higher Education for Catholics* (Gill & Macmillan, Dublin, 1961).

—*Catholic Education: Its Functions and Scope* (Dublin, 1962).

Mac Réamoinn, Seán, 'An tÉadach is an Duine', in Bernard Harris and Grattan Freyer (eds), *Integrating Tradition: The Achievements of Seán Ó Riada* (Irish Humanities Center, Ballina, 1981), pp. 8–11.

Mhac an tSaoi, Máire, 'Letter to the Editor', *Comhar*, Bealtaine 1945, VOL. 4, NO. 2 [reprinted in *Comhar* 1942–1982].

Maher, Denis J., *The Tortuous Path: The Course of Ireland's Entry into the EEC 1948–73* (Institute of Public Administration, Dublin, 1986).

Mair, Peter, *The Changing Irish Party System* (Pinter Publishers, London, 1987).

Mandle, W.F., *The Gaelic Athletic Association and Irish Nationalist Politics 1884–1924* (Gill & Macmillan, Dublin, 1987).

Manning, Maurice, *The Blueshirts* (Gill & Macmillan, Dublin, 1970).

—*Irish Political Parties: An Introduction* (Gill & Macmillan, Dublin, 1972).

—'Women in Irish National and Local Politics 1922–77' in Margaret MacCurtain and Donncha Ó Corrain (eds), *Women in Irish Society: The Historical Dimension* (Arlen House, Dublin, 1978), pp. 92–102.

Manning, Maurice and Moore McDowell, *Electricity Supply in Ireland: The History of the ESB* (Gill & Macmillan, Dublin, 1984).

Mansergh, Nicholas, *The Irish Free State: Its Government and Politics* (Allen and Unwin, London, 1934).

——*The Unresolved Question: The Anglo-Irish Settlement and its Undoing 1912–1972* (Yale University Press, New Haven and London, 1991).

Mansergh, Martin (ed.), *The Spirit of the Nation: The Speeches of Charles J. Haughey* (Mercier Press, Cork and Dublin, 1986).

Marcus, Louis, 'The Ireland of the Sixties' in Bernard Harris and Grattan Freyer (eds), *Integrating Tradition: The Achievements of Seán Ó Riada* (Irish Humanities Center, Ballina and Dufour Editions, Chester Springs, Pennyslvania, 1981), pp. 16–27.

Meenan, James, *George O'Brien: A Biographical Memoir* (Gill & Macmillan, Dublin, 1980).

——*The Irish Economy since 1922* (Liverpool University Press, Liverpool, 1970).

Mills, Michael, 'Fighting the World Slump of the Thirties—Rise and Decline of the Blueshirts', *The Irish Press*, 24 January 1969.

——'Seán Lemass: A Profile', *The Irish Press*, 18 February 1969.

——'Seán Lemass looks back', *The Irish Press*, 24 January 1969.

Mitchell, Arthur, 'William O'Brien, 1881–1968 and the Irish Labour Movement', *Studies*, VOL. 60, NO. 239 (Winter 1971), pp. 311–31.

Mitchell, Arthur and Pádraig Ó Snodaigh (eds), *Irish Political Documents 1916–1949* (Irish Academic Press, Dublin, 1985).

Moody, T.W., *The Ulster Question, 1603–1973* (Mercier Press, Dublin, 1974).

Moynihan, Maurice (ed.), *Speeches and Statements by Éamon de Valera 1917–1973* (Gill & Macmillan, Dublin, 1980).

Murphy, John A., *Ireland in the Twentieth Century* (Gill & Macmillan, Dublin, 1975).

——'"Put them out!" Parties and Elections, 1948–1969' in John J. Lee (ed.), *Ireland 1945–70* (Gill & Macmillan, Dublin, 1979), pp. 1–15.

Murphy, Seamus, *Stone Mad* (Routledge and Kegan Paul, London, 1982).

Ní Dhonnchadha, Máirín and Theo Dorgan (eds), *Revising the Rising* (Field Day, Derry, 1991).

Nowlan, Kevin B., and T. Desmond Williams, *Ireland in the War Years and After, 1939–51* (Gill & Macmillan, Dublin, 1969).

O'Brien, Conor Cruise, *To Katanga and Back: A UN Case History* (Simon and Schuster, New York, 1962).

—'Ireland in International Affairs' in Owen Dudley Edwards (ed.), *Conor Cruise O'Brien Introduces Ireland* (Andre Deutsch, London, 1969), pp. 104–34.

—*States of Ireland* (Hutchinson, London, 1972).

—*Herod: Reflections on Political Violence* (Hutchinson, London, 1978).

—*God Land: Reflections on Religion and Nationalism* (Harvard University Press, Cambridge, 1988).

O'Brien, Flann, 'The Dance Hall', *The Bell*, VOL. 1, NO. 5 (February 1941), pp. 44–52.

O'Brien, John and Pauric Travers (eds), *The Irish Emigrant Experience in Australia* (Poolbeg, Dublin, 1991).

O'Brien, William, *Forth the Banners Go: Reminiscences of William O'Brien* (Three Candles, Dublin, 1969).

Ó Broin, León, *Just Like Yesterday—An Autobiography* (Gill & Macmillan, Dublin, no date).

—*Michael Collins* (Gill & Macmillan, Dublin, 1969).

—(ed.), *In Great Haste: The Letters of Michael Collins and Kitty Kiernan* (Gill & Macmillan, Dublin, 1983).

Ó Buachalla, Séamas, *Education Policy in Twentieth-Century Ireland* (Wolfhound Press, Dublin, 1988).

O'Callaghan, Jerry, *The Red Book: The Hanrahan Case against Merck, Sharp and Dohme* (Poolbeg, Dublin, 1992).

O'Carroll, J.P., 'The politics of the 1983 "abortion referendum debate" in the Republic of Ireland', unpublished paper delivered at European Consortium of Political Research Conferences, Salzburg, April 1984.

O'Carroll, J.P. and John A. Murphy, *De Valera and his Times* (Cork University Press, Cork, 1983).

Ó Coileáin, Seán, *Seán Ó Riordáin, Beatha agus Saothar* (An Clóchomhar Tta., Baile Átha Cliath, 1982).

O'Connell, T.J., *100 Years of Progress: The Story of the Irish National Teachers Organisation 1868–1968* (INTO, Dublin, 1969).

O'Connor, Emmet, *Syndicalism in Ireland 1917–1923* (Cork University Press, Cork, 1988).

O'Connor, Frank, 'Introduction' in *The Tailor and Ansty* by Eric Cross (Mercier Press, Cork 1975 (3rd ed.), pp. 5–9.

O'Connor, Seán, 'Post-Primary Education: Now and in the Future', *Studies*, VOL. LVII, NO. 227 (Autumn 1968), pp. 233–51.

Ó Direáin, Máirtín, *Dánta 1939–1979* (An Clóchomar, Baile Átha Cliath, 1980), reprinted from the collection *Dánta Anair* (1943).

O'Donnell, Peader, 'The Clergy and me', *Doctrine and Life*, VOL. 24, NO. 10 (October 1974), pp. 539–44.

O'Dowd, Anne, *Spalpeens and Tattie Hokers: History and Folklore of the Irish Migratory Agricultural Worker in Ireland and Britain* (Irish Academic Press, Dublin, 1981).

O'Duffy, Eoin, *Crusade in Spain* (Browne & Nolan, Dublin, 1938).

Ó hEithir, Breandán, *The Begrudger's Guide to Irish Politics* (Poolbeg Press, Dublin, 1986).

O'Faoláin, Seán, *The Life Story of Éamon de Valera* (Talbot Press, Dublin and Cork, 1933).

—editorial/review of M.J. MacManus, *Éamon de Valera* (Talbot Press, Dublin, 1945) in *The Bell*, VOL. 10, NO. 1 (April 1945), pp. 1–18.

—*De Valera: A New Biography* (Penguin, London, 1939).

O'Farrell, Padraic, *The Burning of Brinsley MacNamara* (Lilliput Press, Dublin, 1990).

O'Halloran, Clare, *Partition and the Limits of Irish Nationalism* (Gill & Macmillan, Dublin, 1987).

O'Halpin, Eunan, *The Decline of the Union: British Government in Ireland, 1892–1920* (Gill & Macmillan, Dublin, 1987).

O'Leary, Cornelius, *Irish Elections 1918–1977: Parties, Voters and Proportional Representation* (Gill & Macmillan, Dublin, 1979).

O'Malley, Pádraig, *Biting at the Grave: The Irish Hunger Strikes and the Politics of Despair* (Blackstaff Press, Belfast, 1990).

O'Reilly, Emily, *Masterminds of the Right* (Attic Press, Dublin, 1992).

O'Riordan, Michael, *The Connolly Column: The Story of the Irishmen who fought for the Spanish Republic 1936–1939* (New Books, Dublin, 1979).

O'Shea, Finbarr, 'Government and Trade Unions in Ireland 1939–1946: The Formation of Labour Legislation', MA thesis, UCC, 1988.

O'Sullivan, D., *The Irish Free State and its Senate* (Faber and Faber, London, 1940).

O'Toole, Fintan, 'Introduction', in *Three Plays* by John B. Keane (Mercier Press, Cork, 1990).

O'Toole, Michael, *More Kicks than Pence: A Life in Irish Journalism* (Poolbeg Press, Dublin, 1992).

Ó Tuathaigh, Gearóid, 'The Land Question, Politics and Irish Society, 1922–1960s', in P.J. Drudy (ed.), *Ireland: Land, Politics and People* (Cambridge University Press, Cambridge, 1982), pp. 157–90.

—'Religion, Nationality and a Sense of Community in Modern Ireland', in Gearóid Ó Tuathaigh (ed.), *Community, Culture and Conflict* (Galway, Galway University Press, 1986).

—and J.J. Lee., *The Age of de Valera* (Dublin, Ward River Press, 1982).

Patterson, Henry, *The Politics of Illusion: Republicanism and Socialism in Modern Ireland* (Hutchinson, London, 1989).

Peck, John, *Dublin from Downing Street* (Gill & Macmillan, Dublin, 1978).

Power, Vincent, *Send 'em Home Sweatin': The Showbands' Story* (Kilnadore Press, Dublin, 1990).

Prager, Geoffrey, *Building Democracy in Ireland: Political Order and Cultural Integration in a Newly Independent Nation* (Cambridge University Press, Cambridge, 1986).

Puirséal, Pádraig, *The GAA and Its Time* (Purcell Family, Dublin 1982).

Raymond, R.J., 'De Valera, Lemass and Irish Economic Development: 1933–1948', in J.P. O'Carroll and John A. Murphy (eds), *De Valera and his Times* (Cork University Press, Cork, 1983), pp. 113–133.

—'David Gray, the Aiken Mission and Irish Neutrality, 1940–41', *Diplomatic History*, VOL. 9 (Winter 1985), pp. 55–71.

Reich, William, *The Mass Psychology of Fascism* (Pelican, London, 1975).

Roche, Desmond, *Local Government in Ireland* (Institute of Public Administration, Dublin, 1982).

Rosenberg J.L., 'The 1941 Mission of Frank Aiken to the United States: An American Perspective', *Irish Historical Studies*, VOL. XXII, NO. 86, (September 1980), pp. 162–77.

Rothery, Seán, *Ireland and the New Architecture 1900–1940* (Lilliput Press, Dublin, 1991).

Ryan, Liam, 'Social Dynamite: A Study of Early School-Leavers', *Christus Rex*, VOL. XXII, NO. 1 (January 1967), pp. 7–44.

—'Church and Politics: The Last Twenty-five Years', *The Furrow*, VOL. 30, NO. 1 (January 1979), pp. 3–18.

Rynne, Xavier, *Letters from Vatican City* (Faber and Faber, London, 1963).

Salmon, Trevor, *Unneutral Ireland: An Ambivalent and Unique Security Policy* (Clarendon Press, Oxford, 1989).

Sandford, Cedric and Oliver Morrissey, *The Irish Wealth Tax: A Case Study in Economics and Politics* (ESRI, Dublin, 1985).

Sexton, Brendan, *Ireland and the Crown 1922–1936: The Governor Generalship of the Irish Free State* (Irish Academic Press, Dublin, 1989).

Share, Bernard, *The Emergency: Neutral Ireland 1939–45* (Gill & Macmillan, Dublin, 1978).

Sheehy Skeffington, André, *Skeff: A Life of Owen Sheehy Skeffington, 1909–1970* (Lilliput Press, Dublin, 1991).

Smith, Raymond, *Garret: The Enigma* (Aherlow Publishers, Dublin, 1985).

Stephan, Enno, *Spies in Ireland* (Stackpole, Harrisburg, Pennsylvania, 1969).

Sweeney, Garry, *In Public Service: A History of the Public Service Executive Union, 1890–1900* (Institute of Public Administration, Dublin, 1990).

Thomson, David, *Woodbrook* (Barrie & Jenkins, London, 1975).

Tobin, Fergal, *The Best of Decades: Ireland in the 1960s* (Gill & Macmillan, Dublin, 1984).

Trevor, William, *A Writer's Ireland, Landscape in Literature* (Thames and Hudson, London, 1984).

Tweedy, Hilda, *A Link in the Chain: The Story of the Irish Housewives Association 1942–1992* (Attic Press, Dublin, 1992).

Valiulis, Maryann Gialanella, *Almost a Rebellion: The Army Mutiny of 1924* (Tower Books, Cork, 1985).

—*Portrait of a Revolutionary: General Richard Mulcahy and the Foundation of the Irish State* (Irish Academic Press, Dublin, 1992).

Venturi, Lionello, *Rouault: Biographical and Critical Study* (Crown Books, New York, 1972).

Walker, Graham, *The Politics of Frustration: Harry Midgley and the Failure of Labour in Northern Ireland* (Manchester University Press, Manchester, 1985).

Walsh, Dick, *The Party: Inside Fianna Fáil* (Gill & Macmillan, Dublin, 1986).

Waters, John, *Jiving at the Crossroads* (Blackstaff Press, Belfast, 1991).

Weafer, John A., 'Change and Continuity in Irish Religion, 1974–1984', *Doctrine and Life,* VOL. 36, NO. 10 (December 1986), pp. 507–17.

—'The Irish Laity: Some Findings of the 1984 National Survey', *Doctrine and Life,* VOL. 36, NO. 5 (May-June 1986), pp. 247–53.

—'Vocations: A Review of National and International Trends', *The Furrow,* VOL. 39, NO. 8 (August 1988), pp. 501–11.

—'Listening to the Young Church', *The Furrow,* VOL. 42, NO. 1 (January 1991), pp. 18–27.

Whelehan, J.B., 'Ten Coffins', *The Capuchin Annual* (1938), pp. 201–03.

Whitaker, T.K., 'Todhchaí eacnamaíoch agus shóisialta na hÉireann', *Central Bank of Ireland Quarterly Bulletin* (1971).

—*Interests* (Institute of Public Administration, Dublin, 1983).

Whyte, J.H., *Church and State in Modern Ireland 1923–1979*, 2nd ed. (Gill & Macmillan, Dublin, 1984).

Williams, T. Desmond, 'From the Treaty to the Civil War', in T. Desmond Williams (ed.), *The Irish Struggle 1916–1926* (Routledge and Kegan Paul, London, 1966), pp. 117–28.

— (ed.), *The Irish Struggle 1916–1926* (Routledge and Kegan Paul, London, 1966).

—'Ireland and the War' in K.B. Nowlan and T.D. Williams (eds), *Ireland in the War Years and After 1939–51* (Dublin 1969), pp. 14–27.

Woodman, K., *Media Control in Ireland 1923–1983* (Galway, 1986).

Young, Comdt Peter, 'The Way We Were', *An Cosantóir,* VOL. 49, NO. 9 (September 1989), pp. 3–38.

Bibliography to the Second Edition

Primary Sources

Office of Refugee Applications Commissioner (ORAC) Website
ESRI Website
Dublin Archdiocese Website
Ferns Diocese Website
Department of Enterprise, Trade and Employment Website
Department of An Taoiseach Website

Central Statistics Office Economic Series
Central Statistics Office Statistical Yearbook of Ireland 2004
Central Statistics Office, Statistical Abstracts Various Years
ESRI, *Medium Term Review 1994–2000*
Ombudsman, *An Investigation by the Ombudsman of Complaints Regarding Payment of Nursing Home Subventions By Health Boards* (2001)
Department of the Environment and Local Government, *Reifirinn In Éirinn, 1937–1999* (2000, PN 8976)
The Second Interim Report of the Tribunal of Inquiry into Certain Planning Matters and Payments, September 2002
2002 Annual Report of the Comptroller and Auditor General and Appropriation Accounts, Volume 1
The Fourth Interim Report of the Tribunal of Inquiry into Certain Planning Matters and Payments, June 2004
Report of Investigations into the affairs of National Irish Bank Limited and National Irish Bank Financial Services Limited, 23 July 2004
IFSRA, *Investigations in AIB Group on Foreign Exchange and Other Charging Issues &Deal Allocation and Associated Issues*, 7 December 2004
Some of our Children—A Report on the Residential Care of the Deprived Child in Ireland [Tuairim Pamphlet 13] (London, 1966)
Building Trust in Ireland—Studies Commissioned by the Forum for Peace and Reconciliation (Blackstaff Press, Belfast, 1996)
Suicide in Ireland: A National Study, 2001

Secondary sources

Ardagh, John, *Ireland and the Irish* (Hamish Hamilton, London, 1994).

Augusteijn, Joost (ed.), *Ireland in the 1930s: New Perspectives* (Four Courts Press, Dublin, 1999).

Augusteijn, Joost, *The Irish Revolution 1913–23* (Palgrave Macmillan, Basingstoke, 2002).

Barnes, Jane, *Irish Industrial Schools 1868–1908* (Irish Academic Press, Dublin, 1989).

Barton, Brian, *Brookeborough: The Making of a Prime Minister* (Queen's University, Belfast, 1988).

Barton, Brian, *Northern Ireland in the Second World War* (Ulster Historical Foundation, Belfast, 1995).

Bew, Paul, Peter Gibbon and Henry Patterson, *Northern Ireland, 1921–2001: political forces and social classes* (Serif, London, 2002).

Bielenberg, Andy (ed.), *The Shannon Scheme and the Electrification of the Irish Free State* (Lilliput, Dublin, 2002).

Böll, Heinrich, *Irish Journal* (Cologne, 1961; London, 1967).

Boyce, D. George, 'Ireland and British politics, 1900–1939', in Christopher John Wrigley (ed.), *A companion to early twentieth-century Britain* (Blackwell Companions to British History) (Blackwell, Oxford, 2003), pp. 102–17.

Brady, Ciaran (ed.), *Interpreting Irish History: The Debate on Historical Revisionism* (Irish Academic Press, Dublin, 1994).

Breen, Michael J. (ed.), *A Fire in the Forest—Religious Life in Ireland* (Veritas, Dublin, 2001).

Brown, Terence, *Ireland: A Social and Cultural History, 1922–2002* (Perennial, London, 2004).

Brown, Stewart J. and David Miller (eds), *Piety and Power in Ireland 1760–1960: Essays in honour of Emmet Larkin* (University of Notre Dame Press, Indiana, 2000).

Callanan, Frank, *T.M. Healy* (Cork University Press Cork, 1996).

Clinton, President Bill, *My Life* (Hutchinson, London, 2004).

Collins, Stephen, *The Cosgrave Legacy* (Blackwater Press, Dublin, 1996).

Connolly, Linda, *The Irish Women's Movement: From Revolution to Devolution* (Lilliput Press, Dublin, 2003).

Coogan, Tim Pat, *De Valera: Long Fellow, Long Shadow* (Hutchinson, London, 1993).

Cooney, John, *John Charles McQuaid: Ruler of Catholic Ireland* (O'Brien Press, Dublin, 1999).

Corish, P.J., *Maynooth College 1795–1995* (Gill & Macmillan, Dublin, 1994).

Craig, Patricia (ed.), *The Oxford Book of Ireland* (Oxford University Press, Oxford, 1998).

Creaton, Siobhán, *Ryanair: How a Small Irish Airline Conquered Europe* (Aurum, London, 2004).

Cronin, Mike, *The Blueshirts and Irish Politics* (Four Courts Press, Dublin, 1997).

Cronin, Mike and John M. Regan (eds), *Ireland: The Politics of Independence, 1922–49* (Macmillan, Basingstoke, 2000).

Cullen, Bill, *It's a Long Way from Penny Apples* (Mercier Press, Dublin, 2001).

Cullen, Paul, *Refugees and Asylum Seekers in Ireland* (Cork University Press, Cork, 2000).

Daly, Mary, *The buffer state: the historical roots of the Department of the Environment* (IPA, Dublin, 1997).

Daly, Mary, *The first department: a history of the Department of Agriculture* (IPA, Dublin, 2002).

Dalsimer, Adele M. (ed.), *Visualizing Ireland: National Identity and the Pictorial Tradition* (Faber and Faber, London, 1993).

Delaney, Enda, *Demography, State and Society: Irish Migration to Britain, 1921–1971* (Liverpool University Press, Liverpool, 2000).

Delaney, Enda, *Irish emigration since 1921* (Economic and Social History Society of Ireland, Dublin, 2002).

Desmond, Barry, *Finally and in Conclusion: A Political Memoir* (New Island, Dublin, 2000).

Doyle, Paddy, *The God Squad* (Raven Arts Press, Dublin, 1989).

Dudley Edwards, Ruth, *The Faithful Tribe: An Intimate Portrait of the Loyal Institution* (Harper Collins, London, 1999).

Duignan, Seán, *One Spin on the Merry Go-Round* (Blackwater Presss, Dublin, 1996).

Dunn, Joseph, *No Lions in the Hierarchy* (Columba Press, Dublin, 1994).

Dunn, Joseph, *No Vipers in the Vatican* (Columba Press, Dublin, 1996).

Dunphy, Richard, *The Making of Fianna Fáil Power in Ireland, 1923–48* (Oxford University Press, Oxford, 1995).

Durkan, Teresita, *Goldenbridge: A View from Valparaíso* (Veritas, Dublin, 1997).

English, Richard and Graham Walker (eds), *Unionism in Modern Ireland: New Perspectives on Politics and Culture* (Gill & Macmillan, Dublin, 1996).

Fahy, Bernadette, *The Freedom of Angels: Surviving Goldenbridge Orphanage* (O'Brien Press, Dublin, 1999).

Fallon, Brian, *An Age of Innocence: Irish Culture, 1930–1960* (Gill & Macmillan, Dublin, 2000).

Fanning, Ronan, 'The Anglo-American Alliance and the Irish Question in the Twentieth Century', in Judith Devlin and Howard B. Clarke, *European encounters: essays in memory of Albert Lovett* (University College Dublin Press, Dublin, 2003), pp. 185–220.

Farren, Seán, *The Politics of Irish Education, 1920–1965* (Institute of Irish Studies, Queen's University, Belfast, 1995).

Feeney, Brian, *Sinn Féin: a hundred turbulent years* (O'Brien Press, Dublin, 2002).

Ferguson, Harry, 'States of Fear, Child Abuse, and Irish Society', in *Doctrine and Life*, VOL. 50, NO. 1, January 2000.

Ferriter, Diarmaid, *The Transformation of Ireland 1900–2000* (Profile Books, London 2004).

Findlater, Alex, *Findlaters* (A&A Farmar, Dublin, 2001).

Finnegan, Frances, *Do Penance or Perish: A Study of Magdalen Asylums in Ireland* (Congrave Press, Kilkenny, 2001).

Foster, R.F., *The Irish Story: Telling Tales and Making It Up in Ireland* (Oxford University Press, Oxford, 2002).

Fuller, Louise, *Irish Catholicism since 1950: The undoing of a culture* (Gill & Macmillan, Dublin, 2002).

Garvin, Tom, *1922: The Birth of Irish Democracy* (Gill & Macmillan, Dublin, 1996).

Garvin, Tom, *Preventing the Future: Why was Ireland so poor for so long?* (Gill & Macmillan, Dublin, 2004).

Girvin, Brian and Geoffrey Roberts (eds), *Ireland and the Second World War: Politics, Society and Remembrance* (Four Courts Press, Dublin, 2000).

Gorham, Maurice, *Forty years of Irish Broadcasting* (Talbot, Dublin, 1967).

Hanley, Brian, *The IRA, 1926–1936* (Four Courts Press, Dublin, 2002).

Hart, Peter, *The IRA and Its Enemies: Violence and Community in Cork, 1916–23* (Clarendon Press, Oxford, 1998).

Hart, Peter, *British intelligence in Ireland, 1920–21: the final reports* (Cork University Press, Cork, 2002).

Hegarty, Peter, *Peadar O'Donnell* (Mercier Press, Cork, 1999).

Hopkinson, Michael, *The Irish War of Independence* (Gill & Macmillan, Dublin, 2002).

Horgan, John, *Seán Lemass the Enigmatic Patriot* (Gill & Macmillan, Dublin, 1997).

Horgan, John, *Noel Browne: Passionate Outsider* (Gill & Macmillan, Dublin, 2000).

Horgan, John, *Irish Media: a Critical History since 1922* (Routledge, London, 2001).

Hull, Mark, *Irish Secrets: German espionage in Ireland, 1939–45* (Irish Academic Press, Dublin, 2003).

Inglis, Tom, *Moral Monopoly: the Rise and Fall of the Catholic Church in Ireland* (University College Dublin Press, Dublin, 1998).

Jeffery, Keith, *Ireland and the Great War* (Cambridge University Press, Cambridge, 2000).

Jeffery, Keith (ed.), *An Irish Empire? Aspects of Ireland and the British Empire* (Manchester University Press, Manchester, 1996).

Kelly, James and Dáire Keogh (eds), *A History of the Catholic Diocese of Dublin* (Four Courts Press, Dublin, 2000).

Kennedy, Finola, *Cottage to Crèche: Family Change in Ireland* (Institute of Public Administration, Dublin, 2001).

Kennedy, Liam, *Colonialism, Religion and Nationalism in Ireland* (Institute of Irish Studies, Queen's University, Belfast, 1996).

Kenny, Mary, *Goodbye to Catholic Ireland* (Templegate, London, 1997).

Keogh, Dermot, *Ireland and the Vatican: the politics and diplomacy of church and state, 1922–1960* (Cork University Press, Cork, 1995).

Keogh, Dermot, *Jews in Twentieth Century Ireland: Refugees, Anti-semitism and the Holocaust* (Cork University Press, Cork, 1998).

Keogh, Dermot ed., with Ronan Fanning, Michael Kennedy and Eunan O'Halpin, *Documents on Irish foreign policy i, 1919–1922* (1998); *ii, 1923–1925* (2000); *iii, 1926–1932* (2002); *iv, 1932–1936* (2004). Royal Irish Academy/Department of Foreign Affairs, Dublin.

Keogh, Dermot, with Mervyn O'Driscoll, *Ireland in World War Two: Diplomacy and survival* (Mercier Press, Cork, 2004).

Keogh, Dermot, with Finbarr O'Shea and Carmel Quinlan, *The Lost Decade: Ireland in the 1950s* (Mercier Press, Cork, 2004).

Keogh, Dermot, with Gabriel Doherty, *De Valera's Irelands* (Mercier Press, Cork, 2003).

Kirby, Peadar, *The Celtic Tiger in Distress: Growth with Inequality in Ireland* (Palgrave, London, 2002).

Kleinrichert, Denise, *Republican Internment and the Prison Ship Argenta, 1922* (Irish Academic Press, Dublin, 2001).

Laffan, Michael, *The Resurrection of Ireland: The Sinn Féin Party 1916–23* (Cambridge University Press, Cambridge, 1999).

Logan, John, (ed.), *Teachers Union: The TUI and Its Forerunners in Irish Education, 1899–1994* (A&A Farmar, Dublin, 1999).

Luddy, Maria and Cliona Murphy (eds), *Women Surviving* (Poolbeg, Dublin, 1990).

Manning, Maurice, *James Dillon: A Biography* (Wolfhound Press, Dublin, 2000).

Maume, Patrick, *The Long Gestation: Irish Nationalist Life 1891–1918* (Gill & Macmillan, Dublin, 1999).

McCarthy, Conor, *Modernisation: Crisis and Culture in Ireland, 1969–1992* (Four Courts Press, Dublin, 2000).

McCoole, Sinéad, *Hazel: A Life of Lady Lavery, 1880–1935* (Lilliput Press, Dublin, 1997).

McCourt, Frank, *Angela's Ashes: Memoir of a Childhood* (Flamingo, London, 1996).

McCullagh, David, *A Makeshift Majority: The First Inter-Party Government, 1948–51* (IPA, Dublin, 1998).

McDermott, Eithne, *Clann na Poblachta* (Cork University Press, Cork, 1998).

McDonagh, Enda, *Faith in Fragments* (Columba Press, Dublin, 1996).

McKay, Susan, *Sophia's Story* (Gill & Macmillan, Dublin, 1998).

McKittrick, David, Seamus Kelters, Brian Feeney and Chris Thornton, *Lost Lives— The Stories of the Men, Women and Children Who Died as a Result of the Northern Troubles* (Mainstream, Edinburgh and London, 1999).

McGarry, Fearghal, *Frank Ryan* (Dundalgan Press, Dundalk, 2002).

McGarry, Fearghal, *Irish Politics and the Spanish Civil War* (Cork University Press, Cork, 1999).

Mitchell, Senator George, *Making Peace—The Inside Story of the Making of the Good Friday Agreement* (Heinemann, London, 1999).

Moore, Chris, *Betrayal of Trust—The Father Brendan Smyth Affair and the Catholic Church* (Marino Books, Dublin, 1995).

Nevin, Donal (ed.), *Trade Union Century* (Mercier Press, Dublin, 1994).

Ó Gráda, Cormac, *A Rocky Road: The Irish Economy since the 1920s* (Manchester University Press, Manchester, 1997).

O'Brien, John A. (ed.), *The Vanishing Irish* (Allen, London, 1954).

O'Brien, Conor Cruise, *My Life and Themes* (Poolbeg, Dublin, 1998).

O'Connor, Ulick, *The Ulick O'Connor diaries, 1970–1981: a cavalier Irishman* (John Murray, London, 2001).

Ó Corráin, Donnchadh (ed.), *James Hogan: Revolutionary, Historian and Political Scientist* (Four Courts Press, Dublin, 2001).

O'Donoghue, David, *Hitler's Irish Voices—The story of German radio's wartime Irish service* (Beyond the Pale, Dublin, 1998).

Ó Drisceoil, Dónal, *Censorship in Ireland, 1939–45: Neutrality, Politics and Society* (Cork University Press, Cork, 1996).

Ó Drisceoil, Dónal, *Peadar O'Donnell* (Cork University Press, Cork, 2001).

O'Driscoll, Mervyn, *Ireland, Germany and the Nazis: politics and diplomacy, 1919–1939* (Four Courts Press, Dublin, 2004).

Ó Faoláin, Nuala, *Are You Somebody?* (New Island, Dublin, 1996).

O'Leary, Don, *Vocationalism and Social Catholicism in Twentieth-Century Ireland: the search for a Christian social order* (Irish Academic Press, Dublin, 2000).

Ó Riain, Micheál, *On the Move: Córas Iompair Éireann, 1945–95* (Gill & Macmillan, Dublin, 1995).

O'Toole, Fintan, *Meanwhile Back at the Ranch—The Politics of Irish Beef* (Vintage, London, 1995).

Paseta, Senia, *Before the Revolution: Nationalism, Social Change, and Ireland's Catholic Elite, 1879–1922* (Cork University Press, Cork, 1999).

Phoenix, Eamon, *Northern Nationalism: Nationalist Politics, Partition and the Catholic Minority in Northern Ireland, 1890–1940* (Ulster Historical Foundation, Belfast, 1994).

Raftery, Mary and Eoin O'Sullivan, *Suffer the Little Children: The Inside Story of Ireland's Industrial Schools* (New Island, Dublin, 1999).

Regan, John, *The Irish Counter-Revolution, 1921–1936* (Gill & Macmillan, Dublin, 1999).

Robins, Joseph, *The Lost Children—A Study of Charity Children in Ireland 1700–1900* (Institute of Public Administration, Dublin, 1980).

Ruane, Joseph and Jennifer Todd (eds), *After the Good Friday Agreement— Analysing Political Change in Northern Ireland* (University College Dublin Press, Dublin, 1999).

Sweeny, Paul, *The Celtic Tiger* (Oaktree, Dublin, 1998).

Walshe, Eibhear (ed.), *Ordinary People Dancing: Essays on Kate O'Brien* (Cork University Press, Cork, 1993).

Whelan, Bernadette, *Ireland and the Marshall Plan, 1947–57* (Four Courts Press, Dublin, 2000).

Whelan, Gerard and Carolyn Swift, *Spiked: Church-State Intrigue and the 'Rose Tattoo'* (New Island, Dublin, 2002).

Wilson, Andrew J., *Irish America and the Ulster Conflict 1968–1995* (Blackstaff Press, Belfast, 1995).

Index